VIETNAM

An American Ordeal

Third Edition

George Donelson Moss

Prentice Hall
Upper Saddle River, New Jersey 07458

Library of Congress Cataloging-in-Publication Data

Moss, George.
　　　Vietnam, an American ordeal　/　George Donelson Moss.—3rd ed.
　　　　　p.　　cm.
　　　Includes bibliographical references and index.
　　　ISBN 0-13-897083-1
　　　　1. Vietnamese Conflict, 1961–1975.　2. Vietnam—
　　History—1945–1975.　3. Vietnam—Relations—United States.
　　　4. United States—Relations—Vietnam.　I.　Title.
DS557.7.M66　1998
959.704′3373—dc21　　　　　　　　　　　　　　　97-34013
　　　　　　　　　　　　　　　　　　　　　　　　　CIP

Editor-in-Chief: Charlyce Jones Owen
Production Editor: Jean Lapidus
Prepress and Manufacturing Buyer: Lynn Pearlman
Copy Editor: Michele Lansing
Photo Research: Kathy Ringrose
Cartographer: Magellan Geographix
　　　　　　　Santa Barbara, CA
Cover Design: Bruce Kenselaar
Cover Image: Viet Nam War Memorial Wall
　　　　　　　Courtesy of the Smithsonian Institution

This book was set in 10.5/12.5 Times Roman by DM Cradle Associates,
and was printed and bound by Courier Companies, Inc.
The cover was printed by Phoenix Color Corp.

© 1998, 1994, 1990 by Prentice-Hall, Inc.
Simon & Schuster / A Viacom Company
Upper Saddle River, New Jersey 07458

Printed in the United States of America
10　9　8　7　6　5　4　3　2

ISBN 0-13-897083-1

PRENTICE-HALL INTERNATIONAL (UK) LIMITED, *London*
PRENTICE HALL OF AUSTRALIA PTY. LIMITED, *Sydney*
PRENTICE-HALL CANADA INC., *Toronto*
PRENTICE-HALL HISPANOAMERICANA, S.A., *Mexico*
PRENTICE-HALL OF INDIA PRIVATE LIMITED, *New Delhi*
PRENTICE-HALL OF JAPAN, INC., *Tokyo*
SIMON & SCHUSTER ASIA PTE. LTD., *Singapore*
EDITORIA PRENTICE-HALL DO BRASIL, LTDA., *Rio de Janeiro*

To the young Americans who fought the
Vietnam War and for those who opposed it—
they are heroes and victims all.

Contents

Epiphany: Of Black Marble and Memories

Washington, D.C., April 4, 1987. . . . A cold spring rain drenched clusters of visitors filing along the walkway bordering the Vietnam Veterans Memorial. From my vantage point in front of the Lincoln Memorial, I watched them descending slowly, occasionally stopping to read the names etched in the black marble slabs. Some may have sought a name they would remember, of a boy they had known, had loved, from among the 58,201 names of the dead stencilled in the bleak stone. I could feel the grief and anger welling up inside of a young woman as she reached out to touch an inscribed name. As I stood musing amid the afternoon shadows cast by Lincoln's brooding monument, the idea of writing the story of the long and disastrous American involvement in Vietnam first came to my mind. I wanted to answer the question that must have formed wordlessly in the young woman's mind that cold spring day: Why? Why Vietnam?

Preface

This book can be read by anyone curious to know about the American involvement in Vietnam, but it is meant particularly for two large constituencies, one middle-aged and one coming of age. A new generation of Americans has grown up since the end of the American intervention in Southeast Asia that we call the Vietnam War. They join another, older generation now reaching middle age, who were compelled to either fight the war or to oppose it. This book may help the older generation to come to terms with their Vietnam experiences and it may also help the new generation discover the ordeal that anguished their parents' generation.

I have been quite pleased with the reception of the second edition of *Vietnam: An American Ordeal* and I am delighted to have the opportunity to offer this third version. The opening of new records, particularly of the archives in Moscow and Beijing, and the continuing flood of scholarship on the American War in Vietnam in recent years have significantly enhanced our knowledge of all facets of the U. S. experience in Southeast Asia. Where possible I have incorporated much of this new information into the corpus of the book. Each chapter has been carefully reworked, and in many instances extensively revised. The last chapter has been expanded and updated to include recent changes in U.S.–Vietnamese relations and the continuing influence of Vietnam memories on American political life and foreign policy.

While this revised edition includes much new material and my thinking has changed on some of the major issues, I want to emphasize that the basic structure of the book and my basic understanding of the American Indochinese intervention have not changed. The book remains a comprehensive narrative history of the U. S. involvement in Southeast Asia spanning three decades—from the mid-1940s to the mid-1970s. My thesis remains that American involvement in Southeast Asia is best understood as a concerted effort that goes through many phases over a long period of time to thwart the Vietnamese national revolution, which was also a social revolution, backed by the Soviet Union and the Peoples Republic of China.

Within a larger historical context, America's Vietnam entanglement can best be comprehended as a major episode occurring during the long Cold War between the United States and the Soviet Union that raged from the end of World War II until the collapse and disappearance of the Soviet empire during 1989–1991. American leaders, in thrall to Cold War-spawned ideologies, consistently invested the regional conflicts of Indochina with a larger significance—preventing the global spread of Communism, which was equated with Soviet and Chinese imperialism.

Whether supporting the French during the First Indochina war, backing one faction of Vietnamese nationalists during a civil war, fighting a limited war against the NLF and NVA forces, or pursuing a complex and contradictory strategy called Vietnamization, Washington sought to prevent the proliferation of Communist states in Southeast Asia. Following the triumph of the Vietnamese revolution, the United States refused to normalize relations with Vietnam for twenty years. For most of those two decades, American imposed a trade embargo against Vietnam and tried to isolate that country from international life.

It was not until July 11, 1995, that President Clinton, who as a graduate student had opposed the Vietnam War and avoided military service, with Arizona Senator John McCain, a much-decorated former Naval aviator and POW, standing by his side, officially extended diplomatic recognition to the Democratic Republic of Vietnam. On May 9, 1997, Pete Peterson, a former U. S. Air Force pilot shot down over North Vietnam in 1966, who spent $6^1/_2$ years as a prisoner-of-war in Hanoi, arrived at that city's Noi Bai Airport en route to assuming his duties as the new U. S. ambassador to Vietnam. Peterson was the first American envoy ever posted to that Communist country. Ambassador Peterson was greeted by a friendly crowd waving both U. S. and Vietnamese flags. A new era of peace, friendship, and trade had begun between the two nations that had fought America's longest war and the only war that the United States ever lost.

Because of their Cold War beliefs, a succession of American presidents and their senior advisers perceived the Vietnamese national revolution as a potential threat to the security of Southeast Asian nations and ultimately a threat to American security. These successive administrations tried hard for a long time to defeat or at least contain the Vietnamese revolution. Ultimately they failed. And that is the story I have to tell—why Americans tried so hard so long to stop the spread of Communism into Indochina, and why they failed.

The American people have a strong interest in the American Vietnam War and memories of Vietnam continue to have a strong hold on the American psyche. In 1990–91, as the United States prepared to go to war in the Persian Gulf to drive the occupying Iraqi forces out of Kuwait, President Bush reassured anxious citizens by exclaiming that the Gulf War would not be another Vietnam. American forces sent to the Gulf would not have to fight with one hand tied behind their backs. Pentagon officials, believing that defeat in Vietnam derived in large part from uncensored and biased media coverage, made sure that journalists got highly sanitized and favorable stories to write about military action in the Persian Gulf. Americans gave the returning DESERT STORM troopers lavish heroes' welcomes, partly because of guilty memories of the shabby treatment accorded returning Vietnam veterans who got no parades.

Memories of Vietnam have continued to affect the nation's political life during the 1990s. President Bush, seeking to fend off the challenge of the Democratic candidate Bill Clinton in the fall 1992 elections, repeatedly attacked the Arkansas governor for evading the draft during the Vietnam War era and for helping to organize an antiwar demonstration in London. Bush's attacks put Clinton on the defensive, but did not wound him badly nor prevent him from winning the election by a sizeable margin. But the fact that Bush brought up Clinton's Vietnam-era behavior is a testament to Vietnam's continuing power to trouble Americans twenty years after the last U. S. combat soldier left Vietnam.

Two recent episodes demonstrate that the spectre of Vietnam continues to haunt American memories and suggest that many Americans have still not come to terms with those troublesome and ambiguous events that occurred long ago in Southeast Asia. In the summer of 1995, former Secretary of Defense, Robert S. McNamara, the principal architect of the American war in Vietnam, brought out a book, *In Retrospect: The Tragedy and Lessons of Vietnam*. In this book McNamara frankly acknowledged that the U. S. Vietnam War policy was "terribly, terribly wrong." The reaction to McNamara's classic *mea culpa* was quite remarkable. His book was extensively reviewed and discussed, and in every instance McNamara was severely taken to task. It did not appear to matter whether the reviewer was a liberal or conservative, former hawk or dove, veteran or former antiwar activist; their responses were universally negative, often intensely so. McNamara's confessions and apology, which he intended to aid the healing process succeeded only in reviving bitter memories and knocking the scabs off of partially healed wounds. McNamara's chief sin was to remind Americans of a bad time in their lives and to remind them that he was the culprit who bore primary responsibility for those bad times.

In the fall of 1995, the Clinton administration managed to broker a cease-fire in the brutal ethnically-driven civil wars in Bosnia-Herzegovina that had claimed 100,000 lives and generated over a million refugees since 1993. A majority of Congressional members and a large majority of the American people opposed the Clinton administration's decision made in December 1995 to send 20,000 U. S. combat soldiers as part of a 60,000-person NATO contingent assigned to keep the peace in Bosnia-Herzegovina and to try to regenerate a national rebirth in that tortured land. Opponents of the U. S. military intervention repeatedly raised the fear of another Vietnam-like quagmire in which U. S. soldiers get bogged down in an unpopular war that they could neither win nor end.

In our time, Vietnam remains a metaphor haunting the American imagination. It serves as a cautionary tale of the catastrophe that awaits a nation, however rich and powerful, that ever again allows its crusading idealism to override its realistic sense of limits.

It is also important that we understand that the United States was involved not only in a major war in Vietnam, but we also got into wars in Cambodia and Laos. The Vietnam War was, in reality, the Indochina War, or more precisely, the Second Indochina War, following the French effort to reimpose colonialism in Indochina, 1946–1954. The wars in Cambodia and Laos were an integral part of the American entanglement in SE Asia, and they also influenced our involvement in Vietnam, the dominant nation in what was formerly the French possession of Indochina. Because the U. S. venture is best understood as an Indochinese intervention, I have expanded my coverage of events in Cambodia and Laos. Readers of the Third Edition will acquire a more realistic sense of the size and complexity of the U. S. intervention that involved warfare, at times simultaneous, in three Southeast Asian countries.

I believe the principal strength of this book lies in the fact that I have blended Vietnamese and American political, diplomatic, and military history to show the interplay of two national cultures caught in a violent entanglement that lasted the better part of three decades. Most general histories of American involvement in Vietnam are either conventional diplomatic histories or conventional military histories. I have crafted an original synthesis, a hybrid diplomatic-military history that gives much attention to both dimensions of the struggle. I believe the use of this original format enables me to elucidate more of the complexities of the U. S. Vietnam involvement and to write a comprehensive narrative.

Although I focus on the U. S. side of the conflicts, I also devote considerable attention to Vietnamese history and culture. In addition, I write extensively about North Vietnamese and South Vietnamese political and military activity. The book also includes extensive coverage of U. S. domestic politics and the various antiwar movements for they too are an integral part of the U. S. Vietnam story.

My voice is that of ironic detachment from human folly and tragedy. Folly and tragedy appear to me to be about equally shared by people of all races, nationalities, genders, cultures, politics, and ideologies. I have no need to defend or accuse anyone. I have no prior political stance to defend or repudiate. I belong to no "school" of historiography, and have no vested interest in putting any particular interpretation or spin on the events I describe. My single purpose in writing this book, and twice revising it, is to help you acquire as much historical understanding as you can of what we mean when we say "The American Involvement in Southeast Asia, 1942–1975." *I want to help you learn how to think about Vietnam, not what to think.*

Acknowledgments

Perhaps the greatest satisfactions of scholarship derive from the fact that it is so much a collective enterprise. As an industrious member of that small army of scholars working assiduously to discover, write, and disseminate the history of the American Vietnam intervention, I want to thank all of you who have helped with this revision.

Many scholars have read all or parts of the book at one time or another. They have been both generous in their praise and helpful with their constructive criticisms. To mention a few: Jeffrey Kimball, Miami University, Oxford, Ohio; Paul Conway, Oneonta College; Jack Colldeweih, Fairleigh Dickinson University; Stephen Ambrose, formerly at New Orleans University; Robin Winks, Yale University; George Mct. Kahin, Cornell University; Michael Schudson, University of California, San Diego; Daniel Hallin, University of California, San Diego; Diane Shaver Clemens, University of California, Berkeley; David Hollinger, University of California, Berkeley; Douglas Pike, the Indochina Archive, University of California, Berkeley; Ronald Walters, Johns Hopkins University; Lawrence Lichty, Northwestern University; and Larry Berman, University of California, Davis. To you and to all the others who remain unmentioned, I say thanks—for your expert advise and help.

Thanks also to the three reviewers of the Third Edition: Peter Kip Frost, Williams College; John M. Simpson, Pierce College; and Mark W. McLeod, the Univerity of Delaware. It is a far better book as a result of their efforts and I am immensely grateful for their help.

And my last and best thanks to the lovely Linda, who failing to read the fine print among the marriage vows, has nevertheless adapted graciously to life with an obsessive scribbler. Please remember, dear heart: They also serve who only sit in front of the great white bull (or is it a whale?) of a word processor and type, type, type.

George Donelson Moss

The Fall of Saigon:
The End As Prelude

As April 1975 drew to a close, South Vietnam faced extinction: 150,000 battle-hardened Viet Cong and North Vietnamese troops surrounded Saigon, posed to launch an all-out assault on the defenseless capital. Since January, when NVA forces launched what turned out to be the final offensives of the long war, Communist troops had quickly swept through collapsing South Vietnamese defenses. Now they had positioned themselves for the kill.

The North Vietnamese forces had been aided substantially on March 11 when South Vietnamese President Nguyen Van Thieu decided to surrender the strategic central highlands and marshal his remaining forces for a last-ditch defense of Saigon and the Mekong River Delta regions. In the aftermath of Thieu's surrender of the northern half of his country, a disorderly retreat from the highlands turned into panicky flight. Leaderless soldiers, joined by family members and thousands of other frightened civilians, fled the highlands for the coastal city of Tuy Hoa. Many died during the two-week trek that became known as the Convoy of Tears. Tuy Hoa proved to be only a temporary haven for the refugees before it too surrendered to the rapidly advancing foe.

As North Vietnamese forces applied increasing military pressure on the beleaguered South Vietnamese defenders during the spring of 1975, President Thieu urgently requested increased American aid for his imperiled nation. President Gerald R. Ford asked Congress to appropriate an additional $722 million of emergency military aid for South Vietnam. But Congressional leaders, knowing that there was almost no public support for the aid bill and convinced that the United States would only be spending more money on a losing cause, refused Ford's request.

Thieu, who had counted desperately on American aid to enable South Vietnam to survive the fierce Communist assault, was furious at the U. S. government's betrayal of its commitments. The United States had abandoned South Vietnam in its critical hour of need. Thieu, knowing that his armed forces could never fight effectively without U. S. support and despairing of his country's fate, ceased to lead. Discredited, he resigned on April 21. Immobilized by pessimism and indecision at the top, the Saigon government was paralyzed. Its demoralized armies could not stop the Communist forces. Its equally demoralized citizenry fearfully awaited the end that they knew must come.

The sudden collapse of South Vietnam's defenses caught American embassy officials in Saigon by complete surprise. Contingent planning for evacuations had been inadequate. U.S. Ambassador Graham Martin, a fervent supporter of the South Vietnamese cause, was convinced that there would be an eleventh-hour decision by Washington to intervene and save South Vietnam, thus he delayed ordering evacuation procedures to begin until the third week of April.

In addition to evacuating remaining U. S. military and civilian personnel and their dependents, embassy officials removed many third-country personnel and thousands of South Vietnamese citizens, many of whom had formerly worked for American military or civilian agencies and now feared for their lives. But for every South Vietnamese who had a coveted American connection or who could afford to purchase the requisite credentials, there were many others who desperately wanted to leave but could find no way out.

On April 29, President Ford ordered Ambassador Martin to evacuate all remaining Americans. Helicopters from a U. S. fleet standing by about forty miles offshore made the final evacuations, sometimes under fire from North Vietnamese rockets and artillery. By now, order had completely collapsed in Saigon. Crazed mobs roamed the streets. Looters were everywhere, ransacking homes and businesses. During the evening, a large, angry crowd surrounded the U. S. embassy compound. Some were there hoping to find a way out; others came to jeer at the departing Americans. United States Marine security guards used tear gas and rifle butts to prevent hysterical people from climbing over the compound walls. Throughout the night, evacuees made their way to a heliport in the embassy parking lot and their ride to safety. Ambassador Martin wearily boarded one of the last helicopters to leave a rooftop heliport. By the early morning of April 30, all Americans and many of the eligible Vietnamese had safely departed South Vietnam. A few hours after the last Americans and their Vietnamese clients had departed, Communist tanks advanced into the heart of Saigon.

Just before noon, a column of North Vietnamese tanks rumbled up Thong Nhut Boulevard and rolled to a halt in front of Independence Palace, forming a semicircle in front of the capitol. Communist troops quickly moved inside the building and arrested the Republic of South Vietnam officials they found there. A terse announcement over radio Saigon proclaimed the triumph of the revolution. The bitter struggle for control of South Vietnam's political destiny, which had consumed the energies of a generation, had ended at last.

1

Vietnam:
A Place and A People

We must weaken [the enemy] by drawing him into protracted campaigns. When the enemy is away from home for a long time and produces no victories and families learn of their dead, then the enemy population becomes dissatisfied and considers it a Mandate from Heaven that their armies be recalled. Time is always in our favor. Our climate, mountains, and jungles discourage the enemy; but for us they offer sanctuary and a place from which to attack.

Tran Hung Dao, 1284

THE LAND

The Vietnamese say that their country resembles two baskets borne on the ends of a peasant's bamboo carrying pole. The baskets constitute two of the world's most densely populated rice-growing regions: to the north, the Red River Delta, and to the south, the Mekong River Delta. The pole represents the narrow and curving central part of the country composed of jungle-covered mountains and a fertile coastal strip. Vietnam's geographic area of 127,000 square miles makes it about the size of the state of New Mexico. When separated from northern Vietnam from 1954 to 1975, South Vietnam formed an elongated and sinuous country with a coastline approximately as long as California's.

Most of Vietnam's 75,000,000 (1997 est.) people cluster in the two alluvial deltas formed by the Red and Mekong Rivers and in small coastal enclaves lying between them. The people inhabiting these regions comprise the 85 percent of the country's inhabitants who are ethnically Vietnamese. The sparsely populated mountainous regions north and west of the Red River Delta and those of central Vietnam are home to a melange of ethnic minorities, representing about 15 percent of the country's people. They constitute the people the French called "Montagnards," or "mountain people," who inhabit the mountainous terrain that constitutes three-quarters of the country's landmass. In addition to the Montagnards, about 800,000 Cambodians reside in the Ca Mau peninsula region and one million ethnic Chinese live in Vietnam. In southern Vietnam, about 80 percent of the people live on one-fourth of the land; over 40 percent of the terrain is uninhabited. These unpopulated regions of South Vietnam, covered with jungle, elephant grass, and swamps, provided sanctuaries for the Vietcong guerrillas and avenues for invading North Vietnamese forces.

Vietnam lies entirely within the tropical zone. Its northernmost point is the same latitude as Key West, Florida; its southernmost extremity is the same latitude as the Panama Canal. Its climate is determined by monsoon cycles. From November to April, the winter monsoon, coming off the cold, dry steppes of Central Asia, dominates. During these months, it does not rain much in Vietnam, and the climate is moderate throughout the northern half of the country. Between May and October, the summer monsoon blows in from the southwest, coming off the Indian Ocean and bringing with it high winds, heavy rains, and stifling heat and humidity. Vietnam's average annual rainfall is about six feet. The effects of the monsoons vary with the terrain. The Red River Delta enjoys a mild winter, and summertime temperatures rarely exceed 100 degrees. It is hot year-round in the Mekong River Delta. During the winter monsoon, it never rains in the south, but the summer monsoon brings torrential downpours. Some years it rains much more than the normal six feet, causing floods. Other years, far less than normal rainfall occurs, bringing droughts. Cycles of floods, drought, and famine have afflicted the Vietnamese people throughout their long history.

French troops, and later Americans fighting in Vietnam, encountered serious obstacles posed by the summer monsoon. The heat, humidity, rain, and mud exhausted and discouraged the young soldiers carrying sixty-pound packs and struggling through elephant grass, jungle vines, and up mountainous terrain. The French and the Americans also discovered that they could not operate some of their sophisticated military equipment during the summer monsoon season. Highly mobile guerrilla forces often took advantage of the weather conditions to outmaneuver their Western enemies. Summer monsoons also meant special hazards for aviators. Pounding rains, dense ground fog, and treacherous winds caused many fatal aircraft accidents. Weather also determined the cycle of fighting for both the French and American forces. The heaviest fighting in southern Vietnam occurred during the dry season, from February to June, with combat intensity falling off from October to January.

THE FORGE OF HISTORY

The origins of the Vietnamese people are shrouded in the misty realms of prehistory. Thousands of years ago, people from China to the north, Thailand to the west, and Indonesia to the south settled in the Red River Valley. Over the centuries, they intermingled. From their ethnological and biological fusion emerged an ethnically and a racially distinct population, the Viets. A Viet culture based on rice cultivation and feudal principles of social organization was well-established by the second century B.C.E., when the Viets came into contact with their powerful neighbors to the north, the Chinese. The Chinese were destined to play a crucial role in shaping the evolving culture and national identity of the Vietnamese people over the ensuing centuries.[1]

Vietnamese history began in 208 B.C.E. On that date, recorded in Chinese annals, a Chinese war lord, Trieu Da, declared himself ruler of a large area encompassing southern China and Vietnam, as far south as present-day Danang. This new addition was incorporated into the Chinese empire as the province of Giao Chi. The informal name for this region was "Nam Viet," meaning "the land of the southern Viets." Trieu Da ruled his Vietnamese domains indirectly, content to leave Viet feudal lords in charge of affairs. In 111 B.C.E., the great Han emperor, Wu-ti, conquered Nam Viet. It became a province within the Chinese empire, and Chinese officials took over its governance. Wu-ti's conquest began an era of Chinese colonial domination of Vietnam that would last a millennium.[2] The lengthy period of Chinese domination critically influenced Vietnamese culture and the formation of a distinctive national identity.

For the next thousand years, the northern half of present-day Vietnam was controlled by the Chinese. During this long period of colonial rule, the Vietnamese adopted many features of Chinese culture. They incorporated much Chinese technology. The elite Vietnamese classes embraced Confucian social and political values. Chinese became the official language of Vietnam and all writing was done in Chinese characters. The Vietnamese also adopted the Chinese mandarinate, a hierarchical administrative system based on mastery of Chinese literary and philosophic works. To become a Mandarin, candidates had to devote years of study to the Chinese classics, then pass a series of rigorous examinations. Most mandarins came from elite backgrounds, because only the wealthy could afford to allow their sons the years of study and training required to pass the demanding tests. The mandarins incorporated many Chinese institutions into their evolving administrative system, including a centralized tax system and a judicial hierarchy.

Although the Vietnamese admired many features of Chinese culture and benefited in many ways from their long, close association with the magnificent Chinese civilization, they fiercely resented Chinese political domination and economic exploitation. They also resented Chinese efforts to Sinicize them and steadfastly refused to embrace a Chinese identity. In fact, Chinese efforts at forced Sinicization of the Vietnamese provoked the first of their many rebellions against Chinese rule. A rising, long-celebrated in Vietnamese history and led by two noblewomen, Trung Trac and her sister, Trung Nhi occurred in C.E. 39. The Trung sisters led an army that overwhelmed the Chinese garrisons stationed on Vietnamese soil and promptly proclaimed themselves queens of an independent Viet kingdom. Their rule was short-lived, however, for the emperor sent a strong army that restored Chinese rule in C.E. 42.[3]

Over the subsequent centuries of Chinese overlordship, the Vietnamese upper classes embraced much of the Chinese culture based on Confucian principles. But the vast majority of Vietnamese, the 90 percent of the population comprising the peasantry, remained relatively unaffected by this process of Sinicization. They retained many of their traditional customs, a testament to the strength of their indigenous culture nurtured during their long pre-Chinese ethnic past as inhabitants of the Red River Valley, the cradle of Vietnamese civilization.

There was one important Chinese cultural import enthusiastically embraced by the Vietnamese peasantry—the Buddhist religion. Originally founded by an Indian prince in the sixth century B.C.E., Buddhism reached the Vietnamese during the second century C.E. when Chinese Buddhist monks sought political asylum in the land of the Viets. Within a few centuries, Buddhism, particularly its Mahayana sect, had become a pervasive influence in the religious and political life of the Vietnamese peasants. Mahayana Buddhism was a form of religion that stressed moral redemption through salvation and community spirit. Buddhist monks, living among the villagers, played prominent roles in community life.

Even though the Vietnamese elite were thoroughly Sinicized, they retained a strong sense of their Vietnamese identity and remained restive under Chinese rule. Between the sixth and tenth centuries, these Sino-Vietnamese notables led numerous rebellions against their Chinese masters. The Chinese suppressed them all. During most of this era of Chinese dominance, the empire was ruled by a mighty dynasty, the T'angs.

After the T'ang dynasty fell in 907, a series of uprisings in Vietnam eventually ended Chinese dominion. The crucial battle occurred in 939. During that year, a Vietnamese army, led by Ngo Quyen, confronted a far larger Chinese invasion force, led by the heir to the Chinese throne, along a stretch of the Bach Dang River, a tidal waterway in the vicinity of present-day Haiphong. Ngo, knowing his troops were overmatched, resorted to a clever stratagem to defeat the more powerful Chinese. He had his troops drive pilings into the riverbed so at high tide the stakes would lie just below the water's surface, hidden from sight. Ngo then engaged the Chinese in battle and ordered his boats to feign retreat. The Chinese, sensing victory, pressed after Ngo's retreating ships, passing over the undetected pilings. He waited until the tide began to ebb. Timing the maneuver perfectly, Ngo ordered his ships to wheel about, and they drove the Chinese boats against the now-exposed pilings. With their ships impaled, the immobilized Chinese troops were slaughtered by Ngo's warriors. The imperial heir was taken prisoner and later beheaded.[4] The Battle of Bach Dang, which destroyed Chinese colonialism in Vietnam, is commemorated by all Vietnamese as the beginning of Vietnamese national independence.

From the gaining of their independence in 939, the Vietnamese endured a precarious national existence. They were threatened externally by powerful foes, particularly China, the colossus of the North. Internally, Vietnam was frequently ruled by inept leaders, riven by civil wars, and suffered from a fragmentation of power. But the

Vietnamese managed to maintain their independence for over 900 years. They twice fought off Chinese invading armies in the thirteenth century and thereafter stayed free of foreign rule, except for a brief period during the fifteenth century when the Chinese, taking advantage of Vietnamese disunity, reestablished a colonial regime of brief duration.

For centuries, it remained a constant of Vietnamese statecraft to be aware of the colossus to the north, to guard against Chinese intrusions upon their sovereign independence.[5] In modern times, this theme of Vietnamese independence from foreign conquerors has reasserted itself following the defeat of the French in 1954 and again following the withdrawal of the Americans in 1973. In Hanoi's Historical Museum today, a large room is devoted to celebrating the struggles of the Vietnamese people against Chinese invaders.[6]

Until the fifteenth century, Vietnamese expansion south of the Sixteenth Parallel was blocked by the kingdom of the Chams, a people of probable Indonesian origin. The Vietnamese eventually destroyed the Champa kingdom, and under the leadership of Emperor Le Loi, whose reign began in 1427, they began a great march southward. Over the next 250 years, the Vietnamese slowly trekked south. Advancing colonies of Vietnamese peasant-warriors reached the Mekong delta region in the early seventeenth century, about the same time British colonists were settling the Atlantic seaboard of what would become the United States. As the Vietnamese consolidated their geographic gains in the Mekong delta, they either slaughtered or pushed the indigenous population they encountered, the Khmer, who were ethnic Cambodians, up the river into present-day Cambodia. Vietnamese peasants made formidable warriors, as the hard life of rice farming prepared them for the physical rigors of military combat and the group discipline of communal rice farming prepared them for the discipline and esprit de corps of battle. Peasant warriors were tenacious and resourceful in combat, and they were strongly motivated by the high value that traditional Vietnamese culture placed on bravery and victory in war.

History, geography, and economics combined to ensure that the two major regions of Vietnam evolved differently. Life was typically easier and slower-paced in southern Vietnam than in the North. The Mekong River flowed gently and predictably. It flooded in July and again in September, providing rich alluvial soil for abundant rice crops. Ample amounts of arable land were available for enterprising farmers, many of whom became large landholders and established prosperous families. The relative recency of settlement in southern Vietnam created a more rural society, with more individualistic and materialistic personality types than could be found in the older, poorer, and more densely populated region of northern Vietnam. Crop yields were lower in Tonkin and rice had to be imported from the South, the breadbasket of Vietnam. The land was generally less fertile in northern Vietnam and landholdings tended to be smaller. Life was generally harder in the North for most families. There was also a more sophisticated level of political and economic organization and a much stronger sense of community among the inhabitants of Tonkin. Northerners tended to be more aggressive, sophisticated, and urbane than their country cousins to the south.

Figure 1.1   Tran Hung Dao, a great Vietnamese military hero. Dao defeated an invading Mongol Army in 1284 to preserve Vietnamese national independence. Dao's guerilla warfare strategies were used by Vo Nguyen Giap, a history professor turned military commander, to defeat both the French and American invaders. *Source:* Maurice Durand Collection, L'Ecole Française d'Extrème-Orient

Political disunity hampered Vietnamese expansionism during the seventeenth and eighteenth centuries. During this period, Vietnam was ruled by separate, hostile governments, one located in the traditional capital of Hanoi, the other in a new city lying 400 miles to its south, Hue. Their armies clashed repeatedly, but neither was able to prevail over the other. With much of its energy absorbed in fighting the Hanoi regime, the Hue government was still developing the relatively underpopulated southern frontier region of the Mekong delta in the late eighteenth century. From 1771 until 1802, peasant rebellions led by three brothers named Tay-son convulsed Vietnam. Taking advantage of the internal disarray, Chinese armies once again invaded the land of the Viets. The Tay-sons rallied the Vietnamese people to drive the invaders out of their country in 1789. But the Tay-sons, their resources depleted by their battles against the Chinese, were overthrown as the eighteenth century ended.

Nguyen Anh emerged in 1802 as the ruler of all Vietnamese. For the first time in its history, a single ruler governed the region extending from the Chinese border in the north to the Gulf of Siam in the south, the boundaries of the modern Vietnamese state. Nguyen Anh proclaimed himself emperor, made Hue his imperial capital, and called his politically unified nation Vietnam.[7] He took the name Gia Long, founding the last Vietnamese imperial dynasty, the Nguyen. Nguyen emperors were reduced to ruling in name only after 1883 because of the French conquest of Vietnam. Vietnam's last dynasty came to its end in 1955, when Bao Dai was defeated in a rigged election by Ngo Dinh Diem for the presidency of South Vietnam.

The advent of the Nguyen dynasty ushered in an era of political stability and national unity that lasted until the French colonial conquest. It also signaled the attainment of a unique Vietnamese identity. Centuries-long struggles to resist foreign conquerors and internal divisions "had created in Vietnam a distinctly 'national' ethnic spirit, more self-conscious, and more passionate than that found virtually anywhere in Southeast Asia."[8]

By the beginning of the nineteenth century, Vietnam had achieved nationhood. Vietnam's turbulent history since 939, characterized by the use of military force to fend off foreign aggression, overcome internal factionalism, and extend the boundaries of the nation, ensured that a warrior tradition formed an integral part of the Vietnamese national identity. Vietnamese history celebrated military heroes and glorified martial qualities. Vietnamese art frequently depicted soldiers riding horses or elephants into battle. Eternal war was the primal theme of Vietnamese history; but there was the corollary theme as well—the myth of indomitability. It became a staple of Vietnamese belief that they themselves were unconquerable, if they were prudent. If they were patient, if they used the natural advantages provided by geography and climate, and if they avoided a direct confrontation with more powerful foes, they could wear their invading enemies down. When the time was ripe and the enemy was confused and demoralized, when the enemy's fighting spirit was sapped and when the enemy was vulnerable, strike! Mount an offensive and either destroy or drive out the hated foe!

Famous Vietnamese generals used protracted warfare strategy successfully against the Mongols and Chinese invaders over the centuries. Tran Hung Dao used it to destroy the Mongols during the 1280s and wrote a manual on the art of protracted warfare that became a classic of Vietnamese military science. Le Loi used Dao's strategy to beat the Chinese during the early fourteenth century. General Nguyen Hue, the warrior most admired by North Vietnamese Generals Vo Nguyen Giap and Van Tien Dung, used the strategy to drive the last Chinese invasion out of Vietnam in 1789. To gain his victory, Hue violated the sanctity of Tet, the lunar New Year holiday, observed by both sides. He surprised a much larger Chinese army encamped on the outskirts of Hanoi. He attacked at midnight, when the Chinese soldiers were sleeping off the effects of the food and wine consumed in day-long celebrations, and destroyed their army. Nguyen Hue's great triumph is the most celebrated military victory in Vietnam's long history. The strategy of protracted warfare worked well over the centuries against the Chinese. It would work against the French from 1946 to 1954, and it would work against the Americans from 1965 to 1973.

The reign of Gia Long lasted until 1820. During his years of power he reestablished a traditionalist Vietnamese state administered by the Confucian mandarinate that had prevailed for centuries. According to Confucian theory and practice, Gia Long was an absolute monarch whose powers derived from a mandate of heaven. He was the supreme lawmaker, head of all civil and military institutions, and chief justice. The mandarins derived their authority solely from him. The despotism of the regime was modified in two ways. The emperor respected the authority of the head of a family, the most important Vietnamese social institution. Traditionally, submission to the head of one's family was the most important moral obligation facing every Vietnamese. Second, Gia Long partially observed the ancient Vietnamese proverb, "The law of the emperor ends at the village gate." He and his mandarins permitted a certain amount of village self-government. Local officials enforced village laws and customs, dealt with local problems, and collected taxes. Loyalty to one's village was a deeply rooted sentiment and a profound civic obligation for all Vietnamese.[9]

The Vietnamese economy under Gia Long and his successors remained what it had been for ages—a static agrarian system based on the cultivation of rice. The great mass of the Vietnamese people remained peasants, tending their own fields or working as tenants and residing in villages and hamlets concentrated in the great rice-growing regions of the Red River and Mekong River Deltas. True to their Confucian principles, Gia Long and his mandarins discouraged all new economic developments and all modernizing trends. There was little industry, little commerce, and almost no foreign trade. No middle class of manufacturers and tradesmen emerged in nineteenth-century Vietnam. Modern science and technology were forbidden. Few Vietnamese traveled beyond the confines of their native land, or studied abroad.

Gia Long was succeeded in 1820 by his son Ming Mang, who embraced a total Confucian orthodoxy in all matters of governance. He believed Vietnam's national interest was best served by maintaining traditional institutions and ways of life based on the ancient Confucian way. He tried to isolate his country from all Western influences. He resisted all European efforts to open trade and tried to suppress the activities of French Catholic missionaries who had been active in Vietnam since the seventeenth century. Because he and his mandarin advisers rejected all Western contacts—all efforts at modernization—Vietnamese officials by the mid-nineteenth century found themselves virtually powerless to defend themselves against aggressive European imperialists. When the French came to conquer them in the 1860s, about all the Nguyens could muster to resist them was a deep reservoir of nationalist feeling that had been nurtured through centuries of Vietnamese struggles to retain their independence from foreign conquerors. But fierce patriotism and national pride proved to be no match against modern French organizational skills and their military technology.

THE FRENCH COLONIAL ERA

The French came to Vietnam in two major waves, first during the seventeenth century and again in the nineteenth. A Jesuit priest, Alexandre de Rhodes, first arrived in Hanoi in 1627. While there, he not only converted thousands of Vietnamese to Roman Catholicism but also created a Latin alphabet for the Vietnamese language. The Vietnamese twice expelled de Rhodes—in 1630 and again in 1645, but he succeeded in planting the seeds of empire in Vietnamese soil.

The period of Vietnamese political unity achieved under the Nguyens ended with the French conquest of the 1860s. Fearing the political meddling of French missionaries working in his country, Ming Mang and his successors, Thieu Tri and Tu Duc, took strong measures to suppress them. These actions gave French officials a pretext to intervene in Vietnam. French officials, in the service of Emperor Napoleon III, had additional motives for intervention in Southeast Asia. Napoleon III, activated by expansive dreams of imperial glory, wanted to acquire a colony in the region the French called "Indochina" to obtain markets for French manufactures, provide raw materials for their factories, and expand their trade within their sphere of influence in China, which was adjacent to Vietnam. The French also sought a foothold in Southeast Asia to compete with the British, who had conquered a vast colonial empire in the region stretching from India to the eastern half of New Guinea.[10]

Napoleon III sent a French naval expedition, under Admiral Rigault de Genouilly, to establish a French military base at Tourane (Danang) in 1858. De Genouilly's forces occupied the port city but could not reach the Vietnamese leaders residing in the imperial capitol at Hue, seventy-five miles to the north. Stalled at Turin, the French were drenched by monsoon rains and stricken by disease. Realizing his efforts to establish a French base at Turin were failing, de Genouilly sailed south. His troops occupied Saigon in early 1859. The Vietnamese were able to drive the French out of Saigon, but with reinforcements they returned to stay in 1861, enabling the French to add three provinces to their empire in southern Vietnam.

Vietnamese officials tried to drive the French out of their country, but obsolete military technologies fatally handicapped Vietnamese efforts to resist French imperialism. Military deficiencies, not a lack of fighting spirit, forced the imperial court at Hue to sign a treaty giving Saigon and the three southernmost provinces of Vietnam to the French in 1862. Even as they lost their lands, the proud Vietnamese told their French conquerors that while "disorder will be long . . . our cause will triumph in the end."[11] By 1867, growing military strength enabled France to conquer all of southern Vietnam, which they organized politically as a colony called Cochin China.[12] The French required another sixteen years of political maneuvering and military action to complete the conquest of all of Vietnam. The imperial court at Hue was forced to sign a treaty with their conquerors in 1883 that extended French authority over the entire country. Twenty-five years after sending a naval expedition to Tourane, the French acquired control of all of Vietnam. The Vietnamese did not submit to French imperialism easily; it was not until the end of the nineteenth century that the French finally crushed all opposition and secured their hold on Vietnam.[13]

The French, during the years they were conquering Vietnam, also imposed protectorates over neighboring Cambodia (1863) and Laos (1893). All of these acquisitions were formally organized into the French Indochinese Union. After 1893, French Indochina constituted five administrative departments: Cochin China, a colony in southern Vietnam, and the four protectorates of Cambodia, Laos, Annam (central Vietnam), and Tonkin (northern Vietnam). The French ruled their colony directly, initially using military personnel as administrators. In Annam and Tonkin, the French initially ruled through the Nguyen administrative apparatus, which they controlled. But as the years passed, French control over all of its Vietnamese departments became more centralized and more pervasive. The imperial court at Hue and its mandarins were reduced in time to largely ceremonial functions. Hanoi served as the capital of the entire Union, the French governor-general residing in that city and being directly responsible to the Ministry of Colonies in Paris. Residents-Superiors governed each of the five departments. Most French nationals who emigrated to Vietnam settled in Cochin China. Saigon, its capital and commercial center, became known as the "Paris of the Orient." French economic and financial interests were concentrated in southern Vietnam. There they invested most of their capital and their administrative apparatus penetrated most deeply, down to the district and even village levels. Cochin China was the most profitable, therefore the most important, department of the French Southeast Asian empire.

The French conquest of Indochina was part of the larger pattern of European imperialism that imposed Western institutions and values upon much of Africa and Asia during the latter decades of the nineteenth century. Western penetration usually began with missionaries and traders, gradually expanding to include military conquest, political control, and economic exploitation. Europeans rationalized these brutal imperialistic enterprises as benign undertakings—the spreading of "civilization" to "backward" or "savage" peoples.

Figure 1.2 Indochina.

As was typical of European imperialists of this era, the French ruled solely by force, or the imminent threat of force, in Indochina. The Vietnamese never accepted French control as legitimate nor ceased resisting it whenever they could. Although French officials paid lip service to the goals of modernizing and "civilizing" the Vietnamese (what they called their *mission civilisatrice*), in practice, French colonialism remained brutally exploitative. The French viewed Vietnam, its land, natural resources, and people, as existing for the benefit of France, specifically for the enrichment of French economic interests with investments in that country. They expected Vietnam to generate valuable raw materials to feed into the French economy and furnish a tariff-protected market for French manufactures. Many of the French regarded the Vietnamese as an inferior, childlike race, ideally suited for a life of hard work for low wages.

The French invested mainly in Vietnamese rice, rubber, and coal, which became the three leading Indochinese export commodities. The rich Mekong River Delta become one of the world's leading rice-exporting regions. Rice growing in this region was dominated by a class of large landowners, many of them French, joined by a small class of Vietnamese landlords who cooperated with their colonial masters and enriched themselves in the process. During the 1920s and 1930s, rubber became the second most important Vietnamese export. Hundreds of rubber plantations, concentrated in southern Vietnam and all owned by the French, made Vietnam one of the world's leading sources of raw rubber. Vietnamese coal production was centered in Tonkin, where two large French-owned mining companies accounted for more than 92 percent of the country's total coal output.[14]

Under French colonialism, the Vietnamese economy remained what it had always been, predominantly agricultural. The peasantry comprised about 90 percent of the national population, a vast labor force that paid taxes and bought cheap French imports if they could afford them. Industrial development of Vietnam was discouraged, as it was contrary to French neomercantilist policies. However, some internal improvements were constructed during the first three decades of the twentieth century—railroads, highways, bridges, and harbors—and some local light industries evolved. But the French wanted short-run profits, having no interest in the long-run development of the Vietnamese economy.[15]

As a result of French colonial rule, aggravated by the worldwide depression of the 1930s, living standards were lower for most of the Vietnamese people on the eve of World War II than they had been a century earlier under the Nguyens. The concentration of land owning under the French brought the pauperization of millions of Vietnamese peasantry who lost ancestral lands formerly in their possession.[16] These landless families dropped into the ranks of tenants and day laborers, entrapped in a vicious round of hard labor, low income, debt, usurious interest rates, and high taxes.

Before the arrival of the French, the Vietnamese prized a highly developed educational system. Literacy was widespread, and learning, according to the Confucian way, was revered. The French closed the Vietnamese schools, replacing them with schools modeled after the French system of education. The Chinese classics were abolished, and the Chinese ideographic language was replaced with the Romanized *quoc ngu.*[17] After 1878, the French declared that only *quoc ngu* and French could serve as the official languages. But most Vietnamese children were excluded from the new schools. On the eve of World War II, only about 15 percent of Vietnamese school-age children were attending schools of any kind. In 1939, Vietnam had only fourteen secondary schools and one university serving a population of 20 million people. "About 80 percent of the population was illiterate after 60 years of French rule, in contrast to precolonial Vietnam where 80 percent of the people possessed some degree of literacy."[18]

In addition to creating a society made up mainly of landless, illiterate peasants, ruled by a colonial bureaucracy, and a small class of privileged Vietnamese, who joined in the exploitation of their country, French colonialism also disrupted the traditional Vietnamese way of life based on the extended family and the village. French and Vietnamese bureaucrats violated the traditions of village autonomy. Traditional leaders, who neither understood the legal and political systems imposed by the French nor collected enough taxes, were replaced by Vietnamese middlemen. These brokers, who were chosen by French officials, were often without roots or kin in the villages under their control and were an alien force against which there was no recourse nor appeal.

French colonial rule imposed many changes on Vietnam, and most changes brought by the French worked to the grave disadvantage of Vietnamese peasants and workers who comprised the great bulk of the Vietnamese population. The vast profits earned by the French-owned enterprises, the banks, factories, mines and plantations of Vietnam, benefited a relatively small group of investors. Neither the French government nor most French earned a franc from Indochina. Under harsh French governance, the Vietnamese were accorded no political rights. Political parties were proscribed. A combination of neomercantilist economic policies and political repression prevented the rise of a substantial middle class and precluded "the development of a liberal, Western-oriented political movement."[19]

For the majority of Vietnamese families, mass immiseration was the chief consequence of three generations of French colonial rule. The people were enmeshed in a socioeconomic system controlled by French officials and an elite class of Gallicized Vietnamese that allowed almost no opportunity for improvement or escape. The Vietnamese peasantry gradually realized that French colonialism was responsible for their oppression, but they also understood that they had two enemies: the French who ruled them and the privileged Vietnamese elite who exploited them. In time, the struggle to achieve independence after World War II, common throughout Asia and Africa, throughout what would become known during the 1950s as the Third World, became for the Vietnamese a social revolution as well. This intertwining of nationalistic and revolutionary goals made the postwar history of Vietnam unique to Southeast Asia. Only in Vietnam did the struggle for home rule also become a struggle for who should rule at home. Only in Vietnam did the revolutionaries seek to smash French imperialism and dispossess the wealthy Francophilic Asian elite class.

THE RISE OF VIETNAMESE NATIONALISM

Vietnamese resistance to French rule began as the French were establishing their colony of Cochin China in the 1860s and continued, whenever possible, for as long as the French controlled Indochina. The earliest rebellions were led by local mandarins, scholars, and officials from the emperor's court at Hue who detested the European intruders and whose own powers were threatened by the advent of the French. Resistance took the forms of refusals to work, sabotage, and, most commonly, guerrilla warfare. Rebel mandarins appealed to the peasantry, in the name of the emperor and Confucian ideals drawn from Vietnam's precolonial heritage, to join them in efforts to regain their country's independence. A teenage emperor himself, Ham Nghi joined one of these rebellions in Annam in 1885. He was later captured by the French and exiled to Algeria.

For decades, periodic revolts challenged the growing French colonial power. They all failed because of French military superiority and because the Mandarin rebels could offer the people only a return to the imperial past in place of French rule. But for many Vietnamese, the Nguyen dynasty had been discredited. The Court's shortsighted efforts to forestall all progress and isolate Vietnam from Western forces in the first half of the nineteenth century had been responsible for the inability of the Vietnamese to keep the French out. Further, the catastrophe of the loss of political independence was proof to many patriots that the Nguyens had lost the mandate of heaven, the right to rule. In the eyes of many Vietnamese, the Mandarin-led revolts existed on behalf of discredited rulers and ideals.

Other factors contributed to the defeat of the rebellions. No efforts were made to coordinate or unify the various risings. They were local, isolated insurrections—district uprisings—with no chance to inflict permanent defeat on the French or drive them out of Vietnam. The French also were able to call upon some segments of the Vietnamese population for assistance in suppressing the rebellions. Catholic Vietnamese often sided with the French, remembering their persecution under the Nguyens. Various Montagnard tribes, for centuries neglected and despised by the lowland Vietnamese who regarded them as uncivilized, often joined French expeditions against the rebels.[20] The Vietnamese people paid a severe price for these risings; local economies were disrupted, taxes were increased to pay for the police forces required to suppress the insurrections, and thousands of Vietnamese were killed by the French. As the nineteenth century ended, all of the rebels were dead, imprisoned, or exhausted. For a time, social peace settled on the land.

A new generation of Vietnamese nationalists came of age during the first decade of the twentieth century. Their leader was the scholar Phan Boi Chau, who was the recipient of a modern education. Although faithful to the idea of monarchy, Chau embraced Western philosophical rationalism, science, and constitutionalism. Detesting French suzerainty over his countrymen, he called for independence from France and for Vietnam to develop a constitutional monarchy. He hoped to place Prince Coung De, a descendant of Gia Long, on a restored, modernized throne.

An energetic propagandist and organizer, Chau, working with the prince, formed the Association for the Modernization of Vietnam while both were living in Japan. For a time, Chau and the Prince hoped Japanese liberals would support and finance their cause. In 1908, nationalistic followers of Chau, protesting high taxes, staged mass demonstrations in cities throughout Vietnam. The French responded by jailing thousands of demonstrators.[21] In the aftermath of the failure of the protests, and disillusioned by lukewarm Japanese support, Chau moved to China where he became an enthusiastic follower of Chinese revolutionary leader Dr. Sun Yat-sen, who founded the Chinese Republic in 1911.

After World War I, Chau's movement declined. Kidnapped by French agents, he returned to Vietnam and was condemned to death. But the governor-general commuted his sentence to confinement for life at his home in Hue. Phan Boi Chau died in 1940, an obscure figure from Vietnam's turbulent political past. Chau's movement had always lacked mass support, and further suffered from a lack of discipline and the absence of a coherent program; however, Chau had been the first Vietnamese national leader to espouse modern political ideas and to call for the use of more sophisticated resistance tactics against French colonialism than the hopeless rebellions led by Mandarin reactionaries.

French repression hindered the political activities of Vietnamese nationalists. Even moderates who tried to work for independence through legal political activity often found themselves in jail, under house arrest, or forced into exile to China or Japan. Nationalist organizations were forced to go underground to have any chance of political effectiveness. During the 1920s, the Vietnam Quoc Dan Dang (VNQDD), the Vietnamese Nationalist Party, was the major underground organization. The VNQDD's goals were political independence and the creation of a Vietnamese republic. In early 1930, a garrison of Vietnamese soldiers stationed in northern Tonkin, influenced by VNQDD ideas, rebelled against French rule. They hoped their revolt would create similar uprisings everywhere in Vietnam, starting a revolution. They were disappointed when French forces, moving quickly, suppressed their rebellion before it could generate any momentum. The failed uprising meant the end of the VNQDD as a major nationalistic movement. Afterward, French authorities destroyed the VNQDD organization although some of its leaders were able to escape to exile in China.

Following the destruction of the VNQDD, Marxist organizations took over the revolutionary nationalist cause in Vietnam. In 1930, the Indochinese Communist Party was organized by a professional revolutionary and Vietnamese patriot who called himself Nguyen Ai Quoc (Nguyen the Patriot). The world would later know him as Ho Chi Minh.[22] He was born Nguyen Sinh Cung on May 19, 1890, in Kim Lien, a small village in the Nghe An province in central Vietnam, a site of many rebellions against French colonial rule over the years. Most of Nghe An consists of low coastal plains bordered on the west by the rugged Annamese Mountains. Because of its dense population, poor soil, and bad climate, most inhabitants of Nghe An endured harsh lives. Despite its poverty, or perhaps because of it, Nghe An has produced poets and scholars. In fact, much of the artistic and intellectual talent of Vietnam has come from this hard, poor place.

Ho Chi Minh was the son of a minor mandarin who had been a supporter of Phan Boi Chau, later dismissed from government service because of his nationalistic activities. As a boy, Ho Chi Minh had been inspired by Chau and his vision of a modern Vietnam freed from French imperialism. Since his youth, Ho Chi Minh held a passionate hatred of French imperialism, and he would devote most of his life to the great task of reclaiming Vietnam for the Vietnamese people. Ho Chi Minh attended Quoc Hoc lycee in Hue to prepare for a career in government service, but left the school in 1911 without graduating—he shipped out on a French steamer determined to see the world, and he would not set foot on Vietnamese soil again for almost 30 years. For the next several years, Ho Chi Minh traveled widely and worked at a variety of jobs. He made a voyage to the United States, visiting Boston and New York. He later wrote about the abusive, brutal, and often lethal treatment of blacks by white Americans in the American South during the early twentieth century.[23]

Ending up in France during World War I, Ho Chi Minh quickly immersed himself in the political activities of Vietnamese anticolonial nationalists living in Paris. Within the large Vietnamese expatriate community, he soon became a leader. The French secret police then placed him under surveillance. In 1919, while the victorious Allies were meeting at the Versailles Conference, Ho Chi Minh presented a petition to the Big Four demanding that the principle of self-determination embodied in Woodrow Wilson's Fourteen Points be applied to French Indochina.[24] The leaders of the victorious great powers ignored the demands of this bold but obscure Vietnamese patriot.

At about the same time, Ho Chi Minh also joined the French Socialist Party and was a member of the faction that broke off to form the French Communist Party in 1920. He was drawn to Lenin's ideology, especially his *Thesis on the National and Colonial Questions*. In his seminal work, Lenin argued that there were two enemies to be overthrown: Western capitalist imperialists and their elite Asian collaborators. The revolution must smash both classes. Following his conversion to Marxist-Leninism, Ho Chi Minh was to remain a passionately committed Communist revolutionary leader for the rest of his life. But he also was a bone-deep Vietnamese patriot steeped in Confucian culture, practicing the traditional virtues of wisdom, benevolence, sincerity, righteousness, moderation, and harmony. He would prove to be a charismatic leader who inspired both the impatient radical intellectuals and the peasants who comprised most of the population of his native land.

Ho Chi Minh journeyed to Russia in 1923. He lived and studied in Moscow, becoming a specialist on colonial questions and a professional organizer. He went to China in 1925 as an assistant to the Comintern's adviser to the Koumintang during the years of cooperation between Moscow and the Chinese Nationalists. In Canton, Ho Chi Minh organized Vietnamese political exiles into the Vietnamese Revolutionary Youth Movement, a precursor of the Indochinese Communist party. He also edited a political journal called *Thanh Nien* (Youth) and wrote his only book, *The Road of Revolution*. Ho Chi Minh insisted that a revolution would succeed only when it organized the mass of Vietnamese workers and peasants. In China, he met a brilliant Vietnamese nationalist, Pham Van Dong, whose father had been a high-ranking Mandarin involved in anti-French resistance activities. Thirty years later, Dong would become prime minister of the People's Republic of Vietnam.[25] After the Sino-Soviet split of 1927, Ho Chi Minh returned to Moscow for a time. In 1930, he traveled to Hong Kong, where he organized the Indochinese Communist Party. Underground cells were established in Vietnam, and Haiphong became the center for Communist activities in the country.[26] These young militants had all been indoctrinated with Ho Chi Minh's writings, and they eagerly worked to organize peasant associations and trade unions.

The modern Vietnamese revolution began in 1930 and 1931, when peasant rebellions erupted in several districts of central Vietnam, provoked by hard times and high taxes. The newly formed Indochinese Communist Party moved in to furnish leadership for the peasants in those regions. Communist leaders included Pham Van Dong and a brilliant young high school history teacher, Vo Nguyen Giap. Giap was destined to become a resourceful general who planned the campaigns that would bring the Vietnamese military victories over the French, the Americans, and the South Vietnamese forces. The Communists managed to set up people's "soviets" in two provinces of central Vietnam, Ha Tinh and the troublesome Nghe An, Ho Chi Minh's ancestral home. They moved against large landlords and redistributed land to hard-pressed peasant farmers.[27]

But French forces quickly moved into these regions. Police and legionnaires instituted a reign of terror and crushed the peasant insurrections. Suspected agitators were given summary trials en masse and condemned. Thousands of Vietnamese—peasants, patriots, nationalists, liberals, and Communists—were destroyed.[28] Giap's wife and daughter died in a French prison, and Giap had to go into exile to survive. The fledgling Indochinese Communist Party was badly damaged. French authorities tried Ho Chi Minh *in absentia*, convicted him of treason, and sentenced him to death. A rumor spread that Ho Chi Minh had been killed by the secret police. An estimated 10,000 Vietnamese were killed and another 50,000 were deported. In the 1930s, French prisons and penal colonies in Indochina bulged with thousands of political prisoners. Pham Van Dong spent eight years in one of the worst French penal colonies on Con Son Island. French authorities believed they had eliminated the Vietnamese Communist movement while it was in its infancy.

Despite the savage losses, the Communists survived. The Indochinese Communist Party remained the best-organized, strongest, and most popular of the underground nationalist groups in Vietnam. Its key leaders also survived all French efforts to eliminate them.[29] From 1936 to 1939, pressure on the Communists in Vietnam eased as a Popular Front government in France allowed the parties both in France and Indochina an increased freedom for peaceful political activity. Both the French and Vietnamese Communists, following orders from Moscow, moderated their revolutionary programs and sought alliances with liberals and socialists. Many non-Communist nationalists were attracted to the Communist program, which emphasized democratic reform rather than revolution during the Popular Front years. The Indochinese Communist Party assumed unrivaled leadership of the Vietnamese drive for independence.[30] But the fall of the Popular Front government, followed by the signing of the Nazi-Soviet Pact in August 1939, brought renewed French attacks on the Vietnamese Communists.

WAR COMES TO INDOCHINA

When World War II began in Europe with the German invasion of Poland on September 1, 1939, the Vietnamese Communists opposed the French war effort and resumed their revolutionary activity. Within Indochina, the French were still in firm control. The secret police suppressed the Communists and other radicals, but the events of war would break France's hold on its Southeast Asian empire and bring the liberation of the Vietnamese people from colonialism. The unique fusion of nationalism and Communism in Vietnam also imparted a social revolutionary thrust to the Vietnamese drive for self-determination. The war would also propel the United States into Southeast Asian affairs, inaugurating an entanglement in that region that would persist for thirty years.

In the late spring of 1940, Nazi armor rolled to an easy victory over French armies in a stunningly successful campaign, forcing France's surrender after only six weeks of fighting. Their German conquerors chose to occupy only northern France and turned over the government of the rest of the country to a collaborationist regime in Vichy. The Vichy government retained nominal control of French overseas territories, including Indochina. German victories over France and other European powers, British preoccupation with European threats to its interests, and the fact that the United States had declared its neutrality at the outset of war all created opportunities for Japanese expansionists to take over weakly defended European colonial possessions in Southeast Asia.

The Japanese, who had been waging war against China since 1937, exploited France's weakened defenses. They quickly moved into Indochina after Germany defeated France. Indochina was an important component of the expanding Japanese East Asian empire for several reasons. The Japanese wanted to stop the French from sending supplies to the Chinese via a route that wound through the mountains separating southern China from Tonkin. They also wanted to acquire airfields in Vietnam to use for launching attacks against Chinese targets. Further, Vietnam would serve Japan well as a rich source of raw materials, such as rice and rubber. Vietnam's strategic location also would offer the Japanese a staging area for their expansion into Southeast Asian territories, principally the Dutch East Indies and British Malaya. Finally, Vietnam would be a basing area for Japanese troops, and its harbors would serve as trans-shipment points for the resources the Japanese would be extracting from the southeastern territories whose conquests they were planning.

In August 1940, Japanese troops poured out of China into northern Vietnam. Governor-General Admiral Jean Decoux of Indochina offered little resistance to the Japanese presence. By the end of 1941, the Japanese had acquired a free hand in Vietnam. Admiral Decoux granted them permission to station troops anywhere in the country and to use all of the French naval and air bases. He also signed agreements guaranteeing that Japan would receive all Vietnam's exports. In return, the Japanese acknowledged French sovereignty over Indochina and permitted the French to maintain their administrative apparatus. Technically, the Japanese did not occupy Vietnam; the two countries agreed to joint control, a *de facto* dual sovereignty. Militarily and economically, the arrangement favored the Japanese. The French were saddled with the costs of administering territories whose riches were now going to Japan.[31]

The coming of the Japanese gave some Vietnamese nationalist groups unprecedented opportunities to achieve a greater role in political affairs, because now both the French and the Japanese had to compete for the allegiance of the people. French administrators granted the Vietnamese additional political freedoms, upgraded the status of Vietnamese officials, and sought to organize young people into various groupings.[32] Some Vietnamese nationalists sought to work with the Japanese in the hopes of achieving independence from the French, including adherents of two religious sects whose members mostly resided in southern Vietnam, the Cao Dai and the Hoa Hao. The Japanese encouraged these religious groups, playing on their Pan-Asian nationalistic and anti-French sentiments, but they had no intention of granting the Vietnamese their independence.[33] In time, Vietnamese enthusiasm for Japanese assistance in seeking liberation from the Vichy French cooled.

The new French-Japanese arrangement in Vietnam did not favor the Vietnamese Communists or other radical nationalistic groups. They suffered severe repression and were forced to seek sanctuary in southern China to survive. Here, they benefited from the truce in China arranged between the Nationalists and the Maoists, who agreed to curtail their civil war to fight the Japanese invaders of their homeland. The Vietnamese Communists operated freely in southern China during the war. The Chinese government also worked with Vietnamese nationalists, both Communist and non-Communist, to hinder the Japanese war effort being mounted against China from Vietnam. The Chinese tried to unite all Vietnamese nationalists living in China within a front organization dedicated to carrying on sabotage and espionage activities against the Japanese in Vietnam.[34] But only the Vietnamese Communists proved capable of carrying out these dangerous tasks, and the Chinese turned to them.

Ho Chi Minh, still known as Nguyen Ai Quoc to his followers, the leader of the Communist remnants, was residing in southern China in 1941. He understood that the French defeat in the European war and its forced acceptance of the Japanese presence in Vietnam offered his cause a great opportunity if he could exploit it. Japanese dominance in Southeast Asia had destroyed whatever lingering notions of white superiority had survived in the region. Ho Chi Minh knew that these revelations of French weakness had encouraged many Vietnamese, including businessmen, landowners, and urban workers, to join the peasants supporting independence. He also knew these groups needed leadership; they had to be organized and given direction. Further, he knew he had to establish a political base in Vietnam. Independence from both Japan and France could not be achieved by emigres living in China.

Ho Chi Minh set out to achieve both objectives. Vietnamese Communist leaders met on May 10, 1941, on Vietnamese soil in the village of Pac Bo in the Cao Bang province, with Ho Chi Minh chairing the meeting. It was the first time in thirty years that he had set foot in his native land. The participants agreed that the party's main goal was to organize all Vietnamese—peasants, workers, middle-class elements, and landlords—to achieve independence. The social revolution would have to wait. The Communist leaders played down their revolutionary goals of land redistribution and the nationalization of industries. To organize all of these groups, a new organization was created: the Viet Nam Doc Lap Dong Minh (Vietnamese League for Independence). The French and the Americans would come to know this group as the Vietminh.

Under the Vietminh umbrella were gathered organizations of peasants, workers, students, intellectuals, women, and landlords. These associations were organized at the village level. There were also pyramids of associations that paralleled the political jurisdictions of the country, including district and provincial associations. At the top stood the Central Committee, controlled by Ho Chi Minh and his lieutenants, all of whom were Communists. All associations were also controlled by party members, but many non-Communist participants joined the associations because the Vietminh represented the largest and most effective anticolonial movement in Indochina. At the time the Vietminh were forming, Ho Chi Minh wrote a public letter in which he appealed to the nationalistic and antiimperialist traditions of the Vietnamese people:

> National salvation is the common cause of our entire people. Every Vietnamese must take part in it. . . . The hour has struck. Raise aloft the banner of insurrection and lead the people throughout the country to overthrow the Japanese and the French. The sacred call of the fatherland is resounding in our ears, the ardent blood of our heroic predecessors is seething in our hearts.[35]

Ho Chi Minh and his associates created the Vietminh as a national front organization controlled by the Indochinese Communist Party to attract Vietnamese patriots of all political persuasions to a common cause, the struggle to rid their country of Japanese and French rule.[36] Ho Chi Minh and his Vietminh colleagues also viewed their struggle against Japanese and French imperialism as part of the worldwide struggle against Fascism. When the mighty United States entered the war against the Axis powers, Ho Chi Minh associated the Vietnamese nationalist cause with the American war aims embodied in the Atlantic Charter.

In addition to forming the Vietminh front organizations, Ho Chi Minh and his associates established a strong revolutionary base in Cao Bang. Following Maoist strategies, the Vietminh's goal was to liberate this remote mountainous northern province and replace the colonial administration with their own party apparatus. Within six months, they had succeeded. A training site for guerrillas was established near Pac Bo to transform peasant recruits into warriors.

THE ROOTS OF AMERICAN INVOLVEMENT

When Chinese officials selected the Vietminh to take charge of anti-Japanese espionage and guerrilla campaigns in Vietnam, a Chinese general, Chang Fa-K'uei, upon learning of Nguyen Ai Quoc's Communist past, urged him to change his name, lest the Nationalist leaders reject him. To oblige his Chinese sponsors, Nguyen selected the name Ho Chi Minh ("he who enlightens") sometime in early 1943.[37] With Chinese sponsorship, the Vietminh automatically qualified for funding from the U. S. Mission in China, which was bankrolling the entire Chinese war effort against the Japanese.

American involvement in Vietnam reaches back to the days of World War II, when the American China mission found itself bankrolling Communist guerrillas engaged in resistance activities against the Japanese in Tonkin, while American pilots bombed and strafed Japanese installations in various parts of Vietnam. These wartime experiences thrust the United States into a prominent role in Southeast Asia and confirmed the American sense of Vietnam's significance: as a source of foodstuffs and raw materials, and its strategic location astride major shipping lanes linking India, the islands of the southeast Pacific, China, and Japan.

The fall of France in June 1940 created serious diplomatic problems for the United States. President Franklin Roosevelt despised and distrusted the collaborationist Vichyites, but granted them diplomatic recognition to forestall German occupation of their colonies in North Africa and to try to prevent, unsuccessfully, Japanese occupation of Indochina. American officials were angered by French acquiescence in the Japanese penetration of Vietnam. From their perspective, it appeared that French officials made little effort to resist Japanese demands and settled rather comfortably into a joint occupation with them. American officials also were unhappy that possession of Indochina gave the Japanese strategic leverage in Southeast Asia and its continuing war with China. They later attributed many of the Japanese successes in conquering Southeast Asian territories, including the Philippines, from 1941 to 1942, to their ability to use Indochina as a base of operations.

It was the Japanese move into all of Indochina in the summer of 1941 that probably made war between the United States and Japan inevitable. Roosevelt viewed Japanese entry into that strategic region as a clear sign that the Japanese planned further imperialistic moves into the southeast Pacific region. The American response to Japan's takeover of all of Indochina was to cut off Japan's supply of oil. The oil cutoff created a crisis for the Japanese leaders. With only six weeks of oil reserves on hand, the Japanese would have to get the oil embargo rescinded quickly, or find a new source of supply to prevent their war machine and industrial economy from grinding to a halt. U. S. and Japanese negotiators met through the summer and fall of 1941 to try to resolve their conflicts. As a price for restoring Japan's oil supplies and other trade goods that had been embargoed, Washington demanded that the Japanese get out of China and Indochina. These terms proved unacceptable to Japan, who would not consider abandoning their expansionist ambitions. They preferred a war with the United States rather than a surrender of their dreams of an empire. The Japanese response came on December 7, 1941, at Pearl Harbor, which brought the United States into the Asian war. Soon afterward, the Japanese, using Vietnam as a staging area, occupied the East Indies and began extracting oil from this former Dutch colony. The Japanese also made use of Vietnamese ports as depots for the oil and other resources they were getting from their newly conquered empire in the southeast.

The Japanese move into Indochina also brought the first U. S. military intervention into Vietnam in early 1942, about a month after America had entered the war. Cutting the Japanese lifeline from Southeast Asia and denying the Japanese use of air bases in Vietnam for continuing attacks on China became major tactical objectives of the American Volunteer Group, famed as the "Flying Tigers," under the command of General Claire L. Chennault. The Flying Tigers operated under the control of the Chinese Nationalist Army. Flying out of bases in southern China, the Flying Tigers, in early 1942, began attacking Japanese airfields in northern Vietnam. On May 12, 1942, John T. Donovan, a former Navy pilot, was shot down and killed by Japanese anti-aircraft fire while flying his P-40 on a strafing mission over Hanoi. Donovan was the first American to be killed on Vietnamese soil.[38]

As the war progressed, the future political status of Indochina became a diplomatic problem among the wartime allies. It was tied to a larger issue, the postwar fate of the European Asian empires. On the one hand, U. S. officials, faithful to Atlantic Charter war aims, firmly opposed the restoration of colonial imperialism in Asia. Liberation from Japanese occupation was to be followed by independence. The end of colonialism in Asia would liberate subject peoples, open markets to U. S. exports, and bring stability to turbulent regions. On the other hand, President Roosevelt had an understanding with British prime minister Winston Churchill that the Atlantic Charter did not apply to British colonial possessions, particularly the vast Southeast Asian subcontinent, India. But in a private conversation with Secretary of State Cordell Hull, Roosevelt made clear early in 1944 the kind of future he envisioned for Indochina:

France has had the country—30 million inhabitants—for nearly one hundred years, and the people are worse off than they were at the beginning. . . . France has milked it for one hundred years. The people of Indochina are entitled to something better than that.[39]

Charles De Gaulle, the leader of the Free French government-in-exile, whom Roosevelt disliked intensely, joined with Churchill in an effort to thwart Roosevelt and forestall the loss of Indochina after the war. Churchill, linking De Gaulle's attempts to retain France's Asian colonies with his own efforts to cling to empire, supported De Gaulle. The colonial issue created fissures in the wartime alliance's conduct of the war in the Far East. The British tried to claim wartime jurisdiction of Indochina, which the Americans had assigned to the China theater, to restore the colony to France at the conclusion of the war. Roosevelt, perceiving Churchill's strategy, circumvented British efforts by ordering that no U. S. aid would go to French forces in Indochina and forbidding the British to conduct military operations in the region without clearance from the American China command.[40]

Pursuing efforts to prevent a return of French colonialism in Vietnam, Roosevelt asked Chiang Kai-shek, the Nationalist leader of China, if he wanted to govern Indochina. The answer he received was an emphatic no. Chiang, aware of Vietnam's long history of resistance to Chinese colonialism, told Roosevelt that the Vietnamese were "not Chinese. They would not assimilate into the Chinese people."[41] Following Chiang's rejection, Roosevelt proposed the idea of an international trusteeship for Indochina until the people were ready for independence. Churchill strongly opposed Roosevelt's proposal, which he saw as implicitly threatening to British imperial interests.[42] It is significant that Roosevelt, the great liberal statesman, wanted to see Vietnam freed of the burden of French colonialism. He was motivated in part by spite, the desire to punish the French for their wartime capitulation to the Axis, by shearing off one of their prized imperial possessions. He also sensed that the days of Western imperialism in Asia were coming to an end and that colonialism promoted imperial rivalries that led to war. He would make use of a historic opportunity to liquidate French imperialism in Southeast Asia and align U. S. foreign policy with the forces of Asian nationalism.

THE AUGUST REVOLUTION

While international leaders quarreled over the political future of Indochina, Vietminh guerrillas carried out espionage missions and guerrilla raids on Japanese forces occupying northern Vietnam. The Vietminh also used their wartime guerrilla activities and the prestige gained from their American connections to strengthen their leadership of the Vietnamese nationalist movement. In December 1944, in the Cao Bang Province, Ho Chi Minh ordered the creation of a military division of the Vietminh, the Vietnamese Liberation Army. During the winter of 1944 to 1945, under the leadership of Vo Nguyen Giap, Vietminh guerrillas gained control of three northern provinces and engaged Japanese forces in sporadic combat.[43]

Beginning in the spring of 1945, the Vietminh received support from an Office of Strategic Services (OSS) contingent operating out of the U. S. China Mission at Kunming. The Vietminh and OSS units collaborated to hasten the defeat of the Japanese. The Vietminh helped OSS commandos rescue downed U. S. pilots and escaped prisoners, accompanied them on sabotage missions, and provided them with information on Japanese troop movements in Vietnam. OSS officers served with the Vietminh at Ho Chi Minh's headquarters at Pac Bo. The Americans came to know many of the Vietminh leaders and assisted them in their struggle for national independence. The OSS officers who knew him viewed Ho Chi Minh as a Vietnamese patriot who would subordinate his Leninist revolutionary principles to the larger cause of national liberation.[44]

By 1945, U. S. and British forces had reclaimed many of Japan's wartime Southeast Asian conquests. They had liberated important territories, including the Dutch East Indies, Malaya, and the Philippine archipelago. Confronted with their rapidly shrinking assets in Southeast Asia, Japan made a determined effort to hold its vital Indochina positions. American planes from carriers operating with the U. S. Third Fleet in the Tonkin Gulf began attacking Japanese shipping in Saigon harbor. Army Air Corps bombers from Clark Field in the Philippines carried out raids on Saigon and Danang, destroying Japanese warships and freighters. Within a few months, American planes had closed Japanese supply lines from Vietnam to China and their home islands. U. S. strategic bombers, flying from Clark Field, knocked out all railway linkages between Vietnam and China. Indochina was cut off from the remaining Japanese theaters of war.

These American air raids signaled that the end of the Japanese presence in Indochina was fast approaching. Many of the French in Vietnam, who had collaborated with the Axis for years, prepared to join the fight for Vietnam's liberation from Japan. Sensing the changed French attitudes, the Japanese moved to prevent French action against them in their hour of approaching defeat. On March 9, 1945, the Japanese abruptly brought the eighty-year-old French rule over the Indochinese people to an end. In a series of lightning raids that took the French by surprise, Admiral Decoux and many French officials were arrested, and most French soldiers were disarmed and interned. Thousands of French nationals were also interned. Only a few hundred managed to escape to the hills. Some joined the Vietminh guerrillas; others fled to China. Japanese officials seized control of the Indochina government.[45]

In their efforts to retain control of Vietnam, the Japanese also installed a Vietnamese government headed by Emperor Bao Dai, who, prior to the war, had been the French-controlled ruler of Annam for ten years from his palace in Hue.[46] Japanese officials informed Bao Dai that he was the ruler of an "independent" nation that had been "liberated" from the French imperialists. In reality, the Japanese were going through a desperate charade. The new government had neither the resources nor the power to command. Japanese Army officers remained in control of Vietnamese affairs.

Bao Dai also understood that Japan would soon be defeated, and his shadow government would be discredited because of its association with the Japanese, who were no more loved by the Vietnamese people than the French.

Ho Chi Minh understood that the Japanese coup d'etat created a political vacuum in Indochina that he intended to exploit. He also understood that the Japanese defeat of the French, as well as their conquest of former British and Dutch colonies in Southeast Asia, had destroyed the lingering myth of European invincibility that had restrained Asian nationalists. With the French removed from power and the Japanese on the verge of defeat, the Vietminh moved quickly to position themselves to take control of their country. General Giap took command of the Vietnam Liberation Army. Vietminh forces now controlled much of Tonkin, and their influence was spreading rapidly over the country, reaching from the villages into the cities.[47] Within the provinces they controlled, the Vietminh installed revoutionary regimes, recruited guerrillas, abolished taxes, reduced land rents, and redistributed land taken from French landlords to poor peasants.[48] The Vietminh were harnessing the vast energies of a people who were sensing that their moment of liberation from both Japanese and French dominion was fast approaching. Where positive appeals to patriotism and economic self-interest failed, the Vietminh relied on terror to intimidate opponents. Known collaborators with the French or Japanese were liquidated.

The Vietminh also gained followers during the summer of 1945, because they responded effectively to a terrible famine that was especially acute in the northern provinces. The famine had been caused by the Japanese, who, in 1943, had ordered French soldiers to seize the rice harvest for shipment to Japan. Peasants went bankrupt in 1943 and starved in 1944. An estimated 500,000 to 2 million Vietnamese died in the famine. Neither French nor Japanese officials cared much about the plight of the starving Vietnamese, but the Vietminh confiscated rice from landlords and raided granaries containing rice stored for export. The Vietminh turned these precious rice stores over to the people to alleviate some of the misery. They also assassinated local landlords and Vietnamese officials working for the French and Japanese. Vietminh forces continued to work with OSS teams, gathering intelligence on Japanese troop movements, harassing Japanese outposts, and rescuing downed American flyers. Other U. S. groups, including military intelligence units, also worked with Vietminh guerrillas in various parts of Vietnam.

The Vietminh got their opportunity to seize power when the Japanese forces in Vietnam surrendered to Vietminh forces in mid-August, a few days after U. S. planes had dropped atomic bombs on the Japanese cities of Hiroshima and Nagasaki, abruptly ending World War II. Events moved quickly in early August 1945. Vietnam rapidly underwent a nationalist revolution.[49] Everywhere, Vietminh associations took control of local, district, and provincial governments.[50] The Vietminh swept to power. A provisional council in Saigon, comprising religious sectarians, various Communist splinter groups, and several non-Communist nationalist groups, declared their support for the Vietminh.

Figure 1.3 Two men who made a revolution. At the time this photo was taken, August 1945, Vo Nguyen Giap (left) was serving as Minister of the Interior with Ho Chi Minh (right), the head of the new Vietnamese Provisional Revolutionary Government.

Because they headed the only well-organized political and military movement in Vietnam, the Vietminh were able to supplant the deposed French and the beaten Japanese and take power without any significant opposition.[51] On August 19, the Vietminh took Hanoi. On August 23, they claimed Hue, the seat of government of the Nguyen dynasty. Between August 18 and 28, Vietminh supporters took control of some sixty district and provincial capitals. On August 29, the Vietminh formed a national government they called the Provisional Government of the Democratic Republic of Vietnam, with its capital in Hanoi. On September 2, 1945, Ho Chi Minh made a public declaration of Vietnamese independence before 500,000 people assembled in Hanoi's Ba Dinh Square.[52] Ho Chi Minh, who admired the United States because it had defeated the Japanese and because of its official commitment to self-determination for Asian peoples following the war, and who hoped Vietminh cooperation in the war against the Japanese would bring American support of Vietnamese independence, began his speech with words taken from the American Declaration of Independence:

> We hold truths that all men are created equal, that they are endowed by their Creator with certain unalienable Rights, among these are Life, Liberty, and the pursuit of Happiness.[53]

Later in the day, Americans joined the festivities that celebrated Vietnam's independence. A flight of U. S. aircraft overflew the city. U. S. Army officers stood with Giap and other Vietminh leaders on the reviewing stand as Vietminh forces passed in review. A Vietnamese band played *The Star Spangled Banner.*[54] Later a Vietnam-American Friendship Association was formed in Hanoi. Ho Chi Minh, hoping for U. S. support for Vietnam's independence and for economic development, cultivated the friendship of the small American contingent in Hanoi and repeatedly appealed to the U. S. government for diplomatic recognition.

The Vietnamese people had reclaimed their national identity that had been submerged for eighty years under French and Japanese colonialism. For the first time in eighty years, Vietnam was united and independent under a government controlled by the Communist-led Vietminh. Its revolution represented a remarkable merging of a people and a movement that gave expression to the deep yearning of nearly all Vietnamese citizens to be rid of foreign control. In the rush to achieve national independence, factional conflicts and ideological differences among Vietnamese political parties, which were sharpest in southern cities, were temporarily submerged. On August 30, Emperor Bao Dai presented the imperial seal and sword, the twin symbols of Vietnamese sovereignty, to the Vietminh leaders, and then abdicated.[55] Bao Dai promised to support the new provisional government, conferring legitimacy upon it and linking it to Vietnamese political traditions. Most Vietnamese, Communist and non-Communist alike, accepted Ho Chi Minh as the leader of the revolution that had retrieved Vietnamese independence. The Communist revolutionary and devout Vietnamese patriot also symbolized Vietnam's revived nationhood.

But the August revolution was not destined to endure peacefully. As U. S. Army officers joined with Vietminh leaders in Hanoi to celebrate the rebirth of Vietnamese independence, American leaders in Washington were clearing the way for the return of the French to Vietnam. Before he died, Roosevelt had retreated from his support of Vietnamese nationalism. Concerned with maintaining good relations with important European allies at Yalta, Roosevelt did not actively oppose France's announced intention to return to Indochina.[56] Secretary of State Edward Stettinius told the French foreign minister that the United States had never questioned, "French sovereignty over Indochina."[57] Any possibility of an international trusteeship for Indochina ended with Roosevelt's death on April 12, 1945.

Roosevelt's successor, Harry Truman, was overwhelmed by the vast economic, political, and strategic problems resulting from the upheavals of World War II. From Truman's vantage point in August 1945, Vietnam was an insignificant country, and Ho Chi Minh was an insignificant leader for whom he had no time. If there was a historic moment when Washington could have aligned itself with the forces of Vietnamese nationalism, it failed to grasp it. Truman, a more parochial nationalist than the cosmopolitan statesman he replaced, having no interest in Asian self-determination, supported the French goal of reimposing colonialism on the Vietnamese people.[58] State Department officials had urged Truman to placate the French, who were still seething over Roosevelt's efforts to remove Vietnam from their empire. Truman made a point of telling Charles de Gaulle that the United States would not try to undermine the French position in Indochina.

Truman and other Allied leaders, meeting at Potsdam a few weeks before Ho Chi Minh made his declaration of independence, had determined that Vietnam would be divided temporarily at the 16th parallel at war's end. North of that boundary, Chinese

Nationalist troops were to handle the surrender of Japanese forces, arrange for their repatriation to Japan, and obtain the release of all prisoners of war and Allied internees. South of that line, British troops would take charge of these matters. As the Potsdam conferees made these secret agreements, they did not specify the shape the political future of Vietnam would take, but, in effect, they granted the French a free hand to return to Indochina and reimpose colonialism on the Vietnamese people.[59]

Even as the Vietnamese nation made its reappearance, French forces were planning their reentry into Vietnam. The revolution of the summer of 1945 that ended the French colonial era of Vietnamese history also began thirty years of conflict that eventually claimed more than 2 million Vietnamese lives and tens of thousands of French and American lives. For Ho Chi Minh and his Vietnamese compatriots, a moment of celebration would be followed by decades of conflict and turmoil. No one could foresee it during that fateful summer of 1945, but completing the Vietnamese national revolution would take thirty years and exact a dreadful toll in blood and treasure from those who made the revolution and those who tried and failed to defeat it.

NOTES

1. Duiker, William J., *Vietnam: Nation in Revolution* (Boulder, Colo.: Westview, 1983), 13.
2. Le Thanh Khoi, *Le Viet-nam: Histoire et Civilization* (Paris: Editions du Minuit, 1955), 88–97.
3. Duiker, *Vietnam: Nation in Revolution*, 15.
4. Hall, Daniel G. E., *A History of Southeast Asia,* 2nd ed. (New York: St. Martin's, 1955), 199–200.
5. Cady, John F., *Southeast Asia: Its Historical Development* (New York: McGraw Hill, 1964), 103–106; Duiker, *Vietnam: Nation in Revolution*, 18–19.
6. Kahin, George M. and Lewis, John, *The United States in Vietnam: An Analysis in Depth of the History of America's Involvement in Vietnam* (New York: Delta, 1967), 5.
7. Duiker, *Vietnam: Nation in Revolution*, 22–23.
8. Duiker, William, *The Rise of Natrionalism in Vietnam, 1900–1941* (Ithaca, N. Y.: Cornell University Press, 1976), 16.
9. Buttinger, Joseph, *The Smaller Dragon: A Political History of Vietnam* (New York: Praeger, 1958), 283–294.
10. Cady, John F., *The Roots of French Imperialism in Eastern Asia* (Ithaca, New York: Cornell University Press, 1954), 97–102, 136–59, 178–180, 186–191.
11. Buttinger, Joseph, *A Dragon Defiant: A Short History of Vietnam* (New York: Praeger, 1972), 60; also his *Vietnam: A Dragon Embattled*, vol. 1 (New York, Praeger, 1967), 495.
12. Hall, Daniel G. E., *The History of Southeast Asia*, 560–570. Cochin China, Annam, and Tonkin are the Western names given to the three regions of Vietnam. The French also called Vietnam "Annam" and referred to the Vietnamese people as "Annamites" or the "Annamite people," names the Vietnamese despised and rejected. The Vietnamese have

never thought of their country as being divided into distinct regions; they think of it in terms of the whole nation, at the same time recognizing its distinctive regional characteristics. During the colonial period, they called the aforementioned three regions Nam Viet, Trung Viet, and Bac Viet, that is, South Vietnam, Central Vietnam, and North Vietnam.

13. Buttinger, *Vietnam: A Dragon Embattled*, vol. 1, 138–144; Duiker, *Vietnam: Nation in Revolution*, 23–26.

14. Doyle, Edward, Lipsman, Samuel, and the editors of Boston Publishing Company, *Setting the Stage* (Boston: Boston Publishing Co., 1981), 119–120. The first volume of a multi-volume history of Vietnam called *The Vietnam Experience*. The volumes are illustrated and generally well-written.

15. Thompson, Virginia, *French Indochina* (London: Allen & Unwin, 1937), 228–234; Cady, John F., *SE Asia: Its Historical Development* (New York: McGraw-Hill, 1964), part 5, chap. 18, 406–34.

16. Lancaster, Donald, *The Emancipation of French Indochina* (London: Oxford University Press, 1961), 65–66.

17. For most of Vietnamese history, Chinese ideographs were used in writing the language. In the seventeenth century, Portuguese and French missionaries invented a system of writing Vietnamese in the Latin alphabet called *quoc ngu*. During their colonial tenure, the French made *quoc ngu* an official language, along with French. Currently, *quoc ngu* is in general use throughout Vietnam.

18. Buttinger, *A Dragon Defiant,* 68.

19. Hess, Gary R., *Vietnam and the United States* (Boston: Twayne Publishers, 1990), 11.

20. Buttinger, *A Dragon Defiant*, 111–144.

21. *Ibid.*, 151–156.

22. The man the world knows as Ho Chi Minh employed numerous pseudonyms until 1943, when he adopted his final, famous name.

23. Lacouture, Jean, *Ho Chi Minh: A Political Biography*. Translated from the French by Peter Wiles. Translation edited by Jane Clark Seitz. (New York: Random House, 1968), 13–21; Fall, Bernard B. (ed.), *Ho Chi Minh on Revolution, Selected Writings, 1920–1966* (Boulder, Colo.: Westview, 1984), 43–51.

24. Doyle and others, *Setting the Stage* , 156–157.

25. Duiker, William J., *The Communist Road to Power in Vietnam* (Boulder, Colo.: Westview, 1981), 17–18.

26. *Ibid.*, 32–33.

27. Hammer, Ellen J., *The Struggle for Indochina* (Stanford, Calif.: Stanford University Press, 1954), 84–86; Duiker, *The Communist Road*, 33–40.

28. Duiker, *The Communist Road*, 40–43.

29. Duiker, *Vietnam: Nation in Revolt*, 37–38.

30. In 1935, Stalin became alarmed at the growing power of Fascist states in Europe, concluding that they posed a grave threat to Soviet interests. He instructed Communist parties in Western democracies to abandon their revolutionary tactics and form coalitions, "popular fronts," with liberal and socialist parties to combat the Fascist menace. The Indochinese Communist Party, under Ho Chi Ming's leadership, responded to Comintern directives. It moderated its revolutionary program and formed alliances with liberal and socialist groups within Vietnam.

31. Lancaster, Donald, *The Emancipation of French Indochina* (London: Oxford University Press, 1961), chap. 6, 98–104.

32. Buttinger, *Dragon Embattled*, vol. 1, 244–50; Hammer, *Struggle*, 31.

33. Buttinger, *Dragon Embattled*, vol. 1, 250–53.

34. Chen, King C., *Vietnam and China, 1938–1954* (Princeton, N. J.: Princeton University Press, 1969), 44–48.

35. Ho Chi Minh, *Selected Writings, 1920–1969* (Hanoi: People's Publishing House, 1973), 46.

36. Devillers, Philippe, *Histoire du Vietnam de 1940 a 1952* (Paris: Editions du Seuil, 1952), 96–113; Duiker, *The Communist Road*, 64–72; Chen, *Vietnam and China*, 51–55; and Pike, Douglas, *History of Vietnamese Communism, 1925–1976* (Stanford, Calif.: Hoover Institution Press, 1978), 30–51.

37. Lacouture, *Ho Chi Minh*, 78–79.

38. Doyle and others, *Setting the Stage*, 176.

39. Quoted in *Ibid.,* 177.

40. LaFeber, Walter, "Roosevelt, Churchill, and Indochina, 1942–1945," *American Historical Review*, vol. 80 (December 1975), 1277–95.

41. Quoted in Pettit, Clyde Edwin, *The Experts* (Secaucus, N. J.: Lyle Stuart, 1975), 13.

42. Hess, Gary R., "Franklin D. Roosevelt and Indochina," *Journal of American History*, vol. LIX (September 1972), 353–68.

43. Patti, Archimedes L., *Why Vietnam? Prelude to America's Albatross* (Berkeley, Calif.: University of California Press, 1980), 55–56. The Office of Strategic Services (OSS) was a wartime intelligence agency whose agents also engaged in commando operations behind enemy lines. They committed sabotage and aided resistance forces, which often included Communists within their ranks, in both the European and Asian theaters of war. See "Instructions By Ho Chi Minh For Setting Up of the Armed Propaganda Brigade for the Liberation of Vietnam," December 1944, printed in Porter, Gareth, ed., *Vietnam: The Definitive Documentation of Human Decisions* (Stanfordville, N. Y.: Earl M. Coleman Enterprises, 1979), vol. 1, 14.

44. Devillers, *Histoire*, 152; Chen, *Vietnam and China*, 113–4. Chen points out that the Chinese Nationalists only helped the Vietnamese Nationalists, particularly the VNQDD and Dong Minh Hoi. He finds no evidence that the Vietminh received any help from the Chinese Communists. The Soviets displayed no interest in the Vietminh revolution. The Vietminh were on their own, except for some help from their American friends in the OSS.

45. Hammer, *Struggle*, 36–45.

46. *Ibid.*, 46–47.

47. Buttinger, *Dragon*, vol. 1, 292–5; Duiker, *The Communist Road*, 94–100.

48. Woodside, Alexander B., *Community and Revolution in Modern Vietnam* (Boston: Houghton Mifflin, 1976), 225–40.

49. Hess, *Vietnam*, 20.

50. Buttinger, *Dragon*, 296–8; Duiker, *The Communist Road*, 94–100; Porter, ed., *Vietnam Documents*, vol. 1, "Resolutions of the Vietminh Conference to Establish a "Free Zone," June 4, 1945, 47–49.

51. Duiker, *The Communist Road*, 98–99; Chen, *Vietnam and China*, 102–14 is a good brief account of the Vietminh August Revolution; Porter, *Vietnam Documents*, vol. 1, "Appeal By Ho Chi Minh for General Insurrection," August 1945, 60–61.

52. Chen, *Vietnam and China*, 111-112.

53. Smith, R. Harris, *OSS: The Secret History of America's First Central Intelligence Agency* (New York: Delta Books, 1973), 351–55; Ho Chi Minh's Declaration is printed in Porter (ed.), *Vietnam Documents*, vol. 1, 64–66.

54. Herring, George C., *America's Longest War: The United States and Vietnam, 1950–1975*, rev. ed. (New York: Knopf, 1986), 3; quoted in Kahin, George McT., *Intervention: How America Became Involved in Vietnam* (New York: Knopf, 1986), 14–15.

55. Young, Marilyn B., *The Vietnam Wars* (New York: Harper Collins, 1991), 10.

56. Hess, *Vietnam*, 29–30; Kahin, *Intervention*, 5.

57. Gardner, Lloyd C., *Approaching Vietnam: From World War II Through Dienbienphu* (New York: W. W. Norton, 1988), 46–63; Lafeber, "Roosevelt, Churchill, and Indochina," 1289.

58. Kahin, *Intervention*, 19–20; Arnold A. Offner, "The Truman Myth Revealed: From Parochial Nationalist to Cold Warrior," March 1988 unpublished paper presented at the Organization of American Historians Convention; and Herring, George, "The Truman Administration and the Restoration of French Sovereignty in Indochina," *Diplomatic History*, vol. 1 (Spring 1977), 97–117.

59. Kahin, *Intervention*, 15–16; Tuchman, Barbara, *The March of Folly: From Troy to Vietnam* (New York: Ballantine, 1984), 239–40.

2

The Elephant
and the Tiger

It will be a war between an elephant and a tiger. If the tiger ever stands still, the elephant will crush him with his mighty tusks. But the tiger will not stand still. . . . He will leap upon the back of the elephant, tearing huge chunks from his side, and then he will leap back into the dark jungle. And slowly the elephant will bleed to death. That will be the war of Indochina.

Ho Chi Minh

THE FRENCH RETURN

The end of World War II presaged the end of Western imperialism in Southeast Asia. Emergent nationalist leaders took advantage of the sudden surrender of the Japanese and the evident strategic weakness of the European powers to demand independence. The August Revolution of the Vietminh paralleled nationalist revolutions in the Dutch East Indies, Burma, and India.[1] In the Philippines, nationalists urged the United States to fulfill its prewar pledge to grant their country independence. In China, the defeat of the Japanese ended the wartime collaboration of the Koumingtang and the Maoists, and they resumed their civil war.

The French simply dismissed the Vietnamese claim of independence and maneuvered to reestablish their Indochina colony. They did not take seriously the claims of a fragile government struggling to feed its starving people, lacking a powerful army, with limited financial resources, and having no standing or support in the international community. British and Chinese troops entered Vietnam in September 1945 to carry out the Potsdam directives issued the previous month by the victorious Allied powers. In the train of the British troops entering southern Vietnam came French forces. Insertion of these outside military forces triggered a series of conflicts that engulfed Vietnam for decades, delaying the emergence of an independent, unified Vietnamese state for more than thirty years.

In the aftermath of World War II, the French instinct was to hang on to all of their overseas possessions and privileges, and they were willing to use military force if necessary to preserve them in the Middle East, North Africa, and Southeast Asia. Because they were determined to cling to their empire, the French fought a series of disastrous colonial wars from the 1940s to the 1960s and still lost their colonies. The first of these colonial wars occurred in Indochina.

The French were driven by a mix of motives to try to reimpose their rule on the Vietnamese, Cambodian, and Laotian peoples. Economic considerations were important, especially in Cochin China, where the French financial and commercial interests were concentrated. The French also had a politico-psychological motive for returning to Indochina. The quick Nazi conquest of France in 1940, followed by the rigors and humiliations of the German occupation, had dealt French national esteem serious blows, as had Japanese occupation of Indochina and other French possessions in the South Pacific. Permanent loss of their Southeast Asian colonies in the wake of wartime humiliations would be more than the French national psyche could bear.

The most important reason for the French drive to regain control of their former Southeast Asian possessions transcended Indochina and concerned the political cohesion of France's entire overseas empire. French officials had a view of colonialism resembling the subsequent American domino theory: If one colony won its independence, others would then be tempted to stage similar breakaways from French control. If the Vietnam domino fell, not only would the Cambodian and Laotian dominoes follow quickly, but, far worse in the French view, their much more valuable North African possessions, Morocco, Tunisia, and the most valuable of all French overseas territories, Algeria, would rise in rebellion against French colonialism. To safeguard the interests of their 1 million Algerian "colons," the French prepared to reconquer 24 million Vietnamese.[2]

The advance wave of 2,000 British and Indian troops, most of them famed Gurkhas, marched into Saigon on September 13, 1945, under the command of General Douglas D. Gracey. Eighteen thousand additional troops soon joined them. General Gracey did not acknowledge the Democratic Republic of Vietnam's (DRV's) claim of sovereignty. He favored the French returning to Indochina and reacted to the political disorder he encountered within a country in the throes of revolution after a disruptive war by declaring martial law. He also gave orders to disarm all Vietnamese forces, but released and rearmed about 5,000 French troops that the Japanese had interned. These French forces, armed with U. S. weapons and joined by newly arriving French troops carried to Indochina in U. S. and British ships, overthrew the Vietminh government in Saigon on September 23, 1945. The French had forced their way back into Vietnam. The Tricolor once again flew over public buildings in the "Paris of the Orient." The French return was supported by the British and the Americans. At the time of the French reentry into Vietnam, Acting Secretary of State Dean Acheson wrote the American charge d'affaires in China that the, "U. S. has no thought of opposing the reestablishment of French control in Indochina."[3] The French takeover of Saigon triggered a thirty-year war for control of Vietnam that ended only when the DRV troops captured Saigon on April 30, 1975, and placed the remnants of South Vietnam's last government under arrest.

The Vietminh leader in Saigon, Tran Van Giau, ordered a general strike and also ordered counterattacks against the French. Nearly all Vietnamese, determined to prevent a return of the French, joined the resistance, including the religious sectarians and a criminal organization, the Binh Xuyen, the Cochin China "Mafia." General Gracey responded to these actions by releasing and rearming Japanese soldiers! Multinational British, Indian, French, and Japanese forces, many armed with American weapons, undertook the pacification of southern Vietnam in the fall of 1945. For the British, what has been called First Indochina War, from 1945 to 1946,[4] proved to be short; it lasted about one year. As more French troops arrived and as the British completed their assigned task of supervising the repatriation of Japanese troops, their troops were withdrawn. As spring came to southern Vietnam in 1946, the British soldiers were gone.

Most Americans were not aware of the complex political developments taking place in a remote corner of the world at the end of World War II. American media gave little attention to these events or to the major role Americans played in helping the French return to Vietnam. Americans would have been astounded to learn that Allied political maneuvering in Vietnam in the fall of 1945 was preparing the ground for a long U. S. entanglement in that country. But one American knew what was happening in Vietnam, and he did not like it. General Douglas MacArthur, preeminent hero of the Pacific war and newly appointed American proconsul in Japan in charge of the occupation and reconstruction of America's recent enemy, passionately denounced the Allied intervention in southern Vietnam:

> If there is anything that makes my blood boil, it is to see our allies in Indochina deploying Japanese troops to reconquer the little people we promised to liberate.[5]

By February 1, 1946, French forces, under the command of General Jacques Phillipe LeClerc,[6] had brought Cochin China under their control. But Leclerc's troops controlled only the cities, towns, and main roads. Vietminh forces effectively contested French authority in the countryside, where most Vietnamese lived. Ho Chi Minh and his Vietminh associates in Hanoi supported these resistance efforts, but they could not control events in the South, where the strong French position in southern Vietnam derived not only from Allied support, but also reflected the fact that French wealth and influence had been concentrated in that region. The Vietminh had not been able to establish a strong base of support there. While concerned about the French presence in southern Vietnam, Ho Chi Minh remained focused on the Tonkin region, because once again Chinese forces had invaded northern Vietnam.[7]

To carry out his part of the Potsdam bargain, Chiang Kai-shek sent an army of 180,000 troops commanded by General Lu Han into Tonkin. The Chinese generals, like the British, did not recognize Ho Chi Minh's government as legitimate, but treated Vietnam as a conquered territory. The Chinese brought along some non-Communist Vietnamese nationalist politicians, remnants of the VNQDD, the Dong Minh Hoi, and other groups who had been living in exile in China since the 1930s. As the Chinese troops marched through hamlets and villages, they replaced Vietminh officials with the Vietnamese political leaders that they had brought with them. Chiang appeared to be using Chinese troops to destroy the Vietminh revolution in the northern half of Vietnam and to install a government headed by Vietnamese Nationalists who would look to China for guidance and protection. By the end of September, Dong Minh Hoi and VNQDD officials, backed by Chinese troops, controlled the countryside.[8] Posing a further problem for the Vietminh, the Chinese troops behaved more like bandits than soldiers, systematically looting the Vietnamese villagers as they marched through the countryside. The Vietminh, powerless to stem the invasion of the huge Chinese army, remained in power only in Hanoi. Facing a French takeover in the south and Chinese occupation in the north, Ho Chi Minh and his colleagues maneuvered desperately to save their imperiled revolution.

The Vietminh bribed the Chinese generals to keep themselves in power. Requisitioning gold and currency from the Vietnamese people, Ho Chi Minh made Lu Han and his friends rich men. In return, the Chinese were content to leave his fledgling government in power and to avoid conflict with the Vietminh leaders. Ho Chi Minh also appointed VNQDD leaders to positions in the Vietnamese Provisional Government. Soon afterward, the VNQDD split, with half joining the Vietminh coalition. In addition, Ho Chi Minh dismantled the Indochinese Communist party apparatus and introduced a range of democratic reforms that brought Vietnamese Catholic and other non-Communist groups over to his government. Most important, he called for elections to select delegates to a National Assembly to draft a constitution and establish a permanent government for Vietnam. To save his social revolution, Ho Chi Minh was forced to soft-pedal it.

The first national elections in Vietnamese history took place on January 6, 1946. Voter turnouts were massive. Over 90 percent of eligible voters participated, and Vietminh candidates scored an overwhelming victory, winning 206 of the 254 seats.[9] But Ho Chi Minh allowed nationalist delegates seventy slots to guarantee them an important role in his new government. His deft maneuvering had bought off the Chinese generals, coopted the political threat posed by the Vietnamese nationalists that the Chinese had brought with them, and broadened the popular base of support for his Vietminh-controlled government among non-Communist elements who made up the large majority of the Vietnamese population.

The Chinese Nationalists, resuming their civil war with the Maoists in the aftermath of the Japanese defeat, were less interested in taking control of northern Vietnam or in restoring Vietnamese Nationalist political groups to power than in using their temporary occupation of the country to wrest concessions from the French. U. S. officials, committed to the restoration of French sovereignty in Indochina, also pressured the Chinese to "facilitate the recovery of power by the French."[10] But the Chinese refused to permit French troops to enter northern Vietnam until they had extracted major concessions from France.

French and Chinese negotiators concluded a series of important political and military agreements in February and March 1946. The French agreed to give up all of their pre-war trading rights and concessions in China in exchange for China's permitting their reentry into northern Vietnam. Under the terms of the Sino-French accord, French forces could start landing at Haiphong on March 6, 1946. But the return of French troops to the north would require Vietminh permission in the spring of 1946, because the French were not strong enough at the time to simply walk in and overpower Ho Chi Minh's forces without absorbing considerable casualties if the Vietminh chose to resist them. There also was the possibility of the Chinese backing the Vietminh to keep the French out if Ho Chi Minh refused to accept the return of the French.

For his part, Ho Chi Minh was willing to seek a compromise with the French in order to rid his country of the rapacious Chinese whom he believed were a greater long-range threat to Vietnamese sovereignty than the French.[11] Delicate negotiations between the French and Vietminh officials took place at the same time as the French-Chinese talks. Ho Chi Minh headed the Vietminh team of negotiators dealing with the French. Jean Sainteny, the commissioner-delegate for Tonkin and an old friend of Ho Chi Minh, headed the French delegation. Sainteny offered many concessions to obtain Vietminh acceptance of their reoccupation of northern Vietnam. The two sides reached a preliminary understanding signed on March 6, 1946. By its terms, France appeared to be taking its first steps toward decolonizing Indochina. Ho Chi Minh's government was declared to be "a free state within the French Union," with its own government and army. France also agreed to hold a national referendum to determine whether the colony of Cochin China would rejoin Annam and Tonkin in a reunited Vietnam or would remain a separate French territory. In return, the Vietminh agreed that 25,000 French troops would replace Chinese forces north of the 16th parallel and they could remain until 1951. Both sides also agreed that a Vietminh delegation would travel to Paris later in the year to work out the details of the agreement that had been deliberately left vague. The Chinese accepted these arrangements, agreeing to withdraw all of their troops by June 16, 1946. For a hopeful moment, it appeared that moderation and statesmanship had averted both war and colonialism in Vietnam.[12]

But the March 6 agreement soon proved a sham. French officials refused to hold the promised plebiscite in Cochin China and construed the new status of Vietnam as a "free state within the French Union" as being only a facade for continuing French colonial domination of the country. Meanwhile, 15,000 French troops reentered Tonkin, with Chinese and U. S. acceptance.

While these crucial events that set the stage for the subsequent tragic French and U. S. involvements in Vietnam were taking place, the Soviet Union ignored Vietnam. In the early postwar period, the Soviet Union was not a major player in the colonial world. It confined its actions to antiimperialist propaganda, meanwhile conceding Western hegemony in the Third World. The Soviets had no choice. At the time, their reach was limited, and they were preoccupied with consolidating their sphere of influence in Eastern Europe and rebuilding their shattered economy in the aftermath of the war. Even though the Communist revolutionaries in Vietnam were fighting for their lives in 1945 and 1946, Soviet aid to the Vietminh did not begin until the 1950s.

Ironically, in 1946, Stalin favored French Communist officials over a minor Communist leader in Southeast Asia, who appeared from Moscow's perspective to be a Vietnamese nationalist first and a Communist second. Stalin had hopes that the French Communist Party, the largest political party in France, might win the 1946 elections and legally take control of the French government. Although they did not win that election, the Communists came out of it with several cabinet positions, and their leader Maurice Thorez became deputy premier. Fearful that they would lose electoral appeal if they supported anticolonialism, Communist leaders in the government supported the French drive to reimpose colonialism on Indochina, a popular cause in France in 1946 and 1947. Stalin backed the French Communists, leaving Ho Chi Minh and the Vietminh to fend for themselves!

From his vantage point in Hanoi in the spring of 1946, Ho Chi Minh felt isolated and vulnerable. He headed a struggling revolutionary regime in a small country that had almost no money and a poorly equipped army. The major powers were either backing or accepting French efforts to reimpose colonialism in Indochina. The Vietminh had no allies in either the Communist or Western camps as they prepared to face the powerful French alone.[13]

Ho Chi Minh and his associates tried to negotiate agreements with the French to avoid a war and to preserve a measure of autonomy. French and Vietminh officials met at Dalat, a mountain resort in the Central Highlands, to try to define the March 6 agreement. Vo Nguyen Giap led the Vietminh delegates. At Dalat, the French representatives made clear that their interpretation of the phrase "free state within the French Union" meant continuing French colonial domination of Vietnam. Ho Chi Minh refused to accept the outcome of the Dalat conference as final, and he prepared for further negotiations to be held later in France.

In the summer of 1946, French and Vietnamese delegates met for a series of talks at Fontainebleau Palace near Paris. Ho Chi Minh journeyed to France to head the Vietminh contingent. For eight weeks, he tried desperately to achieve the substance of independence for his country and to avoid war. But these talks were also doomed to fail, because the French refused to budge from their Dalat interpretation of the March 6 accords. Trying to obtain help from any quarter, Ho Chi Minh contacted the American embassy in Paris. He promised the Americans that he would open up Vietnam to U. S. investment, and he offered to lease a base at Cam Ranh Bay to the U.S. Navy in exchange for help in keeping the French out. Ho Chi Minh was rebuffed by a low-level State Department functionary. He then met with French Prime Minister Georges Bidault and other top French officials. He pleaded with them to make some concessions that he could take back to his people. On September 14, 1946, Ho Chi Minh also warned Bidault:

If we must fight, we will fight. You will kill ten of our men and we will kill one of yours. Yet, in the end, it is you who will tire.[14]

Despite all of his pleading and threats, all Ho Chi Minh could extract from the determined French was a promise to hold the Cochin China referendum and agree to more negotiations at a later date. They never made good on either commitment. Sick at heart, Ho Chi Minh had to return to Hanoi in October 1946, bringing only a flimsy *modus vivendi* to show for his extensive diplomatic efforts.[15]

The fragile peace in Tonkin was shattered the following month. On November 20, French and Vietminh customs collectors quarreled over who had the right to collect customs duties at the port of Haiphong. That night, squads of French and Vietminh soldiers exchanged fire in the city's streets. "These were the opening shots in the eight-year war between the French and the Vietminh, . . ."[16]

In the aftermath of these skirmishes, French officials decided to teach a hard lesson to the Vietnamese, who did not seem to know their place in the colonial scheme of things. On November 23, after giving the Vietminh only two hours to vacate the Chinese Quarter of Haiphong, the French attacked guerrilla hideouts in that sector. French infantry and armored units swept through the city. French aircraft provided tactical air support for the ground forces. The French cruiser *Suffren* unleashed a sustained bombardment that lasted for hours. When the day ended, much of Haiphong lay in rubble; six thousand people were dead and another 25,000 were wounded, mostly civilians. On November 28, French Commander General Morliere issued an ultimatum demanding that the Vietminh yield control of the city, its suburbs, and the main highway between Haiphong and Hanoi to the French military forces. The Vietminh refused General Morliere's demands. On December 18, the French moved troops into Hanoi and occupied several government buildings. On December 19, General Morliere ordered General Giap to disarm his forces.[17] Giap defied the French general and refused to obey his command.

That night, the Vietminh leaders held a plenary meeting. General Giap ordered that a war of national resistance begin. Later that same evening, Vietminh guerrillas destroyed the Hanoi power plant, plunging the city into darkness. Other guerrilla units attacked the homes of French officials, assassinating several, and planted mines in the streets of Hanoi. All over northern Vietnam, French installations were attacked by guerrilla raiders. As the attacks were taking place, Ho Chi Minh removed himself from Hanoi and set up a temporary government at Ha Dong, six miles to the south.[18]

The war that had begun in Saigon in September 1945 had spread north, engulfing all of Vietnam. In retrospect, the conflict that Ho Chi Minh had tried hard to avoid, appears inevitable because the French were determined to reimpose colonialism on a people who absolutely refused to accept it, who were ready to fight to preserve their revolution if they must, and who had the means to resist French imperialism. Most of all, the Vietnamese nationalists had a charismatic leader in iron-willed Ho Chi Minh, part committed Communist revolutionary and part Confucian philosopher, who was absolutely committed to the cause of Vietnamese independence. Vietnamese nationalists had been dreaming of an independent, unified Vietnam for eighty years. French efforts to shear off Cochin China from the rest of Vietnam also threatened the balance of the national economy in which southern Vietnam exchanged surplus food for industrial products from densely populated northern Vietnam.

As the war that was destined to last eight years and end in France's humiliation began, confident French officials predicted that the conflict would last three months at most. Their modern army faced a native militia force that was both poorly armed and poorly trained. French officials, assuming an easy victory over the forces they contemptuously called "the barefoot army," regretted only that their soldiers would not be home for Christmas.

THE FRANCO-VIETMINH WAR

When the war began in December 1946, the Vietminh could field about 60,000 troops. In addition to these main force units, the Vietnamese had large peasant and youth militia forces. But the poorly prepared Vietminh soldiers could not hope to defeat "a serious French effort to restore colonial rule in Vietnam."[19] In 1946, the French could field a modern well-equipped and well-trained army of 150,000 soldiers, including French soldiers, Legionnaires, and colonial troops. The early phase of the Franco-Vietminh War severely tested Ho Chi Minh's claim that the Vietnamese tiger could survive the French elephant's efforts to crush it.

Ho Chi Minh, who had continued to seek a negotiated settlement until French military actions forced him to accept war rather than capitulate to French colonialism, now called his people to arms:

> Those who have rifles will use their rifles; those who have swords will use their swords; those who have no swords will use spades, hoes or sticks. . . . Long live an independent and unified Vietnam! Long live the resistance![20]

The Vietminh looked to Maoist doctrines of guerrilla warfare for strategic guidance as they planned their campaigns against the French forces. On December 22, 1946, the revolutionary government announced that the struggle against the French imperialists would advance through three stages. Applying Maoist precepts to their struggle, the revolutionaries stated that the first stage of the war would be defensive, during which the Vietminh guerrillas would abandon the urban areas if they had to and retreat into the countryside and to the mountains of northern Vietnam. During this stage, the Vietminh would avoid major battles with the French forces, concentrate on building up their own main force units, and continue political organization in the villages. The second stage would be one of equilibrium, in which the revolutionary forces would be growing in strength and the imperialist forces would be declining. The third stage would feature a general offensive by the revolutionary forces, stronger than their enemies, that would defeat the imperialist armies and drive them from the country.[21] No specific time frames were mentioned in the December 22 announcement; there were no indications how long they expected each phase to last. But it was clear that the Vietminh planned for a protracted war against the French, a war that could go on for years, and one that they were confident they would ultimately win. Protracted warfare had defeated Chinese invaders over the centuries. The Vietminh believed it would also beat the French.

Already controlling Cochin China, the French forces in the early months of 1947 occupied the major cities and towns of Annam and Tonkin. The outgunned Vietminh main force units avoided combat with the more powerful invaders, and what resistance the French encountered in these early campaigns came mostly from local guerrillas. The Vietminh put up their stiffest resistance in Hanoi, and it took the French forces three months to take the city. Beyond the cities, the Vietminh remained in control of much of the countryside, where they retained the loyalty of most of the population. Viet Bac, the mountainous northern provinces, remained a revolutionary stronghold and haven. Near the remote mountain village of Bac Can, fifty miles from the Chinese border, Ho Chi Minh established his headquarters.[22]

In October 1947, the French launched a major offensive designed to destroy the Vietminh main forces and capture the revolutionary leaders in their Viet Bac sanctuaries. The French sent a powerful force of twelve infantry battalions, reinforced by armored units and air support, deep into the northern countryside. French paratroopers staged a surprise raid on Vietminh headquarters in a cave near Bac Can. They missed capturing Ho Chi Minh and other Vietminh leaders by less than one hour.[23] Although they failed to capture the revolutionary leadership, the French military campaign scored major successes. They killed an estimated 10,000 Vietminh main force personnel and forced the rebels to abandon large areas of Viet Bac.

At the same time they launched their military offensive in the north, the French, convinced they could not defeat the Vietminh by force alone, moved to undercut the Vietminh politically by forming alliances with Vietnamese groups that would cooperate with them against the revolutionaries. The heart of the French political strategy involved forming a Vietnamese government in Saigon and persuading former emperor Bao Dai to head it. The French plan was to create a non-Communist Vietnamese state that would offer a political alternative to the Vietminh revolutionary regime and provide a rallying point for non-Communist Vietnamese nationalists. Such a government could pose a threat to the Vietminh. If Bao Dai succeeded in uniting the various non-Communist political factions into a cohesive force, he could create "a serious alternative to the Vietminh Front for the loyalty of the Vietnamese people."[24]

The French political strategy in 1947 failed for two main reasons. The first, a perennial problem of Vietnamese politics, especially southern urban Vietnamese politics, was the inability of various non-Communist nationalist factions to overcome chronic political fragmentation and form a stable coalition government. The second was the French refusal to grant the proposed government anything resembling independence. It promised to be only a puppet regime that most Vietnamese regarded as a cover for French colonialism, and they made a point of shunning it.

Although the French had seized both the military and political initiative in the fall of 1947, they had failed to either destroy the Vietminh army or to create a viable political alternative to Ho Chi Minh's revolutionary nationalism. French leaders failed to realize it at the time, but their effort to reimpose colonialism on the Vietnamese had reached its high-water mark. Given Vietminh control of most of the countryside and the fact that it had the support of most of the people, a French military victory was probably never a realistic possibility, at least not with the force levels they were willing to commit to the war.

Vietminh prospects improved markedly in 1948. In China, the Communists were fast gaining the upper hand against Chiang Kai-shek's Nationalist armies. Mao's victory, which now appeared to Ho Chi Minh and his associates to be only a matter of time, offered the promise of significant economic and military assistance, as well as political support for the struggling Vietnamese revolutionaries.

Emboldened by developments in China and by a sense that the French campaign to destroy their revolution had already reached its limits, General Giap announced that the Vietnamese struggle against the French had progressed to its second stage, the stage of equilibrium. No longer would the rebels be content to remain on the defensive; they would henceforth move to expand both the geographic area and population under their control and to wear down the French main forces. During the second phase of their struggle, they relied mostly upon guerrilla tactics, but occasionally deployed main force units in swift mobile assaults on French forces when they knew they could win.[25] During 1948, both the Vietminh military forces and their political apparatus doubled in size. They regained most of the territory they had lost in the North the previous year and expanded the area in Cochin China under their control. As the year ended, the Vietminh controlled about 55 percent of all Vietnamese villages, north and south. The French, who found themselves bogged down in what one writer called a "quicksand war," mainly controlled the cities and coastal enclaves.[26]

French officials in Vietnam, having failed to defeat the rebels militarily, tried again to outmaneuver them politically. The French also were concerned to attract direct U. S. military support for their increasingly expensive efforts in Indochina that were quickly losing favor with the French public. After a series of negotiations, the French finally persuaded Bao Dai to head a new government that was given the status of "an associated state within the French Union." According to the Elysee Agreement, signed March 8, 1949, the French granted "independence" to the "State of Vietnam," Laos, and Cambodia, all of which became "associated states" within the French Union. The French now claimed that the conflict in Indochina was not a colonial war; it was a civil war between Vietnamese nationalists and Communists, with the French fighting for the nationalist cause.

But all of the new states were to be incorporated into the French Union without most of the attributes of sovereignty. The French retained control over the new

Vietnamese government's foreign affairs, defense forces, and taxes levied on French properties. The new political order constituted a sham, a facade for continuing French domination, and failed to attract the support of most prominent Vietnamese nationalists.[27] For most Vietnamese, there were only two real political choices available in 1949: One could either support the French effort to reimpose colonialism on Indochina, or one could support the revolutionary nationalists resisting the French efforts to reimpose colonialism. The vast majority of the Vietnamese, whatever their politics, opted to support or at least accept the Vietminh.

Perceiving that Bao Dai's government lacked legitimacy, had little real power, and had only a narrow base of support, the Vietminh forces located in the South escalated their revolutionary activity in Saigon and its vicinity. They also infiltrated the new government's police force and its civil service bureaucracies and launched a series of assaults on provincial capitals in the Mekong River Delta. But French troops routed the guerrillas in the Delta, and they were forced to seek refuge in the Plain of Reeds, a huge area of swamps, waterways, and rice paddies fifty miles southwest of Saigon.[28]

By far the most important political event of 1949 influencing the course of the Franco-Vietminh War and the growing U. S. involvement in Vietnam was the Maoist victory in China. The People's Republic of China (PRC) was established in November 1949 as Chiang Kai-Shek, accompanied by remnants of his government bureaucracy and army, fled the Chinese mainland for the island of Formosa (Taiwan). One month later, Chinese Communist military forces appeared at the Vietnamese border. In January 1950, the new Chinese government extended both military assistance and diplomatic recognition to Ho Chi Minh's government, the Democratic Republic of Vietnam (DRV). Moscow soon followed suit, formally recognizing the DRV.[29]

The new relation between China and the Vietminh transformed the Franco-Vietminh conflict both politically and militarily. Until now, Ho Chi Minh had waged his battles with France alone. Now he had a powerful friend and ideological soul brother next door. Responding to the more favorable political situation they found themselves inhabiting, Ho Chi Minh's government also threw off its Patriotic Front trappings. It became openly Communist, and many non-Communist elements were purged. The Indochina Communist Party, which had been dissolved in 1945, reappeared as the Dang Lao Dong Viet Nam (the Vietnamese Worker's Party, or VWP, a.k.a. the Lao Dong).

For the first time since the formation of the Vietminh in 1941, the Vietnamese revolution was cast within a Marxist-Leninist framework.[30] Henceforth, the Vietnamese revolution would be led openly by the Lao Dong. The revolutionaries also made it clear that the socialist revolution, which they had played down for so long for the sake of national unity, would commence as soon as the French were driven out of Vietnam. In fact, the social revolution began before the French were expelled. In 1951, Lao Dong cadres began land reform in various districts in the countryside. Land rents were reduced and rice lands were confiscated from landlords and given to poor peasants. Land reform both restructured rural class relations and strengthened popular support in the countryside for the ongoing war against the French.[31]

Although the political consequences of the new alliance with China were significant, the most important immediate result of the new relationship was to strengthen the Vietnamese Communist military forces tremendously and give them the option of moving to the general counteroffensive, the projected third stage of their protracted struggle against the French.[32] In April 1950, Ho Chi Minh journeyed to Beijing, where he concluded a "lend-lease arrangement" with the Chinese.[33] The Chinese loaned the Vietminh artillery, mortars, and modern rifles. In addition, Chinese instructors and technicians arrived in Viet Bac to train the Vietnamese in the use of more effective weapons and tactics. By the fall of 1950, General Giap had 60,000 regulars organized into five infantry divisions. All of his soldiers were indoctrinated, disciplined, well-trained, and armed with modern weapons. The Vietminh Army had been transformed—from a ragtag band of irregulars into a formidable modern military force.

While the Vietnamese revolutionaries were being strengthened immensely by their Chinese friends, the French effort in Vietnam was sagging, hampered by declining popular support at home. In the eyes of many of the French back home, the Indochina War had become too expensive; they did not like it, and they did not want it. Responding to the war's growing unpopularity, the French government refused to send conscripts to fight in the war and also reduced the number of French troops in Vietnam by nearly 10,000. When Giap took the offensive in 1950, the French forces found themselves with fewer troops having to face the newly enhanced Vietminh units.

Giap's objectives were to clear out a string of French garrisons that reached into the northern countryside along the Chinese frontier. The principal garrison was at Dong Khe, which fell to the aggressive assaults of the Vietminh after two days of tough fighting on September 16, 1950.[34] After Dong Khe had fallen, the French evacuated two other sites, and the Vietnamese battered the retreating columns from these garrisons.

Dong Khe was a major military disaster for the French. It exposed all of the other outposts to attack. They were either overrun or evacuated, and the retreating troops often were hammered by the mobile, aggressive Vietminh units that were using artillery, mortars, grenades, and machine-gun fire. French losses were heavy; some 6,000 were either casualties or captured by the Vietminh. The French also abandoned a huge stockpile of valuable weapons, ammunition, medical supplies, and foodstuffs, all eagerly confiscated by the victorious Vietminh troops.[35] Giap's forces drove the French out of northern Tonkin and pushed them back into the coastal enclaves.

Giap's border offensive during the fall of 1950 constituted a major turning point in the Franco-Vietminh War. For the first time, the Vietminh had attacked and defeated sizeable units of a modern European army. Giap's troops were now positioned to invade the strategic Red River Delta with its large population and rich rice harvests. They also had unrestricted access to China and its resources and growing prospects for aid from the USSR and Eastern Bloc countries. Most of all, the Vietminh could now seize the tactical initiative in the war.[36] French morale sank, and, for the first time, worried French officials had to confront the unthinkable possibility that they could be beaten militarily by their former colonial subjects.

THE FRANCO-AMERICAN PARTNERSHIP

Although the Truman administration had supported the return of the French to Indochina following the defeat of the Japanese, Washington was nevertheless alarmed by the outbreak of the Franco-Vietminh War in 1946. Because the Indochina conflict was only one of several national revolutions occurring simultaneously in Southeast Asia, that economically and strategically significant region, from Washington's vantage point, appeared to be one of the globe's most volatile areas.[37] The State Department was leery of the United States overtly aligning itself with French colonialism. Further, by the end of 1947, Washington officials were skeptical that the French could ever defeat the Vietminh militarily, that Vietnamese nationalism could be subdued by force. They believed the French would have to make some accommodation to satisfy the nationalist aspirations of the Vietnamese people.

But if they were skeptical of French efforts to retrieve their Indochinese empire, acting and later Secretary of State Dean Acheson was appalled at the prospect of an independent Vietnamese nation under the control of Communist revolutionary Ho Chi Minh. Acheson's problem was that U. S. State Department officials serving in Vietnam and those who traveled to that country on official business in the late 1940s could find no credible evidence linking Ho Chi Minh to Moscow, nor any sign that he was carrying out Soviet policies in Indochina. In fact, the Soviets appeared to not have any Indochina policy in the late 1940s. U. S. officials also knew that Ho Chi Minh led and personified the Vietnamese drive for self-determination. Further, they were aware that he and other Vietminh leaders repeatedly appealed to the Americans for support and protection from the French imperialists.

Acheson finally resolved the question of how Communist Ho Chi Minh and his Vietminh colleagues would be perceived in 1949 by asserting what the Secretary of State no doubt regarded as a self-evident proposition: Ho Chi Minh is a Communist, and if Vietnam achieves its independence, he will show his true Stalinist colors. Acheson operated on the assumption that Communism and nationalism were incompatible ideological forces. He refused to consider the possibility that the Vietminh leaders, although surely committed Communist ideologues, also represented the nationalistic aspirations of most Vietnamese, whatever their politics or class interests. Acheson knew little of Vietnamese history or culture and had no understanding of Ho Chi Minh's fierce determination to not only rid Vietnam of French imperialism, but to also remain free of Soviet or Chinese domination. While the Vietminh willingly accepted help from the major Communist powers, they had no intention of exchanging French colonialism for any form of Communist domination. But Washington assumed that Ho Chi Minh and his chief associates were Stalinist agents and therefore believed it was in the best interests of the United States to prevent a Communist revolution from occurring in Indochina that they equated with advancing the imperial interests of the Soviets and Chinese.[38]

In short, U. S. policy makers confronted a dilemma in Indochina in the late 1940s. On the one hand, they rejected imposing colonialism as neither desirable nor possible; on the other hand, they rejected a French military withdrawal that would leave "chaos and terroristic activities" in its wake and open the way to a Communist takeover in Vietnam. Not wanting the French either to win or get out, and unable to implement or even conceive of an alternative policy, State Department officials shrugged their shoulders and for a few years followed a passive policy that included covert support of the French effort to reimpose colonialism in Indochina while fussing about its desirability and feasibility. In the formative years of the Cold War, there could be some flexibility, some space for internal debate, at least some ambiguity and indecision within the State Department about the direction American foreign policy should take in Southeast Asia. Attitudes had not yet been fully formed; ideas had not yet hardened into anti-Communist dogmas. Within a few years, external events, domestic political pressures, and Cold War ideological imperatives had resolved the dilemma. The United States openly supported the French war to reimpose colonialism on the Vietnamese and justified that support in the name of anti-Communism.[39]

America's Indochina policy at the outset of the Cold War with the Soviet Union in 1946 and 1947 was distinctly secondary to U. S. interests in Europe. The Truman administration pursued a Euro-centered foreign policy premised on the view that Soviet expansionism across war-torn Europe represented the principal threat to American vital interests in the postwar world. In March 1947, the president had proclaimed the Truman Doctrine, which committed the United States to a policy of containing Communism in Europe. Within Western Europe, France was the focus of U. S. concerns in the late 1940s because it had a war-shattered economy, an unstable government, and a powerful and popular Communist party. American officials feared the Communists could come to power in France, given its shaky economic and political status.

Committed to keeping France within the Free World orbit, the United States provided France with political, economic, and moral support during the late 1940s. Part of this support took the form of leaving the French a free hand in Indochina. Between 1946 and 1949, the official U. S. position on the Franco-Vietminh War was one of neutrality. Covertly, the United States furnished the French with substantial amounts of financial and military assistance.[40] In late 1946, Washington made $160 million available to the French for use in Vietnam. In September of 1948, the U. S. ambassador to France privately told French officials that Washington would consider it appropriate for the French to spend a portion of their Marshall Plan funds on military operations in Indochina.[41] The American Indochina policy during the late 1940s was hostage to the much more important commitment of building up postwar France to prevent a possible Communist takeover in that crucial European country.

Just as it profoundly altered the political and strategic situation in Indochina, the Chinese revolution induced major changes in America's Indochina policy that, in turn, were components of a general reorientation of U. S. global foreign policy during 1949 and 1950. The French, facing both a much more formidable foe armed and trained with Chinese assistance and the loss back home of popular support for their colonial war, starting in late 1949, began requesting direct assistance from the United States. France warned U. S. officials that without greater amounts of American military and economic assistance they could lose the war and would have to leave Indochina. They found a receptive audience in Washington, where President Truman and his advisers were reappraising American foreign policy in the light of two global disasters that had occurred in the fall of 1949: the Soviet's successful testing of an atomic device that fractured the American nuclear monopoly and the fall of China to the Communists, which took 600 million people behind the "Bamboo Curtain."

In the aftermath of these two major blows to American prestige and power, President Truman and his advisers, convinced that the principal goal of Soviet foreign policy was to dominate the world and that the recent Chinese revolution accorded with Stalinist ambitions for imposing Communism worldwide, looked at a world divided into two hostile camps. In his public utterances, Truman interpreted this political bipolarity in highly charged moralistic terms. He saw the forces of freedom engaging the forces of tyranny. In Truman's Manichaean view, the complex conflicts of interest between the Western powers and the Communist nations pitted the forces of light against the forces of darkness in a mortal struggle for control of the political future of the planet and the destinies of all of its people.[42] Fearing a shift in the balance of power in favor of the Communists and dreading the prospect of global war,

> the Truman administration initiated plans to increase American military capabilities, shore up the defense of Western Europe, and extend the containment policy to the Far East.[43]

Convinced that Europe faced grave danger from an expansionist Soviet Union now empowered with nuclear weapons, the United States moved to shore up French defenses and to propose rearming West Germany. Fearful lest the French not approve the creation of a European Defense Community (EDC), a plan for integrating French and West German forces into a multinational army, the United States met French demands for direct American support for their Indochina campaign. The Truman administration implemented a program of direct military and economic assistance for the French colonial war in Indochina in the hopes that such support would induce the French to cooperate with U. S. strategic designs for Europe and would also free up French resources for the North Atlantic Treaty Organization (NATO).

At the same time the United States was committing itself to underwriting the security of Western Europe, Washington came to the conclusion that, in the aftermath of the Chinese revolution, the strategic security of Southeast Asia itself had become an important U. S. interest. From the American perspective, it appeared that Southeast Asia, with its explosive mix of declining European imperial powers and unstable newly independent states, was vulnerable to pressure from both China and the

U.S.S.R., especially China because of its geographic propinquity. Loss of these rich former European colonies to the Communists would close Western Europe out of major markets. Cutting off sources of vital raw materials such as rubber, tin, and oil would retard Europe's, and particularly Britain's, postwar recovery. Loss of the region would also set back the economic recovery of the nation that had quickly become America's principal Far Eastern ally following the fall of China, the recent World War II enemy, Japan. Such developments would also harm U. S. economic interests. America needed prosperous trading partners in Europe and the Pacific Rim that could earn the foreign exchange convertible to dollars needed to buy the exports that would sustain U. S. economic growth and prosperity in the postwar era.

Within the framework of the new American Southeast Asian policy calculus, U. S. officials regarded Indochina, particularly Vietnam, as the key to the security of the entire region. If Ho Chi Minh's revolution, now backed by both the Chinese and the Soviets, succeeded in driving the French out of Vietnam, it would open the rest of Southeast Asia to Communist penetration.[44] It was this application of the domino theory to the Franco-Vietminh War in the aftermath of the Maoist triumph in China that greatly raised the American stake in Indochina and transformed what had been a comparatively minor appendage of the U. S. Euro-centered goal of shoring up France after World War II into a major foreign policy concern in its own right. The domino theory reflected the American ignorance of the profound differences among Asian nations and societies. It also reflected a failure to appreciate the power of Asian nationalisms.

Washington feared that if Vietnam fell to the Communists, so would Laos, Cambodia, Thailand, Burma, and Malaysia. Perhaps Japan, Indonesia, possibly even the Philippines and the Indian subcontinent, would be vulnerable. Maybe in time even Australia and New Zealand could fall to the Communist juggernaut. Americans feared that severe economic problems and political instability in these countries in the aftermath of war and decolonization made Communism appealing to people and undermined their ability to resist aggression. Interlinking its security to the security of these weak Asian nations, Washington believed the United States could one day be threatened by the expansionist Communist monolith.

What Washington perceived to be at stake in Vietnam by 1950 was no longer merely the outcome of a regional colonial war. Indochina had become one of the front lines in the global Cold War between Communism and Freedom, one of the key links in the security chain. In American eyes, the French were no longer merely fighting to reimpose colonialism on the Vietnamese, they were part of the Western world's concerted effort to contain Chinese and Soviet Communism in Europe and Asia. The United States had to "draw the line" in Southeast Asia by providing economic assistance to friendly governments and helping to reconstruct the Japanese economy. Southeast Asia would be crucial for the Japanese future, as a source of raw materials and as a market for manufactures now that China had been removed from the capitalist orbit.[45]

Another factor, in addition to developments in Europe and Asia, drove Washington to invest the outcome of the Franco-Vietminh War with enhanced strategic significance in 1950. American internal political considerations, particularly the growth of domestic anti-Communism, exerted a strong influence on the Truman administration's new foreign policy design. Conservative Republicans accused Truman's liberal Democratic administration of being "soft on Communism," that is, they accused these officials of not taking the tough, effective measures that they insisted were needed to contain the spread of Communism abroad and to squelch "Red" subversion at home.[46]

The Maoist triumph in China gave the domestic practitioners of the politics of anti-Communism an enormous boost. Many conservative Republicans, and some Democrats, charged President Truman, Secretary of State Dean Acheson, and other high administration officials, with the "loss of China." Chiang fell, these critics asserted, because the Truman administration did not provide the Chinese Nationalists with enough military and economic support, that they, in effect, sold them out to the Communists. Senator Robert Taft of Ohio led the Republican onslaught against the Truman administration for "losing China."

In the aftermath of the fall of China to the Communists, Truman feared that if his administration did not energetically back the French in Vietnam and they subsequently lost their war, the conservative senatorial wolf pack would be after him again, this time for the "loss of Indochina." Such an outcome would cost both him and the Democrats popular support and probably the next election. This domestic political factor that bedeviled Truman and Acheson became "one of the most powerful and enduring factors shaping American policy toward Vietnam."[47] During the early and mid-1960s, the domestic politics of anti-Communism strongly influenced the decisions of the Kennedy and Johnson administrations that gradually committed the United States to its longest war.

Whatever lingering anticolonial scruples American officials may have held were quickly overmastered by the application of the containment doctrine and its domino correlative to Southeast Asia in the aftermath of the Chinese revolution and the Soviet acquisition of a nuclear capability. For the Truman administration, supporting the French war in Indochina had become an urgent necessity, a strategic imperative, vital to the security interests of the United States and its allies. A regional conflict between Asian nationalists and French imperialists that had begun in 1945 had by 1950 become enmeshed in the global Cold War struggle between the East and the West.[48]

The French made it easier for the United States to support directly its Indochina War by creating the Bao Dai puppet regime in 1949. Although the Bao Dai government possessed few attributes of sovereignty and few Vietnamese supported it, it enabled the French to claim, disingenuously, that they were fighting to preserve a non-Communist Vietnamese nation from the forces of international Communism intent on pulling Indochina into the Soviet-Chinese orbit. Although the Bao Dai ploy attracted few Vietnamese, American officials claimed publicly that the French were offering the Vietnamese people a genuine nationalistic alternative to the revolutionary cohorts of Ho Chi Minh. Even if American officials were not certain that the French, with

American help, could defeat the Vietminh, they feared that if they did not lend assistance, the French would surely lose and that the outcome would be ruinous to U. S. interests in Southeast Asia. In February 1950, the United States formally took sides in the Franco-Vietminh War when it extended diplomatic recognition to Bao Dai's "Associated States of Vietnam." By backing the Bao Dai regime, the United States hoped to "avoid the appearance of being an accomplice of French imperialism."[49]

By backing French imperialism and its Vietnamese puppets, the United States had committed itself to a losing cause; it had aligned itself with the losing side in the Franco-Vietminh War. By the time America had committed itself to directly supporting the French military effort, the Vietminh armed forces had gained the strategic initiative and had taken the offensive. The revolutionary nationalists controlled two-thirds of the land and the people of Vietnam. The Chinese were providing Giap's forces with substantial amounts of modern weaponry. The French were on the defensive, clinging to the cities and coastal enclaves. The war had become unpopular in France, and the French government was wavering in its support of the war. Bao Dai himself acknowledged that his pseudo-government was merely a French tool.[50]

The unanticipated outbreak of the Korean War in late June 1950, when North Korean armies suddenly invaded South Korea to try to unify Korea under Communist control, confirmed the Truman administration's belief that the Soviet Union was an expansionist power intent on dominating all of Asia. Although he had no evidence or intelligence data to confirm it, Truman simply assumed that the North Korean troops were Soviet proxies and that Beijing also marched to Stalin's orders. Chinese intervention in the Korean War in late November 1950 raised the specter in Washington and Paris that Chinese troops could also invade Vietnam. These developments reinforced President Truman's and Secretary of State Acheson's sense of the importance of Vietnam and of the vital need for the French to continue their war to prevent Communist expansion into Southeast Asia. Washington linked the French war against the Vietnamese Communists with the U. S. war against the North Korean and Chinese Communists; they were twin fronts in a larger campaign to save Asia from Communist conquest. Initially, U. S. support for the French Indochina War derived from American efforts to shore up the French after the devastation and humiliation of World War II. With the success of the Chinese revolution and the outbreak of war in Korea, support for the French war now took on a far larger purpose: stopping the spread of Communism in Asia. Backing the French Indochina War became part of the U. S. global crusade to contain international Communism.

In the summer of 1950, the first U. S. aid package for the French Indochina War was implemented and a unit of U. S. military advisers, designated the Military Assistance and Advisory Group (MAAG), was sent to Vietnam. The MAAG officials were to coordinate the aid program and instruct the French, and, later, the Vietnamese, in the use of American weapons and tactics. At the same time, U. S. officials inaugurated a program of economic and technical assistance for the Bao Dai government. During 1951 and 1952, the United States provided increasing amounts of military and economic aid to sustain the French war effort.[51] With America backing the French and China backing the Vietminh, the Franco-Vietminh War had become an international affair.

The French also feared a Chinese invasion of northern Vietnam akin to the Chinese intervention in Korea. Knowing their forces could not cope with the Chinese should they come in, the French sought Washington's assurance that American troops would be sent to Indochina to fight the Chinese if they entered Vietnam. Truman, wary of getting into another land war in Asia after Korea, made it clear to French officials that under no circumstances would American ground troops be sent to Indochina. The President apparently considered sending Nationalist Chinese troops from Taiwan to Vietnam to fight alongside the French in the event of a Chinese invasion.[52]

The Americans found themselves repeatedly frustrated by their French partners. Despite receiving large amounts of U. S. military aid, the French forces could never reverse the course of the war. To defeat a guerrilla army, an invader force must have overwhelming military superiority and strong popular support. The French never had either. French forces never seriously considered fighting for a truly independent Vietnam. They paid lip service to the cause of Vietnamese nationalism, but they kept the Bao Dai regime tightly under their control, thus preventing it from ever becoming a credible alternative to the revolutionary nationalists. The French also hampered the U. S. aid programs that furnished economic and technical assistance to the Vietnamese people, because they did not want the Vietnamese people to know that the Americans were helping them.

Any efforts by Americans to pressure a series of weak French governments to fight harder or consider a grant of independence to the Vietnamese were met by French arguments that they could not approve the EDC, or that they might have to leave Vietnam and let the United States confront the results of a Communist takeover. The French could always play their trump card against the Americans: they could threaten to pull out of Vietnam and allow the Communists to take over. Viewing such an outcome as intolerable and having no comparable leverage with the French, Washington, rather than risk such possibilities, acquiesced in the face of these threats. The United States continued to provide ever increasing amounts of aid and let the French call the shots.[53] Consequently, in the eyes of most Vietnamese, the Americans appeared to be supporters of French colonialism, not Asian nationalism, and the French position in Indochina continued to deteriorate.

The new American Southeast Asian foreign policy forged from 1949 to 1950 rested on false premises and misunderstandings. The Vietminh revolution was not inspired or directed by Moscow or Beijing. Washington failed to understand that Vietnamese revolutionary nationalism had indigenous roots and causes; that Ho Chi Minh and his associates represented the cause of Vietnamese nationalism; the powerful and widespread appeal that the drive for independence from European colonialism had with nearly all Vietnamese regardless of their politics; and that Ho Chi Minh was not a Stalinist or Maoist stooge. Truman and Acheson's flawed Indochina policies laid the groundwork for the American ordeal in Vietnam.

It was the U. S. decision to support the French war in Vietnam that drew the Americans into their "initial political commitments in Indochina."[54] Here lie the roots of the subsequent long American involvement in Southeast Asia that culminated in the American Vietnam war. Gradually, by stages, the American commitment in Indochina escalated under a succession of presidencies. Truman made the initial decision to support the French war effort. Eisenhower made the decision to intervene in southern Vietnam to replace the French and support the efforts of Ngo Dinh Diem to establish a non-Communist state to stop the further spread of Communism in Indochina. Kennedy escalated the American effort and inaugurated a small-scale U. S. war in South Vietnam. Johnson made the fateful decision in July 1965 to fight a major U. S. war in Vietnam. All of these major decisions were made by presidents after consultations with their leading civilian and military advisers. These chief executives did not often seek advice from Congress, nor was there extensive public debate about Vietnam at any stage of the gradually expanding American intervention.

Most Americans were neither informed about nor involved in the Vietnam foreign policy process over the long interval during which an initial commitment to support the French Indochina War grew incrementally into a major American war in Southeast Asia. Vietnam did not become an important issue in this country until 1965 and did not become a source of major controversy until 1967, nearly twenty years after American involvement in that region had begun. When Americans awakened one day in the summer of 1965 to find their country fighting a major war in a remote part of the world that most citizens knew scarcely anything about nor could even find on a map, they had no inkling of the long preparation time or the policies or events that preceded it.

THE ROAD TO DIEN BIEN PHU

As the Truman administration, in response to the Soviet possession of nuclear weapons, the Chinese revolution, and the Franco-Vietminh War, devised its expanded foreign policy based on containing Communism around the world, the war in Indochina also expanded. The Vietminh offensive during the fall of 1950 forced the French to face a hard choice. They could either increase their military forces substantially and seek a military victory over the Vietminh, or they could try for a negotiated settlement with their stubborn foes. Neither choice appealed to French officials, and they tried to avoid the dilemma by calling on the United States for military aid and by creating a Vietnamese national army to supplement the French forces; the French called this latter move "the yellowing of the army." American aid was soon forthcoming, and "the new Army of the Republic of Vietnam began to take shape."[55] In addition, the French brought in their best field commander to take charge of the war, General de Lattre de Tassigny, who soon infused the French forces with new determination and confidence. He viewed the Red River Delta as the key to winning the war and built up French defenses in that region by stringing a series of concrete forts along the boundaries of the Delta to prevent infiltration of this strategic region by Vietminh forces.

General Giap, having concluded that the time had come to launch the third stage of the protracted war against the French imperialists, opened a general offensive in January 1951 in the western end of the Delta. Two Vietminh infantry divisions, 22,000 troops altogether, attacked the provincial capital of Vinh Yeh, which was defended by a force of 10,000 French. In two days of hard fighting in which Giap employed a series of human wave attacks, the outnumbered French beat off the Vietminh and inflicted heavy casualties on them by using superior firepower and air attacks. During the ensuing months, the Vietminh attacked other towns at the edges of the Delta, and the outnumbered French fought them off every time and usually inflicted heavy casualties. Giap called off the failed offensive in June after having lost about 15,000 troops, either killed or wounded.[56]

Clearly, Giap's decision to take to the offensive had been premature. The campaigns against de Lattre's soldiers showed that the French were still full of fight and revealed serious weaknesses in the DRV Army's ability to conduct large-scale conventional warfare. But the failed Vietminh offensive in 1951 did not alter the basic military situation. The DRV forces significantly outnumbered the French; they could marshal 225,000 troops against approximately 150,000 French main forces deployed throughout Indochina.[57] The French remained in an essentially defensive position. Substantial amounts of American military aid, the creation of the Vietnamese National Army (ARVN), the presence of General de Lattre, and the bloody losses inflicted on the Vietminh troops could not turn the tide of war in favor of the French.

Between 1951 and 1953, the Vietminh launched several attacks, primarily in northern Vietnam. There was correspondingly little fighting in central and southern Vietnam. French pacification efforts were relatively successful in Cochin China, and, consequently, the Vietminh forces had a much thinner base of popular support in Saigon and its vicinity. In the north, the DRV forces retained the strategic initiative; the French remained in defensive positions, although occasionally de Lattre would send out a strike force to hit the Vietminh. The normal pattern was for the Vietminh to choose the time and place for an assault. Their strategy was to probe the French for weak spots, attack in force, inflict as many casualties as they could, and then break off the engagement and retreat to their mountain sanctuaries in Viet Bac. Their goals were to wear the French down, keep pressure on them, undermine their morale, and weaken their political support in France.

One of the major campaigns fought during this phase of the war took place at Hoa Binh in November 1951. Hoa Binh was a town about fifty miles west of Hanoi, outside the de Lattre line of defense. It sat astride a major supply and communications route of the Vietminh in the hills to the west of the Delta. It was inhabited by the Muouong tribe, a Montagnard people loyal to France. If the French could hold Hoa Binh, it would seriously hamper the ability of Vietminh main forces to mount attacks in the Red River Delta and would extend the French defense perimeter twenty-five miles west. The French occupied the town without meeting much resistance from the Vietminh initially.

Giap, determined to drive the French out of the strategic site, committed several divisions to the battle. The Hoa Binh campaign lasted three months, with many intense battles being fought as Giap sent wave after wave of attackers against the French positions. Both sides were now using modern U. S. weapons. The weapons had been furnished to the French under the U. S. aid program; the Vietminh had acquired them from the Chinese and through theft and capture. The DRV attacks gradually wore the French down, and they were forced to withdraw from Hoa Binh in mid-February.[58] Meanwhile, General de Lattre, who had become seriously ill during the battles for Hoa Binh, returned to France, where he died on February 11, 1952, of cancer.

Hoa Binh was a major victory for the Vietminh. Six months after their victory, Vietminh political cadres had organized most of the villages of the western delta. More important, the victory at Hoa Binh gave Ho Chi Minh, General Giap, and the other DRV leaders a growing confidence that defeating the French was within their grasp.

During the years 1951 to 1953, as the war raged on, the Vietminh political cadres continued their efforts to organize the Vietnamese people in the cities and coastal enclaves still under French control. The DRV leaders had always emphasized the crucial role that political organization played in their revolution to rid Vietnam of the French presence and to implement Communism. They hoped to foment popular uprisings in the cities that would further weaken the declining French grip on Indochina. But Vietminh organizers found little support for their cause among the urban populations.[59] Among the urban classes that they assumed might share an affinity for their movement—students, workers, and intellectuals—they often encountered either opposition or indifference. Disappointed, Vietminh leaders concluded that the major political base of the Vietnamese revolution would have to remain in the countryside.

To solidify their support among the poorer classes of peasants and to strike against landlords who opposed their program, the Vietminh implemented land reform in areas under their control, modeling it after the Maoist program implemented during the Chinese Civil War. In Tonkin and Cochin China, thousands of peasants received land.[60] Land reform strengthened the Vietminh political base in the countryside, weakened the landlord classes, advanced the Vietminh social revolution, and foreshadowed the large-scale land reform programs undertaken in North Vietnam during the mid-1950s, following the defeat of the French and their American backers.

In April 1953, General Henri Navarre assumed command of the French forces in Indochina with orders to win the war. Given the assets available to him, he knew he had been assigned an impossible mission. The DRV forces now totalled 350,000 armed troops, organized into eight infantry and one armored division, and the size of the Vietminh army increased daily as new troops arrived from China where they had been undergoing military training and political indoctrination.[61] French force levels, deployed over the whole of Vietnam, were not sufficient to counter this large DRV army. The new Vietnamese National Army had not developed as expected; its troops had little incentive to fight for the Bao Dai government, which they knew was French-controlled. There was wholesale avoidance of military service in that army, and the quality of its recruits was low. Navarre knew the ARVN could not effectively supplement the French expeditionary forces. In France, by the spring of 1953, public opposition to the war was widespread; many politicians were openly calling for negotiations to end the conflict that its critics called *la guerre sale* ("the dirty war"). Washington, fearing the French might falter and that Indochina would be lost to the Communists, was putting intense pressure on the French government, headed by Premier Joseph Laniel, to step up its war effort.

Feeling the pressure both from his government and the Americans, General Navarre developed a plan to try to improve the French military position in Indochina before any negotiations began. The first phase involved regaining control of the Red River Delta. Navarre attacked Vietminh strongholds in the western delta. Following a strategy that had been worked out the previous January, Giap did not challenge the French forces; his troops retreated in the face of Navarre's assaults. French troops regained delta provinces that had fallen under Vietminh control. While French forces reoccupied parts of the Delta, Giap's forces ranged widely over northwest Vietnam and into Laos, where Vietminh forces threatened a French-supported regime in that lightly defended landlocked country.[62]

General Navarre, concerned for the safety of Laos and wanting to disrupt the Vietminh offensive in northwest Tonkin, decided to take a strategic gamble. In mid-November 1953, he sent his paratroopers to occupy strong points blocking a major Vietminh invasion route into Laos, cutting off one of their supply routes from China. He also intended to tie down a sizeable number of Giap's forces to keep them out of the Red River Delta. He chose a site by a village lying 170 miles northwest of Hanoi, just ten miles from the Laotian border. The town was near two airstrips in a broad valley surrounded by hills and mountains. Navarre assumed Giap would be forced to attack the new fortress. Navarre believed he, having control of the air and possessing superior firepower, would be able to send enough troops to make the French position invulnerable to Vietminh assaults. Navarre intended to force the Vietnamese to fight at a place of his own choosing and then inflict on them a significant defeat that would improve the French military position in Indochina and rekindle domestic support for the war. The site General Navarre selected to make his stand would soon become famous as a symbol of French futility and defeat in Indochina. It was called Dien Bien Phu.

The DRV did not respond immediately to the French thrust into Dien Bien Phu, and they continued their campaign in northwest Tonkin and Laos. Navarre, while building up his defenses at Dien Bien Phu, also launched the second phase of his plan to regain the military initiative in Indochina, a series of operations in northern Annam called "Operation Atlante."[63] These attacks were designed to clear the Vietminh forces out of north-central Vietnam to permit the pacification of this major rice-growing region. Giap chose not to commit any main force units to challenge Operation Atlante, relying instead on local guerrillas to disrupt French efforts to pacify these key coastal provinces. Giap also countered Navarre's move into northern Annam by sending Vietminh main force units into the central highlands regions to the west. Their attacks on French outposts in Kontum Province forced Navarre to disperse his forces and prevented the French from consolidating their position in Annam.

While the DRV and French forces battled each other throughout northern and central Vietnam during the fall of 1953, both sides also moved toward negotiating a settlement. Premier Laniel indicated his interest in finding a compromise solution to the conflict.[64] Ho Chi Minh said he would like to hear the French proposals. In February 1954, the foreign ministers of the major powers scheduled an international peace conference to convene in Geneva in April to consider proposals for the unification of Korea in the aftermath of the armistice agreement that had ended the Korean War the previous August. Despite American objections, the foreign ministers added the settlement of the Indochina War to the proposed conference agenda.

Shortly after the announcement that a peace conference would be meeting in May to settle the Franco-Vietminh War, General Giap decided to attack Dien Bien Phu. He had several reasons for doing so: He wanted to inflict a major military defeat on the French that would coincide with the opening of the Geneva Conference in order to maximize the DRV's leverage at the bargaining table. Dien Bien Phu was the key to the Navarre strategy. If the garrison were taken, the French plan would fail and the Vietminh would retain the military initiative. A defeat at Dien Bien Phu could finish the French in Indochina. Such a devastating defeat might destroy the remaining French will to continue the war.[65]

Giap was confident that he and his staff had devised a strategy that would bring the Vietminh forces victory at Dien Bien Phu. He planned a siege of the French positions. He also planned to destroy the airstrips to cut off French supply sources and prevent them from bringing in reinforcements. He would place artillery and mortars in the hills overlooking Dien Bien Phu, and the Vietminh gunners would bombard the French and wear them down. Infantry assaults would seize their strong points one by one until their center was taken.[66]

For the battle, Giap deployed over 50,000 main force troops, another 50,000 support forces, and 200,000 workers to man his supply lines. The Vietnamese were also joined by an estimated 20,000 to 30,000 Chinese workers, technicians, mechanics, truck drivers, advisers, and artillerymen. The Chinese made crucial contributions to the Vietminh campaign at Dien Bien Phu. In addition to personnel, they supplied ammunition, weapons, gasoline, and foodstuffs. Chinese staff officers also helped Giap plan and implement his tactics. The Soviets provided aid to the Vietminh forces as well as they prepared for the most important battle of the long war. The Soviets furnished trucks and artillery and also established a Soviet Bloc aid pool to support the DRV war effort.[67] Giap and his staff took three months to prepare the battlefield in meticulous detail.

The French had a scant 12,000 troops under Colonel Christian de Castries dug in at Dien Bien Phu to face Giap's carefully prepared forces. The French had arrayed themselves in a coordinated series of strongly defended areas. The main ones were clustered around the larger airstrip; away from these main points were four other defended areas, each guarding an approach to their center.[68]

The Battle of Dien Bien Phu began on March 13, 1954, at sunset, when Vietminh artillery placed in the surrounding mountainsides opened fire on the French positions below. Vietminh infantry also assaulted one of the outlying strong points that first night. Fighting was fierce, and the Vietminh sustained heavy losses. Within two days, Vietminh artillery and mortars had shut down the airstrips. Thereafter, the French defenders could only be reinforced and supplied by parachute drop. Vietminh artillery continually shelled the French positions. Navarre, victimized by faulty military intelligence, had not anticipated that the Vietminh could bring in the firepower that they did. He had counted on his air force silencing the enemy's artillery. But the French planes could not destroy the Vietminh guns, because they had been placed in camouflaged tunnels dug into mountains and were moved around constantly.[69]

In early April, Giap launched a series of all-out infantry assaults in an effort to overrun the outer defenses. The French fought them off and inflicted heavy losses on the attacking Vietnamese. Following the failure of his assault tactics, Giap resorted to tunneling. Vietminh sappers tunneled their way toward the French positions. They dug night and day. Miles of trenches zigzagged toward the strong points. The French perimeter steadily shrank in the face of this antlike labor. French artillery, mortars, explosive charges, and counterattacks slowed, but could never halt, the tunneling process.

As Giap's sappers slowly tightened the noose, Navarre realized Dien Bien Phu was doomed. With the airstrips closed down, he could not extract his soldiers from what had become a trap that he had set for them. Neither could he adequately reinforce and supply his beleaguered force or evacuate his wounded. He concluded that only massive air strikes by American bombers could save the defenders. High French officials urged the Americans to intervene and save them. The United States refused.

Giap ordered a series of assaults beginning May 1. Night and day the Vietminh soldiers attacked the French positions. They came in waves, unrelentingly. The French defenders fought hard and made the Vietminh pay dearly in blood and pain for their victory. On May 7, the Vietminh 308th broke through into the center of the French defenses. On May 8, the French surrendered. They had lost about 7,500 men, killed or wounded. About 10,000 French soldiers were marched off into captivity, over half of whom perished while prisoners of war. During the fifty-five-day battle, the Vietminh sustained an estimated 25,000 casualties.[70]

But they had won a glorious victory, the most important one of the war. Asians had defeated Europeans in a large-scale pitched battle. They also had broken the spine of French military power in northern Vietnam. Whatever lingering popular support for the war still existed in France collapsed, as did any remaining resolve on the part of the French government to continue the bloody, expensive, and futile campaign. The victorious general, Vo Nguyen Giap, defined the historic significance of Dien Bien Phu:

> A colonized people once it has risen up and is united in the struggle and determined to fight for its independence and peace, has the full power to defeat the strong aggressive army of an imperialist country.[71]

The day after the French surrender at Dien Bien Phu, the Indochina phase of the Geneva Peace Conference began.

As the delegates began negotiations at Geneva, the war raged on in Indochina. Pumped up by his great victory at Dien Bien Phu, the Vietminh tiger, with teeth bared and looking for the kill, now went after the weary French elephant. The French withdrew to a restricted area around Hanoi and Haiphong. About 80 percent of the country was now under Vietminh control. They held nearly all of Tonkin, most of Annam,

Figure 2.1   French soldiers in combat at Dien Bien Phu, April 1954. The Vietminh victory at Dien Bien Phu brought an end to French efforts to reimpose colonialism on Indochina. *Source:* USMI Photo Archives

and about half of Cochin China, including much of the rich Mekong River Delta. While the politicians talked at Geneva, the French army battled for its life.

TO THE BRINK OF WAR

President Eisenhower and his energetic Secretary of State John Foster Dulles assumed office in January 1953, committed to continuing the Truman-Acheson policies in Indochina. They shared their predecessors' assumptions and goals, believing that the fall of Indochina to the Communists would cause the loss of all Southeast Asia with disastrous political, economic, and strategic consequences for the United States and its allies in Europe and Asia.[72]

The new administration followed a pattern that would become familiar throughout the years of the long U. S. involvement in Vietnam. It came to office accepting the necessity and importance of the U. S. stake in that country. It was confident it could assert the leadership, avoid the mistakes, and develop the new initiatives required to salvage the deteriorating situation in that region. Each new administration soon discovered to its dismay that its options were limited as was its power to influence the course of events in Vietnam. Each administration also discovered that increasing commitments of American power and prestige, including a large-scale American war that raged in Vietnam for years, while raising U. S. costs and casualties, never empowered a succession of South Vietnamese governments to solve their serious economic, and social problems nor cope with threats to their security posed by revolutionary insurgencies. But the combined efforts of these successive administrations managed to avoid defeat and to achieve a stalemate for a quarter-century. They could delay but they could never develop strategies to defeat the Vietnamese national revolution.

President Eisenhower initially tried to infuse the sagging French war effort in Indochina with new energy, to prod the French to fight the Vietminh more aggressively. He tried to persuade them to grant the Bao Dai government greater powers so it could become a genuine nationalistic alternative to Ho Chi Minh's movement, and Washington substantially increased the amount of military and economic aid to the French and Bao Dai nationalists. Vietnam had become more important to Washington than it was to France.[73] General Navarre's ill-fated strategy derived from Eisenhower's exerting increased pressure on the French government to make another effort to win the war. Ike was disappointed to see that despite the increased American aid and his pep talks, the French military situation continued to deteriorate, and their effort to strengthen Bao Dai's regime foundered. The Vietminh retained the military initiative in Indochina and continued to add territory to its domain in Vietnam and eastern Laos.

Weary of a seemingly interminable war that it no longer had any realistic chance of winning despite increased U. S. aid, the French government sought a compromise solution to the war. Premier Laniel, over American objections, got the Foreign Ministers' Council to place the Indochina War on the agenda of the upcoming Geneva Peace Conference. Reluctantly, the Eisenhower administration acquiesced in the

French decision to seek a political solution to the war. Like the Truman administration that preceded them, Eisenhower and Dulles discovered that they had little leverage with the French, who still had not committed their forces to the European Defense Community (EDC). Too much pressure from Washington to fight harder in Vietnam and the French might then refuse to join the EDC, undermining European unity and playing into the hands of the Soviet Union. American officials also understood that French manpower commitments to the Indochina War significantly reduced the number of soldiers available for NATO assignments or the hoped-for EDC.[74]

As General Giap tightened his grip on the French soldiers trapped at Dien Bien Phu, it became increasingly obvious to both the French and their American sponsors that the French were headed for a major defeat that would spell the end of the war for them and force their humiliating withdrawal from Vietnam. Washington, for the first time, confronted the possibility of direct U. S. military intervention into the Indochina War to try to save the French cause and prevent the loss of Vietnam to the Communists. Washington believed that a Communist victory in Vietnam would threaten the stability, even the survival, of non-Communist governments throughout Southeast Asia.

The French Chief of Staff General Paul Ely journeyed to Washington to request additional U. S. military assistance. Fearful that Dien Bien Phu would soon fall unless the United States intervened militarily, Chairman of the Joint Chiefs of Staff Admiral Arthur Radford proposed a series of U. S. air strikes to save the beleaguered fortress. Code-named Operation VULTURE, the plan included possible use of tactical nuclear weapons. Eisenhower and Dulles showed little enthusiasm for Operation VULTURE or any other use of U.S. air and naval forces to try to save the French. Dulles preferred a diplomatic response to the crisis, the formation of a coalition of powers including the United States, Great Britain, France, Australia, New Zealand, the Philippines, Thailand, and the Associated States to guarantee the security of Southeast Asia. Dulles also hoped the coalition could deter Chinese intervention into Indochina or elsewhere in Asia.

Among the joint chiefs, only Air Force General Nathan F. Twining approved the proposed Operation VULTURE. The other chiefs warned that air intervention entailed many risks and could not save the French cause in Vietnam. Army Chief of Staff General Matthew Ridgway emphatically rejected Operation VULTURE, and he warned his old Army buddy, President Eisenhower, that air power could not win the Franco-Vietminh War and that U. S. ground forces would have to be sent to fight. He also told Eisenhower that if U. S. ground troops were sent into that war, they "would have to fight under the most difficult logistic circumstances and in a uniquely inhospitable terrain."[75] Influenced by Ridgway's caveats, Eisenhower ruled out the use of U. S. ground forces. With the bitter experiences of the stalemated Korean War, which had ended only the previous year, still fresh in the national memory, Eisenhower was not about to send ground troops to Vietnam and risk another unpopular quagmire.

Eisenhower would not consider intervening in Vietnam unilaterally. He insisted that any intervention would have to be an international affair joined by America's

European allies, mainly the British. He also sought a bipartisan congressional resolution of support for any action America might undertake in Vietnam. On April 3, 1954, Dulles and Radford met with the congressional leadership. Both Democratic and Republican leaders told him that without firm commitments from U. S. allies, especially the British, to join any proposed intervention, they, and by extension the American public, would not go along with it. There must be no more Koreas. Since no international support had been forthcoming by this date, Congress, in effect, killed any possibility of a U. S. air attack to save Dien Bien Phu. Two days later, Eisenhower rejected the French request for air strikes.[76]

For the next three weeks, while the battle for Dien Bien Phu raged on and disaster crept closer and closer to the French cause, the United States tried to enlist allied support for some form of united action in Vietnam. President Eisenhower wrote a long personal letter to his friend Prime Minister Winston Churchill, urging him to join an allied coalition to block Communist expansion in Southeast Asia. Eisenhower also held a much-publicized press conference on April 7, during which he tried to rally public support for a possible U. S. military intervention in Vietnam by emphasizing the crucial geopolitical stakes that the United States and the Free World had in the outcome of the Indochina War. He made two major arguments on behalf of Allied interests: First, he stressed that Indochina was a major source of raw materials, such as tin and rubber. Second, he stated that if Indochina fell to the Communists, the rest of Southeast Asia would fall very quickly, like a "row of dominoes." Japan, our most important ally in the Far East, would be threatened; American strategic interests would be undermined: "So the possible consequences of the loss are just incalculable to the free world." Most Americans, who were neither well-informed nor much concerned with the affairs of Indochina, had no discernible response to Ike's press conference pronouncements.[77]

Despite the pleas and pressures emanating from Washington, British Foreign Secretary Anthony Eden, speaking for Churchill, rebuffed the U. S. request to join its crusade to prevent a Communist victory in Vietnam. The British did not share the American faith in the domino theory; they did not share Washington's belief that the loss of Indochina would threaten other members of the international community of nations. They also had no desire to become involved in what they saw as a lost cause. They believed the French were destined to lose their colonial war, and they had no desire to go down with them. The British also believed that outside military intervention on the eve of the Geneva Conference would wreck any prospect for a negotiated settlement of the war and might provoke a Chinese intervention into Indochina. They looked to improving relations with China and the Soviet Union and to the prospect of negotiating with the major Communist powers.[78]

Even if some agreement for intervention had been worked out between the British and the Americans, the terms on which Washington would consider intervening in April 1954 were unacceptable to the French. The United States was willing to try to save the French at Dien Bien Phu, but only if they would reject a negotiated settlement and agree to continue fighting the Indochina War. Both Eisenhower and Dulles agreed that the French would have to make a greater effort to win the war. The French also would have to grant the Americans a greater role in formulating strategy and training indigenous forces. Further, the French would have to agree to Vietnamese demands for complete independence. The exigencies of French domestic politics required that they reject all the strings attached to the American aid proposal.[79] They would risk losing at Dien Bien Phu and take their chances on obtaining an acceptable negotiated settlement at Geneva, rather than accede to the American demands. To the end of the Franco-Vietminh War the two allies sought incompatible goals: The French fought to restore their empire; "the Americans wanted them to liquidate that empire in order to build an anti-Communist nationalist base."[80]

In late April, as the end neared at Dien Bien Phu, French Foreign Minister Georges Bidault made a desperate eleventh-hour plea for a U. S. air strike to save the French. Unable to count on British or congressional support and unhappy with France's continuing unwillingness to accept the U. S. conditions for intervention, Eisenhower once again refused to go to war for the French cause in Indochina. The final refusal of the United States sealed the French fate. On the afternoon of May 7, the Vietminh flag was hoisted over the French command bunker at Dien Bien Phu. Having lost the war in northern Vietnam, France prepared to abandon Hanoi-Haiphong and salvage what it could in southern Vietnam. The day after the French surrendered at Dien Bien Phu, diplomats from nine nations gathered around a horseshoe-shaped table inside the old League of Nations building in Geneva to hold open discussions on the "Indochina problem."[81]

THE GENEVA SOLUTION

U. S. officials reluctantly participated in the Geneva Conference; they would have much preferred that there be no political solution to the Indochina War. They wanted the French, with U. S. support, to continue fighting and ultimately defeat the DRV forces. Washington also feared that the French, given the war-weariness of the French people and the military and political momentum the Vietminh had gained in Indochina, would accept a negotiated settlement that would lead to a Communist takeover of Vietnam, Laos, and Cambodia and open the floodgate of Communist expansion in Southeast Asia. For weeks, Washington kept alive the option of a possible U. S. military action in Vietnam. Eisenhower gave renewed consideration to a possible U. S. military intervention on the side of the French, in the event the conference failed to produce an acceptable diplomatic solution to the war. Adding to American concerns, as the conference dragged on, the DRV armies kept pressure on the French forces and continued to extend their political and military control over the people and territory of Vietnam and Laos. Once again, a possible U. S. military intervention in the Franco-Vietminh War foundered on the inability of U. S. and French negotiators to agree on what terms the Americans might intervene. The French preferred to seek a negotiated settlement rather than accept the strings inevitably attached to any possible American military initiative.

Nine delegations attended the Geneva Conference. There were representatives from Laos, Cambodia, and two delegations from Vietnam, one representing Bao Dai's government and the other representing Ho Chi Minh's. France, of course, attended, as did the Americans, the Soviets, the British, and the Chinese. Soviet Foreign Minister Vyacheslav Molotov and British Foreign Secretary Anthony Eden served as co-chairs of the conference. The Americans, in the awkward position of attending a conference they did not support and whose outcome they feared, played a relatively minor public role in the negotiations. Dulles rarely attended the sessions; the U. S. delegation was headed by Dulles' assistant, Undersecretary Walter Bedell Smith. At one point, Zhou Enlai, the head of the Chinese delegation, offered his hand to Dulles. Dulles, not wishing to recognize a regime he loathed, refused to shake Chou's hand and turned away. Dulles' rude behavior humiliated and infuriated the Chinese leader.

Negotiations at Geneva were dominated by the foreign policy concerns of the major powers who negotiated over the heads of the Vietnamese and imposed an agreement on them. Since they were winning the war and controlled most of the land and population of Vietnam, the DRV should have emerged from Geneva with agreements reflecting their strategic superiority. The Vietminh did not achieve political gains at the conference table commensurate with their military triumphs, because such a resolution of the Franco-Vietminh War did not conform to the vital interests of the major powers dominating the conference.[82]

While the Conference was in session, the United States used the threat of military intervention to strengthen France in relation to the DRV and to lessen Chinese and Soviet support for the Vietminh. Washington was opposed to any agreement that took away territory from Cambodia, Laos, or Vietnam. Dulles got the British to back the American position and tried to persuade the French to avoid making any settlement that would transfer territory to the Communists. But the French negotiated skillfully at Geneva, playing the Soviets and Americans against each other. On the one hand, French officials threatened Washington with rejection of the proposed EDC, the top U. S. priority in Europe, if the United States insisted on their making unrealistic demands at the bargaining table that might torpedo the conference and prevent a political resolution of the conflict. On the other hand, the French held out to the Soviets the prospect of French rejection of the EDC, which the Soviets desired, if the Soviets could persuade the Vietminh to moderate their demands and offer the French terms that they could accept. The Soviet leaders, in the aftermath of Stalin's death, also interested in moderating Cold War tensions and not having major interests in Southeast Asia, played a role in restraining DRV demands.

China, fearful of U. S. intervention in the war if it went on much longer and the French position continued to deteriorate, and wanting to keep American military forces out of Indochina, joined the Soviets in putting pressure on the Vietminh to reach an agreement that was acceptable to the French. China, exhausted after years of civil war and fighting in the Korean War, where its armies sustained a million casualties, wanted to devote its resources to internal development. The Chinese did not care whether the Communist state on its southern periphery controlled all or part of the territory of Vietnam as long as it could protect China's southern flank. Chinese leaders may also have felt that partition of their country would make the Vietminh more susceptible to their influence. The Soviets and the Chinese made it clear to Ho Chi Minh that the repeated U. S. threats to intervene necessitated compromise: Soviet and Chinese pressure forced the Vietminh to moderate their demands and played a crucial role in arranging the final settlements. "The political reality of Vietminh power in Vietnam must yield to the larger reality of its power-lessness in the world at large."[83]

Over the next two months the outlines of a settlement gradually emerged, based on the temporary partitioning of Vietnam to allow the regrouping of military forces following a cease fire; elections to unify the country would be held in two years, in July 1956. Before an agreement could be fully worked out, Laniel's government fell. His place at Geneva was taken by the Socialist leader Pierre Mendes-France, who had assumed office and pledged to achieve a settlement by July 21, or resign. Mendes-France came to Geneva committed to disengaging France from the war as quickly and gracefully as possible.[84] Movement toward a settlement based on partition was evident. With an agreement in sight, the Conference recessed for a few days.

While the delegates rested from their labors, the United States "made the most fundamental decision of its thirty-year involvement" in Vietnam.[85] Washington realized that U. S. military intervention was not possible and that the French would not continue fighting. Despite their concerted efforts to prevent its occurrence, American leaders could also see that a political resolution to the Franco-Vietminh War was imminent and that the Communists were going to gain control of part of Vietnam. Eisenhower and Dulles decided to intervene directly in Vietnam's internal affairs. Washington planned to replace the French in Vietnam and to assume responsibility for the defense of Cambodia, Laos, and southern Vietnam in the aftermath of the French defeat. America would pick up the sword that the French were dropping. They would hold the line against further Communist expansion in that region. It was Eisenhower's fateful decision, made in July 1954 to intervene in southern Vietnam, that directly involved the United States in the Vietnam conflicts that culminated in the American Vietnam war a decade later.

The conference resumed, and agreements were reached on the details of the settlement that would end the Franco-Vietminh War on July 19, 1954. A cease-fire was declared, and Vietnam was partitioned at the 17th parallel of north latitude. Chinese Premier Zhou Enlai had to put enormous pressure on Ho Chi Minh to get him to accept the 17th parallel as a temporary boundary between the two regroupment zones. Ho Chi Minh had wanted the 13th parallel as the boundary. It would have given the French just Cochin China, the southern third of Vietnam and the only region where the French and Bao Dai government could claim to have control and where the Vietminh forces were relatively weak.

The agreements specified that the partition line was to be just a provisional military demarcation, "on either side of which the forces of the two parties shall be regrouped after their withdrawal."[86] The DRV forces were to regroup north of the line. Bao Dai's and the French forces were to regroup south of the line. The conferees made clear that they never intended the line to become a permanent political or territorial boundary. The Geneva accords did not create two states; they only created a temporary military division within a single state. To prevent further fighting, both sides were to have 300 days from the date the document was signed to make all force and personnel transfers to either regroupment zone. People were encouraged to move if they wished. There were to be no reprisals against people for the side they had chosen or anything they had done during the war. Both regroupment zones of Vietnam were prohibited from entering into any military alliances, bringing in any new military forces or weapons, or developing additional military bases.

As neither Vietnamese government would tolerate the permanent division of Vietnamese territory, the agreements provided for consultations between representatives of the two zones to begin July 20, 1955, within a year of the Conference. These consultations were to lead to free elections to be held within another year, in July 1956, supervised by an International Control Commission comprised of inspectors from Poland, India, and Canada. Whichever government won the elections would govern a reunified Vietnam in 1956. The agreements also established cease-fires for Cambodia and Laos and declared these countries to be independent nations under their current governments.[87] The accords also acknowledged the two new nations' right of self-defense, but they were prohibited from entering military alliances or permitting foreign bases on their soil unless their security was clearly threatened. Most of the Geneva participants assumed that the French would remain in Vietnam to supervise the implementation of the settlement that had been worked out at the Conference. During the subsequent two years, Vietnam would constitute two military zones administered north of the 17th parallel by the Democratic Government of Vietnam and south of the 17th parallel by Bao Dai's Associated States, also called the State of Vietnam.

Washington was unhappy with the loss of northern Vietnam to the Communists and refused to be associated formally with the Geneva agreements. Walter Bedell Smith did not assent to them. Instead, he issued a separate protocol stating that the United States acknowledged the agreements and would "refrain from the threat or use of force to disturb them. . . ."[88] President Eisenhower announced that since the United States government did not sign the accords, America did not consider itself bound by them.[89] Bao Dai's new premier, Ngo Dinh Diem, denounced the accords and also refused his assent. The war that had ended in defeat for the French was, by extension, also perceived as a serious setback for the United States.

But Eisenhower and Dulles were not entirely displeased with the outcome of the Geneva conference. In their view, it could have been much worse. They knew that their power politics, adroit French diplomacy, and Soviet and Chinese pressure had forced Ho Chi Minh to accept half a country at Geneva, even though his armies controlled most of the entire country. They also saw that the provisions of the Geneva agreements partitioning Vietnam, permitting a temporary regroupment of forces and people, and calling for nationwide elections within two years to reunify the country, amounted to a face-saving formula permitting the defeated French to make a more or less graceful exit from Indochina. Eisenhower and Dulles saw a window of opportunity in these provisions designed to give the French a delayed exit.

Washington believed that within the two years allotted to them under the Geneva agreements, they could supersede the French and work with the people in southern Vietnam. They would use the two-year interim to turn Bao Dai's government into a nation-state that would provide the people of Vietnam with a genuine alternative to Communism. Perhaps Bao Dai could even win the elections two years hence. They also believed they could effect arrangements that would protect the strategic security of Southeast Asia in the aftermath of the partial Communist victory in Vietnam and that those arrangements would confine the spread of Communism to northern Vietnam. They would hold the line at the 17th parallel and save the rest of Indochina and Southeast Asia from Communist expansionism.

Even before the Geneva Conference had officially ended, the United States was pledging its support to the Bao Dai government and preparing to subvert the accords.[90] Because of U. S. intervention in southern Vietnam, the Geneva accords did not produce a permanent political solution to the Indochina conflict, only a temporary military truce. The "conference was merely an interlude between two wars—or rather, a lull in the same war."[91]

LESSONS LEARNED AND LESSONS NOT LEARNED

There is a kind of symmetry between the reactions of the Americans and the Vietminh to the outcome of the Geneva Conference. Both came away disappointed, but at the same time both perceived opportunities to exploit in the settlement and both expected the future to go their way. Ho Chi Minh had been willing to bow to Soviet and Chinese pressure and to settle for half of Vietnam, because he feared the United States would intervene militarily if a reasonable settlement were not arranged. U. S. forces in Vietnam would seriously impede the Vietminh's planned scenario for Vietnam, so Ho Chi Minh did what he had to do to keep them out. From his vantage point at Geneva in July 1954, the DRV had gained more than it had lost at the Conference. The international community had acknowledged the legitimacy of his government. The DRV was now a member of the world family of nations. Despite partition and the continuing presence of French troops on its soil, Vietnam had officially regained its sovereignty after over eighty years of colonial subjugation. The accords kept the Americans out and also prepared the ground for the departure of the French. Only the discredited Bao Dai regime remained as Ho Chi Minh's political competition. He was confident that he could win the upcoming elections, and looked ahead to governing a reunified Vietnam under Lao Dong control.[92] Within two years, the Vietminh expected to acquire control of all of Vietnam through democratic political processes. Ho Chi Minh did not anticipate that the Americans would soon supplant the French in southern Vietnam and block his plans. Neither side could see it at the time, but Washington and Hanoi had launched themselves on collision courses over who would control the political destiny of southern Vietnam after 1956.

The Communist forces were winning the Franco-Vietminh War at the time of the Geneva conference and had there been no diplomatic solution to the Franco-Vietminh conflict, the DRV forces, barring a major commitment of U. S. forces, would most likely have inflicted a total military defeat on the French within another year. The Eisenhower administration had a simplistic view of the outcome of the war. They thought the French had lost for two reasons: They had not fought hard enough or long enough. They had lacked the determination and firepower to defeat the DRV forces, even with substantial U. S. help. They were also an anachronistic colonial power, trying to cling to the remnants of empire in Indochina, and they could not bring themselves to offer the Vietnamese a genuine nationalistic alternative to the Vietminh. Eisenhower and Dulles both believed that American intervention in southern Vietnam could succeed, because the United States was a vastly richer and more powerful nation that was coming to help Bao Dai build a modern nation-state. American technology, know-how, and good intentions would work where French efforts had failed. The Old World had failed; the New World would redeem Vietnam and light the way to a non-Communist future.

Washington's diagnosis of the French defeat was only partially correct. The French were losing in Indochina in part because they had never sent enough troops to give themselves a realistic chance to win the war, and because most Vietnamese perceived the Bao Dai government as only a cover for continuing French domination. However, there were other, more important, factors that were determining the outcome of that war. To understand what happened to the French in Indochina in 1954, we have to reorient our analysis and our frame of reference. The proper question to ask was not why were the French losing, but why were the Vietminh winning? If we focus on the reasons why the Vietminh were winning the war, we necessarily have to focus on the DRV and what their forces were doing. What the Vietnamese accomplished in their country determined the outcome of the Franco-Vietminh War. The French, backed by the United States, were fighting a war that they could not realistically expect to win in 1954, even if they had been willing to send more troops and offer Bao Dai's government independence. By that late date, Indochina was no longer France's to lose; it had probably been lost by 1945. Local conditions, forces, realities, and historical factors brought about the Vietminh victory over the French, which is to say that Vietnam realities determined the outcome of the Franco-Vietminh War.

Vietnam, during the years of the Franco-Vietminh War, still possessed a colonial society with many serious social and economic problems, all of which contributed to popular support for the revolutionaries. Inflation, high taxes, and usurious interest rates all bore heavily on the people of Vietnam, especially on the rural poor. Government corruption and incompetence coupled with official indifference to the welfare of the rural population strengthened popular discontent and played into Vietminh hands.[93]

In addition to the indigenous social and economic conditions, the organizational strength of the revolutionaries played a crucial role in bringing them their ultimate success. The revolutionary political organization of the Vietminh and the extraordinary leadership of Ho Chi Minh were the decisive determinants. Until the war's end, the party apparatus continued its organizing efforts both in the urban areas and in the villages of Vietnam. Most important, the party succeeded in retaining control of the nationalistic aspirations of most of the Vietnamese people, regardless of their politics. Ho Chi Minh had a rare combination of talents: he was both a skilled organizer and a charismatic figure, a visionary who gave expression to the nationalistic aspirations of most Vietnamese. The revolution's prime strength was always politics, not war.

Ho Chi Minh, Troung Chin, and Vo Nguyen Giap also perceived that in the long run the chief weakness of the French war effort in Vietnam was not that their soldiers could not fight effectively or that they were pursuing a colonial agenda, but that it was undermined by a psycho-political weakness, the declining public support in France for the Indochina War. Lack of popular support proved to be the French's Achilles' heel. The loss of popular support for the war eroded the political will of a succession of French governments to conduct it vigorously, and eventually forced them to the conference table where they negotiated agreements that provided for their departure from Indochina. Vietminh party leaders grasped the importance of this psycho-political factor and developed sophisticated military—political—diplomatic strategies to undermine their enemy's will to fight.[94]

Years later, when the North Vietnamese and the National Liberation Front forces fought another war, this time against the American successors to the French and the Vietnamese successors to Bao Dai, they remembered the lessons that they had learned during the war with France: What the Vietnamese do and what happens in Vietnam are crucial to the outcome of the war. Be patient, they learned, and fight a protracted war. Exploit the social and economic conditions created by a series of corrupt, ineffective, and elite-based governments. Rely on party organization and political discipline. Retain the voice of Vietnamese nationalism. Fight a people's war. Use strategies designed to undermine popular support and erode the political will of the foreign government to continue the war. These strategies enabled the Communists to defeat a

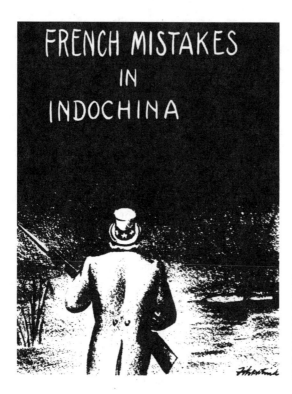

Figure 2.2   Editorial cartoonist Daniel Fitzgerald's prophetic cartoon anticipating the outcome of the American Vietnam intervention. Uncle Sam marches into the heart of darkness to replicate the French disaster. *Source:* St. Louis *Post Dispatch*

more powerful foe, the French. Twenty years later they used the same strategies to defeat an even more powerful foe, the Americans.

The American war in Vietnam, fought from 1965 through 1972, largely replicated the French war. There were, of course, important differences between the two conflicts; there was no American equivalent of Dien Bien Phu. American troops were never defeated in any major battles. Americans made much greater use of helicopters and employed vastly greater airpower. The Americans also used military force on a much larger scale than the French. But the similarities between the two wars were quite remarkable and significant. Their duration and outcomes were similar. Both began with high hopes and ended in disaster for the Western powers and in victories for the Asian Communists. Both the Americans and the French tried to use their technological superiority, which gave them greater firepower, mobility, and control of the sea and air to win their wars of attrition. They found that these advantages were not sufficient to defeat the complex diplomatic-political-military strategies employed by their enemies. Neither the French nor the Americans ever succeeded in creating stable governments that offered the Vietnamese people a viable alternative to the Communists. Both failed to develop pacification strategies that effectively neutralized the efforts of insurgent political cadres to maintain support among the rural population. Neither nation ever developed ARVN forces strong enough to defend themselves against the Communist forces that were receiving support from China, the Soviet Union, and the Eastern Bloc. Both only used Vietnamese forces extensively after domestic public support for the wars had seriously eroded. "The areas that caused the most problems for the French in South Vietnam were also the worst trouble spots for the Americans."[95]

The French and the Americans were eventually defeated and were forced to negotiate agreements that provided for their withdrawal from Vietnam, mainly because the long-running wars had become unpopular among their home populations and their governments no longer had enough political support to continue them. During both wars, the Vietnamese revolutionaries, sensing that the loss of popular support was the fatal weakness that would eventually undermine both the French and the American war efforts, patiently and skillfully employed a variety of political, military, and diplomatic strategies that promoted war weariness on the Western home fronts.

Many French and American war veterans felt they had made sacrifices in vain. They had fought well in a losing war and had returned home to civilian populations that did not appear to care about, understand, or appreciate what they had done. They returned to encounter civilian populations that had lost faith in the war and ignored them, or worse, condemned them. The long, losing wars also had devastating impacts on national morale and national self-esteem in both countries, draining both nations of significant amounts of their wealth.

Eisenhower and Dulles and their successors, enmeshed in the ideology of containment and its domino correlatives, and responding to the political imperatives of domestic anti-Communism, never fully understood nor heeded the lessons of the Franco-Vietminh War. American leaders, heedless of history and contemptuously indifferent to the French analogue, would in time replicate their disaster.

NOTES

1. Hess, *Vietnam*, 33.
2. Kahin, *Intervention*, p. 9.
3. Doyle, Edward; Lipsman, Samuel; and others, *Passing the Torch*, (Boston: Boston Publishing Co., 1981), 16–17; Isaacs, Harold, *No Peace for Asia* (New York: MacMillan, 1947), 152–75. Isaacs was an American journalist in Saigon who wrote a firsthand account of Anglo-French cooperation in the South from 1945 to 1946 to suppress the Vietnamese nationalist revolution. He also documented the Anglo-French use of Japanese troops against the Vietnamese. Acheson is quoted in Young, *Vietnam Wars*, 12.
4. Dunn, Peter M., *The First Vietnam War* (New York: St. Martin's, 1985). Dunn has written a history of the complex political and military conflict in Vietnam during the first year after World War II that he states made up a "First Vietnam War." According to Dunn, the French-Vietnamese conflict, 1946–1954, was the "Second Vietnam War," and the war waged between U. S./ARVN forces and the NLF/PAVN forces, 1965–1973, was the "Third Vietnam War."
5. Quoted in Pettit, *The Experts*, 11.

6. "Jacques Phillipe Leclerc," second only to De Gaulle himself as a war hero in France, was the assumed name of Jean de Hautecloque.

7. Buttinger, *A Dragon Defiant*, 81; O'Ballance, Edgar, *The Indo-China War, War, 1945–1954* (London, Faber and Faber, 1964), 59–60. Ho Chi Minh replaced Giau in early 1946 with Nguyen Binh, who was assigned responsibility for fighting a guerrilla war in southern Vietnam against the French.

8. Hammer, *Struggle*, 135–40; Chen, *Vietnam and China*, 120–29. McAlister, John T., Jr., *Vietnam: The Origins of Revolution* (New York: Knopf, 1969).

9. Doyle, *Passing the Torch*, 18–20; Duiker, *The Communist Road to Power*, 114–18.

10. Quoted in Kahin, *Intervention*, 19.

11. In defense of his strategy of accepting the return of the French for a few years to get the Chinese out of Vietnam, Ho Chi Minh berated a group of VNQDD leaders who wanted to keep the Chinese in Vietnam in order to keep the French out: "You fools! Don't you realize what it means if the Chinese stay? Don't you remember your history? The last time the Chinese came, they stayed one thousand years! As for me, I prefer to smell French shit for five years rather than Chinese shit for the rest of my life." Quoted in Doyle, *Passing the Torch*, 21.

12. A copy of the Preliminary Franco-Vietnamese Convention of March 6, 1946, is printed in Porter (ed.), *Vietnam Documents*, vol. 1, 95–97, Document 59; Sainteny, Jean, *Histoire d'une Paix Manquee* (Paris: Amoit Dumont, 1953) is an insider's account of French Indochina policy, 1945–46; and Chen, *Vietnam and China*, 146–50. The most comprehensive account of the negotiations leading to the March 6 agreement is found in Devillers, *Histoire du Vietnam*, chaps. 11–13.

13. Between August and October 1945, Ho Chi Minh wrote seven letters to U. S. leaders appealing for support for Vietnamese independence. In one letter, Ho Chi Minh even proposed that Vietnam be placed on the same status as the Philippines, that is, he asked that Vietnam be allowed to become an American territory. Because America did not recognize Ho Chi Minh as the head of a legitimate government, all of the letters were ignored. Copies of several of Ho Chi Minh's letters are printed in Porter (ed.), *Vietnam Documents*, vol. 1, 83–86, 95.

14. Quoted in Doyle, *Passing the Torch*, 23.

15. Hammer, *Struggle*, 159–74.

16. O'Ballance, *The Indo-China War*, 75.

17. Kahin, *Intervention*, 23–24; Hammer, *Struggle*, 181–191.

18. Doyle, *Passing the Torch*, 26.

19. Duiker, *The Communist Road*, 127.

20. Quoted in Young, *Vietnam Wars*, 19.

21. Duiker, *The Communist Road*, 128–31; O'Ballance, *The Indo-China War*, 74–85. The Vietminh military treatise was written by Troung Chinh, the leading Vietminh theoretician and ideologist. Chinh borrowed much of his doctrine from Mao's book, *On Protracted War*.

22. O'Ballance, *The Indo-China War*, 79–80.

23. Duiker, *The Communist Road*, 131–32.

24. *Ibid.*, 133.

25. Vo Nguyen Giap, "Activate Guerrilla Warfare," a directive issued by Giap November 17, 1947, printed in Porter (ed.), *Vietnam Documents*, vol. 1, Document 113, 169–71.

26. Duiker, *The Communist Road*, 136.

27. Hammer, *Struggle*, 224–28; Kahin, *Intervention*, 25–26. About the only people supporting Bao Dai's government were some wealthy landowners and businessmen, some Catholics, and some of the religious sectarians. No prominent nationalists of any stripe signed on.

28. Kahin, *Intervention*, 28–33.

29. Duiker, *The Communist Road*, 139–40. The Soviets, not involved in Southeast Asia and still inclined to concede Western hegemony in that region, felt compelled to recognize the DRV so as not to lose influence in the Communist camp to the more militant Chinese.

30. Shaplen, Robert, *The Lost Revolution: The U. S. in Vietnam, 1946–1966*, rev. ed., (New York: Harper & Row, 1966), 69–75; see the Platform of the Vietnam Worker's Party, February 19, 1951: "The primordial task of the Vietnam revolution, therefore, is to drive out the imperialist aggressors to gain complete independence and unity for the people, . . . and root up the vestiges of feudalism and semifeudalism so that there is land for those who till it, to develop the People's Democratic Regime, and to lay the foundations for socialism." A copy of the platform is printed in Porter (ed.), *Vietnam Documents*, vol. 1, Document 212, 337–44.

31. Kolko, Gabriel, *Anatomy of a War, Vietnam, the United States and the Modern Historical Experience*, (New York: Pantheon Books, 1985), 57–61.

32. O'Ballance, *The Indo-China War*, 104–5.

33. *Ibid.*, 106–7.

34. *Ibid.*, 114–15.

35. *Ibid.*, 116–17. Bodard, Lucien, *The Quicksand War: Prelude to Vietnam* (Boston: Little, Brown, 1967), translated from the French, *La Guerre d'Indochine: L'enlisement* (Paris: Gallimard, 1963), and *La Guerre d'Indochine: L'humiliation* (Paris, Gallimard, 1965) both contain accounts of the battle.

36. Duiker, *The Communist Road*, 144–45.

37. National revolutions were occurring in Burma, Malaya, and Indonesia at the same time the Vietnamese were fighting the French.

38. Young, *Vietnam Wars*, 21–24. Telegram from Secretary of State Acheson to the U. S. Consulate in Hanoi, May 20, 1949. A copy is printed in Porter (ed.), *Vietnam Documents*, vol. 1, Document 131, 198–99. Acheson commented on Soviet recognition of the DRV in a State Department bulletin issued February 13, 1950, in which he said; "The recognition by the Kremlin of Ho Chi Minh's Communist movement in Indochina . . . should remove any illusions as to the 'nationalist' nature of Ho Chi Minh's aims and reveals Ho in his true colors as the mortal enemy of native independence in Indochina." The U. S. Department of State *Bulletin*, 22 (February 13, 1950) is also printed in Porter, Document 156, 225.

39. Department of State Policy Statement, September 27, 1948. A copy of this policy statement is found in Porter (ed.), *Vietnam Documents*, vol. 1, 178–81, Document 121.

40. Kahin, *Intervention*, 36–37. Between 1946 and 1949, America provided indirect, covert, and extensive financial and military assistance via metropolitan France for the French colonial war in Indochina. This aid remained hidden to avoid public criticism of both its purpose and cost.

41. *Ibid.*, 37–38. Kahin has found evidence suggesting that of the $525 million in U. S. aid to support the French budget in the fiscal year 1953, almost half came from ECA counterpart funds released for the use of the French military in Indochina. T. E. Vadney, *World*, 133. Young, *Vietnam*, 22.

42. On March 12, 1947, President Truman appeared before Congress to give his most famous and successful speech that called for the enactment of an aid package for Greece and Turkey. The substance of his address has become known as the Truman Doctrine, which announced the first application of the developing U. S. policy of containment of Communism in southern Europe and the rationale for such a policy.

43. Herring, *America's Longest War*, 12. In April 1950, at Truman's request, the State Department and Defense Department jointly prepared a top secret report for the National Security Council, known as NSC-68, which outlined an enlarged U. S. Cold War foreign policy.

44. Kahin, *Intervention*, 29; Hess, Gary, *The United States' Emergence as a Southeast Asia Power, 1940–1950* (New York: Columbia University Press, 1987), 40.

45. Schaller, Michael, "Securing the Great Crescent: Occupied Japan and the Origins of Containment in Southeast Asia," *Journal of American History*, 69 (September 1982), 392–413.

46. Kahin, *Intervention*, 40–41.

47. *Ibid.*, 29–30.

48. Gardner, *Approaching Vietnam*, 80–86.

49. Herring, *America's Longest War*, 15.

50. Shaplen, *Lost Revolution*, 57–69. What Bao Dai said was, "What they call a Bao Dai solution turned out to be just a French solution. The situation in Indochina is getting worse everyday."

51. Morrocco, John, and the editors of the Boston Publishing Co., *Thunder from Above: Air War, 1941–1968* (Boston: Boston Publishing Co., 1984), a volume in *The Vietnam Experience* series. In the summer of 1950, Congress authorized $164 million for arms, ammunition, planes, ships, trucks, jeeps, and tanks for the French war effort in Indochina. At about the same time, the U. S. economic and technical assistance program for the Bao Dai government committed $50 million over a two-year period. The first U. S. military advisers arrived in Vietnam in August 1950.

52. *Ibid.*, 21–22.

53. Shaplen, *Lost Revolution*, 87–91.

54. Duiker, *The Communist Road*, 146; Hess, *Vietnam*, 34.

55. O'Ballance, *The Indo-China War*, 120–139.

56. The two DRV divisions that fought in the Battle of Vinh Yeh were the 308th and the 324th. Both were infantry divisions equipped with Chinese weapons.

57. Duiker, *The Communist Road*, 355.

58. The account of the Battle of Hoa Binh is taken from O'Ballance, *The Indo-China War*, 159–68.

59. Duiker, *The Communist Road*, 152–53.

60. *Ibid.*, 154.

61. Duiker, *The Communist Road*, 154–55; Kahin, *Intervention*, 39. At the time of the Battle of Dien Bien Phu, total French forces in Indochina numbered about 500,000. Only about 80,000 of them were French, over half of whom were noncommissioned and commissioned officers. The rest of the French Indochina Expeditionary Force was comprised of French Foreign Legion forces, French North African troops, Indochinese, predominantly Vietnamese, troops, and Bao Dai's inchoate Vietnamese National Army (ARVN).

62. "Report by Ho Chi Minh of the Fourth Conference of the Party Central Committee," January 25–30, 1953 (extract). Printed in Porter (ed.), *Vietnam Documents*, vol. 1, Document 251, 422–23.

63. O'Ballance, *The Indo-China War*, 208–9.

64. Porter (ed.), *Vietnam Documents*, vol. 1, Document 292, "Speech by Premier Laniel Before the National Assembly," March 5, 1954, (Extracts), 495–97.

65. *Ibid.*, "Report by Giap to Senior Field Commanders on the Dienbienphu Campaign," January 14, 1954 (Extract), Document 292, 493–94.

66. *Ibid.*, "Appeal by Vo Nguyen Giap to All Cadres and Fighters, Units and Services, on Beginning the Dienbienphu Campaign," March 1954, Document 295, 497–98.

67. O'Ballance, *Indo-China War*, 218, 225, and 230; Fall, Bernard, *Hell in a Very Small Place: The Siege of Dien Bien Phu* (New York: Lippincott, 1967), 177–80.

68. O'Ballance, *Indo-China War*, pp, 213–17. Another 4,000 to 5,000 troops parachuted into Dien Bien Phu during the battle to join the defenders.

69. *Ibid.*, 224; Giap's porters had hauled in U. S.-made 105-mm. howitzers that the Chinese had given him. These artillery were larger than most of the French guns. The Chinese Communists had captured these American guns from the defeated Chinese Nationalist forces during their civil war in the late 1940s.

70. Duiker, *The Communist Road*, 162; there is a fine brief account of the Battle of Dien Bien Phu in Doyle, *Passing the Torch*, 62–85. Of the 18,000 defenders of Dien Bien Phu, fewer than half were French. The others included Legionnaires, mainly Germans, Africans, and over 6,000 loyal Vietnamese. There are many books about the Battle of Dien Bien Phu. Two of the best are Fall, Bernard, *Hell in a Very Small Place: The Siege of Dien Bien Phu*, (New York: Lippincott, 1967) and Roy, Jules, *The Battle of Dien Bien Phu*, (New York: Harper and Row, 1983). Giap, Vo Nguyen, *People's War, Peoples Army*, (Hanoi: Foreign Language Publishing House, 1961) presents his version of the famed battle.

71. Giap, Vo Nguyen, *People's War, People's Army*, 187. Giap is also quoted in Young, *Vietnam Wars*, 36.

72. Herring, *America's Longest War*, 29.

73. Kahin, *Intervention*, 42. In the fiscal year 1953, the Eisenhower administration spent $1.3 billion, 61 percent of the total cost of the war for that year. For 1954, America financed 78 percent of the total cost. The total cost to Americans for supporting the French colonial war in Indochina from 1950 to 1954 came to over $2.8 billion. Tuchman, *March of Folly*, 257, states that most of the U. S. aid money "trickled away into the pockets of profiteering officials."

74. Herring, George C. and Immerman, Richard H., "Eisenhower, Dulles, and Dienbienphu: 'The Day We Didn't Go to War' Revisited," *Journal of American History*, vol. 71 (September 1984), 343–63.

75. Kahin, *Intervention*, 45–46; Herring and Immerman, "The Day We Didn't Go to War," 343–63; and Herring, George C., *America's Longest War: The United States and Vietnam, 1950–1975*, 3d. ed., (New York: McGraw Hill, 1996), 33–34. Ridgway quote is cited in Herring, 34.

76. Kahin, *Intervention*, 48; Herring, *Longest War*, ed., 35.

77. Herring, *America's Longest War*, 34–35.

78. Porter, (ed.), *Vietnam Documents*, vol. 1, Document 315, "Telegram from Dulles in Geneva to the State Department," April 25, 1954, 542–43.

79. Herring, *America's Longest War*, 35. It is not true, as has sometimes been written, that the United States offered the beleaguered French the use of two nuclear weapons in the spring of 1954 to save Dien Bien Phu.

80. Hess, *Vietnam*, p.47; Herring, *Longest War*, 3d. ed., p.34.

81. Kahin, *Intervention*, 52–53; Karnow, Stanley, *Vietnam: A History* (New York: Viking Press, 1983), 198; Arnold, James R., *The First Domino: Eisenhower, the Military, and America's Intervention in Vietnam* (New York: Morrow, 1991), says Eisenhower wanted to help the French and only reluctantly bowed to domestic political pressures to keep U. S. forces out Indochina. Herring, *Longest War,* 3d. ed., states that it is difficult to tell what Eisenhower and Dulles wanted to do because they maneuvered so craftily during this crisis. Eisenhower probably did not want to intervene militarily in Vietnam because he did not believe that air power could do the job, and he did not want to get the United States bogged down in another land war in Asia.

82. Kahin and Lewis, *The United States in Vietnam*, 43.

83. Quote is from Young, *Vietnam Wars*, 38–39; Herring, *Longest War*, 3d. ed., 41–42.

84. Kahin, *Intervention*, 63–65.

85. *Ibid.*, 66.

86. Porter (ed.), *Vietnam Documents*, vol. 1, Document 378, "Agreement on the Cessation of Hostilities in Vietnam," July 20, 1954, 642.

87. The armistice agreements, the Final Declaration, the protocol issued by Bedell Smith, and the statement by Eisenhower are found in U. S. Department of State, *American Foreign Policy, 1950–1955: Basic Documents* (Washington, D. C.: U. S. Government Printing Office, 1957), Vol. 1, 750–88. The Geneva Accords consist of two distinct, related agreements: (1) A bilateral armistice agreement signed on July 20, 1954, by Brigadier General Henri Delteil on behalf of the French forces fighting in Indochina and by Ta Quang Buu on behalf of the People's Army of Vietnam that partitioned the country into two temporary regroupment zones. (2) A Final Declaration issued on July 21. It was endorsed by oral assent by all but Walter Bedell Smith, representing the United States, and Ngo Dinh Diem. Both refused to give their approval. Its key provisions include chapter 6, which states that "the military demarcation line is provisional and should not in any way be interpreted as constituting a political or territorial boundary," and chapter 7, which spells out the terms of preparing for and holding elections in order to reunify Vietnam in July 1956.

88. Porter, *Documents*, vol. 1: "Declaration by Walter Bedell Smith, Representing the U. S. Delegation to the Geneva Conference," July 21, 1954, Document 381, 656.

89. Kahin and Lewis, *The United States in Vietnam*, 59–62.

90. Moss, George Donelson, ed., *A Vietnam Reader: Sources and Essays* (Englewood Cliffs, N. J.: Prentice Hall, 1991). See essay by the editor, "An American Entanglement: U. S. Involvement in Indochina, 1942–1975," 5.

91. Karnow, *Vietnam*, 199.

92. Duiker, *The Communist Road*, 163–64; Kahin and Lewis, *The United States in Vietnam*, 47. The Vietminh would never have accepted partition without guarantees of elections within two years to reunify Vietnam being written into the agreements.

93. Duiker, *The Communist Road*, 166–67.

94. *Ibid.*, 168.

95. Thayer, Thomas C., *War without Fronts: The American Experience in Vietnam* (Boulder, Colo.: Westview, 1985); also see Dunn, Peter M., "The American Army: The Vietnam War, 1965–1973" in Beckett, Ian F. W., and Pimlott, John, eds., *Armed Forces and Modern Counter-Insurgency* (London: Croom Helm, 1985), 80–81, 85. Dunn faults the Americans for not seeking the advice of the French or to absorb "their bitterly-learned lessons." The U. S. Army "became, in effect, a large French Expeditionary Corps—and met the same frustrations."

3

An Experiment in Nation Building

There are profound differences between the Vietnamese and American people, in customs, outlook, political training, and philosophy. I hope we can find a bridge between Eastern and Western cultures.

Ngo Dinh Diem

NGO DINH DIEM TAKES CHARGE

During the summer of 1954, the Eisenhower administration firmly committed itself to creating a new nation in the southern half of Vietnam in order to block further Communist expansion in Southeast Asia. The National Security Council (NSC), meeting a month after the Geneva Conference that had worked out the political settlement ending the Franco-Vietminh War, interpreted the Geneva agreements as a serious setback for the United States and a major victory for the Communists that gave them a salient for applying pressure to the nations of Southeast Asia. The NSC report called for the United States to negotiate new international agreements in order to provide strategic security for the new country it was going to create in southern Vietnam, and to protect Laos, Cambodia, Thailand, Burma, and the other nations of Southeast Asia.[1]

To fulfill the policy recommendations of the NSC review, Secretary of State Dulles journeyed to Manila to orchestrate the Southeast Asia Treaty Organization (SEATO). Dulles had been promoting an alliance of Asian powers since the Dien Bien Phu crisis. Washington intended the alliance to evolve into "a regional multilateral defense system."[2] The creation of SEATO was part of a two-pronged U. S. strategy developed during the summer of 1954 to block the further spread of Communism in Indochina in the aftermath of the Geneva settlement. The other prong consisted of strongly backing Ngo Dinh Diem as he created a viable non-Communist state out of the temporary regroupment zone south of the 17th parallel.

The new security arrangements were embodied in the Pact of Manila, signed on September 8, 1954. A loosely constructed alliance including the United States, Great Britain, France, Australia, New Zealand, and three Southeast Asian nations (the Philippines, Thailand, and Pakistan) was created by SEATO. The major neutral nations of the region—Burma, India, and Indonesia—declined to join. Because of restrictions imposed by the Geneva agreements, Laos, Cambodia, and southern Vietnam could not join. But Dulles arranged for a protocol to be attached to the SEATO agreement that projected an umbrella of protection over Laos, Cambodia, and southern Vietnam. This protocol circumvented the provisions of the Geneva Accords, which had tried to neutralize Indochina.[3] Cambodia promptly repudiated the SEATO protocol, and Laos was later excluded by treaty. But the French and Bao Dai accepted the protection offered by SEATO for the temporary military regroupment zone south of the 17th parallel created at Geneva, which the protocol referred to as "the free territory under the jurisdiction of the State of Vietnam."[4]

The Eisenhower administration was happy with the new alliance. Unlike NATO, SEATO carried no military obligations. It called only for members to consult with one another in the event of an attack on a signatory or one of the Indochina countries covered by the protocol. The SEATO agreement allowed the United States a freedom to maneuver and to decide if military intervention was warranted to suppress an insurrection or to thwart aggression. Washington viewed SEATO as a defensive alliance erected to block Chinese expansion in Southeast Asia and to prevent a possible invasion of southern Vietnam across the 17th parallel by the Hanoi regime. SEATO helped promote the diplomatic fictions that the United States was proclaiming, that the southern half of Vietnam had quickly evolved from a temporary administrative zone into a free and independent state and that the 17th parallel had just as quickly metamorphosed from a transient demarcation line into a permanent political boundary. Thus SEATO was part of an American-instigated process of defining a new state at a time when there was only one Vietnam that was prohibited from joining any alliances or entering into any military agreements and whose political future would be determined by free elections scheduled for July 1956. SEATO also proved useful by furnishing a legal justification for American intervention into Vietnam to deter North Vietnamese aggression against South Vietnam when the United States moved to subvert both the letter and the spirit of the Geneva Accords.[5]

The man Washington selected in the summer of 1954 to head the new state that it planned to create in southern Vietnam was a staunch Vietnamese nationalist, Ngo Dinh Diem. The new leader was born near the imperial city of Hue on January 3, 1901, one of nine children of Ngo Dinh Kha. Kha was a wealthy man who had served as court chamberlain to Emperor Thanh Thai. The Ngos were Catholics, and even as a boy Diem stood out for his unusual piety and devotion to religious duties. For a time he considered becoming a priest. He later changed his mind and gave up an opportunity to study in France. He attended Quoc Hoc lycee in Hue, the same school that Ho Chi Minh, another mandarin's son, had attended ten years earlier. Graduating at sixteen, Diem enrolled in the French-run School for Law and Administration in Hanoi, where he performed brilliantly, graduating at the top of his class. Following graduation, Diem moved immediately into government service. Within a few years, he had reached mandarinic rank and was the provincial chief of a district containing 300 villages.[6]

An ardent Vietnamese patriot, Diem early demonstrated an abiding hatred of the French for their domination of his country and of the Communists whom he regarded as enemies of Vietnamese nationalism. In 1932, the young emperor Bao Dai, aware of Diem's energy and administrative talents, appointed him Minister of the Interior. Diem eagerly threw himself into his new job. He proposed a long list of reforms to modernize the ministry and to give it real authority. Neither Bao Dai nor his French masters would accept the reforms, and Diem, angry and disillusioned, resigned.[7] He never held another government position until he became premier under American auspices in 1954.

Scholarly and reclusive by nature, Diem lived in his father's village near Hue. He refused all offers from the Japanese, the Vietminh, and Bao Dai to participate in various governments that were formed after World War II. At one time he was captured by Vietminh guerrillas, who took him to Ho Chi Minh. Ho Chi Minh offered Diem a position in his government, which he declined with the explanation that a Vietminh guerrilla had murdered his older brother. When the French set up Bao Dai's puppet government in 1949, Diem urged the emperor to ask the French for greater autonomy; Diem was disappointed when Bao Dai declined to do so.[8]

In 1951, Diem came to America and lived for two years at a Maryknoll seminary in Lakehurst, New Jersey. From that base, he traveled around the country campaigning for Vietnam's independence. He attracted the support of prominent Americans, including Francis Cardinal Spellman, the leading spokesman for American Catholics. Through Spellman, he met Democratic Senators John Kennedy and Mike Mansfield, and Supreme Court Associate Justice William O. Douglas.[9] In the summer of 1954, when it appeared that France would lose the Indochina War and the Communists might take over Vietnam, Washington decided to intervene to replace the French and to try to save the South. American officials looked for a leader of southern Vietnam whom they could back. They wanted no part of Bao Dai, the titular head of the French-backed regime in Saigon, who preferred living on the Riviera with his mistress to residing in Saigon. Dulles had become aware of Diem, thanks to the efforts of Diem's lobby of prominent supporters. Diem's administrative experience, staunch patriotism, and anti-Communism appealed to the Americans. Since the Americans were planning to replace the French in southern Vietnam, Diem's lifelong hatred and mistrust of the French increased his attractiveness to U. S. officials. Bao Dai appointed him premier in June.[10]

Upon arriving in Saigon on June 25, 1954, Diem discovered that the government he had inherited from the French rested on an inefficient and a corrupt bureaucracy, a demoralized army whose fighting prowess and loyalty to him were both questionable, and a fragmented capital city seething with a bizarre amalgam of fierce political rivalries. Local military and political leaders conspired with the French and Bao Dai to ensure an early demise to Diem's fledgling administration. Diem found he did not control the capital city, much less the country. Compounding his troubles, the Geneva agreements, promulgated on July 21, called for nationwide elections to unify the country within two years. Ho Chi Minh and the Lao Dong were odds-on favorites to win these forthcoming elections and to take over the whole country.

Throughout the fall and winter of 1954 and 1955, Diem was caught in the midst of a bitter conflict between the French and the Americans for influence in southern Vietnam. The French and the American partnership in Indochina had always been riven with tension, mutual suspicion, and resentment. The French bitterly observed that the United States was trying to supplant them in southern Vietnam. Their charges were confirmed when Eisenhower wrote Diem a letter on October 23, 1954, pledging U. S. economic and military assistance.[11] Henceforth, U. S. aid money went directly to Diem rather than through the French legation, which had been the recipient since May 1950 when the United States began providing the French and Vietnamese with economic and military assistance. When the French delayed turning over full powers of governance to Diem until December, American officials suspected that the French were trying to hang on in the South and also build bridges to the Hanoi regime to protect extensive French investments in the country. American officials also knew the French were encouraging Diem's political rivals and trying to undermine Diem because he was strongly pro-American and anti-French. The French supported Prince Buu Hoi, a royal cohort of Bao Dai; they wanted him to supplant Diem as premier of the emergent state. Franco-American Vietnamese disputes were exacerbated by the French rejection of the American plan for a European Defense Community a month after Geneva.[12]

Support from the United States enabled Diem to eventually overcome all of his political foes. Key support came from an American Central Intelligence Agency (CIA) group headed by Air Force Colonel Edward G. Landsdale, a legendary and controversial figure during the long U. S. involvement in Vietnam. An experienced anti-Communist nation-builder, Landsdale had previously helped Philippine President Ramon Magsaysay defeat the Huk rebellion on the island of Luzon. Colonel Landsdale quickly became a close friend and trusted adviser to Ngo Dinh Diem. Landsdale and General J. Lawton "Lightning Joe" Collins, Eisenhower's special envoy to Vietnam, foiled a military coup headed by dissident Army Chief of Staff General Nguyen Van Hinh. Hinh, a French citizen with a French wife, plotted to overthrow Diem in the fall of 1954. Landsdale and Collins saved Diem by informing Hinh's backers that if the coup went forward, the United States would cut off all funding for the Vietnamese army.[13]

American support also helped Diem cope with a massive influx of refugees who fled northern Vietnam in the fall of 1954, following the Communist takeover. About 800,000 civilians, 600,000 of them Catholics, moved south of the 17th parallel under the provisions of the Geneva Accords, permitting free movement between regroupment zones. The Catholic emigrants who went south were mostly peasants who fled their villages in the districts of Phat Diem and Bui Chi in the Red River Delta, south of Haiphong. The refugees also included former soldiers in the Vietnamese National Army, colonial administrators, and businessmen who feared reprisals at the hands of the victorious Vietminh. Whole parishes under the leadership of parish priests left the North. Diem's officials settled them in villages in southern Vietnam in the vicinity of Saigon and in areas of the central highlands that were regarded as strategically significant.[14]

Even though many of these Catholic peasants were uncertain and fearful about life under the Communists, and voted with their feet, the mass migration south was not an entirely spontaneous folk movement. The Catholic Church, American and French officials, and the Diem administration all promoted the migration. The Catholic migrants were urged to come south, both to form a base of support for the Diem government and to serve as compelling symbols of the Cold War. The mass migration of northern Catholics received extensive media coverage in America. U. S. officials and journalists depicted the migrants as pitiable refugees fleeing Communist tyranny for the freedom and religious tolerance they would find in southern Vietnam. Tom Dooley, a navy doctor involved in transporting the refugees, wrote powerfully of a people fleeing from the godless cruelties of Communism. Vivid images of a flight to freedom became ingrained in the American public consciousness. To spur the migration along, Landsdale's CIA agents used propaganda and psychological warfare operations to induce reluctant villagers to flee North Vietnam. The United States played a major role in transporting people south. U. S. naval ships hauled hundreds of thousands of these northerners, and private American religious and charitable agencies helped the migrants resettle in southern Vietnam.[15]

The migrants more than doubled the South Vietnamese Catholic population, which, augmented by the newcomers, totaled about 10 percent of the southern population by 1955. These northern Catholics became an important part of Diem's political base. In return, they generally enjoyed a privileged status under his rule. Educated Catholics often found positions in Diem's government bureaucracies. Diem's government also established hundreds of villages and provided land and financial support for many of the new settlers. More than 400,000 of the newcomers settled in the Mekong Delta, often on land previously worked by the Khmer.[16] The Khmer villagers resented these newcomers from North Vietnam, regarding them in much the same manner as native white southerners had regarded the northern carpetbaggers who had come south after the American Civil War to live and work. The presence of a large and resentful Khmer population in the Delta also ensured that the region would become a fertile recruiting ground for the Viet Cong in a few years.

Figure 3.1   General Joseph Lawton "Lightning Joe" Collins, President Eisenhower's personal representative to the South Vietnamese government, greets Ngo Dinh Diem in March 1955. *Source:* St. Louis *Post Dispatch*

Diem's government nearly fell in the spring of 1955 when he challenged two powerful religious sects and also confronted the Binh Xuyen, the crime lords of Saigon and Cholon, the Chinese suburb of Saigon. Led by a godfather-type crime boss named Bay Vien, the Binh Xuyen controlled a huge underworld empire. In downtown Saigon, the Binh Xuyen operated the Grande Monde, a huge and opulent casino. Down the block from the casino was the world's largest brothel, the Hall of Mirrors. Another block down was an opium factory that supplied all of Indochina with high-grade products. By the early 1950s, the Binh Xuyen had become a powerful political faction in southern Vietnam. They also maintained their own private army of 25,000 thugs and enforcers. Bao Dai accepted bribes from Bay Vien, and in return, with French approval, he made Vien a general in the Vietnamese National Army and appointed him head of the national police, with authority over gambling, prostitution, and opium traffic!

The powerful Buddhist sects, the Cao Dai and the Hoa Hao, claimed millions of followers; both had their own private armies and exercised political control over large areas of southern Vietnam. The Cao Dai sect, founded by Ngo Van Chieu in the late nineteenth century, fused traditional Buddhist and Christian beliefs with a worship of films. Believers prayed to Buddha, Confucius, Jesus Christ, and Charlie Chaplin. The

Cao Dai strongholds were in the Mekong Delta, centered around Tay Ninh, about sixty miles northwest of Saigon. By the 1950s, the Cao Dai claimed 2 million adherents and could field a private army of 25,000 troops. The Hoa Hao had been founded by Huynh Phu So during World War II. Hoa Hao theology blended religious and nationalistic themes. So's followers worshipped heroic figures from Vietnam's past, such as the Trung sisters, Tran Hung Dao, Le Loi, and Nguyen Hue. Vietminh assassins, concerned with the growing power of the Hoa Hao, murdered Huyhn Phu So in 1947. The new leader who stepped forward was Ba Cut. By the early 1950s, the Hoa Hao claimed 1.5 million followers, mostly living in the Mekong Delta, and had raised an army of 15,000 men. The two sects, along with the Binh Xuyen, were strongly anti-Communist. All had enjoyed symbiotic relations with the French, and all had opposed the Vietminh during the Franco-Vietminh War. Long accustomed to autonomy under the French, they refused to submit to the authority of Diem's new national government. After all parties failed to negotiate an acceptable political compromise, the sects, with French support, joined forces with the Binh Xuyen in March 1955. Together, they prepared to destroy Diem's struggling government.[17] Diem appeared to be finished before his government had a chance to take hold.

But Diem moved first. He ordered the Binh Xuyen to close down their opium dens and brothels and to lay down their arms. Bay Vien refused. Diem's army invaded Cholon and opened fire. Civil war raged in the streets of Cholon. Thousands of people, mostly Chinese civilians, were killed. But Diem crushed the Binh Xuyen forces and Bay Vien, with the remnants of his army, was forced to flee into the Mekong Delta.

Prior to Diem's assault on Cholon, General Collins, who had been skeptical of Diem's abilities for months, had flown to Washington to tell Eisenhower that Diem lacked the requisite qualities of leadership to prevent a Communist takeover of southern Vietnam. He told Eisenhower that Diem had been beaten by a cabal of religious sectarians, gangsters, and French officials. Eisenhower accepted Collins's judgment and prepared to withdraw U. S. backing for Diem. While Collins was en route back to Vietnam to inform Diem that he no longer had American support and to seek his replacement, Diem, with Landsdale's support, had taken the actions that saved his government and retained U. S. backing. Landsdale's actions had been critical to Diem's success. He had provided the assurances and moral support that gave Diem the confidence to take military action. Landsdale had also bribed the leaders of the Cao Dai to join Diem, and most of their forces were integrated into Diem's army. Further, Landsdale had used bribe money to induce most of the Hoa Hao soldiers to either join Diem or to remain neutral. Several U. S. military advisers supported Diem's troops who routed the gangster-warriors. With Landsdale's help, Diem had overcome his political enemies and had outmaneuvered the French. Diem was master of Saigon and now controlled his army, which had been augmented by the addition of thousands of sectarian troops. Diem had come back from the edge of disaster to find himself a hero in American eyes. "South Vietnam, it can truly be said, was the creation of Edward Landsdale."[18] Eisenhower shelved his plan to replace Diem, and he and Dulles reembraced the determined leader as the only man who could lead the new U. S.-sponsored state in southern Vietnam. Following Diem's victory, the French abandoned whatever remained of their hopes to retain influence in the South and made preparations to leave. By March 1956, the last French soldiers and civilian officials would depart Saigon, ending nearly 100 years of French colonial rule.

Diem, having vanquished his foes and shaken free of lingering French influence, and confident of the strong backing of the United States, now moved to eliminate Bao Dai, who was still the nominal head of the emerging South Vietnamese state. While the emperor remained in France, Diem arranged a referendum in which people could vote either for Bao Dai or Ngo Dinh Diem as head of state. Even though Diem would surely have beaten Bao Dai in a fair election, he took no chances. His henchmen rigged the election to ensure an overwhelming mandate for himself. Before the vote was held, Diem mounted a propaganda campaign against Bao Dai through the government-controlled press and radio. The referendum was held on October 23, 1955. Diem's soldiers supervised the polling places, and Diem's officials counted the ballots. Diem was urged by his U. S. advisers to settle for a 60 percent majority. But Diem wanted more, and his enthusiastic election managers obliged him. Some districts tallied more votes for Diem than there were voters. The Saigon-Cholon area, with 450,000 registered voters, cast 605,025 votes for Diem. At the end of the day, Diem announced that he had won, with 98.2 percent of the vote.[19] The political career of Bao Dai, Vietnam's last emperor, was at its end. A vote of the people had made Diem sole head of the South Vietnamese government.

As he consolidated his authority, Diem could rely on the political support of four main groups: (1) the sizeable Catholic population, now more than doubled in size by the addition of the northern exiles; (2) a small but influential class of wealthy planters; (3) the Vietnamese serving in the government bureaucracies, the police, and the armed forces; and (4) a new urban middle class created by the massive flow of U. S. funds to South Vietnam. For twenty years, U. S. economic assistance maintained Diem's government and all of its successor regimes. It allowed a generation of enterprising southerners to enjoy a lifestyle that could not be supported by the indigenous economy and one that quickly collapsed in 1975 when the great American money spigot was shut off. The members of this new class fully understood that their affluence was absolutely dependent on the American pipeline, which would continue to pump money into South Vietnam only as long as the United States backed whatever government happened to be in power in Saigon. Aware of these political and economic realities, most of the new Vietnamese bourgeoisie unfailingly backed Saigon, regardless of who ruled, and its American connection.[20]

The major component of the American economic aid program to South Vietnam was embodied in the Commodity Import Program (CIP). The CIP began in January 1955. Originally designed to absorb purchasing power to hold down inflation that would have been ignited by the rapid injection of large sums of money into the relatively small Vietnamese economy, the CIP also enabled the United States to fund the cost of Diem's army, police, and civil service. Diem was relieved of the need to tax the Vietnamese people because, in effect, the American taxpayers were underwriting the costs of his government. The most important part of the CIP was a method of subsidizing imports, whereby the United States furnished dollars to Diem's officials who, in turn, sold them to licensed local importers who bought them with piasters at about one-half the official exchange rate. The importers then purchased American imports with their cut-rate dollars. They imported mostly consumer goods, luxury items, and relatively few capital goods. The piasters government officials collected from the sale of the dollars that had been given to them by American CIP officials were put into a fund used for paying South Vietnam's police, soldiers, and officials, and for meeting other government expenses. Any additional revenues required by the government were raised by taxing the imports subsidized by the CIP. The commodity-import system generated the consumer goods that the new middle class wanted at prices they could afford. It kept taxes down, inflation rates low, and paid for most of the costs of Diem's and his successors' governments.[21] It also purchased the loyalty of the new urban middle classes to Diem and whomever might come after him in Saigon and to their American sponsors.

The Commodity Import Program did have some adverse long-run impacts on the economy and on many of the people of South Vietnam. While the CIP greatly expanded the size of the urban middle classes and made some Vietnamese wealthy, it created a narrowly based prosperity that never reached into the countryside or benefited the rural masses, who made up 85 percent of the southern Vietnamese population. The villagers could never afford to participate in the new consumer economy that American aid dollars sustained. The gap between city affluence and rural poverty widened. Saigon prospered, while mass poverty persisted in the countryside. The CIP, in effect, created an artificial economy that could last only as long as American officials were willing to pump hundreds of millions of dollars of American tax money into South Vietnam each year. The CIP also brought wholesale corruption and graft. Importers eagerly paid huge bribes to government officials to obtain licenses that practically guaranteed their becoming rich. Sizeable black markets flourished. The CIP, which brought in mostly consumer goods, also retarded South Vietnamese industrial development. There were no incentives for Vietnamese entrepreneurs to import capital goods and set up factories to produce items that could be imported cheaply from America and sold for windfall profits.

The South Vietnamese economy never industrialized or moved toward self-sufficiency. South Vietnam remained an economic dependency of the U. S. capitalist juggernaut. In the long run, two of the chief reasons for the failure of Diem and his successors to achieve stable and popular governments in South Vietnam were their failures to promote economic development and establish a popular base of support among the rural masses. The seductive lure of the CIP is partly to blame for both failings.

As the time approached for holding nationwide elections in Vietnam, as called for in the Geneva agreements, Diem made it known that he had no intention of permitting them to be held in his half of Vietnam. The United States backed Diem's actions even though it was inconsistent with America's calls for free elections in other divided countries such as Germany and Korea, and U. S. officials feared that Diem's refusal to hold the elections might provoke a Communist attack across the 17th parallel.[22] Given Ho Chi Minh's countrywide reputation as a nationalist leader and given the fact that northern Vietnam contained 14 million people to only 11 million for Vietnam south of the 17th parallel, the Communists surely would have won the elections had they been held as scheduled in July 1956.

Diem justified his refusal to hold the elections by stating that his government did not "consider itself bound in any respects by the Geneva Agreements which it did not sign."[23] He also contended that the Vietnamese Communists were responsible for the partition of his country and that only his government stood for the fulfillment of the nationalist aspirations of all Vietnamese people to live within a unified, independent Vietnam. Until the Hanoi government permitted genuine freedom and democracy in its territory, there could be no election. Diem also insisted that the Communists would never permit a free election to be held in those parts of Vietnam under their control.[24] Diem failed to mention the most fundamental reason for his refusal to hold elections. President Eisenhower acknowledged that if elections had been held during that summer of 1956 to reunite Vietnam in accordance with the provisions of the Geneva Accords, Ho Chi Minh would have received 80 percent of the votes.[25]

During the mid-1950s, while the United States was backing Diem's efforts to consolidate his power and his refusal to hold scheduled national elections, the major arena of Cold War competition between the United States and the Soviet Union shifted to the Third World, that is, to the emerging nations of Africa, Asia, and the Middle East. This shift in focus occurred primarily because the Soviet Union launched its first important programs of military and economic assistance designed to win friends and influence people in the Third World. The Soviets moved into the Third World arena during the mid-1950s for a mix of motives. They needed to find sources of strategic raw materials, and they were looking for trade opportunities. Favorable trade balances with Third World countries would provide the Soviets with opportunities to accumulate hard currencies (dollars or currencies convertible to dollars) with which to offset their trade deficits with the developed nations of the West.

The fact that a Soviet balance of payment problem had risen testified to the power of Western capitalism as well as to the intrinsic weakness of the Soviet monetary system. The Soviets were forced to play the game of international trade by capitalist rules. Although Soviet penetration of Third World countries during the mid-1950s had powerful economic wellsprings, the most important reasons were geopolitical and ideological. As the Soviets recovered from the devastation of World War II and consolidated their sphere of influence in Eastern Europe, it became possible for them to challenge Western dominance in the Third World. As its capacity to function as a global power increased, the Soviet Union was no longer willing to concede Western hegemony in the Third World. Many of these Third World nations into which the Soviets ventured were similar to Vietnam—newly independent former colonies and protectorates of European imperial powers such as India, Indonesia, and Egypt.[26]

For Washington, this shifting context of the Cold War rivalry brought about by Soviet expansionism into the Third World significantly enhanced the American sense of what was at stake in Vietnam. It confirmed Washington's essentially defensive mentality, a sense of embattlement. It reinforced the U. S. notion of global mission—the urgent need to deflect an aggressive international conspiracy reaching into regions of vital interest to America and her allies. It also reinforced the U. S. tendency to view all diplomatic developments within a global framework, to calculate any shift in the political fortunes of contending Vietnamese factions as a gain or loss for either Communism or Freedom.

By mid-1956, American officials had made fundamental commitments to Vietnam. After Eisenhower had settled in with Diem following his refusal to hold the elections called for in the Geneva protocol, none of Eisenhower's successors found themselves able to get out of Vietnam until America had fought (and lost) its longest war.

SOCIAL REVOLUTION

While Diem was taking charge in the South, Ho Chi Minh directed a Communist version of nation-building in the half of Vietnam that lay north of the 17th parallel. Although the Communists did not have to confront the political challenges to their rule in North Vietnam that Diem had to face in South Vietnam, the serious economic challenges facing the Communist leaders were more daunting than those facing Diem. Most of the fighting during the Franco-Vietminh War had occurred in northern Vietnam; consequently, the damage to the war-torn economy of Tonkin was much greater than any damage done to the southern half of the country.

When the French and non-Communist Vietnamese pulled out in the fall of 1954, they "gutted basic services, and sabotaged or dismantled industries as they withdrew from the North."[27] Much of the technical and skilled manpower in northern Vietnam also left with the French. North Vietnam had fewer resources and more people than South Vietnam. Agricultural productivity was low. The separation of the country deprived North Vietnam of its traditional source of rice. Historically, the North had imported much of the rice its people consumed from the South, and Diem refused to meet with Hanoi's emissaries to discuss economic integration or trade. Only an emergency loan from the Soviets enabled North Vietnam to import rice from Burma in 1955 and avoid a famine.[28] The requirements of reconstruction from war and the need for food forced Hanoi to seek assistance from China and the Soviet Union. External aid was crucial, not only to meet immediate needs, but to realize North Vietnam's long-term objective of building a modern socialist political economy.[29] Although China and the Soviet Union provided significant economic and technical assistance for Ho Chi Minh's revolutionary reconstruction of that portion of Vietnam under Communist control, that aid amounted to only a fraction of the assistance that the United States lavished on South Vietnam during the same period.

The new government that the revolutionaries established in Hanoi in the fall of 1954 was cast in the Marxist-Leninist mold. All power was concentrated within the executive directorate (Politburo) of the Lao Dong, headed by Ho and his senior colleagues. Opposition parties were forbidden on the grounds that non-Communists could not possibly be Vietnamese patriots. This Communist rationale for repression of all opposition represented an inversion of the logic used by American Cold Warriors, and by Diem as well, which held that Communists could not possibly be national patriots because their primary loyalties lay with an external power. The Vietnamese Communists permitted a national legislature to exist and regularly scheduled elections were held, but the legislature had no power independent of the Politburo, who ignored its laws whenever it wanted to and routinely presented it with programs to approve. "People's democracy" in practice meant that the masses were free to obey the edicts of the party directorate who decided all policy. The people of North Vietnam came under the control of a Communist ruling elite whose authority flowed from its monopoly of state power.

Political authority at all levels, down through the levels of urban neighborhoods, rural villages and hamlets, work places, schools, and occupations, was wielded by party members organized into blocs called cadres. These cadres also monopolized local government offices. Through the cadres, both party doctrine and government policy, often one and the same, reached every citizen. When fully articulated, the party apparatus was the mechanism for collectivizing the entire society.[30] The cadres, using a combination of positive incentives and coercion, worked especially hard to impose collectivist discipline on the rural masses.

While Diem, with American help, was maneuvering to overcome his many political rivals in Saigon, Ho Chi Minh announced on January 1, 1955, that the time had come to implement his long-held Communist principles of economic and social organization. He launched a two-point program for rebuilding the northern economy and restructuring it along socialist lines:

> We shall endeavor to restore our economy, agriculture, commerce, industry, and transport, gradually to raise our living standards. We shall continue our work of mobilizing the masses for land rent reduction and land reform. . . .[31]

It was through rebuilding and restructuring the northern economy that the Communist leaders sought to achieve their major objective: a self-sufficient industrializing economy within five years. Socialist reconstruction would be based upon the twin pillars of agricultural reform and industrial development.

When the government turned to the difficult task of rebuilding the war-shattered economy, its first priority was rebuilding the infrastructure. Transportation and communication systems lay in shambles. One of the first projects the government undertook was the rebuilding of the railroad that linked Hanoi with Lang Son at the Chinese border. Under relentless pressure from party officials, 80,000 workers rebuilt the lines in six months. The human costs of this forced labor were high, resulting in deaths, injuries, illness, malnutrition, and exhaustion.[32] Rebuilding the railroad was crucial to the development of the northern economy because it linked Vietnam not only with China but also with the Soviet Union and the East European Communist countries. Over North Vietnam's Hanoi-Lang Son railroad would come over $2 billion of industrial and military equipment that "fueled its recovery and later its war against South Vietnam."[33]

China, the traditional overlord of Vietnam, furnished extensive economic assistance to the North Vietnamese. Ho Chi Minh journeyed to Beijing in 1955 where he was met personally at the airport by the august Mao Zedong himself.[34] Between 1955 and 1960, Chinese aid to North Vietnam totaled about $225 million, and thousands of Chinese technicians worked on various projects all over the country. The Chinese interest in helping Ho Chi Minh modernize his country was to ensure that a friendly regime protected China's southern flank; the Chinese did not want either the United States or the Soviet Union to dominate Indochina. Ho Chi Minh, for his part, was quite willing to accept the Chinese aid on behalf of his desperately poor, war-battered economy; but he also recalled the long history of Chinese domination of his country and took care not to become too dependent on China. He was not about to sacrifice his country's hard-won independence or freedom of action.

Ho Chi Minh traveled to Moscow in 1955, where he was warmly received by the Soviet leaders. He had lived and worked in the Soviet Union during the 1920s and 1930s and had derived his political ideology from Marxist-Leninist doctrines. Ho Chi Minh's goal was for North Vietnam to industrialize along Soviet lines; the Soviet Union served as his model. The Soviets granted the North Vietnamese a wide array of aid programs. Soon, northern Vietnam was swarming with Soviet technicians, engineers, agricultural experts, and managers to help the North Vietnamese industrialize their predominantly rural and agrarian economy.

But Ho Chi Minh was no more likely to become a Soviet puppet than a dependent of China. He rather skillfully extracted much aid and technical assistance from both countries, retained his freedom of maneuver, and played one Communist power against the other, the entire time moving his country in the direction of economic self-sufficiency. By contrast, the Diem government in southern Vietnam, between 1955 and 1960, became ever more dependent on American economic and military aide to finance its government, to keep its consumer economy going, and to protect its security. Contrary to official U. S. views, Diem's regime was much more a creature of U. S. foreign policy than Ho Chi Minh's was a creature of Chinese and Soviet diplomacy.

Ho Chi Minh and his colleagues on the Politburo proceeded to restructure the North Vietnamese economy during the mid-1950s. French-owned coal mines, steel factories, and textile plants were taken over by the government, as were banks and utilities. The former owners were not compensated for their lost properties. Wages and prices were controlled. The commissars permitted some capitalist enterprises to survive; they retained a private sector of commerce and small-scale industries.

Agricultural reform played the crucial role in Communist plans for economic development of their country during the late-1950s. Industrialization would be retarded until they could make their rural economy more productive. Party officials also wanted to drive a sizeable part of the rural population, which made up about 85 percent of the total population, off of the land in order to ease population pressures in the countryside and furnish workers for developing industries. Party planners believed the ultimate solution to the problem of low farm productivity would be the collectivization of agriculture. Large-scale, mechanized collective farms would raise productivity and eliminate surplus rural populations. But to placate the land-hungry peasantry for whom socialism held no attractions, the Communists "preceded collectivization with a program of land reform."[35] Lands belonging to wealthy landlords were seized and turned over to the poor. Since there were not enough rich landowners to satisfy the massive land hunger of North Vietnam's rural poor, roving political cadres of land reformers classified some of the wealthier peasants as landlords. Their lands were confiscated, they were imprisoned, and they were sometimes killed.[36]

Land reform accomplished both its political and economic objectives. About 2 million peasants received land. The old landlord class was destroyed, and a new class of landowners composed of middle peasants strongly supportive of the Hanoi regime took control of the villages. But many abuses and atrocities accompanied the North Vietnamese land reform. Thousands of people were dispossessed, imprisoned, beaten, and murdered.

The excessive brutality of the land reformers provoked a rebellion among Catholic farmers in the Nghe An province in November 1956. The farmers protested to the International Control Commission, which had been created at Geneva to monitor the armistice. Militia forcibly dispersed the peasants who fought back. To halt the spreading violence, Ho Chi Minh sent a division of regular army troops to suppress the rebellion. Thousands of people were killed, injured, or deported.[37] Conditions got so bad that Ho Chi Minh was forced to call a halt to the land reform program, order the release of prisoners, and apologize publicly for the abuses and mistakes that party cadres had committed. Officials responsible for the excesses and atrocities were dismissed. The harsh land reform program and the methods used to implement it left a residue of bitterness and distrust, as well as deep divisions in the countryside between the beneficiaries and the victims of land reform.

Although preoccupied with consolidating his rule, rebuilding the northern economy, and implementing socialism, Ho Chi Minh expected the reunification elections to be held in the summer of 1956 as scheduled. He also expected to win the elections and shortly thereafter to assume leadership of a unified, independent Communist-controlled Vietnam, which had been his lifelong goal. Hanoi assumed that the French, who had pledged to hold the elections, would still be in control of affairs in South Vietnam when it came time to hold them. But by the spring of 1956, the American-backed regime of Ngo Dinh Diem ruled South Vietnam. Bao Dai had been deposed, all French troops had been withdrawn, and French influence in Vietnam had ended.

During 1955 and 1956, North Vietnamese officials repeatedly tried to establish communications with Diem and start consultations in preparation for the elections. Diem ignored them. They also tried to persuade the members of the International Control Commission to get the electoral process underway; its members were not responsive to Hanoi's requests. Neither the Chinese nor the Soviets showed much interest in seeing that the electoral provisions of the Geneva Accords were carried out. As 1956 ended, it was evident that none of the members of the International Control Commission and none of the major powers were going to back North Vietnamese efforts to hold the elections. Diem was able to subvert the provisions of the Geneva Accords that called for the national unification of Vietnam via the political mechanism of free elections in July 1956, largely because the major powers supported the division of Vietnam. The French had departed and were no longer involved in Vietnamese political affairs. The United States backed Diem, but neither the Soviet Union or China considered it to be in their national interest to back Hanoi's efforts to fulfill the terms of the Geneva settlement and to unify their country.[38] As far as the international community was concerned, Vietnam had been permanently partitioned at the 17th parallel, and two de facto states, North Vietnam and South Vietnam, had been created.

Although disappointed and angry, the leaders in Hanoi, preoccupied as they were with implementing their socialist revolution in northern Vietnam and lacking support from the major Communist powers, were not prepared to resort to force to unify their country in 1956. Ho Chi Minh also feared that he might provoke a U. S. military intervention if he sent his troops south of the 17th parallel. Ho could also be patient because he believed the Saigon regime would soon collapse from its own failures and lack of popular support. Perceiving that no one other than Hanoi appeared to be concerned about holding the elections and that the North Vietnamese did not intend to force the matter, Washington was confident that it could build a viable non-Communist nation in the southern half of Vietnam in violation of the Geneva agreements.

BUILDING A NATION

The ambitious American effort to create a non-Communist nation-state in southern Vietnam in the middle and late 1950s took on the aspects of a crusade in Southeast Asia. By 1958, over 1,500 Americans were at work in South Vietnam on various projects. South Vietnam received the largest single share of the American foreign aid budget, and the U. S. mission headquartered in Saigon was the largest in the world. The mission, under the nominal direction of the U. S. ambassador to Saigon, comprised a myriad of government agencies, each with its own personnel, budget, and programs.

In addition to the regular embassy staff, these agencies included the Central Intelligence Agency (CIA), The United States Information Agency (USIA), the United States Operations Mission (USOM), and the Military Assistance-Advisory Group (MAAG). The MAAG was undoubtedly the most important of these agencies, because building up the South Vietnamese Army (ARVN) was the top U. S. priority; about 80 percent of the total American assistance program for South Vietnam went to building up its military forces.[39] Washington believed that before South Vietnam could have a chance to survive and develop its economy, it had to be able to defend itself.

The MAAG had been assigned primary responsibility for training the ARVN. The 342 members of the American advisory group inherited a challenging assignment. They found the South Vietnamese military forces that they were to try to whip into fighting shape to be in a sorry state. The ARVN soldiers were poorly trained and poorly equipped. The ARVN was short in officers, certainly qualified officers. "Diem tended to value political reliability in senior officers far more than military expertise."[40] Consequently, the officer corps, especially at the senior level, was riven with political intrigue. Diem, who functioned as his own minister of defense, frequently bypassed the military chain of command to give orders directly to unit commanders.

The MAAG advisers also discovered that the South Vietnamese army lacked patriotism. Commanders lacked any national feeling for their country. Most of its senior officers had fought with the French Expeditionary Force during the Franco-Vietminh War. Most spoke French better than they did Vietnamese, and many were French citizens. None of Diem's senior commanders had ever been associated with the resistance to French colonialism, the supposed foundation of Diemist nationalism and South Vietnamese patriotism. Insubordination was rampant, and seniors were reluctant to discipline subordinates who had political connections. Army Chief of Staff General Le Van Ty bluntly told General Samuel T. Williams, the MAAG commander, that "many of our units would disappear into the countryside at the very start of the reopening of hostilities."[41]

Corruption in the ARVN was rampant. Many South Vietnamese officers saw their military careers as an opportunity to enrich themselves and their families. Senior officers often developed nonmilitary enterprises on the side that included black marketeering, drug operations, and prostitution. Some regional commanders set themselves up as warlords in outlying districts, and their soldiers collected taxes from the villagers.[42]

General Williams and his advisory teams went to work to try to turn a thoroughly politicized, thoroughly corrupt South Vietnamese army that was incapable of fighting into an effective military organization. American-style training schools and methods were implemented. Thousands of Vietnamese officers were sent overseas to attend U. S. military schools. The ARVN was trimmed from a bloated 250,000-man force to a leaner, more efficient 150,000 troops. Soldiers were equipped with modern weapons and taught modern tactics. The "heart of the American advisory effort was the Combat Arms Training Organization (CATO),"[43] an operations staff that controlled all the

MAAG field detachments assigned to the various Vietnamese commands from the corps level down to the infantry, artillery, or armored battalions in the field. Advisers played key roles in determining the effectiveness of the training and discipline that the ARVN units acquired.

The effectiveness of the American advisers was sometimes hindered by language and cultural barriers. Few Americans could speak Vietnamese (or French), knew anything about Vietnamese culture, and sometimes displayed racist attitudes, calling the Vietnamese "natives." Some American advisers vented anti-Asian stereotypes, viewing their Vietnamese charges as passive, cunning, and incapable of understanding modern technology. For their part, some Vietnamese were slow to learn English, often resented their aggressive, brusque American advisers, and did not always train conscientiously. Many remained suspicious that the Americans had come to replace the French as their new colonial masters. U. S. advisers had to spend much time reassuring their South Vietnamese counterparts that they had not come as conquerors; they had come to help South Vietnam achieve independence, to be able to defend itself against aggression.

By the late 1950s, the American effort to turn the ARVN into a modern and disciplined fighting force had only partially succeeded. The South Vietnamese army still lacked sufficient qualified officers; Diem still insisted on selecting senior commanders on the basis of their politics rather than on their professional competence. Corruption continued to pose problems. But the chief shortcoming of the new-model ARVN was that the MAAG had trained it for the wrong mission.[44] The MAAG advisers, perceiving that Diem appeared to have eliminated all internal political opposition, concluded that an invasion across the 17th parallel posed the chief threat to the security of South Vietnam. The U. S. advisers were also influenced by their Korean experiences, where many of them had helped the South Koreans build up their defenses against another invasion from the North Koreans. The American advisers therefore created a South Vietnamese army with the capability of fighting a conventional main force war that could defeat an external invader, and they were dismayed to discover that the ARVN could not cope with the guerrilla insurgencies that arose in the South Vietnam to challenge Diem's rule in the late 1950s.[45] By training the ARVN forces for the wrong mission, the Americans also revealed that they had failed to understand the lessons learned at such great expense by the French in the Indochina War.

Along with military assistance, America pumped over $1 billion in foreign aid into the South Vietnamese economy during the late 1950s, most of it into the aforementioned Commodities Import Program (CIP) that sustained the South Vietnamese government and created a new class loyal to Diem and his American sponsors. The United States also provided over $150 million in direct economic and technical aid. U. S. money repaired war-damaged roads and railroads, enhanced agricultural productivity, improved schools, and raised public health standards. A group of advisers from Michigan State University improved the performance of South Vietnamese police and public administrators.[46]

Massive U. S. economic, technical, and military aid enabled Diem's government to take hold in Saigon. By 1957, the American experiment in nation building in southern Vietnam appeared to be a stunning success. From unpromising beginnings in the summer of 1954, Ngo Dinh Diem had risen to preside over a stable government protected by a modern army and sustained by a flourishing consumer economy. To confirm South Vietnam's nationhood and to celebrate Diem's political achievements, America's mandarin was flown to Washington in the American presidential jet in May 1957. The U. S. government rolled out the red carpet, and President Eisenhower himself met Diem at the airport:

> You have exemplified in your corner of the world patriotism of the highest order. You have brought to your great task of organizing your country the greatest of courage, the greatest of statesmanship.[47]

Diem was invited to address a joint session of Congress. The *New York Times* profiled Diem as "An Asian Liberator" who had saved his country from disintegration and who was a strong, popular leader.[48] Diem was feted at public gatherings as a miracle worker, who, with American help, had done the impossible: The gutsy little leader had overcome the inveterate political fragmentation of Saigon to create a strong, stable government, a showcase of freedom. South Vietnam was offered to the world as a model of enlightened U. S. Southeast Asian foreign policy in action. A thriving South Vietnam proved that foreign aid worked. America was helping an Asian people help themselves. The South Vietnamese had established a free society and were holding the line against the further spread of Communism in Indochina. Diem was the leader of his people fighting on the front lines of freedom, stemming the Communist tide. Beijing's and Hanoi's expansionist tendencies were being contained north of the 17th parallel, and the Soviet master plan for Southeast Asia was being thwarted. Diem kept his favorable U. S. media image until his government was engulfed by revolution during the early 1960s.

But beneath the brightly shining surface of public celebration, however, all was not going well in Vietnam south of the 17th parallel, even during 1957, Diem's *annus mirabilis*. Diem did not believe in nor did he implement a democratic political system in South Vietnam. He clearly stated his political philosophy:

> Our political system has been based not on the concept of management of the public affairs by the people or their representatives, but rather by an enlightened sovereign.[49]

To please his American sponsors, Diem established a constitutional system in 1956, modeled on the U. S. Constitution with executive, judicial, and legislative branches. Formally his creation, the Republican Government of Vietnam (GVN or RVN) was a constitutional democracy. But Diem was observing the forms, not practicing the substance of democracy. Diem's constitution lodged almost all powers of government in the executive branch. Diem's powers resembled those of the Vietnamese emperors or the French Governors-General, not the limited powers of the American president. The South Vietnamese judiciary never established its independence from the all-powerful executive, and Diem controlled all judicial appointments. Diem also had considerable legislative authority; the National Assembly could only initiate legislature covering comparatively minor matters.

Diem also moved to assert his authority over all of South Vietnam. He extinguished the regional autonomy of Cochin China and southern Annam. He appointed province chiefs for South Vietnam's forty-one provinces and administrators for the nation's 246 districts. Diem also extended his rule to the villages themselves. By decree, he abolished elective village councils and then appointed officials to supervise the affairs of the country's 2,500 villages and 16,000 hamlets, the levels of government with which the peasants identified. Diem was motivated to take control of the South Vietnamese government at all levels for two reasons: It accorded with his conceptions of authoritarian governance, and he was concerned that the Vietminh might win many village elections if they were allowed to take place.[50]

As a result of Diem's centralizing thrust, South Vietnam had the most authoritarian governmental system in its history. Neither the imperial Confucian administrators nor the French colonial administrators had ever completely abolished the tradition and practices of village autonomy. There was also a symmetry between what Diem was doing in South Vietnam and the centralization that Ho Chi Minh's government implemented in North Vietnam through the agency of the Lao Dong. One ironic consequence of ridding Vietnam of French colonialism was that Diem and Ho Chi Minh saddled the Vietnamese people with the most ruthlessly authoritarian governments in their history, in the name of "freedom" in South Vietnam and "people's democracy" in North Vietnam.

Diem also filled government positions with a preponderance of northern and central Vietnamese. The highest-ranking positions contained the highest proportions of northerners and centralists. Diem and his family were from Hue and were Catholics. Many of the northern Catholics who had migrated south in the fall of 1954 filled civilian and military positions in his government. Southerners resented these outsiders, who enjoyed special privileges, did not speak their dialects, and were not familiar with or much interested in their problems. This regional imbalance caused special problems for the Diem government's relations with many southern peasants and prevented the central government from ever winning their trust or loyalty. Southern Buddhist peasants especially resented having northern Catholics, who looked down on them and were indifferent to their welfare, administering their affairs.[51]

Trusting no one, Diem relied heavily on his family to govern South Vietnam. Behind a democratic facade, nearly total power "remained lodged with Diem and his immediate family."[52] The Ngos formed a family oligarchy ruling South Vietnam. The most powerful members, after Diem, included Diem's youngest brother Ngo Dinh Nhu and Nhu's wife Tran Le Xuan, who functioned as South Vietnam's First Lady. (Diem, because he took a vow of celibacy, never married.) Two of Diem's brothers, Ngo Dinh Thuc, the Archbishop of Hue and Catholic primate of Vietnam, and Ngo Dinh Can, ruled central Vietnam. Another brother, Ngo Dinh Luyen, bright and well-educated, served as the international spokesman for the family, roaming the world as a kind of all-purpose envoy. Several other relatives and in-laws held important offices, including Madame Nhu's father, who was South Vietnam's ambassador to the United States for many years.

The Can Lao, a secret political party directed by Nhu, was the chief instrument of family rule. It was the only legal political party permitted in South Vietnam. Cells of the Can Lao reached into every agency of the government, infiltrated the South Vietnamese army, controlled the National Assembly, the police, the militia, the schools and colleges, the media, and entered into every level of the administrative apparatus of the Diem government.[53] The Can Lao cells furnished the sinews that connected all the parts of Diem's authoritarian political system in much the same fashion as the Communist party operated north of the 17th parallel.

Having consolidated its power in Saigon and the other cities in South Vietnam, Diem's family regime moved to eliminate or suppress all remaining opposition in South Vietnam. Their major targets were Vietminh supporters, who had remained in the South following the armistice and who controlled many of the southern villages. In the course of fighting and defeating the French, the Vietminh had established itself in many regions of southern Vietnam. It controlled perhaps one-fourth of the villages within South Vietnam with an estimated 2 to 3 million people. The Vietminh was strongest in the Mekong Delta and in coastal enclaves. Nhu spearheaded a drive to eliminate the Vietminh presence in South Vietnam. During 1955 and 1956, thousands of Vietminh cadres rallied to the Diem government or were imprisoned or killed. Perhaps as many as 50,000 were imprisoned and 12,000 were killed. Diem issued ordinances in 1956 and 1959 that gave government officials virtually a free hand to root out any opposition to his regime.[54] Diem's repression fell most heavily on the countryside, on the peasants. In theory, Nhu's campaign aimed only to root out the Communists, but it also included anyone opposed to or suspected of opposing Diem: religious sectarians, intellectuals, journalists, socialists, and liberals.

During the middle 1950s and after, the people of Vietnam were victimized by twin tyrannies. There was one in South Vietnam, bankrolled by American taxpayers, and another in North Vietnam, granted extensive economic and technical assistance by China and the Soviet Union. Marxism-Leninism had taken root in North Vietnam; in South Vietnam, a Fascistic police state apparatus, directed by Diem's younger brother Nhu, had been implemented.

In addition to destroying their traditional village autonomy, appointing outsiders to administer their affairs, and mounting oppressive campaigns to root out all opponents, Communist and non-Communist alike, the Diem government's approach to

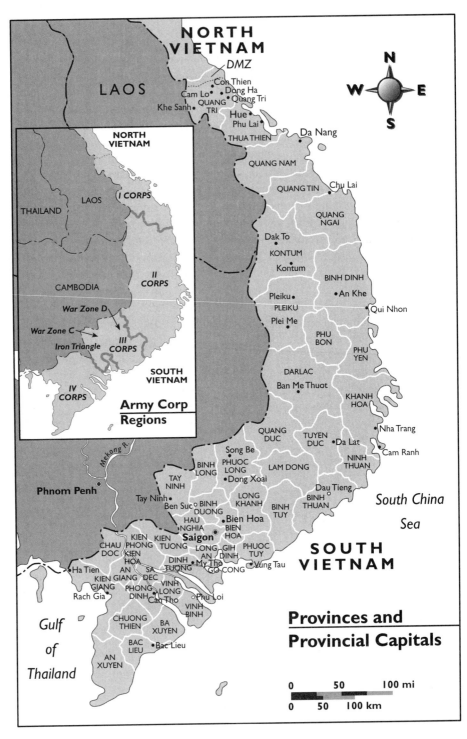

Figure 3.2 Public domain map.

land reform also alienated many peasants. Landlords loyal to Diem were allowed to repossess rice lands that Vietminh cadres had confiscated during the Franco-Vietminh War and had given to poor peasants. Special courts established to adjudicate landlord-tenant disputes were dominated by landlords and officials responsive to landlord interests. Programs designed to hold land rents to no more than 25 percent of the value of the annual crop often were inefficiently administered.[55] A program to settle villagers on abandoned lands in the Mekong Delta promised to be popular, but Diem's insistence that the people buy the land from the government angered many peasants. Another program to distribute rice-growing lands to tenants succeeded in providing some tenants with land; but only about 10 percent of the eligible poor peasantry in southern Vietnam were able to get the land, which came from expropriated French estates that Diem's government had purchased from their former owners, with funds provided by the United States. Landlords also were allowed to retain sizeable landholdings, up to 250 acres, for their own use, further limiting the extent of Diem's land reform efforts.[56]

Starting in 1957, the Diem government initiated a resettlement program for some of the Catholic refugees from North Vietnam and for peasants from overpopulated coastal enclaves. They were resettled on lands in areas within the sparsely populated central highlands. The new settlers were placed in fortified villages on lands claimed by Montagnard tribes who practiced a form of slash-and-burn agriculture. In addition to taking their lands, Diem also attempted to impose his rule on the Montagnards and to Vietnamize them. Long accustomed to autonomy and allowed to retain their cultural identities under French rule, the Montagnards fiercely resented the intrusive Diemist policies. By 1958, some of the Montagnards were rebelling against the government.[57] Later, the Communists were able to win the support of some of the Montagnard tribes by exploiting their grievances against the GVN.

During the years when U. S. government officials and journalists were extolling Diem's triumphs in the South, many of his policies were alienating much of the rural population. In truth, the United States in South Vietnam "devoted little attention to political matters and despite its massive foreign aid program, exerted little influence."[58] Even though Diem's government was absolutely dependent on American aid for its survival, U. S. officials had very little leverage they could use against the strong-willed ruler. Diem was convinced that only he knew what needed to be done and that only he knew how to do it. He sensed that Washington was content just to have a functioning "free," that is, anti-Communist, government in the southern half of Vietnam preventing the spread of Communism. Democracy in South Vietnam would be nice, but it could always be implemented later. Besides, the Americans reasoned, Vietnam lacked an indigenous democratic tradition; the people were accustomed to authoritarian rulers. Diem and Thu also believed the Americans would be forced to go along with them no matter what they did or did not do, as long as the family oligarchy maintained a tough anti-Communist stance in South Vietnam. Diem and his brother were correct, because it was not until the early 1960s, when Diem's government was

rationale for Diem's failings is U.S.

engulfed by revolution, that worried American officials began pressing them to make reforms.

Diem's political ideology, an unwieldy mix of doctrines called "personalism" developed by his brother Nhu to provide an ideological alternative to Communism, blended Confucian, Catholic, and Marxist principles. It added up to a rationale for a species of paternalistic despotism: As the leader-father of his people, Diem knew what was best for his country, and it was his duty to implement the policies that would achieve the Diemist conception of the general good. The people's duties were to respect and obey their leader. Personalistic theory called for a government for the people, but not of the people or by the people. In fact, Diem viewed his people, if by "the people" one referred to the rural masses who constituted 85 percent of the South Vietnamese population, as potential enemies who must be kept under surveillance and tight administrative control. The Ngo family oligarchy was indifferent to the needs of its people and violated their sensibilities. It promulgated policies that alienated much of the rural population. Worst of all, it repeatedly attacked and tried to suppress all of its opponents. Inevitably, its actions provoked resistance. In time, that resistance evolved into armed rebellion. Hanoi took over and directed that rebellion, which evolved into revolution.

THE ROOTS OF REVOLUTION

According to the provisions of the Geneva agreements that arranged an armistice and proposed a political settlement for the Franco-Vietminh War in 1954, the armed forces and supporters of both sides were allowed 300 days in which to withdraw to one of the two regroupment zones, with the French and their supporters retiring to the zone south of the 17th parallel and the Vietminh and their supporters moving north. During the 300-day interim, about 800,000 people moved south. An estimated "50,000 to 90,000 Vietminh sympathizers went to the North, while approximately 10,000 to 15,000 remained in the South."[59] The Vietminh cadres remaining in South Vietnam were under instructions to protect the remaining revolutionary forces in the region, maintain the party apparatus, and retain their influence in the villages sympathetic to the Vietminh program. Neither these "stay-behinds" nor their leaders in Hanoi anticipated the rapid decline of French influence in South Vietnam or the emergence of the Diem government backed by a strong U. S. presence. They also did not anticipate that the elections to unify the country would be aborted. These Vietminh stay-behinds formed the nucleus of the armed rebellion that would erupt within a few years in South Vietnam.

During the first few years of Diem's administration, opposition had come mainly from the Right of the political spectrum, from the sects and the Binh Xuyen. During these years, the Vietminh stay-behinds, following their instructions, involved themselves mostly in political activity, preparing for the upcoming unification elections they expected to win. They were shocked and angry when the promised elections were never held. They also were disappointed that the major powers, including their Communist allies, accepted the cancellation of the elections and that Hanoi was not prepared to force the issue. Some left the Vietminh ranks, but most remained loyal to Hanoi and to its goal of a unified and an independent Vietnamese nation under a Communist government.

Nearly all Vietnamese, northerners and southerners, whatever their political beliefs and affiliations, held to a "concept of a single all-embracing nation." These widely and deeply held nationalistic sentiments were either not perceived or were ignored by American officials who had embarked on a crusade to create a new nation south of the 17th parallel. Disregarding the strong sense of national identity held by most Vietnamese citizens, a succession of American administrations advanced the notion that those Vietnamese who happened to live south of the 17th parallel under a free government had developed "their own sense of nationhood and patriotism" that was distinct from the sentiments held by the Vietnamese living north of that line under a Communist regime. But the idea of a permanently divided Vietnam was no more acceptable to Diem, his successors, or their followers than it was to Ho Chi Minh or his followers. Nor was it any more acceptable to that broad spectrum who did not support either the Communists or the Diemists. "Adherence to the principle of a unified Vietnam was common to almost all Vietnamese; where they differed was under what authority it should be reunited."[60] Both Diem and Ho Chi Minh believed that there should be and could be only one Vietnamese nation, as did their fellow citizens. For the Vietnamese, there was only one homeland; the conflict was over who should rule at home.

These nationalistic aspirations to live within a unified country, embraced by nearly all Vietnamese, explain why no "South Vietnamese" national consciousness ever evolved. There existed only a region cut off from the rest of Vietnam by an arbitrary line drawn by diplomats who never intended for it to become a permanent political boundary. It never did become permanent, except in U. S. foreign policy formulations. What did evolve in the southern part of Vietnam by the late 1950s were three broad political groupings. One was loyal to Diem and his successors and supported their American patrons; a second group supported the Vietminh and looked to national reunification under the leadership of Ho Chi Minh; and a third force evolved, composed of those who held to a goal of wanting to live in a Vietnamese nation governed neither by Saigon nor Hanoi.[61] The rebellion that became a revolution, which in time involved the United States in a major war in Vietnam, was always a struggle for control of one country. For nearly all Vietnamese, there never were nor could there ever be two Vietnamese nations.

In 1956, the head of the southern branch of the Vietnamese Communist Party, Le Duan, a veteran revolutionary leader and member of the Politburo, recommended rebuilding military forces in South Vietnam and reviving guerrilla activities to protect the political cadres. A southerner himself, Duan was concerned for the survival of the Lao Dong political apparatus in South Vietnam because of defections, attrition, and the depredations of Nhu's campaigns to root out Vietminh influences in southern Vietnam.[62] Hanoi was not responsive to Duan's request. The Communist leadership in North Vietnam was fully engaged in nation-building enterprises of its own and had no desire to provoke U. S. military intervention in South Vietnam, especially given the lack of support for Vietnam's reunification from the U. S. S. R. and China. The Soviets, under Khrushchev's leadership, were promoting peaceful coexistence with the Western powers; China, absorbed with its own national development, had no stomach for any more Korean-style military conflicts with the United States. The Soviets even went so far as to propose that the United Nations admit both North Vietnam and South Vietnam in 1957, apparently acknowledging a permanent partition of the country, a position absolutely contradictory to the desires of Hanoi's leaders.

Hanoi's leaders also told Duan that before there could be military action in South Vietnam, the southern party apparatus would have to be reorganized and rebuilt. Consequently, the political directorate strongly reaffirmed its policy of calling for peaceful political activity in South Vietnam. Duan wrote a pamphlet outlining Hanoi's policies to the southern cadres.[63] While affirming Hanoi's contention that the revolution in South Vietnam would develop peacefully and Diem's government would inevitably fall because of its inherent political weaknesses, Duan also advocated a more militant policy that would actively promote reunification and prepare the southern cadres for possible revolutionary activity. Some southerners read into Duan's ambiguous tract a call for more militant actions, including armed struggle. Duan's paper served as Hanoi's policy in South Vietnam until 1959, when fast-developing events in that region forced the political directorate to change it.

The southern Communists did have some successes in 1957 and 1958. They exploited popular dissatisfaction with Diem's methods and policies in some districts. But Diem's drive to root out the Lao Dong was effective in many areas. Cadre members were arrested, imprisoned, and killed. In many districts, the party apparatus disappeared or was reduced to a harried rump scrambling to elude Nhu's "hound dogs."[64] Some cadre members resorted to violence in some districts. They murdered Diemist police and village officials. In such scattered fashion, the rebellion in South Vietnam began a death at a time in 1957 when some cadres took violent reprisals against the GVN minions.[65] But Nhu kept the pressure on and continued to eradicate Communist cells in the South. The worst year for the southern Communists and their cause was 1958. They were reduced to pockets of resistance in a few regions, struggling to survive, without any help from Hanoi, and under tremendous pressure applied by Nhu's Can Lao operatives, the police, and the ARVN units.

"In desperation, local leaders in many areas began to act on their own initiative."[66] They resorted to violent reprisals to survive, to keep themselves and their cause alive. Armed units were formed in response to attacks by Diem's forces, even though these actions violated Hanoi's official policy. Guerrilla units were formed in the Quang Ngai Province, in the U Minh Forest, in the Mekong Delta, and in what U. S. soliders would come to know as War Zone D, a region northwest of Saigon and a long-time Vietminh stronghold. War Zone D would become a key basing area during the revolution, because it was near the Cambodian border and also allowed access to the Mekong Delta and central highlands, two areas of extensive Communist activity. By the end of 1958, the insurgents "had clearly reopened the deferred war of national liberation."[67]

Hanoi began developing a new policy in March 1959 in response to the growing militancy among their southern cadres and fears that Diem's repression would permanently weaken the revolutionary organization in South Vietnam. The Communist leadership also perceived the growing popular discontent in the South with Diem's policies and methods of governance and wanted to exploit it, but they had also concluded that Diem could not be overthrown by purely political means. His overthrow would require military activity. Among the Communist leaders, debates turned on how high a priority to assign the growing southern rebellion and on what combination of political and military strategies should be used in South Vietnam to overthrow Diem and reunify the country. They hoped to continue developing the northern economy and to avoid an overt military strategy that would provoke the United States into direct intervention. If that happened, there would be a full-scale, protracted war that would surely engulf them. Such a prospect Hanoi devoutly wished to avoid, if at all possible. It did not want a full-scale war with the United States.[68]

A Politburo directive issued in May 1959 authorized the formation of a base in the central highlands for political organizing leading to limited guerrilla warfare. A few months later, the Central Committee widened the scope of permissible politico-military activity to include other regions as opportunities developed and circumstances required. It also instructed the North Vietnamese army to establish a special transportation unit with the capability of moving weapons, ammunition, people, and supplies overland from North Vietnam to South Vietnam along an infiltration route that ran through the Laotian panhandle. This infiltration route would become famous during the American Vietnam war as the Ho Chi Minh trail. In addition, Hanoi began to send southern cadres that had regrouped in North Vietnam following the 1954 armistice down the Ho Chi Minh trail to join the southern insurgency. Some of these infiltrators entered the South by crossing the Demilitarized Zone (DMZ) that divided the two countries near the 17th parallel.[69] Many of these "regroupees" had received special training in revolutionary tactics while in North Vietnam and once they returned to South Vietnam, they assumed leadership positions in the developing insurgency.

In 1959 and 1960, the level of conflict between Diem's forces and the revolutionaries intensified throughout South Vietnam. Guerrillas raided ARVN outposts and assassinated thousands of Diemist village officials. The Communists staged significant uprisings in three areas that had been long-time insurgent strongholds: Ben Tre Province in the lower Mekong Delta, in the Tay Ninh Province, northwest of Saigon near the Cambodian border, and in the Tra Bong District in the Quang Ngai Province near the northern coast of South Vietnam. In the Ben Tre Province, armed units overran several government outposts in three districts. These attacks prompted the Saigon government to withdraw its forces from enough areas, allowing the Vietminh cadres to distribute thousands of hectares of land to poor peasants. In the Tay Ninh Province, a Vietminh main force overran a government outpost. In the Tra Bong District, the insurgents were able to fight off Diem's troops and establish "liberated zones" incorporating dozens of villages and thousands of people. Political organizing continued in many districts, and many villages that had formerly been controlled by the GVN now passed into the hands of the insurgents. The fact that these uprisings could occur reflected both the strong hold the Communists had on the villagers and the failure of Diemist policies in the countryside.[70]

Diem struck back hard at his enemies in an effort to contain the rising insurgency. Nhu continued his efforts to break the back of the Communist organizations. The ARVN troops raided guerrilla strongholds. Diem, with strong U. S. backing, implemented a program to isolate villages from the guerrilla forces by relocating the people in areas where the ARVN forces could protect them. A series of fortified villages, called "agrovilles," were constructed in strategic areas, and the peasants were relocated. The agroville program demonstrated how far out of touch Diem was with the rural population of South Vietnam and raised the level of popular antagonism toward his government. The peasants deeply resented being forcibly removed from their ancestral lands. They were not adequately compensated for their losses, and they were forced to work on community projects without pay. Originally, Diem's officials planned to construct eighty agrovilles. But peasant resistance and insurgent attacks led to the abandonment of the program at the end of 1960, after only twenty-two villages had been built. After the war, it was discovered that the architect of the agroville scheme, Colonel Pham Ngoc Thao, was a Communist agent. He had sold the plan to Diem, then designed it in such a way as to ensure that the peasants were angered and alienated from Diem's government. From the revolutionaries' point of view, Thao's agroville program was a smashing success.[71]

As the southern insurgency escalated, the Third Party Congress of the Lao Dong, meeting in Hanoi in September 1960, formally endorsed the revolution. It adopted a resolution stating that the Vietnamese revolution now had two primary goals: completing the socialist revolution in North Vietnam and liberating South Vietnam from the Diemist puppet regime to complete reunification of the country. The resolution stated that the two goals were of equal importance and integrally related.[72]

To achieve its revolutionary goal in South Vietnam, the Party Congress also approved plans to reorganize the developing revolutionary forces in the South and form a new united front. Following the Congress, the military cadres in the South gathered to form a united military command. On February 15, 1961, the People's Liberation Armed Force (PLAF) was formed. Tran Luong, a southerner, was chosen to head the PLAF command, but soon after his appointment several generals arrived in South Vietnam from the People's Army of Vietnam (PAVN) to reactivate the southern command that had directed Vietminh forces during the Franco-Vietminh War. It was known as the Central Committee Directorate for the South (Truong Uong Cuc

Mien Nam). The Americans referred to the southern command as COSVN (Central Office for South Vietnam). The southern command, which had direct ties to the Lao Dong Politburo, in early 1962 took control of the PLAF with its 17,000 main force troops. In addition to its main force units, the PLAF also included regional forces, guerrillas who operated at district levels, and local irregulars who were farmers by day, indistinguishable from other villagers, and terrorists by night.

It was these PLAF forces that American soldiers called the "Vietcong." No revolutionary organization in South Vietnam ever called itself the Vietcong. Ngo Dinh Diem coined the term, a contraction of the phrase, "Viet-nam Cong-san," meaning "Vietnamese who are Communists." Diem had coined the term to disparage all of his political opponents, both Communist and non-Communist alike, by calling all of them Vietcong.[73] Not to be outdone by Diem in the coining of propagandistic epithets, the insurgents promised to liberate the country from "My-Diem," which translated "American-Diem." My-Diem reminded the villagers that Diem's government was so dependent on the intrusive Americans as to be inseparable from them. While Diem and Nhu vowed to rid the land of Vietcong, the rebels promised to rid the land of My-Diem.[74]

As the PLAF was forming, at a secret meeting place near Saigon on December 20, 1960, delegates, responding to the September Party Congress plans, created the National Liberation Front for the Liberation of South Vietnam (NLF or Mat Tran Dan Toc Giai Phong Mien Nam Viet Nam). The NLF was a reincarnation of the Vietminh Front tactic adapted to southern Vietnamese politics. Its Central Committee included representatives of the sects, Catholic and Buddhist organizations, labor, intellectuals, women, nationalists, socialists, and Montagnards. Below the Central Committee, the NLF had various administrative levels paralleling the various levels of government. Its basic units of organization were the village-level associations.[75] The overall structure of the NLF resembled a pyramid, with the Central Committee forming the apex and the village associations forming the base.

At their founding conference, the NLF organizers adopted a ten-point program, which, like its Vietminh predecessor, stressed nationalistic rather than revolutionary goals.[76] Most of its leadership was not recruited from Communist ranks, although some like Chairman Nguyen Huu Tho had close links with the Vietminh. In fact, at all levels, the number of Communist party members who were permitted to assume leadership roles within the NLF was strictly limited. The Hanoi leadership had taken care to disguise its relationship with the National Liberation Front, which had the appearance of an autonomous organization composed of a broad spectrum of southern nationalists whose main political goals were expelling the Americans, replacing Diem's government with a democratic coalition government, and seeking peaceful reunification with North Vietnam.[77] The NLF represented itself as a democratic political alternative to the authoritarian Diem regime. The political composition of the NLF, its program, indeed its very existence, proved to many observers that the rebellion was an indigenous southern uprising.

For many critics of American policy in Vietnam, the NLF was a standing contradiction to Washington's oft-proclaimed charge that the southern insurgency was in reality an invasion from North Vietnam. Was the rebellion in South Vietnam in fact a spontaneous insurgency provoked by Diemist repression? It was true that by 1960 there was throughout South Vietnam a hostility to Diem's government that stretched across a broad political spectrum. This popular antagonism fueled the rising level of insurgency. A potent list of grievances had accumulated from the Diemist terror, the failed land reform program, the loss of village autonomy, and governmental policies that usually favored the landlord class at the expense of the poorer rural classes. But it also is true that Hanoi organized and directed the rebellion in South Vietnam from its inception. Party leaders provided the organizational structure and leadership that gave the southern insurgency the focus and dynamism it needed to mount a serious challenge to the GVN. "The insurgency was a genuine revolt based in the South, but it was organized and directed from the North."[78] The Lao Dong Central Committee's southern branch (COSVN) commanded the revolutionary struggle in southern Vietnam.

The NLF was not a spontaneous formation of dissident southern nationalists. It was inextricably linked to Hanoi and comprised the southern wing of the Vietnamese revolutionary nationalist movement. It was formed in response to and in accordance with directives issued by Hanoi. The Lao Dong political directorate meeting in Hanoi determined the NLF's general policy, its program, and its strategy. But the decentralized structure of the NLF and its communitarian basis gave the southern movement a degree of autonomy and flexibility. It often solved its problems its own way, punished enemies, and promoted land reform, without directives from Hanoi or even at odds with the Political Bureau. The independence exhibited by some NLF elements also served to disguise the role Hanoi played in orchestrating the southern revolution.[79] Hanoi hoped its exercise in political camouflage would enable it to avoid an armed confrontation with the United States.

Hanoi exercised general control of the NLF through the instrumentality of the People's Revolutionary Party (PRP), created in January 1962. The PRP formed the inner core pyramid of the NLF. The PRP, formerly the southern branch of the Lao Dong, was directed by the COSVN and thus connected to the Hanoi political directorate. The PRP cadres operated within all departments and at all levels of the NLF, providing education, administration, coordination, and leadership. The PRP was the hidden government of the NLF.[80] From the Politburo through the COSVN and PRP, the NLF and PLAF were guided by Hanoi, which viewed the developing revolutionary situation in southern Vietnam as a continuation of the national revolution that had been going on in Vietnam since August 1945.

Hanoi did not set out to overthrow the Saigon government in 1956, after the scheduled elections that would have given the Communists control of all Vietnam were aborted. It only gradually and reluctantly embraced revolutionary goals. Initially, party leaders hoped to achieve reunification by peaceful political means. By 1959, they understood that Diem's government, while repressive and unpopular because of its U. S. backing, was too strong to be toppled by political means. By 1960, after years of delay and internal debate, the political directorate in Hanoi, whose hand was forced by the developing revolutionary situation in southern Vietnam and by the demands of the militant southern cadres, decided to support a revolution in South Vietnam as a necessary means to achieve its long-standing goal of a unified Vietnam under its control. But even at that late date, Hanoi still hoped to avoid a war with the American backers of Diem's government. The ever-rising level of conflict between Saigon and the insurgents had forced Hanoi to embrace a revolutionary struggle that they would have preferred to avoid if they could have found an alternative political route to reunification.[81]

While Hanoi directed the formation of the PLAF and the NLF, the insurgency in the southern countryside continued to spread, and the level of violence steadily escalated. The number of districts and villages under rebel control increased rapidly. Hanoi's policy change had removed the restraints on the insurgents' use of violence in the South. The government response to the growing militancy of the revolt in the countryside was to remove its troops from exposed outposts, conceding control of districts and villages to the rebels.[82]

Diem and Nhu had nearly succeeded in eradicating the Vietminh in 1957 and 1958. At one point, the despairing rebels, scrambling to survive, verged on extinction. In 1959 and 1960, they achieved a remarkable comeback. They had forced Hanoi's hand. The Politburo had to support the insurgents and allow the hard-pressed survivors to take military action. Otherwise, Hanoi risked losing control of the movement and perhaps its failure. What saved the insurgency in the South was their own developing militancy, eventual backing from Hanoi, and most important, Diem's lack of support among the villagers in the countryside.[83] The Achilles' heel of the Saigon regime was the alienation of the peasantry.

In November 1960, Diem narrowly averted a military coup. It was led by Colonel Nguyen Chanh Thi, commander of an elite paratroop brigade, and by Colonel Doung Van Dong. The coup may have had the backing of a few American officials who had lost confidence in Diem and had pledged to support the coup leaders if they were successful. The coup attempt, and the fact that it almost succeeded, highlighted the growing vulnerability of Diem's government.[84]

U. S. military advisers, worried about the survival of the GVN, finally began to shift the emphasis of their military training of the ARVN units from conventional warfare to counterinsurgency tactics. Three U. S. Special Forces groups arrived in South Vietnam to train special units of the ARVN for counterinsurgency warfare.[85] The American ambassador to South Vietnam, Elbridge Durbrow, tried to persuade Diem to reform his government and mobilize public support. He suggested that Diem allow greater civil liberties and freedom of the media, restore village elections, and offer more economic assistance to the peasants.[86]

Diem ignored Durbrow's advice and tightened his control of the South Vietnamese government. The MAAG officials, concerned with developing an effective military response to the insurgency, strongly opposed Durbrow's efforts to reform Diem. These military officers felt such pressures to push Diem toward democracy at a time when his government was under stress, both from the rebels and disloyal army elements, could only undermine him and endanger the whole nation-building enterprise. As 1960 ended, even though the American experiment in nation building in South Vietnam was clearly imperiled, Washington did not make any major moves to salvage Diem. Eisenhower was preoccupied with crises elsewhere in the world and was preparing to turn the reins of government over to his successor, elected in November—John Fitzgerald Kennedy.[87]

THE LAND OF A MILLION ELEPHANTS

Even as Diem struggled to control his army and to fight the rebels at the end of 1960, Washington was more concerned about developments in Laos than it was about what was happening in South Vietnam. Even though Laos had not received nearly as much attention in the U. S. media as had Vietnam, Washington considered it a strategically important country and became increasingly involved in its affairs at the same time U. S. officials were pouring funds and people into South Vietnam in support of Ngo Dinh Diem. In July 1954, when the Geneva Accords were promulgated and Laos had received its independence, the Royal Lao government had a mildly pro-Western tilt. The United States, replacing the French, in the name of anti-Communism, lavished economic and military aid on that country. It made Laos its first test of strength in Southeast Asia, the first country in which the line against further Communist expansion in the post-Geneva era would be clearly drawn. By the early 1960s, the United States had invested nearly a half billion dollars, mostly in military aid, in support of a series of right-wing leaders.[88]

In the mid-1950s, Laos, a small, mountainous, and landlocked feudal kingdom, was hardly a nation at all. Until the Americans intervened and pulled it into the cauldron of Cold War, it was a quiet political backwater—a poor, underdeveloped, sparsely populated region. It had been colonized by the French at the end of the nineteenth century as a sort of afterthought to their conquest of Vietnam, with whom it shares a long border. About half of the 3 million inhabitants of Laos consisted of ethnic Lao, who lived on fertile plains near the Mekong River and its tributaries. The remainder of the population constituted a melange of hill tribes who inhabited the mountainous interior. At the time of the American intervention in the mid-1950s, perhaps 2 million people lived in areas nominally controlled by the Royal Lao government. The other million inhabitants lived in areas nominally controlled by a Communist movement that called itself the Neo Lao Hak Sat (Lao Patriotic Front). Americans knew the Laotian Communists as the Pathet Lao, which translates "land of the Lao."[89]

The Pathet Lao, led by Prince Souphanouvong and backed by the North Vietnamese, had taken control of the eastern two provinces of Laos in 1957. Prince Souvanna Phouma, the leader of the royalist forces, had negotiated an agreement with

Prince Souphanouvong, establishing a neutralist Laos under a coalition government. Washington opposed Phouma's effort to form a coalition government with the Communists and pursue a neutralist foreign policy.[90] American officials sought to develop a pro-American orientation among the non-Communist leaders of Laos.

The Eisenhower administration, using the CIA, installed a right-wing, pro-Western government in Laos under the rule of General Phoumi Nosavan. General Phoumi repudiated the coalition with the Communist forces. He ousted Prince Souvanna and had Prince Souphanouvong imprisoned. Washington strongly supported General Phoumi, increasing the amount of U. S. aid going to Laos and sending a military mission. The Rightist government proved to be inept, unpopular, and corrupt. Much of the money for U. S. assistance programs went into the pockets of corrupt government officials.[91] The Pathet Lao, now excluded from power and supported by the Soviets and Hanoi, resumed its guerrilla war against the Laotian government.

One day, in August 1960, while General Phoumi was out of town, a military coup led by paratroop Captain Kong Le seized power. Captain Le invited Prince Souvanna to return to power and form a neutralist government. General Phoumi, reacting to the coup, proclaimed his own government and marched on the capital, Vientiane. Prince Souvanna fled to Cambodia, and Captain Le joined the Pathet Lao forces. The United States continued to back General Phoumi. The CIA recruited tribes from the mountainous regions who supported General Phoumi's forces. The most important of these tribal forces came from the Hmong (Meo), led by General Vang Pao.[92] In December 1960, General Phoumi overthrew the neutralist government and returned to power. Responding to the U. S.-backed coup, the Soviets airlifted supplies to the Pathet Lao-neutralist forces.[93]

As 1960 ended, the crisis in Laos was intensifying. A poor, largely passive population was caught amidst political chaos and a fitful civil war. United States efforts to prevent Laotians from forming a neutralist government in coalition with the Communists had destabilized Laotian politics and provoked Soviet intervention. American efforts, paralleling their efforts in Vietnam to create a strong anti-Communist government in Laos, had failed. United States intervention in that obscure country had created an ominous possibility: a civil war that could bring a Cold War confrontation between the United States and the Soviets. When Eisenhower, on his last day in office (January 19, 1961), briefed Kennedy on Southeast Asian problems, he talked mostly about "the mess in Laos" and the possibility of American military intervention there, never once mentioning Vietnam.[94]

A FAILED EXPERIMENT

When Washington intervened in Indochina at the time of the Geneva agreements to create a new nation in the southern half of Vietnam and to prevent the further spread of Communism in Southeast Asia in the aftermath of the French military defeat, American officials confidently believed that they could succeed where the French had failed. Ignorant of Vietnamese history and culture, and not understanding the breadth and depth of Vietnamese nationalistic feelings, Eisenhower and his advisers did not fully realize the perils and the low potential of the enterprise they had so eagerly embraced. It is hard to imagine their choosing a less promising place than southern Vietnam to try their experiment in nation building. Sixty percent of the Vietnamese population resided in northern Vietnam. Ho Chi Minh was by far the best-known Vietnamese leader. His leadership of the struggle to liberate Vietnam from French colonialism had earned him enormous prestige and a popular following among the rural masses. He and the other Vietminh leaders were committed to unifying Vietnam under their rule. The Vietminh had left between 10,000 and 15,000 of their forces in the South to work for unification. At the time of the American intervention, Bao Dai's government was virtually nonexistent. He remained in France and his new premier, Ngo Dinh Diem, arrived in Saigon, only to discover that he had no popular following. The bureaucracies and army existed mostly on paper. Diem had no money and no real power. The French, still in charge in Saigon, wanted to get rid of him. The political culture of Saigon and its environs was riven with factionalism. The economy, based on exporting rice and rubber, had been devastated by years of warfare.[95]

American officials did not grasp the fundamental political reality of Vietnam—that there was scant basis for erecting a viable nation-state in the southern half of a country whose inhabitants had a strong sense of national identity and a proud tradition of national independence stretching back over 900 years before the coming of the French. The Vietnamese people may have quarreled violently among themselves for years over what kind of government should rule their country, but nearly all Vietnamese agreed that there was only one Vietnam to rule. In addition, conditioned by their history and culture to be wary of outsiders, many Vietnamese resented the American presence, viewing American officials as colonial surrogates for the French. Even if Diem had established a more democratic and popular government than his family despotism, he and his American backers would eventually have been challenged by Ho Chi Minh and his followers, who would not have tolerated forever partition of their country, an alien foreign presence, or a Diemist government. Ho Chi Minh would have sought and received assistance from the Chinese and Soviets. Vietnam was fated for either reunification or perpetual turmoil. As it turned out, neither Diem nor any of his successors, the vast panoply of American aid programs, or American military power were able to create a durable new nation out of a fragment of a nation. The U. S. effort in southern Vietnam was a desperate gamble without realistic prospects of success. Although Eisenhower, Dulles, and other U. S. officials could not see it that fateful summer of 1954, they had undertaken an impossible mission that would eventuate in war.

Ngo Dinh Diem was a man of considerable ability and courage; he was hard-working, conscientious, and patriotic. His nationalistic commitments gave him some claim to the loyalty of his countrymen. He could not be corrupted by money. He was the best available man for the Americans to support in 1954, and he was the ablest of a succession of South Vietnamese leaders that the United States backed during the twenty-year existence of South Vietnam. But South Vietnam was a political contrivance, a figment of American anti-Communist diplomatic and strategic imperatives in Southeast Asia.[96] The United States had created South Vietnam and its leaders. What U. S. officials had labored mightily to produce was not a democratic independent nation-state, but an autocratic family oligarchy held in place by foreign power.[97] The pseudo-nation state of South Vietnam could only be sustained by immense infusions of American economic aid and military power. Diem's power and that of his successors always depended on American support. When U. S. military forces withdrew and U. S. aid declined, South Vietnam was quickly extinguished by the PAVN and Vietcong (VC) forces in the spring of 1975.

Diem as a leader also had numerous flaws and shortcomings. His obsolescent political philosophy and authoritarian methods of governance prevented him from ever achieving a broad base of popular support. Diem's favoritism toward his Catholic co-religionists, the shortcomings of his land reform programs, his failure to promote industrialization, his assault on village autonomy, and his repressive attacks on all of his critics and opponents had alienated the majority of Vietnamese from his regime by the late 1950s. Diem was especially unpopular among the rural populations, whom he distrusted and disliked. He never found the programs or the policies to win the trust and loyalty of much of the peasantry, nor to wean them away from the appeals of the Vietminh and their successors, the National Liberation Front (NLF). The failure of Diem's land reform program doomed his efforts to win a popular base of support among the rural populace and possibly undermine Vietminh support.[98] By 1960, the insurgents in the countryside posed a formidable threat to Diem's rule. He faced a powerful and expanding revolutionary opposition that he could not contain. The insurgency was provoked by his political failings, and it was directed and supported from Hanoi.

Only the caprice of the American electoral calendar saved President Eisenhower from having to face the failure of his nation-building experiment in southern Vietnam and the failure of his policy to shore up anti-Communist forces in Laos as well. It would be the fate of his successor to have to choose between abandoning South Vietnam and Laos to the Communists or significantly raising the American stakes in Indochina. It was a major part of the developing American ordeal that Kennedy felt compelled to raise the American stakes in Vietnam.

NOTES

1. Porter (ed.), *Vietnam Documents*, vol. 1, Document 386, NCS 5492/2 "Review of U. S. Policy in the Far East," August 20, 1954, 666–68.
2. Hess, *Vietnam*, 49.

3. Porter (ed.) *Vietnam Documents*, vol. 1 Document 389, South East Asia Collective Defense Treaty, September 8, 1954, 672-75; Herring, *Longest Day*, 3d. ed., 48–49.

4. *Ibid.*, 675.

5. Tuchman, *March of Folly*, 270–2; Herring, *America's Longest War*, 45. Young, *Vietnam Wars*, 46–47.

6. Bouscaren, Anthony T., *The Last of the Mandarins: Diem of Vietnam* (Pittsburgh: Duquesne University Press, 1965), 11–17; Fitzgerald, Frances, *Fire in the Lake: The Vietnamese and the Americans in Vietnam* (New York, Vintage, 1973), 107–8.

7. Bouscaren, *The Last of the Mandarins*, 17; Shaplen, *Lost Revolution*, 107–8.

8. Shaplen, *Lost Revolution*, 111–12.

9. *Ibid.*, 112–13; Scheer, Robert, *How the United States Got Involved in Vietnam* (Santa Barbara, Calif.: Center for the Study of Democratic Institutions, 1965), 13–16.

10. No one seems to know precisely why Bao Dai was persuaded to appoint Diem as his prime minister. See Cooper, Chester L., *The Lost Crusade: America in Vietnam* (Dodd, Mead, 1970), 120–28. and Karnow, *Vietnam*, 217–18.

11. Porter, (ed.), *Vietnam Documents*, vol. 1, Document 395, "Letter from Eisenhower to President Ngo Dinh Diem," Oct. 23, 1954, 681–82. Eisenhower clearly hedged U. S. aid commitments to Diem. The key sentence reads, "The Government of the United States expects that this aid will be met by performance on the part of the Government of Viet–Nam [sic!] in undertaking needed reforms."

12. Gardner, *Approaching Vietnam*, 327–338; Herring, *America's Longest War*, 49–50.

13. Landsdale, Edward Geary, *In the Midst of Wars: An American's Mission to Southeast Asia* (New York: Harper & Row, 1972), 170–76; Scigliano, Robert, *South Vietnam: Nation Under Stress* (Boston: Houghton Mifflin, 1964), 18. Young, *Vietnam Wars*, 43–46. Eisenhower's and Dulles' decision to back Diem was influenced by the U. S. experience in the Philippines during the late 1940s and early 1950s. In the Philippines, U. S. military forces suppressed the Hukbalahap, a Communist insurgency strongest on Luzon. The Americans later backed the rise to power of Ramon Magsaysay, a popular reform leader who established a stable, pro-American government in the former U. S. colony that had achieved its independence on July 4, 1946. In 1954, Washington saw the challenge it faced in southern Vietnam to find a Vietnamese Magsaysay.

14. Kahin, *Intervention*, 75–77; Scigliano, *South Vietnam*, 52–55.

15. Landsdale, *In the Midst of Wars*, 165–70; Kahin, *Intervention*, 76–77; Dooley, Tom, *Deliver Us from Evil*.

16. Doyle and others, *Passing the Torch*, 141–42.

17. Landsdale, *In the Midst of Wars*, 154–227 and 244–312; Shaplen, *Lost Revolution*, 100–28; James S. Olson and Randy Roberts, *Where the Domino Fell: America and Vietnam, 1945–1995*, 2d. ed., 52–57.

18. Landsdale, *In the Midst of Wars*, 260–312; the quote about South Vietnam being the creation of Landsdale is from Neil Sheehan, *A Bright Shining Lie: Joh Paul Vann and America in Vietnam* (New York: Random House, 1988), 138.

19. Kahin, *Intervention*, 95.

20. *Ibid.*, 84–85.

21. *Ibid.*, 84–88; Scigliano, *South Vietnam*, 125–37. Kahin states that of the $322.4 million dollars in economic aid for South Vietnam spent in 1955, 87 percent of those funds, $280 million, was channeled through the CIP. The flow of CIP funds was large enough to allow Diem to accumulate a dollar reserve of $216.4 million by 1960.

22. Herring, *America's Longest War*, 55.

23. Eisenhower, Dwight David, *The White House Years: Mandate for Change, 1953–1956* (New York: Doubleday, 1963), 372.

24. Porter, (ed.), *Vietnam Documents*, vol. 2, Document 1, Declaration of the Government of Vietnam on Reunification, August 9, 1955, 1–2.

25. *Ibid.*

26. Vadney, *World*, 215–17; Herring, *America's Longest War*, 56.

27. Turley, William S., *The Second Indochina War: A Short Political and Military History, 1954–1975* (New York: New American Library, 1986), 18.

28. Karnow, *Vietnam*, 225.

29. Hess, *Vietnam*, 64.

30. Doyle and others, *Passing the Torch*, 102–3.

31. Quoted in Doyle and others, *Passing the Torch*, 102.

32. *Ibid.*, 103–4.

33. *Ibid.*, 104.

34. When he greeted Ho Chi Minh at the airport, Mao was acknowledging the visit of an Asian revolutionary nationalist of a stature equivalent to his own.

35. Duiker, William, *Vietnam: A Nation in Revolution* (Boulder, Colo.: Westview, 1983), 107.

36. Karnow, *Vietnam*, pp. 225–6; Hess, *Vietnam*, 64.

37. Turley, *The Second Indochina War*, p. 19; Karnow, *Vietnam*, 225–6; also see Moise, Edwin E., *Land Reform in China and North Vietnam* (Chapel Hill, N. C.: University of North Carolina Press, 1983), 178–240, and his article, "Land Reform and Land Reform Errors in North Vietnam," *Pacific Affairs*, vol. 49 (Spring 1976), 70–92. Moise says about 5,000 peasants were executed. Porter, Gareth, *The Myth of the Bloodbath: North Vietnam's Land Reform Reconsidered* (Ithaca, N. Y.: Cornell University Press, 1972). Porter found that about 2,500 people lost their lives.

38. Note from Pham Van Dong to the Geneva Co-chairs, April 9, 1956, insisting that the Geneva agreements required both the French and Diem's government to hold elections, in Porter, (ed.), *Vietnam Documents*, vol. 2, Document 8, 15–16; also see Note from the British Embassy in Moscow to the Soviet Foreign Ministry, April 9, 1956, informing the Russians that the British government did not agree that South Vietnam was required to hold the elections, in *Ibid.*, 17–18; see also Message from the Two Co-chairs of the Geneva Conference to the Governments of the Democratic Republic of Vietnam and the Republic of Vietnam, May 8, 1956, in which the Russians essentially conceded that they would not push for reconvening the Geneva Conference or the holding of elections, in *Ibid.*, 19–20; see also Kahin, *Intervention*, 88–92; Hess, *Vietnam*, 59–60.

39. Herring, *America's Longest War*, 57. Hess, *Vietnam*, 60. Between 1954 and 1959, $1.2 billion in American assistance poured into South Vietnam. The top priority was always military security, and most of the U. S. aid went into military programs.

40. Spector, Ronald H., *Advice and Support: The Early Years, 1941–1960* (Washington, D. C.: Center of Military History, U. S. Army, 1985), 278.

41. *Ibid.*, 280.

42. *Ibid.*, 281.

43. *Ibid.*, 289.

44. *Ibid.*, 268–74; Herring, *America's Longest War*, 58–60.

45. Herring, *America's Longest War*, 61.

46. Scigliano, *South Vietnam*, 102–29.

47. Video clip from "America's Mandarin," part three of the television documentary series "Vietnam: A Television Series," produced by Boston (WGBS) and the Public Broadcasting System (PBS), first shown in October 1983.

48. Young, *Vietnam Wars*, 58.

49. Diem's quote is found in Olson and Roberts, *Where the Domino Fell*, 61.

50. Shaplen, *The Lost Revolution*, 132–34.

51. Scigliano, *South Vietnam*, 51–55.

52. Kahin, *Intervention*, 95.

53. The full name for the Can Lao was Can Lao Nhan Vi Cach Mang Dang.

54. Kahin, *Intervention*, 96–97. On January 6, 1956, Diem introduced Ordinance No. 6. According to its language, anyone considered a danger "to the defense of the state and public order" could be arrested. Diem later promulgated the notorious Law 10/59, which went into effect on May 6, 1959. Under its provisions, anyone who committed or aimed to commit sabotage, or infringed upon the security of the state, or belonged to a subversive organization, would be sentenced to death by special military courts within three days of being charged, and there would be no appeal. Young, *Vietnam Wars*, p. 56, cites figures of 50,000 prisoners and 12,000 killed. In a recent study, H. Bruce Franklin cites evidence that the victim's of Diemist repression may have included as many as 800,000 prisoners. Most of these prisoners suffered torture, and 90,000 were executed.

55. Race, Jeffrey, *War Comes to Long An* (Berkeley: University of California Press, 1972), 55–61. Race documents the failure of Diemist land reforms in Long An.

56. Scigliano, *South Vietnam*, 104–5, 120–4. At the time of Diem's ascension to power in the South, about 40 percent of rice lands were owned by 2,500 people, one-quarter of 1 percent of the rural population. Tenant rentals were commonly 50 percent of the crop, and tenants often had to furnish their own equipment, water buffalo, labor, seeds, and anything else needed to produce the crop. There were 1,584 French landowners expropriated and about 111,000 tenants received the lands, about 10 percent of South Vietnam's tenant farmers.

57. Kahin, *Intervention*, 99.

58. Herring, *America's Longest War*, 63.

59. Duiker, *The Communist Roads*, 172–3.

60. Kahin, *Intervention*, 103.

61. Turley, *The Second Indochina War*, 7–9.

62. *Ibid.*, 21.

63. Duiker, *The Communist Road*, 175.

64. Interview with Dr. Pham Thi Xuan Que on videotape in "America's Mandarin," one of the documentaries in the "Vietnam: A Television History," cited in note 47. She said "hound dogs" was the term for Nhu's secret police.

65. Race, Jeffrey, "The Origins of the Second Indochina War," *Asian Survey* (May 1960), 381 ff.

66. Duiker, *The Communist Road*, 184.

67. *Ibid.*, 184; quote is from Millett, Allan R., and Maslowski, Peter, *For the Common Defense: A Military History of the United States of America* (New York: The Free Press, 1984), 545.

68. *Ibid.*, 186–90.

69. Turley, *The Second Indochina War*, 24–25; Porter (ed.), ed., *Vietnam Documents*, vol. 2, Document 21, "Communique of the 15th Plenum of the Lao Dong," May 13, 1959, 44–46. This communique reflects the crucial decision made by the Communist leaders to permit armed struggle in the south as part of the insurgent strategies to undermine Diem's GVN. The DMZ was created at the Geneva Conference in July 1954. It was a buffer zone five miles wide dividing the northern regroupment zone (North Vietnam) from the southern regroupment zone (South Vietnam). It extended from the South China seacoast to the village of Bo Hu Su along the Ben Hai River, and due west from there to the Laotian border at the 17th parallel of north latitude.

70. Duiker, *The Communist Road*, 190–3. Young, *Vietnam Wars*, 66–68.

71. Doyle et al., *Passing the Torch*, 157–9.

72. Duiker, *The Communist Road*, 194.

73. Turley, *The Second Indochina War*, 30–31.

74. Hess, *Vietnam*, 68.

75. Pike, Douglas, *Vietcong: The Organization and Technique of the National Liberation Front of South Vietnam* (Cambridge, Mass.: MIT Press, 1966), 77–84, 109–18; and Duiker, *The Communist Road*, 197.

76. Porter (ed.), *Vietnam Documents*, vol. 2, Document 37, "Manifesto of the South Viet Nam National Front for Liberation," December 1960, 86–89. The moderate nature of its program was to serve as a bridge linking the Communists and non-Communist nationalists in a common cause, the overthrow of the "disguised colonial regime of the U. S. imperialists" and the American "lackey" "the dictatorial Ngo Dinh Diem administration."

77. Duiker, *The Communist Road*, 196–8.

78. *Ibid.*, p. 198; Kolko, *Anatomy of a Revolution*, 126.

79. Turley, *The Second Indochina War*, 31–32; Kolko, *Anatomy of a Revolution*, 128–9.

80. Pike, *Vietcong*, 136–50.

81. Porter (ed.) *Vietnam Documents*, vol. 2, Document 27, "Address By Lao Dong Party Secretary Le Duan," April 20, 1960, 68–70. Duan's speech is the most authoritative public statement of Hanoi's evolving policy toward the South. It stressed that Hanoi wanted above all else to avoid a war that would bring in the Americans and engulf North Vietnam.

82. Race, Jeffrey, *War Comes to Long An*, 113–30. In his detailed study of the revolutionary dynamics in a crucial province, Race shows how Diemist military forces and local officials could not stem the rising tide of revolutionary violence in Long An. Local officials

were killed, kidnapped, or driven off. Insurgents took control of many districts, gave land to poor peasants, reduced taxes and land rents, established village self-defense forces, and gathered intelligence.

83. Hess, *Vietnam*, 68.

84. Rust, William J., *Kennedy and Vietnam: American Vietnam Policy 1960–1963* (New York: Da Capo Press, 1985), 1–20; Spector, *Advice and Support*, 369–71; and Kahin, *Intervention*, 123–6.

85. Spector, *Advice and Support*, 349–61.

86. Porter (ed.), *Vietnam Documents*, vol. 2, Document 31, 75–78, "Memo from Ambassador Elbridge Durbrow to President Ngo Dinh Diem," October 14, 1960.

87. Herring, *America's Longest War*, 70–71.

88. Isaacs, Arnold R., *Without Honor: Defeat in Vietnam and Cambodia* (New York: Vintage Books, 1984), 159.

89. *Ibid.*, 155–6.

90. Hess, *Vietnam*, 69.

91. *Ibid.*, 69–70.

92. Isaacs, *Without Honor*, 164–8.

93. Hess, *Vietnam*, 70–71.

94. Doyle et al., *Passing the Torch*, 186–7.

95. Herring, *Longest War*, 3d. ed., 49–50.

96. Gravel, Mike, ed., *The Pentagon Papers: The Defense Department History of U. S. Decisionmaking in Vietnam* (Boston: Beacon Press, 1971), vol. II, p. 22; Baritz, Loren, *Backfire: Vietnam—The Myths That Made Us Fight, the Illusions That Helped Us Lose, the Legacy That Haunts Us Today* (New York: Ballantine, 1985), 16.

97. Young, *Vietnam Wars*, 58–59.

98. Hess, *Vietnam*, 60–63.

4

Raising the Stakes

Vietnam represents the cornerstone of the Free World in Southeast Asia, the keystone to the arch, the finger in the dike. . . . Vietnam is crucial to the free world in fields other than military. Her economy is essential to the economy of Southeast Asia; and her political liberty is an inspiration. . . . We must assist the inspiring growth of Vietnamese democracy and economy.

John F. Kennedy

COLD WAR CRISES

When John F. Kennedy took the presidential oath of office on January 20, 1961, the world appeared to be entering the most perilous stage in its history. The ceaseless global Cold War struggle between the United States and the Soviet Union raged on. At several points—Berlin, Cuba, the Congo, and Laos—the two superpowers verged on confrontation. In Asia and Africa, Third World nations were breaking free from colonialism; they struggled to establish stable governments and develop modern institutions. The reckless and erratic Soviet Premier Nikita Khrushchev saw possibilities for advancing Soviet interests in the turmoil and chaos generated within the emerging nations. In a speech delivered a few days before Kennedy's inauguration, Khrushchev vowed his support for anticolonial "wars of national liberation." The Soviet leader, emboldened by Soviet breakthroughs in space and missile technology in the late 1950s, crowed that Communism was superior to capitalism and told anxious Americans that their grandchildren would live under Communism; they would sleep under a Communist moon. Kennedy, sensing the American Cold War angst during his 1960 presidential campaign, had attacked what he called the "horse-and-buggy" policies of the Eisenhower administration that he charged had permitted the American economy to stagnate and had allowed the Soviets to gain the initiative in the Cold War. Kennedy vowed to "get the country moving again" and to regain American primacy in world affairs.

To rally the nation to face the challenges he saw, Kennedy struck an alarmist note in his inaugural address. America approached the Apocalypse: The new president sounded the theme of a nation embattled, facing crises around the world, with the fate of the free world hanging on the outcome of the long twilight struggle between the Soviet Union and the United States. He warned that the time was short, that the perils were grave, and that the news would get worse before it got better. But he also struck a pose of gallant defiance: he welcomed the challenge "of defending freedom in its hour of maximum danger." And he warned the Soviet leaders,

> Let every nation know, whether it wishes us well or ill, that we shall pay any price, bear any burden, meet any hardship, support any friend, oppose any foe to assure the survival and success of liberty.[1]

In responding to what he perceived as Khrushchev's challenge, Kennedy made an unlimited commitment to defend freedom around the globe.

Despite evidence of a growing rift between China and the U. S. S. R., Kennedy and his senior advisers embraced the containment ideology held by his predecessors, Eisenhower and Truman. The New Frontiersmen viewed Communists forces as an interlocked threat that must be checked by the United States around the globe. Kennedy and his men also shared a penchant for action. They eagerly picked up the gauntlet that Khrushchev had apparently thrown down and sought arenas in which to challenge Soviet initiatives. The new secretary of defense, Robert McNamara, a Republican and former president of Ford Motor Company, called for and got the largest peace-time increase in defense spending in U. S. history. The United States immediately embarked on a crash program to build up both its strategic nuclear arsenal and its conventional military forces. Kennedy and his advisers were determined to seize the initiative in the Cold War.

Sensing the need for a greater variety of responses to Cold War challenges, the Kennedy administration broadened its strategic capabilities. It scrapped the Eisenhower doctrine of "massive retaliation," replacing it with the concept of "flexible response," strategic versatility that permitted a calibrated U. S. response to any Soviet-backed uprising without having to risk a nuclear confrontation with the Soviets. Recognizing that the Third World would be the principal Cold War battleground of the 1960s, the new administration worked to developed a counterinsurgency capability to neutralize Soviet support for revolutionary uprisings. President Kennedy also wanted to eliminate the "conditions in which Communism flourished," placing emphasis on developing programs of economic and technical assistance for Third World nations that "would channel revolutionary forces into peaceful, democratic paths."[2]

Kennedy and his advisers shared many of the assumptions and illusions of the Eisenhower administration concerning Vietnam and Southeast Asia. They viewed Vietnamese Communism as an advance arm of Chinese and Soviet Communism that was absolutely dependent on them for its sustenance. They failed to understand that Vietnamese revolutionary nationalism rested on a largely autonomous national foundation.[3] To the New Frontiersmen, South Vietnam remained a domino threatened by external aggression, whose fall would imperil other Southeast Asian nations and threaten vital national security interests of the United States and its allies in Europe and Asia. Like the members of the Eisenhower administration that preceded them, Kennedy and his advisers believed they could develop the programs and take the initiatives necessary to control the political destiny of southern Vietnam. As a senator, Kennedy had been a strong backer of Ngo Dinh Diem; he had consistently supported the Eisenhower policy of keeping Vietnam partitioned and maintaining a non-Communist state in its southern half. Kennedy quickly made ensuring the survival of South Vietnam a top foreign policy priority, confident that the new counterinsurgency forces that he planned to deploy to Vietnam would enable Diem to defeat the insurgents and demonstrate that Soviet-sponsored wars of "national liberation" could not succeed in the Third World. American power, rightly applied, would win in Vietnam.

Other factors increased Kennedy's commitment to retaining a non-Communist government in southern Vietnam. His thin margin of victory in the 1960 election made him vulnerable to Republican charges that he was "soft" on Communism. Ironically, he had leveled similar charges at Eisenhower during the recent campaign, and he knew full well that Nixon and other Republican leaders would be quick to retaliate if he should appear irresolute in the pursuit of anti-Communist foreign policy objectives or if the Communists should make advances anywhere in the world. As a Democratic president, he also felt vulnerable to the legacy of McCarthyism and memories of the "loss of China." Further, the Bay of Pigs fiasco, occurring early in his presidency, probably reinforced his inclination to take a tough anti-Communist stance in Southeast Asia.[4]

But Kennedy's first Southeast Asian challenge came in Laos rather than in Vietnam. Eisenhower had warned his youthful successor that Laos was the most acute Cold War crisis of the moment and told him that if Laos were lost, the entire Far East would soon follow. The old general advised military intervention if necessary to save that country from a Communist takeover.[5] In Laos, the Eisenhower administration had been backing General Phoumi's right-wing government, which was engaged in a small-scale civil war with neutralist and Communist forces that were backed by DRV forces and aided by the Soviet Union. General Phoumi's government verged on collapse as Kennedy took office, and the young president was forced to act quickly to try to salvage it.

Kennedy seriously considered military intervention in Laos in March 1961, then decided against it after conferring with the Joint Chiefs of Staff (JCS). The Joint Chiefs warned the president about the pitfalls of a land war in Asia. They told Kennedy

Figure 4.1   U.S. Army Special Forces on a clear-and-search mission with Montagnard troopers. President Kennedy believed that these "Green Berets," trained to perform counterinsurgency missions, would enable the South Vietnamese government to win the hearts and minds of the people and defeat the Vietcong insurgency. *Source:* USMI Photo Archives

that if America sent troops to Laos, it was likely that China would also send forces. If the United States did intervene militarily, the Joint Chiefs recommended that it be full-bore; hit them with everything we have—60,000 troops, air power, even nuclear weapons; and be prepared to encounter the Chinese. Otherwise, stay out.[6] Kennedy stayed out. Probably Kennedy's failure to intervene in Cuba at the time of the Bay of Pigs disaster killed any possibility of sending troops into Laos. How could Kennedy explain to the American people his willingness to send troops to Laos 9,000 miles away if he was unwilling to send them to Cuba ninety miles away? Kennedy was also aware of the unpromising political situation in Laos. He did not hold General Phoumi and his friends in very high regard; nor did he perceive them as being terribly promising instruments with which to fight America's Cold War battles in Southeast Asia.[7] Renouncing the military option in Laos, Kennedy could only seek a political resolution of the civil war.

The Soviets and the British agreed to reconvene the Geneva Conference and to try to work out a negotiated settlement among the Pathet Lao, neutralist, and pro-Western groups. In May 1961, the three Laotian factions began negotiations at

Geneva. Eventually, they worked out an agreement that created a tripartite coalition government. The agreement was signed on July 23, 1962.[8] According to its terms, Laos became a neutral nation governed by a coalition under Prime Minister Prince Souvanna, with the pro-Western and Communist factions sharing power. The new coalition government was a fragile creature that favored the Pathet Lao and its North Vietnamese backers, who kept thousands of troops in eastern Laos in violation of the Geneva agreement.[9] The Communists controlled the eastern half of the country, including two provinces bordering Vietnam containing major infiltration routes along the developing Ho Chi Minh trail. Kennedy also violated the 1962 Geneva agreement on Laos when he ordered the CIA to expand military operations in that country. The U. S.-sponsored "secret war" in Laos escalated as the CIA recruited 9,000 Hmong tribesmen to strike against the Ho Chi Minh trail complex that ran along the Laotian southern corridor for hundreds of miles.[10]

As he was deciding to seek a political settlement in Laos, Kennedy's concern for South Vietnam was growing because Diem's position continued to deteriorate. Almost as soon as the new president had settled into the Oval Office, he had received a pessimistic report from General Landsdale stating that the southern insurgents were increasing their numbers, extending their control over more and more terrain and villages, and getting closer to their goal of toppling the shaky Diem government. Landsdale called for an increase in U. S. aid to the GVN, a 20,000-man increase for the ARVN, and urged that the South Vietnamese armed forces be taught quickly how to confront the revolutionaries with the "tactics and strategy of unconventional warfare."[11]

Despite their rising worries over Diem's survivability, for most of their first year in office Kennedy officials continued Eisenhower's policies in South Vietnam. In May 1961, Kennedy approved a few actions to try to shore up Diem's deteriorating position. He ordered an increase in the MAAG contingent in South Vietnam by 100 advisers, approved the 20,000-man increase for the ARVN, and he sent in 400 Special Forces troops (Green Berets) to train South Vietnamese forces in counterinsurgency tactics. He also dispatched Vice President Lyndon Johnson to South Vietnam to assure Diem of continuing, strong U. S. support. In addition, the president authorized covert operations against North Vietnam. South Vietnamese paramilitary units were sent into the DRV on espionage, sabotage, and psychological warfare missions. They also attacked enemy supply lines and staging areas. Finally, Kennedy established a task force headed by his Deputy National Security Adviser Walt Rostow to consider additional measures that the United States might have to take if the Communist threats to Laos and South Vietnam increased: bombing North Vietnam, blockading its ports, and sending U. S. combat forces to South Vietnam.[12] The president's actions in the spring of 1961 represented a cautious minimal response that did not move the U. S. commitment in Vietnam much beyond the levels achieved under Eisenhower. They were mainly intended to shore up Diem's government, buy time, keep options open, and enable Kennedy and his advisers to deal with U. S. foreign policy crises elsewhere.

In the fall of 1961, events forced President Kennedy to give greater attention to Vietnam. Hanoi increased the rate of infiltration of regroupees into the South. The insurgents sharply increased the military pressures on Diem's floundering government. The NLF forces escalated their military campaigns, threatening to overrun the Mekong Delta. Vietcong main force units also launched a major offensive in central South Vietnam. They seized Phuoc Vinh, the capital of the Phuoc Long province, sixty miles northwest of Saigon. The NLF regular forces attacked other provincial towns in the central highlands. President Diem, frightened by the rising level of military activity, called for additional American military aid. The JCS considered sending U. S. combat forces to the embattled country.[13]

Kennedy, hesitant to send American combat forces to Vietnam, instead sent his personal military adviser General Maxwell Taylor, accompanied by Walt Rostow, on a fact-finding mission. Taylor's findings, submitted to the president on November 3, were starkly pessimistic. They confirmed the rot in the GVN: Diem's government was ineffective and unpopular. The ARVN forces refused to take the offensive against the insurgents. Taylor recommended that the United States undertake a "limited partnership" with the GVN by significantly increasing its military support for Diem and by upgrading the performance of GVN paramilitary and local defense forces in order to free the ARVN regulars for combat against the NLF forces. He also recommended sending 8,000 U. S. combat troops.[14]

While administration officials were debating Taylor's report, Kennedy received another recommendation, this one written by Undersecretary of State Chester Bowles and Averell Harriman, the chief American negotiator at Geneva. Bowles and Harriman frankly doubted Diem's ability to survive, and they opposed increasing the U. S. commitment to the GVN. They believed that the causes of Diem's decline were primarily political; his failing government could not be saved by U. S. military action. Bowles and Harriman proposed instead that Kennedy seek a negotiated settlement in Vietnam. They called for an expanded agenda at Geneva, currently dealing with Laos, to work out a negotiated solution for Vietnam based on the 1954 Geneva Accords. Other administration voices joined Bowles and Harriman in proposing a negotiated settlement of the Vietnam issue.[15]

Kennedy's advisers had given him clear choices for Vietnam. He could either expand the U. S. commitment in an effort to seek a military solution or he could try for a negotiated settlement. Kennedy quickly ruled out a negotiated settlement for Vietnam. Having already opted for negotiations on Laos, having suffered the Bay of Pigs fiasco, and having accepted the Berlin Wall, Kennedy feared that a decision to seek a political settlement in Vietnam would send the wrong signal to Khrushchev and other Soviet leaders who already believed Kennedy was not tough enough to stand up to Soviet pressure tactics. Adding to his concern, Kennedy had recently met with Khrushchev for a series of talks in Vienna. Kennedy feared the Soviet leader had misread him, that he had mistaken his civility and restraint for weakness. Kennedy also assumed that he would face domestic political reprisals from his conservative anti-Communist flank if he opted for negotiations on Vietnam as well as on Laos.

On the other hand, the president refused to send U. S. combat troops, which would significantly raise the American commitment in South Vietnam. He believed that the introduction of American combat forces might jeopardize the Laotian negotiations at Geneva. Kennedy was skeptical that U. S. combat forces could solve Diem's problems, believing that the South Vietnamese themselves would have to defeat the insurgents. Kennedy also feared that once American soldiers engaged in combat and took casualties, the pressure to send more troops would be intense. Once he started sending troops, where would it end? Diem himself did not welcome combat troops. He wanted increased U. S. financial support and equipment to strengthen his own forces, not U. S. armies fighting in his country.[16]

Rejecting both negotiations and an immediate dispatching of American combat troops, Kennedy tried to solve the Vietnam dilemma by choosing the cautious middle ground. Influenced by a memo from Secretary of State Dean Rusk and Secretary of Defense Robert McNamara, the president rejected Taylor's proposal to send combatants. But Kennedy approved Taylor's proposals to increase significantly the number of U. S. military advisory and combat support personnel going to Vietnam. In addition, Washington sent helicopter, transport, and reconnaissance aircraft to add firepower and mobility to Diem's army. Kennedy authorized the use of napalm and the Air Force began the aerial spraying of defoliants to deny the Vietcong ground cover and food crops. Kennedy also approved funding to increase the ARVN force levels and to upgrade their training and equipment. Further, Washington endeavored to improve the performance of South Vietnamese district forces and local security forces.

The President hoped these actions would arrest the steady political and military erosion occurring in South Vietnam. He also knew that the large increases in the number of U. S. advisory and support personnel would violate the Geneva Accords of 1954. Washington feared the Communists could gain a propaganda windfall from the American violations of the agreements. Accordingly, in December 1961, the State Department issued a White Paper that claimed that renewed aggression by Hanoi being in violation of the Geneva agreements justified U. S. escalatory actions in South Vietnam.[17] Kennedy's decisions in November 1961 formed the basis of the U. S. Vietnam policy for the remainder of his presidency. It also established a pattern of responses. Despite his bold rhetoric, Kennedy was a cautious Cold Warrior in action. He preferred to make short-term responses to immediate problems. He usually tried to split the difference between his hawkish- and dovish-advisers, between the National Security faction and the State Department.

Because many Kennedy administration officials believed the inept and repressive South Vietnamese government itself was a major cause of the insurgency and an obstacle to defeating it, all of their aid increases were approved with the proviso that Diem would take actions to reform his government and broaden his base of support. But Diem stubbornly resisted American pressures to get him to reform his administration and his army. He made it clear to U. S. Ambassador Frederick Nolting that South Vietnam's governance was an internal matter beyond the province of American officials. He told Nolting bluntly that the GVN "did not want to be an American protectorate."[18] The Americans quickly yielded to Diem. But by refusing to confront Diem or make increased American assistance contingent upon his reforming his government, U. S. officials encouraged the South Vietnamese leader to continue traveling down a self-destructive path that would ultimately destroy the limited U. S.-Diem partnership, Diem's government, and Diem himself.

The persistent refusal of Diem and his successors to make reforms that would have made their governments more democratic, and more responsive to the needs and welfare of the peasants, was a major cause of the ultimate Communist victory and the American defeat in South Vietnam. In Diem's case, it was much more than obsolete ideology, stubbornness, pride, and arrogance. He and Nhu believed that they knew how to run their government better than their U. S. advisers, and they resented and rebuffed American efforts to intervene in what they regarded as an internal matter. They also perceived that America had committed itself to their cause and would continue to provide them with support even if they did not make the requested reforms. They understood that the Americans preferred stability and continuity above all else. Further, they knew that the Americans would not pressure them severely to make changes while they were under the stress of insurgent assaults because U. S. officials feared undermining their fragile regime and aiding the rebels.

But there were other, more important, reasons why Diem and subsequent leaders of South Vietnam, mostly army generals, could never make the necessary reforms that might have strengthened their governments and improved their chances for long-term survival. These factors also shed light on the underlying South Vietnamese political limits that continually frustrated U. S. efforts in Vietnam and ensured the eventual U. S. defeat and the demise of South Vietnam. Diem and all of his successors did not respond to U. S. requests for reform because they could not, at least not without grave risk to their survival.

In the first place, they would lose legitimacy, the perceived right to govern, in the eyes of their own people if they appeared to be puppets, doing what their American masters dictated. That was a charge consistently made against them by Hanoi and NLF propagandists. Second, the South Vietnamese governments, whether headed by a civilian or general, were essentially military dictatorships. Their power, their ability to govern, depended mainly on the support of powerful senior military officers whose loyalty had to be purchased. Any effort to move beyond the generals and reach out to other classes with land reform, a wider suffrage, or village autonomy risked provoking a coup d'etat.[19]

There was another restraint, another dilemma, that American officials concerned to reform South Vietnamese governments could never overcome. Genuine reform that might have broadened a regime's popular base also would have risked bringing to power a leader who might have sought a cease-fire, opted for negotiations with NLF officials, formed a neutralist coalition government, and asked the Americans to leave. U. S. officials regarded such possibilities as tantamount to an American defeat because they believed that such a government would soon be dominated by NLF leaders who would eventually seek a reunion with Hanoi. In short, a succession of South Vietnamese governments dared not reform and American officials dared not push them too hard toward reform. These unresolved (and unresolvable) political dilemmas constituted an integral part of the American ordeal in Vietnam.

A LIMITED PARTNERSHIP

Kennedy's November 1961 decisions to violate the military provisions of the 1954 Geneva agreements and to increase significantly American military support levels for the GVN were intended to keep Diem in power, at the same time keeping the American commitment in South Vietnam limited, preserving the administration's freedom of action, and maintaining U. S. control of events in Vietnam. Kennedy was not trying to win in Vietnam; he was doing only enough not to lose. By opting for the limited partnership, he revealed that he was not prepared to make a tough decision to either try to negotiate a settlement and withdraw or send large numbers of American combat forces to try to win the war in South Vietnam.

Instead of biting the bullet, Kennedy took only a few nibbles at it, hoping that they would be sufficient but knowing that if the increased support levels proved inadequate, he would again have to confront the crisis. Kennedy had inherited a commitment in South Vietnam from Eisenhower. He would not abandon it, fearing the loss of American prestige and power vis-a-vis the Soviet Union and political damage to his administration at home if he did. The costs of pulling out appeared to him greater than the costs of getting in deeper.[20] Without fully realizing it, Kennedy had "maintained the momentum of American involvement,"[21] a momentum that neither he nor his successor could arrest before the United States plunged into a large and lengthy war that it eventually lost.

To implement the newly formed limited partnership with the GVN, the United States rapidly expanded its military presence in southern Vietnam. A reorganized and expanded military mission, the Military Assistance Command, Vietnam (MACV), commanded by General Paul Harkins, replaced the MAAG. Thousands of American advisers poured into South Vietnam during 1962. Hundreds of U. S. helicopters, reconnaissance, and transport aircraft arrived, with American pilots and maintenance personnel on board. Giant M-113 armored personnel carriers arrived to haul the ARVN forces into battle. Special Forces units moved into the central highlands to train Montagnards in various kinds of counterinsurgency operations. American advisers accompanied ARVN forces into combat zones, and American helicopter pilots flew ARVN troops into battle. Although American forces were officially limited to advisery and support roles, Americans on the ground and in the air increasingly found themselves in combat situations as the war escalated. By the summer of 1962, American soldiers were fighting and dying alongside of their ARVN counterparts in South Vietnam.[22]

During the first half of 1962, bolstered by the large increases in U. S. advisers, support personnel, and equipment, the South Vietnamese army took the offensive against the Vietcong insurgents. Using helicopters flown by American pilots, ARVN commanders moved into Vietcong strongholds northwest of Saigon and the U Minh forest along the Gulf of Thailand. South Vietnamese Air Force (VNAF) pilots incinerated villages with napalm and made use of defoliation techniques to deny the guerrillas use of crops and livestock. The ARVN 7th Division attacked a guerrilla stronghold in the Plain of Reeds, eighty miles southwest of Saigon, killing scores of Vietcong during three days of fighting. In July, ARVN forces launched a major offensive in the Kien Hoa Province. A month later, ARVN forces, supported by U. S. helicopters, invaded the Ca Mau Peninsula.[23]

The ARVN mounted larger offensives against Vietcong strongholds later in the year. In November, a force of more than 2,000 troops, transported by over fifty U. S. helicopters, launched a full-scale attack in War Zone D, northwest of Saigon. It was the advent of the helicopter more than any other contribution the Americans made to the GVN war effort during the 1962 buildup that enhanced the fighting abilities of the ARVN forces. Helicopters, which began arriving in Vietnam in December 1961, transformed the face of the war. They were flown on combat assault missions, provided transport and ferry services, and supplied Special Forces camps deep in the central highlands. Other important helicopter missions would evolve with experience, including gunships and medevac units.

As the conflict expanded in 1962, U. S. advisers discovered that there was not just one war in South Vietnam, but several, each with its own terrain, methods of warfare, and strategic importance. The Mekong Delta, a watery world of flat expanses, rice paddies, and irrigation canals, dominated by the many tributaries of the Mekong River, constituted one war region. Travel in the Delta regions was mostly by boats and sampans. In 1962, the Vietcong had about 10,000 main force troops and at least that many guerrilla irregulars in the Delta. Operating out of bases located in remote, impenetrable swamps, the insurgents were almost immune from attack and enjoyed uncontested mobility in this strategic region containing 60 percent of the South Vietnamese population and producing about 75 percent of its annual rice crop.[24]

Beginning about fifty miles north of Saigon and running north for almost 200 miles, and varying in elevation from 500 to over 3,000 feet, lay the mountain plateaus of the central highlands. Here, another kind of war raged. Dominating central Vietnam, the highlands were sparsely inhabited by the Montagnard tribes. The Vietcong often recruited the Montagnards, historically hostile to the Vietnamese, who regarded them as primitives. Since troops could not operate effectively in the highlands without Montagnard support, both the Americans and the GVN tried to wean the Montagnards away from the insurgents. By spring of 1962, several ARVN divisions were deployed in the central highlands to try to contain the Communists, because the forces that could control this region held the key to the strategic security of the populated coastal enclaves.[25] North of the central highlands lay the jagged peaks of the Truong Son Mountains, a rugged wilderness of rain forests, steep ridges, roaring rivers, and foul weather. In this region, South Vietnam narrowed to a width of thirty to sixty miles. Lying just below the Demilitarized Zone (DMZ) and bordering Laos to the west, the Truong Son Mountains were a major infiltration route for the Vietcong. The rugged peaks rising to 8,000 feet were almost impenetrable to ARVN forces. The guerrillas dominated the region, frequently overrunning ARVN units and ambushing their reconnaissance patrols.[26]

At the same time that its armies, with enhanced U. S. support, went after the Vietcong, the GVN implemented a "strategic hamlet" (ap chien luoc) program. Strategic hamlets were designed by Eugene Staley and promoted by a British advisery mission headed by Sir Robert Thompson, who had used strategic hamlets to defeat a Communist insurgency in Malaya during the mid-1950s. Through the strategic hamlets, Thompson planned to complement the ARVN military effort by offering the Vietnamese villagers physical security and economic development. Peasants would be removed from areas of Vietcong activity to secure villages defended by ARVN forces initially, and then later by specially trained local militia. Civic action teams would restore village self-government and implement social and economic programs that would benefit the villagers.

American counterinsurgency enthusiasts supported the strategic hamlet program. They understood that the threat the revolutionaries posed to the GVN was more political than military. To defeat the Vietcong insurgency, it would be necessary to cut it off from its popular base in the rural villages. Winning the war in the villages, winning the villagers' hearts and minds, required more than weapons; it required furnishing the peasants with positive economic and social incentives for supporting the South Vietnamese government. Before these programs could be implemented, the GVN would have to guarantee the physical security of the villagers, both to insulate them from insurgent attacks and to deny the guerrillas access to provisions and recruits. Kennedy administration officials believed that the strategic hamlet program promised to separate the Vietcong from the villagers and would thereby kill the rebellion.[27] Washington believed that strategic hamlets would rectify the GVN's most serious political weakness, its lack of support among the peasantry.

Diem embraced the idea of isolating the Vietcong from the rural population. Under the rubric of Operation Sunrise, the first fortified villages were under construction in March 1962 in the Ben Cat district of the Binh Doung Province, a heavily forested Vietcong stronghold forty miles northwest of Saigon. The ARVN forces dispersed the insurgents. By summer, several strategic hamlets had been carved out of the jungle, accommodating over 3,000 people. The new villages were equipped with schools, medical clinics, markets, and a defense force.[28]

Diem hailed the strategic hamlet program as the ultimate solution to the problems of rural pacification and reconstruction. Diem's brother Nhu was particularly enthusiastic and became the driving force behind the program. He saw the strategic hamlets not only as a means of isolating the people from the Vietcong and regaining loyalty to the GVN via social and economic development but also as vehicles for social control, political indoctrination, and ideological transformation. With the villagers under the control of the GVN, Nhu planned to convert all of them to his philosophy of Personalism. During the summer of 1962, Operation Sunrise was expanded to other provinces, and by the end of the year, Diem and Nhu had made it a national program. They declared 1962 to be the year of the strategic hamlet.

SOCIAL REVOLUTION IN THE SOUTH

The initiative seized by the ARVN forces during 1962 proved temporary. Despite using helicopters and having U. S. advisers integrated into the command and staff structure of the South Vietnamese forces at every level, the ARVN forces were prone to operational failures. Vietcong riflemen learned how to bring down helicopters with small arms fire. It proved difficult for the South Vietnamese military to locate and trap the elusive Vietcong guerrillas amidst the swamps and paddy lands of the Delta. Peasants sympathetic to the insurgents would provide intelligence to and warn the guerrillas of ARVN or provincial force movements, giving them ample time to escape. The large-scale ARVN sweeps through Vietcong-infested regions usually netted few casualties, prisoners, or captured weapons and stores. As soon as the South Vietnamese forces withdrew, the Vietcong returned to reestablish their networks. Vietcong tactics could neutralize and occasionally defeat ARVN/U. S. A. technology. The Vietcong also made good use of intelligence and mobility to offset ARVN/U. S. A. firepower. Although frustrated, U. S. military advisers remained confident that the ARVN forces, trained and led by the Americans, and equipped with powerful modern weaponry, could defeat the elusive Vietcong if they would only stand and fight.

During the latter half of 1962, the insurgents built up their forces and continued to make political gains in the northern Mekong Delta region. The Delta was split into northern and southern halves by the Bassac River, one of the many tributaries of the Mekong. Historically, the southern Mekong Delta region had been a Communist stronghold since the days of the Vietminh. During 1962, the Vietcong and GVN forces fought for control of the people and resources of the northern half. The VC gradually gained the ascendancy despite the improved efforts of the ARVN, that was bolstered by U. S. equipment and field advisers.

During this time, the NLF more than compensated for the substantial increase in U. S. military aid going to the South Vietnamese forces. The number of main force units the Vietcong could field expanded. The size of their maneuver battalions increased, and their training, discipline, and operational capabilities improved. Their recruits came mainly from the ranks of the southern peasantry, although their forces were significantly enhanced by about 5,800 infiltrators coming into the south via the Ho Chi Minh trail during 1962.[29] Most of these infiltrators were regroupees, southerners who had gone north in 1954 and 1955, and they constituted highly motivated, thoroughly indoctrinated, specially trained cadres who moved into leadership positions within the Vietcong ranks. Insurgent firepower increased, coming mostly from captured American weapons acquired when the rebels overran ARVN outposts or ambushed small units. The insurgents also purchased U. S. weapons from some ARVN officers who were quite willing to do business with the Vietcong, and they obtained some modern Chinese weapons, automatic rifles, and mortars, which had been brought down the Ho Chi Minh trail. Vietcong planners devised tactics to counter the heliborne assaults of the ARVN forces. As their strength, confidence, and tactical sophistication improved, the guerrillas proved more willing to stand and fight the South Vietnamese forces, who still enjoyed tremendous advantages in firepower and numbers. Despite the infusion of thousands of U. S. military advisers and large amounts of sophisticated military hardware, the South Vietnamese forces remained on the defensive.[30]

The escalating conflict in the vital northern Mekong Delta region came to a head early in 1963 during the Battle of Ap Bac, the most important battle of the developing war in southern Vietnam.[31] ARVN forces learned of the presence of a heavy concentration of enemy troops near the hamlet of Ap Bac, located in the Dinh Tuong Province forty-five miles southwest of Saigon. The enemy was prepared to stand and fight; U. S. advisers got the battle they wanted. A golden opportunity appeared here for the ARVN 7th Division, led by Colonel Bui Dinh Dam and considered one of the finest units in the South Vietnamese army, to attack and destroy a major Vietcong force. Instead, the battle that occurred on January 2, 1963, turned out to be a stunning rebel victory and an ARVN fiasco. It revealed all of the shortcomings of the South Vietnamese armed forces and served as an ominous sign of the future.[32] It also thrust into prominence the senior U. S. military adviser to the ARVN 7th Division, Lieutenant Colonel John Paul Vann, one of the American heroes of the Vietnam era.[33]

The ARVN battle plan called for South Vietnamese forces to launch a three-pronged attack on rebel troops. The Eleventh Regiment Battalion from the 7th Division, helilifted to the battle site, was to attack from the north. Two companies of Civil Guard troops, provincial forces under the command of the Province Chief Major Tho, also a Diem favorite, attacked from the south. In addition, a company of the 7th Division, transported in M-113s and commanded by Captain Ba, another Diem protege, would assault from the west. These attacks were to be supported by artillery fire and tactical bombers, with reserve forces standing by to be helicoptered in, if required. Circling overhead in his Army L-19 spotter plane, Colonel Vann, advising Colonel Dam, would coordinate the attacks.

The planned assault resembled an open claw, and inside the claw, dug into the Ap Bac treeline, was the Vietcong 514th Battalion, a main force outfit of approximately 320 soldiers, reinforced by local guerrillas. Against the 3,000 ARVN and provincial troops, supported by armor, artillery, helicopters, and bombers, the 514th had only automatic rifles, two 30-caliber machine guns, grenades, and a few light mortars. They also had limited stores of ammunition, only enough for about one day of

Figure 4.2 The Ho Chi Minh Trail.

fighting.[34] As the battle began, it appeared that the heavily outnumbered and out-gunned rebels, having no exit, would be quickly overwhelmed and destroyed. The ARVN forces outnumbered their Vietcong enemies nearly 10:1, the classic ratio for success against guerrillas.

The ARVN Eleventh Regiment battalion made their helicopter landings to the north, uncontested. Vietcong forces, probing south, encountered the provincial troops. A fierce firefight ensued before the VC retreated to their tree line. Major Tho ordered his Civil Guards, who had been roughed up by the rebels, to halt their advance. Colonels Dam and Vann then brought in the reserve force to land west of the Ap Bac tree line. The Vietcong riflemen opened fire on the approaching helicopters, ten slow, heavy-bodied H-21s carrying the troops, and five sleek new HU-1 gunships (nick-named Hueys) flying escort. The VC hit fourteen of the fifteen ships, shooting down five helicopters with rifle fire. The reserve forces that landed sustained heavy casual-ties, and the survivors were immediately pinned down in the paddy fields by fire com-ing from the tree line. The company of M-113s, commanded by Captain Ba, was delayed for hours by Captain Ba's caution. When it finally arrived, it was ineffective against the entrenched Vietcong forces.[35] Guerrillas armed only with small arms fire were able to neutralize ten-ton armored behemoths, because the ARVN soldiers lacked effective leadership, discipline, and operational competence.

Colonel Vann, observing from the air, incredulous and outraged by the unwill-ingness of the Saigon forces to attack the VC positions, exhorted Colonel Dam to order both Major Tho and Captain Ba to move their troops forward to assault the tree line. They both refused to obey Dam's orders. Vann then requested an airborne unit from Saigon to be brought in to try to salvage the battle. But the order for the para-troopers had to go through Major General Huynh Van Cao, formerly the 7th Division commander and now the commander of IV Corps, with control over military opera-tions in the northern Mekong Delta. Cao, whose rank owed more to his political con-nections than to his professional competence, delayed calling in the airborne forces for several hours, then landed them at a site that permitted the Vietcong forces to with-draw from the field during the night. Cao, under secret orders from Diem to keep ARVN casualties low, chose defeat at Ap Bac to protect his career rather than seek the victory that could have been his.[36] ARVN politics had snatched defeat from the jaws of victory to the immense frustration of Vann, the other American advisers, and a few ARVN officers who were prepared to fight. The VC casualties were light—eighteen killed, thirty-nine wounded. Sixty-one Saigon troops and three American advisers were killed; one hundred South Vietnamese soldiers were wounded.

What could have been a major ARVN victory turned instead into a significant victory for the NLF and its forces. It was much more than a military success for the Vietcong, who had stood and fought against superior forces. It was a smashing psy-chological victory that NLF propagandists used to recruit more troops and win the allegiance of more hamlets to their cause. Ap Bac also signaled that the momentum of the expanding war had shifted to the NLF. By the summer of 1963, many of the villages of the strategic northern Mekong Delta either supported the NLF or took a neutral stance. The GVN controlled mainly the towns and cities scattered over the region. As the NLF regulars developed larger force units, greater firepower, and tactical sophistication, the ARVN forces grew increasingly reluctant to encounter them.[37]

For the ARVN forces and Diem's government, "Ap Bac epitomized all the deficiencies of the system."[38] The battle served as a paradigm for military failure. For Diem, the political loyalty of General Cao and Colonel Dam represented, above all else, coup insurance. He wanted the 7th Division available to rush to Saigon if necessary to repel possible challenges to his regime by dissident ARVN generals. Diem was determined to keep ARVN battle casualties low, because he and his brother Nhu believed that both the November 1960 coup attempt and another attack on Diem's life that occurred in February 1962, when two disgruntled Vietnamese Air Force pilots bombed his palace, had been provoked by casualties sustained by ARVN forces fighting the rebels. Diem preferred political survival to waging an aggressive war against the Vietcong in the countryside. General Cao and Colonel Dam preferred losing a battle to risking Diem's displeasure and dismissal from their commands. It was a matter of priorities, and Diem considered unhappy ARVN generals more dangerous foes then the NLF insurgents supported by Hanoi. For Diem and his family oligarchs, the key to remaining in power lay in retaining a favorable balance of loyal ARVN forces and in keeping U. S. economic and military support. They probably believed that even if the counter-guerrilla war went badly and most of South Vietnam was ultimately taken over by the insurgents, loyal ARVN units could defend Saigon and the other major cities long enough for Washington to send U. S. combat forces to their rescue. Diem and his brothers assumed that the United States, the world's preeminent power, would never let their anti-Communist government fall to Hanoi's instruments of conquest.

Ap Bac revealed the long-present shortcomings of an army whose leaders were more expert at politics than at fighting battles. According to Colonel Wilbur Wilson, U. S. senior adviser to III Corps, "The generals got to be generals by virtue of their ability in political intrigue, not as a result of their ability to lead men."[39] Further, the officer class of Diem's army came mostly from urban middle- and upper-class families, often Catholic- and French-speaking. They had no nationalistic feelings for their "country" of South Vietnam, nor had they identified with the long hard struggle to defeat French colonialism. Most had served with the French forces fighting the Vietminh. These officers generally held their enlisted troopers, who were mostly peasant conscripts or mercenaries, in contempt.

It dismayed Colonel Vann to discover that ARVN officers were indifferent to the welfare of the troops entrusted to their commands, never associated with them, and did not want to lead them into battle. One ARVN officer told Vann that the reason he became an officer was so that he did not have to go out into the field with the troops. Further, Ap Bac demonstrated the pitfalls of going to war with troops who were afflicted with low morale and whose performance suffered from a lack of training and discipline. Many ARVN soldiers openly admitted that they were afraid of the guerrillas, considered themselves inferior to them, and did not want to engage them in a firefight. The ARVN troops also lacked positive incentives for fighting, and their leaders failed to provide them with any. They were serving time in the South Vietnamese army, not a cause. Colonel Vann and the other American advisers discovered that they were trying to wage war against the Vietcong guerrillas "with an army that suffered from an institutionalized unwillingness to fight."[40]

By contrast, at Ap Bac, the NLF forces had stood their ground against fearsome weapons and troops that outnumbered them ten to one, and they had fought with great skill, tenacity, and courage for a cause in which they believed, a cause for which they were willing to die. Above all, Ap Bac "underlined the limits of U. S. Power" in Vietnam.[41] American wealth, military technology, and advisory leadership could not compensate for the deficiencies of an army that did not want to fight and whose leaders were under orders not to incur many casualties. Vann, who angrily condemned the ARVN performance at Ap Bac, generously praised his enemies for their valor and discipline shown that day along the tree line near Ap Bac.

While Saigon's armed forces were losing ground to the insurgents in the northern Mekong Delta, the much-vaunted strategic hamlet program was coming unraveled in the same region. The program had been hastily conceived and implemented. Most Delta peasants resented being removed from their ancestral lands. They refused to move and had to be forcibly relocated, many to hamlets whose security could not be guaranteed. Few young men of military age moved because they were either avoiding conscription or had joined the Vietcong. Many of these insecure hamlets were infiltrated by the VC. Even in the secure hamlets, many of the programs that were supposed to bind the people to Saigon were never implemented. Promised land reforms were not implemented. Many relocated peasants ended up losing ancestral lands that they had been forced to abandon, for which they received inadequate compensation from GVN officials. Even though the United States provided ample funds for promised strategic hamlet social services, most were never implemented because of official corruption. The funds often ended up in official pockets. U.S. reporters observed that the atmosphere inside some of the strategic hamlets resembled a prison camp. "The strategic hamlets were more akin to concentration camps than communities."[42]

In areas where the strategic hamlets were more successful, Vietcong terrorists often attacked the villages, intimidated the people, and kidnapped or murdered Diemist officials. The fundamental problem with this major initial American-South Vietnamese effort at counterinsurgency, the main reason that the strategic hamlets failed, was that Diem and Nhu viewed them primarily as a means of extending their political control over the rural population, rather than as furnishing an opportunity to provide the peasants with positive incentives for supporting the South Vietnamese state. They were not trying to win the "hearts and minds" of peasants, they were trying to coerce and indoctrinate them. Rural Vietnamese could find little in the strategic hamlet program that worked for their benefit. Even though South Vietnamese officials generated much hype and rigged statistics that vastly exaggerated the number of strategic hamlets constructed and their resident populations, the GVN continued to lose popular support at the rice roots level throughout the latter half of 1962 and into 1963.[43]

The decline in the ARVN's military effectiveness and the failures of the strategic hamlet program reflected the political deterioration occurring in South Vietnam from mid-1962 to mid-1963, despite the large military escalations of the Kennedy administration.[44] The NLF guerrillas continued to grow in numbers and to enhance their military capabilities. More important, Vietcong political cadres continued to gain the support of increasing numbers of villagers in the countryside. The military actions of the guerrillas supported and advanced the political goals of the insurgency. Always, the Vietcong fighters and political cadres worked in tandem, coordinating their activities to achieve their military-political objectives.

There were many reasons why increasing numbers of South Vietnamese peasants chose governance by Hanoi-backed NLF officials over that provided by American-backed GVN officials in 1962 and 1963. In part, the peasants reacted to the political shortcomings of many Diemist officials: their repressiveness, corruption, and ineptitude, as well as their lack of genuine interest in the peasants' needs and problems. The GVN simply never gave many villagers any good reason to support it and often provided very good reasons to reject it. In part, the villagers reacted to the ARVN and provincial troops who failed to provide them with physical security and who sometimes abused the peasants, stole their food, rice crop, tools, and animals. Often, indiscriminate ARVN use of artillery and aerial bombing injured, maimed, and killed civilians, destroying their homes. The abuses and failures of the strategic hamlet program angered and alienated many peasants. In part, the villagers were coerced, intimidated into at least passive support for the rebels. The NLF use of terror, which included kidnappings and selective assassinations of Diemist officials, landlords, collaborators, informers, and spies, often carried out with great brutality, could be very effective. The NLF propagandists also played on the xenophobia of the peasants, invoking bitter memories of French colonialism and linking the Diem government and its American patrons to the hated colonial past.[45]

But skilled and committed NFL organizers also developed many positive incentives with which to win over the villagers whose support was absolutely crucial to their cause. Highly disciplined party cadres often practiced the "three withs": They lived with the villagers, they ate with the villagers, and they worked with them in the rice fields. These cadres were trained to treat the villagers with courtesy, to listen to them, and to respond to their needs. The NLF cadres often brought land reform that gave land confiscated from Diemist landlords to poor, landless peasants. They helped peasants market their crops. They improved public health, sanitation, educational, and maternity services. They restored traditional village autonomy. They organized farmers, women, and young people into village associations under local leadership. They appealed to traditional Vietnamese values of family, communalism, and the strong nationalist feelings of the peasants. In propaganda terms, the VC cadres offered themselves as liberators. They were liberating the people from Diemist taxation, repression, corruption, and subservience to the American imperialists.

In 1962 and 1963, a revolution directed by the Hanoi Politburo was taking root and gathering momentum in many parts of the southern Vietnamese countryside. Villages, although remaining physically within the country nominally governed by Ngo Dinh Diem, had been removed politically from his authority and removed militarily from the control of his army. These villages were now administered by National Liberation Front cadres. The cadres also organized the villagers for self-defense. These "combat villages" provided the basis for the integrated political/military campaign that the NLF waged for over a decade. It was a long and difficult struggle, with many defeats and setbacks, but eventually the revolutionaries prevailed. They forced the Americans to withdraw and overthrew the last South Vietnamese regime at the end of April 1975. The revolution that had been underway in Vietnam since 1945 and had verged on completion in 1954, only to be thwarted by the partition of the country, the subsequent American intervention, and the establishment of the Diem government, had revived as the 1950s ended, and it was clearly gaining momentum in the early 1960s.[46]

Even though the political and strategic situation in southern Vietnam was rapidly deteriorating, Washington saw no reason for reappraising its policy. In Saigon, both Ambassador Nolting and MACV Commander Paul Harkins proclaimed that progress was being made. Secretary of Defense Robert S. McNamara, returning from a trip to Vietnam in November, reported that "every quantitative measure that we have shows that we are winning the war."[47] At a December 12, 1962, press conference, President Kennedy spoke optimistically about the war. Premier Diem pronounced the counterinsurgency program a success and insisted that the GVN military forces were containing the insurgents in the countryside. Diemist officials prepared elaborate color-coded phony maps and fabricated body counts that misled U. S. officials in Saigon and Washington, who were strongly inclined to believe in them.

The wall of U. S. and GVN official optimism was breached by some younger members of the American press corps assigned to cover the Vietnam War. Because these journalists accompanied the ARVN forces into the field and interviewed advisers like Colonel Vann, who talked frankly with them about the outcome of Ap Bac and other engagements, they discovered that Saigon was losing the war in the Delta. The evidence of their own observations was confirmed by the expertise of Colonel Vann. The ablest of these young journalists included David Halberstam of the *New York Times*, Neil Sheehan, a reporter for United Press, Malcolm Brown, and Charles Mohr. Their articles denounced the Diem regime, calling it both inept and corrupt, and they held Diem primarily to blame for the failing GVN effort. The ARVN forces could not fight effectively, despite nine years of American advice, training, and support. They called the strategic hamlet program a sham. They challenged official statistics that inflated both the number of strategic hamlets constructed and the number of Vietcong killed.[48] Halberstam filed stories describing the military and political gains that the rebels were making in the northern Mekong Delta.[49]

To harried U. S. officials in Saigon, and to the Diem family, any stories in the American press that deviated from the official line of optimism and progress toward inevitable victory over the Communists was considered subversion, to be giving aid and comfort to the enemy. Angry and defensive, American officials denied the journalists' accounts and accused them of hurting the American-South Vietnamese war effort. General Harkins, who insisted that Ap Bac had been an ARVN victory, accused Halberstam of being unfair to Diem and of writing lies to make him look bad.[50] President Kennedy, who was trying to hide both the growing American involvement in the civil war in South Vietnam and any bad news emanating from the war zone from the American people, was angered by Halberstam's columns. Kennedy tried to get *New York Times* publisher Arthur O. Sulzberger to recall him. Sulzberger rebuffed the president, and Halberstam stayed in Vietnam.[51] The reporters responded to these attacks and pressures by accusing U. S. officials of deceiving the American people about the growing American involvement in battles that were being lost.[52]

The great irony was that the main reason the young journalists were so critical of the performance of the ARVN forces in the field and of Diem's corrupt and inept government was because these writers believed in the cause and wanted the South Vietnamese and their American advisers to win. They all sought the same goals. The journalists were patriotic supporters of America's Vietnam policies, not adversaries. Browne and Sheehan were Army veterans. Halberstam was an Army reservist. The Marines later awarded Charles Mohr a Bronze Star for bravery during the battle to reclaim Hue in February 1968. Like Colonel Vann, who befriended them, they were Cold Warriors, ideological anti-Communists who believed in the U. S. cause in Vietnam and who wanted the GVN to defeat the NLF insurgents and their North Vietnamese backers. But the journalists could see that the war was being lost. They saw through the lies and phony statistics of Saigon officials and the fatuous American official optimism based on Diemist deceptions. What the reporters were trying to do was warn Washington and the American people that the war was failing. Unless Diem and Nhu were replaced or radically altered their approach to governance and war, the war would surely be lost and the Communists would win.[53]

Behind the declarations of official optimism, internal reports told a more realistic story of growing tension between Diem and U. S. officials, and of a failing war. The relationship between the GVN and Washington deteriorated in 1963. Both Diem and Nhu were alarmed by the rapid buildup of the American advisery apparatus. Diem was infuriated by a policy that gave U. S. military advisers control over the distribution of aid to the provinces; Diem demanded that these advisers be recalled. Diem and his brother also resented the assertiveness of many Americans, which they often interpreted as arrogance and a desire to take over conduct of the war against the rebels. The CIA reports sent to Washington confirmed the political deterioration occurring in the Delta region and elsewhere.[54] Colonel F. P. Serong, an Australian counterinsurgency expert, sent a secret report to General Harkins describing the failure of the ARVN forces to provide security for or to win the support of the rural population.[55] American officials continued to press Diem to make democratic reforms, which he correctly feared would undermine his regime. These U. S. pressures provoked Diem's brother Nhu to public criticism of the pushy Americans. During 1963, the U. S.-GVN partnership became increasingly strained; it appeared more and more to be a marriage of inconvenience. Within the United States, some of Diem's former supporters and some government officials were losing faith in Diem and calling for a coup to rid the country of the failing leader and his family.[56]

Senator Mike Mansfield, an Asian scholar and a longtime supporter of Diem, at President Kennedy's behest, led a fact-finding trip of several senators to Vietnam in December 1962. Upon his return, Mansfield warned Kennedy that the war in Vietnam was becoming an American war that could not be justified by current U. S. security interests in Southeast Asia. He reported that the U. S. escalations had made the Diem regime more unstable and ARVN forces less able to contain the growing NLF insurgency. Further escalation would be a prescription for disaster. Additional efforts necessary for the survival of the GVN would have to come from Saigon, not Washington, and if they were not forthcoming, America should either reduce its commitments to South Vietnam or get out.[57] Kennedy had no intention of walking through the door that Mansfield opened for him. He rejected Mansfield's recommendations and continued the American military buildup during the first half of 1963. Kennedy also continued to support Diem's government, despite the growing rift between U. S. officials and their South Vietnamese clients.[58]

THE DECLINE AND FALL OF NGO DINH DIEM

Suddenly, the Buddhist crisis exploded in Hue, which marked the beginning of the end of the Ngo family oligarchy. The crisis erupted on May 8, 1963, when government troops fired into a crowd protesting a Diemist law forbidding the flying of religious flags celebrating the 2,527th anniversary of Buddha's birth. Nine people were killed. Two days later, thousands of Buddhists took to the streets to protest the shootings and to demand religious freedom. Diem responded by rejecting their demands and jailing the Buddhist leaders. He denied that his soldiers had fired on the demonstrators; he blamed the shootings on the Vietcong. No one was fooled. Diem's rigid and deceptive response provoked additional demonstrations. Major opposition to Diem's floundering regime shifted from the countryside to the cities and came from Buddhist monks, not Communist cadres.

The Buddhist revolt reached a new dimension on June 11, when an elderly Buddhist monk, Thich Quang Duc, immolated himself in front of large crowds at a busy intersection in downtown Saigon. American news photographers and reporters, alerted beforehand by Buddhist leaders, were at the scene, and soon horrific pictures and accounts of the burning monk made the front pages and television news highlights in America and

Figure 4.3   The Buddhist revolt against the Diem family's rule intensified when Thich Quang Duc, an elderly monk, immolated himself by fire on a busy downtown Saigon street on June 11, 1963. Dramatic photographs of the gruesome event made the front pages and television news highlights around the world. *Source:* AP/Wide World Photos

around the world.[59] Americans, appalled by the images of self-immolation, gained insight into the depth and passion of the Buddhist opposition to Diemist rule. World opinion, shocked by the dramatic photograph, criticized Americans for supporting a government that persecuted religious worshippers. Quang Duc's flaming sacrifice had made the political crisis in Vietnam in the summer of 1963 a big story in the American news media. Many of the news stories emanating from Saigon sharply criticized Diem's repressive actions. U. S. officials brought intense pressure on Diem to rescind the ban and conciliate the Buddhists. But Diem was unresponsive to their pleas. His brother Ngo Dinh Nhu continued to denounce and red-bait the Buddhists. Nhu and his wife also advised Diem to ignore the American demands and suppress the Buddhist revolt.[60]

The Buddhist rebellion, which was more a political than a religious uprising, had long been in the making. Its roots lay in the mass emigration from the North following the Geneva agreements of July 1954, when nearly a million Catholics streamed south to form a popular base of support for Diem's emerging government. Under Diem's family rule, Catholics received favored treatment and enjoyed special privileges and opportunities. Priests enjoyed political influence; most district and province chiefs were Catholics. South Vietnam's 1.6 million Catholics constituted a favored minority in a country in which about 11 of its 14 million people were Buddhists.[61]

The Buddhist uprising in Hue reflected not only the passions of the moment, but the accumulated resentments deriving from years of discrimination and social repression. The rebellion also reflected a growing militancy on the part of younger, more political monks, who were determined to challenge Diemist proscriptions and to seek a greater role in public life. Thousands of high school and college students, traditionally apolitical, took to the streets in Saigon and Hue to support the Buddhists. Many ARVN soldiers, themselves Buddhists, sympathized with the protesters. American efforts to reconcile the two warring factions failed.

The Buddhists failed to present a coherent list of demands and there were divisions within their ranks, but generally they called for Diem's removal, an end to American intrusions in Vietnamese affairs, and a neutral South Vietnam governed by a coalition of factions looking toward peaceful reunification with the North. Diem refused all but token concessions.[62] Madame Nhu inflamed the crisis with her shrill denunciations of the Buddhists and ghastly humor when she called Quang Duc's flaming sacrifice "a barbe-cue"[63] and offered to furnish the gasoline and matches for more immolations. By mid-summer, the war against the Vietcong had virtually halted, and South Vietnamese society appeared on the verge of disintegrating. The demonstrations and fiery sacrifices contin-ued. A war inside of a war beckoned. Washington officials were deeply troubled and divided over what to do about this grave crisis.

On the night of August 21, Diem and Nhu perpetrated a series of wanton acts that sealed their fate in American eyes. Nhu's American-trained praetorian guards, assisted by local police forces, raided pagodas in several cities. Temples were dese-crated, 1,420 monks were arrested, and dozens more were killed or injured in these brutal assaults of religious sanctuaries.[64] President Kennedy was stunned and outraged at these latest actions of deranged rulers who appeared bent on committing political suicide. Alarmed ARVN generals began to plot the overthrow of the Ngos before chaos engulfed everyone and the Vietcong won their revolution by default.

Several coup plots were percolating during that tumultuous summer of 1963 in Saigon. Some of them had been underway prior to the pagoda raids. The earliest dated from the end of June and had been started by Tran Kim Tuyen, Diem's national intel-ligence chief. Tuyen was helped by Colonel Do Mau, director of Military Security Services. Other junior officers joined the plot as well, and American agents encour-aged the coup plotters. Nhu's assaults on the pagodas were driving the army officers, many of whom were Buddhists, and the Americans, together.[65]

Nhu, learning of the existence of the plots and sensing the danger to the regime posed by the developing alliance between American officials and dissident army offi-cers, embarked on a bizarre scheme to preserve his family's power. He sought a rap-prochement with the NLF and Hanoi. He tried to reach the NLF leaders through intermediaries and succeeded in making contact with Hanoi. It is impossible to tell from the available evidence whether Nhu was serious about a rapprochement with the Communists; he may have only been trying to outmaneuver the Americans to get them off his brother's back. But he may have been trying to make serious moves toward an accommodation with the enemy and to oust the Americans whom he detested. U. S. officials in Saigon operated on the assumption that Nhu's gestures toward Hanoi were sincere and serious. His weird actions only increased the growing resolve of some

American officials to get rid of him and his outspoken wife, and Diem too, if the president insisted on retaining close ties to his brother and sister-in-law.[66]

The chief planner of the coup who eventually toppled Diem was Major General Tran Van Don, the commander of the ARVN. He worked closely with Lieutenant General Duong Van "Big" Minh, who would head the new government if the coup succeeded. Don made contact with American officials through an old friend, CIA agent Lucien Conein, who became the principal liaison between the generals and American officials as the coup plot developed.

On August 24, a group of anti-Diem officials within the State Department sent a cable to the newly appointed American ambassador to Saigon, Henry Cabot Lodge. Lodge was instructed to give Diem a chance to get rid of Nhu, but, if Diem refused, the message indicated that Diem himself might have to go. Lodge also was instructed to inform the dissident generals that the United States was prepared to abandon Diem if he continued to prove uncooperative and that Washington would support a replacement government. President Kennedy and Secretary of State Rusk approved sending the cable to Lodge.[67]

Ambassador Lodge moved quickly to support the coup plotters. After meeting with the South Vietnamese president several times, Lodge sized up Diem as being rigid and unreformable; he also perceived that Diem would never separate himself from his brother and sister-in-law. In Lodge's view, a coup that rid South Vietnam of the Ngo family rule remained the best hope for winning the war against the Vietcong. Working through Conein, Lodge assured the generals planning Diem's overthrow that they would have U. S. support if the coup d'etat succeeded. Lodge also sent President Kennedy a secret cable on August 28 informing him that the United States "was launched on a course from which there is no respectable turning back; the overthrow of the Diem government."[68] But the generals, unable to gain the support of key officers commanding troops in the vicinity of Saigon, and fearful of Nhu's machinations, aborted the coup in late August, placing it on indefinite hold.

About the time that the coup plotters were temporarily backing off, Kennedy received an unsolicited offer from French President Charles De Gaulle to mediate the crisis in Vietnam. De Gaulle proposed a comprehensive solution that included America's withdrawing its troops, establishing a neutral government for South Vietnam, and having North and South Vietnam resume relations. It was a solution based on the Geneva Accords of 1954. Hanoi and Saigon both expressed an interest in De Gaulle's proposal; Kennedy abruptly rejected the French offer. De Gaulle's proposal represented an ironic reversal; he was suggesting that it was time for America to end the war in Vietnam that it had snatched from the French back in 1954 after failing to get the French to continue the fight.[69] De Gaulle, the seasoned statesmen, tried to warn Kennedy of the pitfalls of imperialism. Kennedy was not interested in being warned, least of all by the imperious Charles De Gaulle. The French record of fighting bitterly to cling to an empire in Southeast Asia and the Maghrib, especially Algeria, was not instructive. In any case, Kennedy was committed to continuing the

American effort to establish a non-Communist state in the southern half of Vietnam, with or without Ngo Dinh Diem and his family rule.

Meanwhile, South Vietnam continued to disintegrate. Diem would not conciliate the Buddhists and their supporters. The Nhus remained in power. The Kennedy administration remained deeply divided over how to handle the deepening crisis that threatened to lose the war and collapse South Vietnam. As was his wont when faced with tough policy decisions, President Kennedy dispatched another fact-finding mission to South Vietnam, this one headed by Marine General Victor Krulak, a counterinsurgency expert working for the Joint Chiefs of Staff, and Joseph Mendenhall, a State Department specialist in Far Eastern Affairs.

Their reports only added to Kennedy's confusion: General Krulak's exuded optimism. He reported that the coup had failed, that the ARVN forces were winning the war in the countryside, and that the United States should continue its support of Diem. By contrast, Mendenhall's report was starkly pessimistic. He reported that South Vietnam was verging on a breakdown, that a religious war between Catholics and Buddhists threatened, and that the war against the Vietcong could not be won by the Diem government. In Mendenhall's view, only the quick removal of Nhu and maybe the replacement of Diem could possibly salvage a nearly hopeless situation. Kennedy, obviously exasperated, asked them, "You two did visit the same country, didn't you?"[70]

Kennedy, frustrated by the inability of American officials to manage the chaotic political life of South Vietnam, nevertheless was not prepared to consider seeking a negotiated settlement or extricating the United States from what increasingly appeared to be a no-win situation. He also did not want to bomb North Vietnam, send American combat forces, or take over the political life of the country. He and his advisers were so preoccupied with the day-to-day crisis management in South Vietnam that they had lost the capacity to think in terms of long-range U. S. interests in Southeast Asia or to confront fundamental issues. Kennedy was not prepared to consider any plan of action that might involve the abandonment of a long-standing American commitment in southern Vietnam or Americanizing the war. "The administration drifted along, divided against itself, with no clear idea where it was going."[71]

Kennedy, following weeks of indecision, in early October sent still another fact-finding team, which was headed by Robert McNamara and General Maxwell Taylor, to appraise the general political and military situation in South Vietnam. Their report "badly misjudged the actual conditions in South Vietnam."[72] They reported that the war effort had made great progress since 1962. It was not true that ARVN was winning the war; the South Vietnamese army was steadily losing territory and villages to the Vietcong at the time McNamara and Taylor made their visit. The NLF controlled much more territory and population in the fall of 1963 in the Mekong Delta region than it had eighteen months earlier. McNamara and Taylor reported that prospects for a coup against Diem were slim, even though the coup planners were again busily at work with American support on the plot that would topple Diem in a few weeks. The report also exaggerated the effectiveness of applying selective pressures to Diem to get him to stop persecuting the Buddhists and to rebuild his base of support among the urban elites. Ambassador Lodge understood that Diem was unreformable and would never separate himself from Nhu, but McNamara and Taylor ignored Lodge's views in their report to the president.[73]

Despite its misperceptions and faulty judgments, Kennedy embraced the recommendations of the McNamara-Taylor report, adopting a policy of applying selective pressures against Diem. Kennedy cut off the funds to support some Special Forces under Nhu's control. He also recalled the CIA station chief in Saigon, John Richardson, who was known to be friendly with Ngo Dinh Nhu. These measures, intended as such by Kennedy, were taken as signals by General Don and the other coup planners to accelerate their plotting and seek greater support from the Americans. Lodge, through Conein, assured the conspirators that the United States would do nothing to hinder the coup and would extend military and economic support to any new regime that broadened its base of popular support, effectively prosecuted the war, and cooperated with U. S. officials.[74]

The Kennedy administration still remained hopelessly divided over whether to support Diem or the coup planners. Vice President Johnson, McNamara, and General Harkins continued to support Diem. State Department officials believed that Nhu and Diem had to go and supported the coup plotters. "Kennedy himself vacillated, adhering to the policy of not overtly supporting a coup, but not discouraging one either."[75] He relied on Lodge, who was on the scene and who backed the coup plot. For several weeks, the coupsters plotted while U. S. officials fretted indecisively. As the coup d'etat became imminent, Kennedy's chief concerns appear to have been that it might fail or that the United States would be implicated. Lodge reassured the nervous president that the coup would succeed and that any new government would be an improvement over Diem and Nhu.[76]

As October 1963 came to an end, Saigon seethed with rumors, plots, and counterplots. General Don and his co-conspirators had planned their coup scrupulously. They had secured the support of key generals commanding troops in the vicinity of Saigon. They neutralized the forces of generals remaining loyal to the Ngos and established a precise timetable of operations. Nhu, knowing a coup attempt was nigh, but not knowing precisely which generals and troop units were involved, schemed furiously to flush out the conspirators, even going so far as to concoct an elaborate fake coup that involved one of the generals who, unbeknownst to Nhu, was part of the real coup.

The coup d'etat that destroyed the Ngo family oligarchy began on November 1 at 1:30 P.M. Saigon time. The coup leaders moved their forces into place, seizing control of key military and communication facilities. Once certain that a coup against them was underway, Diem and Nhu, from a command post inside the presidential palace, tried frantically to contact ARVN units that they thought still remained loyal to them. They quickly discovered that all had either joined the coup, had been jailed or killed, or could not get their forces to Saigon. Generals Don, Minh, and the others had planned the coup well. The Ngo brothers refused the generals' repeated demands

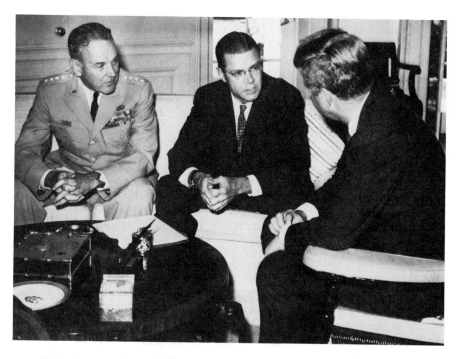

Figure 4.4   As the political crisis in South Vietnam escalated during the fall of 1963, President Kennedy conferred with his two leading advisers, special military representative General Maxwell Taylor and Secretary of Defense Robert McNamara, both of whom had just returned from a fact-finding trip to Saigon. *Source:* National Archives

to surrender. They tried unsuccessfully to lure the coup leaders to the palace for consultations, a stalling device that had worked to thwart the November 1960 coup attempt.

At 4:30 P. M., as the coup went forward, Ngo Dinh Diem phoned Ambassador Lodge, who was staying at the American embassy. The following remarkable conversation ensued:

Diem.   Some units have made a rebellion and I want to know what is the attitude of the U. S.?

Lodge.   I do not feel well enough informed to be able to tell you. I have heard the shooting, but am not acquainted with all the facts. Also, it is 4:30 A. M. in Washington and the U. S. Government cannot possibly have a view.

Diem.   But you must have some general ideas. After all, I am Chief of State. I have tried to do my duty. I want to do now what duty and good sense require. I believe in duty above all.

Lodge.   You have certainly done your duty. As I told you only this morning, I admire your courage and your great contribution to your country. No one can take away from you the credit for all you have done. Now I am worried about your physical safety. I have a report that those in charge of the current activity offer you and your brother safe conduct out of the country if you resign. Had you heard this?

Diem.   No. (pause) You have my phone number.

Lodge.   Yes. If I can do anything for your physical safety, please call me.

Diem.   I am trying to re-establish order. (hangs up)[77]

Lodge, the American point man in Saigon for the coup, had responded disingenuously to Diem's call for help. Diem, who was not obtuse, no doubt inferred the American position from Lodge's offer of asylum: American officials were supporting the coup and would do nothing to prevent it from succeeding. The United States was selling out an ally it had installed in power back in 1954 and 1955, one it had lavishly supported for nearly a decade.

At about 7:00 P. M., Diem and his brother exited the palace through a secret underground passageway and fled to the home of a friend, a wealthy Chinese merchant residing in the Cholon district. Hours later, ARVN troops overwhelmed the guards and occupied the presidential palace. The next morning, Diem and Nhu, after talking with various supporters, phoned General Don's headquarters. They offered to surrender in exchange for pledges of safe conduct. Don accepted their offer, although he told them their surrender would have to be unconditional.

General Minh dispatched two jeeps and an armored personnel carrier to fetch the deposed leaders. He also dispatched his personal bodyguard Captain Nhung, with secret instructions to assassinate Diem and Nhu. They were taken prisoner in front of a small chapel near the house of their friend and placed in the back of the personnel carrier. Their hands were tied behind their backs. Captain Nhung joined the bound brothers in the back of the vehicle. When the armored car returned to coup headquarters, Diem and Nhu were no longer among the living. They had both been shot in the back of the head. Nhu had also been stabbed several times. As Nhung hopped out of the armored car, he saluted General Minh and whispered, "Mission accomplie."

The victorious rebels went after the rest of the Ngo family leaders. Archbishop Ngo Dinh Thuc fled to the Vatican. Ngo Dinh Can was arrested in Hue and executed shortly thereafter by a firing squad. Madame Nhu survived the bloodbath only because she was traveling in the United States when the coup occurred. The coup leaders decided to eliminate the Ngo family because they feared Diem and Nhu still had some populate support and might find a way to return to power if they remained alive. Diem and Nhu were buried in unmarked graves somewhere in Saigon.[78]

In Saigon, news of the successful coup d'etat brought a joyous response. People poured into the streets to celebrate the overthrow of a despised and feared tyrant whose power base, at the time of his downfall, had shrunk to a handful of family members, a few government bureaucrats, some police and military retainers, and the Catholic minority. In Saigon, citizens cheered the ARVN soldiers who had taken part in the coup and, assuming that U. S. officials had ordered the coup, praised all Americans they encountered on the streets.

American official spokesmen in Saigon and Washington claimed to have known nothing about the coup and insisted that they had had no part in it. They said it was an internal political matter involving only quarreling factions of Vietnamese politicians. In fact, the Americans were deeply implicated in the coup. They were aware of it from its inception, and they had encouraged it. Lucien Conein met often with the plotters and functioned as a conduit among the generals, Lodge, and Washington. Conein was with General Don the day the coup was implemented and Diem was overthrown.[79] Without American financial support, promises of noninterference, and most of all, pledges to continue to provide economic and military aid to any replacement government that would emerge from a successful coup, the coup would not have occurred. President Kennedy and the other Americans had not ordered Diem's or Nhu's deaths. Kennedy was shocked and deeply troubled at the news of their murders, perhaps feeling responsible for them. But no one had taken any steps to ensure their survival other than making contingency plans for granting them asylum prior to removing them from the country. No one told Don and Minh that the Americans wanted Diem and Nhu kept alive or that they were not supposed to be killed.

The response in Hanoi to the coup was mixed; the overthrow of Diem both resolved some problems and created new ones for the Communist leadership. The coup had rid South Vietnam of an uncompromising anti-Communist zealot who had also staunchly opposed the French. Diem had been a leader with some claim to rival Ho Chi Minh as a symbol of Vietnamese nationalist aspirations. The successful coup also confirmed Hanoi's claims that the Diem regime was a corrupt, unpopular regime that had lost all right to rule. On the other hand, the Communists had to be concerned because the new government, a military junta led by General Minh, had a potential for achieving a broader base of support. Minh was a southerner and a Buddhist who had been one of the leaders of a coup that had overthrown a tyrant.[80] It would be more difficult to sustain an insurgency that would require greater assistance from the North. Ominously, the new government had the strong backing of the Americans, and General Minh pledged to prosecute vigorously the war against the NLF. Hanoi anticipated an enlarged American presence in the South and a consequent escalation of the conflict. The Communist leadership worried, lest northern economic development be endangered by the costs of a larger war in the South and perhaps U. S. air attacks north of the 17th parallel.[81]

An expanded conflict also posed problems for Hanoi in its relations with the major Communist powers, the Soviet Union, and China. The Soviets had backed off their support of anticolonial "wars of national liberation" and were preaching the doctrine of "peaceful coexistence" with the United States. China, bidding to take over leadership of the Third World, championed the cause of national liberation in the early

1960s. Hanoi's increased involvement in the southern insurgency and possible conflict with the United States appeared to align the Vietnamese Communists with China and against the Soviet Union.[82]

THE COUP AND THE QUAGMIRE

American support for the coup that had made it possible weakened rather than strengthened the security of South Vietnam. It ushered in a protracted period of political instability in South Vietnam that hindered counterinsurgency efforts and was a major cause of large-scale American military intervention in 1965. None of a succession of South Vietnamese governments was as effective as Diem's had been, for all of its flaws, either in governing southern Vietnam or fighting the insurgents. American officials who had supported the coup were so enmeshed in the process that they had given little thought to what kind of leaders might come to power after Diem's downfall. They were so convinced that Diem and Nhu had to be removed from power that they just assumed that whoever replaced them would be an improvement.

Having decided to get rid of Diem and to keep the coup plot from him, American officials did not inform Diem that they were no longer willing to tolerate his rejection of their advice and his repressive methods of governance after Americans had been tolerating them for nearly a decade. Ambassador Nolting said of the coup, "I don't think it was fair, just, or honorable to our ally of nine years standing to do this behind his back."[83] General Harkins condemned U. S. support of the coup while not informing Diem.[84] Madame Nhu, traveling in the United States at the time, attributed American support of the coup that killed her husband and brother-in-law to American "arrogance" and "contempt for the Vietnamese people."[85] Lodge's friendly meeting with Diem on the morning of the coup and his evasive answers to Diem's urgent questions while the coup was underway epitomized the hypocrisy of some American officials in Vietnam toward a patriot who had fought for his country's independence for over twenty years.

American complicity in the coup strengthened the American commitment to South Vietnam and "tied the United States to all succeeding regimes."[86] President Johnson, who had supported Diem and argued against the coup, believed that Kennedy's involvement in the coup was the worst error made by the United States during its long involvement in Vietnam. The coup made the United States directly responsible for the fate of successive South Vietnamese governments. Morally, it locked America deeper into the South Vietnamese quagmire. It also set into motion a train of events that "eventually forced President Johnson in 1965 to choose between accepting defeat or introducing American combat forces"[87]

Three weeks after the coup, Kennedy's assassination overshadowed the murders in Saigon. At the time of his death, Kennedy's Vietnam policy was in disarray and his administration was divided. Kennedy loyalists and some scholars have argued that had Kennedy lived, he was planning to extricate the United States from South Vietnam sometime in 1965 and that there would have been no American war in that country.[88] But in the final months of his presidency, Kennedy repeatedly and publically reaffirmed the American commitment in Vietnam. In a televised interview with Walter Cronkite, broadcast on September 2, 1963, Kennedy told the American people:

> Those people who say that we ought to withdraw from Vietnam are wholly wrong, because if we withdraw from Vietnam, the Communists would control Vietnam. Pretty soon Thailand, Cambodia, Laos, Malaya would go and all of Southeast Asia would be under the control of the Communists and under the domination of the Chinese.[89]

Three days later, in another television interview, Kennedy told David Brinkley that the United States would remain in Vietnam to check Chinese expansionism in Southeast Asia. On the day he died, in a noontime speech Kennedy would have delivered at the Trade Mart to a group of Dallas businessmen, he planned to once again affirm the American commitment in Vietnam. In all of his public statements, Kennedy consistently affirmed a strong commitment to the U. S. effort in Vietnam to the end. He never once suggested to any of his senior civilian or military advisers that he might be thinking about disengaging from Vietnam, a disengagement that would have resulted in a NLF takeover of South Vietnam within six months to a year. Lyndon Johnson never thought that Kennedy had any intentions of pulling out of Vietnam; Johnson always believed that what he was doing in Vietnam was what Kennedy would have done, had he lived.[90]

Had Kennedy lived, he probably would have continued U. S. incremental escalations in South Vietnam to prevent disaster until he was reelected in November 1964. In the summer of 1965, having to face the same crisis that Johnson had to confront and the same stark choices—accept a Communist victory in Vietnam or undertake a major military escalation that amounted to an American takeover of the war to try to defeat the revolutionaries—Kennedy and his senior advisers, most of whom helped forge Johnson's Vietnam policy, would probably have done what Johnson did. Had he lived, President Kennedy probably could not have avoided an American war in Vietnam. It is doubtful that Kennedy was prepared to pull out and present the NLF and Hanoi with an easy victory in Vietnam that would have also given the Chinese and the Soviets a major Cold War victory. At home, the political Right would have exploded in denunciations of a cop-out in Southeast Asia and blamed the Democrats for the "loss of Indochina" to the Communists. A popular backlash would probably have prevented Robert Kennedy from seeking the presidency in 1968, if that was the long-term Kennedy master plan. To believe otherwise is to imbibe a massive dose of Camelot idealism not sustained by the historical record.

Even though Kennedy probably would have taken the United States to war in the summer of 1965 to try to save South Vietnam from a Communist takeover, as Lyndon Johnson did, it is unlikely that he would have escalated the war as rapidly as Johnson or committed so many American troops to Vietnam. Kennedy was too cautious, too skeptical of military power. He probably would have responded to international calls for negotiations much sooner than Johnson and he probably would have been more responsive to Congressional and public opinion than Johnson. Under Kennedy, there probably would have been a Vietnam War, but perhaps it would not have lasted as long or become as severe an ordeal for the American (and the Vietnamese) people as it did under his successor.

What Kennedy might have done can never be known. What can be known is the Vietnam policy of his abbreviated presidency, policies that would eventually have disastrous consequences for the United States and its Vietnamese clients. Kennedy was a conventional Cold Warrior. He embraced a strong anti-Communist ideology; he was committed to containment, and he believed in the domino theory.[91] He and his senior advisers believed unquestioningly that retaining a non-Communist South Vietnam was vital to the strategic security of the United States and its allies in Southeast Asia. Kennedy and his advisers acted on the arrogant presumption that Washington knew best what should be done in Vietnam. In the name of the ongoing struggle with the Vietcong, Americans claimed the right to intervene as they chose. They supported the coup that overthrew the Diem government primarily because it refused to follow Washington's advice—ease up on the Buddhists, reform the government, and more vigorously prosecute the war against the Vietcong.[92] The most important consequence of the Kennedy administration's words and deeds was to increase sharply the American stake in Vietnam from 1961 to 1963.

Vietnam represented President Kennedy's "great failure in foreign policy."[93] "Vietnam stands as the most tragic legacy of the global activism of the Kennedy era."[94] During his abbreviated presidency, Kennedy gave Vietnam only sporadic attention. Vietnam was mostly a marginal issue during his presidency. Vietnam was rarely near the top of his list of foreign policy crises to be managed. The ongoing Cold War with the Soviets, especially showdowns in Berlin and Cuba, preoccupied the young leader. Vietnam policy was often left to advisers, principally McNamara, Taylor, Walt Rostow, and McGeorge Bundy. Kennedy does not appear to have known very much about the country or to have shown much interest in Vietnam for most of his presidency. He never asked hard questions or made tough decisions. Only his brother Robert could do that. Robert Kennedy once asked at a National Security Council meeting, What if no South Vietnamese government could resist a Communist takeover? If it could not, he stated that America should extricate itself from the region.[95] The president never confronted that potentiality; he reacted to Southeast Asian crises and improvised policy on an *ad hoc* basis.[96]

The president preferred to take cautious middle courses. His middle courses of action managed to stave off disaster and increase mightily the U. S. commitment to Vietnam. During Kennedy's presidency, the levels of economic and military aid to the GVN rose significantly. At the time of the coup, South Vietnam was costing the United States $1.5 million per day, and there were 16,500 military advisers in the country, including counterinsurgency forces. Some of these advisory forces engaged sporadically in combat. Over 100 U. S. military advisers were killed in Vietnam during Kennedy's presidency.

When Kennedy took office, there had been about 650 U. S. military personnel in South Vietnam; on the day of his death, about 16,700.[97] When Kennedy took office, the NLF probably controlled half of the villages within South Vietnam; on the day of his death, they controlled many more, especially in the strategic Mekong Delta region. Kennedy "bequeathed to his successor a problem eminently more dangerous than the one that he had inherited from Eisenhower."[98] Johnson soon discovered the quagmire in which Eisenhower and Kennedy had enmeshed America. When Johnson had to choose between accepting defeat or going to war, he chose war by using the flexible response military forces handed down by Kennedy.

Kennedy continued the Eisenhower policies in Vietnam, but he significantly upped the ante and instigated a small-scale American limited war. The Indochina interventions of the Eisenhower and Kennedy administrations revealed an American tendency to think about Vietnam in terms of Cold War abstractions rather than to understand concrete Vietnamese social, political, and strategic realities. American officials gave primacy to global Cold War factors and persistently underplayed particular, local, peculiarly Vietnamese historical forces. Americans tried to understand events in Vietnam using paradigms generated by their exogenous Cold War ideological predilections, not by indigenous Vietnamese realities. U. S. Cold Warriors failed to understand that it was not possible to create a nation out of part of a nation by an act of will if that part of a nation lacked a historical basis for existence. Washington persistently failed to understand that Communism had aligned itself with Vietnamese nationalism, that the national revolution that American officials tried for thirty years to thwart had deep, organic, essentially Vietnamese roots. Revolution in Vietnam was not a Chinese or Soviet Cold War tactic.

Americans also failed to understand the extent to which they were perceived as outsiders meddling in the internal affairs of the Vietnamese people and the consequent liabilities and limits imposed on their actions by that perception. Two thousand years of history had taught the Vietnamese to be wary of, distrust, and fear foreign imperial powers. How could they be expected to perceive Americans differently? U. S. officials persisted in viewing the Vietnamese national revolution as foreign aggression, when in fact the Vietcong insurgency originated as an indigenous southern reaction to misgovernment and repression by the American-backed Ngo Dinh Diem family regime. The Americans were the outsiders in South Vietnam, not the Vietcong. That insurgency and the threat to its survival posed by the Diem government in turn provoked an initially reluctant response from the Communist leaders in Hanoi, who felt compelled to assume command of the rebellion that was occurring in the southern part of their country and to use it as a vehicle to bring about national reunification. In their eyes, Vietnam would have been unified under their control years earlier had it not been for the Americans who unilaterally intervened in Vietnamese affairs, displaced the French, and imposed the

Diem government on the southern part of their country, all in violation of the Geneva Accords.

The fundamental American failing in Vietnam under Truman, Eisenhower, and Kennedy, a failure that would persist throughout the Johnson and Nixon administrations, was a failure of understanding. Americans failed to understand Vietnamese history and culture. The Americans were prisoners of their Cold War ideologies that superimposed a false set of abstractions on Indochina realities. Consequently, the Americans could not only never defeat the Vietnamese national revolution, they could never understand why they were losing, or why a succession of U. S.-backed South Vietnamese governments could never establish their legitimacy, could never win the hearts and minds of the rural population, and could never govern or fight effectively. American officials understood that their mission was to stem the tide of expansionist Communism in Indochina; to many Vietnamese and to much of the rest of the world, Americans appeared to be trying to stop decolonization and preserve Western influence in Southeast Asia.

All of the rage, agony, guilt, death, and destruction associated with the U. S.-Indochina enterprise, the American ordeal in Vietnam itself, derived from this reality: Americans tried to do the impossible in southern Vietnam; they tried to determine the political destiny of its people and change the course of its history. Just as a society of European transplants had created their own nation in the New World, so the Americans would replicate that achievement in the unpromising political geography of southern Vietnam. Such a task was beyond their ken and beyond their strength.

NOTES

1. Excerpts from Kennedy's inaugural address are taken from a copy of the speech printed in Sorensen, Theodore C., *Kennedy* (New York: Harper & Row, 1965), 275–78. Kennedy misread Krushchev's remarks about Soviet support of anti-colonial wars of national liberation. The Russian leader was not flinging down his gauntlet before Kennedy; he was responding to challenges from Mao and trying to assert Soviet leadership in the Third World.

2. Herring, *America's Longest War*, 74–75.

3. Kahin, *Intervention*, 126.

4. *Ibid.*, 127.

5. Porter (ed.), *Vietnam Documents*, vol. 2, Document 38, 90–92, is a memo of the July 19 meeting between Eisenhower and Kennedy; Clifford, Clark, "A Vietnam Reappraisal," *Foreign Affairs*, vol. 47 (July 1969), 604–5; Parmet, Herbert, *JFK: The Presidency of John F. Kennedy* (New York: Penguin, 1983), 81.

6. Schlesinger, Arthur Meier Jr., *A Thousand Days: John F. Kennedy in the White House* (Greenich, Conn.: Fawcett, 1965), 309–11.

7. Cooper, Chester, *The Lost Crusade: America in Vietnam* (New York: Dodd, Mead, 1970), 191–2. Young, *Vietnam Wars*, 78.

8. Protocol to the Declaration of the Neutrality of Laos, July 23, 1962, in Porter (ed.) *Vietnam Documents,* vol. 2, Document 77, 156–60. The nations attending the Geneva Conference signing the protocol included Burma, Cambodia, Canada, the People's Republic of China, the Democratic Republic of Vietnam (North Vietnam), France, India, the Kingdom of Laos, Poland, the Republic of Vietnam (South Vietnam), Thailand, the Soviet Union, Great Britain, and the United States. The protocol reads that all foreign troops and paramilitary forces were to be removed within thirty days; 750 U. S. MAAG forces departed as did a few Russians who were mostly pilots. The 10,000 plus PAVN troops remained in Laos in violation of the protocol.

9. O'Ballance, Edgar, *The Wars in Vietnam: 1954–1980* (New York: Hippocrene, 1981), 28–31.

10. Herring, *America's Longest War*, 78.

11. Doyle and others, *Passing the Torch*, 181. Kennedy, who had a special interest in counterinsurgency, believing it to be the most effective instrument available for checking Third World guerrilla forces, moved to beef up U. S. Special Forces training programs that had begun under the Eisenhower administration in the late 1950s. At the president's direction, special warfare training centers began preparing U. S. soldiers to challenge guerrillas in the jungles and mountains of Laos and Vietnam.

12. Sheehan, Neil, Smith, Hedrick, Kenworthy, E. W., and Butterfield, Fox, *The Pentagon Papers: The Secret History of the Vietnam War* (New York: Bantam, 1971), "National Security Action Memorandum 52," 126–7.

13. Doyle et al., *Passing the Torch*, 191–3; O'Ballance, *Vietnam Wars*, 42–43.

14. Cablegram from General Taylor to Kennedy, Nov. 1, 1961, printed in Porter 4 (ed.), *Vietnam Documents*, vol. 2, Document 70, 140–2. Taylor recommended sending an 8,000-man military force to repair the extensive damage caused by recent floods, forces that could also perform combat missions. Kennedy rejected his suggestion. See also Sheehan and others, *The Pentagon Papers*, Documents 26, 27, 28, and 29, 141–50.

15. Karnow, *Vietnam*, 248.

16. Kahin, *Intervention*, 134.

17. Herring, *America's Longest War*, 84; Berman, Larry, *Planning a Tragedy: The Americanization of the War in Vietnam* (New York, W. W. Norton, 1982), 16–23; Pelz, Stephen, "John F. Kennedy's 1961 Vietnam War Decisions," *Journal of Strategic Studies*, vol. 4, (December 1981), 356–85; Department of State, *A Threat to Peace* (Washington, D. C.: U. S. Government Printing Office, 1961), the State Department White Paper documenting Hanoi's violations of the Geneva Accords exaggerates the amount of Hanoi's support for the NLF and contradicts CIA intelligence findings. The Rusk-McNamara memo, dated November 11, 1961, appears in Sheehan and others, *The Pentagon Papers*, 150–3.

18. Quoted in Herring, *America's Longest War*, 84.

19. Blaufarb, Douglas, *The Counterinsurgency Era* (New York: The Free Press, 1977), 85–88; Gravel, ed., *Pentagon Papers*, Vol. II, p. 123. John Kenneth Galbraith told President Kennedy that Diem would never reform his government because he could not. It was politically naive to expect him to. If he agreed to reforms it would lessen his power and he would be thrown out of office.

20. Gelb, Leslie H., with Betts, Richard K., *The Irony of Vietnam: The System Worked* (Washington, D. C.: The Brookings Institution, 1979), 75–79; Pelz, Stephen, "John F. Kennedy's 1961 Vietnam War Decisions," 356–85.

21. Doyle et al., *Passing the Torch*, 197.

22. Tuchman, *March of Folly*, 299. The Eisenhower administration observed the 1954 Geneva Accords limits on foreign military personnel in South Vietnam. There were about 650 American advisers in South Vietnam in January 1961. By the end of the year, there were over 3,000 advisers and support personnel, 9,000 by the end of 1962. At the time of Kennedy's death, there were about 16,700. America's limited war in Vietnam began in early 1962.

23. O'Ballance, *The Vietnam Wars*, 43–44; Miroff, Bruce, *Pragmatic Illusions: The Presidential Politics of John F. Kennedy* (New York: David McKay, 1976); Maitland, Terrence; Weiss, Stephen; and the editors, *Raising the Stakes* (Boston: Boston Publishing Co., 1982), 19–21.

24. Blaufarb, *Counterinsurgency Era*, 113–15.

25. Maitland et al., *Raising the Stakes*, 23.

26. *Ibid.*

27. Kahin, *Intervention*, 140–1; Herring, *America's Longest War*, 85–86; and Duiker, *The Communist Road*, 201–3; Miroff, *Pragmatic Illusions*, 158–60.

28. Maitland et al., *Raising the Stakes*, 14–15, 18–19.

29. O'Ballance, *The Vietnam Wars*, 43; Hess, *Vietnam*, 74.

30. Sheehan, Neil, "Annals of War: An American Soldier in Vietnam, Part 2, A Set-Piece Battle," *New Yorker*, vol. 64, No.19 (July 1988), 35–36; Halberstam, David, *The Making of a Quagmire: America and Vietnam during the Kennedy Era*, rev. ed. (New York: Knopf, 1988), 56–66; Hess, *Vietnam*, 74.

31. The Vietnamese word for hamlet is "ap." The main action during the Battle of Ap Bac took place in the tree line near the village of Bac.

32. Halberstam, *Quagmire*, 72–73.

33. John Paul Vann arrived in South Vietnam in March 1962, soon becoming the senior adviser to the ARVN 7th Division. He quickly established himself as one of the ablest officers in the U. S. Army. He returned to the states after his year's tour as adviser and retired from the Army. Deeply committed to the American cause in Vietnam, Vann returned in 1965 as a civilian official. Until his death in June 1972, Vann was the most effective American adviser involved in counterinsurgency and pacification activities.

34. For accounts of the Battle of Ap Bac, see Sheehan, Neil, *A Bright Shining Lie: John Paul Vann and America in Vietnam* (New York: Random House, 1988), 203–65; Palmer, Dave Richard, *Summons of the Trumpet* (New York: Ballantine, 1978), 37–51; and Halberstam, *Quagmire*, 67–81.

35. Sheehan, "Annals of War, Part 2," 58–60.

36. *Ibid.*, 60–63; Halberstam, *Quagmire*, 76–81.

37. O'Ballance, *The Vietnam Wars*, 43–47; Duiker, *The Communist Road*, 214–15.

38. Halberstam, *Quagmire*, 79.

39. Colonel Wilson is quoted in Clarke, Jeffrey J., *Advice and Support: The Final Years, 1965–1973* (Washington, D. C.: U. S. Government Printing Office, 1988), 47.

40. Quote is from Sheehan, *A Bright Shining Lie*, 90; see also Halberstam, *Quagmire*, 52–55; Clarke, *The Final Years*, 162–3.

41. Hess, *Vietnam*, 75; Sheehan, "Annals of War, Part 2," 62.

42. Hess, *Vietnam*, 74.

43. Hilsman, Roger, *To Move a Nation* (New York: Delta, 1967), 87–88. Hilsman, a State Department official and counterinsurgency expert, was initially a strong supporter of the strategic hamlet enterprise. By the summer of 1963, Ngo Dinh Nhu claimed that two-thirds of the South Vietnamese population resided in secure strategic hamlets. A more realistic figure would have been 5 to 10 percent; Blaufarb, *Counterinsurgency Era*, 116–27; Pike, *Vietcong*, 61–73. According to Pike, 102, NLF cadres kidnapped 9,000 officials and murdered 1,700 in 1962 and kidnapped 7,200 and murdered 2,000 in 1963.

44. Porter (ed.), *Vietnam Documents*, vol. 2, Document 87, "Short-term Prospects in South Vietnam," extract from a memo by Roger Hilsman, Dec. 3, 1962, 169–74. Hilsman noted the deterioration of internal security in South Vietnam occurring in 1962.

45. Maitland et al., *Raising the Stakes*, 37–41.

46. *Ibid.*, pp. 42–47; Young, *Vietnam Wars*, 84–86.

47. Ball, George, *The Past Has Another Pattern* (New York: W. W. Norton, 1982), 339.

48. Hallin, Daniel C., *The Uncensored War: The Media and Vietnam* (New York: Oxford University Press, 1986), pp. 43–48. Hallin's book is the best study we have of the ways the *New York Times* and the television network nightly news broadcasts covered the Vietnam War.

49. See article entitled "Vietnamese Reds Gain in Key Area," which appeared under Halberstam's byline on the front page of the August 15, 1963, *New York Times*; Rust, *Kennedy in Vietnam*, 81–84; Sheehan, Neil, "In Vietnam, the Birth of the Credibility Gap," *New York Times*, Oct. 1, 1988, 15.

50. U. S. Army Military History Research Collection, Senior Officers Debriefing Program, Conversations between General Paul D. Harkins and Major Jacob B. Cough Jr., recorded at Carlisle Barracks, Penn., 53; Young, *Vietnam Wars*, 90–92.

51. Karnow, *Vietnam*, 296–7.

52. Halberstam, *Quagmire*, chap. 11, 148–55, gives his account of the press controversy; Miroff, *Pragmatic Illusions*, 157–8.

53. Sheehan, "In Vietnam, the Birth of the Credibility Gap," 15; Knightley, Phillipp, *The First Casualty* (New York: Harcourt, Brace, Jovanovich, 1975), 376–83; Sheehan, Neil, *A Bright Shining Lie: John Paul Vann and America in Vietnam* (New York: Random House), 315–16.

54. Kahin, *Intervention*, 143–45; Young, *Vietnam Wars*, 94–95.

55. Maitland, *Raising the Stakes*, 56.

56. Young, *Vietnam Wars*, 94.

57. Extract of Report to the President on Southeast Asia-Vietnam, by Senator Mike Mansfield, Dec. 18, 1962, in Porter (ed.), *Vietnam Documents*, vol. 2, Document 88, 174–76.

58. Kahin, *Intervention*, 146–47.

59. David Halberstam witnessed Quang Duc's self-immolation. He called it a "scene of medieval horror," *Quagmire*, 113.

60. "Thich" means reverend, or the reverend. Madame Nhu's given name was Le Tran Xuan, meaning "beautiful spring."

61. Shaplen, *Lost Revolution*, 191–2.

62. *Ibid.*

63. Videotape, "America's Mandarin," from the television series "Vietnam: A Television History."

64. Kahin, *Intervention*, 152.

65. Shaplen, *Lost Revolution*, 197–201.

66. Kahin, *Intervention*, 153–56. The most thorough study of the coup that destroyed Diem and his brother is by Hammer, Ellen J., *A Death in November: America in Vietnam, 1963* (New York: E. P. Dutton, 1987). See pp. 221–30. Hammer has examined all of the pertinent documents thoroughly and says that she cannot tell whether Nhu was serious about seeking a rapprochement with Hanoi or whether he was trying to outmaneuver U. S. officials whom he detested.

67. Sheehan and others, "Cablegram from the State Department to Ambassador Henry Cabot Lodge in Saigon," August 24, 1963, Document 35, *Pentagon Papers*, 194–5. Its key passages: "U. S. government cannot tolerate situation in which power lies in Nhu's hands. Diem must be given chance to rid himself of Nhu and his coterie. . . . If in spite of all your efforts, Diem remains obdurate and refuses, then we must face the possibility that Diem himself cannot be preserved." Roger Hilsman drafted the cable.

68. Kahin, *Intervention*, 159–60; Hearden, Patrick J., *The Tragedy of Vietnam* (New York: Harper Collins, 1991), 95–96; excerpts from the Lodge cable are quoted in Olson and Roberts, *Where the Domino Fell*, 101.

69. Young, *Vietnam Wars*, 102.

70. Hilsman, *To Move a Nation*, 501–5.

71. Herring, *America's Longest War*, 102; Paul Kattenburg, a State Department expert on Vietnam, recalled attending a National Security Council meeting on August 31, 1963, also attended by Rusk, McNamara, Taylor, Johnson, and Robert Kennedy as they discussed how to handle the crisis in South Vietnam. Kattenburg was appalled at their lack of knowledge about the culture and history of Vietnam, their lack of knowledge of the political situation and the war in Vietnam, and their inability to understand the identification of Nationalism and Communism in Vietnam. They were incapable of fashioning a coherent or an effective Vietnam policy. Kattenburg's observations are taken from an interview cited in Gibbons, William Conrad, *The U. S. Government and the Vietnam War*, vol. 2 (Princeton, N. J.: Princeton University Press, 1986), 161–2.

72. Herring, *America's Longest War*, 103.

73. Porter (ed.), *Vietnam Documents*, vol. 2, Document 109, Extract from "Report of the McNamara-Taylor Mission to South Vietnam," October 2, 1963, 201–3.

74. Kahin, *Intervention*, p. 171; Young, *Vietnam Wars*, 100–1; Giglio, James N., *The Presidency of John F. Kennedy* (Lawrence, Kansas: University Press of Kansas, 1991),

251–2. Giglio has written a good, balanced account of the Kennedy presidency. See 239–54 for his fine brief analysis of Kennedy's Vietnam policy.

75. Herring, *America's Longest War*, 104.

76. Sheehan and others, *Pentagon Papers*. See Documents 48–58, 213–31.

77. *Ibid.*, "Lodge's Last Talk with Diem," Document 59, 232.

78. Shaplen, *Lost Revolution*, 208–11. Shaplen says about $600,000 was funnelled through the U. S. embassy to the coup leaders who used it to bribe key generals stationed near Saigon into supporting the coup.

79. Interview with Lucien Conein recorded on videotape, "America"s Mandarin," from the television series, "Vietnam: A Television History." In 1972, the Senate Committee on Foreign Relations investigated U. S. complicity in the coup that overthrew Ngo Dinh Diem; the committee found extensive U. S. involvement despite the pious disclaimers by U. S. officials. Senate Committee on Foreign Relations, *U. S. Involvement in the Overthrow of Ngo Dinh Diem, 1963*, 92nd Congress, 2nd session (Washington, D. C.: U. S. Government Printing Office, 1972).

80. Duiker, *The Communist Road*, 219–21.

81. Hess, *Vietnam*, 77.

82. *Ibid.*

83. Nolting is quoted on videotape, "America's Mandarin," from the television series "Vietnam: A Television History."

84. U. S. Army Military History Research Collection, Senior Officers Debriefing Program. Conversations between General Harkins and Major Cough recorded at Carlisle Barracks, Penn., 54.

85. Interview with Madame Nhu recorded on videotape, "America's Mandarin," from the television series "Vietnam: A Television History."

86. Berman, Larry, *Planning*, 28.

87. *Ibid.* General William C. Westmoreland agrees with Johnson that Kennedy's involvement in the coup that destroyed Diem was a serious error that locked America into a war to defend South Vietnam.

88. O'Donnell, Kenneth P., and Powers, David F., with Joe McCarthy, *Johnny, We Hardly Knew Ye: Memories of John Fitzgerald Kennedy* (Boston: Little, Brown, 1972), 15–17. Hilsman, *To Move a Nation*, chap. 34: "If Kennedy Had Lived?" 524–37. Hilsman asserts that Kennedy believed in counterinsurgency and was skeptical about using U. S. military power in Vietnam. Hillman says that had he lived Kennedy would probably have opted for a negotiated settlement before he would have Americanized the war. William J. Rust, *Kennedy in Vietnam: American Vietnam Policy, 1960–1963*, believes that had Kennedy lived there would have been no American war in Vietnam. John M. Newman, *JFK and Vietnam: Deception, Intrigue, and the Struggle for Power* (New York: Warner Books, 1992) insists that Kennedy would never have placed U. S. combat troops in Vietnam and that he was planning to withdraw all American military advisers by the end of 1965. Oliver Stone's controversial fiction film "JFK," released in December 1991, suggests that Kennedy was murdered by a conspiracy instigated by national security officials who were unhappy because Kennedy planned to pull out of Vietnam and end the Cold War with the Soviet Union.

89. Quoted on videotape, "Lyndon Johnson Goes to War, 1964–1965," from the television series "Vietnam: A Television History."

90. Those who argue that Kennedy was a closet dove who was planning to disengage from Vietnam and that had he lived there would have been no American war in Vietnam are, in effect, accusing Kennedy of maintaining a persistent and elaborate public deception as well as misleading his senior advisers and successor about his intentions in Vietnam.

91. Giglio, *The Kennedy Presidency*, 240.

92. Herring, *Longest War*, 3d. ed., 119; Hammer, *Death in November*, 211.

93. Schlesinger, Arthur M. Jr., *A Thousand Days* (Greenich, Conn.: Fawcett, 1965), 909–10.

94. Walton, Richard J., *Cold War and Counter-Revolution: The Foreign Policy of John F. Kennedy* (Baltimore: Penguin, 1972), 201.

95. Hilsman, *To Move a Nation*, 501; Schlesinger, Arthur Meier Jr., *Robert Kennedy and His Times* (Boston: Houghton Mifflin, 1978), Vol. 2, 746–7.

96. Rust, *Kennedy in Vietnam*, x. In an oral interview given after his brother's death, Robert Kennedy said that the president never considered either withdrawal or large-scale military intervention in Vietnam. When asked what John Kennedy would have done if the government of South Vietnam appeared about to fall to the Communists (the situation Johnson faced in the summer of 1965), Robert Kennedy, confirming the short-term, ad hoc, and cautious nature of the Kennedy Vietnam policy, said that his brother would have faced that problem when he came to it. Robert Kennedy's remarks carry authority because he knew his brother and his Vietnam policies best. John Kennedy, at the time of his death, probably had not made up his mind about what to do in Vietnam. The President told dovish advisers that he planned to disengage and let hawkish advisers assume that he shared their views and commitments. Meanwhile, he kept his options open.

97. Young, *Vietnam Wars*, 103. Those who believe that had he lived Kennedy would have withdrawn U. S. forces from Vietnam and there would have been no American Vietnam war make much of NSAM 263, issued on October 3, 1963; NSAM 263 announced that the U. S. military mission would be mostly completed by the end of 1965 and that 1,000 troops could be withdrawn by the end of 1963. The primary reason the U. S. military mission was not completed and the troops not withdrawn as scheduled was because the military situation deteriorated. The Vietcong, supported by regular North Vietnamese Army forces, taking advantage of the political chaos reigning in South Vietnam, pressed ever closer to victory in 1964 and 1965. About 1,000 U. S. military advisers did come home, but they belonged to a construction battalion whose mission had been completed, and they were replaced by other soldiers.

98. Herring, *America's Longest War*, 107.

5

America Goes to War

I knew from the start that I was bound to be crucified either way I moved. If I left the woman I really loved—the Great Society—in order to get involved with that bitch of a war on the other side of the world, then I would lose everything at home. . . . But if I left that war and let the Communists take over South Vietnam, then I would be seen as a coward and my nation would be seen as an appeaser and we would both find it impossible to accomplish anything for anybody anywhere on the entire globe.

Lyndon B. Johnson

THE SAME ONLY MORE

Lyndon Johnson and his foreign policy advisers operated within an international diplomatic environment that they perceived to be changing as they turned their attention to Vietnam and Indochina following Kennedy's death in late November 1963. The Sino-Soviet split appeared to be irrevocable; some U. S. officials believed that the two major Communist powers might have a war one day. The Sino-Soviet split also bore directly upon the expanding war in southern Vietnam. Hanoi supported China in its conflicts with the Soviets and "Soviet influence in Vietnam was negligible."[1] America no longer faced an international Communist monolith bent on world domination; the Soviet-Chinese conspiracy had fragmented into quarreling moieties.

Relations between the United States and Soviet Union had improved markedly since their confrontation in Cuba in October 1962 over Soviet efforts to install intermediate range missiles on Cuba. Negotiating a nuclear test ban treaty and grain deals with the Soviets in mid-1963 encouraged some U. S. officials to hope for a lasting *dètente* with the U. S. S. R. But America continued its policy of nonrecognition of China, trying to isolate the PRC from international life. U. S. officials saw China as an expansionist state seeking to assert leadership of revolutionary forces in Southeast Asia and elsewhere among other Third World nations.

To American officials, Southeast Asia appeared especially vulnerable to Chinese intrusions in late 1963. South Vietnam was descending into political chaos in the aftermath of Diem's death. Both Leftist and Rightist forces challenged the fragile neutralist government of Laos. In Cambodia, Prince Sihanouk had cast off both U. S. aid and offers of protection. In Indonesia, Sukarno was seeking Chinese support for his war against a pro-Western government in Malaysia, a country in which China had supported an insurgency during the early 1950s. Washington feared that China might try to exploit the political disorder in countries along its southern periphery and that the food-short Chinese might be tempted to overrun the rich rice baskets of Southeast Asia.

The winds of change blowing in other regions of the world heralded the dawning of a more polycentric world order in late 1963. In Western Europe, De Gaulle was challenging the U. S. dominance of the NATO alliance and was trying to reassert French influence in Vietnam. Rioting, revolution, and rising anti-Americanism in Latin America fueled U. S. fears of a spreading Castroism within a region long dominated by the Yanqui colossus. Birthing pains among African nations emerging from colonialism posed threats to world stability. A superpower confrontation in the Congo had been averted in 1961 by a United Nations intervention. American officials feared that the Communist powers might become involved in some of these Third World trouble spots and that such interventions could bring, *inter alia*, confrontations with the United States and the threat of nuclear war. It is within this context of a more fluid, unstable, and polycentric world order in which the chief threat to American strategic interests appeared to emanate from Chinese expansionism in Southeast Asia that Johnson and his men forged their Vietnam policies.

President Johnson inherited from his late predecessor both a commitment to South Vietnam and a group of advisers who had orchestrated that commitment. A brilliantly successful domestic politician, Johnson was initially neither very knowledgeable about nor confident of his grasp of foreign affairs. The methods that had worked for him at home—a subtle amalgam of strong-arm politics, favors, flattery, and compromise to form coalitions based on a consensus of all interested parties—could not be applied to the international realm. In contrast to his mastery of domestic political processes, Johnson often found himself beyond his depth when conducting U. S. foreign policy. Compounding his difficulties in Southeast Asia, in addition to the frustrating limits on American power to influence events in that troubled region, was Johnson's profound ignorance of the history and culture of the Vietnamese people. He never grasped the dynamics of the Vietnamese revolutionary war strategy that the United States was trying to counter, nor did he ever comprehend the ideologies or psychologies of its leaders. He persisted in trying to understand the peculiarly Vietnamese dynamics of national revolution by applying the Procrustean concepts of the American anti-Communist Cold War ideology.

To a much greater degree than Kennedy, Johnson relied on the knowledge and judgment of his senior foreign policy advisers. From late-1964 to mid-1965, during which time Johnson transformed "a limited commitment to assist the South Vietnamese government into an open-ended commitment to preserve an independent, non-Communist South Vietnam,"[2] and took his nation to war, the men who most influenced the shaping of Southeast Asian policy were a coterie of Kennedy holdovers: Secretary of Defense Robert S. McNamara, National Security Adviser McGeorge Bundy, Secretary of State Dean Rusk, and Ambassador to South Vietnam, Maxwell Taylor. Johnson "had inherited the policy and the men who made it." Of these men, McNamara, through his *ex officio* clout, forceful personality, and a keen analytic mind that absorbed enormous amounts of factual data, exerted the greatest formative influence on Johnson's Vietnam policy."[3]

Vietnam did not dominate Johnson's presidency during his first year as it would later; he had entered the White House committed to fighting another kind of war than the one raging in southern Vietnam. Early in his presidency, he had declared "unconditional war on poverty in America."[4] Johnson intended the fight against poverty to be an integral part of what he labeled a "Great Society," a broad range of welfare, social reform, and civil rights legislation that he would soon propose to Congress.[5] In Johnson's expansive view, his Great Society would fulfill the social vision of the New Deal by eradicating residual poverty and racial injustice. The new president would use the powers of the federal government to bring the 40 million Americans still denied equal access to the American dream into the socioeconomic mainstream. Creating his Great Society would also ensure Johnson, a man of vaulting ambitions and possessor of an outsized ego, an honored place in the national memory.

It is one of the many ironic dimensions of the American Vietnam ordeal that Lyndon Johnson, the man whose highest goal had been to expand the American system in order to include all of its citizens, felt compelled to Americanize the war in Southeast Asia, a foreign war that soon curtailed his domestic war on poverty, slowed the march of civil rights, destroyed the consensus that he had forged to create his "New Jerusalem," and strangled his beloved Great Society before it could be fully realized. The war in Southeast Asia that President Johnson and his advisers set in motion eventually claimed the lives of over 58,000 of their fellow citizens, a disproportionately high number of whom had come from the ranks of the disadvantaged classes whom Johnson had committed himself to helping. From the ranks of the strongest supporters of Johnson's ill-fated Great Society reform program would come some of the most cogent critics of his Vietnam War policies.

Johnson and his advisers quickly embraced the U. S. commitment in Vietnam, considering it an integral part of the Kennedy agenda that the new president, in his first speech to the American people, had pledged to continue.[6] Johnson's immediate goal was to deter aggression in Southeast Asia and give South Vietnam and the other nations on the periphery of Asian Communism the help they needed to maintain their stability and sovereignty. Like Truman, Eisenhower, and Kennedy before him, Johnson considered Southeast Asia a vital strategic interest of the United States. He brusquely dismissed any suggestions that the region might be of only marginal importance or that the United States might consider withdrawing from South Vietnam. Two days after becoming president, he asserted, "I am not going to lose Vietnam. I am not going to be the president who saw Southeast Asia go the way China went."[7]

Although Johnson embraced immediately the U. S. commitment in South Vietnam, he shared Kennedy's reluctance to invest large amounts of American military power in the region. He did not want to fight another land war in Asia, nor did he want to bomb the North. He feared that large-scale American military intervention would undermine the ability of the South Vietnamese forces to fight their enemies aggressively. The new president also feared that the injection of American combat forces into the Vietnam War would provoke adverse reactions throughout the world and trigger uprisings of domestic opposition that could stifle his domestic reform program and cost him the 1964 presidential election. He rejected initial proposals from the Joint Chiefs of Staff to "undertake major air and ground operations against North Vietnam."[8]

Within forty-eight hours of Kennedy's death, Johnson held a full-scale briefing on Vietnam, which was attended by all of his senior foreign policy advisers. The news he got from Indochina was bad. He was informed that the new military government of South Vietnam was struggling; it was not broadening its base of support, and the war was going badly for ARVN forces in many provinces. At this meeting, Johnson opted for a continuation of Kennedy's policy of sending U. S. military advisers to South Vietnam, along with substantial amounts of economic and military aid, and, additionally, he approved the conduct of covert operations against eastern Laos and North Vietnam. The conferees drafted a National Security Action Memorandum (NSAM 273) stressing the continuity of policy between his and his predecessor's administrations:

> It remains the Central Objective of the United States in South Vietnam to assist the people and government of that country to win their contest against the externally directed and supported Communist conspiracy.[9]

The NSAM 273, along with subsequent increases in the number of advisers and the amount of aid going to South Vietnam, and a step-up of covert operations against the DRV, constituted Johnson's Vietnam policy for the first year of his presidency. Johnson adopted a policy of doing the same that Kennedy had done, only doing more of it in hopes of achieving the prime American goal of creating a viable non-Communist state in southern Vietnam.

COUP SEASON

As Johnson reaffirmed the U. S. commitment to Saigon, General Minh, the leader of the Military Revolutionary Council (MRC), the new ruling junta in South Vietnam, rid his country of the last vestiges of Ngo family rule. General Minh unshackled the press, emptied Ngo Dinh Nhu's political prisons, and restored Saigon's vibrant cafe and night life. Saigon once again became a cheerful and noisy cosmopolitan city. And once again, the city's fragmented political life erupted. Religious sectarians, socialists, and especially the Buddhists and Catholics, quarreled heatedly over the political future of their fragile state.

In the South Vietnamese countryside, the Vietcong continued to enhance its control of people and territory.[10] In December 1963, meeting in Hanoi in a special session, the Central Committee of the Lao Dong, after much debate and disagreement among the delegates, enacted a series of resolutions that decisively influenced the course the insurgency in South Vietnam would take over the next eighteen months. The Committee issued a directive calling for an escalation of the southern insurgency and for increased support for the revolution from the DRV. The Communist leaders knew that they were running out of regroupees to send south and that they could not win the war without a major commitment of their own military forces. They issued new directives stressing that winning the insurgency in the South was not only a task for southerners, it was a task for all the Vietnamese people, North and South. Preparations were made to improve the Ho Chi Minh trail complex and to infiltrate PAVN units into southern Vietnam.

The Communist leadership decided that the time had come to move toward the final stage of the revolutionary struggle, a general counteroffensive paralleled by popular risings in the cities that would topple the fledgling South Vietnamese government. They realized their escalations ran the risk of a war with the United States, but they hoped their efforts would bring about the rapid collapse of the South Vietnamese government and the forced withdrawal of their American patrons without a fight. The aging revolutionary leaders in Hanoi made a huge miscalculation; they gambled and lost. Their efforts to bring about a more rapid demise of South Vietnam and force the Americans out provoked a major war with the United States that delayed the completion of the Vietnamese national revolution for more than a decade and brought massive death tolls and physical destruction to their nation.[11]

The new Saigon government alarmed American officials when it quickly demonstrated a penchant for acting independently. It soon proved to be more interested in seeking a negotiated settlement of the conflict than in fighting the PLAF forces. Hoping to move the conflict in South Vietnam from the military to the political plane, the MRC sought the support of rural elements, the sects, Buddhists, and even some of the factions within the NLF. The Saigon generals opposed any proposals by Americans to increase the U. S. advisory role in the conduct of ARVN operations or to expand the war against the NLF. They also opposed American plans for taking the war to the North, especially a bombing campaign against North Vietnam.

General Minh and his colleagues believed that the appeal of the Vietcong had been lessened by Diem's overthrow and that the rural population would be more responsive to government programs administered by local officials independent of the Americans. A conciliatory approach that had the villagers' interests at heart would be more effective than Diemist corruption, repression, and the strategic hamlets. They would strive to form a government of reconciliation that would seek to coexist peace-fully with Hanoi. Most members of the Military Council, including generals Minh and Don, had formerly served in the French colonial forces, and they were responsive to French President Charles De Gaulle's offers to help the Vietnamese achieve a peace-ful reunion of their country, free of external influences, including America influence. Ultimately Minh and most of his colleagues would have looked to a neutralist coali-tion government with the NLF.

Johnson administration officials, both in Saigon and Washington, were angry at the prospect of French intrusion into Vietnamese politics, a cease-fire, negotiations with NLF elements, and the formation of a neutralist coalition government that might ask the Americans to leave. Such possibilities risked the collapse of the American rationale for intervention in southern Vietnam that had prevailed for a decade. Washington held neutralization of South Vietnam in anathema; in their view, it would be tantamount to defeat, because it would leave the Communists in a dominant posi-tion throughout Indochina, "a situation that would have adverse effects throughout Southeast Asia."[12] Johnson and nearly all of his senior civilian and military advisers rejected neutralism out of hand.

It is intriguing to speculate on the possibility of an American withdrawal from Vietnam, indeed from all of Indochina, during the first few months of Johnson's pres-idency. Johnson is on record as having said that he would have much preferred to con-centrate on domestic social reform, not fight a war in Vietnam. No doubt he was sincere in expressing his preferences, although it is also a matter of historical record that withdrawal from Vietnam at the outset of his presidency was an option that Johnson and nearly all of his senior officials never seriously considered. In late 1963 and early 1964, America was not involved in Cambodia, the neutralist government, albeit fragile, was holding in Laos, and in Vietnam the Minh-Don group appeared to be trying to form a broad-based coalition government that would incorporate the NLF, end the insurgency, seek a peaceful coexistence with Hanoi, and adopt a neutralist stance in international affairs. The generals also indicated that they wanted to ease the Americans out of their affairs. Johnson, as a new president, had a certain freedom of maneuver and options that he could have considered. Vietnam had not yet become a major issue with the Congress or the American people; neither great amounts of men and material nor powerful popular emotions were yet committed.

Chances are the Minh government would have failed in its undertakings; during its brief existence, it never established a stable or popular government, fought effec-tively, or impressed the Americans with its political capabilities. Chances are the National Liberation Front, with Hanoi's backing, would have dominated any Saigon coalition government, and sooner or later, probably sooner, would have sought reuni-fication with Hanoi on the Communists' terms. Vietnamese Communists found coali-tions useful for rallying non-Communists to support their revolution against ruling elites; once the Communists achieved power and became the ruling elites, they, like the good Marxist-Leninists they were, would have opted for a monopoly of state power and proceeded to impose state socialism on the South as they did after 1976. Even so, the Minh government might have survived long enough to permit a more or less graceful American extrication from the developing quagmire of Vietnam. Those first few months of the Johnson presidency would be the last time Washington had at least a theoretical option of getting out of Vietnam without a major war. Considering how that long, painful, and disastrous experience turned out, it appears in retrospect an American tragedy that Johnson and his advisers, prisoners of their ideological preconceptions, could not seriously consider cutting their losses and opting out of Vietnam without a major war.

From the American perspective, the political and strategic situation in southern Vietnam deteriorated rapidly in the months following Diem's demise. The Buddhists and Catholics, the most powerful political factions in Saigon, waged bitter internecine warfare. In the rural areas, provincial government verged on collapse. The remaining strategic hamlets were being dismantled, often by their peasant occupants who viewed them more as internment camps than havens.[13] The NLF continued to expand its influence in the South. The MRC proved incapable of governing the fractious politicians of South Vietnam and unwilling to fight the Vietcong.

The coup that had destroyed Diem had also deepened the divisions among American officials concerned with the conduct of Vietnam policy. U. S. military officials, particularly MAC-V Commander General Harkins, who had opposed the coup, in turn opposed the new government because of its unwillingness to fight the NLF aggressively. Ambassador Lodge, who had spearheaded the American support of the coup that destroyed Diem, backed Minh and the other MRC leaders and tried to isolate Harkins from policy affairs.

Minh's junta was not destined to remain in power for long, nor to have much of an opportunity to try its conciliatory approach in the countryside. During the brief reign of the MRC, tensions and rivalries persisted among ARVN leaders, including members of the ruling council. One of these leaders, Major General Nguyen Khanh, who had supported the coup but was not a member of the ruling Council, began plotting his own coup to overthrow the Minh-Don group. Khanh was motivated by his fears that the current leaders could not manage the war against the PLAF. He was supported by General Harkins and some members of Harkins' military advisory group, particularly Colonel Jasper Wilson. Wilson helped shift the balance of power among ARVN commanders toward Khanh and kept Harkins informed of the plot's progress. Khanh's coup also enjoyed the tacit support of Taylor and McNamara, who wanted to be rid of leaders they perceived as inept, pro-French neutralists unable to either fight or govern.[14] The bloodless coup that brought Khanh to power occurred on January 30, 1964. President Johnson, himself having opposed the overthrow of Diem, was pleased with the advent of Khanh, who appeared eager to cooperate with American officials and get on with the war.

Khanh's bid for power opened the coup season in southern Vietnam. There would be five more coups during the next year, and South Vietnam would have seven governments in 1964 alone. As the succession of coups and rickety governments made a travesty of South Vietnamese political processes and poisoned political life, American officials pleaded with their charges to maintain at least a semblance of political stability. Without a stable government in Saigon, the war against the Vietcong would surely be lost.

Hoping that he was the man to rally his people and turn the war around, American officials strongly backed General Khanh. Khanh also appealed to the Americans because he promised to accept their advice. McNamara and Taylor accompanied Khanh on a barnstorming tour of South Vietnam, a public relations effort designed to sell the little-known new leader to his own people. The trio appeared at rallies in several cities, with Khanh standing in the middle, flanked by Taylor and McNamara, both raising Khanh's arms in triumphalist displays of Allied unity. At these rallies, McNamara liked to shout "Vietnam Muon Nam" (Vietnam a thousand years), but he failed to achieve the proper pitch and pronunciation so crucial to speaking Vietnamese correctly. To many Vietnamese in the audience, McNamara's shoutings sounded like "Southern duck wants to lie down."[15] These rallies may very well have had the opposite effect from that intended by the Americans. They made Khanh, a short, squat man standing between two tall American officials, appear inconsequential, even undignified. Khanh appeared to be a small puppet serving U. S. foreign policy interests.

Back from his dubious efforts at promoting General Khanh, McNamara submitted a starkly pessimistic report to Johnson on March 16, 1964. In his report, McNamara noted the deterioration of the political and military situation in the South, occurring since Diem's downfall. He estimated that the Vietcong now controlled about half the population and half the territory of South Vietnam. He also noted that in many areas administered by Saigon, much of the population had no interest in supporting the ARVN cause. Village defense forces refused to fight, deserted, and joined the Vietcong. The ARVN desertion rates and draft dodging were high, while the Vietcong were energetically recruiting new forces in many provinces. Displacing Minh with Khanh had not arrested the growing antiwar and neutralist sentiment among people residing in Saigon-controlled areas, especially among the Buddhists. To revive the sagging war effort, McNamara recommended increasing the size of ARVN forces, augmenting U. S. economic and military aid, and beginning to plan for taking the war to North Vietnam.[16]

The next day, Johnson met with the National Security Council to try to solve the seemingly intractable problems of Vietnam and to consider McNamara's recommendations. After a brief debate, Johnson decided to implement many of McNamara's proposals, a decision that amounted to continuing the U. S. advisory role in South Vietnam on an expanded scale. National Security Action Memorandum 288 (NSAM 288), issued on March 17, restated the American goal: to preserve an independent, non-Communist South Vietnam, which was necessary to prevent all Southeast Asia from turning Communist and to prove to the rest of the world that Communist wars of national liberation could be curtailed. The NSAM 288 called for a national mobilization plan to put South Vietnam on a war footing and for major increases in the number of ARVN forces. The memorandum also approved increases in various U. S. aid programs and in the number of American military advisers serving in South Vietnam.[17]

At the same time that Johnson implemented McNamara's recommendations, an interagency study group working under State Department auspices proposed a series of military operations against North Vietnam. The study group's most important recommendation was aerial bombing. Bombing would put military pressure on the North, threaten to destroy their nascent industrial economy, and demonstrate U. S. power and resolve to the Khanh government, Hanoi, Beijing, Moscow, and the rest of the world. William Bundy, a member of the interagency group, also drafted a proposed Congressional resolution authorizing the president to wage war against North Vietnam.[18]

Understanding that a lack of progress in South Vietnam might require various kinds of punitive responses against North Vietnam, the Joint Chiefs, in late May, proposed a sequence of carefully graduated military operations against North Vietnam. The Joint Chiefs' scenario incorporated many of the recommendations of the State Department's interagency group. These proposals included bombing missions and the mining of North Vietnamese ports. The Joint Chiefs also recommended that these military operations be accompanied by consultations with U. S. allies and that Congress enact a resolution authorizing the president to do "whatever is necessary with respect to Vietnam." The proposed scenario stressed the gradualist, restrained, and limited nature of these military actions. The operations were not designed to destroy North Vietnam; they were only intended to persuade Hanoi to stop supporting the insurrection in South Vietnam by threatening the Northerners with ever greater punishment if they did not desist. How much punishment the North received would be up to them, because at each step of the way they would be given a chance to reconsider and surrender, that is, to call off their support of the southern insurgency.[19] The bland language of the scenario masked a stern reality: However modern and reasonable it sounded, the logic of calibrated response was the logic of the rack, articulated in the language of games theory and the accountant's spreadsheet.[20] The Joint Chiefs' scenario also revealed a growing tendency among American officials to look to North Vietnam for a solution that continued to elude them in South Vietnam. Further, the proposals showed a growing tendency to try to resolve South Vietnam's serious social, economic, and political problems by military means.[21]

By June 1964, Johnson had available a scenario prepared by the Joint Chiefs, recommending a carefully calibrated series of military operations against North Vietnam designed to force them to abandon their support of the revolution raging in South Vietnam or gradually incur extensive damage to their industrial infrastructure. In addition to these contingency plans prepared by his senior military advisers, the president also had a draft copy of a proposed Congressional resolution authorizing him to take the war to North Vietnam. Johnson, who believed that Harry Truman had made a serious mistake when he failed to seek Congressional approval for the Korean intervention in 1950, planned to seek a Congressional authorization if and when he decided to take the war to North Vietnam.

But Johnson was not ready to widen the war in Vietnam at that time. He continued to be reluctant to shift his emphasis from social reform at home to waging a major foreign war. He doubted that military might alone could solve South Vietnam's many serious problems. He could not be certain that the proposed military measures would cause North Vietnam to abandon the southern insurgents. Even if Hanoi did stop supporting the NLF, the Vietcong might be able to continue their rebellion indefinitely unless the Khanh government mounted an effective counterinsurgency campaign. Johnson could not count on strong Congressional, media, or public support for making war on North Vietnam without advance preparation or clear cause. Rather than adopt the Joint Chiefs' scenario for war against North Vietnam in June 1964, Johnson authorized instead an increase in the covert campaign against North Vietnam that he had approved at the outset of his presidency. These operations, code-named Operations Plan 34-Alpha (OPLAN 34-A), included air and naval surveillance missions and commando raids against radar sites and coastal military installations. In addition, Johnson also ordered U. S. pilots to attack Pathet Lao positions along the Laotian panhandle to disrupt North Vietnamese supply lines that ran through that area.[22]

As he authorized the step-up in covert operations against North Vietnamese targets, Johnson also sent a warning to Hanoi via Blair Seaborn, the Canadian representative on the International Control Commission (ICC). Seaborn was instructed to tell the North Vietnamese leadership to stop supporting the Vietcong effort in South Vietnam, or the United States would attack North Vietnam with devastating results. The DRV Premier Pham Van Dong, meeting with Blair, defiantly told him to tell the American leaders that the DRV would continue to support the NLF until it prevailed. He also emphatically told Seaborn that the American choices in Vietnam amounted to either continuing indefinitely a war they could not win, or accepting a neutral south Vietnam and withdrawing.[23]

From Johnson's perspective during the summer of 1964, Vietnam must have appeared as a series of problems that stubbornly resisted solutions. Despite the escalations—the increased American military presence, the additional economic and military support for the Khanh government, and the increased covert operations against North Vietnam—and despite the diplomatic initiative to warn Hanoi about the dangers it faced if it continued to support the insurgency in the South, the situation continued to deteriorate.

Despite the great expectations of McNamara, Taylor, and his other American sponsors, General Khanh quickly showed himself as an ineffective leader and a war manager. The people did not rally to his leadership in the towns and cities. Saigon's numerous political factions continued their quarrels with each other and with Khanh. In the countryside, the Vietcong continued to maintain the initiative, and their military forces became bolder and more aggressive. The insurgents, as they continued their assaults on ARVN forces, also launched terrorist attacks against U. S. advisers. The North Vietnamese continued to support the revolutionaries in the South.

By the summer of 1964, Johnson was gearing himself up for a reelection battle at a time when there was growing concern within the Congress and among segments of the American public about Vietnam. A documentary produced by CBS Television reflected rising public worries about what the Johnson administration intended to do in Vietnam if the Vietcong continued to gain ground and the Saigon government continued to decline. Johnson decided to wait until after the election to confront the Vietnam conundrum and to decide if a major American military intervention might be necessary to defeat the revolution in South Vietnam, which he understood to be Communist aggression from the North. Delay would also permit him to seek reelection as a moderate but firm peace candidate offsetting the appeal of his belligerent hawkish challenger, conservative Republican Senator Barry Goldwater. Besides, any major commitment of U. S. military forces in Vietnam could only be sold to the American people as a response to overt acts of war against American forces by the North Vietnamese or the National Liberation Front, and none appeared forthcoming.[24]

IN DUBIOUS BATTLES

During the first few days of August 1964, a series of controversial incidents took place in the Gulf of Tonkin involving U. S. and North Vietnamese naval forces. These incidents brought about the implementation of many of the proposed military actions against North Vietnam, including the first U. S. bombings of North Vietnamese targets. They also brought about the enactment of a resolution that granted President Johnson a blank check to wage war in Vietnam. The bombing raids and rapid passage of the Congressional resolution convinced the Communist leaders in Hanoi that the United States was planning to wage a major war in Vietnam, a war against them as well as against the National Liberation Front forces in South Vietnam.

On Sunday morning, August 2, three North Vietnamese patrol boats suddenly attacked the destroyer USS *Maddox*, which was engaged in an electronic surveillance mission, code-named DESOTO patrol, off the coast of North Vietnam. Two nights earlier, South Vietnamese patrol boats had attacked North Vietnamese military and radar installations on the offshore islands of Hon Me and Hon Nieu, in the vicinity where the *Maddox* was patrolling when it was attacked. The South Vietnamese raids were part of the series of OPLAN 34-A covert operations that the CIA and military intelligence groups periodically conducted against North Vietnam to harass and confuse the North Vietnamese. The North Vietnamese naval command, probably linking the DESOTO patrol with the earlier night's OPLAN 34-A assaults, ordered its boats to attack the *Maddox*, whose patrol route at times brought it to within eight miles of North Vietnam's mainland coast and within four miles of its offshore islands.[25]

In a brief and intense encounter, *Maddox* opened fire with its three-inch and five-inch guns, badly damaging one of the attacking boats. Naval aircraft operating from the nearby carrier USS *Ticonderoga* strafed the patrol boats, inflicting damage as the crafts sped back toward their bases. The *Maddox* sustained very minor damage (one enemy 12.7mm. machine-gun bullet pierced one of its aft electronic gunfire directors).[26]

In Washington, 10,000 miles away, President Johnson reacted angrily but with restraint to the news of an attack on an American warship. Some of his advisers called for retaliatory air strikes against North Vietnamese targets. One of those officials who favored this course of action was the newly appointed U. S. Ambassador to South Vietnam, General Maxwell Taylor. South Vietnam's ruler, General Khanh, also called for air strikes against North Vietnam.[27]

Resisting pressures to bomb North Vietnam, Johnson instead directed the Navy to order the *Maddox* to resume its patrols, this time joined by another destroyer, the USS *Turner Joy.* The destroyers continued to cruise close to North Vietnamese shores. The Pentagon put U. S. combat forces on alert and a U. S. fighter-bomber squadron in Thailand was strengthened. Johnson also took the precaution of using a recently installed "hot line" to tell the Soviets not to be alarmed by the presence of two U. S. warships in international wars just off the coast of North Vietnam. The president took these military actions to assert traditional U. S. claims to freedom of the seas and to demonstrate to the North Vietnamese officials that the United States was not intimidated by the patrol boat assaults. Johnson had been notified that additional OPLAN-34-A raids were scheduled for the same general area the night of August 3. His advisers had also informed him that they believed that the North Vietnamese patrol boats had attacked the *Maddox* because their leaders apparently connected the DESOTO patrol with the OPLAN-34-A attack. Even though U. S. officials denied that there were any connections between the patrols and the commando raids, Johnson knew that ordering the destroyers to resume their patrols risked additional attacks on the American warships. The president felt it was necessary to run risks in order to send North Vietnam's leaders a message. Johnson was not trying to provoke a fight with North Vietnam, but he was not going out of his way to avoid one either.[28]

At 7:15 P. M., on the evening of August 4, Captain John J. Herrick, on board the *Maddox*, the commander of the DESOTO operation, received a warning from the National Security Agency (NSA) that three North Vietnamese boats operating in the vicinity of Hon Me Island were preparing to attack the two destroyers. At 8:35 P. M., the *Maddox* picked up three radar contacts traveling at high speeds about thirty-five miles to the north. Shipboard analysts evaluated the blips on their radar screens as North Vietnamese patrol boats attempted to set an ambush for the destroyers near the island where the U. S. warships had been steaming the previous night. The two ships wheeled about and headed southeast in the direction of the *Ticonderoga,* about 200 miles away. About thirty minutes later, both destroyers, spotting three more radar contacts, went to general quarters and called for air support. Four jets soon arrived overhead from *Ticonderoga,* having been dispatched fifty minutes earlier, and searched the area but could find no enemy boats. At 9:40 P.M., the confusion began. Both destroyers, now sixty

Figure 5.1 The USS *Maddox*: The U. S. Destroyer was engaged in electronic surveillance along the coast of North Vietnam when it was attacked by North Vietnamese torpedo boats on August 2, 1964. *Source:* AP/Wide World Photos

miles from the North Vietnamese coast and 180 miles north of the DMZ, began shooting at radar targets. Herrick also began sending messages stating that his ships were under attack. The sonar operator on board the *Maddox* reported many torpedoes in the water. Crewmen on board both ships reported that they saw torpedo wakes in the water.[29]

The weather was bad that night in the Gulf. There were clouds, rain storms, heavy surface fog, and it was a moonless night. Twenty-knot winds churned the sea. Surface visibility was near zero. Herrick's attack reports were based on evaluations of radar and sonar contacts. Neither ship suffered any damage. Naval aircraft flying cover over the two destroyers at low altitude and searching for the alleged attacking boats could never find them, nor did the pilots ever see any torpedo wakes, even though they could easily spot the wakes of the destroyers.[30]

For two hours, the two destroyers zigged and zagged furiously around an area of the Gulf in efforts to avoid what their officers and most crewmen thought were torpedo attacks. They fired hundreds of rounds of three- and five-inch shells at their invisible targets, laid depth charges at shallow depths, and even tried to ram their unseen attackers. The Navy pilots, on orders from the destroyers, fired missiles into the ocean at unseen targets. Herrick, trying to evaluate the confusing situation, dispatched a later message expressing his doubts that either of the U. S. warships had been attacked the night of August 4. He stated that he believed that enemy patrol boats had attempted an ambush earlier in the evening, but that it never occurred because Herrick had maneuvered his ships away from the ambush area. He urged a complete evaluation of the night's events before any further action was taken. He attributed the radar and sonar contacts to weather effects, and to his crew's inexperience and anxiety.[31]

While the two destroyers raced around firing at unseen targets, in Washington, Johnson, informed that a second attack had in as many days been made on U. S. ships on the high seas, angrily ordered retaliatory air strikes against North Vietnamese targets. The President concluded that the North Vietnamese were trying to make the United States look weak and ineffectual, like a "paper tiger." President Johnson also decided that it was a propitious moment to have his long-awaited Congressional resolution enacted. McNamara, the chief architect of Johnson's evolving war policy, eager to strike at the North Vietnamese, took charge of preparing the reprisal attacks. While the Joint Chiefs of Staff readied a strike execute order, McNamara sought confirmation that the second attack had occurred. He discounted Captain Herrick's cautionary message. He asked Admiral U. S. Grant Sharp, Commander of the Pacific Fleet (CINC-PACFLT), about the latest reports from the destroyers. Admiral Sharp, who had not read Herrick's cautionary message at the time McNamara called him, told McNamara that there was little doubt that a second attack had occurred. The evidence that convinced McNamara that there had been a second attack came from NSA radio intercepts of North Vietnamese naval communications, which had been made during the battle. While the military prepared the air strike plan and McNamara sought his confirmation, other officials finalized the wording of the resolution to be sent to Congress. Johnson meanwhile met with Congressional leaders to inform them of the incidents and to solicit their support for the resolution that would sanction the retaliatory attacks.[32]

Three years after America had gone to war in Vietnam, the Senate Foreign Relations Committee conducted a full-scale investigation of the Gulf of Tonkin incidents. Several of its members challenged the validity of the August 4 attack. McNamara, testifying before the Committee, insisted that the NSA intercepts proved that the attack in question had taken place. The U. S. government has refused numerous requests to declassify the NSA intercepts, but electronic intelligence experts who have seen them have refuted McNamara's contention. Ray S. Cline, former CIA deputy director of intelligence, who carefully analyzed the contents of the NSA intercepts, concluded that the messages received at the time of the second attack, because of the time differences involved, were after action reports on the first attack occurring on August 2.[33] Louis Tordella, a former deputy director of the NSA, after a careful analysis of the same intercepts, reached the same conclusion.[34]

Years later, James B. Stockdale further undermined McNamara's credibility concerning the Tonkin Gulf incidents. On August 2, 1964, Commander Stockdale was the flight leader of the aircraft that had driven off the patrol boats attacking the *Maddox*. On August 4, when the second attack was supposed to have occurred, Stockdale also led the flight that provided supporting cover for the two destroyers that dark and stormy night in the Gulf of Tonkin. Stockdale was later shot down over North Vietnam and consequently spent eight years in a Communist prison camp. He endured brutal tortures with extraordinary courage and strength. He finally returned home to a hero's welcome and later rose to the rank of vice admiral. Admiral Stockdale has written a revealing account of the events of that controversial night in the Gulf of Tonkin:

I had the best seat in the house from which to detect boats—if there were any. I didn't have to look through surface haze and spray like the destroyers did and yet I could see the destroyers' every move vividly. Time and time again I flew over the *Maddox* and the *Joy*, throttled back, lights out, like a near-silent stalking owl, conserving fuel at a 250-knot loiter speed. . . . When the destroyers were convinced that they had some battle action going, I zigged and zagged and fired where they fired. . . . The edges of the black hole I was flying in were still periodically lit by flashes of lightning—but no wakes or dark shapes other than those of the destroyers were ever visible to me.[35]

Ironically, on August 5, 1964, Stockdale led one of the raids against North Vietnam retaliating for an attack that he believed never occurred. He remembered thinking at the time that Washington officials had acted hastily and irrationally. Five days later, Stockdale was visited by two of McNamara's assistants, who asked him if there had been any boats attacking the destroyers on the night of August 4! He told them that he never saw any. President Johnson voiced his doubts that a second attack had occurred a few days after ordering the retaliatory raids when he told an adviser, "Hell, those dumb, stupid sailors were just shooting at flying fish." Johnson did, however, order the DESOTO patrols to continue, but he also separated them from OPLAN 34-A raids. On the night of September 18, there occurred a replay of the August 4 incident, complete with radar and sonar contacts, reports of torpedoes in the water, ships firing at unseen targets, aircraft flying overhead unable to spot any enemy boats, and advisers calling for more retaliatory raids. LBJ, cautious this time, refused to order more sorties against North Vietnamese targets.[36]

But McNamara, in the crisis atmosphere prevailing in Washington on August 4, 1964, preferred quick action to restrained, thoughtful analysis. At a short National Security Council Meeting, McNamara confirmed the second attack for the president, and plans for the retaliatory raids were finalized. President Johnson wanted the reprisal raids timed so that they would be occurring at the same moment he would be explaining to the American people why he had ordered the bombing of North Vietnamese targets. He told the American people that he had ordered the raids to retaliate for "open aggression on the high seas against the United States of America." He also reassured the public, by noting that "We seek no wider war."[37]

But the air raids, code-named PIERCE ARROW, were delayed because of weather conditions and did not occur until several hours after the president's speech. Naval aircraft from the *Ticonderoga* and *Constellation* flew sixty-four sorties against four North Vietnamese patrol boat bases and a supporting oil supply facility. The raiders destroyed or damaged twenty-five patrol boats and about 90 percent of the oil storage complex. During the strikes, two U. S. aircraft were shot down. One pilot, Lt. (j.g.) Everett Alvarez, was captured. He was the first of 826 American pilots and air crewmen known to have been captured by the North Vietnamese, and he spent eight and one-half years as a prisoner of war.[38]

On August 5, the resolution was sent to Congress. The next day, the senate committees on Foreign Relations and Armed Services met in joint session to consider it.

Senator William J. Fulbright, chairman of the Foreign Relations Committee, presided over the hearings. Fulbright was Johnson's close friend and political ally; Johnson urged Fulbright to move the resolution through quickly so it would have the maximum impact. The president assured his friend that he planned no wider war after the retaliatory raids. At the committee hearings, McNamara presented the administration's version of the events. McNamara portrayed the complex and ambiguous incidents occurring in the Gulf of Tonkin as clear and simple acts of aggression: they were unprovoked attacks against American ships engaged in routine patrols in international waters. He made no mention of the OPLAN-34-A raids, and he did not tell the senators that the destroyers were on spy missions. Although he was aware that the North Vietnamese had presumed a linkage between the OPLAN-34-A raids and the DESOTO patrols, McNamara told the senators that he could give no rational explanation for the attacks. He portrayed them as mindless and suicidal acts of aggression.[39]

All but one of the senators on the two committees accepted McNamara's duplicitous version of the Gulf of Tonkin incidents. The lone challenge came from Oregon's Wayne Morse. An anonymous Pentagon leaker had informed Morse of the OPLAN-34-A raids and DESOTO patrols. The Senator tried to link the clandestine raids with the attacks on the ships. McNamara categorically denied that there could be any connection and reiterated that the *Maddox* was on a routine patrol in international waters both times it was attacked.[40] No other senators were interested in pursuing Morse's line of questioning or challenging McNamara's testimony. The committees voted thirty-one to one to send the resolution to the full Senate; Morse cast the lone dissenting vote.

The next day, Fulbright, who would turn against the war within a year and become the Senate's most prominent dovish critic, guided the resolution rapidly through the full Senate, allowing only perfunctory debate. Long accustomed to routinely approving presidential foreign policy initiatives and sharing the administration's view that the United States had to respond to acts of aggression against its armed forces, nearly all of the senators approved the resolution unquestioningly. And nearly all appeared unconcerned about the possible uses a president might make of it. Maryland Senator Daniel Brewster asked Fulbright if the resolution would approve sending armies to fight in Vietnam. Fulbright told him that it would. Wisconsin Senator Gaylord Nelson proposed an amendment making it clear that Congress, by passing the resolution, was not authorizing a change in the U. S. advisory role in Vietnam, nor approving an expansion of the American commitment in South Vietnam. Fulbright, who agreed in principle with Nelson, talked him out of adding the amendment by telling him that it would only cause confusion and delay. Kentucky's John Sherman Cooper asked Fulbright if the resolution would grant the president the power to take the country to war. Fulbright, who would come to repudiate the role that he played in rushing the Gulf of Tonkin resolution through the Senate, replied that it would.[41] Senator Morse continued to oppose the resolution. He was joined by eighty-three-year-old Alaska Senator Ernest Gruening, an aged liberal New Dealer who opposed the broad grant of power to the president conveyed by the resolution. Greuning had earlier denounced the American efforts in southern Vietnam:

> All Vietnam is not worth the life of an American boy. . . . The United States is seeking vainly in this remote jungle to shore up self-serving corrupt dynasties or their self-imposed successors, and a people that has demonstrated that it has no will to save itself.[42]

Gruening called the resolution "a predated declaration of war." Morse, knowing that the resolution would soon clear the Senate overwhelmingly, told his colleagues that they were in effect giving the president the power to wage war in the absence of a declaration of war.

With only Morse and Gruening dissenting, the Senate approved the resolution, eighty-eight to two. The House passed it unanimously, 416 to 0, after a forty-minute discussion. The news media accepted official versions of the events and editorialized in support of the retaliatory raids. A public opinion poll released on August 10, the same day Johnson signed the resolution, showed that 85 percent of the public supported the air strikes. Johnson's approval ratings in the polls shot up from 42 percent to 72 percent immediately following the retaliatory attacks. All of the indicators denoted a nation that was unified in its support of the attacks on the North Vietnamese.[43] The resolution that Johnson would later use as a Congressional authorization for the Vietnam War had an Orwellian official title: The Joint Resolution to Promote the Maintenance of International Peace and Security in Southeast Asia. It soon became known as the Gulf of Tonkin resolution. The key language in the 300-word document that granted Johnson the constitutional authority he later used to wage a war in Vietnam follows:

> The Congress approves and supports the determination of the President, as Commander-in-Chief, to take all necessary measures to repel any armed attacks against the forces of the United States and to prevent further aggression. . . . The United States is therefore prepared, as the President determines, to take all necessary steps, including the use of armed force, to assist any member or protocol state of the Southeast Asia Collective Defense Treaty requesting assistance in defense of its freedom.[44]

Johnson intended that the reprisal raids and prompt Congressional passage of the resolution serve several political purposes. The Administration sent General Khanh and his South Vietnamese critics a message that America was determined to back his shaky government. At home, by demonstrating that the president could defend U. S. interests in Vietnam without expanding the war, Johnson silenced Republican presidential challenger Arizona Senator Barry Goldwater, who had previously urged the escalation of the war. Goldwater had no choice but to support the air strikes and vote for the resolution. By neutralizing Goldwater, Johnson effectively removed the war issue from the upcoming election campaign. The first Congressional debate on Vietnam had brought "a near-unanimous endorsement of the president's policies and provided him an apparently solid foundation upon which to construct future policy."[45]

Washington also intended that the air raids send Hanoi a message: the United States stood firm in support of its ally, General Khanh. They were also a warning to Ho Chi Minh and his colleagues, that if the North Vietnamese continued to support the southern insurgency, they could expect to lose their fledgling industrial economy to American bombs.

But Hanoi did not react as Johnson and his advisers expected. They read the retaliatory raids as a sign that the United States intended to try to extricate itself from its failed policy in South Vietnam by expanding the war to the North. The men in Hanoi viewed the raids as a prelude to a major American war. They believed that the Americans were preparing to send ground troops to the South and to bomb the North and perhaps to invade North Vietnam as well. Although unhappy about the prospects of a war with the United States that they had hoped to avoid, the Communists leader affirmed their continuing support of the southern insurgency. Pham Van Dong met with Seaborn for a second time on August 10; angry at the American bombings, Dong told Seaborn to tell Johnson that the DRV would fight the United States if war came. Hanoi also decided to send regular combat forces to South Vietnam. Soon, three regiments, about 4,500 men, were on their way to war. These regiments represented the first PAVN regulars to be sent South.[46]

Although they successfully rallied popular support for the reprisal raids, Johnson and McNamara had misled both the Congress and the public. Later, when Senator Fulbright and other Congressional leaders realized they had been deceived, they turned angrily against a war they now believed Johnson and McNamara had tricked them into approving. Fulbright was especially bitter, believing Johnson had deliberately misled him by indicating, at the time the president asked him to run the Gulf of Tonkin resolution through the Senate, that his administration had no intentions of subsequently taking America to war.

The DESOTO missions, aligned with the OPLAN 34-A raids, were provocative to the North Vietnamese, whether their alignment was deliberate or inadvertent. The incident of August 2, when North Vietnamese gunboats attacked the *Maddox*, lasted fifteen to twenty minutes and caused only minimal damage. The August 4 incident may not have occurred; it may have only been imagined by nervous, inexperienced sailors who thought they were being attacked on a moonless and stormy night in the Gulf. In light of these modest realities, the Americans overreacted; the response was excessive. But the Gulf of Tonkin events were timely and served Johnson administration purposes. They provided an opportunity for Washington to demonstrate its resolve in Vietnam and to try to intimidate Hanoi.[47]

The president had also expanded the U. S. commitment in Vietnam to include not only defending South Vietnam, "but also to responding to North Vietnamese provocations."[48] The long-standing barrier against taking the war north of the DMZ had been breached. PIERCE ARROW represented both a culmination and a prologue: it was the capstone of the U. S. policy that limited American involvement in Vietnam to an advisory role that had been in place for a decade; it also foreshadowed the abandonment of that advisory role and the escalations that led to direct intervention in Vietnam.[49] The American response to the Gulf of Tonkin incidents, characterized by official confusion, faulty judgment, and duplicity, was a crucial link in the chain of events that eventually plunged the United States into a full-scale war in Vietnam. With the air raids, followed by Hanoi's decision to send regular troops south, both "the United States and North Vietnam had moved toward the brink of conflict."[50]

Johnson did not, as many Americans later suspected, seek the Congressional resolution as a blank check for bringing the United States into a war to which he had already committed himself after his reelection. In August 1964, Johnson still hoped that the United States could sustain a non-Communist government in southern Vietnam without having to fight an American war in that region. He rejected his advisers' periodic suggestions that he should order more bombings of North Vietnam. He clung to that hope throughout his fall campaign for reelection. Johnson did not want to be a war president. Following his election, he intended to concentrate on implementing that wide range of social legislation that he had earlier labeled the Great Society. He feared that a war would divide Americans and undermine his reform program. But Johnson's hope of avoiding a major war in Vietnam rested on two illusions: that the latest South Vietnamese leader could build a stable government and defeat the Vietcong, and that Hanoi would renounce the August 1945 revolutionary vision of a united Vietnam free of Western influence.[51]

Vietnam was not a prominent issue in the 1964 presidential campaign, in part because of Johnson's politically adroit reaction to the Gulf of Tonkin incidents, but also because public interest in Vietnam was still relatively slight. The news media rarely gave the events of Vietnam extensive coverage in the fall of 1964. The conflict to date had been characterized by relatively small-scale, low-intensity warfare. The American role was limited; costs and casualties were light. Most Americans were relatively uninformed and unconcerned about *la guerre sale* occurring in a small, poor country located in a remote corner of the globe.[52] The 1964 election campaign focused on domestic issues and on the question of which candidate would make the better leader.

The president made few campaign appearances until late September, and when he made speeches, he made only a few references to Vietnam. Johnson hoped these scanty remarks about Vietnam would persuade the American public that he did not intend to expand the U. S. role in Southeast Asia, that he did not seek a wider war. He appeared to commit himself to not sending American combat troops to fight a land war in Asia. At Eufaula, Oklahoma, on September 25, he said,

> We don't want our American boys to do the fighting for Asian boys. We don't want to get involved in a nation with 700 million people and get tied down in a land war in Asia.[53]

At Akron, Ohio, on October 21, he said,

> But we are not about to send American boys nine or ten thousand miles away from home to do what Asian boys ought to be doing for themselves.[54]

These remarks, taken out of context, would appear to be explicit promises by Johnson not to Americanize the Vietnam war. In the years that followed, after America was enmeshed in a controversial war and Johnson had become a controversial leader, these remarks, made during the heat of the 1964 campaign, would provoke bitter accusations that the president had lied to the American people about his intentions in Vietnam in order to achieve his reelection.

But if we read these and other speeches closely, we can discern that Johnson injected qualifiers and other ambiguous remarks into his texts. In his campaign speeches, Johnson also stated that America would not abandon its commitments in Vietnam. He hinted that he might change his mind later about bombing North Vietnam and that he might even send U. S. combat troops.[55] These rhetorical escape hatches represented the efforts of a canny politician who knew that he had obtained the necessary authority from Congress to commit America to war in Vietnam if he determined that he must. Johnson also knew that if the situation in South Vietnam deteriorated further, he might decide that he had to bomb North Vietnam and even send U. S. combat troops. Hence, the escape hatches carefully allowed for those contingencies. At the same time, to ensure his reelection by a landslide margin, Johnson gave his audiences false assurances that he would never take the nation to war in Indochina when he knew that he might have to in the near future. While he did not talk about this possibility during the reelection campaign, he knew that the situation in South Vietnam was deteriorating. He was also involved with the contingency planning by his advisers for bombing North Vietnam and for sending U. S. combat troops to South Vietnam.

Johnson's rhetorical subterfuges worked. He obtained his landslide victory in November, crushing the conservative crusade of Barry Goldwater. The Democrats rolled up their largest Congressional majorities since the glory days of the New Deal and prepared to implement Johnson's Great Society program. But the master manipulator from the banks of the Pedernales River would later pay a high price for the methods that he used to gain his easy political victories in the summer and fall of 1964: Many Americans would later turn against the war, in part because they no longer trusted the man in the White House who appeared to have plotted war while talking peace. He also would have to sacrifice his beloved Great Society on the altar of the Vietnam War and renounce a bid for another term as president of the United States.

ROLLING THUNDER

During the months between the Gulf of Tonkin incidents and Johnson's landslide victory on November 3, 1964, political turmoil prevailed in South Vietnam. The NLF forces continued to take control of more and more of the country. On August 16,

General Khanh, taking advantage of a period of euphoria generated in Saigon by the U. S. retaliatory attacks on North Vietnam, tried to acquire dictatorial powers. Buddhists and students took to the streets to protest this power grab and forced Khanh to back down. In September, Lam Van Phat, an ARVN general who formerly had been a waiter in a Paris restaurant, attempted to overthrow Khanh. Ambassador Taylor intervened in the chaotic South Vietnamese political process to deflect Phat's bid for power. With Taylor's blessing, a countercoup, led by a group of younger officers called the "Young Turks," which included Nguyen Cao Ky, Nguyen Van Thieu, and Nguyen Chanh Thi, restored Khanh to power. In October, the generals selected a civilian, Harvard-educated Tran Van Huong, former mayor of Saigon, as prime minister. General Khanh stepped down to become commander-in-chief of the South Vietnamese armed forces in return for his promise to stay out of politics. Despite his pledge, Khanh and the Young Turks remained the powers behind the new civilian leadership. Huong, when asked at a press conference who the best man was to lead South Vietnam effectively, paused, smiled, and said, "You got me there."[56] Huong's frank response was eloquently expressive of the political confusion prevailing in Saigon and other South Vietnamese cities.

While the political turnstiles were spinning in Saigon during the fall of 1964, the PLAF was escalating the war. On October 11, three Vietcong battalions attacked ARVN forces in the Tay Ninh Province, northeast of the capital city, and they inflicted heavy casualties. On November 1, Vietcong guerrillas attacked Bien Hoa Airport on the outskirts of the capital city. Mortar shells rained down on the airfield, killing four and wounding seventy-two Americans. The VC also destroyed five B-57 bombers and damaged eight other U. S. aircraft. The Vietcong assault on the Bien Hoa Airport amounted to a major shift in guerrilla tactics. For the first time in the developing war, they directly attacked a U. S. military installation. Ambassador Taylor noted the shift in tactics and notified the president. Taylor called the attack "a deliberate act of escalation and a change in the ground rules." He recommended that Johnson should order an appropriate act of reprisal against a DRV target. But Johnson, with the elections still two days away, reacted cautiously. He did not order any retaliatory strikes. Later in the month, the NLF forces mounted their largest offensive of the war to date. In two weeks, two Vietcong regiments occupied most of Binh Dinh, a key populous coastal province and long-time insurgent stronghold.[57] As November 1964 ended, President Johnson and his advisers had to confront a major crisis in Vietnam: the failure of the policy of the same only more that he had inherited from Kennedy.

As 1964 approached its end, the Communists were close to victory in Vietnam for the third time in twenty years. They had been there in August 1945 when the Japanese occupation came to an end, only to have the French return. They got close again in June 1954, following Dien Bien Phu, only to be denied victory by major power diplomacy and American intervention in southern Vietnam. They would be denied victory once again by the U. S. decision to Americanize the war during the first half of 1965. Direct American intervention forced Hanoi "to resort to a higher level of revolutionary war, but it did not substantially resolve the underlying political problems in the GVN or arrest the seemingly inexorable slide of the South toward Communism."[58] Another decade would pass before the Communists would again approach victory. In 1975, there would no longer be anyone able and willing to deny them their long-sought goal.

As the political coherence and military capability of the South Vietnamese government rapidly eroded in late 1964, it was evident to Johnson's advisers that the policies they had been shaping since they had come to office with Kennedy in 1961 had failed. But since their reputations were so closely tied to these policies, it was extremely difficult for them to detach themselves from them and conceive of other policy tracks, such as distancing the United States from the Saigon regime, reducing the American commitment, seeking a negotiated settlement, or even withdrawing and permitting the collapse of South Vietnam. Even if these advisers could have imagined such alternatives, and even if such policies might have been seen as serving the national interest, such proposals would have shown their previous counsels to have been incorrect, and it might have cost some of them their jobs. In addition, by the end of Johnson's first year in office, many of the skeptics who might have tried to warn the president about the futility and dangers of military escalation were no longer in government service. Since Kennedy's death, they had either resigned or Johnson had dismissed them from office. Thus, Johnson heard fewer dissenting voices and was exposed to a narrower range of options than was his predecessor.[59]

As South Vietnam's political crisis deepened, the erroneous assumptions and misperceptions upon which the U. S. advisory policy was based were never seriously questioned or reexamined. Most of Johnson's advisers concluded that the way to rescue a failed policy was by doing more, not less. They called for military escalation, specifically for bombing North Vietnam. They could not be sure that bombing would succeed, but they hoped it might. They preferred escalation to negotiations, withdrawal, or continuing the present policy. Johnson's advisers perceived escalation as the only way to protect the U. S. commitment in which they all had a personal stake.[60]

By the end of November, Johnson's senior advisers had formed a consensus to bomb North Vietnam. According to its various advocates, bombing the DRV could achieve a variety of goals. In their judgment, it would interdict the infiltration of men and material into South Vietnam, boost morale in Saigon, and induce Hanoi to abandon the insurgency in the South by punishing North Vietnam so severely that its leaders would soon understand that they could not hope to support the PLAF, except by incurring unacceptable losses.[61]

There also was a schism among Johnson's advisers about the kind of bombing campaign proposed for North Vietnam. This division pitted the president's civilian advisers against his military advisers. The civilians, led by McNamara and the Assistant Secretary of Defense for International Security Affairs John T. McNaughton, called for a limited air war, for gradually applying air power to North Vietnam.

Starting with a few carefully selected minor targets, this kind of air war was devised to send Hanoi a signal that it must either stop supporting the NLF or face the gradually increasing destruction of its country. The controlling assumption among the gradualists was that at some point the increasing pain inflicted upon the North Vietnamese by the bombing would induce Hanoi to abandon its support of the revolution in South Vietnam rather than see its military facilities, infrastructure industries, and industrial sectors destroyed. Gradualist bombing was designed to give Johnson maximum flexibility; he could increase or decrease the pressure in response to Hanoi's behavior. The gradualist campaign was also perceived as safer; its advocates believed it would not provoke Chinese or Soviet entry into the conflict.[62] It would be a "slow squeeze," designed to save South Vietnam from North Vietnam.

Military advocates of bombing, led by Air Force Chief of Staff General John P. McConnell and Admiral Ulysses S. Grant Sharp, urged Johnson to launch a "fast squeeze" from the beginning. They wanted full-scale air attacks on North Vietnam's military bases, transportation systems, and industrial infrastructures. They argued that only a massive and intense bombing campaign could force Hanoi to the bargaining table on American terms. They believed that only fear of national extinction would force Hanoi to abandon the revolution in South Vietnam.[63]

As Johnson's civilian and military advisers quarreled among themselves about how best to escalate the war, one adviser strongly opposed bombing North Vietnam. George Ball, Undersecretary of State, the number-two man in the State Department, had previously studied the effects of strategic bombing on Germany during World War II and knew its limitations. Ball did not believe bombing would either weaken North Vietnam's war-making ability or demoralize its population. He had also served in the French embassy during the Franco-Vietminh War and understood the nature of the political-military struggle in Vietnam. He doubted that bombing North Vietnam was the proper counter to Hanoi-supported revolution in South Vietnam. He also doubted that bombing North Vietnam could raise morale in South Vietnam. Strategic bombing could not, in Ball's view, accomplish its political objectives in Vietnam.

Ball raised some challenging questions: Suppose, he asked, that Hanoi stopped supporting the NLF. Could the ARVN forces, given the current disarray in Saigon, defeat them, even if the Vietcong had to go it alone? He pointed to the risks entailed by bombing: Suppose, in retaliation for the bombing, the North Vietnamese invaded South Vietnam in force? The United States would either have to send its armies or accept a Communist victory. No matter how it was done, gradually or all-out from the start, he warned Johnson that bombing could bring the Chinese and the Soviets into the war; it could also heal the rift between the two major Communist powers. Most important, Ball warned Johnson that once he started down the escalatory road, the United States would not be able to control events. Ball also told Johnson that as wars expand, they tend to outpace the ability of leaders to control them. He suggested that negotiations, with all of their risks, including their leading to a neutral government in the South and an American departure, better served the national interest than any scenario likely to come from bombing. For Ball, the wiser course for Washington to take, however painful it might appear to Johnson's hawkish advisers, was to seek a political solution and get out of Vietnam.[64]

Ball made no headway either with Johnson or his other advisers. While conceding that bombing might not work, Johnson and his advisers discounted all of Ball's arguments and warnings. Rejecting withdrawal or negotiations, they insisted that bombing was necessary to avert a complete collapse in Saigon; "The administration turned to air power as the only acceptable solution to an urgent problem."[65] Johnson's civilian advisers also prevailed over the military proponents of all-out bombing. On November 27, 1964, an interagency Working Group of the National Security Council, headed by William Bundy, developed a gradualist bombing campaign to be implemented in two stages. Phase one, which would last for thirty days, called for air strikes along the major infiltration routes in eastern Laos and for reprisal strikes against North Vietnam in response to NLF attacks on U. S. installations or personnel. While phase one bombings were being carried out, Ambassador Taylor would try to get South Vietnam's squabbling politicians to resolve their differences. Once Saigon's politics were stabilized, phase two would kick in: it would be a systematic aerial war of rising intensity carried out against North Vietnamese military targets that would last for several months or until Hanoi abandoned the insurgency in southern Vietnam.[66]

Johnson delayed implementing phase one bombing mainly because of the persisting political instability in South Vietnam. He told his advisers that he would not order any bombing of North Vietnam until the South Vietnamese politicians had put their political house in order and were able to carry on the war against the insurgents. Johnson's reluctance to order the bombing reflected his lack of confidence in the shaky Saigon government. Why should Americans take the war north if the RVN was on the verge of collapse or about to be taken over by a coalition of neutralists? Why should Americans fight for an unstable, unpopular, and unrepresentative regime whose own armed forces appeared unwilling to defend it with any enthusiasm or conviction? Perhaps Johnson's hesitation was also a sign of Ball's influence, perhaps a yearning for a way out of the Vietnamese quagmire with honor and minimal political damage at home and abroad?

Ambassador Taylor conveyed Johnson's concerns to the top echelons of Saigon's military and civilian leadership: There would be no bombing of North Vietnamese targets until South Vietnam had a stable government. Some of the generals apparently did not receive or understand Taylor's message, because in mid-December Air Marshal Nguyen Cao Ky and General Nguyen Chanh Thi made a bid for power that amounted to another coup attempt. President Johnson, informed that yet other coup was underway in Saigon, angrily exclaimed,

> I don't want to hear anything more about this coup shit! I've had enough of it, and we've got to find a way to stabilize those people out there![67]

Taylor, furious at Ky's and Thi's blatant display of political irresponsibility in the face of imminent danger, gave the South Vietnamese generals a traditional Army-style chewing out,

> I made it clear that all the military plans which I know you would like to carry out are dependent on government stability. Now you have made a real mess. We cannot carry you forever if you do things like this. . . . You people have broken a lot of dishes and now we have to see how we can straighten out this mess.[68]

The South Vietnamese generals were both humiliated and infuriated by Taylor's tactless and condescending reproach, although he did persuade them to support Huong's government. Meanwhile, the Buddhists, sensing the war-weariness and desires for a negotiated settlement among many segments of the population, launched a new wave of protests, including more immolations by fire. The Buddhists also called for Ambassador Taylor to resign. In Hue, riotous students attacked the U. S. Information Service Library.[69] The protests had taken on a distinctly anti-American as well as an anti-government cast. American officials once more feared that a government that would be willing to negotiate with the NLF and favor the expulsion of Americans might arise from the chaos that had become the political norm in Saigon. General Khanh fed these fears by making overtures to some of the Buddhist factions and parroting some of their anti-American sentiments. The CIA reported that Khanh also made contact with NLF elements, further alarming his American patrons, who had become increasingly skeptical of both his reliability and competence.

While confusion reigned in the streets of Saigon, Vietcong forces continued their terrorist attacks on American installations and inflicted a series of defeats on ARVN forces. On Christmas Eve 1964, the Vietcong bombed the Brinks Hotel in downtown Saigon in which U. S. officers were billeted. Two officers were killed and dozens were injured by the blasts. On New Year's Day, at Binh Gia, about forty miles southeast of Saigon, two of ARVN's elite units, a Ranger battalion and a Marine battalion, were chewed up by forces of the Vietcong 9th Division, the first PLAF main force unit to reach divisional size.[70] At Binh Gia, there were 445 South Vietnamese and sixteen American casualties against only thirty-two confirmed VC casualties.[71] On January 6, 1965, Ambassador Taylor sent an extremely pessimistic assessment of the situation in South Vietnam to President Johnson. To Taylor, the Saigon government was growing weaker day by day. He feared that a political collapse was imminent and that a neutralist government reflecting a Khanh-Buddhist alliance could come to power in Saigon that would negotiate with the NLF unless a bombing campaign were implemented immediately.[72]

For more than a year, Hanoi had been pursuing a strategy in southern Vietnam designed to win the war in the countryside, foment popular uprisings in the cities, and bring down the struggling South Vietnamese government. They intended to supplant the RVN with a coalition dominated by the National Liberation Front that would adopt a neutralist stance internationally, tell the Americans to get out of Vietnam, and seek a peaceful reunion with the North. In early 1965, it appeared to the Communist leadership that they were close to achieving their goals. Political chaos reigned in Saigon, and the ARVN forces were increasingly demoralized and ineffective. Since Johnson authorized the retaliatory air strikes in early August following the Gulf of Tonkin incidents, he had been restrained, unwilling to order further air raids for any of the Vietcong attacks, even attacks on American installations and advisers. American restraint encouraged Hanoi's leaders to believe that they might be able to achieve their objectives without a major war with the Americans, that Johnson would adhere to the campaign pledges he made during the recent presidential campaign in which he appeared to promise the American people that he sought no wider war in Vietnam.

But Johnson's advisers, including Taylor, in a classic inversion of logic, now argued that the reason for delaying the bombing, Saigon's chronic political instability, had become the main reason for implementing it immediately! Bombing might not win the war but it could fend off political collapse in southern Vietnam. George Ball has commented sardonically on his colleagues' reasoning processes:

> I was not surprised when my colleagues interpreted the crumbling of the South Vietnamese government, the Vietcong's increasing success, and a series of defeats of South Vietnamese units not as proving that we should cut our losses and get out, but rather that we must promptly begin bombing to stiffen the resolve of the corrupt South Vietnamese government. It was classical bureaucratic casuistry. A faulty rationalization was improvised to obscure the painful reality that America could arrest the galloping deterioration of its position only by the surgery of extrication: We must, they argued, commit our power and prestige ever more intensely to stop the South Vietnamese government from falling completely apart, negotiating covertly with the Liberation Front or Hanoi, and ultimately asking us to leave. It was Catch-22 and the quintessence of black humor.[73]

Despite the mounting pressure being applied by both his civilian and military advisers, Johnson continued to delay implementing the bombing campaign against North Vietnam. Guided by his political intuitions, he was not convinced that it should be undertaken as long as the South Vietnamese political situation remained so unstable and unpromising. However, Pleiku changed Johnson's mind. Early on the morning of February 7, 1965, the Vietcong attacked a U. S. airfield at Pleiku and a nearby helicopter base at Camp Holloway in the central highlands. The VC inflicted heavy casualties. They killed nine and wounded 137 Americans.[74] Twenty-two helicopters and fixed-wing aircraft were destroyed or damaged during the insurgent assault. Within a matter of hours, Johnson had ordered the JCS to implement FLAMING DART, a series of reprisal air strikes against preselected North Vietnamese targets. For two days, naval and South Vietnamese aircraft flew retaliatory strikes against DRV sites, just north of the DMZ in North Vietnam.

Undeterred by the air strikes, the Vietcong struck again on February 10. They attacked a hotel that housed members of the 140th Maintenance Detachment, an Army aircraft repair unit, at Qui Nhon, a coastal city eighty-five miles east of Pleiku. After the assaults, rescuers pulled twenty-three bodies and twenty-one wounded soldiers from the rubble.[75] Again, Johnson retaliated, this time with heavier air strikes against military targets in North Vietnam. This time Washington did not characterize the air strikes as tit-for-tat reprisals, but called them generalized responses to a continuing pattern of aggressive acts. "The administration had moved from reprisals to a continuing, graduated program of air attacks against North Vietnam."[76]

McGeorge Bundy, who was visiting Vietnam at the time of the Pleiku attack, wrote Johnson a long memo calling for the implementation of sustained bombing. Bundy asserted that if a systematic bombing campaign were not undertaken, the South Vietnamese cause would be lost within six months to a year and the Communists would control all of Vietnam. He admitted that the bombing campaign might fail, but Washington had to try it in order to preserve its credibility as a great power in world affairs. Johnson found Bundy's arguments persuasive. On February 13, Johnson authorized ROLLING THUNDER, a systematic, gradually expanding bombing campaign using both American and VNAF aircraft to strike at North Vietnamese targets.

Figure 5.2   The establishment dove: George Ball, shown here being sworn in by Chief Justice Earl Warren as the U. S. ambassador to the UN, had been a senior adviser to both President Kennedy and President Johnson. Ball consistently opposed Americanizing the Vietnam War. *Source:* National Archives

It began on March 2, ten months after the Joint Chiefs had recommended to the President that he initiate a gradually expanding air war against North Vietnam to force them to abandon their support of the southern insurgency.[77] ROLLING THUNDER represented a major U. S. escalation of the expanding war.

But Pleiku served more as a pretext than as a cause.[78] Ultimately, Johnson's change of heart occurred because his advisers had finally convinced him that if the bombing campaign were not undertaken, the GVN would simply collapse. Johnson conceded that taking the war north could provide the Saigon government with a reprieve and give it a chance to stabilize itself. Beginning with sporadic strikes against minor targets just north of the DMZ, Johnson gradually expanded the air war against North Vietnam until it became a systematic, large-scale effort that struck major targets all over the country. ROLLING THUNDER, the U. S. and VNAF air war against North Vietnam, had begun. It would continue, with occasional bombing halts, for over three years. In time, it would become the largest campaign in the history of aerial warfare.

As Washington made its decisions to initiate an air war against North Vietnam, the political sands in Saigon shifted once again. On February 14, General Khanh appointed Phan Huy Quat, a physician, as prime minister. Quat quickly selected a new cabinet that included four other doctors. American officials soon dubbed Quat's government the "medicine cabinet." A few days after the medicine cabinet took office, another coup attempt erupted, led by Colonel Pham Ngoc Thao and General Lam Van Phat, who had been the instigator of the failed coup attempt in September 1964. They intended to oust General Khanh from his position as commander of the ARVN. But Air Marshal Ky used his control of the Air Force to disperse the coup forces. Both Thao and Phat quickly disappeared from public view.

But Marshal Ky and General Thieu, the leaders of the "Young Turks," hitherto aligned with Khanh, then convened a meeting of the Armed Forces Council. The Council voted to remove Khanh from his position as commander-in-chief of ARVN and to affirm its support for Quat and his medicine cabinet. Khanh tried to rally ARVN generals to his support, but he failed. Colonel Wilson, who had helped Khanh come to power thirteen months earlier and whom Khanh trusted, persuaded him to resign and leave the country. The Young Turks, who wanted to depose Khanh because of his growing alliance with the Buddhists and his efforts to establish contacts with NLF elements, brought Khanh's erratic one-year reign to an end.

Ambassador Taylor, who had backed the Young Turks, had also wanted to be rid of Khanh because he was skeptical that a Khanh-controlled government could be relied on to support the air war against North Vietnam. Ambassador Taylor feared that Khanh might seek a neutralist alternative to continuing the war.[79] General Westmoreland, the MAC-V commander who also backed the coup, believed that Ky and Thieu had staged a mock coup in order to depose Khanh: a farce to humiliate Khanh and show the other generals that he no longer had control of the South Vietnamese army.[80] Khanh's departure cleared the way for the Young Turks, who, with

American blessings, would soon become the military rulers of South Vietnam. After a long period of turmoil and chaos, Washington believed that a government was finally emerging in Saigon that would follow American advice and enthusiastically support the widening American war.

DAHLIAS AND GLADIOLI

When ROLLING THUNDER began, administration officials confidently expected that it would quickly bring Hanoi to its senses. It would take only a few weeks, at most a few months, of bombing before the North Vietnamese Communists abandoned the southern insurgents. Ho Chi Minh and his associates, awed by the power and destructive potential of America's arsenal of high-tech air weapons systems, would quickly capitulate rather than risk losing their industrial and transportation infrastructures. But the high hopes of the Americans in the efficacy of their aerial campaign were soon dashed. The air war quickly proved ineffective. ROLLING THUNDER achieved none of its expected goals. Its failure rebutted the predictions of Johnson's senior advisers that a gradualist bombing campaign against North Vietnam would save the GVN from impending military defeat and political collapse. It failed to bring Hanoi to the bargaining table on American terms. Supplies from North Vietnam for the PLAF continued to pour into many parts of South Vietnam. A State Department Intelligence Note on the effects of bombing found that the air strikes had not diminished the morale of the North Vietnamese people. In fact, State Department analysts found that the U. S. bombing had increased North Vietnamese resolve and enabled the North Vietnamese leaders to tighten their control over the populace.[81] Bombing North Vietnam also failed to bolster morale in South Vietnam, failed to halt the entropic tendencies of Saigon politics, and failed to grant a reprieve to the GVN from the steadily increasing NLF military and political offensives. "The military and political fabric of the southern regime continued to unravel even more rapidly than before."[82]

President Johnson had hoped that bombing North Vietnam would obviate the sending of American combat forces into South Vietnam, but the restrained manner in which he implemented the air war against North Vietnam ensured that it could not. Gradually taking the war to North Vietnam increased rather than decreased the pressures on Washington to send troops into South Vietnam. Soon after the bombing campaign had begun, Johnson's advisers pressed him to move to the second escalatory stage, sending in U. S. combat forces. The troops were needed to protect U. S. air bases in South Vietnam from NLF attacks. More ominously, bombing had also provoked the introduction of additional PAVN forces into South Vietnam.[83]

> ROLLING THUNDER was a fateful U. S. decision in Vietnam primarily because it brought about what its opponents feared, massive ground retaliation by the North Vietnamese, without bringing about what its proponents sought, the DRV to the conference table on terms then acceptable by the U. S.[84]

There is a direct linkage between the gradually expanding bombing campaign against North Vietnam and Washington's decision to send the first American combat troops to South Vietnam. General Westmoreland, fearing PLAF attacks against the large American air base at Danang, which was essential for conducting the air war, requested two battalions of Marines to provide ground security for that facility.[85] The MACV commander had no faith in ARVN forces that had been assigned to protect the air field.

Ambassador Taylor initially opposed Westmoreland's request for troops on several grounds. Citing the French experience, Taylor questioned whether American troops could fight a guerrilla war successfully in Southeast Asian jungles. He also believed that the introduction of U. S. combatants would tempt the ARVN commanders to unload more of the burden of the fighting onto the Americans. He could foresee American combatants taking full responsibility for the war "amid a population grown as hostile to [the] American presence as it had been to the French."[86] Most of all, Taylor worried that the introduction of even a small contingent of U. S. combat forces with a specific and limited mission would remove an important limit on U. S. involvement in South Vietnam, a limit that U. S. officials had observed since the beginning of the Indochina wars. It would be a foot in the door to an ever-widening commitment, and once that first step was taken, it would be very difficult to hold the line.[87]

Washington ignored Taylor's prophetic objections; Johnson promptly approved General Westmoreland's request for security forces that had previously been endorsed by Admiral Sharp, the man in charge of the air war and Westmoreland's immediate superior in the chain of command. Johnson's crucial decision to send American ground combat forces to South Vietnam was made without much deliberation, planning, or thought about its possible consequences.

The landing of American troops that transformed the Vietnam War and the U. S. role in it occurred on the morning of March 8, 1965, at a beach south of Danang. At 9:03 A.M., Marine Corporal Garry Powers leaped from his amphibian landing craft, waded through ankle-deep water, and jogged up the wet sand. He was the first of the more than 2.7 million young men and women who would serve in South Vietnam over the next seven years. As wave after wave of Marines streamed ashore in full battle gear that warm spring morning, they encountered throngs of pretty Vietnamese girls who placed leis of yellow dahlias and red gladioli around their necks. The mayor of Danang made a welcoming speech celebrating the festive occasion. Overhead, helicopter gunships searched for Vietcong snipers in the nearby jungle-covered hills.[88]

Just as Taylor had predicted, a few weeks after the Danang landings, military commanders were urging Johnson to take the next step. Westmoreland, fearing security threats to other U. S. military installations and disturbed by intelligence reports that the NLF planned "to seize a large sector of the Central Highlands, there to establish a government to challenge Saigon's, and drive eastward to the coast to cut South Vietnam in two," asked Washington for two Army divisions, one to deploy in the highlands, the other to send to the Saigon area.[89] Admiral Sharp, Army Chief of Staff Harold Johnson, and other members of the JCS, impatient with what they viewed to be Johnson's too-cautious approach to the war, all aggressively endorsed General Westmoreland's request.

President Johnson had come face to face with the dilemma that his predecessors who had previously involved the United States in Vietnam—Truman, Eisenhower, and Kennedy—had all managed to evade: either accept the collapse of the South Vietnamese government and the defeat of the American cause or send large numbers of U. S. combat forces into that country. He had arrived at the crunch point. Johnson and his advisers had trapped themselves. They had ruled out the options of withdrawal, negotiations, or an all-out air war against North Vietnam. Knowing that the gradualist air war was not producing the desired results, nor was it likely to do so any time soon, Johnson and his advisers knew that if they did not send combat forces quickly, the GVN would probably go under before year's end. Having convinced themselves that defeat for the South Vietnamese regime would result in unacceptable diplomatic disasters for America and would activate a vicious right-wing political assault on their liberal Democratic administration at home, Johnson and his men could only accept the ineluctable logic of their policy formulations and agree to send more combat forces, albeit fewer than the military leadership wanted.

On March 29, a gray Renault sedan stalled on Saigon's Vo Di Nguy, a street running alongside the American embassy. Within minutes, 300 pounds of plastic explosives packed in the trunk of the car erupted into a giant fireball. The powerful blast extensively damaged the embassy. It killed twenty and injured over 100 people, who were either working in the embassy, were passersby, or were dining in restaurants across the street from the American headquarters. As dazed and bleeding embassy staff members stumbled out of the wrecked building, only to encounter the litter of bodies in the street, Saigon police shot and killed the Vietcong terrorist who had deliberately stalled the explosives-laden car near the embassy.[90]

Two days later, President Johnson met with members of the National Security Council to review U. S. Vietnam policies. On April 2, he made a series of decisions that moved America closer to war: 20,000 additional troops would be sent to Vietnam and the air war against the North would be expanded. A major effort to create a multilateral force to intervene in South Vietnam would be mounted. South Korea, Australia, and New Zealand would be asked to send troops to Vietnam. Most important, additional Marine combat units would be deployed in the vicinity of Danang, and their mission would be expanded to include offensive operations against Vietcong forces within a fifty-mile radius of the Marine bases.[91] The Marine mission had made a crucial transition—from static defense to offensive mobile operations.

On April 6, 1965, with Taylor's reluctant approval, McGeorge Bundy issued NSAM 328, implementing Johnson's decisions. On that date, there were about 27,000 American troops in South Vietnam, most of them noncombatants. Within a few weeks, thousands of combat troops would be pouring "in country." Confronted with a choice,

Figure 5.3 U. S. Marines storm ashore on March 8, 1965, at Da Nang Beach in South Viet Nam. They were the first of more than 2.7 million young men and women who would serve in South Vietnam over the next seven years. The Marines landed in Viet Nam to strengthen the defenses of Da Nang Air Base against communist forces. *Source:* AP/Wide World Photos

as he put it in his own words, "of running in or running out of Vietnam," Johnson chose to run in. While he expanded the American military presence and changed its mission from advice and static defense to limited offensive operations against the NLF forces, Johnson chose not to inform the American people of those important moves. At a press conference, he stated, "I know of no far-reaching strategy that is being suggested or promulgated."[92]

As the air war against North Vietnam expanded and the first ground combat troops were being sent into South Vietnam, public opinion polls showed that a large majority of Americans supported the continuing U. S. efforts in Vietnam.[93] Johnson's continual escalations drew broad popular support; influential media editorials all supported the President's actions. But it was also during the spring of 1965 that vocal critics of Johnson's war policies surfaced: not only those who criticized him for doing too much, but those who attacked him for not doing enough. The words "hawk" and "dove" entered the growing public discourse on the war. The words were not precise descriptive terms, but they identified the two emerging strands of public opinion critical of the administration's war policies. Hawks favored a stronger military effort, an all-out airwar and the sending of more U. S. combat forces. Doves called for an end to the bombing of North Vietnam and opposed the sending of American combat forces to South Vietnam. Many doves also wanted a negotiated settlement of the conflict, followed by U. S. withdrawal.

The first vocal opposition to the war appeared on university campuses. Professors at the University of Michigan, Harvard, and the University of California at Berkeley staged "teach-ins," featuring speakers who condemned Washington's war policies. Academics opposed to the war staged a national teach-in modeled on those held on university campuses: Telephones linked 122 colleges to a national debate on the war staged at the Sheraton Hotel in Washington, D. C. The highlight of the national teach-in was a debate between Professor Robert Scalapino, a political scientist from the University of California (UC), Berkeley, who defended U. S. policy in Vietnam, and George Kahin, director of Southeast Asian studies at Cornell, who mounted a dovish critique of that policy.[94] On April 17, a New Left group, the Students for a Democratic Society (SDS), organized the first antiwar protest march; about 15,000 people, mostly college students, gathered in the nation's capital to demonstrate their opposition to the developing war in Vietnam.

Aware of the developing hawkish and dovish criticisms of his Vietnam policies, President Johnson, on the evening of April 7, delivered a major speech at Johns Hopkins University in which he reaffirmed the American commitment to South Vietnam. Johnson attempted to silence his critics on both the Left and the Right. He tried to appear tough enough to satisfy the hawks, but soft enough to give the doves hope. He told the American people, "We are there because we have promises to keep. . . ," "We are also there to strengthen world order. . . ," and "We are there because there are great stakes in the balance. . . ." He forcibly stated that the United States would remain in Vietnam as long as it was necessary to protect

South Vietnam and that he would use whatever force was necessary to repel aggression. But he also stated that the United States remained ready for "unconditional discussions" if they would lead to a peaceful settlement. Johnson's talk of his readiness for unconditional negotiations was mostly rhetoric, a public relations gesture. Neither he nor his advisers had given any thought to the form or substance of such talks if they had occurred. The President added that when the war was over and South Vietnam could live in peace without fear of aggression from North Vietnam, America would sponsor a billion-dollar developmental program for the Mekong River Valley, a kind of TVA for Southeast Asia that would include North Vietnam.[95] In his speech, Johnson was trying not only to persuade Americans to support his Vietnam policies, but to find the right mix of sticks and carrots that would persuade Ho Chi Minh to settle on U. S. terms. Concerning Johnson's offer of developmental funds to the North Vietnamese, Presidential Aide William Moyers later said, "If Ho Chi Minh had been George Meany, Lyndon Johnson would have had a deal."[96]

The public responded favorably to the president's speech at Johns Hopkins. Reactions in Congress were mostly supportive. Media editorializing was generally enthusiastic. The thousands of letters and telegrams sent to the White House ran five-to-one in favor of the president. But his words failed to satisfy or silence most hawks or doves. Soon after the speech, the term "credibility gap" appeared in the media to describe the skepticism voiced by some journalists and politicians over whether the Johnson administration was being entirely candid about its present Vietnam policies.[97]

On April 8, unexpectedly responding to Johnson's offer of unconditional discussions put forth in the Johns Hopkins speech, North Vietnam's premier, Pham Van Dong, offered Hanoi's basis for negotiations. It consisted of four points: (1) The United States would have to accept the 1954 Geneva Accords: stop all acts of war against North Vietnam and withdraw all of its forces from South Vietnam, (2) Until Vietnam was reunified, the Geneva Agreements must be strictly observed; that meant no alliances with any foreign power for either zone, no foreign bases, and no foreign military personnel in either zone, (3) The internal affairs of South Vietnam must be settled in accordance with the program of the NLF, and (4) the peaceful reunification of Vietnam would be achieved by the people of both zones without any foreign interference.[98] This four-point program would remain Hanoi's basic negotiating position for the next three years.

Washington regarded Hanoi's terms as unacceptable. Johnson and his advisers were especially concerned about point 3, which they understood as calling for a NLF takeover of the South Vietnamese government. Notwithstanding their rejection of specific DRV proposals, it is doubtful that the Johnson administration was seriously interested in a negotiated settlement of the conflict in April 1965. Washington feared that the South Vietnamese government was too weak militarily and politically to risk a negotiated settlement, although for political reasons they knew they had to appear to want a settlement. Johnson understood that if two-thirds of the American population supported his Vietnam policies in the spring of 1965, two-thirds also favored a negotiated settlement of the war. But at that time, Johnson intended to apply more military power in hopes of strengthening the position of the GVN to a point at which future negotiations could promise a settlement on terms acceptable to Washington. In the meantime, Washington sought to buy time. A short bombing pause from May 13 to May 18 did not elicit any reduction in PLAF activity, nor did it entice Hanoi into modifying its negotiating stance. But it defused some of Johnson's domestic critics, who accused Washington of not wanting negotiations, which may have been its main purpose.

Hanoi was probably not serious about negotiations either in April 1965; it probably did not anticipate Washington's accepting its four-point program as a basis for negotiations any time soon. The North Vietnamese leaders were proposing terms more to improve relations with the Soviet Union, who had endorsed the four-point peace program and whose economic and military assistance would be crucial in a protracted war with the United States, than to settle the conflict in Vietnam. Washington and Hanoi had reached a diplomatic impasse; both sides, regardless of what they said for political and public relations purposes, made non-negotiable demands that each knew were unacceptable to the other: The United States would not compromise on its insistence that an independent non-Communist South Vietnamese state be allowed to exist in the southern part of Vietnam. Hanoi would not compromise its goal of a NLF-dominated coalition government taking over in South Vietnam, which they believed would lead inevitably to the peaceful reunification of Vietnam under Communist control. By summer, both sides had abandoned their diplomatic sparring and were going after each other on the battlefield.[99]

On April 20, McNamara, Taylor, the Joint Chiefs, and other high-ranking American officials met in Honolulu to chart the next phase of the American military buildup in South Vietnam. Since Washington had agreed to send some combat forces to South Vietnam, Taylor had opposed increasing their numbers and had been trying to confine those troops "in country" to security patrols in the immediate vicinity of coastal air bases. General Westmoreland's staff challenged Taylor's enclave concept. They asserted that his enclave strategy represented "an inglorious static use of U. S. forces in overpopulated areas with little chance of direct or immediate impact on the outcome of events."[100]

In Honolulu, Westmoreland, backed by the Joint Chiefs, requested seventeen additional Army maneuver battalions, specifically, the 173rd Airborne Brigade, and all necessary support forces; he also wanted authorization to deploy them in unrestricted offensive operations. With McNamara leading the way, the conferees worked out a compromise. Taylor abandoned his opposition to further combat deployments. Westmoreland got his infantry battalions plus an additional 40,000 troops, including 7,000 "Third Country" forces from South Korea and Australia. But the MACV commander accepted Taylor's proposal that the troops would be assigned to four enclaves that would be established at Chu Lai, Qui Nhon, Quang Ngai, and Bien Hoa.[101] The next day, President Johnson approved the troop increases and their assignment to the four enclaves. Altogether, an additional 82,000 soldiers were ordered to join the 33,500 already serving in South Vietnam. The Honolulu decisions, although they did not meet all of the military's operational demands, significantly increased the number of U. S. combat troops in South Vietnam and "marked a major step toward a large-scale involvement in the ground war."[102]

As the Johnson administration made the decisions that brought America closer to war in the spring of 1965, Washington responded to a crisis in the Dominican Republic, a small and poor Caribbean nation with a long history of U. S. domination. In late April, Johnson, told that pro-Castro elements had infiltrated a revolutionary movement making a bid for power in the Dominican Republic, sent 23,000 U. S. Marines and Army infantrymen to suppress the revolt. U. S. forces blocked the rebellion and succeeded in stabilizing the politics of the country. The explanation Johnson gave to the American people for the military intervention was to protect American lives that were endangered by the uprising. The Organization of American States (OAS) later sent a peace-keeping force and U. S. forces were withdrawn. Elections were held in the Dominican Republic in 1966, and a moderate-conservative government came to power that protected U. S. strategic and economic interests in that country. Washington was satisfied that the Dominican Republic was not going to become another Cuba.

Polls taken at the time of the intervention showed that public opinion strongly supported the U. S. military incursion, although liberals and foreign critics denounced the intervention that violated the charter of the OAS and abrogated the long-standing U. S. pledge to refrain from direct military intervention into any Latin American country. The Dominican campaign was limited in duration, and only twenty-six American lives were lost (about 3,000 Dominicans died during the fighting). Success in the Dominican operation probably encouraged Johnson to try more of the same in Vietnam, and he assumed that similar success there would ultimately silence any domestic or foreign detractors who might protest his policies. He ignored the implications of the liberal protests; he did not see them as possible harbingers of opposition to his escalatory Vietnam policies.[103]

On May 4, Johnson asked Congress for $700 million to support the American military operations in Vietnam. Johnson made it clear to the lawmakers that he would regard a vote for the money as an endorsement of his Vietnam policies. Even though Johnson's evasive and ambiguous rhetoric made it difficult for many legislators to understand just what Johnson's Vietnam policies were at this time or what his future intentions might be, they could not vote against funding for American boys already in the field. Both houses approved the appropriation quickly, without debate. Johnson would later insist that this vote and the Gulf of Tonkin resolution refuted dovish critics who claimed that he never gave Congress a chance to pass judgment on his Vietnam policies.[104]

In South Vietnam, despite the bombing, increased U. S. aid, and the introduction of U. S. combat forces, ARVN forces verged on disintegration. Desertion and draft avoidance rates were high. The politicized ARVN officer corps had virtually given fighting the war over to the Americans and were concentrating on doing what they did best—engaging in constant political intrigue and using their military positions to enrich themselves. The PLAF forces, strengthened by the addition of PAVN regulars now fighting in South Vietnam, went on the offensive. In the Phuoc Long Province, northwest of Saigon, VC regiments attacked a Special Forces camp at Dong Xoai and also attacked Song Be, the provincial capital. At Ba Gia, in the coastal province of Quang Ngai, another VC regiment destroyed two ARVN battalions. In the central highlands, NLF forces overran several district towns and besieged a Special Forces camp at Duc Co, a remote site in the Pleiku Province. With ARVN losses running high and its military organization nearing collapse, General Westmoreland concluded that only the rapid, large-scale introduction of U. S. combat forces could avert defeat.[105]

If the South Vietnamese military situation was bad, its political condition was worse. The fifth Saigon government within a year came to power when the Young Turks overthrew the "medicine cabinet" of Phan Huy Quat in early June. Taylor and Westmoreland were pleased to see Quat go. His supporters included a faction of Buddhist monks who wanted to end the war. Quat also opposed the introduction of large-scale U. S. combat forces into his country. The new government was headed by a military directorate of ten senior ARVN officers led by a triumvirate: Air Marshal Ky, General Thieu, and General Nguyen Chanh Thi. All were pro-American and all favored Americanizing the war. Ky became prime minister and Thieu became head of the military forces.[106]

Logically, the Ky government represented the *reductio ad absurdum* of the South Vietnamese political process. The regime was hardly a government at all; it was a committee of generals who did not represent any South Vietnamese groups in the political sense. Having no political base and with much of its armed forces incapable of fighting, the new government could survive only with massive American economic, diplomatic, and military support. In the name of self-determination and to ensure the continuation of the war against the NLF and the PAVN forces in South Vietnam, Washington supported a political facade in Saigon that was devoid of any meaningful popular support, and to survive in power, was forced to surrender control of its war to American officials.

DECISIONS FOR WAR

In early June, Westmoreland and the JCS requested an additional 150,000 troops. They also called for abandoning the modified enclave strategy and supplanting it with an offensive strategy. They warned that anything less than a rapid, large-scale commitment of U. S. forces with the freedom to fight aggressively risked imminent defeat in South Vietnam. Among Johnson's senior civilian advisers, only George Ball opposed a major commitment of U. S. ground combat forces to Vietnam. Ball continued to press for disengagement, but he was outnumbered and outranked. In mid-July, Robert

McNamara, after another of his many trips to Saigon, confirmed the military leaders' warnings that a failure to act decisively would probably mean defeat for the GVN within a few months. He also told Johnson that vigorous U. S. involvement in the war could avoid defeat in the short run and produce victory in the long run. McNamara recommended sending an additional forty-four battalions, which would bring the total U. S. force level in Vietnam to 179,000 by year's end.[107] McNamara's recommendations triggered a week of intensive discussions among the President and his advisers, stretching from July 21 to July 28, during which

> Johnson made his fateful decisions, setting the United States on a course from which it would not deviate for nearly three years and opening the way for seven years of bloody warfare in Vietnam.[108]

Although he made the momentous decisions that Americanized the Vietnam War, that transformed both the character of the conflict and the U. S. role in it, Johnson rejected the military's call for an all-out air war, mainly because he feared it would provoke Chinese military intervention as it had happened in Korea. He committed 175,000 (later raised to 220,000) combat troops to South Vietnam. Johnson also granted Westmoreland the authority to commit American troops to combat in any situation where the MACV commander deemed their use necessary to strengthen the GVN forces.

Still another important threshold had been crossed. A new course had been set, the end of which was not in sight. The decision to build up and use American combat forces amounted to an open-ended commitment to defend South Vietnam. The amount of force required and the length of time needed to defeat the enemy would depend on Hanoi's response to the U. S. buildup and the Communists' willingness to raise their own stake in the war's outcome. Johnson, without fully realizing it, had committed his country to a war of indeterminate size and duration.[109]

These presidential decisions, most strongly influenced by McNamara's memos and the Secretary of Defense's oral arguments made in the sequence of discussions held over several days in late July, are among the most important decisions ever made during the long history of U. S. involvement in Southeast Asia. During the last week of July 1965, the president decided that American boys would henceforth have to do what Johnson, during his presidential campaign in 1964, had told his fellow citizens that he believed only Asian boys should do for themselves: they would fight a land war in Southeast Asia. These July decisions, the nearest thing to a formal decision for war in Vietnam, represented the culmination of a year and a half of debate and indecision over America's Vietnam policy. They derived ultimately from Johnson's persistent refusal to even consider the possibility of cutting U. S. losses and withdrawing from Vietnam.

Chairman of the Joint Chiefs Earle Wheeler urged President Johnson to put the nation on a war footing by calling the Reserves and National Guard to active duty. The president refused to mobilize the Reserves and National Guard because he feared that such an act might precipitate a divisive Congressional debate that would undermine the coalitions he was forming to enact Great Society legislation. McNamara, the *primus inter pares* among Johnson's senior advisers, urged him to declare a state of national emergency, seek a tax raise, and place the July decisions squarely before the American people. Johnson refused to take any of these actions because he did not want to alarm the major Communist powers, threaten his domestic reform agenda, and stir the passions of the American people. He chose to take the nation to war by stealth, without calling attention to his actions.[110]

Johnson's failure to seek a declaration of war from Congress, to tell the American people plainly that the United States was going to war against both North Vietnam and the National Liberation Front that it controlled, and his failure to mobilize the Reserves and National Guard limited the American war effort and hastened the rise of opposition to the conflict among the public and within the halls of Congress. Johnson decided to fight the Vietnam War on the sly, to avoid raising taxes, and to use the Gulf of Tonkin resolution as the functional equivalent of a war declaration.[111]

As Johnson and his top echelons made their decisions for war, they ignored the supposed object of everyone's concern—America's South Vietnamese ally. The generals in Saigon were never involved in nor even consulted about the fateful decisions to inaugurate ROLLING THUNDER or to send large contingents of U. S. ground combat forces to South Vietnam. The generals would be briefed on the steps being taken and their acquiescence would be expected. Indeed, Generals Ky and Thieu had no choice but to support these decisions, since their survival in power depended on the Americans maintaining a strong military presence in South Vietnam and on their continuing high levels of military and economic assistance. "The Americans came in like bulldozers and the South Vietnamese followed their lead without a word of dissent."[112]

On the morning of July 28, Johnson met with Congressional leaders. At noon, he held a televised press conference. He continued to mislead Congress, the media, and the American people about his Vietnam decisions. The president insisted that he had not authorized any change of policy, implying that the American role in Vietnam continued to be that of advising and supporting the South Vietnamese forces, when in fact he had committed the United States to a major war. While acknowledging that he was sending 50,000 more troops, doubling draft calls, and bringing the total U. S. forces in South Vietnam to about 125,000, Johnson downplayed his intention to send more soldiers later. He also made no mention of his agreement to allow General Westmoreland to deploy U. S. forces into any combat zone that the U. S. field commander deemed necessary. The United States was taking over the ground war from the ineffectual ARVN forces.

President Johnson quietly took the nation to war during the fourth week of July 1965, by indirection and dissimulation. At the time, most Americans probably did not realize that their nation was headed for war. Most of those who understood that America was entering a war probably did not give it much thought, assuming that now that the United States was in it, it would be a relatively short, small-scale affair with the powerful, well-equipped, and well-trained U. S. combat forces gaining an easy victory over the Communists.

"Displaying the consummate skill that had become his trademark, Johnson in the last week of July [1965] shaped a consensus for his Vietnam policy in his administration, in Congress, and in the country."[113] The president saw himself as rejecting both the extremes of withdrawal and rapid escalation. Instead, he believed that he was taking the middle course of measured escalation, solidly supported by a large majority of Americans. But beneath the consensual surface, relatively few Americans understood or strongly supported his Vietnam War policies. Many people probably supported the war at the time simply because President Johnson appeared to be a capable and strong leader; they trusted his leadership and also anticipated quick victories at minimal cost. When war costs and casualties vastly exceeded anticipated levels and the conflict endured far longer than anyone had expected, Johnson's carefully crafted consensus collapsed into quarreling factions of hawks and doves surrounding increasingly disillusioned, confused, angry, and frustrated middle Americans.

Johnson and his advisers forged a Vietnam War policy that rested upon a number of myths and misperceptions, some of which they had inherited from previous administrations. Some of Johnson's advisers knew that international relations were more complex and dynamic in 1965 than they had been in the 1950s. They understood the implications of the Sino-Soviet split, and they sensed that emerging polycentrism heralded a breakup of the bipolar world dominated by the United States and the U. S. S. R. But the president and his advisers remained thralls of the containment ideology and its domino correlative, just as the Truman, Eisenhower, and Kennedy administrations before them. Most of Johnson's aides perceived Ho Chi Minh as an agent of Chinese expansionism. They believed the line against Communism had to be drawn and held in southern Vietnam, lest all Southeast Asia become vassal to the Asian colossus and American and Allied interests in that crucial region be undermined. They believed America would be humiliated if it withdrew from Vietnam. The United States would be exposed as a "paper tiger." They feared China and the U. S. S. R., emboldened by an American debacle, would support Third World insurgencies wherever they appeared. Wars of national liberation could not be suppressed or contained. America would lose credibility in the world; its allies would be demoralized, and they would no longer trust the United States to honor its commitments.

Additional considerations underpinned Washington's determination to hold the line in Southeast Asia to prevent the fall of the dominoes to Communism. Johnson administration officials did not want the economic resources of Southeast Asia to fall into Communist hands. They intended to preserve the rice lands and raw materials of that region for integration into the world economic system, particularly for access by the Japanese and America's NATO allies. American officials also retained a sense of mission about their country's special role in world affairs. America, by its very existence, had set an example for the world of a free and prosperous people for nearly two centuries. From time to time in the past, America had been called upon to use its power to advance the cause of democracy elsewhere in the world. Once again, it would now use its righteous power to preserve freedom and thwart Communism, this time in

Vietnam. American officials saw themselves as champions of a noble cause destined to triumph in Southeast Asia.[114] Perhaps an implicit cultural racism also influenced official Washington as it forged its interventionist Vietnam policy: Americans, given their superior know-how, noble intentions, vast wealth, and advanced technology, would take over the fighting; they would show their Vietnamese wards how to fight and win a major war, and how to establish a stable, modern state.

Johnson and his advisers also embraced the McCarthyite myth that had haunted liberal Democrats since the Chinese revolution of 1949. To Johnson and his aides, it was axiomatic that the loss of any additional territory in Southeast Asia to Communism spelled political disaster for them and their party. The loss of southern Vietnam to the Communists would galvanize a Rightist political backlash that could destroy Johnson's beloved Great Society and cost him the upcoming election. Johnson was determined not to replicate the fate that had befallen Truman in the early 1950s.

Johnson's ignorance of Vietnamese history and culture, shared by his senior advisers, and coupled with his habit of thinking in terms of simplistic Cold War cliches, caused him to misread the nature of Vietnamese nationalism and misunderstand the nature of the revolutionary insurgency in southern Vietnam. Johnson apparently never understood that Ho Chi Minh and his revolutionary Communist movement embodied Vietnamese nationalism much more so than did the succession of corrupt and inept military dictatorships that the United States backed. He did not understand that the Hanoi-backed insurgency in southern Vietnam enjoyed widespread popular appeal, in part because it expressed Vietnamese nationalistic aspirations to be free of foreign influences. All the president could see was Communist aggression orchestrated from Hanoi in service of the foreign policies of Beijing and the Kremlin that he felt compelled to stop. Had Johnson and his bureaucratic experts in Washington been better acquainted with Vietnamese history and culture, they might have known that Vietnam's national identity was rooted in resistance to foreign domination. They might have known that Vietnam struggled for 1,000 years to throw off Chinese suzerainty. They might have known that Ho Chi Minh in 1946 was even willing to tolerate a temporary return of the French to his nation to be rid of voracious Chinese armies.

Although Johnson and his senior advisers made pivotal decisions during the last week of July that meant America's taking over the Vietnam War, they did not develop a coherent war strategy. Thus, the future roles in the war of the South Vietnamese forces and the future roles of the U. S. forces remained ill-defined:

> Boiled down to its essence, American "strategy" was simply to put more U. S. troops into South Vietnam and see what happened.[115]

Johnson and his aides also made a series of faulty judgments as they took the nation to war. They seriously underrated their enemy. They underestimated Hanoi's popular support, ferocious determination, political discipline, fighting ability, and diplomatic skill. They could never bring themselves to admit that a small, poor Asian nation, even with substantial assistance from China and the Soviet Union, might withstand a large-scale application of U. S. military power for years. Likewise, they overestimated the strategic capabilities of the American military forces, both in air and ground operations. Without accurately accessing the capabilities of their enemies or the particular limitations and obstacles U. S. military forces would encounter in Vietnam, Johnson and his advisers simply assumed that the mere application of sizeable amounts of U. S. military force would be sufficient to bring victory. In addition, having drastically underestimated the future size, cost, and duration of the war that they began in July 1965, the administration necessarily overestimated the willingness of the American people to go on year after year passively paying in lives and dollars for a military stalemate.[116]

Johnson understood his Vietnam War strategy to be a holding action that was essentially defensive in nature. He was not trying to defeat North Vietnam or destroy the NLF. But he would punish the North Vietnamese from the air, and the American combat forces in South Vietnam would prevent the Communists from winning the revolution. He believed that, in time, Hanoi would reach its threshold of pain, would grow weary of punishment and persistent failure and agree to let South Vietnam live in peace. Without fully considering the consequences, Washington had chosen to wage a limited defensive war against a determined foe waging an unlimited strategic offensive for the highest of stakes, national reunification, and independence from foreign influences.

In the short run, Johnson's centrist leadership was brilliantly successful in forging a consensus among his advisers, Congress, the media, and the American people in support of Americanizing the Vietnam War in July 1965. At the same time, he also succeeded in pushing landmark Great Society measures through Congress, among them Medicare, the Voting Rights Act, and federal aid to education. Johnson gambled that a measured escalation of the bombing of North Vietnam and a limited commitment of ground combat forces to South Vietnam would enable him to achieve his military and political goals in Southeast Asia, soon enough to allow him to fulfill his commitment to social justice at home. He believed America could afford to fight a limited war in Vietnam at the same time it completed the New Deal at home. He refused to choose between the Great Society and the war in Vietnam; he refused to choose between being a leader of war and a leader of peace. Johnson's frontier faith in American omnicompetence led him to believe that the United States could afford both "guns and butter." In his own words, "I wanted both, I believed in both, and I believed that America had the resources to provide for both."[117]

But in the long run, the price paid for seeking this middle-of-the-road consensus was military stalemate in Vietnam and political stasis at home, "a middle road of contradictions and no priorities for action."[118] Johnson, who went to war in Vietnam to save the Great Society, later had to sacrifice the Great Society to pay for the Vietnam War.

In the summer of 1965, Washington began sending its armies to fight a major land war in Asia.

NOTES

1. Herring, *America's Longest War*, 113.

2. *Ibid.*, 108.

3. Halberstam, David, *The Best and the Brightest* (Greenwich, Conn.: Fawcett, 1969), 424–7. Halberstam affixed his ironic label, the best and the brightest, to the men who crafted America's disastrous Vietnam policy. His best and brightest included Rusk, McGeorge Bundy, McNamara, Taylor, and Westmoreland, as well as Kennedy and Johnson; quote that Johnson inherited both a Vietnam policy and the men who made it is from Young, *Vietnam Wars*, 105.

4. Gelb and Betts, *The Irony of Vietnam*, 97. The Johnson quote is from the videotape "Lyndon Johnson Goes to War, 1964–1965," from the television series "Vietnam: A Television History."

5. Leuchtenburg, William, *A Troubled Feast: American Society Since 1945* (Boston: Little Brown, 1983), 138.

6. Moss, George, *America in the Twentieth Century* (Engelwood Clifts, N. J.: Prentice Hall, 1989), 340.

7. Halberstam, *Best and Brightest*, 364.

8. *Ibid.*, 116.

9. Sheehan et al., *Pentagon Papers*, "Excerpts from National Security Action Memorandum 273," Nov. 26, 1963, Document 60, 232–3; Bornet, Vaughn Davis, *The Presidency of Lyndon B. Johnson* (Lawrence, Kansas: University of Kansas Press, 1983), 66–68. The substance of NSAM 273 had previously been prepared as a reaffirmation of Kennedy's Vietnam policy before his death.

10. Maitland and others, *Raising the Stakes*, 94–96.

11. Turley, *The Second Indochina War*, 57–60; Duiker, *The Communist Road*, 221–3; and Doyle, Edward; Lipsman, Samuel; Maitland, Terrence; and the editors, *The North* (Boston: Boston Publishing Co., 1986), 40–43; Hess, *Vietnam*, 77; Herring, *Longest War*, 3d. ed., 122.

12. Quote taken from Hess, *Vietnam*, 78; Kahin, *Intervention*, 183–91.

13. Hess, *Vietnam*, 74.

14. Kahin, *Intervention*, 194–207.

15. Quoted in Maitland and others, *Raising the Stakes*, 100–1.

16. Sheehan et al., *Pentagon Papers*, "McNamara Report on Steps to Change the Trend of the War," March 16, 1964, Document 63, 277–83. In the report, McNamara identifies the greatest weakness in the present situation as "the uncertain viability of the Khanh government."

17. *Ibid.*, "Excerpts from National Security Action Memorandum 288 'U. S. Objectives in South Vietnam,'" March 17, 1964, Document 64, 283–5. By the end of 1964, there were 23,300 U. S. advisers in South Vietnam, an increase of about 7,000 for the year.

18. Young, *Vietnam Wars*, 109–10.

19. *Ibid.*, p. 113; Clodfelter, Mark, *The Limits of Air Power: The American Bombing of North Vietnam* (New York: The Free Press, 1989), 42–43. President Johnson prohibited military actions that might threaten North Vietnam's survival or might appear to the Chinese and

Soviets to threaten North Vietnam's survival. Johnson and other administrative spokesmen repeatedly announced publicly that the United States had no intention of destroying the Hanoi regime; they also gave repeated assurances through private and diplomatic channels.

20. Quoted from *Ibid.*, 113.

21. Porter (ed.), *Vietnam Documents*, vol. 2, "Draft Resolution on Southeast Asia," June 11, 1964, Document 151, 283–5. The resolution was written by William Bundy, assistant secretary of state for Far Eastern Affairs.

22. Hess, *Vietnam*, 79.

23. Porter (ed.), *Vietnam Documents*, vol. 2, "Notes by Canadian ICC Representative Blair Seaborn on Meeting with Pham Van Dong," June 18, 1964, Document 155, 291–2. Blair noted that Dong told him that the choices in Vietnam were either a *guerre a outrance*, which the United States could not win, in any event, or neutrality; Herring, George (ed.), *The Secret Diplomacy of the Vietnam War: The Negotiating Volumes of the Pentagon Papers* (Austin, Texas: University of Texas Press, 1983), 8–9; and Goodman, Allen E., *The Lost Peace* (Palo Alto, Calif.: Hoover Institution Press, 1978), 19–20.

24. The CBS television documentary "Vietnam: The Deadly Decision" was broadcast on April 1, 1964.

25. The main primary source for the Tonkin Gulf incidents occurring between August 1 and August 5, 1964, is the U. S. Congress, Senate, Committee on Foreign Relations, "Hearings on the Gulf of Tonkin, the 1964 Incidents," 90th Congress, 2nd Session, February 1968 (Washington, D. C.: GPO, 1968). The most authoritative secondary account is Marolda, Edward J., and Fitzgerald, Oscar P., *The U. S. Navy and the Vietnam Conflict*, vol. 2: *From Military Assistance to Combat, 1959–1965* (Washington, D. C.: GPO, 1986), chaps. 14 and 15, 393–462.

26. *U. S. News and World Report*, "The 'Phantom Battle' that Led to War," *U. S. News and World Report* (July 23, 1984), 59–60.

27. Kahin, *Intervention*, 214–15.

28. Porter (ed.), *Vietnam Documents*, vol. 2, "Telegram from Rusk to Taylor," August 3, 1964, Document 163, 301–2. Rusk told Taylor, "We believe that present OPLAN 34A activities are beginning to rattle Hanoi, and the *Maddox* incident is directly related to their effort to resist these activities."

29. *Ibid.*, "Chronology of Events Relating to the Gulf of Tonkin Incidents By Joint Reconnaissance Center, U. S. Navy," August 10, 1964 (Extract), Document 170, 313–15; "The Phantom Battle," 61–62; Davidson, Phillip B., *Vietnam at War: The History, 1946–1975* (Novato, Calif.: Presidio, 1988), 317–20.

30. *U. S. News and World Report*, "The Phantom Battle," 62–63.

31. *Ibid.*, 63; Maitland and others, *Raising the Stakes*, 159.

32. Kahin, *Intervention*, 222.

33. Interview recorded on videotape, "Lyndon Johnson Goes to War, 1964–1965," from the television series "Vietnam: A Television History."

34. *U. S. News and World Report*, "The Phantom Battle," 64.

35. Stockdale, James B., and Stockdale, Sybil, *In Love and War* (New York: Harper and Row, 1984), 3–36. Stockdale is quoted in Kahin, *Intervention*, 223.

36. *U. S. News and World Report*, "The Phantom Battle," 66. Hanoi has always denied that there was a second attack; it insists that it was fabricated by the U. S. National Security Agency.

37. Kahin, *Intervention*, 223–5; Johnson quoted in Olson and Roberts, 117.

38. *U. S. News and World Report*, "The Phantom Battle," 65.

39. Maitland et al., *Raising the Stakes*, 160–1.

40. *U. S. News and World Report*, "The Phantom Battle," 65–66.

41. Gelb and Betts, *Irony of Vietnam*, 103–4; Hoopes, Townsend, *The Limits of Intervention: How Vietnam Policy was Made—and Reversed—During the Johnson Administration* (New York: W. W. Norton, 1987), 26.

42. Quoted in Olson and Roberts, *Where the Domino Fell*, 118.

43. Eighty-five percent of the public approved of Johnson's decision to order retaliatory air raids against North Vietnamese targets. Polls cited in *Ibid.*, 39, and Herring, *America's Longest War*, 123; O'Keefe, Kevin J., in an unpublished paper on print media coverage of the Gulf of Tonkin incidents, found that most newspaper and news magazine accounts of those events were uncritically accepting of official versions and were nearly unanimous in their editorial support of President Johnson's actions.

44. Porter (ed.), *Vietnam Documents*, vol. 2, "The Gulf of Tonkin Resolution," August 7, 1964, Document 167, 307.

45. Herring, *America's Longest War*, 123.

46. Young, *Vietnam Wars*, 123.

47. Gelb and Betts, *Irony of Vietnam*, 101.

48. Davidson, *Vietnam at War*, 322.

49. Herring, *America's Longest War*, 125.

50. Hess, *Vietnam*, 80.

51. *Ibid.*, 81.

52. Herring, *America's Longest War*, 126.

53. Quoted in Goldman, Eric, *The Tragedy of Lyndon Johnson* (New York: Dell, 1968), 279.

54. Quoted in *Ibid.*, 281.

55. Goldman calls Johnson's rhetorical insertions "escape hatches."

56. Maitland et al., *Raising the Stakes*, 162–3; Huong's quote is recorded on videotape, "Lyndon Johnson Goes to War, 1964–1965," from the television series "Vietnam: A Television History."

57. Davidson, *Vietnam at War*, 323; Taylor quote is found in Olson and Roberts, *Where the Domino Fell*, 12.

58. Duiker, *The Communist Road*, 233.

59. Kahin, *Intervention*, 245–6; Thomson, James B., "How Could Vietnam Happen? An Autopsy," *Atlantic*, vol. 221 (April 1968), 50–52. Officials who resigned or were dismissed included Paul Kattenburg and Roger Hilsman. Thomson, and East Asia specialist, left the government for Harvard in 1966.

60. Thomson, "How Could Vietnam Happen?", 52; Gallucci, Robert, *Neither Peace nor Honor: The Politics of American Military Policy in Viet-Nam* (Baltimore: The Johns Hopkins University Press, 1975), 35–58.

61. Herring, *America's Longest War*, 124; Duiker, *The Communist Road*, 236.

62. Davidson, *Vietnam at War*, 336–9.

63. *Ibid.*, 339–40; Millett and Masloski, *For the Common Defense*, 549.

64. Ball, George W., "A Light that Failed—Top Secret: The Prophecy the President Rejected," *Atlantic*, vol. 230 (July 1972), 33–49. The substance of the article is a memo Ball wrote on October 5, 1964, which Johnson later read. Ball hoped to get Johnson and his advisers to examine the erroneous assumptions underlying U. S. Vietnam policies and to realize that there were other options available besides escalation. Ball failed, and left office in 1966.

65. Herring, *America's Longest War*, 126.

66. Sheehan et al., *Pentagon Papers*, "Final Draft Position Paper Produced by Working Group," Document 88, 373–8. Key members of the group besides William Bundy included John McNaughton, George Carver, Marshall Green, and Vice Admiral Lloyd Mustin.

67. Remarks attributed to Johnson by Jack Valenti in an interview recorded on videotape, "Lyndon Johnson Goes to War, 1964–1965," from the television series "Vietnam: A Television History."

68. Sheehan et al., *Pentagon Papers*, "Account of Taylor's Meeting with Saigon Generals on Unrest," December 24, 1964, Document 89, 379–81.

69. Herring, *America's Longest War*, 129.

70. Davidson, *Vietnam at War*, 333–4.

71. Kahin, *Intervention*, 262.

72. *Ibid.*, pp. 263–5.

73. Ball, George W., *The Past Has Another Pattern* (New York: W. W. Norton, 1982), 389–90; Ball is quoted in Kahin, *Intervention*, 275; Berman, *Planning a Tragedy*, 45–52.

74. Davidson, *Vietnam at War*, 335–6.

75. Maitland et al., *Raising the Stakes*, 170–1.

76. Herring, *America's Longest War*, 129. Young, *Vietnam Wars*, 137–8. The maze of memos generated by Johnson's senior civilian and military advisers between November 1964 and February 1965, as they forged U. S. Vietnam policy that culminated in the decision to initiate an air war against North Vietnam, reveals a bureaucratic worldview that increasingly had few points of reference to Vietnamese social, political, and strategic realities. The terms of the paper debate waged among these high echelons, George Ball excepted, were defined by the prime goal they had set for themselves in Vietnam, and this goal in turn derived from the Cold War ideological consensus they all embraced. The goal, of course, remained the creation of a non-Communist state south of the 17th parallel to stop the spread of Communism in Southeast Asia. To U. S. foreign policy-making elite, nothing Vietnamese would be permitted to prevent them from ordering that part of the world in accordance with the principles and practices of the American liberal capitalist system.

77. Sheehan and others, *Pentagon Papers*, "McGeorge Bundy Memo to Johnson on Sustained reprisal' policy," February 7, 1965, Document 92, 423–7. The tone of Bundy's memo is grim. Even as he advocates bombing, he concedes that it might

fail to improve the situation in South Vietnam; Clodfelter, *Limits*, 58–63. On February 27, 1965, the State Department issued a White Paper rationalizing the bombing campaign as a response to North Vietnamese aggression against South Vietnam.

78. McGeorge Bundy referred to incidents such as Pleiku as "streetcars." If you don't catch it, another will come along soon.

79. Kahin, *Intervention*, 294–305.

80. Westmoreland, William C., *A Soldier Reports* (New York: Dell, 1976), 123–4.

81. The State Department note is cited in Berman, *Planning a Tragedy*, 51.

82. Quote is from Kahin, *Intervention*, 306; Sheehan et al., *Pentagon Papers*, "McCone Memo to Top Officials on Effectiveness of Air War," Document 97, 440–1.

83. Davidson, *Vietnam at War*, 324–5.

84. Kattenburg, Paul, *The Vietnam Trauma in American Foreign Policy, 1945–1975* (New Brunswick, N. J.: Transaction, 1980), 131–2. Kattenburg is quoted in Berman, *Planning a Tragedy*, 51–52.

85. Westmoreland, *A Soldier Reports*, 157.

86. *Ibid.*, 157–8.

87. Porter (ed.), *Vietnam Documents*, vol. 2, "Telegram from Taylor to Rusk," March 18, 1965, Document 195, 364–5.

88. Maitland et al., *Raising the Stakes*, 174–5; Corporal Powers was assigned to the Third Marine Amphibious Force. Its 3,500 personnel, under the command of General Lewis Walt, came ashore along Danang's beaches on March 8, 1965.

89. Westmoreland, *A Soldier Reports*, 161.

90. Maitland et al., *Raising the Stakes*, 183–4.

91. Sheehan et al., *Pentagon Papers*, "Order Increasing Ground Forces and Shifting Mission," April 6, 1965, Document 98, 442–3. According to Item 11: "The actions themselves should be taken as rapidly as practicable, but in ways that should minimize any appearances of sudden changes in policy, . . . The President's desire is that these movements and changes should be understood as being gradual and wholly consistent with existing policy."

92. Quoted in Maitland et al., *Raising the Stakes*, 184.

93. Poll cited in Turner, *Dual War*, 116.

94. Goldman, *Tragedy of Lyndon Johnson*, 476–7; Young, *Vietnam Wars*, 156–7.

95. Johnson's statements from his Johns Hopkins speech are cited in Turner, *Dual War*, 128–9.

96. Moyers' quote is from an interview recorded on videotape, "Lyndon Johnson Goes to War, 1964–1965," from the television series "Vietnam: A Television History."

97. Turner, *Dual War*, 131–2.

98. Hanoi's Four Points are reprinted in Gettleman, Marvin E.; Franklin, Jane; Young, Marilyn; and Franklin, Bruce, (eds.), *Vietnam and America: A Documented History* (New York: Grove, 1985), 274–5.

99. Kattenburg, *Vietnam Trauma*, 130–3; Duiker, *The Communist Road*, 241–2.

100. Quoted in Westmoreland, *A Soldier Reports*, 166.

101. Porter (ed.), *Vietnam Documents*, vol. 2, "Memorandum for the President by McNamara," April 21, 1965, Document 198, 370–1; Doyle, Edward; Lipsman, Samuel, and the editors, *America Takes Over* (Boston: Boston Publishing Company, 1982),10–11, from the series, "The Vietnam Experience."

102. Herring, *America's Longest War*, 132.

103. Moss, *America in the Twentieth Century*, 348–9. Young, *Vietnam Wars*, 153.

104. Herring, *America's Longest War*, 135.

105. Morrocco, John, and the editors of the Boston Publishing Co., *Thunder from Above: Air War, 1941–1968* (Boston: Boston Publishing Co., 1984), 81–83, a volume in the series, "The Vietnam Experience;" Westmoreland, *A Soldier Reports*; Clarke, *The Final Years*, 48. By June 1965, ARVN was suffering about 2,000 battle casualties per month and losing an additional 10,000 men a month from desertions. Total manpower losses outstripped gains from recruiting and conscription.

106. Clarke, *The Final Years*, 22–23. According to Clarke: During 1964–1965, a rising group of younger officers, most in their late thirties and early forties, displaced the older generals who had overthrown Diem. These Young Turks emerged as the new arbiters of power in Saigon. Thieu, Ky, and Chi were the leaders of these new men of power.

107. Westmoreland, *A Soldier Reports*, 179–82; Sheehan et al., *Pentagon Papers*, "McNamara's Memo on July 20, 1965, on Increasing Allied Ground Force," Document 105, 456–8. The memo was drafted on July 1 and revised on July 20.

108. Herring, *America's Longest War*, 138–9.

109. There are detailed accounts in Kahin, *Intervention*, 366–401, and in Berman, *Planning a Tragedy*, 105–53, that anatomize the decision-making process of July 21 to July 28, 1965, that plunged America into a land war in Asia. Clark Clifford, a friend of Johnson's, and Senator Mike Mansfield, joined with George Ball to try to warn the president of the perils of getting involved in a major war in Southeast Asia. He rejected their advice. See also Schandler, Herbert Y., *The Unmaking of a President: Lyndon Johnson and Vietnam* (Princeton, N. J.: Princeton University Press, 1977), 30–31.

110. Herring, *America's Longest War*, 139–40.

111. Summers, Harry G. Jr., *On Strategy: A Critical Analysis of the Vietnam War* (New York: Dell, 1982), 49–50; Young, *Vietnam Wars*, 160.

112. Herring, *Longest War*, 3d. ed., 153–4.

113. *Ibid.*, 142.

114. Hess, *Vietnam*, 87–88.

115. Quoted in Clarke, *The Final Years*, 106.

116. Summers, *On Strategy*, 142–3.

117. Johnson quoted in Young, *Vietnam Wars*, 158.

118. Gelb, Leslie, "Vietnam: The System Worked," *Foreign Policy*, vol. 3 (Summer 1971), 164.

6

The Chain of Thunders

Front line combat in Vietnam was remarkably similar to the battles fought by those soldiers on the point who charged the Bloody Angle at Spotsylvania, who stormed the Nazi fortifications along the Siegfried Line, who broke through the Japanese defenses before Manila, and who assaulted the Chinese and North Korean entrenchments on Pork Chop Hill. The casualty figures tell the story.

Harry G. Summers Jr.

LIMITED WAR

Americans went to war during the summer of 1965, confident that the Vietnamese insurgents could not withstand for long the application of U. S. military might. They assumed that the United States, the world's richest and most powerful nation, needed to do little more than flex its high-tech military muscles and it would triumph in Southeast Asia. President Johnson expected a relatively quick and cheap U. S. victory that would save South Vietnam, implement his Great Society, and preserve his broad-based consensus supporting containment of Communism abroad and social reform at home.

Two and one-half years later, the nation found itself mired in a frustrating and costly war. As 1967 drew to a close, America had committed 486,000 troops to Vietnam and was spending over $2 billion per month on the conflict. Despite these large investments of their nation's manpower and wealth, far in excess of what anyone had anticipated when the war began, many Americans feared the United States was not winning the war in Vietnam. To them, the conflict appeared to be stalemated; they faced the dismaying prospect of a protracted war with ever-mounting costs and casualties. Many citizens concluded that it had been a mistake for the United States to have become involved in the Vietnam War.

During most of 1967, support for the conflict and for Johnson's leadership was declining among the Congress, the media, and the public. A debate between the hawks and the doves over Johnson's war policy was building in Congress and echoing in the streets. Within the White House, presidential advisers were dividing into hawkish and dovish factions. Facing rising war costs, Congress was abandoning Johnson's Great Society reform program. Widening social fissures heralded the breakdown of consensus. In Newark, Detroit, and elsewhere, angry black rioters torched entire blocks of cities. Violence in Vietnam bred violence at home.

The prime cause of America's entanglement in a stalemated war of increasing magnitude was the failure of America's leaders to develop effective strategies for achieving national political objectives in a limited war milieu of the kind that the United States had gotten itself into in Vietnam.[1] Traditionally, U. S. military leaders have not devoted themselves to the development of grand strategy, specifically with the development of the military means required to achieve particular national goals. "The Americans had won every war since (and including) the Civil War by an overwhelming combination of superior manpower and weight of materiel, a superiority which minimized the importance of strategy."[2]

As the rivalry between America and the Soviet Union intensified in the aftermath of World War II, both sides built up potent thermonuclear arsenals. Strategists in both nations spawned new strategic theories as they struggled to control these extraordinarily powerful weapons. Within America, given the absence of military theorists, strategic analysts for the nuclear age were recruited from civilian ranks, many from academia. At institutes and "think tanks," civilian theorists fashioned strategic concepts for the nuclear era. For the most part, military professionals ignored the theories propounded by civilian strategists, considering them arcane, intellectual exercises irrelevant to solving the practical problems of war-fighting in the atomic age.

One of the fashionable theories developed for the nuclear age by civilian strategists was the concept of limited war. It rested on two beliefs: first, that a nuclear war with the Soviet Union (later expanded to include China) had to be avoided at all costs, for it could never be won given the immense destructive power of the nuclear weaponry possessed by both sides; and, second, that the United States must contain Communism, which was spreading in the Third World via local, small-scale revolutionary wars, backed by the Soviets and the Chinese. Limited warfare assumed the gradual application of economic and military assistance, diplomatic pressure, covert operations, and military force at the site of Communist or Communist-inspired insurrections. Limited-war doctrine called for the employment of these instrumentalities with restraint and skill. A deft touch was required to use just enough and the right mix of persuasion, money, aid, and force necessary to defeat a rebellion and contain the spread of Communism, without provoking a response from the U. S. S. R. or China that could escalate to a nuclear confrontation.

The theory of limited war received its first real-world application during the Korean conflict. That war started when North Korea, seeking to bring the entire country under its control, invaded South Korea on June 25, 1950. President Truman, assuming that the North Korean invasion was supported, perhaps directed, by the Soviet Union to further Soviet expansionist ambitions in Asia, quickly made the decision to intervene militarily. American objectives were not only to defend South Korea against Communist aggression but to contain the spread of Communism without provoking a confrontation with the Soviets that could lead to World War III.

Reacting to the Chinese intervention into the Korean War five months later that caught him by surprise, U. N. Commander General Douglas MacArthur wanted to undertake military initiatives against China. He ran up against the civilian proponents of limited war who insisted on confining the U. N. forces to the Korean battlefield.[3] MacArthur and his supporters chafed at the limitations placed on U. N. forces, while their Chinese adversaries freely used their homeland for logistics support, basing aircraft, and sanctuaries.

A dispute over the objectives for which the Korean War was being fought lay at the core of the conflict between MacArthur and Truman. MacArthur wanted to inflict a major defeat on China and liberate all of Korea from Communism. Truman sought the limited political objective of restoring the status quo, of ensuring the survival of a non-Communist South Korea below the 38th parallel. Truman's overriding concern was the avoidance of a confrontation with the Soviets, then aligned with China. Truman removed MacArthur from his command when MacArthur publicly criticized the Truman administration's limited war strategies and political objectives. This dispute between civilian and military leaders, which erupted during the Korean War over strategies and objectives, foreshadowed similar conflicts during the Vietnam War.

Following the end of the Korean War, a decade would pass before America would again resort to limited war in order to contain the spread of Communism in Asia. But, in Vietnam, American limited war strategists came up against a sophisticated and complex revolutionary war strategy employed by the North Vietnamese and the NLF. In the Korean War, American forces had only engaged in conventional war against the North Korean and Chinese armies. During 1962 and 1963, President Kennedy cautiously pursued a small-scale limited war policy in Vietnam, based on furnishing the South Vietnamese government with diplomatic, economic, and military assistance, accompanied by the use of covert operations, counterinsurgency tactics, and the deployment of thousands of U. S. military advisers. Following Kennedy's assassination, Lyndon Johnson immediately embraced the limited U. S. commitment in Vietnam and gradually expanded it.

During the first half of 1965, to stave off the imminent collapse of the South Vietnamese government, Johnson rapidly escalated the conflict, first by bombing North Vietnam, and when that strategy quickly proved ineffective, then by sending large numbers of American combat forces to fight the Vietcong and PAVN forces in southern Vietnam. Johnson chose to expand drastically the limited war, which he had inherited, rather than to accept the Kennedy administration's failure to develop an effective strategy that would have enabled the South Vietnamese government to survive. From Johnson's vantage point, the fall of Saigon would have meant intolerable disaster—the failure of the U. S. strategy of limited war to contain Communism in Indochina, a failure that threatened to crumble the entire U. S. Cold War foreign policy edifice that had been constructed since 1945 and increase the likelihood of thermonuclear war.

At the time that Johnson made these escalatory decisions, he could not know that he had committed U. S. forces to a long, costly, and ultimately losing war. One of the many causes of that eventual disaster would be defects inherent in the American concept of limited war, as well as in its application to Indochina. American efforts to fight a limited war in Vietnam were also complicated by disputes among Johnson's civilian and military advisers over how best to implement military strategy, disputes that added ambiguities to Washington's conduct of the war. The architects of America's limited war in that region never improvised a grand strategy that could counter the sophisticated strategy used by their determined foes and achieve U. S. objectives.

In August 1965, an operations study prepared for the Joint Chiefs defined four major American objectives in Southeast Asia. They included enabling the GVN to extend its control over all of that country lying south of the 17th parallel, defeating the PLAF and NVA forces fighting in South Vietnam, forcing Hanoi to withdraw its forces from the South and renounce its support of the southern insurrection, and deterring Chinese expansion into Vietnam, Indochina, or anywhere in Southeast Asia.[4]

But U. S. policy makers never generated the strategies to accomplish most of these objectives. One reason for their failure was their unwillingness to order a total mobilization of U. S. human and economic resources. Vietnam would be a limited war for limited ends, using limited assets.[5] Another cause of failure lay in the fact that U. S. military strategies in Vietnam were incompatible. On the one hand, Johnson limited the American military effort in Vietnam so as not to provoke Chinese or Soviet military intervention. On the other hand, he counted on a comparatively quick and easy victory over the NLF and Hanoi. Having limited the use of U. S. military power to avoid war with China and a possible nuclear confrontation with the U. S. S. R., and having seriously underestimated their enemy's capacity to resist American power, Washington "did not confront the crucial question of what would be required to achieve its goals until it was bogged down in a bloody stalemate."[6] Bound by their doctrine of limited war to contain Communism in southern Vietnam while avoiding confrontations with China and the U. S. S. R., and concerned with limiting the war for domestic political reasons, American officials never developed the means to defeat their enemies and save their allies before popular support for the war collapsed.

When the United States was eventually forced to curtail the air war and withdraw its ground combat forces from Vietnam because public opinion would no longer support a war that involved sustaining massive American casualties and costs for a lengthy and ultimately indeterminate period of time, the GVN remained totally dependent on U. S. economic and military aid, military advisers, and air and logistics support for its survival. After the U. S. aid programs were reduced and military support was withdrawn, PAVN forces overwhelmed the demoralized GVN army, and South Vietnam was extinguished at the end of April 1975.

Having surrendered the formulation of limited war strategy to civilian analysts and having failed to conceive of any alternative, Johnson's military advisers had no choice but to go along with it. But his military advisers resented the restrictions civilian officials imposed on the air war against North Vietnam, restrictions they believed prevented them from inflicting enough damage to force Hanoi to stop supporting the southern insurgency. They continually pressured Johnson to intensify the air war against North Vietnam. But the President feared that the military's call for full-scale bombing attacks risked Chinese military intervention, a risk Johnson, with vivid memories of Korea, refused to run. In 1967, Johnson eased his controls and permitted an expanded air war.

Although they exercised tight control over the selection of targets for the air war against North Vietnam, civilian leaders in Washington, other than confining the ground war to the territory of South Vietnam, left the framing of strategies for its conduct to the Joint Chiefs and to General Westmoreland.[7] Initially, Johnson's military advisers accepted these geographic limits imposed on the ground war because Westmoreland did not have enough combat forces or a sufficiently developed logistics support system for conducting operations within South Vietnam and simultaneously undertaking cross-border operations into Laos, Cambodia, and southern North Vietnam. In time, military leaders would also challenge some of the civilian restrictions clamped on the ground war, which they viewed as needlessly delaying the achievement of U. S. objectives in Southeast Asia.

WAR OF ATTRITION

General William Westmoreland was the "key American military actor in the Vietnamese drama."[8] As commander of the Military Assistance Command—Vietnam (COMUSMACV), Westmoreland held tactical command over the American war that began in the summer of 1965. He and his staff devised the strategy of attrition that was in place from July 1965 until President Nixon supplanted it with Vietnamization in August 1969. During his tenure of duty in Vietnam, General Westmoreland won the most important campaign of the American Vietnam war, the Tet-68 Offensive, a series of battles in which RVNAF and U. S. forces destroyed the PLAF and severely damaged the Vietcong's political infrastructure in many districts. Westmoreland was also the principal adversary of the commander-in-chief of the North Vietnamese Army, General Vo Nguyen Giap, who, after defeating the French, ultimately defeated American efforts to control the political destiny of South Vietnam.

Westmoreland has been called the "inevitable general."[9] From the outset of his military career, he appeared destined for distinction. Westmoreland compiled a superb World War II record, serving as an artillery officer with the 9th Infantry Division, which saw extensive action in North Africa, Normandy, and Germany. He also fought in Korea, where he reached the rank of brigadier general at the relatively youthful age of thirty-eight. After Korea, he continued to advance his career with choice assignments, including a tour as superintendent of the Military Academy. Westmoreland assumed command of U. S forces in Vietnam in June 1965. The Vietnam War proved to be a difficult and frustrating experience for the inevitable general. He became a controversial figure, often the target of criticism, most often from doves, but also from hawkish critics who believed his strategy of attrition could never produce victory in Vietnam.[10]

Westmoreland quickly decided to use an attrition strategy. It was the traditional American way of war that had produced victories in all major U. S. wars since the American Civil War. Attrition played to the American strengths—firepower and mobility—and it minimized U. S. casualties. Attrition warfare also promised an opportunity for winning the war more quickly than protracted counterinsurgency operations. Denied by the exigencies of the American limited-war policy of an opportunity to wage a war of annihilation by invading North Vietnam, Westmoreland believed that attrition campaigns in South Vietnam were the next best strategy available. Westmoreland also felt he had no choice but to use an attrition strategy, because North Vietnam was committing its main force units to the war in South Vietnam.[11]

Westmoreland's attrition strategy was quickly endorsed by Army Chief of Staff Harold Johnson, by the Joint Chiefs, and by civilian leaders, including Secretary of Defense McNamara and President Johnson. If Westmoreland were the inevitable general, attrition was the inevitable U. S. war strategy in South Vietnam. But "the Army applied the doctrine and force structure it had developed for conventional contingencies in Europe and Korea against insurgent forces practicing a form of revolutionary warfare."[12] A major reason for the failure of the Americans to gain more than a military stalemate in the Vietnam War after years of large-scale warfare was their reliance on a conventional strategy against adversaries who employed unconventional revolutionary war strategies that enabled them to avoid defeat at the hands of a much more powerful army.

As Westmoreland and his staff planned it, his strategy of attrition was to unfold over three phases, anticipating a U. S. victory by the end of 1967. During phase one, U. S. troops would be used to protect the developing American logistics system, that is, military bases, air fields, and lines of communication. Westmoreland also believed that U. S. combat forces would have to be committed to battle during this first phase, because enemy main force units operating in the vicinity of Saigon and in the central highlands continually attacked GVN forces. Westmoreland viewed the military situation in the summer of 1965 as precarious. The Vietcong controlled half the territory and population of South Vietnam. The VC offensives launched in May were destroying ARVN units at the rate of one battalion per week, and the insurgents were overrunning many district headquarters. The PAVN offensives in the central highlands sought to take control of that vital region and threaten the coastal cities. Typically, political chaos reigned in Saigon. A South Vietnamese political collapse and a

Figure 6.1   The inevitable general: William C. Westmoreland, the American field commander in Vietnam from 1965 to 1968. Here, COMUSMACV addresses some of the U. S. troops.
Source: U. S. Marine Corps

Vietcong victory before the end of the year both appeared possible. Westmoreland's objectives during phase one were to protect the populated areas, thwart enemy operations, and halt the downward slide of the war in the South.[13]

Assuming that the military situation could be stabilized by the end of 1965 and that the South Vietnamese would have stopped losing by then, Westmoreland's planners called for phase two to begin in 1966. American forces would take the initiative and, wherever possible, eliminate the enemy's base camps and sanctuaries. These large-unit sweeps into enemy basing areas were to be the tactical operations that came to be known as "search-and-destroy" missions. Westmoreland assumed that by attacking key enemy basing areas, he could force the Vietcong main units to fight, giving the U. S. forces an opportunity to use their superior firepower to "find, fix, and finish the enemy." U. S. forces would also provide security for an expanded pacification effort. The length of phase two would depend on American force commitments and the enemy's reaction to the U. S. efforts. General Westmoreland estimated that phase two would last about a year. It was assumed that the back of the insurgency would have been broken by the end of phase two. Phase three would begin in 1967; it would essentially be a mopping-up exercise. Remaining insurgent forces would be destroyed or pushed back to remote areas, where they would pose no threat to village security or GVN forces. During phase three, the pacification program would be extended throughout South Vietnam.[14]

U. S. planners assumed that the tasks of pacification and building up the GVN military forces would be pursued during all three phases. They expected that by the time the U. S. war of attrition was completed, most of the people of South Vietnam would be living in villages free of Vietcong pressure. They also assumed that the GVN military forces would be strong enough to handle any lingering security threats to South Vietnam. With the VC forces neutralized and PAVN units forced back into North Vietnam, Hanoi would have to negotiate on U. S. terms. American combat forces would be withdrawn.[15] As the American war in Vietnam unfolded, Westmoreland's strategic plan would prove easier to draft than to implement; in fact, it proved impossible to implement fully for many reasons.

As Westmoreland began deploying U. S. combat units during the summer of 1965, his operations were hampered seriously by inadequate logistical support systems. President Johnson's failure to mobilize the Reserves and National Guard and to rely completely on increased draft calls and enlistments to meet the expanding manpower needs of the rapidly escalating war created serious problems for Westmoreland. The regular U. S. Army had few engineering, logistics, and service units on active duty. Military planners had assumed that in the event of war, Reserve and National Guard units would be mobilized to provide these crucial support services. When Johnson, ignoring the advice of the Joint Chiefs, refused to call the Reserves to active duty for political reasons, Westmoreland faced a crisis in supplying and supporting the combat units that were pouring into the war zone.[16] Many units found their ammunition in short supply. Other combat units arrived under strength and without all of their weapons, equipment, or supplies.

At the time the American war in Vietnam began, South Vietnam possessed only one deep-water port, the commercial docks located fifty miles inland at Saigon. Since warehouse and storage areas were not equipped to handle the massive influx of war material, military supplies piled up on Saigon docks. Vietcong sappers destroyed huge quantities of the arriving U. S. supplies. South Vietnamese workers stole equally large quantities of material for their use, for sale on the black markets, or to sell to the Vietcong. For the rest of 1965, Westmoreland had to delay the tactical deployment of maneuver units because of inadequate logistics support.[17]

Working furiously under adverse conditions, the Seabees, the Army Corps of Engineers, and civilian contractors constructed additional deep-water ports, warehouses, jet-capable air fields, roads, and bridges. The world's most productive economy was soon sending a cornucopia of equipment and supplies over 9,000 miles to its warriors fighting in Vietnam; the 1st Logistical Command developed a superb supply system that not only kept American soldiers supplied with ammunition, guns, tanks, and planes, but also with toilet paper, shaving lather, fresh socks, beer, soft drinks, and ice cream.[18] Within a year, Westmoreland had accomplished "what has properly been called a logistics miracle. The Americans who fought in Vietnam were the best fed, best clothed, best equipped army the nation had ever sent to war."[19]

Serious problems also were inherent in the magnificent logistics success story. American troops were so well supplied with luxuries that many of them quickly lost enthusiasm for the hardships of extended field operations. The supply system was also colossally expensive and wasteful. Sometimes soldiers expended enormous amounts of ammunition to kill one enemy soldier. The promiscuous use of firepower was also responsible for many accidental deaths. A disturbingly large number of troops were killed by "friendly fire" from U. S. aircraft, artillery, mortars, and machine guns. Many other U. S. troops were also killed in the numerous accidents involving the handling, transporting, storing, and guarding of ammunition. Bombs and bullets intended for use against their enemies all too often accidentally killed Americans. Most of all, the effort necessary to make the U. S. Army the best-supplied in history tied up large numbers of military personnel in noncombat activity.[20]

SEARCH AND DESTROY

Although Westmoreland had few combat units and U. S. logistics were still in the chaotic stage, he felt he had to attack Vietcong units operating in some areas in order to take the pressure off beleaguered ARVN forces. On June 28, troops of the 173rd Airborne Brigade, the first Army unit to see combat in Vietnam, climbed aboard helicopters at the Bien Hoa air base on the outskirts of Saigon. They were accompanied by a battalion of Australian soldiers and several battalions of ARVN infantry. Westmoreland was sending the 173rd and their allies on the war's first "search-and-destroy" mission. They were flown into War Zone D, a jungle-infested area thirty-five miles northwest of Saigon that had long been a Vietcong stronghold. The VC chose not to engage the green U. S. sky troopers or their allies on that operation. After two days of inconclusive skirmishing, the troops returned to Bien Hoa. "This American foray 27 June locked the United States into a ground war in Asia."[21]

The 173rd Airborne Brigade made several more incursions into War Zone D during the ensuing months, each of them ending much like the first: withdrawal after a few days of skirmishing, with an elusive enemy not much interested in a real fight. In early November, the troops of the 173rd once more helicoptered into War Zone D. One of the soldiers gave the operation the sarcastic name of HUMP. ("Hump," "humping," and "humping the boonies" were the soldiers' terms for long and exhausting marches over rugged jungle-covered terrain in hot, humid weather under the heavy weight of rucksacks crammed with extra rations, water, and ammunition.) But Operation HUMP turned out to be a fierce and brutal campaign. In a remote region of War Zone D, several Airborne platoons ran into a large force of Vietcong hiding in the thick jungle. This time, the VC wanted a fight. The combat was intense, some of it savage hand-to-hand fighting. The noise level from rocket, machine gun, and automatic rifle fire was so high that officers and noncoms had to convey orders to their men by hand signals. Both forces sustained heavy casualties in a day-long battle that ended when the VC broke contact and disappeared into the jungle.[22]

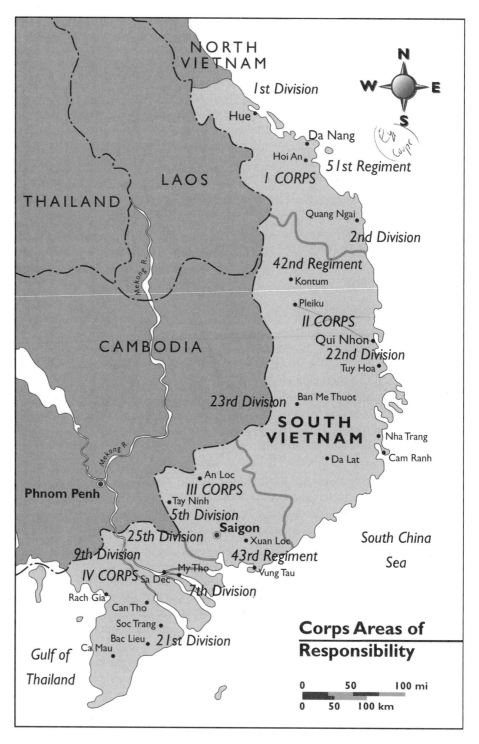

Figure 6.2 Public domain map.

The first big battle of the developing American war occurred in I ("Eye") Corps, the northernmost combat sector controlled by the 3rd Marine Amphibious Force, under the command of General Lewis Walt.[23] On August 15, 1965, Marine intelligence learned from a VC deserter the exact location of the 1st Vietcong Regiment. It was holed up in hamlets on the Batangan Peninsula, fifteen miles south of the new Marine base at Chu Lai in the Quang Ngai Province. General Walt concluded that the regiment posed a threat to Chu Lai, and he ordered the Marines to attack it.[24]

Quickly, the Marines organized a large-scale amphibious assault, code-named Operation STARLITE,[25] on the Vietcong positions. An assault battalion of the 3rd Marines landed on the sandy peninsula to pin the enemy against the sea. Another battalion came ashore in the enemy's rear. The two Marine battalions slowly worked their way forward over several days, squeezing the black pajama-clad Vietcong between them. As the Marines advanced, tactical aircraft strafed and naval gunfire bombarded the VC positions. The Vietcong regiment was destroyed; about 700 enemy troops were killed. The Marines lost fifty dead and 150 wounded. Operation STARLITE was considered a major American victory.[26]

Operations STARLITE and HUMP served as preliminaries for the most important battle of phase one of the war of attrition. It occurred in a remote region of the central highlands between October 18 and November 24, 1965. Westmoreland's chief worry during the summer of 1965 was that a PAVN offensive would conquer the central highlands, drive to the coast, and sever Saigon from the northern provinces, in effect cutting the country in half. He planned to counter the NVA drive with the 1st Air Cavalry Division (air mobile) based at An Khe. Westmoreland wanted the Air Cavalry to beat back the PAVN thrust and keep open Route 19, the main highway running from Pleiku to Qui Nhon.

The 1st Cavalry brought a new concept to warfare; it combined infantry, artillery, and aviation functions into one unit possessing 435 helicopters. Because rugged terrain and remote locations posed no obstacles for the Air Cavalry, they appeared to be the best force to use to blunt the PAVN offensive. The stage was set for the first battle pitting North Vietnamese regulars against an elite American combat force. Both sides were sending in their first strings for a campaign that was to have a decisive impact on the American conduct of the entire war.[27]

By early October, General Giap had committed three NVA regiments to the campaign, the 320th and 33rd, with the 66th held in reserve in Laos. These units were joined by some crack Vietcong main forces. On October 19, the 320th and 33rd struck a U. S. Special Forces camp at Plei Me on the Cambodian border, twenty-five miles southwest of Pleiku, and ambushed an ARVN relief column sent to help the embattled defenders. The NVA regiments then lay siege to the Special Forces camp. Their objective was to destroy Plei Me, perhaps other camps in the area, and capture Pleiku. The North Vietnamese would then be positioned to strike east toward the coast. Westmoreland countered with the Air Cavalry, which supported the ARVN relief force with air and artillery attacks. U. S. firepower inflicted heavy casualties on the enemy and broke the siege of Plei Me.[28]

With their opening gambit checked, the PAVN forces retreated to the west. Westmoreland ordered the 1st Air Cavalry to search out and destroy the NVA forces. He was taking a gamble. The air mobile concept had never been tested in combat. The 1st Cavalry was under strength. Many of its soldiers were weakened from bouts with malaria, and many of their helicopters were not operational. The Air Cavalry would have to operate in unfamiliar and rugged terrain dominated by jungle-shrouded mountains. Even the open spaces between the jagged peaks were covered with shrubs and elephant grass as high as a man's head. The search area, the Ia Drang Valley, covered about 1,500 square miles of desolate country inhabited only by a Montagnard tribe, the Jarai.[29] To add to the danger, the inexperienced 1st Cavalry was also going after the regiments of one of the finest light infantry in the world.

The first phase of the Battle of the Ia Drang lasted for two weeks, from late October to November 14. It consisted of searches punctuated by brief and violent clashes whenever the Americans located NVA units. The largest of these battles occurred on November 6, when two Air Cavalry companies ran into an NVA ambush. Both sides were bloodied in a brief but brutal firefight.[30] Another week of sporadic clashes preceded the major battles of the Ia Drang campaign.

By November 10, the PAVN forces had eluded their pursuers and had made their way to the sheltering crevices of the Chu Pong massif, a mountain range at the southern end of the Ia Drang Valley near the Cambodian border. There they planned to rest and regroup for another assault on the camp at Plei Me. As the NVA forces took refuge in the Chu Pong Mountains, Major General Harry W. O. Kinnard, the Air Cavalry commander, ordered air searches of the area around the massif. After aerial reconnaissance, Kinnard ordered the 1st Battalion, 7th Cavalry, to attack the largest landing site in the valley at the foot of the mountains, named "Landing Zone X-ray."[31] The 1st Battalion helicoptered in on November 14. Inadvertently, the 1st Cavalry had launched its attack right in the midst of an NVA staging area. The PAVN tactical commander, General Chu Huy Man, instantly ordered the 66th and 33rd NVA regiments to counterattack. The climactic phase of the Battle of the Ia Drang was joined.

Within a few hours, the 1st Battalion was engulfed "in fighting as fierce as any ever experienced by American troops."[32] Lieutenant Colonel Harold G. Moore Jr., commanding the embattled battalion, brought in air strikes and artillery support and also urgently requested reinforcements. The NVA rained rocket and mortar fire on Landing Zone X-ray in an effort to deny the 1st battalion its reinforcements. Despite heavy fire, another battalion landed at Landing Zone X-ray to join the fight. For three days, fighting raged in the vicinity of Landing Zone X-ray, an area about the size of an American football field. The two U. S. battalions beat back repeated attacks by one of the NVA regiments that was trying to overrun their perimeter. The combat was intense, "resulting in savage, close quarter fighting, sometimes in hand-to-hand combat. One U. S. soldier was found dead, his hand clutching the throat of a dead enemy infantryman."[33]

Figure 6.3   Elements of the 7th Cavalry fighting during the Battle of the Ia Drang, October–November 1965, the first major battle of the American Vietnam War. *Source:* U. S. Army photo

Air Cavalry pilots flew in and out of the landing zone under heavy fire, bringing in ammunition and supplies and hauling out wounded and dead soldiers. Air Force tactical bombers bombed and strafed enemy positions. Artillery, hauled to nearby firebases by powerful CH 47 Chinook cargo helicopters, rained thousands of rounds on the North Vietnamese, as B-52 strategic bombers flying out of Guam, each carrying a 36,000-pound payload, used for the first time in support of ground operations, pounded the NVA positions.[34]

The battle for Landing Zone X-ray ended on November 16. Having failed to break through the U. S. perimeter and having sustained huge losses from American artillery and bombs, the North Vietnamese withdrew from the battle site and retreated into Cambodia. Forbidden by the rules of engagement then in place from pursuing a retreating enemy in neutral territory, General Kinnard had no choice but to let them go. Over the next few days, occasional firefights ensued between the air cavalrymen and straggling NVA units, the last occurring on November 24. The Battle of the Ia Drang was over. Soon afterward, the Americans also withdrew from the river valley and were flown back to their base at An Khe. American officials estimated that the North Vietnamese lost 3,561 soldiers killed and more than 1,000 wounded of the 6,000 that they had committed to battle. The three enemy regiments were decimated. They did not return to action for more than six months. The PAVN threat to the central highlands had been eliminated;

305 American soldiers had been killed during the five weeks of fighting around Plei Me and in the Ia Drang valley.[35]

U. S. forces won a significant victory at Ia Drang. General Westmoreland and his Chief of Operations General William Depuy, both strongly committed to an attrition strategy, found confirmation for their views in the favorable ratio of U. S. to enemy losses which they fixed at 12:1. Both leaders were convinced that search-and-destroy missions would eventually defeat both the Vietcong and PAVN forces fighting in South Vietnam. Seasoned in the meat-grinder battles of World War II, Westmoreland and Depuy were convinced that they could bleed the enemy to death over the long haul of attrition warfare. The Battle of the Ia Drang locked the attrition strategy in place for nearly four years.[36]

The campaign also vindicated the air mobile concept; henceforth, helicopter assaults would be the mainstay of U. S. tactics in Vietnam.[37] Over the years of America's longest war, over a million soldiers would ride into battle aboard Huey helicopters, and the familiar "whup, whup, whup" of their whirling rotors would become the most enduring soundtrack of the Vietnam War. Westmoreland was also impressed by the performance of the green U. S. sky troopers, fighting a tough foe under egregious conditions.

But military analysts concerned themselves with some of the implications of the Battle of the Ia Drang. They wondered about the accuracy of the estimates of enemy casualties that, according to some skeptical soldiers on the scene, were merely WEGs (wild-eyed guesses) that probably drastically inflated the numbers.[38] They also wondered why the 1st Cavalry so quickly abandoned the Ia Drang Valley after weeks of hard fighting, leaving the region vulnerable to future PAVN infiltrations. They were not reassured by the Army's explanation that the Valley had no strategic significance and that the chief purpose of the operation had been to kill as many enemy soldiers as possible.

The Ia Drang campaign also signaled that the Vietnam War was entering a new phase; it had evolved into two parallel wars. The long-standing conflict between the GVN forces and the Vietcong for control of the countryside continued. "Superimposed on the older war was the more recent and more conventional struggle between the NVA and the Allied forces."[39] In the future, there would be fewer small-scale, low-intensity campaigns between South Vietnamese forces and Vietcong guerrillas and more large-scale conventional warfare between invading NVA main force units and American troops. Future battles would require more U. S. forces and would portend higher U. S. casualties. "A major part of the war in Southeast Asia had thus become Americanized, as vividly demonstrated by the Ia Drang campaign. . . ."[40]

The Battle of the Ia Drang also indicated that the Air Cavalry had a serious tactical limitation. Once out of their helicopters and on the ground, American combat units were immobilized. The lightly armored NVA troopers used their foot mobility to outmaneuver the Americans. Only if the NVA attacked could the Americans engage them in battle. And only then could the Americans, using their far greater firepower, inflict more casualties than they took. But if the enemy chose to elude American assault units, as the Vietcong troops did repeatedly in War Zone D earlier in the year, and as the retreating NVA troops did for two weeks in the Drang River Valley, the Air Cavalry troops could not force a fight because they were not willing to leave their landing zones to go plunging off into the jungle in pursuit of their more mobile enemy. Throughout the Ia Drang campaign, the NVA had retained the initiative. If the PAVN forces wished to evade the U. S. forces or engage in brief, small-scale firefights, they had the maneuverability to do so. Having learned the hard way what U. S. firepower could do to their regiments if they chose to go to battle with the Americans, PAVN forces could be expected to adjust their tactics to reduce combat losses in future campaigns. How would U. S. search-and-destroy missions attrite a mobile enemy that could control the terms of engagement?[41]

Senior NVA commanders in Hanoi took note. Their infantry had gone up against the most modern weapons system the high-tech superpower could throw at them, and they had survived. They could use their foot mobility to evade the U. S. firestorm and could retreat to the Cambodian sanctuaries to avoid annihilation. For them, Ia Drang amounted to a victory. The outcome of the Battle of the Ia Drang also convinced General Giap and his associates that North Vietnam would win the war eventually. Protracted warfare, the people's war strategy, would inevitably defeat air mobile tactics. The NVA would avoid catastrophic defeat, and they would avoid taking unsustainable casualties. They would be patient; they would retain the tactical initiative. In time, they would wear the Americans down. The war would become unpopular with the American people, and the U. S. soldiers would have to leave South Vietnam—just like the Chinese and the French had been forced to leave previously. Once the Americans were gone, the NVA and Vietcong forces would then quickly dispatch the puppet forces of the GVN, and victory would be theirs.[42]

The civilian leader directing the American Vietnam War also derived lessons from the Battle of the Ia Drang. Secretary of Defense Robert S. McNamara was briefed by Generals Westmoreland and Kinnard in the aftermath of the campaign. What he grasped was the most important message coming out of that crucial battle: Vietnam was going to be a long and difficult war. "The Vietnam War had just exploded into an open-ended and massive commitment of American men, money, and materiel."[43] Following his briefings, McNamara drafted two secret memos for President Johnson in which he stated that in the aftermath of the Ia Drang campaign, the United States had two options in Vietnam. It could arrange for a negotiated settlement and withdraw, or it could drastically increase the number of U. S. combat forces currently in Vietnam to try and win the war. If America opted for escalation, there could be 600,000 U. S. troops fighting in South Vietnam by 1967 and U. S. casualties could exceed 1,000 per month. Even so, in McNamara's estimation, the chances of defeating the North Vietnamese and Vietcong forces would be no better than one in two or one in three.[44] McNamara, concerned about the failure of the gradualist bombing campaign against North Vietnam to date, and having grasped the full implications of Ia Drang, was fast losing any expectations he may still have retained about a relatively quick and easy victory in the Vietnam War.

At year's end, General Westmoreland had achieved the objectives of phase one of his strategic war plan. The military situation had stabilized. He had 184,000 U. S. troops in South Vietnam and more were on their way. The Vietcong found they could not sustain the momentum they had built up earlier in the year. The PAVN offensive in the central highlands had been blunted. The ARVN forces had stopped losing the war. Since the advent of American combat forces during the summer of 1965, most war news had been favorable to the U. S. side. Within the United States, the war continued to enjoy widespread popular support. *Time* magazine named General Westmoreland its "Man of the Year" for 1965.

If it was true that the Allies had stopped losing by year's end, it was also true that they were far from winning the war. Even as security in South Vietnam had been strengthened in many areas, enemy infiltration had increased. About 20,000 NVA troops were fighting in South Vietnam, constituting one-third of the enemy's combat effectives. U. S. intelligence officials put the total enemy strength at year's end at 221,000, far more troops than ever before. The Vietcong/PAVN forces were matching the U. S. escalations. Intervention had saved the GVN from imminent collapse; it also transformed a revolutionary conflict into a prolonged and lethal international war.[45]

There were few major battles in South Vietnam during 1966, although there were many small-scale firefights all over the country. Although fighting occurred everywhere, it was concentrated in the areas where the Vietminh and their successors in the NLF were strongest: in the northern provinces and in the areas northwest and southwest of Saigon. In the northern sector, American Marines engaged frequently in combat operations against Vietcong forces and also defended the region just below the DMZ from NVA attacks. Westmoreland could not implement phase two of his attrition strategy according to the schedule for 1966, primarily because manpower shortages delayed his buildup of combat forces. His policy of limiting soldiers to a one-year tour in the combat zone also delayed the U. S. buildup and was a continuous source of manpower instability throughout the war. Further, most of the arriving troopers and their officers had never seen a moment's combat. Their training in the states before arriving "in country" had not prepared them for the rigors of warfare. Westmoreland spent most of the year acclimating, training, and building up the U. S. combat force levels. He was preparing his troops for the large-scale operations that would characterize the fighting during 1967.

American troops also had to adapt to the unique conditions of the Vietnam battlefield. Unlike World War II or Korea, the Vietnam conflict was a frontless war. There were no territorial objectives to be taken. There was no vital center of enemy resistance to be destroyed; all of South Vietnam was a fluid battlefield. Military operations had to be highly mobile, multilinear, and nondirectional.[46] Battles occurred throughout the entire country. They could occur wherever and whenever the VC or PAVN forces picked a fight. They could occur in remote, sparsely populated highlands or borderlands, or amid the populous Mekong Delta and coastal regions. The American objective in these sporadic encounters was to attrite as many of the enemy as possible while using their superior air mobility and firepower to minimize their own casualties. Westmoreland never had enough combat effectives to occupy an area after a battle, so, inevitably, the American forces would be withdrawn after a campaign had ended. Enemy forces often returned to these areas soon after the American pullout because there were no available ARVN forces to secure and pacify them or because the ARVN forces available were ineffective in securing and pacifying the areas from which the enemy had been cleared. In such a formless war, the only measures of progress, of "winning," were statistics: the number of enemy soldiers killed, captured, or persuaded to surrender, of enemy weapons captured, and of enemy equipment, supplies, and food stores destroyed. It was not an orderly war with territorial goals, but a ragged war of numbers, numbers that never added up to a U. S. victory before American public support for the war collapsed and time ran out.

In the fall of 1966, the United States mounted the largest search-and-destroy mission to date, Operation ATTLEBORO, which prefigured the big-unit war of 1967. In late October, General Westmoreland sent a large Allied force consisting of the 1st Infantry Division, units from two other U. S. infantry divisions, the 173rd Airborne Brigade, and a large contingent of ARVN troops into War Zone C. War Zone C was an area northwest of Saigon in the Tay Ninh Province that bordered Cambodia. It had been a Vietcong stronghold for years. The Vietcong 9th Division, accompanied by a NVA regiment, had attacked a Special Forces outpost in that region and then overran a relief column sent to assist it.[47] In a series of battles spread over a month, the 22,000-man allied force, supported with B-52 strikes and artillery, killed over 1,100 enemy soldiers and captured tons of supplies before driving their adversaries across the border into Cambodia.[48]

As 1967 dawned, Westmoreland was more convinced than ever that large-scale search-and-destroy missions such as Operation ATTLEBORO provided the means for the destruction of North Vietnamese regular forces and Vietcong main force units. He believed subsequent ATTLEBORO-type operations would be the keys to eventual Allied victory. He "forged jumbo operational plans as the dominant pattern of strategy for the upcoming year."[49] Even though hundreds of small-scale operations would continue all over South Vietnam during the year, 1967 would be the year in which Westmoreland vigorously pushed his big-unit war.

Westmoreland had at his disposal 390,000 U. S. soldiers, including seven divisions, two airborne and two light infantry brigades, an armored regiment, and a Special Forces group. They were supplemented by "third country" forces from South Korea, Australia, and New Zealand. In addition, ARVN, which had expanded rapidly in 1966, could field eleven divisions. Total RVNAF (Republic of South Vietnam Forces), in addition to the ARVN units, included territorial forces, security forces, local troops, and irregulars. Westmoreland's Combined Campaign Plan for 1967 assigned RVNAF the tasks of securing and pacifying areas under their control, while the U. S. forces carried the brunt of the fighting against the Communists. His goals included securing South Vietnam's borders and beating back NVA attacks across the DMZ, neutralizing the VC forces in War Zones C and D, eradicating Vietcong sanctuaries in the vicinity of Saigon, defending the strategic central highlands against PAVN incursions, driving the VC and PAVN forces back from the populated regions, and providing security for the populated regions of South Vietnam. It was an ambitious plan.[50]

The first of the 1967 big-unit campaigns occurred in a region about thirty miles northwest of Saigon, in a strategic area sandwiched between War Zones C and D called the Iron Triangle, which served as a staging area for VC attacks against GVN installations in the vicinity of Saigon. The Iron Triangle, bounded on two sides by rivers and on a third by a jungle, incorporated about forty square miles of nearly impenetrable territory covered by trees, vines, bushes, and shrubs. Underneath the dense forest and jungle growth lay miles of tunnels, caverns, and chambers, some of which dated from the Vietminh campaigns against the Japanese during World War II. Thousands of insurgents could inhabit this subterranean labyrinth, an inviolable sanctuary, seemingly immune from counterattacks or efforts at destruction. On the fringe of the region, nestled in a loop of the Saigon River, lay the village of Ben Suc, many of whose estimated 3,500 residents had been Vietcong or Vietcong supporters for years.[51]

Wanting to eliminate once and for all the threat to the Saigon regime posed by the Vietcong redoubt buried within the recesses of the Iron Triangle, General Westmoreland in early January 1967 launched a massive operation, code-named CEDAR FALLS, lasting three weeks and involving 30,000 U. S. and ARVN forces.[52] The first phase of the operation was to dispose of the threat posed by the villagers of Ben Suc. If, according to Vietcong doctrine, itself derived from Maoist theory, the people are the "sea" in which the guerrilla "fish" must swim, MACV strategists concluded that permanently eliminating the threat posed by the Vietcong forces marshaled in the Iron Triangle necessarily involved "draining the sea" by removing the villagers and razing the village.

On January 8, 1967, an armada of U. S. transport helicopters suddenly descended upon Ben Suc. Instantly, a force of hundreds of American and ARVN soldiers surrounded the village. They met with little resistance from the sullen villagers. Although the arrival of the helicopters caught them by surprise, most of the Vietcong fighters in the village at the time escaped. All of the villagers were rounded up and transferred to a refugee camp at Phu Loi, near Phu Cuong, fifteen miles downriver. Specially trained destruction teams then moved in. Giant caterpillar tractors, called Rome plows, fitted with wide bulldozer blades, cleared huge swatches of jungle, exposing the tunnel complexes. Demolition teams destroyed the houses above the ground and the tunnel complexes below. Within a few days, "the village of Ben Suc no longer existed."[53]

While Ben Suc was being demolished, U. S. combat forces ranged across the Iron Triangle searching for Vietcong units. Because the Vietcong commander chose not to engage the American forces, most of the VC scattered and fled. Despite the corps-sized operation, the superior American mobility, and the vastly greater U. S. firepower, the tactical initiative remained with the Vietcong commander. He could choose to fight or not to fight; he could therefore control both the scale of the fighting and his casualty rate.

During the three weeks of the CEDAR FALLS operation, about 700 Vietcong were killed and another 700 were either captured or turned themselves in under the "chieu hoi" (open arms) program, run by the GVN that granted amnesty to Vietcong defectors. American forces also destroyed enemy structures, equipment, and food supplies. Volunteers from the 1st Infantry Division's special chemical unit, nicknamed the "tunnel rats," combed the nearly twelve miles of tunnels that were exposed at various locations in the Iron Triangle. Among their discoveries were a power station, a fully equipped field hospital, a weapons factory, and a regional PLAF headquarters.[54]

The entire region was then bombed, shelled, strafed, and burned to destroy any remaining structures or tunnels that could be of use to the Vietcong. In an effort to deter Vietcong reentry into the Iron Triangle, the area was declared a "free fire zone," which meant that artillery and air strikes could be made in the region without prior approval of GVN officials and without warning to its inhabitants. As the Allies departed the Iron Triangle, they were convinced that they had dealt the Vietcong a serious setback. They had rendered one of the enemy's long-time bastions and staging areas unusable and had severed the Vietcong military and political connections with the people inhabiting its vicinity. They had permanently removed a serious security threat to the GVN. They soon discovered that "they were wrong."[55]

The VC quickly returned to the Iron Triangle. They rebuilt and resupplied their base and once again threatened the region around Saigon. The razing of Ben Suc and the forced relocation of all of its residents amounted to an admission that the ARVN forces were failing to pacify the peasants. Some villagers were killed and others were brutally treated by ARVN soldiers in the process of relocating them. Most of the villagers of Ben Suc were angry about their forced move. They lost their homes, their ancestral lands, and all of their possessions except for what they could carry with them. They found conditions in the refugee camp at Phu Loi miserable; initially, each family was allotted only ten square feet of living space in hastily constructed shelters. About all CEDAR FALLS brought the Saigon government "was a devastated forest and a horde of hostile refugees."[56]

Using the same forces and more, the United States mounted a larger operation called JUNCTION CITY against War Zone C, about a month after CEDAR FALLS. The American soldiers made special efforts during JUNCTION CITY to trap Vietcong combat units and force a fight with them, thus avoiding a repetition of CEDAR FALLS, when most of the VC slipped through their grasp. But mostly the Vietcong avoided combat during JUNCTION CITY, and the bulk of their forces fled across the Cambodian border. Even so, over a three-month period, American officials reported about 3,000 enemy soldiers killed.[57] But War Zone C was not neutralized, the Vietcong

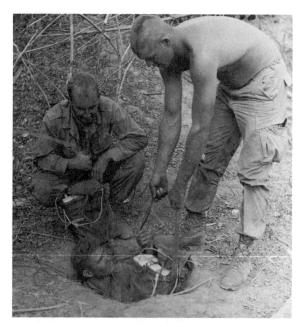

Figure 6.4   Soldiers prepare to destroy one of the many Vietcong tunnels that were exposed during the campaigns in the Thanh Dien Forest region of the Iron Triangle during Operation CEDAR FALLS, January 1967. *Source:* U. S. Army photo

9th Division was not put out of the war, and no serious efforts were made to pacify the villagers living in the region. War Zone C continued to be used as a VC basing area after the Allied withdrawal.

One dimension of the ground war that limited the effectiveness of JUNCTION CITY was the rules of engagement civilian leaders imposed on American troops fighting in Vietnam. Even though both the VC and the NVA forces repeatedly violated Cambodian neutrality, U. S. forces were never allowed to pursue their enemies into Cambodia or attack any Cambodian-populated areas. The Vietcong 9th Division commander, aware that U. S. mobility and firepower had eliminated the inviolability of VC basing areas inside of South Vietnam, and wishing to evade the mounting American pressure on his forces, took his troops into adjacent Cambodian sanctuaries where they joined PAVN combat units.

But Westmoreland's powerful forces had to stop at the Cambodian border. The rules of engagement in effect confined them to defensive efforts aimed at attriting a resourceful, highly maneuverable enemy who could escape beyond the fixed boundaries of the ground war in southern Vietnam to rest, resupply, regroup, replenish ranks, and then renew attacks on GVN targets in South Vietnam. U. S. military commanders vainly sought to modify these rules of engagement to permit U. S. troops to pursue opposing forces to their destruction or until they surrendered, even if that meant some fighting on Cambodian soil and inflicting damage and casualties on that neutral nation.[58]

While Operations CEDAR FALLS and JUNCTION CITY were being conducted in III Corps Tactical Zone in the vicinity of Saigon, to the north, in II Corps Tactical

Zone, battles for control of the central highlands raged. Units of the 4th Infantry Division under the command of Major General William R. Peers, operating out of their base camp at Pleiku, battled forces from the 1st and 10th NVA divisions. In the Kontum Province, small units from both sides engaged in fierce firefights of short duration amid "some of the most difficult tropical terrain in the world."[59] There, among huge trees, as tall as 250 to 300 feet, where little sunlight filtered through a tropical rain forest and triple-canopied jungle even at midday, PAVN regulars chose where and when to attack U. S. forces. The Americans counterattacked, trying to kill as many of the enemy as they could, often sustaining heavy losses themselves. Both sides lost many soldiers in vicious jungle-mountain warfare.

In other action in the central highlands, General Peers deployed units of his 4th Division along the South Vietnamese border in western Pleiku. His objective was to deny invading PAVN forces access to South Vietnam's strategic heartlands. From April to October, U. S. and NVA troops fought a series of battles in the rolling tropical plains of western Pleiku near the Cambodian border. The hard-fighting U. S. forces succeeded in beating back numerous NVA thrusts. By October, General Peers discerned that the major Communist push would be an invasion of the Kontum Province, directly north of Pleiku.[60] There, one month later, occurred the Battle of Dak To, a decisive battle that determined the outcome of the campaigns waged for control of the central highlands during 1967.

Dak To was the site of a U. S. Army Special Forces camp set amid towering mountains in the central Kontum Province. The camp lay in a valley ringed by 6,000-foot peaks and ridges. Fighting had begun during the summer, when NVA forces had entrenched themselves in bunker complexes along the hilltops and ridgelines above the camp. For months, grueling battles took place in the vicinity of Dak To between forces from the 24th NVA Division and Allied forces that included the 3rd Brigade of the 1st Cavalry Division and some elite ARVN ranger units. In early November, a battalion of the 173rd Airborne and a brigade from the 4th Infantry Division were flown in to join the battle. The Allies prepared to locate and assault the NVA positions.

During the first two weeks of November, U. S. patrols made contact with the NVA units, enabling the American troops to call in artillery barrages, tactical aircraft, and high-flying B-52s to pound the enemy positions. On November 17, the fighting around Dak To intensified when a patrol from the 173rd Airborne Brigade came upon the 174th NVA Regiment entrenched in bunker complexes running along the eastern slope and the summit of a peak known on American maps as Hill 875. Hill 875 lay twelve miles west of the Special Forces camp, about two miles from the point where the borders of South Vietnam, Cambodia, and Laos merge.[61] "The fight for Hill 875 would ultimately climax the Battle for Dak To, as well as the 1967 campaign for the highlands."[62]

The 2nd Battalion, 503rd Infantry, of the 173rd Airborne was ordered to move in and clear the enemy from Hill 875. It took five days of hard fighting to secure the mountain. During the battle, the paratroopers of 2nd Battalion lost so many men that another airborne battalion and units of the 4th Infantry Division had to be brought in. On November 23, the Americans reached the summit of Hill 875, only to discover that the defenders had abandoned their positions during the night. The 174th had accomplished its mission, which had been to cover the withdrawal of the NVA forces retreating into Cambodia and Laos.[63]

The taking of Hill 875 ended the Battle of Dak To. U. S. officials estimated that during the campaign, the North Vietnamese lost about 1,400 KIA (killed in action) compared to 289 American and 49 ARVN dead.[64] The Battle of Dak To was also the last of the border campaigns in the central highlands for the year. The Allied forces had repulsed the NVA invaders. The strategic central highlands remained under South Vietnamese control.

As the border battles raged in the Pleiku and Kontum Provinces for control of the central highlands, to the north in I Corps Tactical Zone the Marines held the line against efforts by the NVA units to infiltrate across the DMZ into northern South Vietnam. Along Route 9, a dirt road that ran east-west across the country's northernmost province of Quang Tri, from the sandy coastal plains to the mountainous border with Laos, the Marines had constructed a series of fire support and patrol bases at Dong Ha, Cam Lo, Khe Sanh, and Lang Vei. The facility at Khe Sanh already served as a Special Forces camp. Teams of Montagnards, involved in the secret war in Laos that aimed at interdicting enemy supplies coming down the Ho Chi Minh Trail, operated out of Khe Sanh. Route 9 roughly paralleled the DMZ, and most of the Marine firebases lay ten to fifteen miles south of the DMZ. Forward of these fire bases, perched on a hill three miles south of the DMZ near Con Thien (Hill of Angels), the Marines had constructed their most important fire base.[65]

Artillery batteries from the NVA 325th C Division shelled the northern fire bases sporadically. In April 1967, a regiment from the 325th occupied several hills in the vicinity of Khe Sanh in preparation for an attack on the camp. The Marines, in a series of vicious hill fights, drove the PAVN forces from the heights and ended that threat to Khe Sanh.[66] In September, NVA forces besieged Con Thien. Artillery and rocket barrages on Con Thien and a nearby base at Gio Linh were followed by infantry assaults that tried to overrun the Marine perimeters.

U. S. forces eventually broke the sieges of Con Thien and Gio Linh with a combination of massed firepower and aggressive ground tactics. A combination of artillery and naval gunfire, tactical aircraft strikes, and B-52 bombings hit the enemy positions along the DMZ. Marine troopers, using claymore mines, machine guns, and automatic rifles, beat back the PAVN charges, inflicting severe casualties. The hellish Battle of Con Thien ended on October 20. American estimates of NVA losses for that battle were 2,000 KIA. Over 200 Marines died in the conflict.[67] At year's end, the Marines still retained all of their forward bases. They had withstood sieges, repelled infantry assaults, and blocked all NVA efforts to infiltrate units across the DMZ.

Within a few months, the Americans would discover that the bloody campaigns initiated by the NVA forces at Dak To and Con Thien in the fall of 1967 were part of

Figure 6.5 U. S. troops engaged in combat. Firefights between small units erupted suddenly and were fierce while they lasted. *Source:* U. S. Army photo

a strategic plan to lure American forces into remote border regions in northern and central South Vietnam in preparation for the surprise Vietcong/PAVN assaults on the country's cities and towns during the Tet campaign of early 1968.

Westmoreland's attrition strategy during 1967 had accomplished major objectives. American troopers had pushed many of the VC main force units and guerrillas away from populated areas, forcing them to flee to remote regions of the country, or seek refuge in Cambodian sanctuaries to avoid destruction. Vietcong-controlled areas in South Vietnam had been significantly reduced. The Vietcong found they no longer had any safe havens inside South Vietnam; nowhere were they safe from the reach of American firepower. The NVA forces were driven out of the central and northern border provinces of South Vietnam, often with heavy casualties. As 1967 ended, American officials estimated that 180,000 enemy soldiers had been killed since 1965. Assuming a sizeable official inflation of body counts, it is clear that American forces had inflicted severe losses on the enemy while keeping their own losses relatively light. The number of PLAF volunteers declined, forcing the NLF to rely on conscription, which many villagers resented. U. S. combat forces and Westmoreland's aggressive tactics prevented a GVN collapse and Vietcong victory, both of which probably would have occurred before 1965 ended, if not for the massive American intervention.

But the U. S. attrition strategy also had limits, and it was grounded on some dubious assumptions. Westmoreland assumed that American forces would be able to use their superior firepower and mobility to destroy enemy forces at a greater rate than they could be replaced, at the same time keeping U. S. casualties low and within politically acceptable limits. But despite Westmoreland's big-unit campaigns of 1967, the war remained essentially one of small-unit warfare. For these small-unit battles, the VC and NVA units usually retained the tactical initiative. They avoided pitched battles when the odds were not in their favor and deftly sidestepped major U. S. sweeps. If the odds favored them, they launched attacks at times and places of their choosing. They determined where and when they wanted to fight and for how long; thus, they controlled the tempo of their losses. If their casualties reached unacceptable levels, they broke off battles and melted into the jungle. The U. S. forces could use their massive firepower to inflict heavy casualties, but they could not annihilate their enemies. "The pace of fighting was dictated by the North Vietnamese and by the Vietcong, not by the United States."[68]

They also exploited the restrictions placed on U. S. forces. They knew that American troops could not pursue them and that U. S. aircraft could not strike them whenever they sought the safety of their cross-border sanctuaries in Cambodia and Laos. They also took advantage of the weather, when heavy rains, thunderstorms, and thick fog hampered American air operations. When retreat was impossible, both the Vietcong and PAVN troops found they could nullify the U. S. firepower advantage by swiftly closing with the American troops and fighting at close quarters.[69] The MACV planners did not anticipate the remarkable ability of the Communists to absorb huge manpower losses and continue the war. Despite suffering proportionately far greater

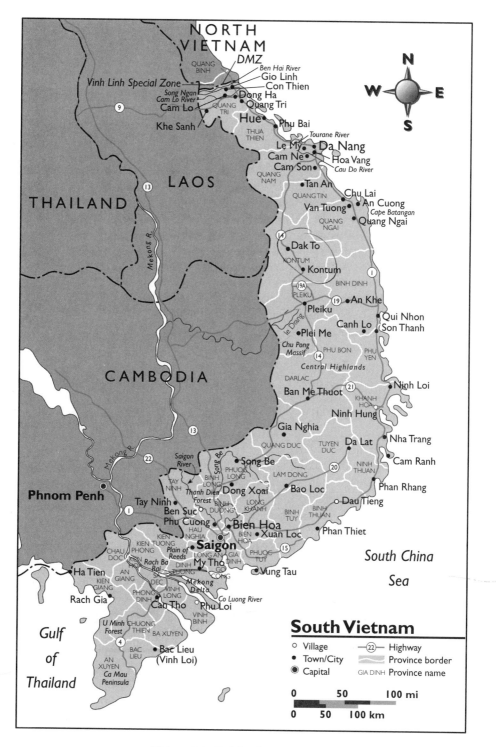

Figure 6.6 Public domain map.

casualties than the armies of most nations that have lost wars in the twentieth century, the Vietcong and NVA forces carried on the fight year after year. The MACV planners also could not foresee that their pursuit of victory via attrition amounted to an open-ended U. S. military commitment that might eventually require more forces than President Johnson would find politically acceptable to send. Finally, they failed to anticipate that rising American casualties, although proportionally and absolutely far lower than the losses of either the NLF or PAVN forces, would become a major cause of the Vietnam War's growing unpopularity in the United States.[70]

Although the Americans frequently inflicted serious damage on the enemy forces, they had not defeated the Communists as 1967 ended. Nor were the NVA or Vietcong anywhere close to being defeated. Despite substantial losses, the Vietcong and NVA forces not only survived, but increased in numbers. Because Westmoreland never had enough U. S. combat-effectives to occupy an area following a large-unit search-and-destroy sweep and the ARVN forces were usually unable to secure or pacify these areas, the Vietcong returned and reestablished their bases following Allied withdrawals. In addition, Westmoreland never had enough forces both to fight the enemy main force units and secure all of the rural areas where most of the villagers lived.

Many Vietcong guerrillas retained their capability of operating within the populated regions. The NLF's political infrastructure remained intact. Many of the NLF political cadres retained their ties to the villagers. In South Vietnam, as 1967 ended, thousands of insurgent "fish" continued to swim in the South Vietnamese "sea." America had won all of the major battles since the Battle of the Ia Drang, but it was not close to winning the war. In the summer of 1965, General Westmoreland had estimated that the war could be won by the end of 1967. By the end of 1967, he had nearly 500,000 soldiers fighting a stalemated war.

Attrition warfare also had several adverse consequences that hindered the U. S. effort at nation-building in South Vietnam. The massive use of firepower disrupted the South Vietnamese economy, diminished rice production, inadvertently killed civilians, and generated millions of refugees. The refugees were herded into squalid camps or else they fled to the cities, where they survived as an uprooted fringe population representing potential Vietcong fifth columns.[71] The U. S. war thus weakened the social fabric of a fragmented nation and further alienated people from a fragile government that had never enjoyed the support of much of the rural population. The American takeover of the war represented an explicit expression of U. S. officials' lack of confidence in the South Vietnamese military forces and further undermined the resolve of the ARVN troops that were all too willing to let the Americans take the offensive in major campaigns.[72]

THUNDER FROM THE AIR

ROLLING THUNDER, the strategic air war waged by the U. S. Air Force, the air attack arm of the U. S. Navy, and the VNAF against North Vietnam that began on March 2, 1965, paralleled the ground war raging in South Vietnam. Initially, the air war against the North was a strictly limited affair. President Johnson himself selected the targets on a weekly basis, allowing air commanders to choose the specific times for the raids during that time span. During the first weeks of ROLLING THUNDER, attacks were confined to military targets, mostly south of the 20th parallel. In time, the air war against North Vietnam evolved in phases. "During each phase, a different emphasis was placed upon targets, and the scope and intensity of the attacks varied as well."[73] During the first phase implemented in the spring and summer of 1965, allied planes also attacked infiltration routes in North Vietnam, just above the DMZ to try to destroy the ability of the North Vietnamese to infiltrate men and supplies into South Vietnam in support of the Vietcong insurgency.

It quickly became evident to the planners of ROLLING THUNDER that the gradualist bombing campaign of limited scope had failed to reduce appreciably North Vietnam's ability to infiltrate men and supplies into South Vietnam. Hanoi also gave no indication that it was ready to negotiate an end to the war on anything like American terms. Conceding the air war's ineffectiveness, General Earle Wheeler, chairman of the Joint Chiefs, advised President Johnson to intensify the aerial campaign, order more sorties, and strike at key North Vietnamese military and industrial targets. After a brief debate in July 1965 among senior administration officials in which George Ball, the hawks' nemesis, was the only adviser to oppose escalating the air war, Johnson ordered major increases in the number of air strikes. He also expanded the target list. For the rest of 1965, Johnson and McNamara gradually expanded the air war against North Vietnam, although they refused to order an all-out air assault to try to destroy the war-making ability of North Vietnam, as called for by the Joint Chiefs and Admiral U. S. Grant Sharp, Commander-in-Chief of the Pacific Fleet (CINCPACFLT) and commander of ROLLING THUNDER.[74]

As 1965 ended, it was evident to both U. S. civilian and military leaders that the air war had failed to accomplish its strategic goals, even though it had expanded into a large-scale operation involving thousands of sorties monthly. The target list had expanded to include military bases, transportation systems, and supply depots, as well as intensified bombing of the major infiltration routes out of North Vietnam. Intelligence data confirmed that Hanoi was infiltrating more men and supplies into the south than ever before, and North Vietnam also continued its strong backing of the southern insurgency. Further, U. S. intelligence sources showed that the bombing, far from hurting the morale of the North Vietnamese people, had united them with their government.[75]

Johnson's military advisers blamed the continuing failure of the air war on the self-imposed restrictions of civilian leaders. But Secretary of Defense Robert McNamara remained confident that at some point the gradually escalating bombing campaign would cross a threshold, would reach a point where Hanoi would stop supporting the southern insurgency rather than continue to absorb punishment and risk losing their painstakingly constructed industrial base. President Johnson still believed in the air war as a means to secure his political goals in Vietnam, but he realized that bombing could not bring him the relatively quick and easy victory he had anticipated.[76]

After Johnson ordered a bombing pause from December 24, 1965, to February 1, 1966, in a futile effort to get negotiations going, both the air war and the debate over it resumed. Once again the Joint Chiefs pressured McNamara to escalate the bombing, but they changed their plan from interdiction to bombing North Vietnam's POL (petroleum products, i.e., gasoline, oil, and lubricants) storage facilities located near the cities of Hanoi and Haiphong. The Joint Chiefs understood oil to be the vital element in North Vietnam's ability to infiltrate men and materiel into South Vietnam. By early 1966, U. S. intelligence estimates had placed five NVA regiments in South Vietnam. Supplying these forces required the DRV to expand its truck fleet. By destroying North Vietnam's oil supply, the Joint Chiefs reasoned that they could stop the trucks and thus stop them from supplying the NVA and NLF forces fighting in South Vietnam. Since North Vietnam possessed no oil wells and no refineries, all of their oil was imported, most of it via Soviet tankers that docked and offloaded their cargoes at the port of Haiphong. Prior to distributing it, most of the oil was stored in giant tank farms on the outskirts of the city. The Joint Chiefs insisted that destroying these storage tanks and those near Hanoi would cripple North Vietnam's ability to sustain the revolution in South Vietnam. Admiral Sharp concurred.[77]

Pentagon analysts thoroughly studied the POL bombing proposals for months. Since the sites were located near cities, there was a high risk of civilian casualties. The oil storage areas were also heavily defended by anti-aircraft batteries, surface-to-air missiles (SAMs), and North Vietnamese air force fighters. The danger of heavy U. S. aircraft losses was great. Johnson also worried that such a major escalation of the war might provoke Hanoi to expand the war in South Vietnam, or worse, it might bring the Chinese and the Soviets into the conflict. After months of discussion, a consensus of Johnson's military and civilian advisers finally convinced him that raids on North Vietnam's POL facilities were necessary. Johnson approved them, although he retained misgivings. On the day the first attacks were carried out, a distraught president, fearful that they might somehow go wrong, told his daughter, Luci, "Your daddy may go down in history as having started World War III."[78]

On June 29, 1966, Navy fighter-bombers from USS *Ranger* on Yankee Station in the Gulf of Tonkin and Air Force fighter-bombers flying out of bases in Thailand struck three POL sites "in the heart of North Vietnam."[79] American military and civilian leaders considered these initial attacks highly successful. They were the first air strikes near Hanoi and Haiphong, and they caught the enemy by surprise. Facilities near the two cities accounting for about 60 percent of North Vietnam's POL storage capacity were destroyed, with the loss of only one American plane. Polls showed the American public strongly backed the POL raids, and Johnson's popularity rating jumped twelve points, from 42 percent to 54 percent. America's European allies were less enthusiastic about the POL raids, and Prime Minister Harold Wilson of Great Britain publicly dissociated himself from the attacks.[80] The Soviet Union and China both condemned the air strikes and promised increased aid to North Vietnam, but made no gestures toward intervention.

Delighted with the bombing results and the public's response to them, and relieved that the Chinese and Soviets reacted moderately, Johnson ordered additional POL strikes. During July and August 1966, Navy and Air Force planes attacked oil storage facilities in the North Vietnamese heartland. By the time the POL campaign ended on September 4, 75 percent of Hanoi's oil storage capacity had been destroyed. Soviet-bloc tankers that hauled in Hanoi's POL supplies could no longer offload their cargoes in Haiphong because American bombers had destroyed the port's pumping equipment.[81] But North Vietnamese air defenders made American pilots and aircrewmen pay a high price for the July and August POL campaigns. Anti-aircraft batteries and SAMs downed over seventy U. S. aircraft during those two months. Hoa Lo Prison in Hanoi, given the ironic nickname of "the Hanoi Hilton" by the Americans flyers, became the residence for years for dozens of American pilots and crewmen shot down over North Vietnam while flying POL missions.

Analysts monitoring the POL operations concluded that the attacks constituted a strategic failure. Having anticipated the raids long before President Johnson finally ordered them, the North Vietnamese had decentralized their POL supply systems. Stored in fifty-gallon drums in small camouflaged sites near major transportation arteries, dispersed POL supplies proved hard to find and extremely costly to destroy. Although the air strikes knocked out a high percentage of Hanoi's oil storage capacity, they destroyed only a small amount of their POL stores. The POL imports via rail from the Soviet Union through China quickly replaced the losses. Analysts also discovered that only a small percentage of North Vietnam's POL requirements were needed to keep the supply trucks rolling south, and the NVA had more than enough oil and gasoline for themselves.[82]

At the conclusion of the U. S. POL campaign, a joint CIA-DIA (Defense Intelligence Agency) report found that Hanoi retained "the capability to continue support of activities in South Vietnam at even increased combat levels."[83] McNamara also commissioned a study of the second phase of ROLLING THUNDER by the Institute for Defense Analysis (IDA), an independent agency from outside of the government, composed of forty-seven distinguished American scientists. The IDA report, known as the Jason Summer Study, was bluntly critical of strategic bombing. Whatever damage ROLLING THUNDER had done to North Vietnam's facilities and equipment had been more than offset by the increased flow of economic and military aid from the Soviet Union and China. The scientists not only found the POL campaign to have failed, they doubted that any amount of strategic bombing could either appreciably reduce North Vietnam's infiltration of men and supplies to the southern war theater or induce Hanoi's leaders to call off their strong support of the revolutionary war in South Vietnam:

It must be concluded therefore, that there is currently no adequate basis for predicting the levels of U. S. military activity that would be required to achieve the stated objectives—indeed, there is no firm basis for determining if there is any feasible level of effort that would achieve these objectives.[84]

The failure of the POL raids ended Robert McNamara's advocacy of increased bombing. He now viewed the Vietnam War as a stalemate and became convinced that President Johnson should seek a negotiated end to the conflict. For the remainder of his tenure as Secretary of Defense, McNamara refused or scaled back the military's subsequent requests for additional troops.[85] He began to identify with the small but growing number of Washington officials who were becoming disenchanted with the American war policy in Vietnam. In time, these doves came to outnumber the hawks among Johnson's advisers. Following the Tet offensive, Johnson would abandon his failed policy of gradual escalation in pursuit of military victory in Vietnam. Just as the architects of ROLLING THUNDER had predicted, the bombing campaign did eventually find a breaking point, but that threshold turned out to be Washington's willingness to continue a costly air war for marginal gains, not Hanoi's willingness to back the southern insurgency.

To substitute for the bombing campaign that they perceived as a failure, the scientists who had drafted the Jason Study proposed building an electronic barrier of wire, mines, and sensors across the DMZ and the segment of the Ho Chi Minh trail complex that wound through the Laotian panhandle as the most effective way of reducing infiltration into South Vietnam.[86] McNamara became an advocate of the electronic barrier, which was later partially built, as an alternative to the bombing of North Vietnam.

McNamara's move toward dovishness set off another debate in Washington over the effectiveness of the bombing campaign against North Vietnam. The Joint Chiefs, wedded to the belief that if enough bombing were done against enough targets soon enough it would be effective, continued to call for escalating the air war against North Vietnam. Since the POL raids had failed to diminish North Vietnam's ability to supply its forces and the Vietcong fighting in the South, the military leaders shifted their advocacy. They now called for a vastly expanded bombing campaign to destroy North Vietnam's electrical industry, port facilities, and locks and dams. "They aimed to wreck the enemy economy to produce a prostrate foe."[87]

McNamara assumed the leadership of the advocates of scaling back the bombing campaign. Johnson was caught in the middle of his advisers' intramural dispute. By the spring of 1967, after the failure of another bombing pause to start the negotiations process, Johnson, siding with his military advisers, escalated the air war. ROLLING THUNDER entered its third phase, the most intensive and important, which included air strikes against hitherto exempted major industrial targets: electrical production plants and North Vietnam's only steel factory. American aircraft also mined North Vietnamese harbors and estuaries and bombed previously off-limits targets near the Chinese border. "ROLLING THUNDER grew fangs."[88] Polls showed the American public strongly supported the expanded air war that aimed to destroy North Vietnam's industrial economy, thus its ability to prosecute the war.[89]

For the rest of 1967, U. S. aircraft attacked industries supportive of the war effort, including electrical-generating plants, petroleum storage facilities, military installations, transportation support facilities, and air defense systems. ROLLING THUNDER spared few North Vietnamese targets of any economic or military consequence. The air war raged at peak intensity as measured by the scope of permissible targets, numbers of sorties flown, and bomb tonnage dropped. Johnson had granted the Joint Chiefs and Admiral Sharp permission to hit most of the targets that they had been demanding to attack since ROLLING THUNDER began in March 1965. President Johnson, many of his civilian advisers, the Joint Chiefs, Admiral Sharp, and the air commanders all believed that the damage inflicted by the air war, coupled with the success of Westmoreland's big unit war in South Vietnam, would eventually "cause Hanoi to yield to American terms."[90] The third phase of ROLLING THUNDER would last until April 1, 1968, when, in the throes of a political crisis created by the Tet-68 campaigns, President Johnson deescalated the air war.

The Tet-68 offensive mounted by the Vietcong and PAVN forces proved dramatically that the bombing campaign "to interdict the flow of men and supplies to the South had been a signal failure."[91] Most of the resources necessary for the enemy to mount and sustain a large-scale campaign had flowed down the Ho Chi Minh Trail, despite the intensive bombing of North Vietnam. The magnitude of the Tet-68 offensive stunned the advocates of ROLLING THUNDER and shattered their conviction that the air war curtailed North Vietnam's ability to infiltrate men and materiel to the South and weakened their will to fight.[92] Tet-68 was also a major element in the conversion of Lyndon Johnson to the cause of deescalating the bombing.

ROLLING THUNDER, the gradually expanding air war waged against North Vietnam for three years, from March 2, 1965 through March 31, 1968, failed. It failed to interdict North Vietnamese supply routes to the South, and it failed to weaken either North Vietnam's fighting capabilities or its determination to support the war in South Vietnam. The Joint Chiefs, Admiral Sharp, and the air commanders always insisted that political restrictions imposed by civilians caused the air war to fail. But during the third phase of the air war, most of the targets in North Vietnam that the Joint Chiefs claimed to be of economic or military significance were either destroyed or damaged before Tet-68 occurred. ROLLING THUNDER, even when waged at its maximum intensity for months, neither stopped the flow of goods to South Vietnam nor broke Hanoi's will.[93]

Johnson's military advisers also insisted that had the bombing campaign been intense from the outset, North Vietnam would not have had time to develop its air defenses, disperse its industries and POL stores, or prepare its people to withstand the air war. Hanoi would have been forced to abandon its support of the southern revolution, or risk national extinction. Although it necessarily remains forever in the realm of counterfactual speculation, it is possible to maintain that an all-out effort from the start might have rendered ROLLING THUNDER more effective. But it is also true that when ROLLING THUNDER began, Hanoi's leaders expected that U. S. aircraft would soon attack industrial targets and bomb population centers. They quickly mobilized all of their resources to defend against an unrestricted air war. They also prepared for an American invasion of North Vietnam and for a protracted war. They prepared for far worse than they ever got or that the Joint Chiefs and Admiral Sharp ever proposed delivering, and never did they indicate that they were prepared to end their support of the southern rebels or that they could not infiltrate the supplies and people into South Vietnam that the war in that region required. Further, an all-out air assault that threatened to destroy North Vietnam could have provoked Chinese or even Soviet intervention, a peril that no responsible policy maker in Washington dared ignore. Finally, an all-out air assault would have created more international and domestic opposition to the war:

> There is no basis to saying with any certainty that air power unfettered by political considerations would have 'won' the air war in Vietnam. Various outcomes of a more rapid escalation [were] possible, not all of them favorable to victory.[94]

Military analysts have suggested additional reasons for the failure of ROLLING THUNDER besides the political controls clamped on U. S. air operations over North Vietnam by civilian officials. The unconventional type of warfare waged by the enemy contributed to the failure of the air war. A conventional air war waged against North Vietnam could not defeat an enemy waging guerrilla warfare in South Vietnam. There were three major reasons why the effort to interdict Hanoi's supply efforts failed: the minimal needs of the NVA and NLF forces fighting in South Vietnam, North Vietnam's excess resupply capabilities, and the supplies pouring into North Vietnam from China via rail and from the Soviet Union and eastern Bloc countries via ship.[95] Destroying North Vietnam's primitive industrial economy had no discernible effect on either its capacity or its will to wage a guerrilla war against the RVN.

Between 1965 and 1968, aircraft flying ROLLING THUNDER sorties dropped 643,000 tons of bombs and inflicted an estimated $600 million worth of damage on North Vietnam.[96] It crippled the country's nascent industrial sector and disrupted its agriculture. Several cities in southern North Vietnam were leveled, and others sustained severe damage. The government diverted thousands of people from agricultural work to air defense activities and to repairing roads and bridges. Food supplies diminished, and only extensive aid from the U. S. S. R. and China enabled millions of North Vietnamese to maintain even a subsistence-level diet. The quality of available education and health care in North Vietnam declined. Although Washington never adopted a policy of directly targeting civilians, the bombing campaign nevertheless claimed approximately 50,000 civilian casualties out of a population of 17 to 18 million.[97]

ROLLING THUNDER eventually proved to be exceedingly costly. Before Johnson ordered the bombing of North Vietnam halted on October 31, 1968, America lost 950 planes costing about $6 billion. A Pentagon study found that in addition to manpower and aircraft losses, every dollar's worth of damage inflicted on North Vietnam cost the American taxpayers $9.60 in 1966.[98] There were other costs: Captured U. S. pilots and air crewmen provided Hanoi's leaders with a bargaining chip that they later used in negotiating with American officials. ROLLING THUNDER also gave the Communists a propaganda advantage that they exploited to influence world and American public opinion. Robert McNamara, disillusioned by the failure of the air war, wrote in a memo to President Johnson:

> The picture of the world's greatest superpower killing or seriously injuring 1,000 noncombatants a week, while trying to pound a tiny, backward nation into submission, . . . is not a pretty one.[99]

Although opinion polls showed that a large majority of Americans consistently supported the air war against North Vietnam for its duration, the growing number of domestic opponents of the war seized on ROLLING THUNDER, denouncing it as expensive, futile, and wrong. By the summer of 1967, President Johnson had to confront a sizeable antiwar movement that derived much of its furious energy from its reactions to the air war. Both the civilian and military advocates of ROLLING THUNDER had assumed that the destruction or the threat of destruction of North Vietnam's industrial sector would cripple Hanoi's ability to supply the insurgents fighting in South Vietnam and persuade it to negotiate an agreement permitting South Vietnam to survive as a stable, non-Communist state. That assumption proved to be one of the grave errors in judgment made by those who led the nation to war.

AERIAL ATTRITION WARFARE

While ROLLING THUNDER unfolded against North Vietnam, America waged a large-scale air war in South Vietnam against the Vietcong. Air operations in South Vietnam were an integral part of the U. S. attrition strategy. Although the American media gave the ground war in South Vietnam far more coverage, the war leaders in Washington considered the accompanying air war to be just as important. The southern air war reflected the same logic that underlay the aerial campaign against North Vietnam: that America would use air power extensively to force Hanoi to stop its aggression in South Vietnam. The air war in South Vietnam also suffered from the same misjudgments: underestimating the enemy's determination and the enemy's ability to counter U. S. air power.[100] The air war in South Vietnam was also much larger, lasted far longer, and was much more diversified than the bombing campaign against North Vietnam.

Strikes against guerrilla bases and supply routes constituted two-thirds of the U. S. air operations undertaken in southern Vietnam. These preplanned attacks, based on aerial reconnaissance and intelligence reports, attempted to deny the Vietcong "safe havens where they could train and rest troops, store ammunition and food, and plan offensive operations."[101] Giant B-52 Stratofortresses from the Strategic Air Command (SAC) often participated in these air strikes against guerrilla strongholds and supply lines. Code-named ARC LIGHT, the flights of B-52s, initially flying from Andersen Air Force Base on the U. S. island territory of Guam, 2,800 miles away, approached their targets at altitudes varying from 30,000 to 36,000 feet. The giant bombers were both invisible and inaudible to observers on the ground; they combined the element of surprise with devastating power. A flight of six B-52s, each plane capable of carrying from eighteen to twenty-seven tons of bombs and using a carpet bombing technique in which all of the bombs were released according to a predetermined pattern, could saturate a target area in a matter of seconds. "Carpet bombing could change the face of the earth."[102] The ARC LIGHT strikes often caused enormous destruction and heavy casualties. The B-52s constituted the most frightening weapon in the U. S. arsenal deployed in the Vietnam War. After surviving a B-52 assault, a terrified Vietcong guerrilla called carpet bombing "the chain of thunders."[103]

If U. S. air strikes were scheduled for populated areas or sites near populated areas, clearance had to be granted by South Vietnamese officials, either by the province chief or by the military commander responsible for the area. Friendly populations were supposed to have advance warning that the area in which they resided had been designated a target area. Although American officials denied it, air attacks in or near populated areas claimed civilian casualties, as proven by examinations of hospital admissions records. Advance warning was not always provided and not always understood when furnished.[104] Subject to approval by South Vietnamese officials, areas known to be controlled by the Vietcong and not inhabited by friendly villagers were designated "free fire zones." These areas could be bombed without clearance from local officials or without warning to any inhabitants who might be in the area.[105]

After the preplanned strikes against guerrilla sanctuaries and supply lines, the most frequent kind of missions flown in South Vietnam were close air support operations carried out by Air Force, Marine, and Army pilots who usually flew from air fields in South Vietnam. These strikes provided crucial added fire power for ground combat forces locked in battle with Vietcong units.[106] These missions also helped keep down U. S. casualties. These close-in attacks were called in by ground commanders or forward air controllers (FACs) flying over the combat area. The FACs would mark the location of enemy forces with smoke flares to guide the pilots as they roared in to fire rockets, 20mm. cannons, air-to-ground missiles, or to drop iron bombs, phosphorous bombs, or napalm canisters on their targets. The B-52s also flew support missions in South Vietnam, often with devastating results.

Along with its preplanned strikes and close support missions, the Air Force also conducted an extensive campaign of aerial defoliation, code-named Operation

RANCH HAND, in South Vietnam to deprive the guerrillas of their forest cover and to destroy Vietcong food crops. Defoliation was a civilian counterinsurgency program initiated by President Kennedy on a small scale in 1962, over the objections of his senior military advisers who feared the United States might be accused of resorting to chemical or biological warfare.[107] As the war escalated, Operation RANCH HAND expanded rapidly. Air Force C-123s, specially fitted with 1,000-gallon tanks and bars of spray nozzles attached to the undersides of their wings, flew hundreds of sorties during the years 1965 to 1967. Over the door of the RANCH HAND briefing room at Tan Son Nhut Air Base hung a plaque with the sardonic inscription, "Only You Can Prevent Forests."[108]

Crews aboard the RANCH HAND C-123s used a variety of color-coded herbicides on their missions. The most effective herbicide proved to be Agent Orange. It contained an extremely toxic chemical agent, 2,4,5-T (Dioxin). One C-123 could haul 11,000 pounds of Agent Orange that it dispensed over a 300-acre target area in about four minutes. Within a few weeks, all of the plants, shrubs, and trees in the sprayed area had withered, turned brown, and died. Lush, green forests turned quickly into barren, brown moonscapes following a RANCH HAND spraying. During 1967, the peak year of Operation RANCH HAND, Air Force crews sprayed about 1.5 million acres, 40 percent of which were croplands. Before the defoliation campaign ended, more than 100 million pounds of chemicals were sprayed over millions of acres of South Vietnamese forests and crops. Operation RANCH HAND destroyed an estimated one-half of South Vietnam's timberlands and left behind unknown human costs.[109]

Operation RANCH HAND in time became controversial. On June 26, 1969, a report appeared in a South Vietnamese newspaper alleging that a toxic ingredient

Figure 6.7 Giant B-52 strategic bombers were the most feared weapon in the American arsenal. Here, a cell of Stratofortresses release their bombs over a suspected Vietcong stronghold. *Source:* U. S. Air Force photo

found in Agent Orange caused birth defects in children born to women who had been exposed to the herbicide. Later that year, a study by the National Institute of Health presented evidence that Dioxin caused malformed babies. A study done under the auspices of the American Association for the Advancement of Science to investigate the effects of spraying in Vietnam found that some of the forested areas that had been sprayed with Agent Orange had not regenerated. On April 15, 1970, the Defense Department suspended the use of Agent Orange. The last RANCH HAND mission, using other herbicides, flew from Tan Son Nhut air field on January 7, 1971.[110]

Years after the Vietnam War had ended, scientific researchers were still trying to determine the specific effects that exposure to Dioxin could have on people. Veterans, exposed to Agent Orange during the war, have reported recurring health problems. These problems included skin rashes, breathing dysfunctions, various kinds of cancers, and birth defects in their children, which they believe came from their exposure to Dioxin. A class action suit against the Veterans' Administration brought by veterans who were exposed to Agent Orange while serving in Vietnam was settled out of court in 1985.[111]

Another facet of the U. S. air war in Indochina entailed air operations within neutral Laos. At the beginning of 1965, the southern panhandle of Laos, which shared a 450-mile-long border with Vietnam, had been turned into a supply corridor supporting Vietcong military operations in South Vietnam. The heart of that supply corridor was the Ho Chi Minh trail.[112] A few months before ROLLING THUNDER began against North Vietnam, President Johnson ordered American aircraft to interdict traffic coming south along the Ho Chi Minh trail running through the Laotian corridor. The bombing campaign in Laos gradually expanded until it reached a volume of 3,000 sorties per month during the fall of 1967.

The air war waged in Laos from 1965 through 1967, like its counterpart waged against North Vietnam, also failed strategically. Bad flying weather and rugged jungle-covered mountainous terrain continually hampered U. S. air operations. Because the Ho Chi Minh trail through Laos consisted of a vast web of small roads and trails, most of which were invisible from the air, U. S. pilots could only interdict a portion of the weapons, military supplies, and soldiers coming into South Vietnam. Enemy countermeasures and self-imposed restrictions on the bombings further reduced the effectiveness of the air war in Laos. At the height of the U. S. campaign against the Ho Chi Minh trail along the Laotian corridor, enemy forces were infiltrating more supplies into South Vietnam than ever before.[113]

THE OTHER WAR

While drastically escalating the Vietnam War and transforming America's failed advisory role into a full-scale military effort to suppress the Vietcong insurgents and to discourage their North Vietnamese backers, American officials strongly supported the Ky regime's efforts to build a new nation in southern Vietnam. Ky's performance as prime minister pleasantly surprised Washington. He managed to survive in office and the

Figure 6.8   An Air Force C-123 on a defoliation mission over jungle terrain in South Vietnam during Operation RANCH HAND. *Source:* U. S. Air Force photo

chronic instability that had plagued South Vietnamese politics since the anti-Diemist coup of November 1963 ebbed. In fact, the June 1965 coup that brought Ky to power would prove to be South Vietnam's last. In February 1966, to evade growing opposition to the Vietnam War among senators led by William Fulbright, who was holding hearings before his Senate Foreign Relations committee on all aspects of administration war policy, Johnson traveled to Honolulu with his senior advisers to meet with General Ky and other high South Vietnamese officials.

On February 6, in Honolulu, Johnson publicly embraced Ky and urged him to emphasize what Johnson called "the other war" in South Vietnam: building a South Vietnamese nation, developing the South Vietnamese economy, improving the lives of the Vietnamese people, and winning the allegiance of the villagers.[114] Ky, who had been briefed by U. S. officials before coming to Hawaii, made a speech replete with ambitious plans for implementing a social revolution throughout South Vietnam that would revitalize its economy and ensure a prosperous and free South Vietnamese nation for the future. Johnson, delighted by Ky's speech, put his arm around the South Vietnamese leader and told him, "Boy, you speak just like an American!"[115] At the conclusion of the conference, through a joint communique, Johnson and Ky pledged to work for the welfare of the ordinary people and bring about the end of poverty, disease, and ignorance in South Vietnam. The communique read like a South Vietnamese version of Great Society. It gave pacification a high priority and a momentum that lasted for the duration of the American war in Vietnam.[116]

Ky, emboldened by Johnson's public show of support at Honolulu, returned to Vietnam determined to strengthen his grip on the South Vietnamese government.

Backed by U. S. officials, Ky persuaded the Military Directorate to dismiss a powerful rival, one of the triumvirs, General Nguyen Chanh Thi, the I Corps commander. The I Corps area included Danang and Hue, South Vietnam's second and third largest cities. Ky's firing of Thi provoked a major political crisis in South Vietnam, resulting in a brief civil war that occurred inside the war already raging in South Vietnam.

The Buddhists, quiescent for nearly a year under the leadership of Thich Tri Quang, who had formed a loose confederation of dissidents called the Struggle Movement, suddenly erupted. Their revolt quickly spread to Danang, Saigon, and other South Vietnamese cities. The Buddhists also revived their demands for free elections and a restoration of civilian rule. Other disaffected groups joined their movement, including students, trade unionists, some religious sectarians, and even some dissident army and police elements. Several Buddhist monks and a nun committed self-immolation by fire in support of the movement. Although they were careful not to make their ultimate political goals explicit, the Buddhists hoped that the elections would bring a coalition government to power in South Vietnam that would end the war, negotiate a settlement with the NLF, and expel the Americans. Above all, the Buddhists wanted the political destiny of South Vietnam to be determined by the Vietnamese.[117]

Henry Cabot Lodge, having replaced Maxwell Taylor, was back in Saigon for another stint as the U. S. Ambassador. Lodge feared that free elections could bring a neutralist government to power that would proceed to negotiate an end to the war and throw the Americans out. Lodge endorsed Ky's efforts to suppress the Buddhists and their supporters, as did General Westmoreland and President Johnson, both of whom were alarmed by the outbreak of civil unrest in the midst of an expanding war.

When the Buddhists had risen against the Diem regime three years earlier, the American officials had supported them, mainly because the Kennedy administration perceived Diem and his brother Nhu as being uncooperative. The Ngo brothers had rejected American advice and had been unwilling either to reform their government or prosecute vigorously the war against the PLAF. But in the spring of 1966, with the U. S. stake in the Vietnam war far greater than it had been in the Diem era, Ky cooperated with American officials, sought and followed their advice, and strongly supported the expanded U. S. war effort against the NLF and the North Vietnamese.

Assisted by General Westmoreland, Ky moved against the Buddhists. On the morning of April 5, 1966, U. S. C-130 transports flew 2,000 ARVN troops into the Danang air field. Ky, personally leading two battalions of ARVN Marines, announced that he had come to "liberate Danang." Ky's show of force, designed to overawe his opponents, only provoked them. General Thi and the local ARVN commander, General Nguyen Van Nhuan, joined the rebels. General Nhuan used his troops to confine Ky's forces to the Danang Air Base. He also warned Ky that if he tried to move his troops out of the air base there would be fighting. Ky, embarrassed, was forced to back down. He announced that he would withdraw his troops from Danang and seek a rapprochement with the Buddhists. After meeting with Buddhist leaders, General

Figure 6.9 President Johnson confers with the leaders of the Republic of South Vietnam at Honolulu on February 6, 1966. The man in the middle is Prime Minister Nguyen Cao Ky. To his left is President Nguyen Van Thieu. *Source:* National Archives

Thieu, Ky's chief of state, announced that elections for a constituent assembly would be held within a few months and that civilian government would soon be restored. Reacting to these concessions from the military government, Tri Quang and the other Buddhist leaders called off their protests.[118]

By canceling their protests, the Buddhists played into the hands of the wily Ky and Thieu, who never intended to keep their promises. Confident of U. S. support, they were stalling for time until they could mount a larger effort against the rebels. On May 15, 1966, Ky launched another assault on Danang. With U. S. aircraft again providing logistic support, Ky sent in larger forces armed with tanks, artillery, and other heavy weapons. Ky's forces took control of the mayor's office, the radio station, I Corps headquarters, the police station, and key military installations. There followed two days of bitter and intense fighting in the streets of Danang, during which hundreds of soldiers and protesters were killed. Ky's heavily armed forces crushed the revolt.[119] His forces also suppressed the dissident movement in Saigon, but Hue, the center of the Buddhist resistance movement, remained in rebel hands.

The Struggle Movement's actions took on a decidedly anti-American coloration in Hue. Angered by the U. S. backing of Ky as well as by his betrayal, the dissidents sacked the U. S. consulate and burned the United States Information Service (USIS) library there. They also unfurled banners demanding the ouster from Vietnam of all foreign influences, including American. Soon thereafter, Ky's forces assaulted the dissident positions in the former imperial capital. By June 19, Hue was once again under government control. Tri Quang was arrested along with hundreds of bonzes, students, and other protesters. The Buddhist political movement was crushed. Ky and Thieu, rescinding their promises to hold elections within a few months, announced that the military junta would remain in power until elections took place sometime in 1967. The Buddhist revolt was finished. The Ky-Thieu regime, with American backing, had proven too powerful for the Struggle Movement to bring down.

American soldiers were both baffled and angered by the internecine struggle occurring at a time when the U. S. military effort in Vietnam was rapidly expanding, American troops were doing most of the fighting, and American casualties were growing. One U. S. soldier angrily asked, "What are we doing here? We're fighting to save these people, and they're fighting each other!"[120] But the Buddhist revolt had little impact on the continuing war between the RVNAF and PLAF. The Vietcong were caught by surprise by the Struggle Movement and did not support it or take advantage of it. Ky and Thieu were able to suppress the revolt without causing major turmoil.

The suppression of the Buddhist uprising signaled the end of the Buddhists as a major factor in the South Vietnamese political calculus. Their movement lost its political coherence. The ARVN generals had defeated their last major political rivals; the possibility of a civilian alternative to military rule in South Vietnam no longer existed. After three years of political conflict that had begun with the coup that brought down the Diem regime, during which none of a succession of governments could provide even the rudiments of political leadership, a measure of stability was returning to South Vietnam's civic life. Following the suppression of the Buddhists, the Vietnamese people living under the control of the RVN perceived that the rule of the generals could not be challenged as long as the Americans maintained such a powerful presence in their country and stood solidly behind the military rulers:

> The middle ground that the Buddhists had been building up between the Saigon military and the NLF was cut away and prospects destroyed for anything resembling a viable "third force."[121]

Politics in South Vietnam had been polarized. The people's practical choices were reduced to either rule by the ARVN generals or by the NLF-Hanoi forces, a prospect that dismayed millions of South Vietnamese citizens who were neither Communists nor supporters of military dictators.

U. S. officials, in addition to committing more troops to the expanding war against the PLAF and NVA forces, had to inject American power into the areas of South Vietnam under the RVN's administrative control. Given the absence of indigenous support for the RVN, it was necessary for American forces to provide guarantees

Figure 6.10   Buddhists in Saigon protesting the policies of the Thieu-
Ky government in May 1966. *Source:* U. S. Army photo

that the governmental apparatus would remain in the hands of Vietnamese willing to support American policies and goals. U. S. officials often staffed RVN agencies and programs at the provincial and district levels. The RVN took on more of the attributes of a neocolonial American dependency in 1966.

Following the suppression of the Buddhists, both American and Vietnamese officials tried to implement effective pacification programs among the rural population of South Vietnam. To American officials, pacification had become a catch-all term that referred to all of the nonmilitary aspects of the war. As U. S. ground combat forces took over the bulk of the fighting in South Vietnam using General Westmoreland's attrition strategies, the South Vietnamese armed forces, both ARVN and territorial troops, were assigned major responsibility for the nonmilitary aspects of the war, that is, pacification support. In practice, pacification support usually meant using local South Vietnamese forces to provide area security for the villagers, while the American forces engaged Vietcong main force units. Sometimes American combat forces, especially Marines assigned to I Corps in the North, provided area security for the villagers. Pacification could also refer to the myriad of civilian programs that provided the rural population of South Vietnam with schools, health services, economic assistance, and political indoctrination—whatever might improve the quality of their lives, wean them from the allure of the NLF, and bind them to the government of South Vietnam.

At the Honolulu conference in early February 1966, President Johnson made pacification a top priority. Johnson personally identified with the people of South Vietnam and what he assumed to be their desires to live in a free, peaceful, and prosperous society. He also believed military action alone could never defeat the Vietcong. The Saigon government would have to win the allegiance of the villagers, and Johnson thought that the best way to win them over was to provide social programs that improved the quality of their lives.

Responding to the American pressure, with funding and expert advice provided by American officials, the Ky government implemented a Revolutionary Development program (RD). Consciously imitative of the NLF cadres, fifty-nine-person revolutionary development teams were sent into South Vietnamese villages. Team personnel were trained to provide physical security for the villagers, assist in government reorganization and political development, establish schools and literacy programs, and aid in social and economic development.[122] They lived among the people and "carried out hundreds of tasks to build popular support for the government and to undermine the Vietcong."[123]

As had been the fate of earlier pacification efforts, Revolutionary Development failed. The inept and corrupt RVN never developed an adequate program. Cadres were hastily trained, and there were never enough teams available to service all of South Vietnam's hamlets and villages. District officials sometimes undercut the revolutionary developmental teams' efforts; sometimes ARVN troops extorted money from the villagers and stole their pigs and chickens. Wary villagers, knowing from experience that RVN promises often exceeded its ability to implement them, were slow to cooperate with the RD teams. The most serious problem was the absence of physical security. Since U. S. troops were preoccupied with the war against the Vietcong main force units, providing village security devolved upon the ARVN forces. But they were incapable of supplying adequate security in many areas. In some locales, ARVN troops were the security problem. In insecure areas, the Vietcong often terrorized the revolutionary development teams. The VC terrorists kidnapped and murdered thousands of RD cadres in 1966 and 1967.[124]

The failure of Revolutionary Development also raised three fundamental questions about the RVN's approach to pacification: (1) Pacification could not succeed as long as corrupt officials and rogue ARVN units continued to prey upon the villagers. There was no evidence that Ky's regime seriously intended to reform itself and eliminate these abuses. (2) Given the peasant preoccupation with land owning, land reform would have to form the heart of any long-range pacification program that hoped to win the allegiance of the peasantry. Ky's lack of commitment to land reform and his responsiveness to the interests of large local landowners ensured the continuing failure of Revolutionary Development. (3) To overcome the fragmentation of South

Vietnamese society and the alienation of the rural masses from the ruling urban elites, villagers would need to have been given a sense of participation, an active involvement in the government for pacification to work. The peasants would have had to see people from their villages rising to positions of authority within the government system to identify with the GVN, to connect its operations to their interests and welfare. Ky's government never tried to breach the profound divisions existing within the South Vietnamese social structure by recruiting district or provincial officials from the villages.

President Johnson, in April 1967, to promote pacification, folded it into Westmoreland's command (MACV). All civilian and military agencies involved with pacification now came under the administrative control of a hybrid agency called Civil Operations and Revolutionary Development Support (CORDS). The MACV deputy placed in charge of CORDS was Robert Komer, an energetic civilian bureaucrat nicknamed "Blowtorch" because of his aggressive management style. An able bureaucrat, Komer completely reorganized and revitalized the American approach to pacification. He improved the liaison with South Vietnamese civilian and military officials responsible for pacification programs. He also established the Hamlet Evaluation System (HES), a computerized reporting system to monitor and quantify the progress of pacification in the countryside. Komer also worked closely with CIA officials and the RVN district and provincial leaders to put greater emphasis on identifying and neutralizing the Vietcong political infrastructure that enabled the insurgency to maintain its ties to the villagers.[125]

While it pursued the will-o'-the-wisp of pacification following the suppression of the Buddhists, the South Vietnamese military regime also implemented democratic political reforms, but in carefully limited fashion to ensure that the generals retained control of the government. Pressure for drafting a constitution and holding elections came mainly from the Johnson administration. Washington wanted to legitimatize the South Vietnamese government in American eyes and thereby gain increased domestic support for the expanding war. In early 1967, South Vietnamese voters elected a constituent assembly. The newly elected assembly, assisted by U. S. constitutional scholars, proceeded to draft a new constitution modeled on the American Constitution. It created a bicameral legislature, but it granted the executive branch most of the powers of government and permitted the president to assume dictatorial powers in the event of an emergency that could be declared at his discretion. Further, the president needed only to obtain a plurality of the votes to be elected. This provision prevented opposing candidates from joining together in a runoff to defeat the government's candidates.[126]

Elections under the new constitution were held in September 1967. The most serious political conflict that occurred during the campaign pitted the supporters of Ky against the supporters of Thieu to see which man would head the government ticket. Ky eventually gave way, and Thieu ran for president with Ky as his vice presidential running mate. They were challenged by ten civilian candidates. Since Communists and neutralists were barred from seeking office, Buddhists were boycotting the election, and the opposition consisted of obscure men with small local followings, Thieu and Ky were running under conditions that made their defeat extremely unlikely. Even so, the Thieu-Ky ticket received only 35 percent of the vote. They were also embarrassed by the electoral performance of a political unknown, Truong Dinh Dzu, an obscure civilian candidate running on a platform calling for negotiations with the National Liberation Front, who came in second with 17 percent of the vote.[127] Their slender electoral victory did not give the Thieu-Ky regime greater legitimacy, a broader political base, or increased political power. Two-thirds of South Vietnam's carefully circumscribed electorate preferred alternatives to Thieu and Ky. It is possible that if all of the South Vietnamese people had been permitted to vote in a genuinely free election, they might have registered a preference for a government that would have sought to negotiate an end to the war and to expel the Americans. Thieu and Ky survived in power not because their government was popular or intrinsically powerful but because it had the backing of the Americans.

American officials convinced themselves that the September 1967 election showed that democratic government had come to South Vietnam and that the Thieu-Ky regime had achieved a popular base of support. Most South Vietnamese voters held a different view. They understood that they had participated in a carefully arranged, essentially meaningless political ritual mainly to please their American patrons. "Many Vietnamese regarded the entire process as 'an American-directed performance with a Vietnamese cast.' "[128] But the Thieu-Ky victory, however dubious it might be within a Vietnamese political context, meant that the military junta would remain in power, Americans would remain in South Vietnam, and the war would go on.

From mid-1965 to the end of 1967, while the Americans escalated both the air war against North Vietnam and the ground war in South Vietnam, albeit only achieving a stalemate with their enemies, the South Vietnamese government failed to eliminate its underlying political weaknesses. Pacification floundered, and the Thieu-Ky regime remained a narrowly based military directorate dependent on continuing American support to remain in power. In the long run, the large-scale U. S. military effort could not compensate for the continuing failure of the South Vietnamese to erect a strong, stable, and popular government or to build a viable nation. The American war proved either irrelevant to nation-building or exacerbated its problems. The continuing political failures of the Saigon regime were a major cause of the eventual U. S. defeat in Vietnam.

The impact of the U. S. war with its half million troops, thousands of civilians, and billions of dollars strained and disrupted the South Vietnamese economy.[129] Saigon became a boom town whose prosperity was based on a single industry—war. The former "Paris of the Orient" became a crowded, noisy metropolis, its streets clogged with traffic and its hotels, restaurants, bars, nightclubs, casinos, and brothels teeming with American soldiers, civilian advisers, journalists, and tourists. Many Saigonese found work providing services to the Americans and to their fellow Vietnamese who profited from the war economy. Crime and corruption flourished on a grand scale. The black market became a big business, trafficking in stolen American consumer goods, weapons, and illegal currency exchanges.[130] For years, one could buy anything in Saigon, anything that is, but hearts and minds, victory, or peace.

As the American presence in South Vietnam expanded, tensions between the Americans and Vietnamese increased. Because of their profound cultural differences, the Americans and Vietnamese had to struggle to understand each other across a vast chasm of mutual ignorance and misperceptions. The exigencies of fighting a war and building a nation exacerbated the already tense relations between the two allies. Because the Vietcong had infiltrated every echelon of both the government's civilian agencies and its armed forces, security leaks posed chronic problems. U. S. commanders were forced to keep all Vietnamese off of their major bases and to withhold details of major military operations from their ARVN counterparts to maintain security.

"The paradox arose of the Americans fighting on behalf of an army (and a government) that they treated with disdain, even contempt." Many U. S. troops were fighting to save people that they did not regard as worth saving from Communism. American soldiers often spoke openly and contemptuously of their South Vietnamese allies. They wondered why the enemy's soldiers always seemed braver and fought harder than the ARVN forces. A stark contradiction evolved between the official political objectives for which Americans were fighting in Southeast Asia—the freedom and independence of the South Vietnamese people—and the reality of a war in which Americans often bypassed both the RVN and its military forces as they designed and carried out U. S. campaigns aimed at defeating the Vietcong and the NVA.[131]

The apparent indifference of many Vietnamese to the welfare of U. S. soldiers who were dying in battle trying to protect them infuriated American troopers. The uncanny ability of the villagers to avoid mines and booby traps that killed and maimed U. S. soldiers led many troopers to assume that these people cooperated with the enemy or that they were the enemy. American soldiers, upon entering a village after taking fire from it or its vicinity, unable to tell which of its inhabitants were "friendlies" and which were Vietcong or Vietcong sympathizers, tended to assume that all of the villagers were either real or potential enemies. Such assumptions, when held by frightened and angry young soldiers armed with automatic rifles, machine guns, and pistols, could have tragic consequences.[132]

DIPLOMATIC CHARADES

As the Vietnam War expanded, pressures for a negotiated settlement of the conflict also escalated. From mid-1965 until the end of 1967, White House officials estimated that as many as 2,000 individual efforts were made to begin peace talks between Washington and Hanoi. President Johnson claimed in his memoirs that he personally followed seventy-two negotiation initiatives.[133] Neither side dared to ignore the many diplomatic efforts initiated by third parties concerned with bringing together American and North Vietnamese negotiators to halt the war, but they consistently refused to make the concessions necessary to initiate serious peace talks. The more both sides invested in the conflict, the less willing they were to consider negotiating. The escalating military stalemate bred a diplomatic impasse that could not be resolved by well-intentioned diplomatic middlemen.

Hanoi repeatedly denounced U. S. involvement in Vietnam as a violation of the 1954 Geneva Accords. North Vietnamese leaders insisted that the United States would have to cease all acts of war against Vietnam, dismantle its bases, and remove all of its military forces before any talks could begin. They further insisted that the political destiny of South Vietnam would be determined in accordance with the program of the National Liberation Front. The Saigon regime would be replaced by a coalition government dominated by the NLF. Hanoi's leaders clearly indicated that they considered the question of Vietnam's unity to be fundamental and nonnegotiable: "The unity of our country is no more a matter for negotiations than our independence."[134]

According to the view from Hanoi, there was no role for the United States to play in determining the political destiny of South Vietnam. America would have to withdraw all of its troops from that country, after which the RVN would doubtless collapse or be overthrown, and Hanoi would proceed to unify Vietnam under its control. Ho Chi Minh believed that great power diplomatic interests and the U. S. intervention in South Vietnam after Geneva had deprived the Vietminh of the political dividends that should have accrued from their military victory over the French, which was control of an independent and unified Vietnam.

Ho Chi Minh and his associates were determined never to entrust their political future to others again. This time, they and they alone would determine the political outcome of the latest Vietnam war, that is, the current phase of a war that had been going intermittently since 1946. Hence, they made American withdrawal from Vietnam a precondition for negotiations and declared the unity of Vietnam to be a nonnegotiable item. Given the battlefield realities existing during the 1965 to 1967 period, Hanoi's diplomatic stance did not represent the negotiating position of a nation seriously concerned with a diplomatic resolution of the Vietnam War; it reflected the diplomatic posture of leaders who were determined to win the war and confident that in time they would.

Washington promulgated its negotiating position at the beginning of 1966. Johnson, planning to escalate the air war against North Vietnam, halted the bombing during the Christmas holiday. He combined the bombing halt with a diplomatic offensive, sending administration officials around the world and across America to explain that the United States was ready to negotiate with Hanoi without insisting that they meet any preconditions. But the United States offered to halt the bombing of North Vietnam only after Hanoi had stopped infiltrating men and supplies into South Vietnam. American would withdraw all of its troops from South Vietnam only after an "acceptable political settlement" had been reached.

While agreeing that the political destiny of South Vietnam would have to be worked out by the South Vietnamese themselves, Washington refused to allow the

NLF to join any South Vietnamese government. They would allow their views to be represented, but only after Hanoi stopped all "acts of aggression. Beneath these ambiguous words rested a firm determination to maintain an independent, non-Communist South Vietnam."[135] Johnson's insistence that he favored unconditional negotiations masked a U. S. diplomatic stance that was no more acceptable to Hanoi than its stands were to Johnson. McNamara also acknowledged that part of Johnson's motivation for halting the bombing was to prepare American and world public opinion for more escalations.[136] Johnson did not expect Hanoi to accept his overtures.

Hanoi promptly denounced the U. S. bombing pause as a sham and rejected Johnson's terms for negotiations. The North Vietnamese, regarding Vietnam as one country and dismissing as a species of political fiction the American claim that a sovereign nation with a legitimate government existed in the southern half of Vietnam, sharply differentiated between what they regarded as illegitimate American interventions into the affairs of their country and their own legitimate involvement in Vietnam's internal affairs. Hanoi refused to consider performing any reciprocal acts to get the Americans to halt the bombing and insisted that only their negotiating positions offered bases for a correct political settlement of the war.[137] Johnson, anticipating the rebuff, resumed the air war against North Vietnam on January 31, 1966.

In 1966 and 1967, even though both sides remained far apart and neither country appeared willing to make the kinds of concessions that might have brought them closer to negotiations, various third parties tried to bring Hanoi and Washington to the bargaining table. One of these initiatives involved the Polish diplomat Januscz Lewandowski, who persuaded U. S. officials to offer North Vietnam a proposal that he claimed would circumvent Hanoi's refusal to consider reciprocal actions in return for a bombing halt: in exchange for the United States halting the bombing, Hanoi would have only to give private assurances that they would stop their infiltration into South Vietnam within a reasonable time. When American officials could verify that the infiltration had in fact stopped, Washington would freeze its combat forces at current levels, and negotiations between the two sides could begin.[138]

Lewandowski's initiative, code-named MARIGOLD, never had a chance. A few days before the Polish envoy was scheduled to meet for talks with Communist leaders in Hanoi, Johnson ordered U. S. aircraft to bomb rail yards near the center of the capital. Some of the planes inadvertently bombed nearby residential neighborhoods and caused civilian casualties. Hanoi, assuming that Johnson was combining a new negotiating proposal with an expanded bombing effort, refused to meet with Lewandowski. It is unlikely that Hanoi was prepared to accept the Polish diplomat's formula had the air attacks not occurred; however, the bombing killed whatever prospects MARIGOLD may have had, because the North Vietnamese refused to be pressured into negotiations, or to give the appearance of being pressured into negotiations. Lewandowski had to abandon his efforts, and "the Polish initiative ended in fiasco."[139] In 1967, a peace initiative developed by British Prime Minister Harold Wilson that attempted to employ the good offices of Soviet President Alexei Kosygin met a similar fate.

During the period when both sides were expanding their war effort, all third-party initiatives, however well-intentioned or balanced, were destined for failure. Starting negotiations between Washington and Hanoi depended mainly on the willingness of the belligerents to compromise. Neither was prepared to do so because each side remained confident that it was going to win the war and that it would then be in a position to force the other side to make concessions that would be tantamount to accepting political defeat. Leaders in Washington and Hanoi both strove to appear responsive to all serious peace proposals. They also tried to exploit those proposals for propaganda purposes to make it appear that their adversary was the one pressing the war, was not interested in genuine negotiations, and was the aggressor.

In 1967, as both international and domestic pressures for a negotiated settlement intensified, each side became slightly more flexible. Hanoi suggested that reunification might occur over a long period of time. Johnson, in a speech in San Antonio, Texas, on September 29, indicated that he would stop the bombing if it would lead to productive peace talks. But both sides remained far apart.[140] Johnson remained committed to maintaining a pro-Western government in power in South Vietnam. Hanoi remained committed to unifying all of Vietnam under its control. Negotiations could not bridge that gulf in 1966 or 1967.

Both countries continued to try to win the war to control the political destiny of South Vietnam. There is no reason to assume that any of the peace initiatives could have succeeded no matter how adroitly they were handled, given the unwillingness of the belligerents to make concessions. Because both sides indulged in diplomatic charades, "the search for negotiations with Hanoi between 1965 and 1968 is one of the most fruitless chapters in U. S. diplomacy."[141] Johnson's judgment was essentially sound when he concluded that Hanoi was not willing to negotiate an end to the war on terms that he could accept, and therefore the many diplomatic initiatives undertaken in 1966 and 1967 were destined for failure.[142]

WAR AT HOME

When the Johnson administration made its fateful decisions during the spring and summer of 1965 to mount an air war against North Vietnam and to send ground combat forces to fight in South Vietnam, decisions that committed the United States to fighting a major war in Southeast Asia, it also simultaneously called forth domestic opposition to its war policies. A diverse peace movement recruited from left-wing radical and liberal groups that had coalesced in the mid-1950s to try to defuse the Cold War and to ban atmospheric testing of nuclear weapons formed the core of the emerging opposition to the Vietnam War. Between 1963 and 1965, peace advocacy in this country was reoriented from "ban the bomb" rallies to protesting the growing U. S. war in Vietnam.

To call the various organizations and activities comprising the opposition to the expanding war in Vietnam during 1965 to 1967 a "movement" can be misleading, for the term implies a coherency of organizational structures and a congruency of tactics, strategies, goals, and ideologies that never existed among the diverse antiwar groups. Typically, they were action-oriented gatherings of people committed to ending the war in Vietnam and often were involved in other reform causes such as civil rights and women's liberation. Some organizations, such as the Students for a Democratic Society (SDS), generated a sophisticated political analysis and ideological rationale for their antiwar activities, but most antiwar activists did not. Few antiwar protesters had well-defined institutional affiliations or embraced a coherent ideology or politics. However, all protesters felt a strong personal commitment to the cause, to the movement, and it was that commitment that gave the antiwar movement what political cohesion it possessed. Antiwar organizations did not usually recruit members nor did citizens affiliate with them in any formal sense. "There was no way to join; you simply announced or felt yourself to be a part of the movement—usually through some act like joining a protest march."[143] It was this sense of a purposeful togetherness, of belonging to a community organized for political action, that attracted many young New Left militants who were enrolled in the nation's universities to become involved in antiwar activities.

A schism quickly appeared between liberal and radical antiwar activists and persisted for the duration of the movement. Protesters divided over both strategies and goals. Liberals sought to strengthen U. S. international leadership for peace in the world; radicals indicted the United States as the major source of war and injustice in the world. Liberals called for the rule of international law and the strengthening of the United Nations; radicals wanted to liberate and empower poor people, both at home and abroad. Liberals sought to change American foreign policy; radicals wanted a fundamental transformation of the structures of power and wealth within the United States and the world. Liberals were committed to political action, to working within the established political system via electoral action and citizen lobbying; radicals were committed to direct action and acts of civil disobedience against an unjust state. Liberals sought a negotiated settlement of the Indochina conflict—a settlement that would end the fighting, phase out the American involvement, and restore political stability to that part of the world. Radicals demanded an immediate U. S. disengagement from Indochina: "America—Out of Vietnam—NOW!" became their rallying call.[144]

At a deeper level, the divisions within pacifist ranks between liberals and radicals turned on a debate over America, over American values and institutions, and over the meaning of American culture itself. Could American institutions be reformed? Radicals thought not. They believed that American politics had to be radically transformed; some radicals thought it was time for a second American revolution. In combination with angry African Americans, radicalized students, and other malcontents, militants sought to create new political structures and build a new political movement outside of the mainstream political institutions. They believed that only a new radical politics, acting in fundamental opposition to the established order, could redeem America. Just as the Vietcong, whom they supported, were resisting illegitimate authority in the jungles of Southeast Asia, domestic radicals would liberate the American people from homegrown tyrannies. The radical antiwar movement was inextricably linked with the cultural revolution that swept America during the late 1960s. The domestic political and cultural upheavals and the radical antiwar activism reciprocally energized one another.

Liberals, by contrast, believed the problem was not with America or with American culture, but with the American Vietnam war policy. Liberals did not want to remake America; they only wanted to end a war they believed was futile and unnecessary. They did not take sides in the war, but sought to end it. Liberal antiwar activists did not try to restructure American politics; they tried to work within a political system they regarded as sufficiently flexible and open, which could be used to bring about a change in the government's Vietnam War policy.[145] Liberal antiwar activists, who were always much more numerous than their radical counterparts, considered the radical analysis of American culture and politics flawed. They also considered radical calls for a new American revolution as unnecessary and quixotic. For their part, militants considered liberal pacifists superficial and naïve, believers in a bankrupt political system that caused wars and exploited poor people within America and the Third World.

As the American conflict in Vietnam expanded, hawkish critics of Johnson's war policies occupied a prominent place in the developing debate over the war. Hawks, a mix of conservative Republicans, southern Democrats, and Cold War liberals, devout believers in the containment ideology, viewed the conflict in Vietnam as a crucial component of the global struggle with Communism for control of the planet's political future. Hawks felt strongly that America must hold the line against Communist aggression, lest an important ally in Southeast Asia succumb to the Red tide. Hawks believed that if South Vietnam fell to the Communists, the Soviets and Chinese would press their advantage elsewhere in that strategically important region. Additional allies and neutral nations would fall to Communism, and the security of America itself would be undermined in time. Hawks, convinced that America possessed the military power to demolish the Vietcong and North Vietnamese forces if the wraps were removed, were frustrated by the restraints that civilians had clamped on U. S. military forces. They demanded that President Johnson "do whatever was necessary to attain victory."[146] During the first three years of the American war in Vietnam, 1965–1967, Johnson was much more responsive to hawkish critics of his war policies than he was to dovish protesters; he viewed hawks as more influential politically and more likely to reflect mainstream public opinion than liberal and radical antiwar protesters.

Opposition to the war took various forms from 1965 to 1967. The earliest protests were the aforementioned teach-ins and the first antiwar demonstration staged in the nation's capital by SDS in the spring of 1965. It was the bombing of North Vietnam that aroused antiwar activists more than any other aspect of the government's war policy. It was the air war against the North that energized the antiwar movement in 1965. During that year there were comparatively few antiwar activists and few protest demonstrations. Public opinion polls taken during the first year of the American war in Vietnam consistently showed strong popular support for the conflict. Polls also reflected intense popular resentment of the antiwar protesters.[147] Most Americans still expected a U. S. victory; no one dreamed of a Communist victory. One factor that provoked intense negative responses to antiwar demonstrations was the participation of youthful adherents of the 1960s counterculture in some of the protest movements. These "hippies," with their outlandish costumes and bizarre forms of protest, added a satirical quality to the antiwar movement, sometimes turning it into street theater of the absurd. Hippies sometimes disrupted antiwar demonstrations, provoked police reprisals, and further alienated the peace movement from the American society they proposed to change.

In February 1966, Senator Fulbright held televised hearings on all aspects of the administration's war policy before his Foreign Relations Committee. Fulbright and his dovish colleagues grilled administration defenders, such as Secretary of State Dean Rusk, and provided George Kennan, General James Gavin, and other prominent critics of the war a national forum for vetting their dissenting views. Millions of Americans watched the hearings. Fulbright's investigations gave antiwar sentiment a legitimacy that it had previously lacked and strengthened the ranks of critics of U. S. war policy.[148]

Within the nation there was less antiwar activity in 1966 than in 1965. Public opinion polls continued to show strong popular support for the war. The antiwar movement remained small, internally divided, local, diverse, and diffuse. Peace liberals organized for political action during the fall 1966 elections. In Berkeley, California, antiwar activist Robert Scheer challenged a Democratic Congressional incumbent who supported the war. Scheer lost badly, and most liberal antiwar political efforts failed. The antiwar movement continued to operate at the political margins and had no measurable impact on public opinion, Congress, or administration war policy.[149] The big winners in the fall 1966 elections were the Republicans, coming back from the debacle of 1964, who gained nationally. In California, a newcomer to electoral politics, former screen actor Ronald Reagan, was elected governor by a landslide margin. Reagan, a Goldwaterite Republican, attracted enthusiastic popular support by running on a conservative platform that called for victory in Vietnam and condemned black militants, student radicals, antiwar protesters, and hippies.

For most Americans during 1966, the Vietnam War was not yet a major cause for concern. It was still a faraway war that was financially profitable, and it gratified the American penchant for anti-Communist crusades. The U. S. economy was booming, living standards for most Americans had never been higher, and few Americans had to make any sacrifices for the war. American youngsters were much more involved with rock 'n' roll music than a war in some faraway Southeast Asian country most had never heard of. A large majority of Americans united in support of the war to maintain an anti-Communist government in Saigon, although they disagreed over whether the goal could be better-achieved by military escalation or negotiations.[150] But as 1966 was ending, the first signs of war weariness appeared and there was growing dissatisfaction with the government's war policy.

By the spring of 1967, any illusions Americans had about achieving a quick and easy victory in Vietnam had largely receded—America found itself mired in an escalating military stalemate in Indochina. Nor could the United States get an acceptable political solution to the conflict, given the battlefield realities, the grave political weaknesses of the RVN, and the negotiating stance taken by Hanoi. U. S. casualties announced on March 10, 1967—232 killed in action and another 1,381 wounded, over 1,600 casualties in all—were the highest yet for any week of the war. A few days later, Congress passed a $20 billion supplemental appropriations bill to pay for the rising costs of the war.[151] At the time, polls showed that a majority of the American public was still supportive of the war, and the prominent national media continued to back the government's policy.

Figure 6.11 By 1966, opposition to the escalating American war in Vietnam was increasing. In February, Senate Foreign Relations Committee Chairman William Fulbright (pictured right) held hearings on the war. Fulbright and his dovish colleagues subjected administrative leaders such as Secretary of State Dean Rusk (pictured left) to hours of grilling about all aspects of the war. *Source:* National Archives

But opposition to the war was growing, and public support for the conflict was declining. Press coverage of the war was becoming more objective, more independent of government influence, and more critical of U. S. policy. Antiwar rallies, marches, and demonstrations increased in size, occurred more frequently, and developed more militant tactics during 1967, the first year of significant nationwide protest against the Vietnam War. On April 15, the Spring Mobilization Committee, a coalition of liberal and radical protest leaders, staged large antiwar demonstrations in San Francisco and New York City. About 50,000 people participated in the San Francisco demonstration and as many as 200,000 people converged on New York's Central Park for an afternoon of speeches and music.[152] Protesters gathered daily in front of the White House to chant, "Hey, hey, LBJ, how many kids have you killed today? "and "Ho, Ho, Ho Chi Minh, [the] NLF is going to win."[153]

The most prominent civil rights leader, Dr. Martin Luther King Jr., joined the antiwar ranks during the spring of 1967, adding greatly to the peace movement's sense of growth and momentum. In a sermon delivered at New York's Riverside Church on April 4, 1967, the Nobel laureate established himself as a leading spokesman for the peace cause. He blamed America for the war and called for a speedy end to the fighting. He urged all men of humane conviction to protest the war in whatever way was appropriate. He declared that Vietnam was "a symptom of a far deeper malady" that caused the United States, in the name of anti-Communism, to oppose the rightful demands of oppressed people everywhere who were seeking freedom and dignity. King claimed that anti-Communism had caused America to stray from its commitments to brotherhood and peace, and he called upon his country to return to its rightful home.[154]

Another prominent African American also defied the government's war policy. Heavyweight boxing champion Muhammad Ali, a devout member of the Nation of Islam sect, refused induction into the Army on religious grounds. Government attorneys argued successfully that "Black Muslims" were not eligible for conscientious objector status because they did not oppose all wars, only particular wars. Ali's draft board pronounced his religious views "insincere" and refused his request for a deferment. Ali replied:

> It would be no trouble for me to accept on the basis that I'll go into the armed services boxing exhibitions in Vietnam, or traveling the country at the expense of the government, if it wasn't against my conscience to do it. I wouldn't give up the millions that I gave up and my image with the American public, . . . If I wasn't sincere.[155]

Ali was convicted of draft evasion in June 1967, stripped of his heavyweight title, and sentenced to five years in prison. He stayed out of prison on bond until the Supreme Court overturned his conviction on a technicality. Ali lost five of his prime years as a professional athlete for his refusal to be drafted. He became one of the controversial symbolic personalities of the Vietnam War era, venerated by opponents of the war and despised by its supporters.

Alarmed by the rising antiwar protest activities taking place in the spring of 1967, government officials struck hard at their critics. They charged that the antiwar movement was funded and led by Communists and that antiwar protest demonstrations encouraged America's enemies to continue fighting. Johnson ordered the FBI and the CIA, in violation of its charter, to investigate prominent antiwar organizations and individuals. The Secret Service, the IRS, and the Justice Department were also involved in probing protest organizations and prominent individuals. Although CIA agents later told Johnson they could find no evidence that either foreign or domestic Communists controlled the antiwar movement, the President falsely claimed that they had.[156] FBI agents infiltrated many antiwar organizations. The FBI also used agents provocateurs to provoke violent confrontations with police and to take other violent actions that discredited antiwar organizations in the public's eyes.[157] The government's public relations strategy was to try to diminish the significance of the antiwar demonstrations by emphasizing how few people were involved in protest activities and by depicting them as a radical fringe of hippies and Communists. Most of the national news media followed the government's lead in redbaiting and belittling the antiwar movement.

By the summer of 1967, public opinion polls were getting harder to read; they also revealed both mass citizen apathy and ambivalence concerning the war. Nearly half of the citizens polled did not know enough about the Vietnam War to express an informed opinion. Although still supportive of the war effort, a majority of Americans no longer expressed confidence in Johnson's leadership nor expected the war to end any time soon. For the first time, a majority of respondents said American involvement in the Vietnam War was a mistake. More and more Americans revealed a yearning for an end to the war and liked the idea of turning the conflict over to the South Vietnamese.[158] Most Americans in the summer of 1967 were neither hawks nor doves: "If any bird symbolized the growing public disenchantment with Vietnam, . . . it was the albatross." A housewife succinctly expressed the contradictory attitudes generated by the war: "I want to get out but I don't want to give up."[159]

Press editorials and Congressional leaders increasingly voiced criticisms of U. S. Vietnam policy. Polls registered a widening "credibility gap," as a pervasive mistrust of government spread through the body politic. Some Americans saw the Vietnam War as only the most dramatic symbol of a spreading malaise infecting American society, a society increasingly marked by race riots, street demonstrations, and violent crime. The Vietnam War was coming home during that long hot summer of 1967. As the American consensus fractured and civility disappeared from public life, people feared that the Great Society might become a sick society.[160]

One of the earliest forms of antiwar protest was expressed in opposition to the draft. Attacking conscription offered protesters a dramatic way to show how the war directly touched Americans. Radical pacifists staged the first public draft card burning ceremony in New York's Foley Square on October 28, 1965.[161] As the Vietnam War expanded in 1966 and 1967, the size of monthly draft calls grew larger, and the number of conscripts being sent to fight in Vietnam increased, the number of young people resisting conscription also increased. Voluntary associations offering draft counseling proliferated. A new do-it-yourself literary genre, manuals and handbooks instructing readers how to apply for conscientious objector status and other kinds of deferments and exemptions from military service, appeared. A radical historian, Staughton Lynd, emerged as a leader of the militant anti-draft movement, urging young men to oppose conscription and support draft resistance. The SDS also supported draft resistance as an effective means of attacking the Vietnam War.[162]

The draft had become a generational obsession by 1967. Opposition to conscription was widespread; there were many means available and young men resisted, evaded, or avoided the draft for a variety of reasons. A large majority of young men who came of draft age during the Vietnam War era avoided military service.[163] Most of these evaders found legal means of avoiding the draft. They obtained deferments or exemptions by exercising their legitimate rights under the prevailing conscription system. Others manipulated the system to achieve their deferments or exemptions. Motivated primarily by a desire to avoid the Vietnam-era draft, they went to college, got married and fathered children, or obtained jobs in "critical" (exempted) occupations. Medically fit young men, aided by draft counselors and sympathetic doctors, found ways to obtain deferments, often on psychological grounds.

The success of millions of mostly middle- and upper-middle-class young men, in evading the conscription system either legitimately or illegitimately, shifted the burden of fighting the war to youths from lower-middle-class, working-class, minority, and poor backgrounds. The vast majority of U. S. conscripts who fought in the Vietnam War were from the lower rungs of the American social ladder. They were the young men who were either too poor, too uneducated, too unskilled vocationally, or too lacking in political influence to avoid the war. The draftees who had to fight the U. S. Vietnam War were a cross section, not of the entire society, but of its disadvantaged classes. Going to Vietnam was the price paid by many young men who lacked the connections and resources to avoid conscription.[164]

Other draft-eligible young men chose drastic methods of avoiding the draft and the war. Thousands of young men refused to register for the draft upon turning age eighteen. Hundreds of thousands refused induction when called. About 40,000 fled the country, mostly to Canada, to avoid military service. Some, in desperation, maimed and mutilated their bodies to disqualify themselves from military service. A handful of young men, adopting the protest method of South Vietnam's Buddhist monks and nuns, publicly immolated themselves.[165]

Many draft-age young men joined the Reserves or the National Guard to avoid active duty and a possible tour in Vietnam. But during the peak years of the war, when monthly draft calls ranged between 30,000 and 50,000 selectees, nearly all Reserve and National Guard units had filled up and most had long waiting lists. Applicants usually needed political clout to get into one of those draft sanctuaries. It was always possible that the Reservists and National Guardsmen could be called to active duty and be shipped off to Vietnam at any time. But Johnson, rejecting the advice of his senior military advisers and Secretary of Defense McNamara, refused to activate most of these forces. His refusal accorded with his desire to fight a limited war that would have a limited domestic impact. Had he activated the Reserves and the Guard, he would have provoked a firestorm of protest from many influential citizens and lost the support of many members of Congress. Most Reserve and National Guard units remained havens for affluent draft evaders for the duration of the war. A high percentage of draft-eligible college graduates and professional athletes could be found in the ranks of the Reserves and the Guard during the Vietnam War.[166] A future vice president, J. Danforth Quayle was one of the many affluent young men who obtained a coveted National Guard assignment and sidestepped a possible tour of duty in Vietnam.

In California, several antiwar organizations planned a Stop the Draft Week for mid-October 1967. On Monday, October 16, as newly drafted young men arrived in buses for their physical examinations and induction into the Army, a peaceful sit-in was held at the entrance to the Oakland Induction Center at 5:00 A.M. After the group refused orders to leave, the police moved in and arrested over 100 demonstrators. The next day, by 6:00 A.M., 3,500 militants, many affiliated with the SDS, surrounded the entrance to the induction center. After refusing police orders to disperse, they were attacked by the police. The entrance to the induction center was cleared within a few hours. Scores of demonstrators were injured and over twenty people were hospitalized. On Friday, perhaps 10,000 militants showed up and for hours blocked the entrance to the induction center. They were confronted by a force of over 2,000 police. Some demonstrators blocked streets, fought with police, and disrupted traffic over a twenty-block area of the city. Many demonstrators and police were injured during the day-long melee.[167]

A week after the demonstrations at the Oakland Induction Center, the nation witnessed the largest-yet antiwar demonstration held in the nation's capital. On October 21, the National Mobilization Committee and other antiwar organizations staged a rally in front of the Lincoln Memorial in Washington, D. C., attended by an estimated 100,000 people. It was a warm and sunny fall afternoon and the atmosphere was festive, like a picnic. Many people gave speeches; bands played and people sang. The protesters were mostly young, white, and middle class. Some 50,000 demonstrators marched slowly across the Arlington Memorial Bridge to a large parking lot north of the Pentagon, where they held another rally. A group of perhaps 4,000 militant protesters attempted unsuccessfully to "invade" the Pentagon, the nerve center of the American war effort. Most of the demonstrators, disinclined to engage in civil disobedience, disruptive tactics, or provoke confrontations with soldiers and police, left the area after a few hours. That night, government troops attacked the remaining militants in the parking lot and reclaimed the area. Hundreds of protesters were arrested and scores were hospitalized.[168]

Administration officials and most political leaders fiercely assailed the demonstrators as did most news media commentators. Polls taken at the time showed that Americans overwhelmingly agreed that antiwar demonstrations hurt the American war effort, aided the Communists, and harmed the antiwar cause. Even though the antiwar movement remained weak and marginalized, there was little pro-war enthusiasm. Most Americans may not have liked antiwar activists, but they increasingly did not like the Vietnam War either, and polls showed that they were pulling away from it.[169]

The growing public controversy over the war paralleled deepening divisions within Johnson's administration over his war policy. The Joint Chiefs and General Westmoreland had joined forces in the spring of 1967 in an effort to enlarge the war. Westmoreland, confident that his war of attrition would eventually produce victory, requested 200,000 additional troops to expand the ground war against the VC/NVA forces. The Joint Chiefs strongly endorsed his troop request. At the same time, they called for additional escalations of the air war against the North, and again for a mobilization of reserve forces. They also sought authorization for cross-border operations into Cambodia and Laos to clean out the VC/NVA sanctuaries in these neutral nations. They further proposed an invasion across the DMZ. In addition, they asked for an expanded air campaign against North Vietnam and for permission to mine North Vietnam's major ports. Only such measures, they argued, could defeat the rebels and force Hanoi to abandon its support of the southern insurgency.[170]

These escalatory requests by the military collided with moves by some of Johnson's civilian advisers, led by McNamara, to curtail the bombing of North Vietnam, hold the line on ground troops, and seek a negotiated settlement of the conflict that would allow the United States to extricate itself gracefully from the Vietnam quagmire. McNamara and other civilian officials in the Defense and State Departments had been disillusioned by the failure of both the air war against North Vietnam and the ground war against South Vietnam to defeat the Vietcong, discourage Hanoi, or strengthen the Saigon regime.

Johnson found himself caught amidst the divisions among his senior advisers. His political instinct was to seek a middle course between the hawks and doves. He refused most of the requests of the Joint Chiefs, except for expanding the air war against North Vietnam, but he agreed to send Westmoreland 55,000 additional troops. He rejected McNamara's suggestion to scale back the U. S. war effort, having lost confidence in his secretary of defense's judgment.[171] Johnson's war policy decisions were based more on domestic political considerations than they were on strategic criteria. His decisions amounted to a continuation of his policy of graduated escalation. He perpetuated the military stalemate without confronting the flaws within the U. S. strategy of limited war.

Following the October protest demonstrations, Johnson mounted a vigorous public relations campaign designed to bolster popular support for his war policy. He believed that American forces were winning the war. The reports Johnson received from MACV headquarters constantly reported news of progress: of the large numbers of the enemy killed, of the supplies captured, and of the villages pacified. Johnson discounted the critics of the war among the Congress, the media, the antiwar groups, and the general public. He regarded them as uninformed, lacking in nerve, and, in the case of antiwar activists, disloyal. Johnson tended to personalize criticisms of his war policy, and he deeply resented them. He believed the criticisms to be unfounded and unfair and felt that if his critics only understood what he was trying to do, they would support him enthusiastically.[172]

Presidential aides formed a citizens committee headed by former presidents Truman and Eisenhower to rally public opinion behind the war. Johnson met with an informal advisory group composed of elder statesmen. These former top officials, dubbed the "wise men," endorsed Johnson's war policy, although they voiced concern about spreading public disenchantment with the war. Johnson also brought General Westmoreland and Ambassador Ellsworth Bunker home to make upbeat speeches about Vietnam. Both officials exuded confidence and optimism. Westmoreland told a National Press Club audience, "We have reached an important point when the end begins to come into view." In answer to a question following his speech, Westmoreland said he believed America could begin phasing down the level of U. S. forces and turn more of the fighting over to the ARVN.[173] Soon after Westmoreland's speech, Johnson held a press conference, passionately defending his war policy, insisting that America must honor its commitments, and stating that U. S. forces were making progress.[174] He exhorted the American people to stay the course and hang tough, that victory was in sight. Westmoreland, back in Vietnam, announced that the enemy had suffered such severe losses that he could no longer mount an assault anywhere in Vietnam.[175]

As Johnson and other government officials appealed for support of the Vietnam War and told Americans that victory was coming, dovish critics, most of them academic experts, attacked the government's war policy. In lectures, speeches, essays, articles, and books, these unrelenting experts indicted a war policy they thought was wrong, counterproductive, and not serving the national interest in Southeast Asia. They constantly proposed alternatives: halt the bombing of North Vietnam, recognize the National Liberation Front, and seek a negotiated solution to the problem of who should rule in South Vietnam.

Although publicly vowing to continue to press for victory in Vietnam and exhorting his fellow Americans to stay the course, Johnson began privately to consider a change in his Vietnam strategy during the fall of 1967. Influenced by McNamara, other civilian advisers, and the "wise men," Johnson began to reappraise his war policies with an eye toward reducing U. S. casualties and transferring greater responsibility for the ground war to the South Vietnamese armed forces. He still remained committed to winning the war and to saving South Vietnam from a Communist takeover, but his thoughts pointed toward a shift in strategy that an official in President Nixon's administration would one day call "Vietnamization."[176]

President Johnson, whatever he may have been thinking in the privacy of his study, in all of his public appearances and pronouncements concerning his Vietnam War policy, remained committed to winning the war in Vietnam. As 1967 ended, the Administration appeared to be winning the propaganda campaign for the hearts and minds of the American people. The audience for the dovish critique of the war consisted mainly of a relatively small educated elite who embraced liberal or radical politics. Efforts by liberal Democrats to challenge Johnson's war policy from within the government were ineffective. Even though it was cracking at the edges, Johnson's centrist consensus still held. Polls showed that hawks significantly outnumbered doves. Johnson remained determined to prevail in Vietnam and was confident that he would. He also remained confident that he could hold the center and hold Congress.[177] But the American people would continue to support the war only as long as President Johnson could convince them that victory was nigh. Neither Johnson nor the American people could know that for six months the Communists had been planning a major offensive designed to "liberate" South Vietnam and force the Americans out of that country. As 1967 ended, they readied their forces to launch it. The Tet-68 Offensive would be the most important military campaign of the American war in Vietnam. It would shatter all hope of imminent American victory, transform the American political scene, and provoke a major crisis in Washington.

NOTES

1. Thompson, James Clay, *Rolling Thunder: Understanding Policy and Program Failure* (Chapel Hill, N. C.: University of North Carolina Press, 1980), 10–11; Summers, *On Strategy*, 18.
2. Davidson, *Vietnam at War*, 337.
3. *Ibid.*, 338.
4. Clarke, *The Final Years*, 106.
5. Thompson, *Rolling Thunder*, 11.
6. Herring, *America's Longest War*, 145.
7. Krepinevich, Andrew F. Jr., *The Army and Vietnam* (Baltimore, Md.: The Johns Hopkins University Press, 1986),165; Palmer, Bruce Jr., *The 25-Year War: America's Military Role in Vietnam* (New York: Simon and Schuster, 1985), 174–7.
8. Davidson, *Vietnam at War*, 369.
9. Furguson, Ernest B., *Westmoreland: The Inevitable General* (Boston: Little, Brown, 1968).
10. *Ibid.*; Davidson, *Vietnam at War*, 369–86; essay in Summers, Harry G. Jr., *Vietnam War Almanac* (New York: Facts on File, 1985), 357–9.
11. Westmoreland, *A Soldier Reports*, 186–93.
12. Krepinevich, *Army and Vietnam*, 164.
13. Westmoreland, *A Soldier Reports*, 187–8; Clarke, *The Final Years*, 102.
14. *Ibid.*; Clarke, *The Final Years*, 102.
15. *Ibid.*
16. Stanton, Shelby L., *The Rise and Fall of an American Army: U. S. Ground Forces in Vietnam, 1965–1973* (New York: Dell, 1985), 21.
17. *Ibid.*, 23.

18. Palmer, Dave Richard, *Summons of the Trumpet* (New York: Ballantine, 1978), 111–3.

19. Herring, *America's Longest War*, 151.

20. Stanton, *Rise and Fall*, 23; Palmer, *Summons of the Trumpet*, 169–70. The ratio of non-combat to combat effectives within the American force structure in Vietnam was six to one. In early 1969, American troop levels in Vietnam peaked at 543,000. At the time, only about 75,000 of these troops directly engaged in combat.

21. Quoted in Davidson, *Vietnam at War*, 349–50. Doyle et al., *America Takes Over*, 40; Stanton, *Rise and Fall*, 44.

22. Stanton, *Rise and Fall*, 45–46.

23. General Walt in turn was under COMUSMACV's (Westmoreland's) command authority. South Vietnam was divided into four combat sectors: I (Eye) Corps, II Corps (the central highlands), III Corps (Saigon and vicinity), and IV Corps (the Mekong Delta). The MACV directly controlled U. S. combat operations in Corps II, III, and IV. The South Vietnamese army also had a corps commander in each zone and the U. S. Army and ARVN generals and their staffs coordinated operations in each corps zone.

24. Stanton, *Rise and Fall*, 34–35.

25. Operation STARLITE was originally named SATELLITE.

26. Boettcher, Thomas D., *Vietnam: The Valor and the Sorrow* (Boston: Little, Brown, 1985), 317–19; Stanton, *Rise and Fall*, 34–39.

27. Summers, Harry G. Jr., "The Bitter Triumph of Ia Drang," *American Heritage Magazine* (Jan.-Feb. 1984), 56–58.

28. Palmer, *Summons of the Trumpet*, 119–20.

29. Herring, George C., "The 1st Cavalry and the Ia Drang Valley, 18 October–24 November 1965," in Heller, Charles E., and Stofft, William A., *America's First Battles* (Lawrence, Kansas: University Press of Kansas, 1986), 313–14; "Ia" was the Jarai word for river; Moore, Lt. Gen. (Ret.) Harold G. Jr. and Galloway, Joseph, *We Were Soldiers Once . . . And Young: Ia Drang—The Battle That Changed the War in Vietnam* (New York: Random House, 1992), 29–34.

30. *Ibid.*, 315.

31. Summers, "The Bitter Triumph of the Ia Drang," 53.

32. Westmoreland, *A Soldier Reports*, 204.

33. Herring, "The 1st Cavalry and the Ia Drang Valley," 318; Westmoreland, *A Soldier Reports*, 204–5; and Davidson, *Vietnam at War*, 360–62.

34. Morrocco, *Thunder from Above*, 88–93; Palmer, *Summons of the Trumpet*, 128–30; Moore and Galloway, *We Were Soldiers Once*, 124–39.

35. Herring, "The 1st Cavalry and the Ia Drang Valley," 319; Westmoreland, *A Soldier Reports*, 204; Moore and Galloway, *We Were Soldiers Once*, 402–3. Major General Harry W. O. Kinnard, commanding officer of the 1st Air Cavalry, stated, "I was always taught as an officer that in a pursuit situation you continue to pursue until you either kill the enemy or he surrenders."

36. Harry G. Summers Jr., "The Bitter Triumph of Ia Drang," 58, suggests that, ironically, the victorious campaign at Ia Drang contributed to the eventual American defeat in Vietnam. It gave American soldiers a sense of invincibility; after Ia Drang, they believed

that all they had to do was keep fighting battles and they would inevitably win the war. They failed to see that the war was changing, failed to focus on the major enemy, and failed to see the connection between the Ia Drang campaign and defeating the NVA. They forgot that tactics are no substitute for strategy. They lost sight of the major objective of the war and eventually lost the war.

37. Krepinevich, *The Army and Vietnam*, 168–9; Stanton, *Rise and Fall*, 57–58; Morrocco, *Thunder from Above*, 171.

38. Herring, "The 1st Cavalry and the Ia Drang Valley," 323.

39. Palmer, *Summons of the Trumpet*, 140.

40. Clarke, *The Final Years*, 124.

41. Thompson, W. Scott, and Frizzel, Donaldson D. (eds.), *The Lessons of Vietnam* (New York: Crane, Russak, 1977), 73–74; Palmer, *The Summons of the Trumpet*, 323.

42. Moore and Galloway, *We Were Soldiers Once*, 399.

43. *Ibid.*, 400.

44. *Ibid.*, 400–1.

45. Duiker, *The Communist Road*, 239; Turley, *The Second Indochina War*, 66.

46. Stanton, *Rise and Fall*, 76–77.

47. Westmoreland, *A Soldier Reports*, 234; Krepinevich, *The Army and Vietnam*, 190–1.

48. Rogers, Bernard W., *Cedar Falls-Junction City: A Turning Point* (Washington, D. C.: U. S. Government Printing Office, 1974), 73–74; Stanton, *Rise and Fall*, 101–2.

49. Stanton, *Rise and Fall*, 125.

50. *Ibid.*, 126. The MACV officials estimated total enemy combat strength at 285,000 at the end of 1966.

51. Schell, Jonathan, *The Real War* (New York: Pantheon, 1987), 59–74; Morrocco, *Thunder from Above*, 172; Palmer, *Summons of the Trumpet*, 168–71.

52. Westmoreland, *A Soldier Reports*, 268–9.

53. Schell, *Real War*, 86–121; Doyle et al., *America Takes Over*, 105.

54. *Ibid.*, 107–8.

55. Palmer, *Summons of the Trumpet*, 176.

56. Schell, *Real War*, 133–188; quote is from Doyle et al., *America Takes Over*, 108.

57. Rogers, *Cedar Falls-Junction City*, 154–7; Westmoreland, *A Soldier Reports*, 269.

58. Stanton, *Rise and Fall*, 127–9.

59. O'Ballance, *Wars in Vietnam*, 108; Stanton, *Rise and Fall*, 150.

60. Stanton, *Rise and Fall*, 161.

61. Westmoreland, *A Soldier Reports*, 313; hills on U. S. Army maps are designated according to their height in meters. Hill 875 was 875 meters high.

62. Stanton, *Rise and Fall*, 164.

63. *Ibid.*, pp. 165–8; Doyle et al., *America Takes Over*, 182.

64. Westmoreland, *A Soldier Reports*, 312–13; Davidson, *Vietnam at War*, 469.

65. Stanton, *Rise and Fall*, 170–1.

66. Westmoreland, *A Soldier Reports*, 263–4.

67. *Ibid.*, 265–6; Doyle et al., *America Takes Over*, 160–1; O'Ballance, *Wars in Vietnam*, 107.

68. Thompson, Robert, *No Exit from Vietnam* (New York: David McKay, 1969) 135; Gibson, *Perfect War*, p. 109, cites a National Security Council study stating that throughout 1966 and 1967, 75 percent of all battles were the enemy's choice of time, place, and duration.

69. Krepinevich, *The Army and Vietnam*, 167. Krepinevich believes that the fatal flaw of Westmoreland's attrition strategy was that it could not force the enemy to engage in big unit fights.

70. Mueller, John E., "The Search for a 'Breaking Point' in Vietnam: The Statistics of a Deadly Quarrel," *International Studies Quarterly*, vol. 4, (December 1980), 497–519. General Giap has estimated PAVN manpower losses for the war at 600,000 soldiers killed. If his guess was accurate, North Vietnam lost about 3 percent of its prewar population. For America to have sustained an equivalent loss, its battle deaths would have had to reach about 7,000,000.

71. Herring, *America's Longest War*, 155–6. By 1968, the American war in the countryside had created an estimated 5,000,000 refugees. The urban population of South Vietnam swelled from 15 percent in 1964 to 40 percent by 1968.

72. Schandler, *The Unmaking of a President*, 31–32; Herring, *America's Longest War*, 155.

73. Thompson, *Rolling Thunder*, 35; Clodfelter, *Limits*, 63–64.

74. Morrocco et al., *Thunder from Above*, 64–65.

75. Palmer, *Summons of the Trumpet*, 156–7.

76. Thompson, *Rolling Thunder*, 45–48; Clodfelter, *Limits*, 71–72.

77. Clodfelter, *Limits*, 92–93.

78. Quoted in Morrocco et al., *Thunder from Above*, 127.

79. *Ibid.*, 128; Mersky, Peter B., and Polmar, Norman, *The Naval Air War in Viet-Nam* (New York: Kensington, 1981), 118–21.

80. Clodfelter, *Limits*, 98.

81. Morrocco et al., *Thunder from Above*, 130–1.

82. Clodfelter, *Limits*, 99.

83. Porter, (ed.), *Vietnam Documents*, vol. 2, "Intelligence Memoranda By the Directorate of Intelligence, CIA," May 12 and May 23, 1967, Documents 261 and 262, 466–70. Gallucci, *Neither Peace nor Honor*, 64–70; Thompson, *Rolling Thunder*, 51–53.

84. Sheehan et al., *Pentagon Papers*, "Vietnam Bombing Evaluation By Institute for Defense Analysis," *Pentagon Papers*, Document 117, 506–7.

85. Clodfelter, *Limits*, 99–100.

86. Turley, *The Second Indochina War*, 97; Stanton, *Rise and Fall*, 174–5.

87. Quote is from Clodfelter, *Limits*, 101.

88. Palmer, *Summons of the Trumpet*, 162; Porter, (ed.), *Vietnam Documents*, vol. 2, "Memorandum for McNamara By the Joint Chiefs of Staff," JCSM-30767, June 2, 1967, Document 263, 470–2.

89. Clodfelter, *Limits*,105. A Harris poll taken on February 13, 1967, showed that 67 percent of the American public supported the ROLLING THUNDER campaign.

90. Quote is from *Ibid.*, 112.

91. Thompson, *Rolling Thunder*, 64; Clodfelter, *Limits*, 84.

92. Clodfelter, *Limits*, 112.

93. Sharp, Ulysses S. G., *Strategy for Defeat: Vietnam in Retrospect* (San Rafael, Calif.: The Presidio Press, 1978). Admiral Sharp argued that an intensive bombing campaign could have won the war. But in 1965, the rate of infiltration into South Vietnam had been 1,500 men per month; in 1966, 4,500 men per month; in 1967, as the air war intensified, the rate of infiltration increased to 6,000 men per month. In January 1968, on the eve of the Tet Offensive, 20,000 men infiltrated into South Vietnam.

94. Littauer, Raphael, and Uphoff, Norman (eds.), *The Air War in Indochina*, rev. ed. (Boston: Beacon, 1972), 36. The passage is also quoted in Thompson, *Rolling Thunder*, 64; Lewy, *America in Vietnam*, 389–96. By 1967, China was undergoing its Cultural Revolution; it was less able to intervene in North Vietnam, but Johnson would never rule out that possibility.

95. Clodfelter, *Limits*, 117–18. The ROLLING THUNDER campaign led to the destruction of 65 percent of North Vietnam's oil storage capacity, 59 percent of its power plants, 55 percent of its bridges, 9,821 vehicles, and 1,966 railroad cars. In the fall of 1967, when the air war raged at its most intense level, there were about 55,000 NVA troops in South Vietnam and about 250,000 Vietcong forces. These forces engaged in battle infrequently, and the PLAF got much of its required supplies from southern villagers. The NVA and Vietcong required 34 tons of supplies per day from North Vietnam. Seven 2$\frac{1}{2}$ ton trucks could haul that daily requirement, which represented less than 1 percent of the daily tonnage imported from China and the Soviet Union by rail and sea. An all-out air-war waged indefinitely could never have seriously hindered Hanoi's resupply capability, given the small needs of the troops fighting in the South and Hanoi's huge excess resupply capacity made possible by Chinese and Soviet assistance.

96. *Ibid.*, 134–6.

97. Turley, *The Second Indochina War*, 95–96.

98. Enthoven, Allen C.; and Smith, K. Wayne, *How Much is Enough? Shaping the Defense Program, 1961–1968* (New York: Harper and Row, 1971); Coldfelter, *Limits*, 131. One of the major operational controls that limited the effectiveness of ROLLING THUNDER missions was the formidable air defense system gradually developed by the North Vietnamese. It included 200 surface-to-air (SAM) missile sites, 7,000 anti-aircraft guns, and 80 MiG fighters. American pilots had to operate against the most sophisticated and deadliest air defense system ever erected in the history of aerial warfare.

99. Sheehan et al., "Secretary McNamara's Position of May 19 on Bombing and Troops," *Pentagon Papers*, Document 129, 580.

100. Thayer, *War Without Fronts*, 79–86; Morrocco, *Thunder from Above*, 74.

101. Morrocco et al., *Thunder from Above*, 84.

102. *Ibid.*, 88–89.

103. *Ibid.*

104. Thayer, *War Without Fronts*, 129–32.

105. *Ibid.*

106. *Ibid.*, 83–84.

107. Morrocco, *Thunder From the Air*, 85.

108. Buckingham, William A. Jr., *Operation Ranch Hand: The Air Force and Herbicides in Southeast Asia, 1961–1971* (Washington, D. C.: GPO, 1982).

109. Herring, *America's Longest War*, 151.

110. Boettcher, *Vietnam: The Valor and the Sorrow*, 258–9; Morrocco et al., *Thunder from Above*, 180.

111. Jacobs, James B., and McNamara, Dennis, "Vietnam Veterans and Agent Orange," *Armed Forces and Society*, vol. 13 (Fall 1986), 57–79.

112. Morrocco, *Thunder from Above*, 180.

113. *Ibid.* Weather hampered air operations over North Vietnam as well as over the Laotian panhandle.

114. Sheehan et al., "Johnson's Remarks to Officials of U. S. and Saigon at Honolulu," *Pentagon Papers*, Document 111, 495–6.

115. Quoted in Karnow, *Vietnam*, 444.

116. Blaufarb, *Counterinsurgency Era*, 232–3.

117. Kahin, *Intervention*, 413–14; Clarke, *The Final Years*, 128–9.

118. *Ibid.*, 423–5.

119. Doyle & others, *America Takes Over*, 78–79; Clarke, *The Final Days*, 136.

120. From interviews with soldiers on videotape, "America Takes Charge, 1965–1967," from the television series "Vietnam: A Television History."

121. Kahin, *Intervention*, 432.

122. Blaufarb, *The Counterinsurgency Era*, 225–9.

123. Herring, *America's Longest War*, 158.

124. *Ibid.*, 158–9; 3,015 RD personnel were kidnapped or murdered during a seven-month period in 1966.

125. Blaufarb, *The Counterinsurgency Era*, 229–31; Herring, *America's Longest War*, 159; Davidson, *Vietnam at War*, 431–2; Clarke, *The Final Years*, 209–12; Andrade, Dale, *Ashes to Ashes: The Phoenix Program and the Vietnam War* (Lexington, Mass.: Lexington Books, 1990), 58–63.

126. Herring, *America's Longest War*, 159–60.

127. Karnow, *Vietnam*, 451–2.

128. Shaplen, Robert, *The Road from War: Vietnam, 1965–1971* (New York: Harper & Row, 1971), 151; also quoted in Herring, *America's Longest War*, 160.

129. Herring, *America's Longest War*, 161.

130. *Ibid.*, 162. In 1954, Saigon had a population of 550,000; in 1961, 1,000,000. In December 1967, U. S. officials estimated that 2,200,000 people lived within the city and another 1,000,000 in the suburbs of the Gia Dinh Province.

131. Schandler, *The Unmaking of a President*, 31–32. Interviews with soldiers recorded on videotape, "America Takes Charge, 1965–1967," from the television series "Vietnam: A Television History."

132. *Ibid.*

133. Goodman, *The Lost Peace.* 23–26.

134. Quoted in Gareth Porter (ed.), *A Peace Denied: The United States, Vietnam, and the Paris Agreement* (Bloomington, Ind.: Indiana University Press, 1975), 29; also quoted in Herring, *America's Longest War,* 165.

135. Herring, *America's Longest War,* 166.

136. Goodman, *The Lost Peace,* 28.

137. *Ibid.,* 35–36.

138. Karnow, *Vietnam,* 493–4; Goodman, *The Lost Peace,* 39–42.

139. Herring, *America's Longest War,* 167.

140. Turner, *Lyndon Johnson's Dual War,* 191–8; Doyle et al., *America Takes Over,* 136–7.

141. Goodman, *The Lost Peace,* 24.

142. *Ibid.*

143. Quoted in DeBenedetti, Charles, Charles Chatfield, Assisting Author, *An American Ordeal: The Antiwar Movement of the Vietnam Era* (Syracuse, N.Y.: Syracuse University Press, 1990), 75.

144. *Ibid.,* 25–26, 97.

145. *Ibid.,* 117.

146. Herring, *America's Longest War,* 170.

147. Debenedetti, *American Ordeal,* 119–27, 135–6; Small, Melvin, *Johnson, Nixon, and the Doves* (New Brunswick, N.J.: Rutgers University Press, 1988), 31–33. Most Americans thought opposition to the war to be illegitimate. They viewed the protesters as aiding the enemy and undermining American troops fighting in Vietnam. They especially resented male university students who joined the ranks of antiwar activists, considering them a privileged elite of cowards and traitors.

148. Doyle et al., *America Takes Over,* 141–52.

149. Debenedetti, *American Ordeal,* 151–2, 157; Small, *Johnson, Nixon, and the Doves,* 75.

150. *Ibid.,* 162.

151. Schandler, *The Unmaking of a President,* 49.

152. Debenedetti, *American Ordeal,* 175–6.

153. Quoted in Herring, *America's Longest War,* 173.

154. King's April 4, 1967, sermon was published as "A Declaration of Independence from War" in *Ramparts,* vol. V; no. 11 (May 1967), 33–37.

155. Moss, George, "The Vietnam Generation, 1964–1973," unpublished essay, 1984, 13; Baskir, Lawrence M., and Strauss, William A., *Chance and Circumstance: The Draft, the War and the Vietnam Generation* (New York: Random House, 1978), 63, 79, 97.

156. DeBenedetti, Charles, "A CIA Analysis of the Antiwar Movement: October 1967," *Peace and Change,* vol. 9 (Spring 1983), 31–41. According to the CIA report to Johnson on the peace activists, "Many have close Communist associations but they do not appear to be under Communist direction." Despite the report, Johnson met with a bipartisan Congressional group, including House minority leader Gerald Ford on October 24 and

told them that he had a "secret" report that documented Communist control of the October 21 march on Washington.

157. Gitlin, Todd, *The Whole World Is Watching: Mass Media in the Making and Unmaking of the New Left* (Berkeley, Calif.: University of California Press, 1980), 186–9.

158. DeBenedetti, *American Ordeal*, 179.

159. Both quotes are from Herring, *America's Longest War*, 174.

160. Oberdorfer, Don, *Tet! The Turning Point in the Vietnam War* (New York: The Da Capo Press, 1971), 79–81; Herring, *America's Longest War*, 174–5; Mueller, *War, Presidents, and Public Opinion*, 112–13. Three times during 1967, the Gallup Poll asked people, "Do you think the Johnson administration is or is not telling the public all it should know about the Vietnam War?" Each time, only 21 to 24 percent answered "yes," and 65 to 70 percent answered "no."

161. DeBenedetti, *American Ordeal*, 128–9.

162. *Ibid.*, 165–7.

163. Moss, "The Vietnam Generation," 3–7. Between August 10, 1964, when President Johnson signed the Gulf of Tonkin Resolution formally making the Vietnam conflict an American war, and March 28, 1973, when the last American soldier exited Vietnam, about 27 million young men reached draft age; 16 million of them avoided military service. Of these 16 million, 9 million obtained deferments or exemptions, 4 million drew high lottery numbers during the two years that the lottery draft operated, and the other 3 million avoided military service because Selective Service lost or mishandled their files.

164. *Ibid.*, pp. 5–6; Baskir and Strauss, *Chance and Circumstance*, 8–10.

165. Baskir and Strauss, *Chance and Circumstance*, 62–90.

166. Moss, "The Vietnam Generation," 9.

167. Powers, Thomas, *Vietnam: The War at Home* (Boston: G. K. Hall, 1973), 236–8; DeBenedetti, *American Ordeal*, 196.

168. *Ibid.*, 238–40; DeBenedetti, *American Ordeal*, 197–8; and Norman Mailer, *The Armies of the Night: History as a Novel, the Novel as History* (Cleveland: World Publications, 1968).

169. DeBenedetti, *American Ordeal*, 198–9. Americans, by a three to one margin, thought antiwar demonstrations were acts of disloyalty against American boys fighting in Vietnam and encouraged the Communists to fight harder. Seventy percent thought the demonstrations hurt the antiwar cause.

170. Sheehan et al., "Westmoreland Cable to Joint Chiefs on Troop Needs," March 28, 1967, *Pentagon Papers*, Document 123, 560–5; "Joint Chiefs Report to McNamara on Troops Needs," April 20, 1967, Document 124, 565–7; and "Notes on Johnson's Discussion with Wheeler and Westmoreland," April 27, 1967, Document 125, 567–9.

171. Karnow, *Vietnam*, 507–8.

172. Oberdorfer, *Tet!*, 98–99.

173. Quoted in Karnow, *Vietnam*, 514; Schlandler, *The Unmaking of a President*, 62; Small, *Johnson, Nixon, and the Doves*, 120–4. Neither Westmoreland nor Johnson ever used the

phrase, "We can see the light at the end of the tunnel." It was coined by Henry Cabot Lodge.

174. Quoted in Turner, *Lyndon Johnson's Dual War*, 205.

175. Dougan, Clark; Weiss, Stephen; and the editors of Boston Publishing Company, *Nineteen Sixty-Eight* (Boston: Boston Publishing Co., 1983), a volume in the series, *The Vietnam Experience*.

176. Herring, *Longest War*, 3d. ed., 200–1.

177. Small, *Johnson, Nixon, and the Doves*, 178. Polls showed a 6 percent increase in public support for Johnson's war policy at year's end.

7

The Year of the Monkey

For twenty years first the French and then Americans have been predicting victory in Vietnam. But for twenty years we have been wrong. The history of conflict among nations does not record another such lengthy and consistent chronicle of error. It is time to discard so proven a fallacy and face the reality that a military victory is not in sight, and that it probably will never come.

Robert Kennedy

SURPRISE ATTACK!

Taking advantage of the cease-fire called to celebrate Tet, the beginning of the lunar new year and Vietnam's most important holiday, some 84,000 Vietcong and NVA soldiers launched simultaneous attacks during the early morning hours of January 30, 1968,[1] extending from the demilitarized zone in the north to the Ca Mau Peninsula in the south. They attacked the national capital, five of the six largest cities, thirty-six of forty-four provincial capitals, and sixty-four of 242 district capitals. Within South Vietnam's beleaguered towns and cities, ARVN forces, its ranks depleted by the absence of many soldiers who went home for the holidays, fought to defend governmental and military installations, the major targets of the enemy assaults. The offensive caught the Allied commands by surprise. Convinced that any enemy assaults would occur on the northernmost provinces and the Marine base at Khe Sanh, the Allied leaders "could not conceive of an attack of the magnitude of what occurred during the Tet holiday."[2]

Although caught by surprise, RVN and U. S. troops quickly recovered and counterattacked effectively. Using their superior firepower and mobility, they were able to expunge the Vietcong and PAVN forces from the towns and cities. Nearly everywhere they repulsed the attackers quickly, usually inflicting severe losses. Almost nowhere did the attackers have time to secure their positions, and they did not receive any significant support from the residents. General Westmoreland quickly judged the Communist offensive to be a complete military failure.[3] Tet-68, the largest and most important campaign of the American Vietnam war, amounted to a major tactical defeat for the Vietcong and NVA forces.

But news of the Tet *coup de main* broke like a thunderclap across America. The fact that the enemy could mount a major military effort all over South Vietnam and catch the allies by surprise shattered all illusions of impending American victory in the war. Tet suggested that all the years of bombing, attrition warfare, pacification, body counts, and computer printouts that claimed, by all quantitative measures, that the United States was winning the war, had not meant a thing. In the wake of Tet, many shocked, angry, and confused Americans came to the realization that America had involved itself in a stalemated war in Southeast Asia. Although suffering major tactical reverses, Hanoi scored a decisive psychological and thus a political victory over the United States and its RVN allies.[4] Tet constituted a major turning point in the Vietnam War. After Tet-68, President Johnson felt compelled to scale down the bombing of North Vietnam and put a ceiling on the number of U. S. troops committed to South Vietnam. After Tet-68, America could not win the Vietnam War on any politically acceptable terms. Because the Communists offensive forced Washington to confront the reality that it was fighting a war that it was not winning, nor was likely to win at any reasonable cost, and because President Johnson was eventually forced to abandon the strategy of graduated escalation to resolve a political crisis, the first few months of 1968 are the most important in the entire history of the long U. S. involvement in Vietnam. The January–March 1968 period proved to be pivotal in America's longest war.

Hanoi had been planning the Tet campaign since the spring of 1967. Tet-68 was a belated response to the Americanization of the war that had occurred in the summer of 1965. Washington's decisions in July 1965 to escalate the conflict in South Vietnam posed a severe challenge to the Vietnamese revolution. Given American firepower, the Communist leaders understood that any effort on their part to match Westmoreland's strategy of attrition would cost them heavy casualties and would also run the risk of extending the war to North Vietnam. But if they did not respond vigorously to the American threat, the Communist leaders feared that the southern insurgency could be slowed, postponing the achievement of Hanoi's goals of revolution and reunification of the country.[5]

The decision to respond to the U. S. military buildup was made in December 1965 at the Twelfth Plenum of the Central Committee of the Lao Dong meeting in Hanoi, which took place soon after the Ia Drang campaign. Knowing they probably could not defeat the Americans militarily, Hanoi's leadership opted for a strategy of protracted struggle, of "people's warfare." Eschewing the possibility of military victory in the near future, they discerned two enemy political weaknesses they believed

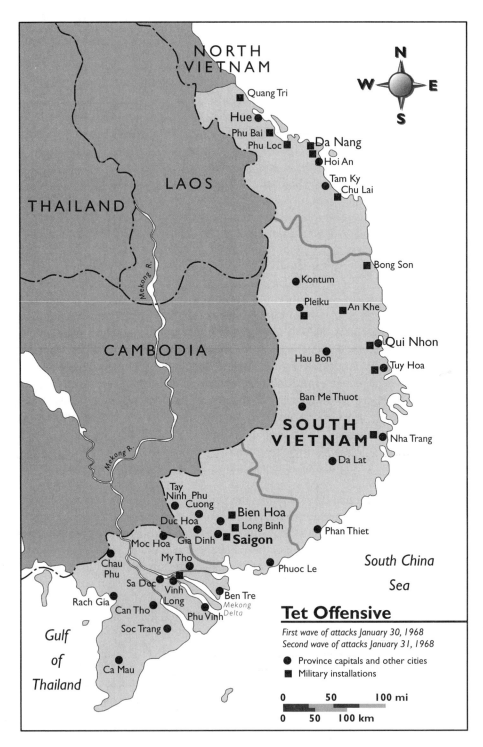

Figure 7.1. Public domain map.

they could exploit: the inherent instability of the Saigon regime and the potential softness of public support for the Vietnam War within the United States.[6] Hanoi's leaders knew that the introduction of American combat forces had not eliminated the underlying political weaknesses of the GVN, and they expected that their propaganda efforts would fan the flames of antiwar sentiment within the United States that had surfaced at the time Johnson took America to war.

To exploit these perceived weaknesses, the directive issued at the close of the Twelfth Plenum called for the Lao Dong to mobilize the armed forces and the Vietnamese people to

> foil the war of aggression of the U. S. imperialists. . . , so as to defend the North, liberate the South, complete the national people's democratic revolution in the whole country, advancing toward the peaceful reunification of the country.[7]

Senior NVA military commanders, including General Giap, publicly endorsed the Politburo's strategy of protracted warfare, which amounted to countering Westmoreland's strategy of attrition with an attrition strategy of their own. They aimed at keeping the tactical initiative, keeping pressure on both the American and GVN forces, and inflicting a high level of costs and casualties on both. The implementation of Communist-style attrition warfare in the South was the prime responsibility of one of its chief advocates, General Nguyen Thi Thanh, the aggressive commander of the PLAF forces.[8]

Throughout 1966 and into 1967, General Thanh vigorously pursued Hanoi's protracted warfare strategy. It proved a disappointment. The Communists incurred severe losses, while attaining few desirable strategic or political results. U. S. and RVN forces won all major battles. American troop levels continued to increase, and Westmoreland aggressively pursued his big-unit style of attrition warfare. The U. S. antiwar movement had no discernible impact on Johnson's determination to bomb North Vietnam or on his decision to fight a gradually escalating ground war. Thanh's strategy also failed to induce Washington to seek a negotiated solution. The GVN, with all of its deficiencies, appeared to be more stable in the spring of 1967 than when Hanoi had implemented the protracted war strategy. Many Vietcong units and some NVA units fighting in South Vietnam had been decimated. Others had been driven out of South Vietnam into Cambodia or Laos, or were forced to take refuge in sparsely populated peripheral areas in the central highlands. The NLF infrastructure controlled fewer villages and less territory in South Vietnam than it had at the time the Twelfth Plenum decided to fight attrition with attrition.[9]

Disappointed with the results of the protracted war strategy and convinced that victory could come only from a combined general offensive and popular rising of the South Vietnamese, Hanoi's leaders, in the spring of 1967, decided that a major offensive should be launched the following year. General Thanh took charge of the planning until his death, which might have resulted from U. S. bombing on July 6, 1967.

Planning for the new strategy continued under his successor, General Pham Hung. Final approval of the General Offensive/General Uprising was given at the Lao Dong's Fourteenth Plenum, in November.[10]

Hanoi's leadership persuaded itself that the political situation in South Vietnam had evolved to a point where a revolutionary uprising could occur in response to a successful Communist offensive. They viewed the Buddhist revolt that had taken place in Danang and Hue during the spring of 1966 as an indicator that the Saigon government was ripe for overthrowing. The Communist leaders expected the military victories achieved during the intended offensive to trigger an uprising that would be led in the towns and cities by Vietcong organizers.[11] If the general uprising succeeded, the RVN would be overthrown. It would be replaced by a coalition government dominated by the NLF. There would be a cease-fire, and the Americans would be forced to withdraw from South Vietnam. The country could then proceed toward reunification and the completion of its national revolution the Vietminh had begun in 1945.

The Lao Dong leaders believed the offensive strategy had a reasonable chance of success. Even if it fell short of total victory, they expected it to discourage the United States and shake the foundations of the RVN by undermining the faith of the South Vietnamese in the ability of their own government to protect them, "thus increasing the likelihood of a negotiated settlement favorable to the revolutionary cause."[12] Perhaps a successful offensive could stop the steady escalation of the American war effort. They hoped to send a message to the Americans that they had involved themselves in a war that they could not win, at least at any reasonable price. Neither desperate nor overconfident, the Communist leaders saw their strategy of the General Offensive-General Uprising (Tong Cong Kich-Tong Khoi Nghia, or TCK-TKN) as a calculated gamble. It would replace the strategy of protracted warfare that had shown little promise of achieving desired goals after more than two years of bloody efforts. Most of North Vietnam's aging revolutionary leaders viewed the new strategy as a risk worth taking.

The Communists launched phase one of TCK-TKN in October 1967 with a series of assaults along the periphery of South Vietnam. They struck at Song Be and Loc Ninh near the Cambodian border, at Dak To in the central highlands, and at Con Thien, just south of the DMZ. Their goals were to inflict casualties and draw U. S. forces away from populated areas to these sparsely populated border regions, which would leave the urban populations of South Vietnam unprotected from the Tet assaults planned for phase two. These peripheral attacks were powerful, fighting was fierce, and casualties were heavy on both sides. In every area, the Communists were beaten and forced to retreat to their cross-border sanctuaries. Communist losses, though substantial, achieved their purpose; they induced Westmoreland to move U. S. and ARVN forces away from populated areas.[13]

By late fall 1967, the U. S. military command in Saigon, noting that the rate of infiltration down the Ho Chi Minh trail had increased sharply, suspected that the Communists were preparing for a major offensive early in 1968. Captured enemy documents and interrogations of VC and NVA defectors confirmed these suspicions.

Westmoreland concluded that the main enemy offensive would occur in I Corps, just south of the DMZ. He believed the Communists would try to capture the two northernmost provinces of South Vietnam, Quang Tri and Thua Thien, which were separated from the rest of South Vietnam by mountains reaching to the sea. Westmoreland strengthened the U. S. forces at Khe Sanh and other forward bases near the DMZ. He did not consider Saigon or the other cities of South Vietnam to be facing any serious dangers. As a show of confidence in the improving South Vietnamese forces, the MACV had entrusted the defense of Saigon and other urban areas to the ARVN.[14]

On January 10, Lieutenant General Frederick Weyand, commander of III Corps, warned Westmoreland that intelligence data indicated that the enemy was shifting his forces from the border regions to Saigon and to other cities in South Vietnam. Weyand's views were confirmed by General Philip Davidson, the head of the MACV's intelligence division. In response to these warnings, Westmoreland moved some U. S. forces to the vicinity of Saigon and placed others in the corridors running from the Cambodian border toward the capital. He also persuaded General Thieu to keep half of his ARVN forces on duty during the Tet holidays. These precautionary moves possibly saved Saigon from an enemy takeover during Tet. But Westmoreland remained convinced that the major enemy push would come in the North and that it would occur before the Tet holidays.[15]

Phase two of TCK-TKN, which Americans knew as the Tet-68 Offensive, began shortly after midnight on January 30, when PLAF/NVA forces launched a nationwide assault on South Vietnam's cities and towns. At 2:45 A.M., a team of Vietcong commandos on a suicide mission blasted a hole in the wall surrounding the U. S. embassy compound in downtown Saigon, and then entered the courtyard. They battled a detachment of American military police for the next six and one-half hours in the courtyard before all of the VC were killed or captured. By 9:00 A.M., the embassy was secure. Bodies littered the compound. At 9:30 A.M., standing amid the rubble and litter of bodies, General Westmoreland held an impromptu press conference. He insisted that the Allied forces had everything under control; Communists all over South Vietnam were being beaten back and slaughtered. Some journalists wondered how Westmoreland could be so confident of victory when Vietcong commanders had managed to get inside the U. S. embassy, the citadel of American power in Vietnam and supposedly the most secure place in the whole country. Although it was of no tactical consequence and it resulted in a quick defeat for the Vietcong, as did most of the Tet battles, the firefight inside embassy walls had a dramatic impact within the United States. Americans were shocked to learn that an enemy supposedly on its last legs could bring the war to the symbolic heart of American power within South Vietnam's capital. The Vietcong attack on the embassy had achieved an important psychological objective. General Westmoreland, standing amid the litter of battle inside the embassy compound, became one of the enduring images in American minds of the Tet-68 campaign.[16]

Within hours of the embassy assault, other Vietcong forces attacked targets in or near Saigon, including the presidential palace, the headquarters of both the MACV and the South Vietnamese joint general staff at Tan Son Nhut Air Base, the RVN's radio station, and the air base at Bien Hoa. In every instance, the attackers were driven off and suffered heavy losses. Some ARVN units, under severe pressure, fought effectively. They were reinforced by U. S. troops, who used their superior firepower to inflict severe casualties on the outgunned Vietcong. Nothing remotely resembling a popular rising occurred in Saigon.[17]

But the Vietcong's attacks left Saigon's inhabitants shocked and dazed. Their sense of security, of invulnerability, their feeling that they were safe from a remote conflict that only engulfed the countryside, had been shattered as they experienced the contagion of war firsthand. The fighting within the city, particularly the use of American firepower, did extensive damage to sections of Saigon. Thousands of families were left homeless in the wake of the fighting that had saved them from a possible Communist takeover.

Everywhere in South Vietnam, local Vietcong units attacked urban centers in force. In Nha Trang, a coastal city of 120,000 about 180 miles north of Saigon, enemy soldiers attacked a naval training center. The VC forces struck targets in Kontum and Pleiku, two central highlands cities. At Danang, ARVN and U. S. forces, alerted by a VC defector that an attack was imminent, met the enemy on the outskirts of the city. In none of these assaults did the attackers accomplish their missions. They were driven back everywhere, with heavy losses.[18]

In the Mekong Delta, that vast, flat, green, and watery expanse that constituted South Vietnam's rice bowl, the Vietcong attacked thirteen of sixteen provincial capitals and many of the district capitals. The ARVN forces generally performed ineffectively in the Delta region, and American forces had to be rushed to many towns and cities to drive out the attackers. An estimated 5,000 VC were killed and hundreds were captured during the fighting in the Delta. Most of the local guerrillas and political cadres were wiped out during phase two.[19]

Figure 7.2   The hole in the wall of the U. S. Embassy compound in downtown Saigon blasted by a suicide squad of Vietcong sappers at the start of the Tet-68 Offensive. Americans, led to believe that the enemy was on the verge of defeat, were shocked by this violent assault on the American citadel. *Source:* U. S. Army photo

The ferocity of the fighting during Tet-68 climaxed at Hue. In a battle lasting a month, two NVA regiments and two VC elite battalions battled eight American and thirteen ARVN battalions in one of the most savage battles of this or any other war. "The furor of the Tet-68 Offensive would become symbolized by the catastrophic destruction incurred in this grim city struggle."[20]

?. Hue.

Hue, located near the coast midway between Danang and the DMZ, had an official population of 100,000, swollen by the influx of thousands of war refugees, at the time of the Tet-68 Offensive. The Perfume River runs through the city, with two-thirds of the population living north of the river, mostly within the walls of the Citadel (Old City), and one-third residing south of the river in the westernized New City. Until Tet, Hue had remained free of war. Both sides had treated it with respect, and Hue was considered an open city.[21] There was a sizeable U. S. presence in Hue, and many other foreigners lived and worked there. It was the most beautiful of Vietnam's cities, with its unique blend of traditional and cosmopolitan cultures.

On the morning of January 31, 7,500 Communist troops, achieving complete tactical surprise, overwhelmed the ARVN defenders and took control of the Citadel and much of the New City within a few hours. Two U. S. Marine companies from Phu Bai, a few miles south of Hue, joined with ARVN forces to counterattack the next day. The counterattack stalled in the face of determined NVA/VC resistance. Over the next few days, both the Americans and South Vietnamese augmented their forces in Hue. Starting on February 5, naval gunfire from ships of the Seventh Fleet, which was positioned offshore, pounded targets inside the Citadel from a range of fifteen miles. Both VNAF and U. S. aircraft napalmed and strafed targets within the Old City. On the ground, Marine rifle companies advanced from house to house in savage fighting.[22]

By February 9, the Marines had reclaimed the sectors of the city lying south of the river, and the ARVN units had reclaimed much of the Citadel. But in the southeastern sector of the Citadel, including the Imperial Palace, the NVA/VC forces held a series of strong points. The Communists inflicted heavy casualties on the attacking South Vietnamese. The hard-pressed ARVN troops were joined by elements of the 1st Battalion, 5th Regiment, U. S. Marines, on February 12. For days, the carnage of close combat took a deadly toll on both the ARVN forces and the Marines of the 1st/5th. On February 24, elements of the 3rd ARVN Regiment raised the RVN flag over the Citadel and the battered remains of the Palace of Perfect Peace. It took the Allies another week of scattered fighting to crush isolated pockets of resistance and round up NVA/VC stragglers. The Battle of Hue ended on March 2, 1968. Over 8,000 soldiers on both sides died in the month-long battle. Seventy-five percent of the city's population was rendered homeless. The stench of death hovered over the littered landscape. The exhausted survivors gazed in horror at the remains of Hue, the once-proud and lovely imperial city, which had been blasted into corpse-strewn rubble. "The beautiful city . . . was a shattered, stinking hulk, its streets choked with rubble and rotting bodies."[23] Hue had been saved, but destroyed.

Concurrent with the Battle of Hue, the Communists had occupied Gia Hoi, a sector of the city lying north of the Perfume River and east of the walled Citadel. Within Gia Hoi, the Communists established a provisional government and set about implementing their revolution. Cadres held rallies, made speeches, and organized groups of students, workers, and teachers into administrative units. The Communists used terror to destroy the established government of the city. They purged Gia Hoi of all "reactionary elements" by liquidating anyone who had an affiliation with the Saigon regime. They executed about 2,800 people, often in brutal fashion, or they buried them alive. They sent a stark message: No one associated with the RVN was safe from insurgent reprisals anywhere in South Vietnam.[24]

The victims of NLF "hit squads" included officials of the national government, city officials, civil servants, community leaders, military personnel, police, priests, and teachers. Foreign victims included many Americans, Germans, Filipinos, Koreans, and nationals of other countries. In November 1969, President Nixon cited the Communist mass murders committed during their Tet-68 occupation of Hue as a justification for his policy of gradually withdrawing American troops from South Vietnam. He asserted that if the U. S. withdrew its forces precipitously, as many Americans were demanding, the massacre at Hue would become a prelude for a nightmare, a bloodbath of massive proportions.[25]

Figure 7.3   A Marine emerges from a blown wall during hand-to-hand fighting in the streets of Hue on February 6, 1968. *Source:* U. S. Marine Corps photo

Phou'i
Khe
Sanh.

Before the Battle of Hue ran its course, the Communists had launched phase three of TCK-TKN in a remote corner of the Quang Tri Province, sixty miles northwest of the battered former imperial city. Two elite PAVN divisions, the 304th and 325-C, lay siege to the U. S. Marine base at Khe Sanh. The base, perched on a plateau near the corner formed by the DMZ and the Laotian border, blocked enemy infiltration along Route 9. It could also be used to stage an invasion of Laos to cut the Ho Chi Minh trail at a key choke point near Tchepone if America chose to expand the war. Four Marine battalions of the 26th Marines, under the command of Colonel David E. Lownds, reinforced by one battalion of ARVN Rangers, 6,000 men total, defended the main base and surrounding hill strong points at Khe Sanh. They faced an estimated 30,000 to 40,000 PAVN troops.

General Giap had planned phase three to be the capstone of TCK-TKN. If the phase-two attacks on the cities succeeded in bringing about popular uprisings and the collapse of the Saigon regime, Giap's divisions would try to drive the U. S. Marines out of Khe Sanh. If the NVA forces succeeded, they could end the Second Indochina War with a stunning military victory.[26]

The Battle of Khe Sanh received extensive media coverage within the United States. Americans feared for the lives of the Marines, who were crowded into their isolated outpost, subjected to intensive artillery and mortar bombardments, and seemingly in danger of being overrun. Journalists noted uneasily that Khe Sanh resembled Dien Bien Phu, the French fortress the Vietminh had isolated and overrun in May 1954. The fall of Dien Bien Phu had been a catastrophic defeat for the French. It had destroyed their will to continue the Franco-Vietminh War. Would history repeat itself at Khe Sanh? Would the United States suffer its first major defeat of the Second Indochina War? If such a military disaster occurred, would it be the end of the American Vietnam war? President Johnson fretted that Khe Sanh might be lost to the Communists. Asserting that he did not want "any damn Dinbinfoo" on his watch, Johnson anxiously raised the possibility of using tactical nuclear weapons to save Khe Sanh if the enemy verged on overrunning it.[27]

The fears of the journalists and President Johnson were exaggerated. Khe Sanh bore only a superficial resemblance to Dien Bien Phu. According to General Westmoreland, there was never any serious danger of the NVA forces overrunning the base or driving out the Marines. General Giap had been able to defeat the French at Dien Bien Phu in 1954 for two major reasons: He had had superior firepower, and he had been able to cut the aerial lifeline to the fortress. But, at Khe Sanh, the combination of American air power and artillery fire gave the Americans a vast superiority over the NVA forces, and Giap's forces could not interdict Westmoreland's air supply system to the base. In fact, one of the reasons Westmoreland had installed the Marines at Khe Sanh was because he hoped to lure Giap into a set-piece battle. Confident that the Marines, supported by artillery and bombers, could hold the base against whatever forces the NVA committed to battle, Westmoreland viewed Khe Sanh as the ideal place to call the awesome American firepower into play. If Giap's forces took the bait and tried to overrun Khe Sanh, Westmoreland believed they would be cut to pieces by artillery fire and bombing.[28]

The siege of Khe Sanh began on the morning of January 20, when NVA forces hit the base and its hilly outposts with barrages of artillery, rocket, and mortar fire. The Battle of Khe Sanh developed as a full-scale conventional campaign fought between two national armies in an important arena of the war. The I Corps Tactical Zone, consisting of the five northernmost provinces of South Vietnam (Quang Nam, Quang Tin, and Quang Ngai, in addition to Quang Tri and Thua Thien) was the largest and most complex combat area in South Vietnam. Within that region, the enemy mounted a potent mix of insurgent and conventional tactics that often put severe pressures on the allied forces. During 1967, the fighting in I Corps accounted for half of the enemy KIAs, with the Marines suffering half of the U. S. KIAs for that year.[29]

Westmoreland reacted to Giap's siege of Khe Sanh by executing Operation NIAGARA, which had been prepared for use against the NVA in the event they attacked the base. Operation NIAGARA represented a mighty concentration of firepower composed of B-52s, tactical aircraft, and artillery directed at the enemy positions.[30] As the Battle of Khe Sanh unfolded, artillery duels between PAVN and Marine gunners, round-the-clock air raids on the NVA positions, and periodic vicious firefights whenever enemy units attacked one of the surrounding strong points were daily occurrences. On February 7, a Special Forces camp at Lang Vei, south of Khe Sanh, was destroyed by NVA forces using Soviet PT-76 light tanks. It was during the Khe Sanh campaign that the enemy first used armor in South Vietnam. The loss of Lang Vei enabled the NVA to put more pressure on the Marines defending Khe Sanh. Three weeks later, the key battle of the Khe Sanh campaign took place. From February 29 to March 1, following the heaviest enemy artillery barrage of the campaign, a regiment of the NVA 304th attacked Khe Sanh from the east. But U. S. artillery and bombers decimated the regiment before any of its units reached the base perimeter.[31]

The destruction of the 304th regiment marked the turning point in the battle. Although there were harassing attacks made by the enemy over the next several days, the NVA mounted no more major assaults on Khe Sanh. The PAVN forces began withdrawing by March 11. Giap apparently decided to pull his forces back from Khe Sanh because of the failure of the phase-two campaigns and because he had concluded that the U. S. forces could not be beaten at Khe Sanh. There would be no replication of Dien Bien Phu if that had been Giap's objective. Scattered fighting occurred in the vicinity of the base until the end of the month. A relief force of Marines and Air Cavalry troops reached Khe Sanh on April 8, allowing Colonel Lownds and his Marines to leave the base. Their ordeal had ended. The siege of Khe Sanh had lasted seventy-seven days; it had claimed the lives of more than 200 Marines. Estimated NVA losses exceeded 10,000 killed or wounded.[32]

In addition to their losses at Khe Sanh, the mostly futile countrywide assaults during the Tet-68 Offensive cost the attackers horrendous casualties. From January 29 through March 31, 1968, combined Vietcong and PAVN losses may have exceeded

Figure 7.4 Khe Sahn: A panoramic view of the sandbagged perimeter bunkers. U. S. Marine defenders held on to the remote outpost lying below the DMZ during a 77-day seige by North Vietnamese regulars. *Source:* U. S. Air Force

58,000 KIA, nearly 70 percent of the forces committed to the campaigns! The Vietcong, who had staged most of the attacks, "were largely destroyed as an effective military menace to the South Vietnamese government."[33] The PLAF main force units had to be reconstituted, using NVA regulars who infiltrated south down the Ho Chi Minh trail.

In many provinces, many of those in the Vietcong political infrastructure, which had been painstakingly erected over the years, were also killed or captured during the Tet-68 battles. The VC cadres had come out into the open to organize and lead the uprisings that were expected to follow the assaults on the towns and cities. The expected uprisings never materialized, and the VC cadres were eliminated. Nowhere in South Vietnam cities and towns were the Vietcong attackers welcomed by the South Vietnamese people, nor did any defections from GVN political or military ranks occur. In fact, many of the ARVN forces fought well, despite being caught by surprise.[34] After Tet, there was no chance the Saigon regime would be overthrown by a revolution from within South Vietnam. After the spring of 1968, the Vietnam War became, for the most part, a conventional war between the main forces units of the allies and the NVA/PLAF. U. S. military leaders in Washington and Saigon considered Tet-68 the greatest tactical victory of the war for the American and ARVN forces. In the wake of his greatest success, having taken advantage of an opportunity to hurt badly the enemy, General Westmoreland was eager to mount a major counteroffensive and win the war.[35]

But the Tet-68 campaigns proved to be the great paradox of the American Vietnam war. Tet-68 turned out to be a short-term tactical U. S. victory that prepared the way for the long-run strategic defeat of the American cause in Southeast Asia. Although few on either side of the war perceived it at the time, Tet-68 was the beginning of the end of the American intervention in Southeast Asia.

POLITICAL CRISIS

The scope, scale, and intensity of the Vietcong Tet offensive shocked most Americans, who had been led to believe that the Vietcong were about finished. Nightly, television news beamed the sights and sounds of fierce battles in the streets of Saigon and Hue into American living rooms. Viewers watched Vietcong commandos fighting inside the American embassy compound; they watched General Westmoreland's impromptu press conference held in the embassy courtyard amidst the rubble and dead Vietcong sappers; and they witnessed the summary execution of a Vietcong terrorist by General Nguyen Ngoc Loan, chief of South Vietnam's National Police, on a cobblestone street in Saigon. Daily press reports filed from cities all over South Vietnam highlighted the surprise attacks and extensive destruction they caused. Initial wire stories, later corrected, exaggerated the Communist successes, and contributed to the confusion and widely shared sense that Tet had been an allied disaster.[36]

A quotation from an Associated Press (AP) report had tremendous impact. On February 7, Air Force Major Chester I. Brown conducted a press tour through the shattered Mekong Delta town of Ben Tre. The town had been occupied by the VC. American troops were called in to reclaim the town. To eject the VC, the Americans used heavy artillery and helicopter gunships that leveled most of the town's buildings and killed many of its inhabitants. Surveying the remains of Ben Tre, Brown matter-of-factly told AP reporter Peter Arnett, "It became necessary to destroy the town to save it."[37]

Major Brown's phrase encapsulated a basic contradiction of the U. S. war effort in South Vietnam. Americans were fighting in Vietnam to protect the freedom of the South Vietnamese people and enable them to build a nation. But American weaponry was destroying part of the South Vietnamese society in the process of trying to liberate it. The military means overwhelmed the political ends. For many of the residents of Ben Tre, the real-world alternative to rule by the Vietcong was death and destruction at the hands of their saviors. If America had to destroy its friends in order to save them, of what use was the war to us, or, *a fortiori,* to our friends? Major Brown's remark "seemed to epitomize the purposeless destruction of the war."[38] The phrase gained wide currency in the United States and became one of the staples of antiwar discourse for years.

While the media stressed the surprising power of the enemy offensive, official cables to Johnson and other leaders in Washington presented a more realistic account of Tet-68. From his reading of the secret cable traffic, Johnson knew the Vietcong had suffered heavy casualties, the ARVN troops were fighting effectively, the urban populace was not rallying to the NLF banner, and the enemy attacks were failing almost everywhere. Johnson, knowing Tet was a significant allied tactical victory, tried to counter the sensational media coverage and reassure the American people.[39] He held a press conference on February 2 to pronounce the Communist offensive a complete failure. Administrative officials appeared on public affairs programs and made speeches around the country to convey the message that Tet was a great allied victory and a disastrous Communist defeat.

The Johnson administration's public relations efforts to salvage popular support for the U. S. Vietnam War policy in the aftermath of the Tet assaults failed. Much of the press and the public continued to regard Tet as a disaster. What administration spokesmen did not understand was that it was not that journalists or the American people thought Communists were winning the Tet battles. That was not the major problem. The public was shocked by the fact that the Tet offensive had occurred, *that it could occur.* The very fact that it had occurred made Tet a psychological disaster in this country, that the enemy could mount and execute a surprise offensive of massive proportions all over the country. Tet-68 exploded all of the official reassurances that the U. S. was winning the war, the Vietcong were on their last legs, and the war would end soon. To many Americans, Tet confirmed what they already suspected, that the Johnson administration had not been telling the truth, that the United States had locked itself into an endless war that was consuming ever-rising numbers of lives and dollars. Public opinion polls showed that public discontent with the war and opposition to Johnson's war policy increased sharply in the aftermath of the offensive.[40]

Figure 7.5 Brig. General Nguyen Ngoc Loan, head of the South Vietnamese National Police, summarily executes a Vietcong terrorist on a street in Saigon during the Tet-68 Offensive. NBC television also broadcast the execution on its nightly newscast on February 2, 1968. Photographer: Eddie Adams. *Source:* AP/Wide World Photos

Despite their outward show of confidence, Johnson and his senior advisers had been shaken by the scale, scope, and intensity of the Communist Tet-68 Offensive. They also were alarmed by the prospect of further offensives in South Vietnam and by Communist initiatives in other parts of the world. On January 23, just before Tet, the North Koreans had suddenly seized an intelligence-gathering ship, the USS *Pueblo*, operating near their coast, after having tolerated such espionage operations for years. At about the same time, South Korean police discovered an assassination plot against South Korean President Chung Hee Park, which was masterminded in North Korea. CIA operatives warned that the Soviets might provoke another crisis over Berlin, a perennial Cold War flash point. Washington also received reports of increased unrest in the Middle East.[41] Johnson worried that the Tet-68 attacks, including the siege at Khe Sanh, constituted parts of a worldwide Communist effort to score Cold War victories over America and its allies.

Johnson's military advisers responded to Tet by proposing to widen the war. The Joint Chiefs wanted to expand the bombing campaign against North Vietnam. But Johnson, concerned above all with holding Khe Sanh, refused to take any additional military actions against North Vietnam. He asked General Westmoreland if he needed any additional troops to prevent a defeat at Khe Sanh. Westmoreland, confident he could hold the fort with what he had, replied that he did not need any more combat troops. But he was concerned about his logistic ability to support the forces that he had committed to I Corps, and he requested some additional airlift and helicopter support.[42]

In early February 1968, General Earle Wheeler, the chairman of the Joint Chiefs, had much on his mind besides Vietnam. In Johnson's willingness to send Westmoreland whatever additional forces he might need to avoid a politically damaging defeat at Khe Sanh, Wheeler saw an opportunity to rebuild the American strategic reserve and replenish U. S. military forces stationed elsewhere in the world. The deployments to Vietnam had not been based on the military demands of the situation, but on the forces available without calling up the Reserves and the National Guard. The NATO forces assigned to Germany and the forces committed to South Korea had all been been skeletonized and stripped of their best officers and noncoms in order to send more troops to the Vietnam War.[43]

Faced with Communist threats in North Korea and Berlin, and perhaps elsewhere, the Joint Chiefs had concluded that U. S. strategic assets had been stretched too thin by Vietnam. General Wheeler, believing Tet would force Johnson's hand, thought he could persuade Johnson to take the politically risky step of mobilizing the Reserves and of putting the country on a full war footing. Wheeler maneuvered Westmoreland, who had initially declined Johnson's offer of more combat troops, into requesting additional forces. Then the Joint Chiefs put pressure on Johnson to provide the forces not only for Vietnam, but to restock the stateside strategic reserve so the military would be better-positioned to meet Communist threats to U. S. interests elsewhere. They were especially concerned that American NATO commitments not be sacrificed on the altar of Vietnam.[44] They were disappointed when Johnson deferred their request to mobilize the Reserves and agreed to send General Westmoreland a force of only 10,500 troops, which could be provided without calling up the Reserves.

Wheeler pursued his goal of a reserve mobilization, which he believed was necessary to enable the United States to meet the military demands of the Vietnam War and to fulfill its other strategic commitments in a dangerous world. He obtained Johnson's approval to travel to Vietnam to assess General Westmoreland's immediate and future manpower needs. After conferring, Westmoreland and Wheeler came up with a planned troop request designed to meet both the MACV's Vietnam needs and defend other American interests in the world. The troop request was composed of three force packages: The first increment of 108,000 men would be sent to Vietnam by May 1, 1968. Additional increments of 42,000 and 56,000 men would be sent by September 1 and December 1, respectively, 206,000 men total. But only the first increment would be sent to Vietnam for sure. The other two increments would constitute the strategic reserve in the United States, which was not to be deployed in Vietnam unless the North Vietnamese mounted a successful offensive.[45]

Wheeler presented the troop request to Johnson and his advisers on February 28, 1968. He accompanied his report with a pessimistic appraisal of the military situation in Vietnam that contradicted General Westmoreland's previous optimistic appraisals. Wheeler told Johnson that the initial Tet attacks nearly succeeded in a dozen places, that the ARVN forces had been thrown on the defensive, and that pacification had suffered serious setbacks. "In short it was a very near thing."[46] Wheeler also told Johnson and his advisers that Westmoreland would need to augment his forces significantly if he was to respond effectively to the challenges posed by Tet-68: to counter the enemy offensive, to eject the NVA forces fighting in I Corps, to restore security to the towns and cities, to restore security in the populated regions of the countryside, and to regain the initiative with a counteroffensive of his own. To accomplish all of these objectives, Wheeler insisted that Westmoreland would require large numbers of additional troops.[47] By accentuating the negative aspects of the military situation in Vietnam, Wheeler tried to frighten Johnson and other senior civilian officials into supporting a call-up of the Reserves, part of which would be used to replenish depleted U. S. force levels elsewhere.

The magnitude of the troop request stunned Johnson and his civilian advisers, and Wheeler's pessimistic assessment of Tet alarmed them. Departing Secretary of Defense Robert McNamara, the *bete noire* of the hawks to the end, "in his valedictory meeting as a member of the cabinet," strongly opposed sending more U. S. troops to Vietnam. McNamara said that feeding another 200,000 soldiers into combat would merely be doing more of the same. The North Vietnamese, as they had previously, would simply match the American escalation with one of their own. McNamara pointed out that bombing had consistently failed to impair the Communists' ability to infiltrate whatever men and supplies they required. He believed the key to improving the situation in South Vietnam was not to send more U. S. troops but to increase the resources and responsibilities of the South Vietnamese army.[48]

At the February 28 meeting, General Wheeler confronted the president with two bitterly unattractive choices. If Johnson met the Army's request for an additional 206,000 troops, it would mean transcending the parameters of limited war that the president had set. The Reserves would have to be mobilized to provide the manpower, and the economy would have to be put on a war footing to meet the vastly increased expenditures. That would mean tax increases and probably economic controls. Worse, Johnson would have to take these politically unpalatable actions in an election year, and at a time of rising domestic opposition to the war and his leadership. But if he refused the Wheeler-Westmoreland request to increase troops levels in Vietnam by 40 percent, he would be sending a clear signal to friends and foes alike that the upper limits of the American military commitment in South Vietnam had been reached. He would be acknowledging that American strategic goals had either been abandoned or pushed far into the future.[49] Further, with U. S. military forces stationed around the world, having already been stretched dangerously thin to provide the 536,000 troops currently in Vietnam, failure to meet the Army's request for 206,000 additional soldiers might render the U. S. government incapable of responding effectively to threats to its strategic interests elsewhere.

Johnson, shocked by General Wheeler's report, refused to make such a critical decision on the spot. He asked his new Secretary of Defense Clark M. Clifford, who was attending the meeting, to head a study group to examine all facets of the troop request. Johnson solemnly told Clifford to study the matter thoroughly and carefully, then to give him "the lesser of evils."[50]

Johnson's directive to Clifford inaugurated the most important debate over what action to take in Vietnam ever undertaken within any administration during the long history of U. S. involvement in Southeast Asia. For the first time, there would be a reappraisal of all aspects of the U. S. Vietnam War policy. During the reassessment process, hawks and doves waged a bureaucratic war for the heart and mind of Lyndon Johnson. Everyone at the meeting that day sensed that a decisive moment in the war had arrived. They also knew Clark Clifford was the man who more than any other was going to determine on which side of the historic divide President Johnson would choose to walk. Would Johnson decide to escalate or back off? The outcome of a war hung in the balance.

Clifford, although he was a newcomer to Johnson's inner circle, also was a seasoned Democratic party insider and elder statesmen. He had managed Harry Truman's 1948 campaign when the feisty president had scored his famous upset over the consensus favorite, Thomas Dewey. Clifford also had been a valued adviser of President John F. Kennedy. Prior to appointing him to replace McNamara, Johnson had often sought Clifford's advice on a whole range of issues.[51] Clifford was an establishment centrist who had embraced the Cold War ideology characteristic of his generation of political leaders. He had supported Johnson's Vietnam War policy since its inception. Johnson brought Clifford on board as McNamara's replacement, primarily because he had assumed that his new defense secretary would continue to back his war policy.

Unknown to Johnson, Clifford had already begun to have doubts about the validity of the domino theory, which was the chief ideological prop for the American war effort in Vietnam. In September 1967, Johnson had sent Clifford to accompany Maxwell Taylor on a trip to Asia to persuade several of the American allies in that region to increase their troop commitments in Vietnam. Clifford was surprised to learn that the leaders of Thailand, the Philippines, South Korea, New Zealand, and Australia neither wished to send more troops to Vietnam nor felt particularly threatened by the fact that North Vietnam had over 100,000 troops in South Vietnam. Clifford asked himself, If these Asian and Pacific island nations proximate to the Vietnam War felt no fear of Communist expansion, could it be that U. S. officials had exaggerated the potential threat to the stability of these countries posed by the Communist revolution in Vietnam?

Clifford also had kept in touch with influential friends in corporate board rooms and law offices across the land. Until Tet, these powerful men had generally supported the administration's war policy. After the Communist offensive, many had turned dovish. Worried about the stalemated war, political disunity, and signs of economic decline, they opposed any further escalations of the war. Some thought it was time for America to cut its losses and get out of Vietnam. Their opinions had an impact on Clifford.[52] The man Johnson thought was a hawk was already questioning the U. S. war policy as he replaced McNamara. When he had completed his reappraisal of the Vietnam War policy, Clifford, the putative hawk, had been transformed into a dove.

To help him complete the task Johnson had given him, Clifford quickly formed a task force, which included several of the president's senior civilian and military advisers: Dean Rusk, Secretary of the Treasury Henry H. Fowler, Undersecretary of Defense Paul Nitze, the Director of the CIA, Richard Helms, National Security Adviser Walt Whitman Rostow, General Wheeler, and General Taylor. The Clifford Task Force turned immediately to examining the Army's request for 206,000 additional troops, as well as the means by which it could be met. The major problem was that all previous troop requests had been fulfilled without mobilizing reserve forces. But it was precisely this political barrier that would have to be broken to meet the military's latest demands. Such a large troop increase also would have an adverse impact on the economy and require large cuts in Great Society programs. Foreign aid would be gutted.[53] Several task force members further pointed out that in their judgment, sending large numbers of additional troops would probably be futile. North Vietnam would match our escalation with one of their own, as they had previously. Besides, by the time the new contingents of American combat troops could be deployed to Vietnam, the outcome of the crucial battles of the Tet-68 campaign would have long since been decided.

As the task force members studied the troop request problem, officials from the Defense Department, the CIA, and the State Department systematically destroyed the rationale for the Joint Chiefs' troop request and began to challenge the Vietnam War policy itself. A Department of Defense official, Alain Enthoven of Systems Analysis, called the troop request another "payment on an open-ended commitment." In his view, sending additional U. S. combat troops to South Vietnam would not bring an earlier end to the war, attrite the enemy, or erode Hanoi's will to fight.[54]

Clifford began to ask fundamental questions about the American Vietnam policy, many of which were questions Johnson had never raised, questions that were exceedingly difficult to answer precisely. By raising these basic issues, Clifford broadened the task force's focus. Although the task force had been formed to study the military's request for more troops, it began to reappraise the entire American Vietnam war effort. To Clifford, the most important question was not how to send 206,000 more troops to Vietnam, rather, should America continue on its present course in Vietnam? Clifford raised other fundamental questions about the American war policy and discovered that senior civilian and military officials either could not provide answers or furnished him with dismaying answers:[55]

1. Will 200,000 more troops win the war? No one could be sure.
2. If not, how many more will be needed to win and when? No one knew.
3. Can the enemy respond with a buildup of their own? They could and they probably would.
4. What would be involved in committing 200,000 more men to Vietnam? A reserve call-up of up to 280,000 men, increased draft calls, and an extension of tours of service for most men on active duty.
5. How much would it cost to meet the latest troop request? An estimated $2 billion per month.
6. What would be the impact on the economy? Credit restrictions, tax increases, and probably wage and price controls. It would also worsen the balance of payments and lower the value of the dollar.
7. Can the bombing stop the war? No, not by itself.
8. Would stepping up the bombing decrease U. S. casualties? Very little, if at all.
9. How long must we keep sending U. S. troops and carrying the main burden of combat? Nobody knew. The South Vietnamese forces are far from ready to replace the U. S. forces.

During his review, Clifford asked General Wheeler for a presentation of the military plan for attaining victory in Vietnam. General Wheeler told him that there was no military plan for victory. Astonished, Clifford asked him why. Wheeler told him that there was no plan because U. S. forces operated under three major political restrictions: They could not invade North Vietnam because such action would possibly bring the Chinese into the war. They could not mine Haiphong, North Vietnam's principal port, because Soviet ships might be sunk. They could not pursue the enemy into Laos and Cambodia because such initiatives would widen the war, both politically and geographically. Clifford then asked, given these restrictions, how could America hope to win the Vietnam War? Wheeler replied, without enthusiasm, that eventually the enemy would reach a point when it would decide it could not continue the war because it could no longer tolerate the damage that the strategy of attrition was inflicting. Clifford then asked General Wheeler how long he thought it would take for the current attrition strategy that was in place to induce Hanoi to abandon the insurgency in South Vietnam? Wheeler would not attempt an estimate.[56]

Following days of analysis of the American Vietnam war policy, Clifford concluded with a series of observations that starkly revealed the bankruptcy of the American strategy of limited war in Southeast Asia:

> I could not find out when the war was going to end; I could not find out the manner in which it was going to end. I could not find out whether the new requests for men and equipment were going to be enough, or whether it would take more and, if more, how much; I could not find out how soon the South Vietnamese forces would be ready to take over. All I had was the statement, given with too little self-assurance to be comforting, that if we persisted for an indeterminate length of time, the enemy would choose not to go on. And so I asked, "Does anyone see any diminution in the will of the enemy after four years of our having been there, after

Figure 7.6 The man who turned the Vietnam War around. In March 1968, Clark Clifford, the new Secretary of Defense, helped persuade Lyndon Johnson to abandon his bankrupt policy of graduated escalation and replace it with an early version of Vietnamization. *Source:* National Archives

enormous casualties, and after massive destruction from our bombing?" The answer was that there appeared to be no diminution in the will of the enemy.[57]

Following his extensive discussions with many officials, Clifford concluded that the most probable outcome of sending 206,000 more troops to Vietnam would be to raise the level of combat and casualties. "I was convinced that the military course we were pursuing was not only endless, but hopeless."[58] Sending more troops would only raise the level of devastation, further Americanize the war, and leave the United States farther than ever from its goal of achieving an independent South Vietnam. Clifford therefore concluded that the United States should send no more troops to South Vietnam. Instead, the American goal "should be to level off our involvement and work toward gradual disengagement."[59] Having made his decision, Clifford set out to try to convince Johnson that the time had come to alter course in Vietnam. Clifford knew Johnson would have to abandon his policy of gradual escalation because it was not working, nor showed any promise of ever working. It also was limiting America's ability to meet strategic commitments elsewhere in the world, weakening the economy, and dividing the American people.

JOHNSON AGONISTES

Johnson received the Clifford Task Force's report on March 4. It contained General Wheeler's recommendation that the troop request should be met. But to achieve the goal of 206,000 additional troops in Vietnam during 1968, the report made clear to Johnson that he would have to call 262,000 Reservists to active duty, increase draft calls, and extend the tours of most men currently serving on active duty.

More significantly, the task force's report also called for a reassessment of the U. S. Vietnam policy, especially in relation to U. S. global strategic interests. It hinted that America would have to establish a limit for its involvement in Vietnam and abide by it. The report also asserted that no amount of additional U. S. troops in Vietnam could achieve American objectives there unless the South Vietnamese government achieved a broader popular base and fought more effectively.[60] Clifford hoped the report would cause Johnson to focus on the fundamental questions of U. S. Vietnam policy raised by the Wheeler-Westmoreland troop request issue. He also hoped to sow seeds of doubt in Johnson's mind about the wisdom of continuing to escalate the war.

The president carefully read and pondered over the report for several days. He discussed what he should do in Vietnam with several advisers, including members of the task force. Rostow urged him to go all out and make a maximum effort to win the war. Johnson's initial reaction to the Communist Tet Offensive had been to do just that. He was angry, and he wanted to strike back. Johnson also believed that an aggressive post-Tet counteroffensive, coupled with an intense bombing campaign, could break Hanoi's will. He felt ready to mobilize the Reserves, not only for Vietnam but to strengthen the overall American strategic posture in the world. He wanted to unleash

Westmoreland and have him pound the Vietcong remnants and battered North Vietnamese forces into submission.

What partially deterred him from striking back hard was the Clifford Task Force's report. Johnson was persuaded to make any further commitment of American forces to Vietnam contingent upon the South Vietnamese government improving its capabilities for governing and fighting. Johnson agreed that the South Vietnamese leaders should be informed that continued American support for their cause would depend on their willingness to assume a greater burden of the fighting. Johnson's willingness to send the message to Thieu and Ky that they would have to do more of the fighting indicated that there was significant movement in Washington's policy toward the concept of Vietnamization that would later be embraced by the Nixon administration. Johnson also knew that Westmoreland was already taking the offensive against the enemy with the U. S. forces he had on hand.[61] The MACV did not appear to have an immediate need for additional forces to take the fight to the Communists and hold Khe Sanh. Johnson also responded positively to a proposal from Rusk to consider curtailing the bombing of North Vietnam. Rusk persuaded Johnson that a partial bombing halt might offset some of the domestic opposition to the war, and it could even elicit a favorable response from the North Vietnamese that would move both sides closer to negotiations.[62] By March 7, Johnson was moving toward two new positions: setting a troop ceiling for Vietnam and ordering a partial bombing halt. In the "Battle for Lyndon Johnson," Rostow, Wheeler, and the other hawks appeared to be losing ground to Clifford and the growing number of doves among them.

Whatever possibility remained of Johnson sending large numbers of additional troops to Vietnam diminished when *New York Times* reporters Hedrick Smith and Neil Sheehan broke the story on March 10 that Johnson was considering a troop increase of 206,000 troops.[63] The impact of the *Times'* scoop, which penetrated the veil of secrecy Johnson had draped over the top-secret deliberations, was dramatic. White House spokesmen denied, unconvincingly, that the president was considering such a large troop request from General Westmoreland. Johnson's credibility gap widened. A storm of public criticism erupted. If Tet were such a great allied victory, people demanded to know, why did General Westmoreland need 200,000 more troops? Other influential print and electronic media voices editorialized against the proposed troop increase and called for changes in the Vietnam War policy. The day after the *Times* broke the sensational story, Senator Fulbright, on live television, grilled Rusk for hours about the Administration's plans for sending more troops to Vietnam. Fulbright ended his interrogation by warning Rusk that any further escalations of the war had better be cleared with Congress. Tet had convinced many wavering congressmen and senators that the United States was not winning the war, that it had locked itself into a stalemated conflict in Vietnam.

Dramatic evidence of flagging Congressional support for the Vietnam War surfaced shortly after the *Times* story broke. Clark Clifford and General Wheeler conferred with hawkish leaders on the House and Senate Armed Services Committee.

These people, mostly conservatives, all Cold Warriors and staunch supporters of the war effort to date, told Clifford and Wheeler that they could not support a reserve call-up or a large increase in the number of U. S. troops fighting in Vietnam. Senator Richard Russell, a close friend and mentor of Johnson, and one of the most powerful and conservative senators on Capitol Hill, made a profound impression on Clifford when he told him and General Wheeler that he believed the United States had made a serious mistake by involving itself in Vietnam in the first place. Clifford wondered, if Senator Russell and his fellow hawks did not support a troop increase, who would?[64]

> The Tet Offensive, . . legitimated the Vietnam War as a political issue. It "liberated politicians, journalists, and commentators from their previous commitments to the war."[65]

The search for alternative war policies became a legitimate, even obsessive, political preoccupation. Because 1968 was a presidential election year, the war became an integral part of the national electoral process. The search for alternatives, for a way out of a war that had become unpopular and seemingly unwinnable—unpopular mainly because it appeared unwinnable—had become the leading issue of the embryonic presidential race. Presidential candidates from both parties began to criticize Johnson, his war policy, and the proposed troop increase.

The first of these candidates to challenge the president was an obscure Democratic senator from Minnesota, Eugene McCarthy. McCarthy had no money, no organization, and apparently no serious ambition to be president. He was an introspective, philosophical, even mystical personality, more comfortable writing poetry or discussing profound questions of human existence with close friends than roaming the Senate corridors or campaigning for votes. But McCarthy felt compelled to offer his presidential candidacy to opponents of the Vietnam War as a conduit through which their opposition to that war could flow into the developing presidential election. When the Minnesota senator entered the New Hampshire presidential primary, scheduled for March 12, the pundits wrote off his quixotic challenge. They expected the upstart maverick to be crushed by the master politician in the White House who, despite his credibility gap and the albatross of war, retained all of the powers of presidential incumbency and the skill to use them.[68]

McCarthy, running on a single issue, opposition to the Vietnam War, surprised everyone with a strong showing in New Hampshire. Aided by hundreds of young volunteers who went door-to-door on his behalf, McCarthy came within 500 votes of defeating President Johnson in a state where the electorate had hawkish inclinations. McCarthy's surprise showing came as a political revelation. Analysts read the New Hampshire results as evidencing far greater public dissatisfaction with the war and with Johnson's leadership than anyone had realized. McCarthy's strong showing exposed Johnson's political vulnerability at the outset of the presidential campaign. If a political lightweight like McCarthy could almost beat President Johnson in a hawkish state, what might a more formidable antiwar candidacy do nationwide? The

Democratic primary election results "buoyed the hopes of the president's critics in both parties."[67]

At the time, everyone interpreted McCarthy's strong showing in New Hampshire as a peace vote, a vote for disengaging from Vietnam. But post-election studies have solved the mystery of how an unknown dovish candidate could have done so well in a hawkish state against the president. Among McCarthy voters in the 1968 New Hampshire primary, a three-to-two majority favored escalating the American war effort. In November, more New Hampshire voters who had cast their votes for McCarthy in the Democratic primary voted for the hawkish third-party candidate George Wallace than for Hubert Humphrey or Richard Nixon.

The hawks of New Hampshire voted for the dovish McCarthy, either because he was the only protest candidate running and they did not care about his ideology, or because they misunderstood McCarthy's position and thought he was a hawk.[68] McCarthy's strong showing in New Hampshire lured a much more powerful dovish presidential candidate into the political arena four days later—New York Senator Robert F. Kennedy. Kennedy could mount a formidable challenge: he had plenty of money, an experienced and savvy campaign organization, name recognition, and a vast personal following among the American electorate. With Kennedy's entry into the 1968 Democratic presidential race, Johnson knew he now faced a long and divisive battle for his party's nomination. Even if he managed to beat back Kennedy's challenge and win renomination, Johnson would be taking a divided Democratic party into the general election against Richard Nixon, the probable Republican nominee, who could be expected to make the increasingly unpopular war and the growing disorders in American society the leading issues. Public opinion polls, taken at the moment Kennedy and McCarthy began their challenges to his leadership, showed Johnson at the lowest point of popularity since he had assumed the presidency.

After New Hampshire came the Wisconsin primary, set for March 19. All three candidates's names would be on the Wisconsin ballots. Johnson's political advisers informed him that recent polls taken in that midwestern state showed both McCarthy and Kennedy positioning themselves to beat him. The Wisconsin voters, more dovish than New Hampshire's electorate, viewed McCarthy and Kennedy as peace candidates and saw Johnson as a war candidate. If the president wanted to retrieve his candidacy, he was told he would have to make a dramatic gesture toward peace in Vietnam.

On top of the disturbing political news in New Hampshire and Wisconsin, Johnson also heard some disconcerting economic news. The inflation rate was rising because of increased war spending and Congress's continuing refusal to enact the President's proposed surtax to reduce the deficit. The consumer price index in 1967 rose more than it had in any year since the Korean War. Increased federal spending for the Vietnam War also exacerbated the nation's spiraling balance-of-payments deficit. A gold crisis loomed during late 1967, when the British were forced to devalue the pound sterling. Many currency speculators sold their dollars, causing a run on the gold markets. During the first half of March 1968, the central banks of various countries

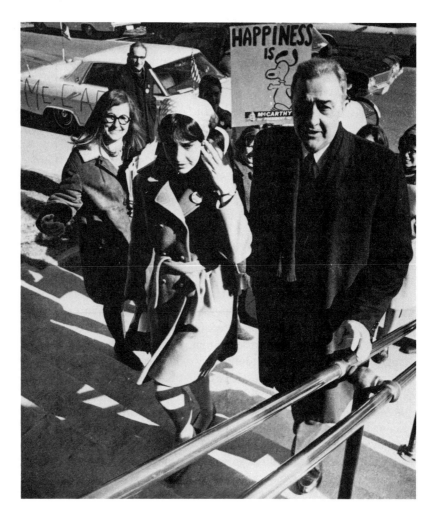

Figure 7.7   The antiwar candidate: Senator Eugene McCarthy of Minnesota entered the Democratic presidential race in early 1968. His surprisingly strong showing in the New Hampshire primary in March 1968 sent shock waves through the American body politic. *Source:* National Archives

had to supply almost $500 million in gold to help stabilize the dollar's value to which all other currencies were pegged. American banks alone had sold over $300 million worth of gold by March 14. The Administration had to grapple with the worrisome gold crisis at the same time it struggled with its failed Vietnam War policy.

A financial crisis was averted only by an emergency joint effort by the treasurers and central bankers of several countries, who created a system of monetary exchanges that temporarily curtailed gold selling on the free market.[69] The jittery international gold market sent a signal to Treasury Secretary Henry Fowler. Fowler told Johnson that if the United States were to send 206,000 additional troops to Vietnam, as requested, it would cost $2.5 billion in 1968 and $10 billion in 1969. These war expenditures would add another $500 million to the balance-of-payments deficit, require a major tax increase, and force deep cuts in funding for many Great Society and foreign aid programs. He warned the President that if the requested troops were sent to Vietnam and Congress did not take the painful political medicine of major tax increases and deep spending cuts in an election year, the United States would be risking the collapse of the dollar and a serious international financial crisis. International trade would be disrupted; the U. S. economy and those of its major trading partners could suffer serious damage.[70]

By mid-March, a combination of strategic, political, and economic considerations convinced Johnson that he could not approve the deployment of 206,000 additional troops to Vietnam. Domestic opposition to any large increase in U. S. forces in Vietnam was both widespread and deeply entrenched, even among many hawks. Meanwhile, Allied forces were holding their own. The NVA assault on Khe Sanh was ending, Hue had been reclaimed, and intelligence data indicated that there was little likelihood of further PLAF/NVA assaults against South Vietnamese cities.

President Johnson also continued to consult with his advisers, including Rostow and Rusk, who supported his war policy. On March 17 and March 18, Johnson made two speeches in which he defended his war policy and attacked his critics. He stated his determination to press on, to win the war, and he urged all Americans to support the U. S. soldiers fighting in Vietnam. The speeches failed to elicit any noticeable popular support. Johnson's political advisers told him that the two speeches had damaged his reelection prospects in Wisconsin and that he must make some conciliatory gestures toward peace if he hoped to salvage his presidency. Johnson and his speech writers also worked on a major speech to be delivered to the American people on March 31, in which he would both announce his decision on the troop request and inform the nation of his policy for the post-Tet phase of the Vietnam War.

Meanwhile, the "wise men," who included some of the principal architects of America's Cold War foreign policy, based on the principle of containing Soviet expansionism in Europe that had been forged in the years immediately following World War II, had decided that Johnson's Vietnam War policy was threatening to harm seriously the national interest. These distinguished and powerful men had given Johnson a vote of confidence at their November 2, 1967, meeting. But the Tet-68 Offensive and the sharp fall-off in popular support for the war, coupled with the gold crisis, had convinced them to press for disengagement from Vietnam before the war did irreparable harm to the nation's global security interests.

The most influential of the "wise men," Dean Acheson, Averell Harriman, and Paul Nitze, wanted a "review of Johnson's war policy within the larger context of America's global national security concerns."[71] They were convinced that Washington had committed too many assets to an area of only peripheral importance and was in danger of neglecting vital U. S. interests in Europe. The limited war in Vietnam had gotten out of control, and it was time to restore the limits. It was time to phase down our commitments and better yet, get out. It was time to refocus on our top priorities; it was time to restock U. S. NATO forces, save the dollar, and stabilize the European gold markets. The old Cold Warriors joined forces with Clark Clifford and together they worked behind the scenes to try to change administration war policy.

Johnson also was inclined to move in two new directions: to send only token American troop increases to Vietnam, which could be raised without necessitating a major Reserve call-up, and to take actions to build up the military forces of South Vietnam. On March 22, the President officially rejected General Westmoreland's request for 206,000 troops. For the first time, Johnson had to put a cap on the number of American forces he would commit to Vietnam; he closed the open-ended commitment he had made in July 1965. On March 24, Johnson approved sending Westmoreland a mere 13,500 additional troops. They would turn out to be "the last increment of American military manpower committed to the Vietnam War."[72] In South Vietnam, the generals were responding to U. S. pressures. Draft calls were raised, and Thieu announced that ARVN forces would be augmented by adding 135,000 men.

The President also announced that he was recalling General Westmoreland from the field. He was bringing him back to Washington to become the Army's new Chief of Staff. To replace him, Johnson appointed General Creighton W. Abrams, Westmoreland's deputy, as the new MACV Commander. Although Johnson's removal of Westmoreland from his command was widely construed as a dismissal, it was not. In fact, Westmoreland was promoted. He would henceforth be the most senior general in the U. S. Army. Although Westmoreland had come under criticism for his prophecies of victory and for failing to anticipate the Communist Tet-68 offensive, he still retained Johnson's trust. Having placed limits on the number of troops he was willing to commit to the war, and having decided to curb any further escalations, Johnson's removal of Westmoreland, the general who wanted a large increase in combat forces and who wanted to undertake an offensive campaign designed to win the war, was inevitable. Johnson's removal of Westmoreland from the war zone put an exclamation point on his decision to end the policy of gradual escalation.

Clark Clifford, convinced the United States could never win the Vietnam War because of the powerful political and economic forces that were imposing limits upon U. S. military activity, was determined to set the United States on a deescalatory course in Vietnam. Clifford also was alarmed by the growing domestic unrest and loss of support for the war among the nation's legal and financial elite with whom he customarily socialized. Clifford worked with Acheson and Harry McPherson, Johnson's head speech writer. Together they "waged an unrelenting battle for the president's mind."[73]

On March 25, the "wise men" gathered at the State Department. They had come to try to salvage America's global foreign policy that they had constructed in the years following World War II—an elaborate network of military bases around the world, regional alliances, and global commitments—that had been stretched to the breaking point by the American war in Vietnam. The Tet-68 offensive and gold crisis had exposed American vulnerabilities and defined limits to American power to order world affairs. The "wise men" spent the day in meetings with Rusk and Rostow from the State Department, with CIA Director Richard Helms, and with Generals Wheeler and Depuy. These officials briefed the "wise men" on the current diplomatic, military, and nation-building dimensions of the Vietnam War.

The next day, the "wise men" assembled for lunch in the White House to present their views to Johnson. The President had previously met with their most influential member, Dean Acheson. Acheson, who also had held extensive discussions on the war with Clifford and some of Johnson's other senior advisers, told the President that neither the time nor the assets were available to accomplish American military objectives in Vietnam. The force of 500,000-plus Americans currently in South Vietnam could neither expel the NVA nor subdue the Vietcong. Acheson also told the president that public opinion would never support an expanded war effort, nor would it support the present level of military activity indefinitely. Acheson further stated his judgments that the ineffective ground war had to be changed, that the bombing of North Vietnam had to be halted, and that the war must be ended as soon as possible without sacrificing the American commitment to South Vietnam.[74] Acheson's frank remarks, however unpalatable, no doubt made an impression on Johnson.

The President went around the table, holding conversations with many individual "wise men" at the March 26 luncheon. While a few still supported Johnson's war policy, most sounded variations on Acheson's themes: They were convinced action had to be taken to reduce U. S. commitments in Vietnam and find a way out of the quagmire. They agreed that a troop increase would be folly and that the South Vietnamese military must shoulder a greater burden of the fighting. They told the President that they believed that the war was stalemated, that the United States could not afford to commit any more assets to Vietnam without doing serious harm to its national economy and global interests. They also told him that neither Congress nor most of the American people would support any further escalations of the conflict.[75] Following their individual conversations with the President, McGeorge Bundy then summed up the collective wisdom of the "wise men" for Johnson:

> The majority feeling is that we can no longer do the job we set out to do in the time that we have left. . . . We must begin to take steps to disengage. When we last met we saw reasons for hope. We hoped then there would be slow steady progress. Last night and today the picture is not so hopeful.[76]

Many of the "wise men," including Bundy, had advised Johnson for years to pursue the war policy that they were now counseling him to abandon. Tet-68 and the gold crisis had turned the once-formidable U. S. foreign policy establishment into a flock of cooing doves. They now saw Johnson's war policy as hopeless and advised him to cut his losses and get out. The Republic of South Vietnam would have to learn to defend itself. The American foreign policy establishment was attending its last hurrah. It was not only abandoning the Vietnam War, it was abandoning its role in the formulation and implementation of U. S. foreign policy. Walt Rostow pronounced the American establishment dead. Lyndon Johnson put it more crudely: "The Establishment bastards have bailed out."[77]

For Johnson, who had become personally involved in this profound political crisis, the remarks of the "wise men" came as excruciating revelations. During the final week of March, Johnson tasted bitter medicine; he had to shoulder personally the responsibility for the greatest American foreign policy failure in the nation's history that also constituted the failure of the foreign policy the political elite, represented by Acheson and Clifford and the other "wise men," had forged to achieve U. S. objectives in Southeast Asia.

Johnson's dramatic meeting with the "wise men" on March 26, finally persuaded him to accept the realities he had resisted for weeks: The Tet Offensive had significantly increased and intensified opposition to the war in America among elite groupings, including emboldened clergy, prominent laymen, influential media editorial writers, and members of Congress. Further escalation of the war was politically impossible. The gold crisis of March 1968 convinced Johnson that further escalation of the war could bring economic disaster. It could both unhinge the dollar and undermine trade between the United States and its major European partners. Johnson would either have to scale down the war or court political and economic disaster.[78]

Following the March 26 meeting, Johnson worked on his speech, which was scheduled to be delivered to the nation on March 31. Clifford was involved in the speech-writing process, working with Harry McPherson. During the final days before it was to be given, Clifford played a key role in determining both the content and tone of the most important speech about the Vietnam War Johnson ever delivered.[79]

Johnson delivered his speech on Sunday evening, March 31, from the Oval Office. He appeared haggard; he spoke more slowly and more softly than usual. The weary president announced four major decisions that changed the course of the Vietnam War and had a decisive impact on American political life.

1. Johnson repeated the offer of negotiations that he had made the previous September at San Antonio. He would halt all bombing of North Vietnam, whenever that action would lead to productive negotiations. As a conciliatory gesture and as a first step to deescalate the Vietnam War, Johnson announced an unconditional partial bombing halt. All bombing north of the 20th parallel would be stopped immediately.

2. Johnson told the American people of his decision to send only 13,500 additional support troops to Westmoreland over the next five months. He was rejecting Westmoreland's request for a major troop increase. There would be no further escalation of the ground war in South Vietnam.

3. Johnson stated that the U. S. effort in Vietnam would henceforth focus on expanding and improving the military capabilities of South Vietnam's armed forces and that they would gradually assume a greater responsibility for defending themselves.

4. As Johnson approached the end of his forty-seven-minute speech, he acknowledged that there was disunity in the country. He warned Americans of the perils of disunity and then concluded his speech with a stunning pronouncement that he said he hoped would restore unity:

> With America's sons in the fields far away, with America's future under challenge right here at home, with our hopes and the world's hopes for peace in the balance every day, I do not believe that I should devote an hour or a day of my time to any personal partisan causes or to any duties other than the awesome duties of this office. . . . Accordingly, I shall not seek, and I will not accept, the nomination of my party for another term as your president.[80]

Even though Johnson had been seriously considering retiring from office long before the Tet-68 and gold crises occurred, he had not discussed that possibility with any of his associates, friends, or journalists. He had suffered a near-fatal heart attack in 1955, and he knew heart disease ran in his family on his father's side. The President, if he were to seek reelection and win, feared he would not live out his second term. He had no desire to join the bruising battle for renomination with Eugene McCarthy and Robert Kennedy, which would divide his party. He also had no desire to join the even more brutal battle with Richard Nixon, the likely Republican party nominee, which would exacerbate the deep divisions within the nation created by the controversial war. But the embattled President had kept these thoughts and misgivings to himself. Almost no one—foreign observers, political commentators, hawks, doves, Clifford, nor most of Johnson's other advisers—had anticipated his resignation. Everyone had assumed the inevitability of his candidacy for reelection. Johnson had caught the nation and the world by surprise.

Three days later, Hanoi declared its readiness to have its delegates make contact with American representatives so that they could both decide how and when to end all bombing and other acts of war against the DRV. Although surprised by Hanoi's prompt response, Washington responded positively to Hanoi's gesture. Talks between Washington and Hanoi opened in Paris on May 13. These negotiations began a diplomatic process that would, years later, bring the U. S. war in Vietnam to a close.[81] On April 4, the Pentagon formally denied Westmoreland's request for 206,000 more troops and placed a ceiling of 549,500 on U. S. troop deployments to South Vietnam. There would be no more requests for American troops from MACV commanders in South Vietnam.[82] The open-ended military commitment had been officially closed.

The Tet-68 Offensive, although it left the Communists with devastating tactical defeats and horrendous casualties, and cost them a good deal of their political infrastructure in South Vietnam, also brought them a tremendous psychological and political victory within the United States that eventually forced President Johnson to abandon his strategy of graduated escalation. He replaced it with an early version of what would later be called Vietnamization by his successor Richard Nixon. Tet-68 was the major turning point of the American Vietnam war. In its wake there occurred a fundamental shift in U. S. war policy that brought the first steps toward the deescalation of American involvement in Indochina. Johnson's dramatic change of direction had been brought about by domestic political developments, by economic and financial considerations, and by the efforts of Clark Clifford and the "wise men," who persuaded him to change course during their discussions held with the president in the latter half of March. Tet-68 had forced the U. S. foreign policy-making elite to confront the stark reality that their limited war strategy of graduated escalation could not achieve U. S. objectives in Southeast Asia. Tet-68 was for them a wake-up call, a reality check. Understanding that the Vietnam War could not be won at any reasonable price that the American public was willing to pay, and that if the administration were to escalate the conflict, serious and permanent damage could occur to the American economy and to the U. S. global foreign policy based on containing Communism, the "wise men," in the weeks following Tet-68, persuaded the president to abandon his failed war policy. "March 31, 1968, marked an inglorious end to the policy of gradual escalation."[83]

The combination of Johnson's March 31 speech and the opening of negotiations with the Communists in Paris two weeks later gave many Americans the sense that the war in Vietnam was coming to an end. No doubt they expected that there would be more battles and that negotiations would be strained at times. Peace would not occur immediately, nor would the American troops be coming home that spring. But a subtle shift in thinking occurred. Americans began to talk about the war in the past tense; they began to think of the Vietnam conflict as history. Public approval of Johnson's conduct of the war rose sharply in the wake of his speech. Johnson appeared to have joined the ranks of his dovish advisers and now sought peace in Vietnam rather than military victory. The fact that he had also announced his intention to retire at the end of his current time and not seek reelection reinforced the widespread public perception that the end of the American war in Vietnam was coming.

But Tet amounted to a serendipitous historical transition for Lyndon Johnson. He had not suddenly turned dovish. The president never intended nor could he foresee that his March 31 decisions would alter the course of the war or determine its outcome. He did not see himself as abandoning U. S. goals nor initiating any fundamental policy changes. He remained powerfully committed to stopping North Vietnamese aggression and to achieving an independent non-Communist state in southern Vietnam. He viewed the partial bombing halt, the leveling off of the American military role in South Vietnam, and the building up of the South Vietnamese armed forces as being steps toward the achievement of U. S. goals in South Vietnam, while at the same time placating public opinion at home.

At the time, Johnson did not believe the North Vietnamese would respond positively to the partial bombing halt any time soon so he would have the option of resuming the air war against North Vietnam in the future when perhaps the political climate at home would be more supportive of such actions. Johnson viewed his actions announced in the March 31 speech as political accommodations that were needed to buy time for his policies to work. He was shifting tactics to save a policy that had come under concentrated attack and had lost popular support. Johnson was repositioning himself politically to persevere in a righteous cause that he believed protected the vital security interests of the United States in Southeast Asia. For the remainder of his presidency, despite what he may have said or implied in his March 31 speech, Johnson prosecuted the war as vigorously as he could in a continuing effort to win a military victory. Clark Clifford, in tandem with the "wise men," had persuaded Johnson to alter his war policy on March 31, but they failed to shake his commitment to an American military victory in South Vietnam or to undermine his belief that his strategy of limited war would one day achieve it.

Johnson did not understand that his March 31 decisions set in motion a process that eventually "unraveled our Vietnam commitments."[84] Tet was a watershed. After Tet, an American military solution was no longer possible in South Vietnam, primarily because the American people no longer had the patience or willingness to continue furnishing the vast resources still required to attain it. Although Johnson did not realize it, after Tet, only a political solution to the Vietnam War was possible.[85] Johnson's partial bombing halt also inaugurated a diplomatic process that would one day bring an end to the American war in Vietnam, a denouement that would open the door to an eventual Communist victory. In the short run, Tet proved to be a major U. S. tactical victory and a severe Communist defeat. But in the long run, Tet-68 turned out to be a crucial Communist political victory and a fatal U. S. strategic defeat.

At the time Johnson made his fateful decisions to end the policy of graduated escalation of the Vietnam War, the United States retained over 1,000,000 troops stationed abroad in more than forty countries. Since 1945, America had enmeshed itself in a global network of treaties and military alliances. By March 1968, the military forces required to defend U. S. strategic interests around the globe had been stretched dangerously thin to send 536,000 troops to South Vietnam. The Joint Chiefs were especially worried about the military's ability to meet its NATO commitments, which remained the key American strategic interest in the world. The powerful U. S. economy that sustained both American global commitments and the war in Vietnam manifested symptoms of decline. The gold crisis threatened to undermine the value of the dollar and disrupt world commerce. The practical limits on the total military assets that the world's richest and mightiest nation-state could afford to commit to its limited war for limited goals in Southeast Asia had been reached by March 1968, the pivotal month of the entire war.

America, a nation whose per capita gross domestic product (GDP) was at least 100 times larger than Vietnam's, one of the poorest countries in the world, whose thermonuclear arsenal had the capability of obliterating Vietnam and its people, could not apply enough of its awesome military power to achieve the strategic goals it had set for itself. In addition to competing global strategic commitments, economic and financial strains, and rising domestic opposition, the refusal of America's SEATO allies to commit more troops to the Vietnam cockpit during the fall of 1967 further limited the U. S. Vietnam war effort.

The inefficient and class-biased conscription system strained to furnish the 40,000 to 50,000 young men required monthly for military service in 1968 because of exemptions and deferments factored into Selective Service and because of the wholesale draft avoidance and resistance occurring at the time. The number of soldiers provided by the draft was insufficient to meet the replacement needs of the U. S. Armed Forces stationed around the world in 1968, much less to continue a large-scale military buildup in South Vietnam had one been ordered in the aftermath of Tet.[86] The insufficiencies of the draft, combined with Johnson's refusal to mobilize the Reserves, deprived the American military services of the manpower needed to meet global strategic commitments and simultaneously fight a major war in Vietnam.

Nor could the United States use nuclear weapons to augment its conventional firepower, because American leaders feared both the domestic and worldwide reaction to their using atomic bombs on a nation of poor Asian peasants who posed no direct threat to U. S. security interests. American public opinion polls showed consistent and overwhelming popular opposition to resorting to nuclear weapons in Vietnam. In addition, U. S. military planners did not see any need to use nuclear weapons because of the adequacy of their conventional weaponry, because of the absence of suitable targets, and because they were reluctant to inflict mass casualties on civilian populations. Another inhibition on the possible use of nuclear weaponry was the desire not to alarm or anger the Soviets and Chinese, who might feel compelled to intervene militarily in Vietnam, or worse, to respond in kind. No doubt an extremely remote threat, but one that could not be absolutely discounted.

In March 1968, a confluence of powerful historical forces forced Washington to abandon its policy of graduated escalation in pursuit of military victory in Vietnam. Given the limits imposed on the size of the war effort America could mount in Vietnam in the spring of 1968 and after, and given the protracted warfare strategy employed by a resourceful and resolute enemy supported by China and the Soviet Union, it appears in retrospect that military victory in Vietnam was beyond available American strength. Given such circumstances, a U. S. military victory in Southeast Asia was probably never a realistic possibility, even if the American limited war strategy had been used with greater rapidity, efficiency, and effectiveness.

THE TELEVISED WAR

Television coverage of some of the fierce Tet battles highlighted the fact that Vietnam was America's first televised war, the first war to be shown night after night in American living rooms. For years, color video brought Americans the sights and sounds of men at war. The Vietnam War was also the first major war the United States ever lost. Many Americans believe that television was a major cause of the American defeat in Southeast Asia. That is, they believe America lost history's first televised war precisely because it was televised. They embrace a myth for which there is no empirical data to sustain it and which cannot withstand critical scrutiny.

There are two versions of the myth that television news coverage caused America to lose the war. The first version, a liberal or dove view espoused mainly by journalists and some left-wing intellectuals who opposed the Vietnam War, holds that television news coverage of the conflict exposed the American viewing public to the brutal realities of an unjust war. It brought Americans news of war crimes committed by U. S. soldiers; it exposed the tyrannical, corrupt, and incompetent governments in Saigon that the U. S. backed for twenty years; and it exposed efforts by American leaders to mislead the American public about the war. In this dovish view of television coverage of the war, journalists braved the wrath of their own government to help bring a halt to an unjust and a futile war. The other version of the myth, the conservative or hawkish view embraced by many Americans, including General Westmoreland and journalist Robert Elegant, insisted that America lost a war in Vietnam that it could have and should have won.[87] These hawks have blamed the defeat on the mass media, particularly the television news networks, for turning American public opinion against the war and eventually forcing an American withdrawal from Vietnam, which allowed the Communists to overwhelm the South Vietnamese defenders and take over the entire country in the spring of 1975.

Westmoreland has stated that the news media, especially television, snatched defeat from the jaws of victory in the aftermath of Tet-68, just when the allies had a battered enemy on the ropes and was ready for the kill. He has asserted that a golden opportunity to mobilize U. S. military resources for a maximum effort to win the Vietnam War in a year or two was lost because television news coverage of the Tet campaigns turned the public against the war in early 1968 and prevented Johnson from escalating the conflict.[88] Westmoreland's stab-in-the-back thesis holds that powerful and hostile media, particularly television news coverage, were primarily responsible for the American strategic defeat in Vietnam.[89]

The thesis that the media, particularly television, were responsible for losing the Vietnam War, or were a major cause of the American defeat in Vietnam, whether advanced by doves or hawks, is groundless and untenable for many reasons. Most historians of the Vietnam War and most analysts of mass media coverage of the war dismiss it as being without merit.[90] Television news coverage of the Vietnam War up to the time of Tet was overwhelmingly favorable; television journalists consistently represented American soldiers as fighting aggressively and winning every major battle en route to inevitable victory in the war.[91] During the first few years of television coverage of the war, the networks rarely showed American soldiers getting killed or wounded. Remarkably little American blood got spilled on television prime-time news. Typical video sequences of combat action showed U. S. troops moving across rice paddies or showed an air strike from a distance. Sometimes one heard the muted sounds of rifle fire or the rhythmic whup-whup-whup of helicopter rotors. Often the televised reports direct from the field were after-action accounts; stories filed after firefights had occurred. Americans got to see a rather sanitized, carefully edited version of war.[92]

The only public opinion poll that ever asked people how watching television news coverage of the Vietnam War influenced their attitudes toward the war found that 83 percent of the respondents said they felt more hawkish after watching the news.[93] At the time this poll was taken—July 1967—other polls showed that 50 percent of Americans believed that U. S. entry into the war had been a mistake.[94] These polls showed that opposition to the Vietnam War and to Johnson's war policy was growing *despite, not because of*, television news coverage, which was highly favorable at the time.

Television news coverage of the war became more critical during the Tet battles, and, for the first time, television provided viewers with a steady diet of live-action coverage of the carnage. Viewers witnessed the destructiveness and brutality of war, of American soldiers fighting and dying in the streets of Saigon and Hue. But evidence from public opinion polls taken soon after the Tet attacks have undermined Westmoreland's thesis. At a time when the media exaggerated the tactical gains made by the enemy, portrayed Tet as a great shock and disaster for America, and showed American soldiers being killed in combat, public opinion polls registered temporary rises in popular support.[95]

Proponents of the stab-in-the-back thesis often cite Peter Braestrup's writings to substantiate their charges. Braestrup, a former Marine officer, Vietnam journalist, and media scholar, produced a massive study of the media coverage of Tet. He found that during the first few days of the Tet Offensive, the public was misled into thinking that the Vietcong were winning, when in fact they were losing, and losing badly, almost everywhere. He has criticized journalists for their inaccurate and misleading stories. To Westmoreland, Braestrup's critique proved that distorted media coverage misled Americans and turned a tactical victory into a major defeat that eventually cost America a war.[96]

But a careful reading of Braestrup's study has shown that he furnishes the proponents of the stab-in-the-back thesis neither aid nor comfort. Braestrup himself did not embrace the thesis and has challenged those who did.[97] He took pains to make clear that he did not charge either print or television journalists with biased coverage during Tet. He has never said that Tet-68 coverage by either the print or television journalists, however deficient in the early stages, turned public opinion against the Vietnam War. In fact, he believed such claims were impossible to substantiate: "No empirical data exist to link news coverage with changes in public opinion."[98]

Braestrup contended that skewed media coverage of the Tet campaigns exacerbated a growing political crisis in Washington that would have occurred even if those journalistic accounts had been clinically accurate. He believed it was Johnson's indecisive leadership in the weeks following Tet that caused the fall-off of popular support for the war that occurred in March. For Braestrup, changes occurring in public opinion of the Vietnam War in the weeks following Tet were caused by failures of political leadership, not by television news or other media coverage of the battles.[99] Ironically, the administration's propaganda efforts in the fall of 1967, which were aimed at convincing Americans that the United States was winning the war, the Vietcong verged on defeat, and the conflict would end soon, magnified the public shock and disillusionment that occurred during the Tet campaigns and widened the credibility gap.

When trends in public opinion on the Vietnam War have been matched with trends in television news coverage of the conflict, it has been shown that a majority of the American people turned against the Vietnam War *before* television news coverage of the conflict became predominantly negative. Despite their shift to a more negative emphasis in their television coverage of the war during and after Tet, on the whole, the network television news coverage continued to be more positive than negative until the fall of 1969. A majority of Americans had developed dovish views on the Vietnam War long before then.[100] Television coverage of the war lagged behind public opinion.

The increasingly critical television coverage of the war that occurred at the time of Tet and after represented a response by media journalists to public opinion, not an effort to shape it. What turned television coverage against the war after Tet-68 was growing antiwar sentiment among U. S. soldiers serving in Vietnam, increasing numbers of public officials speaking out against the war, and growing disillusionment with the war among the American people. The stab-in-the-back theorists, in their haste to make the media into a scapegoat, have inverted the relationship between television news coverage of the Vietnam War and public opinion concerning the war and presidential leadership. Westmoreland, Elegant, and many others failed to understand that it was public opinion that influenced television news coverage of the war much more than it was television coverage that influenced public opinion on the war.

As public support for the war dropped, television news coverage became more critical. But the news networks were merely catching up to what their viewers were already thinking about the war and the U. S. leadership; they were not telling them what to think. When Walter Cronkite, the most popular and influential television anchor during the Vietnam War era, declared at the end of his newscast on the evening of February 27, 1968, that the war was a stalemate, the erstwhile supporter of the war was aligning his views with those of his Middle American constituents. Numerous public opinion polls show that Cronkite told Americans nothing that a large majority of them did not already believe.

The stab-in-the-back theorists also faced another difficulty. Westmoreland's insistence that victory was within the U. S. grasp following Tet, if Johnson had only sent the requested troops and taken the other escalatory steps called for at the time, was dubious. At the time, Clark Clifford, most Pentagon analysts, and the "wise men" had concluded that Hanoi had both the political will and military assets to match any and all U. S. post-Tet escalations. Hanoi could also count on the Chinese, who might have intervened militarily if the North Vietnamese ever faced military defeat or national extinction. Had Johnson escalated the war after Tet, had he sent the 206,000 troops requested by the Pentagon, and had he ratcheted up the air war, he most likely would not have achieved strategic victory within a year or two. Most likely, Washington would only have attained a continuing military stalemate at a far higher level of costs and casualties. Such a continuing costly stalemate in Vietnam would have brought intensified opposition, political polarization, and violent conflict within the United States that could have seriously undermined American political stability. It might also have raised taxes, jacked up the inflation rate, weakened the dollar, worsened the gold crisis, and serious damaged U. S. global foreign policy interests.

The basic problem with the stab-in-the-back thesis is that it represents a lamentable failure of historical understanding. Powerful economic, political, and strategic forces determined the outcome of the Vietnam War and caused the eventual American strategic defeat. The role of the media, including television news coverage, in determining that outcome was so inconsequential it cannot be measured. Television news coverage of the war did not turn the American people against it. It was the course taken by the Vietnam War—the United States had locked itself into a stalemated conflict of rising casualties and costs—coupled with a loss of confidence in the integrity and competence of the government, all of which was highlighted and intensified by the surprise Tet-68 Offensive—that turned most Americans against the Vietnam War.

Public opinion turned the media, particularly television news, against the war. Had the cathode ray tube never been invented, had censorship been imposed on Vietnam War news, and had all of the journalists covering the war in Southeast Asia been cheerleaders for the Allied side, public opinion would have turned against the Vietnam War just as it did against the Korean War. The Korean War was popular when the U. N. forces appeared to be rolling toward an easy victory over the North Koreans in the fall of 1950. Following the surprise Chinese intervention in late November 1950 and the subsequent stalemated warfare that went on for years, public opinion polls consistently showed that a majority of Americans did not support the Korean War. Yet television news was in its infancy, most U. S. households did not have television sets, war news from Korea was heavily censored, and U. S. war correspondents were all supportive of the U. N.'s effort.[101]

Those who praise or blame the television networks for the American defeat in Vietnam promulgate a myth that may serve hidden political and ideological agenda, but they do not explain why the United States lost the war.

TALKING AND FIGHTING

The talks between American and North Vietnamese representatives that began in Paris on May 13, 1968, deadlocked instantly. President Johnson, doubting the talks could be productive, and wary of Communist propaganda, demanded concessions from Hanoi in

Figure 7.8 Members of the 101st Airborne Division carry a wounded man to a Uh-ID Medevac helicopter during the assault on Hill 937 in the A Shau Valley. U. S. troops fighting in Vietnam received the finest medical support services ever available in war. *Source: U. S. Army photo*

exchange for a complete bombing halt. The American delegation, led by Averell Harriman, refused to accept any cease-fire terms that would require the withdrawal of American forces from South Vietnam while allowing the Ho Chi Minh trail to remain open and allowing PAVN forces to remain in South Vietnam. The Americans also refused to consider any political settlement of the conflict that did not guarantee the continued survival of a non-Communist government in South Vietnam. The North Vietnamese delegation, headed by Xuan Thuy, quickly rejected the American demand for a reciprocal deescalation to completely stop the bombing. Hanoi also rejected any cease-fire proposals that would limit its ability to support the war in South Vietnam and refused to consider any political solution that allowed the Thieu-Ky regime to survive.

Given the fact that the military initiative in South Vietnam had passed to the Allies in the months following the Tet Offensive, the North Vietnamese probably were not interested in conducting substantive negotiations at that time. They preferred to wait until the political and military balance shifted toward their side. Hanoi's approach to the Paris talks was to use them as part of a larger strategy of talking while fighting. It intended to use the negotiations underway in Paris to achieve a complete bombing halt, to highlight differences between the Americans and South Vietnamese in an effort to drive the allies apart, and to exploit the antiwar sentiment within the United States that was growing rapidly in the wake of Tet.[102] Hanoi coordinated its diplomacy with its war effort. For the Communists, negotiations were not a means for ending the war, they were part of an integrated military-political-diplomatic strategy designed to achieve their major objectives: the withdrawal of the Americans, the overthrow of Thieu, and the creation of a coalition government in South Vietnam; that is, to win the Vietnam War. They had agreed to the Paris talks to try to achieve objectives via negotiations that they could not achieve by fighting, particularly obtaining a complete bombing halt.

Since both sides refused to make the necessary compromises required to move the negotiations forward, the Paris talks proved sterile for months. Meanwhile, the United States pressed its war in South Vietnam: 1968 was the bloodiest year of the American Vietnam war. More U. S. combatants fought in more battles that year than in any other. During 1968, more than 14,000 American soldiers were killed and 150,000 were wounded, the highest totals for any year of the war. The number of battle deaths would have been far higher if it had not been for the remarkable medical support American Vietnam combat soldiers received for the entirety of the long war. "American servicemen and women fighting in Vietnam received the best medical care in the history of warfare."[103] The key to success in saving the lives of often badly wounded soldiers, many of whom would have died in previous wars, lay in the excellent support system the Army established and the hard work of the doctors, nurses, and other medical personnel. Helicopter crews, often flying into the teeth of an engagement and at great risk, would retrieve the wounded warriors, quickly transporting them to evacuation hospitals. There they would be treated for shock and infection and would be stabilized and resuscitated. Their wounds would be stitched up, burns would be treated, and amputations would be performed if required. After a stay of from three to five days, patients would be transferred to rear hospitals, usually in Japan.[104] In a war in which many aspects of the U. S. military's performance has been severely criticized, there has been only praise for the admirable record of performance compiled by doctors and nurses.

Thousands of American women served in the Vietnam War, some 80 percent of them as Army, Air Force, and Navy nurses. All nurses were officers, and they had to be at least twenty-one years old to be assigned to a combat zone. Their tour of duty was usually one year, and like all military personnel during the Vietnam War, they were rotated in and out of Vietnam on an individual rather than a unit-by-unit basis. Although they were never legally assigned to combat roles, women serving as nurses in forward hospitals often came under enemy fire. Eight American women were killed in Vietnam and dozens were wounded.[105]

Shortly after Tet, Westmoreland mounted the largest search-and-destroy operation of the war: forty-two American and thirty-seven ARVN armored and infantry battalions scoured the countryside around Saigon trying to locate and eliminate the VC/NVA units that had survived Tet. Eventually, the 110,000 allied troops involved in the gigantic operation formed a ring of steel around Saigon.[106]

Figure 7.9   The U. S. Army 45th MUST (Mobile Unit, Self-Contained, Transportable) Surgical Hospital Staff serving in Tay Ninh Province, 1968. Thousands of women served in the American Vietnam War, many as army nurses. *Source:* USMI Photo Archives

During the latter half of 1968, the American Vietnam war was characterized by hundreds of battalion-sized operations and thousands of actions involving companies and platoons. In countless small unit operations, American forces attempted to find, fix, and destroy enemy forces all over South Vietnam. While these land battles raged, specially trained Army and Navy units waged riverine warfare against Vietcong guerrillas amid the watery wastes of the Mekong Delta.[107]

Although the air war against North Vietnam had been curtailed, aerial warfare in South Vietnam reached a new intensity during 1968. The number of air strikes flown against guerrilla sanctuaries and supply lines increased as Air Force and Navy bombers that had been committed previously to raiding North Vietnam's military and industrial sites joined the air war in South Vietnam. After Tet, carpet bombing raids on enemy positions by cells of giant B-52s trebled. American planes also stepped up their bombing of the Ho Chi Minh trail running through the Laotian corridor. As the air war against North Vietnam diminished, the air wars in South Vietnam and Laos intensified.[108]

U. S. military action also included assaults into the border regions adjacent to many of the South Vietnamese cities that the Vietcong and PAVN forces had attacked during Tet. One of the most spectacular operations occurred in the I Corps Tactical Zone following the vicious fighting to reclaim Hue. U. S. forces struck NVA staging areas in the A Shau Valley, which lay in the southwestern corner of the Thua Thien Province adjacent to the Laotian border. Remote and rugged, the A Shau Valley had been a Communist stronghold for years. It was from that region that NVA forces had attacked the northern provinces as well as the city of Hue. MACV officials feared that the enemy might use the A Shau to launch additional attacks, so they mounted an operation to destroy the PAVN bases in the valley, code-named Operation DELAWARE. Two battalions of the U. S. 7th Cavalry, the 1st and the 5th, helilifting in to attack the NVA, ran into the fiercest air defenses encountered in South Vietnam. Ten assault helicopters were shot down and another thirteen were severely damaged by deadly fire coming from antiaircraft batteries lodged in the hills and mountains that ringed the valley.[109] In addition to the air defenders of the A Shau, helicopter and fixed-wing aircraft pilots had to contend with some of the most hazardous flying weather of the entire war. Dense fogs, thick clouds, and driving rainstorms generated by the summer monsoons often reduced visibility in the target areas to near zero.

Sweeps by the 7th Cavalry troops failed to find many NVA forces. The NVA had chosen not to fight and had slipped into cross-border sanctuaries in nearby Laos. But the Americans captured sizeable amounts of food and stores the departing enemy had left behind. After the 7th Cavalry was pulled out, elements from Major General Melvin Zais's elite 101st Airborne, the famed "Screaming Eagles," air-assaulted into the A Shau Valley in an effort to catch the NVA returning to their bases. The 101st also failed to find many PAVN soldiers who wanted to stand and fight.[110] By the end of August 1968, the Americans had withdrawn from the A Shau Valley, and the North Vietnamese had returned.

In addition to action in the A Shau Valley, U. S. troops also fought along the northern border in the vicinity of the DMZ. The Marines' main objective in this region, following their successful defense at Khe Sanh, remained sealing the border against enemy infiltration. Marine units patrolled Route 9, attacking and counterattacking any North Vietnamese forces trying to infiltrate the northern provinces. One of the fiercest of many battles occurring in this area took place near Con Thien, on October 25. In a seven-hour fight, an armored company completely destroyed a North Vietnamese bunker complex.[111] The NVA suffered many losses during the latter half of 1968 in the vicinity of the DMZ, but they nevertheless managed to achieve a stalemate. The NVA units continued to infiltrate the region and continued to battle the Marines and other American forces.

Extensive fighting also occurred in the southern part of I Corps, in the Quang Ngai Province. One of the most gruesome tragedies of the Vietnam War occurred in this region when American soldiers, using pistols, automatic rifles, and machine guns, massacred an estimated 300 to 400 civilians at two hamlets, My Lai and My Khe, on the morning of March 16, 1968. Both hamlets comprised part of Son My village, near the coast in the Son Tinh district of the Quang Ngai Province. The soldiers who massacred the women, children, and old men of My Lai belonged to the 1st and 2nd Platoons of Charlie Company, 1st Battalion, the 11th Infantry Brigade, which was attached to the Americal Division under the command of Major General Samuel Koster.[112]

> The Americal Division suffered from grave command and control problems, stemming from poor training and a lack of leadership, from division down to platoon level, which permitted civilian mistreatment. Some elements of its 11th Infantry Brigade were little better than organized bands of thugs, with the officers eager participants in the body count game.[113]

After the perpetration of the atrocities, members of the brigade and divisional staffs succeeded in covering it up for a time. The American people were not to learn of the hideous incident for over twenty months, until late November 1969, and then from independent media sources who exposed the Army's attempted cover-up.[114] An official Army board then conducted a thorough sixteen-month-long investigation of the incident and its cover-up. Fourteen officers were found to be complicit in covering up war crimes. Additionally, thirteen soldiers—four officers and nine enlisted men— were charged with committing war crimes and crimes against humanity. Subsequently, all of the soldiers accused of war crimes either had the charges against them dropped, or they were acquitted, except Lieutenant William Calley. Calley's 1st Platoon was estimated to have killed over 200 of the villagers that lethal morning in My Lai. A court martial convicted Calley of mass murder.[115]

The mass murders at My Lai and My Khe were a grotesque consequence of many factors: a formless war of attrition in which military success was measured statistically by counting corpses; small-unit actions fought in populated regions against an enemy that relied on village support to sustain its insurgency; the frustrations of fighting a war that appeared both unpopular and unwinnable; race prejudice, which encouraged many U. S. soldiers to regard Vietnamese peasants as "mere gooks," as less than fully human; the fear, rage, and hatred arising from fighting an enemy that set mines and home-made booby traps that maimed and killed GIs and then melted into the jungle or merged into the rural population; paranoia arising from the inability of U. S. soldiers to tell friendly villagers from enemies and therefore to assume that they all were real or potential foes; and the poor leadership, inadequate training, lack of discipline, and thuggery that characterized the 11th Infantry Brigade.

After learning of the massacre, some Americans worried about how many other My Lais might have gone undetected. They feared that perhaps the only unique feature of the My Lai massacre was its discovery. Some also wondered if the American military might have had a policy of targeting civilians suspected of aiding the enemy. In various forums, hundreds of Vietnam veterans claimed they had participated in, witnessed, or heard of mass atrocities committed against civilians in South Vietnam. Some people found cold comfort in the fact that the Vietcong and NVA forces were guilty of systematic atrocities and the cold-blooded murders of thousands of civilians. There also was a troubling inconsistency in finding one young junior officer guilty of mass murder in a war where long-range artillery fire and aerial bombing had killed thousands of civilians since the Americanization of the war. In the eyes of many Americans, William Calley was more a scapegoat than a war criminal.

"The extent of American atrocities in Vietnam cannot be established with any precision."[116] According to available evidence and testimony, American soldiers frequently committed atrocities against Vietnamese civilians, and they became more frequent in the years after Tet as discipline and morale plummeted. However, the MACV never had an official policy of targeting civilians nor even of informally sanctioning attacks under certain circumstances. Killing, attacking, or using unnecessary force against civilians in situations where they posed no danger to U. S. military personnel was illegal, and always in violation of extant rules of engagement. Even the thugs of the Americal Division knew that what had occurred at My Lai and My Khe was both illegal and wrong, which is why they covered it up with falsified reports and sham inquiries. Most U. S. combat soldiers serving in Vietnam did not commit atrocities against civilians, nor is there hard evidence that there were any other My Lai-type massacres where American troopers deliberately murdered hundreds of old men, women, and children.[117]

Six weeks after the massacres at My Lai and My Khe, the Vietcong launched another wave of attacks against Saigon and other South Vietnamese cities. The fighting in and near Saigon was vicious and lasted for weeks. It was not until early June that the ARVN and U. S. forces crushed all remaining enemy resistance. Like its vastly larger predecessor, the Vietcong mini-Tet Offensive also failed tactically. There was a third, even weaker, round of Vietcong urban assaults in August, that Allied intelligence anticipated and an American preemptive strike easily crushed.[118]

Figure 7.10   Bodies of women and children lying in a ditch near the village of My-Lai-4. *Source:* U. S. Army photo

These subsequent enemy offensives showed that the Vietcong were feeling the effects of their terrible losses sustained in February. They fought in smaller units, avoided direct attacks on American installations, and were forced to use younger and less-experienced fighters. More and more NVA troopers had to be fed into the deplet-ed Vietcong main force units. In the aftermath of their defeats at Tet, the North Vietnamese Politburo had to refashion its military strategy. It abandoned offensive operations and reverted to defensive tactics. The Communists resumed a version of protracted warfare. During the latter half of 1968, enemy actions were largely con-fined to sporadic standoff rocket and mortar attacks on Allied positions.[119]

In the fall of 1968, General Abrams abandoned the strategy of attrition warfare that had been in place since 1966 in South Vietnam. He shifted the American focus from small-scale combat operations to pacification and Vietnamization. With negotia-tions underway in Paris, American and South Vietnamese officials launched an accel-erated pacification program to bring as many of South Vietnam's villages as possible under the control of the Saigon government. American combat forces formed securi-ty shields to prevent Vietcong forces from entering populated areas. Allied officials focused their efforts in the areas where the Vietcong had suffered their worst losses and could not thwart the accelerated Allied pacification efforts. The CORDS and South Vietnamese officials also stepped up the Chieu Hoi program that offered amnesty to Vietcong defectors and, with assistance from CIA officers, they implemented the PHOENIX program, an intelligence-gathering operation aimed at exposing and neutralizing the Vietcong infrastructure.[120] Pacification made little progress for the rest of 1968. Saigon controlled only a few more villages at year's end than it had before the Tet Offensive erupted, and there was no way to tell for sure whether all of the people living in "friendly" villages genuinely supported the GVN and the U. S. military effort.

Simultaneously with its enhanced pacification efforts, the United States pressed forward with Vietnamization. Efforts were made to expand and modernize the South Vietnamese armed forces. Authorized force levels were increased from 685,000 to 850,000, and South Vietnamese soldiers were provided with more modern weapons. There was a noticeable improvement in the performance of the ARVN forces by the end of the year, but fundamental deficiencies persisted. Draft evasion and desertion remained both chronic and massive. There was also no discernible enthusiasm for Vietnamization on the part of South Vietnamese leaders. Having become quite comfortable with American soldiers doing most of the fighting and dying for them, Thieu and Ky appeared to be in no hurry to alter the situation.[121] Part of the problem with implementing Vietnamization derived from the fact that South Vietnam's leaders had not been consulted before Johnson decided that Vietnamization would be the new focus of the post-Tet American effort.[122] Neither the GVN political desires nor the RVNAF military capabilities had anything to do with the U. S. decision to begin the process of Vietnamization. Johnson had been forced to turn to Vietnamization because of American domestic political exigencies.[123]

The surprisingly effective performance of some of the ARVN units during the Tet battles had given U. S. leaders in Washington and Saigon some grounds for hoping that Vietnamization might work, that the South Vietnamese government would, in time, develop the capacity to defend itself. But there was never any realistic basis for believing that the RVN could ever carry out Vietnamization successfully. The main reason American soldiers were fighting in Vietnam was because Washington did not believe the South Vietnamese could defend themselves against the insurgency directed from Hanoi. Nothing had really changed since Tet. Most of the ARVN troops who had fought hard during the Tet battles did so because they were fighting for survival, not because they had suddenly become patriots or brave, aggressive warriors. They displayed the "back-to-the-wall courage of the cornered."[124]

The fundamental reality that foreclosed any possibility of a successful Vietnamization program lay in the fact that General Thieu's and Marshall Ky's power depended on maintaining the loyalty of a coterie of ARVN generals who held their commands because of their political reliability, not because they were competent, honest, or patriotic warriors. The price that the leaders of the RVN would have had to pay for eliminating incompetence and corruption within their civilian and military bureaucracies would have been a fall from power. Insistence on reform would have amounted to committing political suicide. Because the South Vietnamese government and army remained rotten at their cores, and because American leaders neither had the leverage nor will to impose radical reforms on South Vietnam's leadership, no amount of American economic and military support could ever make Vietnamization work well enough to defeat their powerful, resourceful, and implacable enemies.[125]

Despite the stepped-up Allied military activity, the accelerated pacification program, and the beginnings of Vietnamization, the military and political balance in South Vietnam had changed little as 1968 ended. The Vietcong forces had suffered severe losses, were much weaker, and controlled fewer villages and a smaller portion of the South Vietnamese population than they had before the Tet Offensive. But much of the Vietcong infrastructure remained intact. American military operations after Tet inflicted heavy losses on the enemy, destroyed staging areas, and disrupted supply lines; but the NVA/VC main force units remained intact, a formidable foe at year's end.

As historian Ronald Specter has noted of the Tet-68 campaigns and the fighting that continued throughout the year, "The battles of 1968 were decisive . . . because they were so indecisive."[126] Stalemate on the battlefield favored the North Vietnamese. Popular support for the war within the United States continued to decline: Congressional opposition grew stronger. Morale and discipline within the U. S. Army continued to erode. The Communists rebuilt their military and their political infrastructure. The U. S. position in Vietnam deteriorated.

The Saigon government's performance improved somewhat during 1968. It was stronger and more stable after Tet than it had ever been. Many of the South Vietnamese people, angry at the Communists for violating the Tet truce and for attacking their cities, turned to the Thieu government. Many city residents, hitherto smug in their sense of safety from the ravages of war and apathetic toward the government, now felt vulnerable and understood that their security depended on the ARVN forces. Thieu's government actively involved citizens in repairing the extensive damage incurred by South Vietnam's cities during Tet. His government also launched new programs to combat corruption and curb rampant inflation.

By mid-summer 1968, Thieu, with U. S. support, had gained the upper hand over his arch-rival, General Ky. Thieu's anti-corruption program was one-sided; it aimed chiefly at the corruption of Ky and Ky's supporters and ignored the corrupt practices of Thieu loyalists. Thieu gradually replaced cabinet members and province chiefs loyal to Ky with military men loyal to him. The political savants, who frequented the sidewalk cafes of Tu Do Street, began calling Thieu "the little dictator."[127]

But chronic political weaknesses persisted in South Vietnam. Tet generated nearly a million new refugees to add to the millions already inhabiting the slums, back-alley labyrinths, and suburban hovels of Saigon and other cities. The massive needs of the war refugees went largely unattended. Land reform in South Vietnam stalled because Thieu favored large landowners. Corruption at all levels of the Saigon government and military persisted. The Buddhists, the sects, and other non-Communist political groupings refused to support the RVN. The Saigon regime, despite a few cosmetic gestures toward civilian rule, remained, in essence, a narrowly based military dictatorship. Another of the Tu Do Street savants commented on the status of the RVN after Tet: "The dung heap is the same. Only the flies are different."[128] There were other problems stemming from the fact that Vietnamization and the U. S. negotiations with Hanoi exacerbated tensions between American and Saigon officials. The South Vietnamese feared and resented what appeared to them as U. S. efforts to impose a settlement on them and then get out, leaving the RVN at the mercy of the Vietcong and the NVA forces.[129]

THE POLITICS OF WAR

The tensions in South Vietnam paralleled the political turmoil in the United States during that turbulent year. The 1968 presidential election evolved amidst a backdrop of the worst violence, social conflict, and political polarization seen in America since the Civil War. The Vietnam War had combined with domestic insurgencies to create profound schisms between white and black, affluent and poor, young and old, "hippies" and "straights," hawks and doves, and practitioners of the so-called new politics and the political establishment. Political and cultural warfare raged in the streets of many of America's cities. Robert Kennedy, seeking the Democratic nomination as an antiwar candidate, and Richard Nixon, seeking the Republican nomination, both feared the institutional framework of the world's oldest democracy might not be able to contain the powerful centrifugal forces threatening to spin out of control.[130]

Racial tensions increased sharply during the first few months of 1968. More race-related disturbances occurred then than for any previous year, and authorities braced themselves for another summer of urban rioting. The Southern Christian Leadership Council (SCLC), headed by Dr. Martin Luther King Jr., began as a Poor People's campaign to protest poverty, discrimination, and the Vietnam War that was draining funds from civil rights and anti-poverty programs. On the evening of April 4, King, the apostle of nonviolent social change and gentle critic of the Vietnam War, was assassinated as he stood on a balcony outside of a Memphis motel room. That night the ghettos of America exploded in fury as news of King's murder reached them, and 75,000 federal troops and National Guardsmen joined thousands of local police and sheriffs to suppress the uprisings in 130 cities. Forty-six people, mostly African Americans, shot by police and the National Guard, were killed, and thousands of people were injured. In Chicago, Mayor Richard Daley ordered police to "shoot to kill" arsonists and looters. In the nation's capital, the site of some of the worst rioting, looting, and burning, barbed-wire barriers and machine gun emplacements surrounded government buildings to protect them from any attacks.[131] Machine-gun mounts on the steps of the nation's capitol building eloquently expressed the torment of a profoundly divided people.

Until Tet-68, the large majority of the nation's nearly 7,000,000 college students had been apolitical, and unquestioningly patriotic and prowar. In its aftermath, many were in a rebellious mood. Dozens of demonstrations convulsed college campuses during the spring of 1968, most of them related to the Vietnam War. Students protested the presence of ROTC programs. Recruiters from the military services, the CIA, and corporations with Pentagon contracts were harassed and picketed. The most violent uprising occurred in April at Columbia, one of the most distinguished universities in the country. On this prestigious Ivy League campus, black militants joined with antiwar radicals to protest both the university's complicity with the Vietnam War and its plans to construct a new gymnasium in an area that would require the relocation of African Americans living in apartments on the building site. During the demonstration, students occupied campus buildings and refused orders to vacate them. University officials called in the New York City police, who forcibly removed the students. In the process, hundreds of students were arrested, and about 150 were injured. Following the police action, student protesters called a strike that forced the university to curtail its spring 1968 semester. Student uprisings also occurred in other countries during 1968. A worker-student revolt in France nearly brought down the government.[132]

From April to early June, Eugene McCarthy and Robert Kennedy waged a spirited primary campaign for the Democratic presidential nomination in the aftermath of Johnson's withdrawal speech. A third candidate for the Democratic nomination, Vice President Hubert Humphrey, knowing he had no chance against McCarthy and Kennedy in many of the primaries because of his support of Johnson's Vietnam War policy, quietly lined up delegates from the states that did not hold primaries. Johnson, who hated Kennedy and did not believe McCarthy had the qualifications to be president, promoted Humphrey's candidacy.

Kennedy, passionate and charismatic, beat McCarthy in most of the primaries because of his remarkable ability to appeal to voters across class and cultural boundaries: black voters, Hispanics, and the disadvantaged generally, as well as to ethnic working-class voters and activist liberal intellectuals. McCarthy, cerebral and cool, who appealed mainly to well-educated middle class liberals who constituted the traditional reform elements in American politics, beat Kennedy once, in the Oregon primary on May 25.

Next up was the important California primary. After a hard fight, Kennedy won a narrow victory. But shortly after delivering a victory speech to his supporters in the ballroom of the Biltmore Hotel in Los Angeles in the early morning hours of June 5, he was assassinated by Sirhan Sirhan, a Arab nationalist who said he was angry at Kennedy's strong support of Israel.[133] Another senseless killing once again intensified widely shared fears that anarchy and civil conflict would overwhelm the American political process. Kennedy's murder appeared to show that the last lines of reason and restraint within American politics had been breached. With his murder, the antiwar forces within the Democratic party lost any chance to capture their party's presidential nomination.

Political violence in America during the tormented year of 1968 climaxed in Chicago at the time of the Democratic Convention. Radical elements within the antiwar movement, the National Mobilization to End the War in Vietnam (MOBE) and the Youth International Party (Yippies) planned a series of demonstrations in Chicago to protest the Vietnam War. The demonstrations were timed to coincide with the Democratic Convention, to be held during the last week of August. Chicago's Mayor Daley, the host of the Democratic Convention, vowed that antiwar demonstrators would not disrupt his city or its convention. The stage was set for the most violent confrontation between antiwar protesters and police of the entire Vietnam War era. Ironically, Daley himself was a strong opponent of the Vietnam War and had been a backer of the late Robert Kennedy, but he was committed to suppressing the antiwar activists.

In the days preceding the convention, thousands of youthful antiwar activists filtered into Chicago, gathering mainly in Lincoln Park, far from the convention site, which was the International Amphitheater, near the stockyards. To meet the anticipated threat to law and order, Mayor Daley mobilized his entire 12,000-man police force. In addition, the governor of Illinois assigned 5,649 members of the National Guard to round-the-clock duty in Chicago, and President Johnson ordered 5,000 federal troops to be flown to Chicago if they were needed. The assembled police, National Guard, and federal troops outnumbered the protesters, whose numbers never exceeded 10,000 to 12,000.[134]

Tension built during the days of the Democratic Convention, which convened at the Amphitheater on Saturday, August 24. There were skirmishes in the parks between protesters and police. For several days, the police and National Guard succeeded in keeping the demonstrations miles from the convention site and nearby hotels, where

Figure 7.11   A martyr for freedom: Senator Robert Kennedy during his final campaign against the Vietnam War abroad and for social justice at home. His murder in Los Angeles the night of June 5, 1968, destroyed any chance of the antiwar forces winning control of the Democratic Convention. *Source:* National Archives

the delegates were staying and where various candidates for the presidential nomination had set up their headquarters.

The convention was controlled by Humphrey's supporters. They easily defeated efforts by a coalition of antiwar delegates to adopt a peace plank for the party platform. After a few hours of emotional debate, the convention adopted a plank that endorsed President Johnson's war policy. Humphrey was nominated on Wednesday evening, August 28. The major antiwar candidate, Senator Eugene McCarthy, finished a distant second.

Chicago exploded that night; there occurred the "Battle of Chicago." About 5,000 protesters gathered in Grant Park across the street from the Hilton Hotel, where most of the delegates were staying. Encircled by National Guardsmen, mobs of demonstrators broke through barriers at various points and fanned out into the nearby Loop. They in turn were attacked by mobs of police, using clubs, mace, and tear gas. The violent scene was illuminated by spotlights and recorded by television cameras and news photographers. Protesters taunted the police by shouting, "The whole world is watching, the whole word is watching." Some of the police chanted "kill, kill, kill" as they charged the crowds. Police also indiscriminately attacked luckless tourists and passsersby caught in the melee, as well as television cameramen and newspaper photographers who were recording the orgy of violence. The entire Walpurgis Night of horrors was telecast to a nation that watched in amazed disbelief. Senator Abraham Ribicoff, viewing the nightmare scenes on a television monitor inside of the convention hall, condemned Mayor Daley's use of "Gestapo tactics." The forces of law and order won the "Battle of Chicago," but there were a lot of casualties on both sides. Over 1,000 people were injured, including 192 policemen, and 662 people were arrested.[135]

Many who witnessed the violence on television were everlastingly horrified and fearful that American fascism might be wearing the blue uniform of the Chicago police. A far larger number of viewers endorsed the police attacks on demonstrators, whose radical politics and countercultural lifestyles they perceived as intolerable threats to the good order and public morality of American civilization. The violence surrounding the Democratic Convention dramatized the ominous fact that there could be no peace in America until peace came to Vietnam. Journalist I. F. Stone observed, "The war is destroying our country as we are destroying Vietnam."[136]

The violent events in Chicago shattered the radical antiwar movement and strengthened the political conservatism that had been making a comeback from the Goldwater debacle of 1964. The Battle of Chicago also played into the hands of Republican presidential candidate Richard Nixon, who had been nominated at an orderly convention in Miami three weeks before the Democrats' tumultuous gathering. In his acceptance speech, a poised and confident Nixon had sounded the themes that would highlight his fall campaign: the need for national unity, the demand for "law and order," and the urgent need for peace in Vietnam, although not peace at any price.[137] These themes would resonate across the land. They would have strong appeal to millions of voters yearning for the return of social peace and for an end to a hated war.

A strong third party candidate with a large popular following, Governor George Wallace of Alabama, the American Independence Party leader, also entered the race for the presidency in 1968. Although he voiced hawkish sentiments, Wallace called for a negotiated settlement of the Vietnam War. He also championed traditional values and the work ethic. When the general campaign began in September, polls gave Nixon a 15 percent lead over Humphrey, and also showed that Wallace commanded considerable popular support.

The 1968 fall presidential campaign turned only partly on the issue of the Vietnam War. The conflict in Vietnam "was enmeshed in a web of racial tensions and barely articulated discontents."[138] None of the three major candidates had a clearly defined stance on the war; all took carefully qualified and nuanced positions that ultimately differed little from one another. All favored a negotiated settlement of the conflict that would end the fighting and preserve a pro-Western government in South Vietnam. Neither the millions of American hawks nor the doves who favored an immediate U. S. pull-out of Vietnam had a candidate to vote for. Nixon, well ahead in all of the polls, refused to discuss Vietnam for fear of complicating the Paris talks. Nixon and especially his vice presidential running mate, Maryland Governor Spiro T. Agnew, spent much time calling for "law and order" and denouncing antiwar activists, black militants, and hippies.

Humphrey, whose candidacy had emerged from the political ruins of Chicago, appeared to have no chance when the electoral contest began. He headed the ticket of a party profoundly divided over the Vietnam War. He had little money and no national campaign organization. He was repudiated by the antiwar liberals who had been defeated at the Democratic Convention. His campaign slogan, "The Politics of Joy," sounded absurdly inappropriate to the joyless mood prevailing in the country. For weeks, his campaign floundered along.

But as the 1968 election entered its final month, Humphrey's campaign suddenly sprang to life. Eugene McCarthy belatedly endorsed Humphrey, and many antiwar Democrats returned to the party fold; they apparently preferred a flawed liberal to their nemesis Nixon. As Humphrey's campaign gained momentum, Nixon's hitherto smooth-running campaign appeared to stall. Nixon, worried by Humphrey's late surge, hinted that he had a secret plan for ending the Vietnam War, but claimed he could not disclose its details lest he compromise its future effectiveness. Wallace's popular support in the North declined as trade union leaders campaigned vigorously for Humphrey. Polls taken throughout October showed Humphrey steadily closing the gap, with Nixon and Wallace fading. Humphrey appeared to have an eleventh-hour chance to win.

Johnson, who despised Nixon and wanted to help Humphrey beat him, and knowing that a dramatic peace gesture could put the Democratic candidate over the top, spoke to the American people on Thursday evening, October 31. The President announced a complete halt of all bombing of North Vietnam effective at midnight on October 31, five days before the election, and he implied that a peace settlement was coming soon. Peace talks were scheduled to begin on November 6, the day after the election. Johnson was persuaded to halt all bombing of North Vietnam by Harriman, who had told Johnson that a bombing halt would clear the way for the start of substantive negotiations with Hanoi. The Communists had indicated informally that they were prepared to begin serious peace discussions within a few days of a complete bombing halt, and that they would also accept the Saigon government's presence at the Paris talks. (The United States, had, in return, agreed to accept a representation from the NLF.) General Abrams assured Johnson that a bombing halt would pose no threat to Allied forces in South Vietnam, especially since Johnson had promised Abrams that he would shift the aircraft engaged in bombing North Vietnam to the aerial war against the Ho Chi Minh trail in Laos.[139]

Johnson's election-eve speech propelled Humphrey's candidacy forward. Public opinion polls taken over the final weekend before Tuesday's scheduled vote showed Nixon's lead had evaporated. The pundits pronounced the election "too close to call." A Harris poll released on Monday, November 4, the day before the election, showed Humphrey ahead of Nixon by 43 to 40 percent.[140] Humphrey appeared poised to pull off the biggest political upset since Harry Truman had defeated Thomas Dewey twenty years earlier.

But the Vietnam War, which appeared to have eliminated Humphrey early, then brought him back to the verge of victory, intruded at the last moment to deprive him, narrowly, of the presidency. On November 1, General Thieu, aware that the unilateral U. S. bombing halt had not required any reciprocal deescalations by Hanoi, announced that South Vietnam would not attend the Paris talks. Thieu's rubber-stamp National Assembly condemned President Johnson's "betrayal of an ally." Americans sadly realized that the killing would go on in Vietnam despite the bombing halt, and that Johnson's peace initiative was not going to halt the war any time soon. Another Harris poll, taken on Monday, showed Nixon had regained the lead. Although it is impossible to calculate precisely the impact of the collapse of the peace initiative on the presidential vote, and no doubt a myriad of domestic issues influenced the outcome, Thieu's last-minute demurral may have given Nixon his thin victory. Out of 73 million votes cast, his winning margin was a scant 500,000. Nixon received 43.4 percent of the vote, Humphrey 42.7 percent.

But it is not likely that American voters viewed the election as a referendum on Johnson's war policy. That policy itself was perceived, erroneously, by most voters as having become dovish in the aftermath of Tet. Voters could not discern much difference among Nixon, Humphrey, and Wallace's policy positions on the war. Nixon may have been narrowly preferred because he was viewed as being better qualified for the presidency and because the nation was becoming more conservative in the wake of the war and social disorder. The antiwar movement was a casualty of the politics of war in 1968. Its radical wing shattered and disintegrated into many extremist, violent, and quarreling factions; its liberal wing was mostly coopted by the Democrats into supporting the ambiguous war policy of Hubert Humphrey.[141]

Following two weeks of intense U. S. pressure and promises of continuing support, Thieu reluctantly agreed to send a delegation to the Paris talks. There followed a debate that went on for weeks over the shape of the negotiating table and the positioning of the four delegations at the table. By the time negotiations involving the four concerned parties began, Johnson's administration had entered its final days. Although it may have cost Humphrey his chance to win the 1968 presidential election, "It seems highly doubtful that South Vietnamese intransigence sabotaged an opportunity for a peace settlement."[142] Hanoi's new flexibility coming toward the end of 1968 did not extend beyond getting the bombing halted, which it managed without having to make any concessions in return. On the substantive issues, Hanoi would have probably accepted nothing less than a U. S. withdrawal and the end of the Thieu regime, both of which were unacceptable to Johnson. In the fall of 1968, neither Washington nor Hanoi was prepared to make the kinds of concessions that might have brought peace to Vietnam. The Tet Offensive and its aftermath had only hardened the diplomatic impasse over the key issues that had prevailed for years.

Johnson's March 31 speech had announced the abandonment of a strategy that had failed and no longer commanded majority support, but the President had not abandoned his objective of securing an independent South Vietnam that could stand as a barrier to the further spread of Communism in Southeast Asia. Despite the widespread public perception that Johnson had become a dove, it was only the strategy that had changed, not the policy or its objective. Johnson had pressed the war as vigorously as he could throughout 1968, at least until election eve.

In the short run, Tet-68 had been a massive tactical defeat that shattered the Vietcong forces and battered the NVA forces fighting in the South. But whatever its costs, Tet-68 represented a decisive political victory for the enemy, because it convinced "most Americans that the war could not be won in an acceptable time at an acceptable cost." Although Johnson refused to allow U. S. delegates to the peace talks to make any concessions that might have broken the diplomatic impasse and continued to try to win the war, he had inadvertently set in motion "what turned out to be an irreversible process of deescalation that would in time work in North Vietnam's favor."[143]

In the larger context of the America's post-World War II global foreign policy, Tet-68 marked both the peak of American hegemony and the beginning of its decline. The political crisis generated in Washington by Tet-68 and the gold crisis convinced the "wise men" that there were limits to American power to order world affairs. They perceived that the limited war in Vietnam had gotten out of control and further escalation of that conflict threatened to do irreparable harm to American global foreign policy interests, particularly in Europe. They understood that America's global commitments had exceeded its ability to pay for them.[144]

As the Year of the Monkey ended, most Americans yearned for an end to the bloody and stalemated war. Those who expected the incoming administration of Richard Nixon to bring an early end to the conflict would be bitterly disappointed to discover that their Vietnam ordeal was destined to endure another four years.

NOTES

1. Tet is a celebration of the beginning of the lunar new year. It is the most important Vietnamese holiday. During the Vietnam War, it was customary for both sides to observe a 36-hour cease-fire during Tet, and 1968, the year of the Monkey, was to be no exception.

2. Stanton, *Rise and Fall*, 220. Palmer, Bruce, Jr., *The 25-Five War: America's Role in Vietnam* (New York: Simon and Schuster, 1985), 78–79. One of the reasons the MACV was surprised by the size of the enemy forces involved in the Tet-68 attacks was because their intelligence reports had underestimated both enemy strength and the rate of infiltration into South Vietnam. Adams, Samuel, "Vietnam Coverup: Playing with Numbers," *Harper's magazine* (May 1975), 41, accuses Westmoreland of deliberately undercounting the Vietcong to deceive civilian leaders in Washington into thinking America was winning the Vietnam War. A CBS video documentary, "The Uncounted Enemy: A Vietnam Deception," broadcast on January 23, 1972, leveled the same charge. In response, General Westmoreland filed a libel suit against CBS that was eventually settled out of court. Larry Berman has shown in *Lyndon Johnson's War: The Road to Stalemate in Vietnam* (New York: W. W. Norton, 1989), 111–113, that there was no conspiracy by Westmoreland to deceive Johnson, McNamara, or any other high officials. Quote is from Hess, *Vietnam*, 106.

3. Oberdorfer, *Tet!*, 34.

4. Brodie, Bernard, "The Tet Offensive," Frankland, Noble, and Dowling, Christopher (eds.), *Decisive Battles of the Twentieth Century* (London: 1976), 319–21.

5. Duiker, *The Communist Road*, 240.

6. Porter (ed.), *Vietnam Documents*, vol. 2, Document 222, "Letter from Le Duan to Nguyen Chi Thanh, Commander-in-Chief of the PLAF," March 1966, 416; Duiker, *Communist Road*, 242.

7. Quoted in Duiker, *Communist Road*, 242–3.

8. Doyle, Edward; Lipsman Samuel; Maitland, Terrence; and the editors of Boston Publishing Company, *The North* (Boston: Boston Publishing Co., 1986), a volume in "The Vietnam Experience" series, 52–56; Duiker, *The Communist Road*, 248.

9. Davidson, *Vietnam at War*, 434–41.

10. Duiker, *The Communist Road*, 263–4; Oberdofer, *Tet!*, 42–43.

11. Porter (ed.), *Vietnam Documents*, vol. 2, Document 268, "Directive from Province Party Standing Committee to District and Local Party Organs on Forthcoming Offensive and Uprisings," Nov. 1, 1967, 477–80. This document shows the Communists were not depending on spontaneous risings of the people in the towns and cities at the time of the TET-68 general offensive. The directive reveals detailed plans for coordinating military attacks on RVN offices with organized political activity by cadre leaders.

12. Duiker, *The Communist Road*, 264–5.

13. Krepinevich, *The Army and Vietnam*, 237–8; Duiker, *The Communist Road*, 265–6.

14. Westmoreland, *A Soldier Reports*, 411–16.

15. *Ibid.*, 410–21.

16. Oberdorfer, *Tet!*, 2–40; Olson and Roberts, *Where the Domino Fell*, 184.

17. Stanton, *Rise and Fall*, 208–16.

18. *Ibid.*, 228–33; Oberdorfer, *Tet!*, 122–31.

19. Stanton, *Rise and Fall*, 231–3.

20. Quote is from *Ibid.*, 221.

21. Summers, Harry G. Jr., *Vietnam Encyclopedia*, 199–200.

22. Stanton, *Rise and Fall*, 228.

23. Quote is from Palmer, *Summons of the Trumpet*, 228–9; 9,776 of Hue's 17,134 houses were destroyed and another 3,169 were seriously damaged. Thousands of civilians were killed during the month-long battle for Hue. Young, *Vietnam Wars*, 217–19.

24. Krepinevich, *The Army and Vietnam*, 250; Oberdorfer, *Tet!*, 232. The 2,800 assassinations (other sources suggest much lower numbers of killings, some much higher) were carried out by the NLF execution teams.

25. President Nixon made his remarks during a speech delivered to the American people on the evening of November 3, 1969.

26. Palmer, *Summons of the Trumpet*, 215–16; Davidson, *Vietnam at War*, 551–4.

27. Johnson is quoted in Pisor, Robert, *The End of the Line; The Siege of Khe Sanh* (New York: Ballantine, 1982), 100, and 121–2; Westmoreland, *A Soldier Reports*, 444–5; Davidson, *Vietnam at War*, 564–6, all discuss the possible use of tactical nuclear weapons at Khe Sanh.

28. Davidson, *Vietnam at War*, 552–3.

29. Stanton, *Rise and Fall*, 235–8; Davidson, *Vietnam at War*, 552–3.

30. Davidson, *Vietnam at War*, 558–9. During the battle for Khe Sanh, U. S. planes dropped over 115,000 tons of bombs, rockets, and napalm, denuding an eight-square-mile area and inflicting thousands of casualties on the enemy.

31. Stanton, *Rise and Fall*, 238–42.

32. Davidson, *Vietnam at War*, 559–61; Pisor, *End of the Line*, 233–8.

33. Stanton, *Decline and Fall*, 233.

34. Pike, Douglas, *War, Peace, and the Vietcong* (Cambridge, Mass.: The M. I. T. Press, 1969), 125–7; Schandler, *The Unmaking of a President*, 77–78.

35. According to Oberdorfer, *Tet!*, who cites official U. S. and South Vietnamese figures, 58,373 PLAF and PAVN soldiers died between January 29 and March 31, 1968. During that time, 4,954 RVNAF soldiers and 3,895 Americans from all branches of the Armed Forces were killed.

36. Oberdorfer, *Tet!*, 158–71; Schandler, *The Unmaking of a President*, 80–81.

37. Quoted in Oberdorfer, *Tet!*,184. Arnett was the only journalist to hear Major Brown's remark, and it was Arnett's wire service account that put the famous quote into circulation. Kendrick, Alexander, *The Wound Within: America in the Vietnam Years, 1945–1974* (Boston, Little Brown, 1974), 251.

38. Quote is from Herring, *America's Longest War*, 192.

39. Schandler, *The Unmaking of a President*, 83.

40. Hess, *Vietnam*, 109.

41. Johnson, Lyndon, *The Vantage Point*, 382–6.

42. Schandler, *The Unmaking of a President*, 92–97.

43. Davidson, *Vietnam at War*, 492–6.

44. *Ibid.*, 497–8; Kolko, Gabriel, *Anatomy of a War: Vietnam, the United States, and the Modern Historical Experience* (New York: Pantheon Books, 1985), 313–15.

45. Schandler, *The Unmaking of a President*, 105–11; Davidson, *Vietnam at War*, 497–505.

46. Porter (ed.) *Vietnam Documents*, vol. 2, Document 279, "Report of the Chairman, Joint Chiefs of Staff, General Earle G. Wheeler, on the Situation in Vietnam," February 27, 1968, 501–4; Sheehan *et alia, Pentagon Papers,* 615–21.

47. Porter (ed.) *Vietnam Documents,* vol. 2, Document 279, "Report of the Chairman, Joint Chiefs of Staff, General Earle G. Wheeler, on the situation in Vietnam," February 27, 1968, 501–4.

48. Schandler, *The Unmaking of a President*, 118–19. The quoted material is on 119.

49. *Ibid.*, 120.

50. Johnson, *The Vantage Point*, 392.

51. *Ibid.*, 235–6.

52. Clifford, Clark M., "A Viet Nam Reappraisal: The Personal History of One Man's View and How It Evolved," *Foreign Affairs*, vol. 47 (July 1969), 606–7.

53. Schandler, *The Unmaking of a President*, 138–40.

54. Alain Enthoven's quote is found in Herring, *Longest War,* 3d. ed., 213.

55. Questions and answers are taken from Clifford, "A Vietnam Reappraisal," 610–11.

56. *Ibid.*, 611.

57. *Ibid.*, 611–12.

58. *Ibid.*, 613.

59. *Ibid.*, 613.

60. Porter (ed.), *Vietnam Documents*, vol. 2, Document 230, "Memorandum for the President from the 'Clifford Group,'" (Extract), 505. Schandler, *The Unmaking of the President*, contains a detailed description of the draft memo for the president, 167–76. The draft was written by William Bundy and Paul Warnke.

61. Johnson, *The Vantage Point*, 396–8.

62. *Ibid.*, 398–401.

63. Sheehan, Neil, and Smith, Hedrick, "Westmoreland Requests 206,000 More Men, Stirring Debate in Administration," *New York Times*, Sunday, March 10, 1968, p. 1.

64. Schandler, *The Unmaking of a President*, 211.

65. Both quotes come from *Ibid.*, 220.

66. McCarthy, Eugene J., *The Year of the People* (New York: Doubleday, 1969), 67–72; White, Theodore H., *The Making of a President, 1968* (New York: Atheneum, 1969), 83–85.

67. Schandler, *The Unmaking of a President*, 223.

68. Converse, Philip E., Miller, Warren E., Rusk, Jerold G., and Wolfe, Arthur C., "Continuity and Change in American Politics: Parties and Issues in the 1968 election," *American Political Science Review*, vol. 63 (December 1969) 1,083–1,092; Moss, *News or Nemesis*, 95–96.

69. Collins, Robert M., "The Economic Crisis of 1968 and the Waning of the 'American Century,'" in *American Historical Review* (vol. 101, no. 2) April 1996, 396–422. See also, Johnson, *The Vantage Point*, 314–18.

70. Collins, "The Economic Crisis of 1968," 407–18; Joseph, Paul, *Cracks in the Empire: State Politics in the Vietnam War* (Boston, 1981), 265–6.

71. Herring, *Longest War*, 3d. ed., 223.

72. Schandler, *The Unmaking of a President*, 236.

72. Clifford, "A Vietnam Reappraisal," 613–14; Schandler, *The Unmaking of a President*, 243–6, 251.

73. Herring, *Longest War*, 3d. ed., 224–5.

74. Johnson, *The Vantage Point*, 409–13; Oberdorfer, *Tet!*, 294–5.

75. The "wise men" present at the March 25 White House meeting included Dean Acheson, George Ball, McGeorge Bundy, Douglas Dillon, Cyrus Vance, Arthur Dean, John J. McCloy, General Omar Bradley, General Matthew Ridgway, General Maxwell Taylor, Robert Murphy, Henry Cabot Lodge, Abe Fortas, and Arthur Goldberg; Kolko, *Anatomy of A War*, 313–20.

76. McGeorge Bundy quote found in Olson and Roberts, *Where the Domino Fell,* 192–3.

77. Johnson is quoted in Morris, Roger, *An Uncertain Greatness: Henry Kissinger and American Foreign Policy* (New York, 1977), 44.

78. Johnson, *The Vantage Point*, 417–18; Sheehan, *A Bright Shining Lie*, 721–2; and Kolko, *Anatomy of a War*, 318–20; Melvin Small, *Johnson, Nixon, and the Doves*, 129–161, argues that the activities of the antiwar movement strongly influenced Johnson's decision to abandon his strategy of graduated escalation.

79. *Ibid.*, 420–1.

80. Johnson's March 31 speech is printed in *Public Papers of the President of the United States, Lyndon B. Johnson, 1968–1969*, vol. 1 (Washington, D. C.: GPO, 1971), 469–76; key passages, with analysis, are in Schandler, *The Unmaking of a President*, 282–7. Johnson resigned mainly because if he had not stepped down then, neither the American people or Hanoi would have believed his proposals were anything more than election-year ploys.

81. Goodman, *The Lost Peace*, 65–67. Peace talks began on May 13, but they were unproductive for months.

82. Schandler, *The Unmaking of a President*, 288–9; Kolko, *Anatomy of a War*, 333–7. The Communist leaders had not anticipated the great uproar that the Tet-68 campaigns caused within the United States, nor their political impact. When they realized that even though they had suffered major losses, the American political defeat was even greater, they were euphoric. They also realized that they had been lucky, that the timing of the attacks coincided with the dollar crisis that together caused the American political elite to lose its stomach for the Vietnam War and to persuade Lyndon Johnson to abandon his policy of graduated escalation. Tet-68 demonstrated that the revolution could not be defeated. The Communist leaders have always maintained that the Tet-68 Offensive was the turning point of the war with the Americans, the decisive triumph of their war effort.

83. Quote is from Herring, *America's Longest War*, 207.

84. Schandler, *The Unmaking of the President*, 319.

85. Kissinger, Henry, "The Vietnam Negotiations," *Foreign Affairs*, vol. 47 (January 1969), 214–16.

86. Moss, "The Vietnam Generation," 6–8, 10–12.

87. Westmoreland, *A Soldier Reports*, 427–8, 438–9, 471–2, 554–7; Elegant, Robert, "How to Lose a War: Reflections of a Foreign Correspondent," *Encounter* (August 1981), 73–74.

88. Westmoreland, *A Soldier Reports*, 427–8, 438–9.

89. Kimball, Jeffrey P., "The Stab-in-the-Back Legend and the Vietnam War," *Armed Forces and Society*, vol. 14 (Spring 1988), 438–9.

90. There is a large and generally excellent literature on the media coverage of the Vietnam War. Daniel C. Hallin, *The Uncensored War: The Media and Vietnam* (New York: Oxford University Press, 1986). and George Donelson Moss, "News or Nemesis: Did Television Lose the Vietnam War?" in *A Vietnam Reader: Sources and Essays* (Englewood Cliffs: Prentice Hall, 1991), both show that television news coverage of the Vietnam War did not turn people against the war. William Hammond, a historian at the Army's Center of Military History has written two books about the military and the media: *Public Affairs: The Military and the Media 1962–1968* (Washington, D. C.: U. S. Gov't. Printing Office, 1989) and *Public Affairs: The Military and the Media, 1968–1973* (Washington, D. C.: U. S. Gov't. Printing Office, 1996). Hammond does not believe that media coverage of the war, whether favorable or unfavorable, had much influence on public perceptions of the war.

91. Hallin, Daniel C., *The Uncensored War*, 110.

92. Patterson, Oscar, III, "An Analysis of Television Coverage of the Vietnam War," *Journal of Broadcasting*, vol. 28 (Fall 1984), 401–2.

93. The poll appeared in *Newsweek*, vol. 70 (July 10, 1967), 20–24.

94. Mueller, *Wars, Presidents, and Public Opinion*, 88–89.

95. See Table 4.6 showing policy preferences in Vietnam appearing in Mueller, *Wars, Presidents, and Public Opinion,* 107. Public opinion polls taken in early February, immediately after the Tet attacks, showed that the number of people calling themselves hawks rose from 56 percent to 61 percent, and the number calling themselves doves dropped from 28 percent to 23 percent.

96. See Braestrup, Peter, *Big Story: How the American Press and Television Reported and Interpreted the Crisis of Tet 1968 in Vietnam and Washington*, 2 vols., (Boulder, Colo.: Westview, 1977).

97. Braestrup, Peter, "The Press and the Vietnam War," *Encounter* (April 1983), 92.

98. Braestrup, Peter, "The Tet Offensive—Another Press Controversy: 2," in Harrison Salisbury (ed.), *Vietnam Reconsidered: Lessons from a War* (New York: Harper & Row, 1984), 167–8.

99. *Ibid.*, 171.

100. Mueller, *War, Presidents, and Public Opinion*, 91, cites a poll taken in September 1968 showing that 48 percent of Americans favored a dovish position, and 43 percent favored a hawkish position. This is the first time any poll showed that doves outnumbered hawks. Popular support dropped sharply, both for the war and for Johnson's war policy, reflecting the public's perception that Johnson's leadership was indecisive in a time of crisis. It was Johnson's indecisive leadership that caused the sharp drop in public support for the war.

101. *Ibid.*, 23–114; Moss, *News or Nemesis*, 35–43.

102. Goodman, *The Lost Peace*, 65–68; Karnow, *Vietnam*, 566.

103. Quote is from Sasaki, Dr. Clarence T., "Holding Death at Bay," *Vietnam*, vol. 5, no. 2 (August 1992), 35.

104. *Ibid.*, 35–40. Between January 1965 and December 1970, 133,447 wounded personnel were admitted to medical treatment facilities in Vietnam. Another 150,375 soldiers received wounds not serious enough to require hospitalization. Of the 97,659 who received serious wounds, the mortality rate was 2.5 percent, compared to 4.5 percent for World War II and 4.0 percent for Korea.

105. Marshall, Kathryn, *In the Combat Zone* (New York: Penguin Books, 1987), 3–13. Many American women, both civilian and military, served in Vietnam, an estimated 33,000 to 55,000 according to Marshall. While 80 percent of military women served as nurses, they also did non-medical work. They were secretaries and clerks, air traffic controllers, photographers, and cartographers; they worked in intelligence, communications, and some worked on classified projects requiring top-secret clearances.

106. Stanton, *Rise and Fall*, 259–60.

107. *Ibid.*, 255, 259, 262–3.

108. Morrocco, *Thunder from Above*, 184–6.

109. Doughan, Clark; Weiss, Stephen; and the editors of Boston Publishing Company, *Nineteen Sixty-Eight* (Boston: Boston Publishing Co., 1983), 142–4, a volume in the *Vietnam Experience*; Stanton, *Rise and Fall*, 248–9; Palmer, *Summons of the Trumpet*, 263–4.

110. Stanton, *Rise and Fall*, 249–50.

111. *Ibid.*, 251–4.

112. Lewy, *America in Vietnam*, 324–5; Dougan, *Nineteen Sixty-Eight*, 79.

113. Stanton, *Rise and Fall*, 258.

114. An independent journalist, Seymour M. Hersh, exposed the Army's cover-up of the My Lai massacre. See his book, *Cover-Up: The Army's Secret Investigation of the Massacre at My Lai 4* (New York: Random House, 1972).

115. "Conversations between Lt. General William R. Peers and Lt. Colonel Jim Breen and Lt. Colonel Charlie Moore," in Oral History collection of U. S. Army Military History Institute, Carlisle Barracks, Penn., 33–44, 56–58; Peers, William R., *The My Lai Inquiry* (New York: W. W. Norton, 1979), *passim*; Palmer, Bruce, *25-Year War*, 85–86, 170–1; Stanton, *Rise and Fall*, 258. Calley was initially sentenced to life imprisonment at hard labor. Following lengthy reviews of his case in both military and civilian courts, his sentence was reduced to ten years. After serving twenty-six months, he was paroled in 1974.

116. Lewy, *America in Vietnam*, 311.

117. *Ibid.*, 324–31. Lewy has carefully studied the issue of American war crimes and atrocities committed during the Vietnam War. See his chapter 9, "Atrocities: Fiction and Fact," 307–42, and chapter 10, "The Punishment of Atrocities and War Crimes," 343–73; also see Westmoreland's views, *A Soldier Reports*, 494–501.

118. Porter (ed.), *Vietnam Documents*, vol. 2, Document 285, "COSVN Directive," June 10, 1968, 512–16; Palmer, *Summons of the Trumpet* 264–5; Stanton, *Rise and Fall*, 259–63.

119. Duiker, *The Communist Road*, 276–8; Davidson, *Vietnam at War*, 540–4. During the first six months of 1968, Hanoi lost an estimated 100,000 PLAF and NVA troops, about half of their entire strength at the beginning of the year.

120. Blaufarb, *Counterinsurgency Era*, 266–74; Herring, *America's Longest War*, 212; Andrade, *Ashes to Ashes*, 81–97. The Phoenix program, 1968–1972, that operated in South Vietnam to neutralize the Vietcong political infrastructure in the villages, became controversial. Its critics, testifying before Congressional investigating committees, accused the CIA and its South Vietnamese counterparts of operating a barbarous assassination program outside of the framework of law, morality, and bureaucratic accountability. Andrade, a careful student of the Phoenix program, has refuted these charges. He concedes that there were plenty of abuses; people were often imprisoned, tortured, and murdered without cause. But he shows that the intent of the program was to identify and neutralize the VCI. In 1969 and 1970, the Phoenix program achieved considerable success in eliminating or disrupting the revolutionary infrastructure in some districts of South Vietnam. But it was too small, too inefficient, and never got the support it needed from RVN officials to cripple significantly the insurgency. Like all pacification programs, Phoenix was too little too late.

121. Clifford, "A Vietnam Reappraisal," 614; Herring, *America's Longest War*, 212–13.

122. Davidson, *Vietnam at War*, 531.

123. Herring, *America's Longest War*, 208.

124. Davidson, *Vietnam at War*, 531.

125. *Ibid.*, 532; Bluefarb, *Counterinsurgency Era*, 302–5.

126. Spector, Ronald H., *After Tet: The Bloodiest Year in Vietnam*, New York, 1933.

127. Quoted in Dougan and others, *Nineteen Sixty-Eight*, 126; Davidson, *Vietnam at War*, 544–7; Lipsman, Samuel, Doyle, Edward, and the editors of Boston Publishing Co., *Fighting for Time* (Boston: Boston Publishing Co., 1983), 88–90.

128. The unidentified Saigonese is quoted in Dougan and others, *Nineteen Sixty-Eight*, 123.

129. Herring, *America's Longest War*, 214–15.

130. Schlesinger, Arthur M. Jr., *Robert Kennedy and His Times*, vol. 2 (Boston: Houghton Mifflin, 1978), 930–1.

131. DeBenedetti, *American Ordeal*, 217–18; Moss, *America in the Twentieth Century*, 370.

132. O'Neill, William L., *Coming Apart: An Informal History of America in the 1960s* (New York: Quadrangle, 1971), 289–91; DeBenedetti, *American Ordeal*, 217–18.

133. Schlesinger, *Robert Kennedy*, 955–6.

134. Moss, *News or Nemesis*, 96–99.

135. Hodgson, Godfrey, *America in our Time: From World War II to Nixon: What Happened and Why* (New York: Vintage, 1976), 370–2; DeBenedetti, *An American Ordeal*, 223–8. Immediately after they broadcast images of the violence taking place in the streets of Chicago, the three television networks were deluged by letters, telegrams, and phone calls from irate viewers. By an eight-to-one margin, the viewers condemned the demonstrators and what they perceived as biased television reportage favoring the protesters. During the ensuing two weeks, Mayor Daley received 75,000 letters from all over the country; 90 percent of them praised his police. Public opinion polls showed that 56 percent of the people approved of Daley's handling of the disorders and 71 percent thought his security measures were justified.

136. Dougan et al., *Nineteen Sixty-Eight*, 175; Stone is quoted in DeBenedetti, *An American Ordeal*, 228.

137. Dougan et al., *Nineteen Sixty-Eight*, 176. During 1968, antiwar sentiment was growing within the U. S. Armed Forces. Desertion rates increased. Riots in brigs and stockades became more numerous. Racial tensions magnified. Forty-three soldiers stationed at Fort Hood, Texas, refused to go to Chicago during the Democratic Convention. Antiwar coffeehouses and underground newsletters appeared on U. S. military installations.

138. Quote is from DeBenedetti, *An American Ordeal*, 235.

139. Johnson, *The Vantage Point*, 513–29; Goodman, *The Lost Peace*, 69–73. The eventual scaling back and cessation of the air war against North Vietnam had ominous consequences for the inhabitants of Laos, where for years Washington had been waging a secret war. Bombing sorties against targets in the Laotian panhandle and the Plain of Jars, an area in northeastern Laos controlled by the Pathet Lao, escalated in 1968.

140. Dougan et al., *Nineteen Sixty-Eight*, 180.

141. *Ibid.*, 180–2; DeBenedetti, *An American Ordeal*, 235–6. Some accounts of the 1968 election state that Nixon, to ensure his election, contacted Thieu through an intermediary, Anna Chinnault, to have her tell him to refuse to attend the peace conference and to promise him that he could get a better deal from Nixon after he won the election. Some Humphrey supporters believe Nixon's meddling cost them the election. They also accuse Nixon of sabotaging the peace talks to win an election. If Nixon did make contact with Thieu, the candidates' efforts probably had little effect on either the election or the peace talks, as there was no peace settlement to sabotage and Thieu did not need Nixon to tell him to boycott the peace talks. Thieu had already concluded that he could get better terms later, from either Nixon or Humphrey.

142. Quote is from Herring, *America's Longest War*, 219.

143. Both quotes are from Herring, *Longest War*, 3d. ed., 241.

144. *Ibid.*

8

A War to End A War

We designed a war we were going to lose, and we managed to lose it the way we designed it.

Newt Gingrich

AMERICAN DILEMMAS

Tet-68 transformed American politics and also transformed the American Vietnam war. President Johnson, his leadership discredited and heading a party badly split over an increasingly controversial war, was forced to remove himself from politics, in effect resigning at the end of March 1968. Amidst the most turbulent backdrop since the Civil War, a divided electorate chose a resurrected Richard Nixon to lead the nation out of the morass of Vietnam and to restore peace both at home and abroad.

Nixon, since 1954, had been a hawk on the Indochina wars. As vice president, he had called for U. S. military intervention in May 1954 to save the French at Dien Bien Phu. In 1955, he had stated that expansionist China posed the greatest threat to U. S. strategic interests in Southeast Asia and that it might become necessary to use nuclear weapons to halt Chinese aggression. Nixon strongly backed the Johnson administration when it committed America to war in Vietnam during the summer of 1965. In 1966, and again in 1967, Nixon opposed calls for negotiations with Hanoi. He believed that such calls only encouraged the Communists to continue fighting. Nixon insisted that negotiations should occur only after all NVA forces had been driven from South Vietnam.[1]

During the 1968 presidential campaign, Nixon had frequently criticized Johnson's gradualist use of military force in Vietnam because it had produced neither military victory nor a negotiated settlement of the war. Conceding that a military victory was no longer possible, Nixon suggested that the road to a negotiated settlement of the Vietnam War ran through Moscow, not through Hanoi. Because Nixon believed North Vietnam could not continue its war in South Vietnam without Soviet backing, Americans should work for "a broad political accommodation with the Soviet Union—for detente—"[2] to reduce or to end Soviet aid to North Vietnam. He stated that if the Soviets wanted Hanoi to end its war in South Vietnam, the North Vietnamese would have no choice but to negotiate its conclusion.

Asserting that ending the Vietnam War was necessarily the top national priority, Nixon stressed the importance of ending the war honorably and in such a fashion that the U. S. withdrawal from Vietnam would never be or even appear to be an American defeat. For him, the maintenance of an independent non-Communist South Vietnamese government was crucial. Ensuring a free South Vietnam was a major American commitment and a vital national interest. Preserving South Vietnam was also necessary for the United States to maintain its credibility as a great power with both friends and foes. How America ended its war in Vietnam would determine if there would soon be another war or if the world would enjoy a generation of peace.

As his campaign for the presidency developed, Nixon had suggested that if he were elected, he would move on a variety of nonmilitary fronts, that he had a plan, which he did not disclose in detail, for ending the war.[3] But once in office, it became evident that President Nixon did not have a plan, secret or otherwise, for ending the Vietnam War. He brought to the White House only a few general principles pertaining to a settlement that he had formulated over the years.

The new president gradually improvised a Vietnam strategy during his first year in office. Some of Nixon's ideas concerning the Vietnam War were similar to the views of Henry A. Kissinger, who became Nixon's National Security Adviser. Kissinger, a former Harvard professor who had written extensively on foreign policy and national security issues during the 1950s and 1960s, shared Nixon's view that the first order of foreign policy business must be the phasing out of the American Vietnam war and that it had to be done in an honorable fashion. But Kissinger had never been an enthusiastic supporter of the American military intervention in Vietnam. He believed Johnson and his advisers had made a serious error in geopolitical judgment when they decided to send American combat forces to Vietnam in 1965; they sought a military solution to a political problem. However, Kissinger argued in 1969, how or why America got into the war no longer mattered, because "ending the war honorably is essential for the peace of the world."[4]

Nixon's approach to Vietnam "was an integral part of an effort to redefine America's global strategy."[5] Both Nixon and Kissinger envisioned a world in which the major powers, including the major Communist powers, maintained a stable world order, in which they would all have a vested interest. Nixon and Kissinger both believed they could provide the leadership and the vision that would enable the United States to maintain its primacy within this new world order that they would bring about. The two American leaders sought to improve relations with the Soviet Union and to move toward normal relations with China, ending twenty years of hostility and isolation between the Peoples Republic and the United States. Both Nixon and Kissinger, who quickly became Nixon's chief foreign policy adviser and envoy, shared the conviction that they must extract the United States from what had become a major liability.[6]

They also believed that to accomplish their major foreign policy goals they would have to concentrate the power to conduct American foreign policy into their hands. Achieving such power required bypassing the National Security Council and the bureaucracies in the Defense Department, the State Department, and the CIA. They believed that an energetic and decisive foreign policy could come only from the new partnership forming in the White House, from themselves, in consultation with a few senior advisers. Early in his presidency, Nixon told Kissinger, "You and I will end the war."[7]

Nixon and Kissinger felt that Johnson's *modus operandi*, decision-making by consensus, had been a slow and cumbrous process. Further, consensus required a variety of lowest common denominator decisions, which often reflected the bureaucratic interests of senior officials. Consensus decisions were expressions of the power balance within Johnson's administration among members of the Joint Chiefs, the State Department, the Defense Department, the CIA, and the National Security Council, whether or not such decisions made strategic or diplomatic sense. Nixon and Kissinger both were certain that they possessed the requisite expertise to rise above the miasma of bureaucratic consensus politics. They believed that they, and only they, could make the bold, decisive moves ending the American war in Vietnam, reorienting American relations with the major Communist powers, and achieving a stable and peaceful world order that accorded with U. S. strategic interests.

Nixon and Kissinger came to power sharing the illusions held by their predecessors in the three previous administrations. They believed they were unique, that they brought to office the requisite knowledge, boldness, and imagination required to achieve a satisfactory outcome to the long American Vietnam involvement. They would devise strategies for making Hanoi accept terms that the North Vietnamese had consistently rejected for years; they would use Soviet leverage to get a settlement.

Consequently, Nixon and Kissinger were doomed to replicate the experience of their predecessors. Once in power, they discovered they had inherited intractable problems in Vietnam. They also found that their power and options were more limited than they had supposed, and that many of their assumptions and ideas proved invalid. They discovered that they had limited freedom of maneuver, even less than their predecessors, because of a multiplicity of factors: the stalemated war, Hanoi's protracted war strategy and absolute refusal to modify its objectives, Soviet unwillingness to prod Hanoi to end the war, General Thieu's fears that any settlement that America might make with Hanoi threatened his country's prospects for survival, and powerful domestic constraints.

Nixon's narrow victory in the November 1968 election carried with it no mandate whatsoever. Because of the presence of a strong third-party candidate, George

Wallace, Nixon won the presidency by only a plurality (with 43 percent of the popular vote). Fifty-seven percent of the voters preferred a candidate other than Richard Nixon for president of the United States. Congress remained firmly in the control of large Democratic majorities. Many liberal Democratic congressman and senators were now freed from the inhibitions of having to support Johnson's war. They could be expected to prod Nixon to seek a negotiated end to the war and challenge any initiatives he might undertake to expand or widen the war.[8]

Public opinion polls taken in early 1969 showed that large majorities of Americans wanted a quick end to the U. S. war and favored an early withdrawal of all American forces. But most Americans did not want to see the United States defeated in Vietnam, and they believed that it was important to stop the spread of Communism in Southeast Asia. They also wanted the South Vietnamese to take responsibility for their own defense and survival. The same people who wanted a quick end to a war that they neither wanted to lose nor see escalated while also stopping the spread of

Figure 8.1   U. S. sea power had a major role in the American Vietnam War. Here, the battleship USS *New Jersey*, lying offshore in Gulf of Tonkin waters, fires a salvo from one of its 16-inch guns, the largest guns in the world. *Source:* U. S. Navy photo

Communism in Southeast Asia exhibited little genuine concern for the welfare of the South Vietnamese people or much regard for the survival of their government.[9] Such a tangle of views may have defied logic, but they set limits to what Nixon and Kissinger could do as the two labored to forge a new American strategy for Vietnam.

The new president and his chief adviser confronted dilemmas as they struggled to improvise a U. S. Vietnam policy and strategies to make it work: any terms acceptable to Hanoi for ending the war were unacceptable to them, to their allies in South Vietnam, to the U. S. Congressional majority, and to a majority of the American people. Domestic criticism of the costs of the war put pressure on the president to withdraw American troops, but unilateral American force withdrawals also encouraged Hanoi to refuse to make any concessions to achieve a settlement Nixon could accept.

Johnson had passed on to his successors a war that could neither be won nor ended, except on terms that amounted to a major American defeat, terms Nixon and Kissinger would not accept in 1969. In fact, the Nixon administration and the American people would endure four more years of war in Indochina before they could accept the unacceptable, accept what had been inevitable since Tet-68, perhaps inevitable since the American intervention in southern Vietnam in the summer of 1954: eventual strategic defeat. Washington finally accepted it in January 1973, only by disguising that defeat within the rhetoric of "peace with honor." "Peace with honor" glossed over the ineffable strategic reality of the American Vietnam War:

> American withdrawal from the war and the survival of the South Vietnamese government . . . had always been contradictory objectives.[10]

VIETNAMIZATION

True to his campaign promises to the American people, Nixon turned his attention immediately to Vietnam. As the new president set out to end the war, he ruled out the two extreme solutions—immediate withdrawal or massive escalation. Nixon understood from the beginning of his presidency that his only feasible option was an American withdrawal.[11] For Nixon, the only significant question concerned the way America withdrew. Would it be precipitous, an ignominious American defeat, or would it be measured and honorable, assuring the survival of South Vietnam? Nixon did not believe he could not just cut and run out of Vietnam. He had joined the conservative Republican assault on the Truman administration for "losing" China during the early 1950s and, like his predecessor Lyndon Johnson, the new president "feared the domestic upheaval that might accompany the fall of South Vietnam to communism."[12] Nixon never deluded himself with fantasies of winning a military victory over North Vietnam. He knew that was not possible. He did not delay ending the war because he was trying to win it, as some radical and liberal antiwar critics have charged. The long delay in ending the war arose from Nixon's preoccupation with how the war was to be terminated and with what consequences, domestic and international. The long delay in ending the war also ensued because for years the North Vietnamese leadership stubbornly adhered to their goals of bringing down the South Vietnamese government, replacing it with one dominated by the NLF, forcing the Americans out, and reuniting the country under their control. They had no interest in negotiating an end to the war on any terms that Nixon and Kissinger could accept. Although Nixon never tried to win the war, he fought ferociously for years not to lose it, or at least to appear not to lose it. For four years, from January 1969 to January 1973, Nixon and Kissinger waged a long, slow, costly, and bitter American retreat from Indochina.

Shortly after assuming office, Nixon sent a letter to the North Vietnamese leaders expressing his desire for peace. He proposed as a first step the mutual withdrawal of "external forces" (American and NVA) from South Vietnam and the restoration of the DMZ as a boundary between the two countries of North Vietnam and South Vietnam. He also proposed, at Kissinger's suggestion, that the Paris negotiations follow a two-tiered approach, with Washington and Hanoi concentrating on mutual troop withdrawals while Saigon's representatives and the NLF negotiated a political settlement of the civil war. At the same time Nixon sent his letter to Hanoi, he sent Kissinger to tell the Soviet ambassador to the United States, Anatoly Dobrynin, that a peace settlement in Vietnam must precede any accommodation between the United States and the Soviet Union. That is, the American Vietnam war must end before détente could occur. To signal to both Hanoi and Moscow that his administration would not be bound by the old limits, Nixon accompanied these diplomatic initiatives with bombings of VC/NVA sanctuaries in the eastern provinces of Cambodia bordering southern Vietnam.[13]

The bombing also represented a response to another Communist offensive carried out in many districts and provinces of South Vietnam on February 22, 1969, and it also fulfilled a long-standing request of the Joint Chiefs to strike at VC/NVA bases in Cambodia that lay beyond the reach of Allied troops. Johnson had always rejected the Joint Chiefs' request out of his fear of widening the war. The bombing operation, code-named MENU, began on March 18, with B-52s bombing VC/NVA Cambodian sanctuaries in several locales. The MENU operation began with a BREAKFAST phase. As the war went on and the bombing of Cambodia continued, BREAKFAST was followed by LUNCH, LUNCH by SNACK, SNACK by DINNER, DINNER by DESSERT, and DESSERT by SUPPER. Nixon ordered intermittent bombing raids on Cambodia through August 1969. Sometimes the bombing raids were followed by lightning cross-border raids by teams of Special Forces operatives. The air raids and ground attacks had the combined effect of driving the North Vietnamese deeper into the Cambodian interior. After August, the secret bombing continued on a regular basis until May 1970, when air strikes in Cambodia began openly in support of Allied ground operations against North Vietnamese bases.[14]

Fearing an adverse reaction from Congress and the American people because the bombings occurred in a neutral country and represented a widening of the war, both geographically and politically, the Nixon administration went to great lengths to try to keep them hidden. Air Force officials in charge of the bombings constructed elaborate systems of phony records of sorties supposedly flown against authorized targets in South Vietnam to account for the expenditures of fuel and ordnance on the secret raids into Cambodia. An elaborate system of dual bookkeeping was set up, which made it appear that the bombs hitting the Cambodian sanctuaries of the enemy were instead falling on targets inside of South Vietnam.[15]

When an account of the secret bombing of Cambodia appeared in the *New York Times* on May 9, 1969, Nixon suggested to Kissinger that the informant could have been someone on the National Security Council staff. Kissinger concurred. The next day, the president, with Kissinger's approval, ordered FBI director J. Edgar Hoover to wiretap the phones of eleven National Security Council staff members and four members of the news media whom he suspected of leaking information about the bombing to the paper.[16]

In May 1970, at the time of the American incursion into Cambodia, Nixon ordered the bombing of target sites in North Vietnam and also tried to keep this action secret. After another press leak, the *New York Times* ran a story about the renewed bombing of North Vietnam. Once again, Nixon ordered wiretaps put on the phones of suspect officials and journalists. In July 1971, the *New York Times* began publishing the "Pentagon Papers," a secret Defense Department internal history of the long U. S. involvement in Vietnam, leaked to them by former Defense Department official Daniel Ellsberg, and Anthony Russo. To stop further press leaks and to discredit Ellsberg, White House officials formed a special unit, the "Plumbers."

President Nixon, increasingly frustrated by his inability to end the Vietnam War, and convinced that his policies, even his ability to govern, were under attack from his "enemies" in the federal bureaucracies, in Congress, in the media, and in the universities, ordered the "Plumbers" to take whatever actions were necessary to stop press leaks. Wiretapping had led to the formation of the "Plumbers." It was a natural progression from the actions of the "Plumbers" to the "dirty tricks" of the 1972 presidential election, one of which was the Watergate burglary and its attempted cover-up. The genesis of the Watergate scandals that eventually destroyed the Nixon presidency lay in Nixon's siege mentality arising from his inability to forge a rapid end to the Vietnam War, which led him to countenance illegal measures intended to squelch his political opponents. When Nixon ordered the wiretapping of the phones of NSC staffers and journalists in May 1969, he unwittingly began the process that would destroy his presidency and mar his historical reputation five years later.

None of Nixon's and Kissinger's initial efforts to end the Vietnam War produced any noticeable results. Neither the VC/NVA February offensive nor the secret U. S. bombing of Cambodia changed the military balance in Vietnam. The stalemate on the battlefield was matched by a continuing diplomatic standoff in Paris. The Soviets did not cooperate as expected; they made no effort to persuade Hanoi to end the war. Both the North Vietnamese and South Vietnamese governments rejected the U. S. proposal for a mutual withdrawal of American and PAVN forces from South Vietnam. The Saigon government refused to recognize or negotiate with representatives of the NLF. The war went on. "At the heart of the U. S.-North Vietnamese conflict remained the status of South Vietnam."[17]

Perceiving that his initial efforts to end the war had failed, Nixon used a televised speech on May 14, 1969, to propose a comprehensive eight-point Vietnam peace plan that he hoped would break the diplomatic logjam. Most of the eight points referred to the proposed troop withdrawal and other military matters. The president also tried to resuscitate the two-tier formula, separating the military and political dimensions of the struggle, by stating that "the political settlement is an internal matter that ought to be decided by the South Vietnamese themselves. . . . "[18]

Nixon followed his speech with a trip to Midway Island in early June, where he met with General Thieu. After conferring with Thieu, Nixon announced on June 8 that he was recalling immediately 25,000 American troops from Vietnam. The U. S. disengagement from Southeast Asia had begun. The large-scale withdrawal of American forces from Vietnam was part of a new "Nixon Doctrine" of limited U. S. involvement in Third World revolutionary wars. Henceforth, the United States would provide economic and military assistance, but the host country would have to furnish its own troops. The United States would help, but it would have to defend itself. Implementation of the Nixon Doctrine meant there would be no more Vietnams. In a larger context, the Nixon Doctrine represented an effort to downsize American global foreign policy commitments, to align U. S. commitments with its ability to meet them. Lest Hanoi or the Soviets read the wrong message into the troop pull-out, Nixon followed his Midway Island pronouncements with several speeches attacking antiwar critics and affirming that his administration would keep America's commitments abroad.[19]

These additional diplomatic and military moves also failed to extract the slightest concession from Hanoi. The Communists could neither be pressured nor lured into altering their basic negotiating stance. They reiterated the peace terms they had maintained since talks had begun in May 1968: the total and unconditional withdrawal of all U. S. forces from Vietnam and the replacement of the Thieu government with a provisional government.[20] On the battlefield, the VC/NVA continued its protracted war strategy. The war went on, although the scale and intensity of fighting declined during the year, casualties dropped, and Hanoi pulled some of its forces back across the DMZ. The North Vietnamese were prepared to wait out the Nixon administration, confident that declining domestic support for the war would eventually force Washington to withdraw the American forces just as the loss of support at home had forced the French to withdraw their forces from Indochina during the previous war.[21] Hanoi's leaders understood that if the U. S. forces did not win, in time, they would lose; the North Vietnamese had only not to lose, and in time they would win. Hanoi confidently embraced General Tran Hung Dao's dictum, which he expressed in 1284 as his forces outlasted the invading armies of the reigning superpower of that era, "Time is always in our favor."[22]

Figure 8.2   President Nixon and General Thieu met for the first time on Midway Island on June 8, 1969. After conferring with the South Vietnamese leader, Nixon announced that he was immediately recalling 25,000 troops from Vietnam. Henry Kissinger, National Security Adviser, appears in the background. *Source:* National Archives, Nixon Collection

By the summer of 1969, it was evident that the strategies Nixon and Kissinger had brought to Washington to end the American Vietnam War had failed to deliver the promised result. Nixon had never set a specific date for ending the war, but he and Kissinger expected that their mix of threats, secret diplomatic maneuvers, and efforts to involve the Soviets would bring an end to the American Vietnam War within a year from the date they took office. But by the summer of 1969, Congressional criticism of the continuing war was on the rise, and the peace movement, quiescent since the violence in Chicago, geared up for fall demonstrations. Fearful that domestic discontent would undermine his efforts to get Hanoi to negotiate an acceptable agreement, Nixon turned to what he called his "go for broke" strategy, an all-out effort to end the war, either by a diplomatic agreement or by the use of military force. Through French intermediaries, the president sent a personal message to Ho Chi Minh urging a settlement, but with the added warning, amounting to an ultimatum, that if no progress were made by November 1, he would have no choice but to resort to "measures of great consequence and force."[23] Nixon sent Kissinger to see Dobrynin again to warn him that there remained little time for a peaceful solution to the impasse at Paris.

Nixon also directed Kissinger to form a select National Security Council study group to develop plans for a "savage, punishing" blow aimed at North Vietnam.[24] Nixon and Kissinger sought that one decisive stroke that would destroy the will of the North Vietnamese to continue the war in South Vietnam. Kissinger told the select group at their first meeting in early September, "I can't believe that a fourth-rate power like North Vietnam doesn't have a breaking point."[25] By the end of the month, the group had developed a thick loose-leaf notebook of attack plans, code-named DUCK HOOK. DUCK HOOK included mining Haiphong, North Vietnam's major port, implementing a naval blockade of the North Vietnamese coast, and saturation bombing of both military targets and major cities. In addition, the planners considered the options of invading North Vietnam, bombing the Red River dikes to flood the major rice-growing region of North Vietnam, and closing down the rail supply lines to China. The DUCK HOOK planners also analyzed possible uses of tactical nuclear devices in North Vietnam.[26] Not averse to using press leaks himself if they could advance his policies, Nixon let journalists know he was considering a range of military options. He probably intended the leaks as warning signals to Moscow and Hanoi, that the time left for diplomacy had grown short and that his patience had worn thin. Nixon also vowed to a group from Congress that he would not be the first president ever to lose a war.[27]

Nixon's "go for broke" strategy failed. Hanoi could not be intimidated, although the Communists did agree to hold secret talks with the Americans outside of the framework of the Paris negotiations. On August 4, 1969, Kissinger met privately with Xuan Thuy for the first of what proved to be a long series of secret talks between Kissinger and DRV envoys, lasting until the Paris Agreement was negotiated in January 1973. At that first meeting, Thuy rejected all of Kissinger's proposals, dismissed Nixon's epistolary ultimatum to Ho Chi Minh, and repeated Hanoi's refrain that there could be no agreement until the United States had removed all of its troops from Vietnam and had sacrificed the Thieu government.[28] On August 15, Ho Chi Minh formally replied to Nixon's letter. The North Vietnamese leader ignored the ultimatum, rejected Nixon's overtures, and restated Hanoi's basic position, insisting that it was the only correct formula for peace. Hanoi radio added to Nixon's chagrin by wishing the American peace movement splendid success with its upcoming demonstrations.[29]

By fall 1969, Nixon, infuriated by Hanoi's intransigence and by dovish antiwar critics whom he believed encouraged North Vietnam's resistance to his diplomatic overtures, faced stark choices: He could undertake a major military escalation of the war, or he could beat a humiliating diplomatic retreat. His gut reaction was to strike back at his enemies. He wanted to hurl U. S. air power at the North Vietnamese and blockade their ports. But he was advised by Secretary of State William Rogers and Secretary of Defense Melvin Laird not to escalate the war because such action would doubtless arouse the doves in Congress, the press, the academies, and the streets. More important, Kissinger's select group of military planners concluded that air strikes and

Figure 8.3   President Nixon visited South Vietnam on July 30, 1969. Here, he chats with soldiers of the 1st Infantry Division at Dian, near Saigon. The 1st, "The Big Red One," served in South Vietnam from October 1965 to April 1970 and fought in most of the major battles occurring in III Corps Tactical Zone. *Source:* USMI Photo Archives

a blockade would probably not wring any concessions from Hanoi nor diminish its ability to support the war in South Vietnam. A strong American military operation directed against North Vietnamese targets would also suggest that Nixon was trying for a military victory in a war that he had promised to phase out. Nixon, with great reluctance, had to give up his plan to strike a decisive blow against the Communists. Nixon's hoped-for "savage, punishing" blow could not be found; it was, in reality, a phantasm. Discovering that military escalation would not be effective, unwilling to make concessions that would mean compromising his notion of peace with honor, and facing rising domestic opposition and impending peace demonstrations, Nixon found himself bereft of a Vietnam policy.[30] All of his secret plans for ending the war had failed.

Caught in a bind largely of his own making, Nixon could only fall back on Vietnamization, the policy he had inherited from Johnson. Having discovered that his and Kissinger's strategies could not end the war, Nixon convinced himself that Vietnamization could. The United States would withdraw its military forces from South Vietnam while continuing to provide substantial military and economic assistance to the GVN to build it up to a point where it could deflect the VC/NVA attacks and survive on its own. Nixon believed that if he could rally the American people behind him, accelerate the buildup in South Vietnam, and persuade Hanoi that

America would never abandon Thieu, then he might be able to convince North Vietnam's leaders that it would be to their advantage to negotiate an acceptable settlement with the United States in the short run, rather than have to deal with a strong South Vietnamese government in the long run.

Vietnamization was attractive to Nixon and Kissinger as their fall-back route to an honorable peace. The real-world results of Vietnamization would be three more years of war for Americans, thousands of additional U. S. battle deaths, additional multi-billion dollar expenditures, continuing domestic turmoil, and, in the end, the collapse of the South Vietnamese state and a victory for the North Vietnamese and Vietcong. En route to those tragic outcomes, Nixon's presidency would be destroyed, the second U. S. administration to fall victim to the ordeal of Vietnam.

While Nixon groped for a Vietnam War policy, liberal antiwar activists organized the Moratorium and the New Mobilization, the largest antiwar demonstrations ever staged in American history. The leadership of the Vietnam Moratorium Committee (VMC) was liberal; many of its organizers had worked for Eugene McCarthy or for Robert Kennedy during the 1968 Democratic presidential campaign. The VMC leaders like Sam Brown wanted to reach beyond the college campuses and into the cities, towns, and workplaces of America, hoping to mobilize the broadest possible coalition of antiwar citizens to get them to engage in legal and traditional protests all across the country. People were encouraged to take the day off from business as usual to discuss the war with fellow workers and what might be done to end it. Brown and his fellow organizers believed that the sheer size and variety of protests would put maximum pressure on the Nixon administration to bring the Vietnam War to a speedier conclusion. Many older liberals, leading intellectuals, and prominent dissidents supported the Moratorium. Twenty-four Democratic senators and Averill Harriman added their support to the cause. The Moratorium also had the support of most of the peace movement, except for its most militant factions.[31]

On M-Day, October 15, 1969, demonstrations occurred all over the country. Between 500,000 and 1,000,000 people participated; 100,000 citizens gathered in Boston Common to hear speeches and listen to music. In a large parade in Manhattan, Wall Street financiers walked alongside housewives, civil rights leaders, hippies, and disillusioned Vietnam veterans. Philadelphia hosted a myriad of antiwar events. The Moratorium was widely observed in the Midwest, largely ignored in the Deep South. In Denver 3,000 marchers braved falling snow and chilling winds to march on the state capital. In California, 20,000 citizens gathered on the sunny U. C. L. A. campus for a day of antiwar programs. The major Moratorium events around the country received live and generally fair media coverage. In Vietnam, groups of U. S. soldiers stationed at various sites wore black armbands to show their support for Moratorium Day. For the first time, the antiwar movement had joined the war.[32]

In between the Moratorium and the New Mobilization, scheduled for November 13–15, the Nixon administration launched its counteroffensive against its antiwar critics. The President unleashed his feisty vice president, Spiro T. Agnew. Agnew, an energetic and articulate polemicist, went on the oratorical warpath. In a series of fighting speeches, he stridently attacked administration foes. He called antiwar politicians "eunuchs" and labeled antiwar protesters "an effete corps of impudent snobs who characterize themselves as intellectuals."[33] Agnew also lambasted what he termed the "liberal establishment press," accusing the media of biased and negative coverage of Nixon administration activities and its Vietnam War policy.

Nixon followed Agnew with a major televised address to the nation the evening of November 3. It was the longest and most important speech of his presidency to date. He timed the speech so it fell midway between the Moratorium and the New Mobilization. His chief goals were to declare war on the antiwar movement and to rally the American people in support of his Vietnam War policy.

The president vigorously attacked his antiwar critics. He called them an irrational minority trying to thwart the will of the large majority of the American people. He defended U. S. intervention in Vietnam and defended the American Vietnam war. He cited the commitments to Vietnam made by three previous administrations, and he vowed to stay in Vietnam until America achieved an honorable and lasting peace. Nixon also used the speech to spell out his Vietnamization policy. He insisted that it would produce an honorable peace by enabling the South Vietnamese to save themselves while he withdrew U. S. forces and reduced American casualties. Citing the Communist mass murders at Hue during the Tet-68 campaign and the thousands of deaths in North Vietnam that had accompanied land reform during the mid-1950s as precedents, the president invoked the chilling specter of a bloodbath facing the South Vietnamese, especially the 1.5 million Catholics among them, if the U. S. precipitously pulled out its forces and left the South Vietnamese people at the mercy of the Communists. He appealed powerfully to the American people's patriotism, to their sense of honor, and to the ideal of American greatness. He concluded his speech with a stirring call for support for Vietnamization by the mass of the American people, whom he called "the great silent majority," ending with "North Vietnam cannot humiliate the United States. Only Americans can do that."[34]

Nixon's Vietnamization speech proved to be shrewd and successful. The president had regained the initiative and put his critics in the Congress, the press, and the peace movement on the defensive. Nixon had sold the American people a policy that he claimed would produce an honorable peace and save American lives. By calling attention to and labeling the "silent majority," Nixon broadened his base of support and gave millions of Americans a new political identity. Pro-Nixon rallies appeared in a number of cities. Polls taken soon after his speech showed that 77 percent of the American people supported Vietnamization. Another poll showed that by a 6:1 margin the American people agreed that antiwar demonstrations harmed prospects for peace in Vietnam.[35] Congressional and media criticism of the war waned, as many antiwar senators and Congressmen climbed aboard the Vietnamization bandwagon. Nixon, delighted with his success, boasted that he:

"had floored those liberal sons of bitches with the TV speech," and "we've got those liberal bastards on the run now; we've got them on the run and we're going to keep them on the run".[36]

Nixon and Agnew's successful counteroffensive complicated preparations for the New Mobilization. Organization was further hindered by endemic factional infighting among radical and liberal antiwar activists. Eventually a slate of various activities was scheduled to take place across the nation, November 13–15. One of the first demonstrations was the March Against Death. Marchers began near the Arlington National Cemetery, led by drummers playing a funeral roll. Marching across the Memorial Bridge solemnly, in single file, each participant carried a lighted candle and a placard inscribed with the name of one of the 45,000 American soldiers who had died in the Vietnam War. They marched to the White House; as they passed, each parader paused to shout the name of of the dead warrior inscribed on his placard. The procession then continued down Pennsylvania Avenue to the Capitol, where each marcher placed his placard in a waiting coffin and blew out the candle. For thirty-six hours, the procession wound its mournful way until all 45,000 of the dead had been honored.[37]

In addition to the March Against Death, many other antiwar activities occurred from November 13–15 as the New Mobilization unfolded. The Reverend William Sloane Coffin led an ecumenical prayer service for peace held at the National Cathedral in Washington. In San Francisco, an estimated 150,000 people paraded for peace. On Saturday, November 15, the largest protest demonstration in American history took place in the nation's capital. A huge crowd of perhaps 500,000 people gathered at the Mall. This human wave then flowed down Pennsylvania Avenue past the White House, which was barricaded by a huge circle of busses, and onto the grounds of the Washington Monument. This huge assemblage of mostly white, mostly young demonstrators appeared to pay fitful attention to a parade of speakers. The protesters were much more interested in the cast from the hit Broadway musical "Hair," who showed up to sing a medley of their songs. The highlight of the demonstration occurred when the vast assemblage joined Peter, Paul, and Mary to chant John Lennon's haunting refrain, "All we are saying/is give peace a chance." For ten or more minutes, the crowd was caught up in the hypnotic power of the chant.[38]

Despite the large numbers of participants and the spectacular events themselves, the New Mobilization appeared to have minimal impact on public opinion and none on the war policy of the Nixon administration. There was no live television coverage of the events, and the events of the New Mobilization received limited coverage on the nightly network newscasts. Public opinion polls revealed that three-fourths of Americans disapproved of the protest demonstrations. Polls also showed that 60 percent of Americans agreed with President Nixon, that antiwar demonstrations aided the enemy and made Washington's efforts to achieve peace in Vietnam more difficult.[39] Most Americans, however, frustrated and angry they might be with the war, resented antiwar demonstrators even more. Part of the popular disgust with antiwar activists was the public's yearnings for an end to controversy. After nearly a decade of upheaval, most Americans longed for a return to domestic tranquility. Many of the protesters themselves were fatigued. They were weary from too many protests of a seemingly endless war and exhausted from challenging a government that harassed, rebuked, or ignored them.

It proved to be much easier for Nixon to manipulate American public opinion by slamming the antiwar movement and by claiming that Vietnamization would produce peace with honor than for U. S. and South Vietnamese officials to turn it into an effective policy. There was some improvement in RVNAF forces in 1969 and 1970. Force levels were increased, from about 820,000 soldiers in 1968 to over 1,000,000 by 1970. They were also equipped with modern and sophisticated weapons, including M-16 rifles and more powerful artillery. Some ARVN units, when properly led, and even some district and local forces, fought effectively. The South Vietnamese air force and navy were both enhanced. Pay and conditions of service were improved for all branches of the South Vietnamese armed forces.

But the improved version of the RVNAF still had many serious problems. Systematic corruption and mass desertion persisted. Paper force levels looked impressive, but they were inflated by 15 to 20 percent because ARVN commanders padded unit rosters with the names of nonexistent soldiers to collect additional money. The ARVN generals also collected large sums of money from affluent Vietnamese, who paid bribes to avoid military service. In addition, Vietnamization required a modern South Vietnamese army. A modern army required large numbers of competent officers, experienced noncommissioned officers, and skilled people to perform a wide variety of tasks and missions. Furnishing the RVNAF with all of the officers and manpower demanded by the Vietnamization process required an elaborate network of training installations, skilled instructors, and equipment. Neither the skilled personnel nor good training facilities were available in sufficient numbers to give Vietnamization a chance to succeed. "ARVN remained an inept instrument riddled with political intrigue and corruption."[40]

Another fundamental problem plagued Vietnamization. The backbone of the ARVN was supposed to be its infantry divisions, but these divisions lacked mobility. Each division served in its home area, and most of its personnel were recruited from its home area. Often, family and dependents accompanied the soldiers into the field, resulting in hovels and tent cities that appeared alongside division cantonments. The ARVN infantry divisions were essentially static territorial units, unavailable for offensive operations or counterattacks. With soldiers' families clustered around the camps, an enemy attack guaranteed disaster, mass desertions, and incredible confusion as soldiers fled their units to help their wives and relatives to safety.[41]

Although Nixon did not realize it, Vietnamization rested on a fantasy, that these motley home guards masquerading as maneuver units could be molded into a modern strike force that would be able to hold its own against the disciplined battle-tested units of the NVA. Possibly, with enough time, at least some of the RVNAF deficiencies—its lack of capable officers and noncoms, its lack of skilled manpower, its lack of training facilities, and its lack of maneuverability—could have been corrected. However, irresistible political pressures on Nixon to end American involvement in the war guaranteed that Vietnamization could never have nearly enough time to succeed. "Vietnamization can be seen in its true light—an American self-serving illusion."[42]

During 1969 and into 1970, one aspect of nation-building appeared to be flourishing—the accelerated pacification program under the direction of William Colby, who had replaced Robert Komer as head of CORDS. General Abrams strongly backed pacification and deployed American units to help provide village security. General Thieu also enthusiastically supported many pacification programs. Additional villages and hamlets were reclaimed from the Vietcong. By the end of 1969, an estimated 80 percent of the rural population lived in secure or relatively secure areas. In many areas of South Vietnam, the threat posed by the insurgency receded. The number of Vietcong defectors, both soldiers and cadres, rose significantly. Project PHOENIX neutralized the VC infrastructure in some areas. Members of the clandestine apparatus were identified, imprisoned, often tortured during interrogations, and in many cases, killed. Both the number and quality of the VC/NVA forces appeared to decline. Many villages developed their own local governments and self-defense forces. Traditional village councils were reinstated in many locales. Roads were opened, bridges were repaired, schools were established, and hospitals were built. Thieu instituted a major land reform program called "Land to the Tiller," which reduced the size of maximum holdings and redistributed thousands of hectares of excess lands to landless peasants. New strains of livestock were introduced; peasants received tractors, steel plows, and other modern farm equipment. The rural economy improved; rice production increased in 1969 in South Vietnam, for the first time in years.[43]

But a closer look at pacification during its heyday reveals its serious shortcomings and limitations. Much of the so-called progress in various pacification programs derived from inflated or phony statistics compiled by corrupt South Vietnamese bureaucrats. Hence the numbers of villages considered under the control of the South Vietnamese government, the number of VC defectors, the number of VC infrastructure neutralized, and the number of landless peasants given land were all exaggerated. Pacification efforts from 1969 to 1970 suffered from two related problems: Most programs represented belated efforts to achieve a quick-fix. There was never enough time to implement programs designed to provide long-term solutions to fundamental problems, and there were never enough honest, competent, and committed South Vietnamese officials to make these programs work. Pacification programs were always vitiated by the corruption and incompetence that riddled the South Vietnamese bureaucracies.[44]

On the battlefield, the scale and intensity of fighting declined during 1969. Because Hanoi continued its defensive protracted war strategy and deliberately avoided large-scale combat, General Abrams assigned more of his forces to the tasks of pacification and to the support, training, and advisory missions involved in preparing the RVNAF forces to take over responsibility for defending themselves. The MACV commander also dismantled his divisions, breaking them down into small platoon and company-sized task forces to assign them patrol, reconnaissance, and territorial security missions. He ordered small-scale offensives mounted against enemy basing areas near the DMZ and along the Laotian and Cambodian borders. These offensives attacked NVA supply depots and supply lines; their objective was to attrite the enemy's logistics system and thereby keep them on the defensive.

General Abrams succeeded in uniting the disparate dimensions of the U. S. war effort in Vietnam. He fused the war of attrition, previously a big-unit war aimed at destroying enemy bases and personnel, with Vietnamization and nation-building. For the first time since the American war in Vietnam had begun, U. S. forces implemented an integrated strategy. They were fighting one war now instead of two.[45]

Most of the fighting in the Vietnam War after 1969 consisted of small-unit combat occurring in the more remote and sparsely populated regions of South Vietnam, involving South Vietnamese and North Vietnamese forces. Because they retained the tactical initiative, the NVA forces usually controlled the scale and tempo of the fighting. They initiated most of the combat and usually inflicted heavier casualties on the South Vietnamese forces than they incurred. American battle deaths decreased sharply in 1969; however, RVNAF casualties remained high.[46]

One of the most notorious battles of the American Vietnam War occurred in late spring 1969. It has passed into history as the Battle of Hamburger Hill, a name appar-

Figure 8.4   A U. S. Army rifle company moves through defense forest cover. Much of the fighting in Vietnam involved small unit warfare-intense firefights that suddenly erupted when enemy squads made contact. *Source:* USMI Photo Archives

ently provided by the soldiers who had to fight it. In March, the MACV intelligence officers had noted that the NVA forces were again building up their logistics systems in the forbidding A Shau Valley, ostensibly preparing for offensive operations in I Corps. General Zais's "Screaming Eagles," the 101st Airborne (Air Mobile), were ordered back into the area to destroy them. During April and early May, soldiers from units of the 101st that had been helilifted into the A Shau Valley found several new supply caches and other evidence of a PAVN logistical buildup taking place in the area.[47]

On May 10, a combined force of U. S. Marines, an ARVN regiment, and the 101st Airborne's 3rd Brigade, 187th Infantry, air assaulted into a rugged area of thickly jungled mountains along the west side of the A Shau Valley near the Laotian border. The next day, soldiers in B Company of the 187th Infantry discovered that the NVA forces had fortified a series of ridges cloaked in thick jungle. These ridges appeared on American maps as Hill 937. Hill 937 was known to the Vietnamese as Dong Ap Bia (Mount Ap Bia). As B Company troops advanced up the slopes of Dong Ap Bia, they were hit by concentrated machine-gun fire coming from enemy bunkers dug into the crests of the montane ridges. B Company was forced to withdraw; artillery and air strikes were called in to pound the NVA positions. Thus began a fierce ten-day battle for Dong Ap Bia, which the world would soon know as Hamburger Hill.[48]

On May 13, two companies of the 187th's 1st Battalion tried to take the hill, only to be driven back by withering rocket and machine-gun fire from the bunker occupants, two battalions of the 29th NVA Regiment. The men of the 187th were reinforced, and they attacked again, only to be driven back once more. There was a pause in the fighting while the enemy bunkers were subjected to intensive artillery fire and air strikes for thirty-six hours. On May 18, two battalions made another assault of the hill, one going up the southern slope, the other up the northern slope. The weather halted this attack. Heavy rains had turned the hillside, denuded of foliage by the artillery fire and air attacks, into mud; the soldiers, as they tried to advance up the mountain, kept slipping and sliding back down the slopes. Finally, on May 20, following another sustained artillery and air bombardment of the enemy positions, a four-battalion force reached the crest of Dong Ap Bia, only to discover that the NVA troops had abandoned the bunkers during the night. A few days after the hill had been taken, orders came down to abandon it because it had no tactical or operational significance.

The Battle of Hamburger Hill received extensive press coverage and quickly ignited public controversy. The men of the 101st had fought hard and taken heavy casualties for an objective that was quickly abandoned. Many troopers bitterly criticized the command decision that had required the seemingly pointless sacrifice of many men. Journalists vetted the soldier's complaints. Senator Edward Kennedy of Massachusetts called the battle "senseless and irresponsible."[49] General Zais defended the action; he stated that the 101st Airborne's mission had been to seek out the enemy and destroy them wherever they found them. Zais pointed out that the enemy had lost an estimated 650 KIA during the ten-day fight, whereas U. S. battle deaths at Dong Ap Bia totalled fifty-six, a kill ratio of better than ten to one.[50]

Hamburger Hill turned out to be the last campaign of the now-abandoned attrition strategy, and it was also the last battle of the Vietnam War in which victory was determined by a body count. In reaction to the controversy aroused by the battle, President Nixon ordered General Abrams to hold down American casualties in future battles. At the heart of the controversy over Hamburger Hill were not so much questions of tactics or casualties, but of what kind of war Americans were now waging in Vietnam and for what goals. The conflict was no longer a war of search and destroy, of attrition. It had mutated into a war based on a new strategy of small-unit warfare aimed at destroying enemy logistics systems, fused with pacification and nation-building efforts. The Battle of Hamburger Hill had occurred during the transitional period. Shortly after the controversial battle, President Nixon announced the first U. S. troop withdrawals from the Vietnam War.

AN ARMY IN DECLINE

"Not only were American troops leaving South Vietnam, but the offensive spirit was leaving the American army."[51] The bitterness expressed by some of the soldiers of the 101st Airborne over the fighting at Dong Ap Bia was a sign that America was beginning to reap a pernicious harvest from its lengthy and inconclusive war in Southeast Asia—the progressive demoralization of the U. S. Army ground forces serving in Vietnam. Until 1968, the U. S. armed forces in Vietnam had fought well. The Army that America sent to fight the Vietnam War was the best the nation ever had and was undoubtedly the best army in the world. The troops were the strongest and healthiest, the most intelligent, the best-educated, and the best-trained in U. S. military history. They were equipped with powerful and effective high-tech weapons, and they were supported by a remarkable logistics system that made them the best-fed and best-supplied soldiers in the history of warfare. Wounded soldiers received better medical treatment quicker than any soldiers who had ever fought a war. They were led by competent professionals at all levels, from sergeants to generals. Troops fought aggressively, with great tenacity, in pursuit of their objectives. Their morale was high, their discipline taut. They believed in the cause for which they fought, and they remained confident of victory. They won every major battle they fought, and they nearly always inflicted far heavier casualties on their enemies than they sustained.

The decline of the American Army that began in 1968 and got progressively worse in 1969, 1970, and 1971 was caused by a multiplicity of factors and circumstances.[52] Nixon's Vietnamization policy was a major cause of the breakdown in morale and discipline. The president emphasized his commitment to seeking a negotiated peace, of not trying to win a military victory. U. S. troop withdrawals reinforced the notion that America was pursuing a no-win policy in a war that would probably end soon for the United States. Soldiers began asking themselves, Why fight? Why get

Figure 8.5   Air assault troopers of the elite 101st Airborne "Screaming Eagles" debarking their helicopter at a landing zone in the A Shau Valley in May 1969. *Source:* USMI Photo Archives

wounded or killed in a war that Washington is not trying to win? A sardonic rhetorical question gained wide currency after 1969: Who wants to be the last soldier to die in Vietnam? As American troops were being pulled out of Vietnam, many soldiers cared only about surviving their year in "'Nam" and returning to the "real world" (the United States) alive. "Short-timer's fever," especially among soldiers with a few weeks to go on their year's tour, became widespread by 1969. Its symptoms included an acute fear of being killed or seriously wounded, a reluctance to engage in combat, a generally poor performance of all duties, a rebellious attitude toward military authority, and withdrawal from social activities with buddies. Short-timers were obsessed with trying to survive their final few weeks in Vietnam.

By 1969, the class-biased Selective Service had delivered an army of conscripts to Vietnam, who were plucked mainly from working-class and disadvantaged backgrounds. The fact that most middle-class youths were avoiding the war was itself a source of resentment and declining morale among the troops in the field. The soldiers manning rifle companies in Vietnam understood that the price they were paying for being poor, poorly educated, without employable skills, and possessing no influence or political clout was having to fight a war that most of their more affluent countrymen were avoiding, that a majority of the American people no longer believed in, and that their government no longer was trying to win.[53]

By 1969, the quality of both the officer and noncommissioned officer corps had declined. In 1965, the officer corps had been made up mainly of career professionals and Reserve Officer Training Corps (ROTC) graduates. The unpopularity of the Vietnam War caused a severe reduction in ROTC enrollments, and, by 1969, dozens of ROTC programs had been expelled from college campuses. To make up the shortages, the Army was forced to turn to Officer Candidate School (OCS) products, who generally possessed lower educational attainments and leadership abilities.

The noncommissioned officer corps had severe shortages of experienced sergeants by 1969. Promising young privates were hurried through twenty weeks of stateside advanced training and given sergeants' stripes. These young, inexperienced buck and staff sergeants, called "Instant NCOs" or "shake n' bakes," were then rushed to Vietnam and thrown into combat. Platoons of "grunts" (the most frequently used nickname that Army and Marine combat infantrymen gave themselves), sometimes found themselves going into combat led by twenty-two-year-old second lieutenants who were just out of OCS and inexperienced twenty-year-old "shake n' bake" sergeants who had just arrived from stateside.[54]

Army personnel practices during the Vietnam War era exacerbated problems created by assigning young and inexperienced officers and noncoms to combat units and undermined unit cohesion. The Army wanted to build up a large pool of officers with combat experience; captains and majors were given six-month tours as company and battalion commanders. Many of these inexperienced officers proved to be ineffective leaders in combat; sometimes their mistakes cost soldiers fighting under their commands their lives. Just about the time these officers had acquired battlefield experience and were becoming effective leaders, their six-months' tour of duty had expired and they were shipped back to the States. Because of the constant turnover in the company and battalion commander positions, there was an instability in these critical leadership positions. Worse, some of these officers were concerned only with advancing their careers, with "getting their tickets punched." These officers did not care about the welfare of the men they were assigned to lead. When ordering the men under their commands to fight, they hovered over the battlefield in command helicopters, safely above the fray. Soldiers sometimes refused to put their lives on the line for such uncaring and unprofessional officers whose principal combat goal appeared to be compiling a good dossier.[55]

The growing unpopularity of the war and the activities of antiwar protesters also undermined the morale of soldiers serving in Vietnam. Grunts loathed college antiwar protesters, viewing them as a privileged class of cowards and traitors. But the knowledge that millions of Americans no longer believed in the war or supported it with any enthusiasm caused resentment and confusion among many troops, who came to doubt the purpose of the war and whether the sacrifices they were making were worthwhile or even appreciated. They felt abandoned by a nation that was abandoning the war that they still had to fight. By 1969, some soldiers serving in Vietnam had turned against the war and wore the symbols of the stateside antiwar protesters—love beads and peace medallions—on their uniforms. Some soldiers grew their hair long and sprouted full beards, in violation of military dress and appearance codes that increasingly went unenforced in the field. Soldiers sometimes saluted one another with the two-fingered peace sign.[56]

The Army's switch from aggressive big-unit search-and-destroy missions to small-scale holding actions in support of Vietnamization and pacification in 1969 also undermined soldiers' morale and discipline. They grew reluctant to expose themselves to danger on operations they knew were only intended to buy time until the South Vietnamese took over and the Americans went home. The war became not just unfinished business, but unfinishable business, therefore, to be avoided whenever possible. "Search-and-evade" operations were added to the tactical repertoires of squads and platoons. Soldiers sent on patrols were careful to search only areas where they knew the enemy would not be found. Sometimes they did not patrol at all, and they filed a faked report of a search that never took place. Combat refusals increased in 1969 and became more frequent in 1970 and 1971.[57] The cumbersome and overloaded military justice system could not handle the increasing incidence of combat refusals in Vietnam. Punishment for refusing a lawful order to fight was often left to field commanders, who in many cases meted out light punishments or ignored the incidents.

From 1969 on, the U. S. Army appeared to be at war with itself. As morale and discipline ebbed, as search-and-avoid tactics and combat refusals increased in frequency, both officers and noncoms who took an aggressive approach to combat or who enforced rules and regulations strictly risked assassination at the hands of rebellious troops. Such assassinations had occurred in previous wars, but never so frequently. A new term came into use: "fragging" (derived from fragmentation grenade, a weapon that was readily available, easy to use, and left no fingerprints or other incriminating evidence when used to kill an unpopular officer or a noncom). The Army reported ninety-six fragging incidents in 1969 and 209 incidents in 1970. In those two years, seventy-five officers and noncoms lost their lives to assassins who in most cases were never apprehended. Court martials were held in fewer than 10 percent of fragging cases because of the lack of evidence and witnesses. Most soldiers who committed fraggings in Vietnam literally got away with murder.[58]

In addition to fragging, racial violence occasionally racked military installations in Vietnam, starting in 1969. Army life in Vietnam had become a racial pressure cooker. Many African American soldiers, angry over the discrimination and prejudice they had encountered in civilian society and in the Army, often denounced white attitudes and sometimes denounced whites as well. Whites frequently replied in kind. Some black soldiers, influenced by black nationalist doctrines, developed an African American style of appearance and behavior that white officers, often southerners with traditional racial attitudes, found threatening. Racial animosity was generally suppressed in combat situations, but in rear basing areas racial enmities sometimes exploded. Race riots, even racially motivated firefights, occurred.[59] Black-white racial conflict was a social pathology that the Army inherited from the American society it served. Racial tensions in Vietnam were exacerbated after 1968 by the pressures generated within an army that was trying to fight a war that it was not allowed to win, one that was afflicted with serious internal problems.

Desertion was another indicator of declining morale and discipline. Thousands of Vietnam-era soldiers deserted in 1969, 1970, and 1971. Desertions were comparatively rare in combat areas, and very few American soldiers defected to the enemy. Neither the Vietcong nor the NVA forces encouraged Americans to desert, nor did either usually offer deserters sanctuary.[60] The Communists wanted the Americans to get out of their country, not to join them.

But for every soldier who deserted, many more troops tried to escape through psychological withdrawal, by using drugs. By 1969, drug abuse had become a serious problem for the Army in Vietnam. A Defense Department survey conducted in 1969 found that about 25 percent of U. S. soldiers serving in Vietnam were using marijuana.[61] Far worse, U. S. troops began using hard drugs in late 1969 and early 1970, particularly heroin. The heroin came from the mountainous region stretching across northern Laos, northern Thailand, and northeastern Burma, known as the Golden Triangle.[62] High-grade heroin, 80 to 90 percent pure, flowed into South Vietnam via illicit conduits controlled by high officials in the South Vietnamese government. These officials garnered huge profits from selling the severely addictive drug to American GIs. U. S. officials tacitly accepted the South Vietnamese officials' involvement in drug operations, refusing to investigate them or to make any effort to get them to curtail the drug trade. South Vietnamese pushers aggressively sold the nearly pure heroin to soldiers for $2.00 to $3.00 a vial, a fraction of the price that diluted heroin sold for on the streets in American cities. By 1970, an estimated 7 percent of U. S. soldiers in Vietnam used heroin regularly; by 1971, between 10 and 15 percent. The Army discovered to its dismay in 1971 that it had a heroin plague on its hands, with an estimated 25,000 to 37,000 addicted users.[63]

The gleaming American sword, honed to a keen edge, which had been thrust into South Vietnam in 1965, had become dull and corroded by 1971. The confusions inherent in Nixon's Vietnamization policy, the class-biased conscription system, the decline in the quality of officers and noncommissioned officers, dubious Army personnel policies, the antiwar movement and declining domestic public support for the war, racial tensions, and the contagion of drug use had combined to undermine morale, erode discipline, and sap the Army's fighting spirit. Other branches of the U. S. Armed Forces serving in Southeast Asia—the Navy, the Air Force, the Marines, and the Coast Guard also suffered similar problems of declining discipline and morale, racial conflict, and drug abuse, but on much smaller scales. One of the reasons Nixon accelerated the recall of U. S. forces from Vietnam in 1970 and 1971, over the protests of General Abrams and General Thieu, was because of his awareness that the fighting machine in

South Vietnam was disintegrating. It became necessary to remove the Army in order to save it.

WIDENING THE WAR: CAMBODIA

During the spring of 1970, Nixon had to confront the contradictions inherent in his Vietnam War strategy. At home he faced declining popular support for his policies, rising Congressional opposition, and more peace demonstrations. Negotiations in Paris remained sterile. Vietnamization proceeded slowly. To appease domestic dissent, Nixon announced a phased withdrawal of 150,000 troops from Vietnam over the next twelve months. Both General Abrams and General Thieu strongly protested the size of Nixon's proposed troop withdrawal. They insisted it would leave the RVN vulnerable to VC/NVA attacks and that it would retard both Vietnamization and nation-building. The Vietnamese were not consulted, either for planning or implementing Vietnamization. Although President Nixon publicly announced that General Thieu had recommended the proposed U. S. troop withdrawals, Thieu had strongly opposed them. The South Vietnamese leaders, having no choice, reluctantly went along with Vietnamization; they saw it for what it was,

> a political expedient for the United States. Some Vietnamese dismissed Vietnamization as a U. S. Dollar and Vietnamese Blood Sharing Plan. Most saw it as a fig leaf to cover U. S. abandonment.[64]

Both Nixon and Kissinger also knew that accelerated American troop withdrawals could only stiffen Hanoi's resolve to make no concessions at Paris and to wait until all of the Americans had been forced to leave South Vietnam. On the battlefield, the NVA continued their patient defensive strategy of protracted small-scale warfare. Only when most Americans had departed would General Giap shift to the offensive and move in to destroy the South Vietnamese forces and eliminate the Saigon government.

But an event occurred that caught both Washington and Hanoi by surprise, changing the shape of the Vietnam War. The neutralist leader of Cambodia, Prince Norodom Sihanouk, was overthrown by his pro-Western Prime Minister General Lon Nol on March 18, 1970. For years, Sihanouk had attempted to keep Cambodia at peace by playing the Chinese Communists and the North Vietnamese off against the Americans and the South Vietnamese. He rejected American offers of military aid and severed diplomatic relations with the United States in 1965. He had allowed the NVA to establish bases in the Cambodian provinces bordering South Vietnam, and he had also granted Hanoi the use of the port of Sihanoukville from which they supplied their forces fighting in the southern half of South Vietnam. In exchange for these privileges, the North Vietnamese looked the other way when Sihanouk used his army to suppress brutally an indigenous Communist insurgency called the Khmer Rouge.

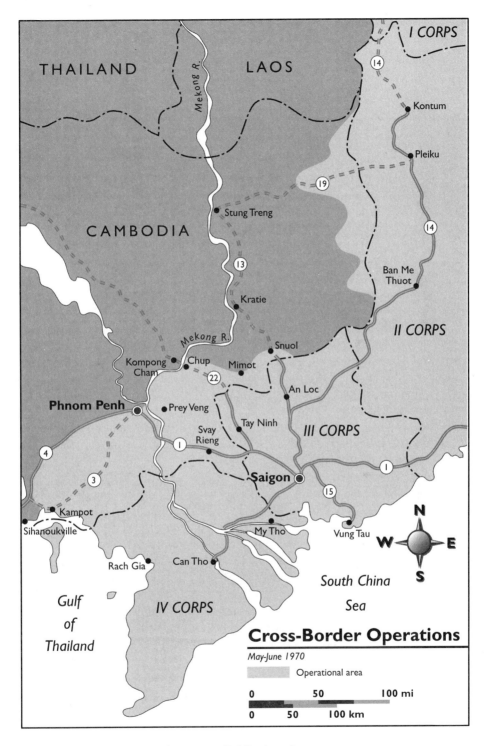

Figure 8.6 Public domain map.

Sihanouk had allowed American and ARVN forces on occasion to pursue fleeing VC/NVA forces into Cambodia. Sihanouk also tolerated the secret American bombing of the NVA bases and sanctuaries in Cambodia that Nixon initiated in March 1969.[65] For years, the Cambodian leader had been able to spare his country and its people from the conflict by accommodating both sides. But with Sihanouk's overthrow, Cambodia's delicate charade of neutrality would soon be replaced by murderous involvement in war.

Although caught by surprise, Nixon and Kissinger welcomed the overthrow of Sihanouk, whose behavior had become increasingly erratic; also, Sihanouk's control of events had slipped, and his neutrality policy appeared to be increasingly anti-American in tone. Washington quickly recognized the Lon Nol government and extended American military and economic assistance to Cambodia. The United States also approved South Vietnamese cross-border raids into Cambodia. Lon Nol barred Hanoi from further access to the port of Sihanoukville, and he ordered the Communists to vacate their bases on Cambodian soil and to get out of his country.

Determined to stay in regions that were crucial to its conduct of its war in South Vietnam, Hanoi promptly sent the NVA forces in Cambodia on a drive to the west in the direction of Phnom Penh, the Cambodian capital, to overthrow the Lon Nol government. A CIA report to President Nixon warned that the Communist forces could overthrow the new Cambodian regime; without strong American action, a domino might fall in Southeast Asia. With Cambodia in Communist hands, the port at Sihanoukville would be reopened and the entire country would become an enemy basing area outflanking the Allied forces in South Vietnam. "The United States had to intervene in Cambodia decisively or see the war change dramatically for the worse."[66]

The deposed Sihanouk quickly cast his lot with the Communists. From Peking, he called for the overthrow of Lon Nol's "illegal" regime, for a Pathet Lao victory in Laos, and for a VC/NVA victory in South Vietnam. China backed Sihanouk's new movement. In Paris, Kissinger met privately with Le Duc Tho, a member of the North Vietnamese Politburo who had replaced Xuan Thuy as Hanoi's chief negotiator in the secret talks. In conversations with Kissinger, Le Duc Tho made it clear that Hanoi had linked the overthrow of Lon Nol's government with the ongoing revolutionary war in South Vietnam. Within Cambodia, to enhance their campaign to overthrow the Lon Nol government, China and Hanoi backed the Khmer Rouge, which had revived in the late 1960s following Sihanouk's efforts to suppress it. The Khmer Rouge, armed and trained by the North Vietnamese, would overthrow Lon Nol's government in the spring of 1975.[67]

Reacting to the widening war, Nixon believed that the time had come to make a decisive move in Indochina. For years, MACV, backed by the Joint Chiefs, had called for ground invasions of Cambodia to destroy the VC/NVA border sanctuaries. Nixon decided that it was now time to hit them. Two areas were targeted for attack: the Parrot's Beak, a section of Cambodian land that jutted into South

Vietnam to a point only thirty miles west of Saigon, and the Fishhook, a point of land lying fifty-five miles northwest of Saigon. The president approved General Abrams' proposal that American forces attack the Fishhook area, while the ARVN forces, supported by American air strikes, attacked the sanctuaries in the Parrot's Beak.[68]

Nixon's decision to send U. S. forces into Cambodia was one of the most controversial actions of his presidency. He sent in the troops to serve a variety of military, political, and diplomatic purposes. They would shore up Lon Nol's regime and help keep Cambodia out of Communist hands. They would buy more time for Vietnamization to work in South Vietnam. Nixon decided that the strategic advantages to be gained from the Cambodian incursion outweighed its political liabilities, particularly the domestic controversy he anticipated would be aroused by the action. He also hoped the invasion would put pressure on Hanoi to consider negotiations as an alternative to facing a wider war.

Nixon also placed the Cambodian crisis in a larger context. He saw it as one of those decisive moments in the Cold War, when the will and character of the American people and its leaders were being tested by events and by their enemies. Nixon vowed to meet the challenge; he would show his mettle in the ongoing struggle between the Communist world and the free world. It was time for the big play that might bring victory in the big game. He would yield neither to domestic critics nor to foreign adversaries. Nixon was determined to maintain American credibility with both U. S. friends and foes.[69]

Nixon announced his decision to invade Cambodia, and he explained the reasons for the incursion in a televised speech given to the American people on the evening of April 30. He stated that the invasion did not represent a change in American policy or direction, that it was not an effort to widen the war; rather, it was to protect and facilitate Vietnamization. Nixon claimed the invasion was necessary to save a friendly government from Communist aggression and that it was necessary to protect American forces still remaining in South Vietnam after the scheduled withdrawal of another 150,000 troops. He also told Americans that one of the major reasons for the invasion was to capture COSVN, the PLAF command center for South Vietnam, located in the Fishhook area. Nixon's tone throughout his speech was belligerent and provocative. In a fighting mood, he defied his critics in the press, the academies, and the Congress:

> I would rather be a one-term president than be a two-term president at the cost of seeing America . . . accept the first defeat in its proud 190-years' history.

He concluded his speech with some vintage Nixonian Cold War hyperbole:

> If, when the chips are down, the world's most powerful nation acts like a pitiful, helpless giant, the forces of totalitarianism and anarchy will threaten free nations and free institutions throughout the world.[70]

Figure 8.7 The helicopter war: The Vietnam War was the first in which helicopters were used extensively to airlift men into combat. Here, riflemen of the 25th Infantry Division prepare to board a squadron of "Hueys" (Bell UH-1Ds) for an assault on Communist positions. *Source:* U. S. Army photo

As the MACV staffers planned the Cambodian campaigns to destroy the enemy bases in the areas of the Fishhook and Parrot's Beak, and any enemy troops that might try to defend them, they knew that many American combat units had already redeployed to the United States or were scheduled to be redeployed soon. The Cambodian incursion would be the last opportunity for the Allies to mount a large-scale combat operation involving American assets. It would also put the ARVN units to the ultimate test of combat against enemy forces on a foreign battlefield. The Cambodian invasion would therefore furnish an excellent opportunity to measure the progress that Vietnamization had achieved to date.[71]

On April 29, 1970, the ARVN forces, with American air and artillery support, penetrated the Parrot's Beak area. They captured some enemy supplies, but the enemy forces in the region eluded the invaders. They did not engage the enemy in much intensive combat. On May 1, following artillery barrages and heavy bombing by B-52s, a task force of 15,000 U. S. and ARVN armored and infantry battalions entered the Fishhook region accompanied by helicopter gunships and fighter-bomber strike aircraft. The operation was code-named TOAN THANG 43. It was the largest tactical operation involving U. S. forces in over a year. The fighting was not intensive, because the VC/NVA forces chose to abandon their bases and supply depots in the region rather than stand and fight against overwhelming forces. Further, the American forces operated in Cambodia under tight ground rules. They had orders to travel no farther than nineteen miles beyond the Vietnamese border, and U. S. commanders had been told to keep U. S. casualties down. The Americans forces also had orders to be out of Cambodia by June 30.[72]

All American forces had withdrawn from Cambodia by June 29. Operation TOAN THANG 43 had been a tactical success. Large quantities of enemy ammunition, weapons, and rice had either been captured or destroyed. All enemy installations and basing facilities had been destroyed. The COSVN operations had been disrupted. But most of the main enemy units had avoided battle. They had retreated to the interior and survived intact.

The pressure on Lon Nol's forces had been eased, and the Cambodian army had gained time to build up its strength. An endangered domino was saved for a time, but the temporary U. S. incursion could not remove the long-run threat to Lon Nol's survival posed by the Khmer Rouge. The VC/NVA losses of men, facilities, weapons, and supplies, plus the closing of the port at Sihanoukville, probably set back their offensive timetable twelve to fifteen months. The Cambodian incursion bought time for Vietnamization, for the staged withdrawal of U. S. forces from South Vietnam, and for pacification and nation-building programs. It also put increased pressures on the Ho Chi Minh trail because it was the sole remaining source of supply for the VC/NVA forces fighting in southern South Vietnam. The Cambodian invasions also eased the danger to the remaining American forces in Vietnam. But the Allies failed to inflict a decisive defeat on the VC/NVA forces; they disrupted but did not end their use of Cambodian territory.[73]

But the tactical gains the Americans and South Vietnamese made from Toan Thang 43 were largely offset by the liabilities of a wider war in Southeast Asia. Even though Nixon had committed himself to winding down the American war in Vietnam, he had expanded the theater of military operations to include another country. Further, the United States had acquired another fragile client in Indochina, Lon Nol's fledgling government, and Nixon committed significant American economic and military resources to help Cambodia defend itself against the VC/NVA and Khmer Rouge attacks, at the same time he was pulling American forces out of South Vietnam. The American Vietnam War had been expanded; it had become the Second Indochina War. It now encompassed Vietnam, Laos, and Cambodia.

Although American aviators and armored units involved in the Cambodian incursion had fought aggressively when they had the opportunity, some American infantry companies indulged in search-and-evade tactics to avoid combat during TOAN THANG 43. One company briefly refused a direct order from its commanding officer to march down a road thought to be infested with enemy soldiers. Most ARVN units involved in the Cambodian incursions performed poorly. They failed to fight aggressively. Their armored units developed severe maintenance problems because they lacked competent maintenance personnel and sufficient spare parts. They had persistent command and control problems. For example, they failed to coordinate artillery fire with their mobile operations and had to rely on American artillery. Further, any improved ARVN performance was premised on having strong U. S. air support, support that they were not always going to have. Insofar as the Cambodia operation had been a test of Vietnamization, ARVN flunked the test. That failure had ominous implications for the future survival of South Vietnam after all of the Americans had departed and the GVN would have to face its foes alone.[74]

In addition to its many consequences for the Indochina War, the Cambodian incursion had many domestic impacts. It accentuated the growing dissatisfaction with the pace of U. S. troop withdrawals, aroused mistrust of the Nixon administration, brought into the open the latent issue of executive authority to make war, and triggered waves of demonstrations that reverberated for months.[75] Antiwar activists took to the streets, and scores of college campuses from Maryland to California erupted in demonstrations, all protesting the sudden widening of a war that the president had promised to phase out quickly. On May 2, radical students at Yale issued a call for a nationwide student strike to demand an immediate U. S. withdrawal from Vietnam. Two days later, Ohio national guardsmen fired into a crowd of protesting students at Kent State University, killing four and wounding thirteen. The killings ignited anger and intensified the anguish over the war and its domestic effects. Within days of the shootings, more than a million college students walked out of their classes and shut down about one-fifth of the nation's campuses. Governor Ronald Reagan ordered the multi-campus University of California system to close for a week. Nearly half of the nation's colleges and universities recorded protests. The Cambodian invasion, coupled with the killings on the Kent State campus, had provoked the most massive protests in the history of American higher education.[76]

Aroused by the Cambodian incursion and the killings at Kent State, on May 8, more than 100,000 young protesters descended on the nation's capital. Antiwar rallies occurred in other cities. Twenty-four ROTC buildings on various campuses were either bombed or torched. Anti-draft actions commonly occurred at various Selective Service sites. Bombs were set off at various federal government installations and military recruitment centers. A bank in Isla Vista, a suburban community near the Santa Barbara branch of the University of California, was burned to the ground. An Army research center on the campus of the University of Wisconsin was bombed.[77] These random terrorist acts represented a kind of chaotic guerrilla warfare being waged against the American war machine by campus-based radicals.

The outbreak of antiwar opposition during May 1970 provoked a backlash among supporters of the administration's war policy. On May 8, construction workers in New York City attacked antiwar demonstrators in New York's financial district. Two weeks later, an estimated 100,000 construction workers and white-collar officer workers staged a march through Manhattan in support of President Nixon and his war policy. The "hard hats" waved American flags and sang "God Bless America" as they strode along the streets of New York. Nixon's "silent majority" was no longer silent. Trade unionists in other cities organized rallies and parades in support of the war. A

Figure 8.8   Tragedy struck at Kent State University on May 4, 1970. Troops of the Ohio National Guard fired into a crowd of student protesters, killing four. In this photo, students attend to one of their fallen classmates. *Source:* National Archives

grateful president held a well-publicized meeting at the White House with union leaders who were supportive of Washington's war policies. This eruption of pro-war support revealed the class divisions among Americans created by the Indochina War. Antiwar activists were recruited from the ranks of the educated middle classes.[78] Pro-war activists came from the ranks of the hard hats, from men who embraced traditional patriotic ideals and moral values. It pitted those who worked with their hands against those who worked with their minds, the proletariats against the professionals, or aspiring professionals. Ironically, the sons and daughters of the Establishment were turning against the war, while the working classes continued to support it.

The Cambodian invasion also provoked dissent within the Nixon administration and an outburst of Congressional criticism. For the first time, it appeared that Congress might seriously challenge Nixon's power to wage war in Indochina. Content since the rise of the Cold War to let presidents control foreign and strategic policy, the Senate, the more dovish branch of Congress, voted to repeal the Gulf of Tonkin resolution, which had been enacted in August 1964. Many senators believed the resolution had served as a retroactive declaration of war. The Senate's gesture was purely symbolic, however. President Nixon claimed he possessed the authority to wage war based on the war powers clause of the Constitution, and no one challenged him. The Senate also enacted the Church-Cooper amendment, which cut off all funding for military operations in Cambodia, effective on June 30, 1970.[79] The House of Representatives failed to enact the Church-Cooper amendment; hence, it never became law. Republican Senator Mark Hatfield and his Democratic colleague George McGovern introduced an amendment to a military appropriations bill that would have cut off all funding for U. S. military operations in Indochina at the end of the year. It also failed to pass. None of these Congressional actions in 1970 seriously impeded the president's power to wage war, but as harbingers of rising Congressional opposition, these actions increased the pressure on Nixon and Kissinger to find a way to phase out the American war in Indochina or risk having Congress slowly, clumsily, even ambivalently, end it for them.[80]

Nixon was neither inclined toward nor capable of reconciling his critics. Instead, he attacked them—hard. He called the student protesters "bums who were blowing up college campuses." He accused his Congressional critics of prolonging the war and told them that if they restricted his war-making powers, they would be responsible for an American defeat in Indochina. Nixon empowered the FBI, the CIA, and military intelligence agencies to use illegal surveillance techniques against radical antiwar groups.[81] By the summer of 1970, the Nixon White House was exhibiting many of the attributes of a beleaguered fortress. The president and the president's men increasingly held the partisan and perhaps paranoiac view that it was them against all of the administration's enemies in the press, the Congress, the universities, and the antiwar movement who were trying to undermine Nixon's policies and his power to govern. The siege mentality that led to Watergate and the eventual self-destruction of the Nixon presidency had taken root in the White House.

As the embattled president confronted the firestorm of protest provoked by the Cambodian incursion, any hope that he may have held out for breaking the diplomatic deadlock at Paris was dashed. If the Cambodian operation had been intended to pressure the North Vietnamese into making concessions, then it had the precisely opposite effect of hardening Hanoi's position. The North Vietnamese and NLF delegates walked out of the Paris talks in protest over the American invasion of Cambodia and refused to return until all U. S. troops were pulled out of Cambodia. Le Duc Tho broke off the secret talks with Henry Kissinger. Nixon's announced withdrawal of 150,000 more American forces in April, coupled with the uproar provoked in the United States by the Cambodian incursion, strengthened Hanoi's determination to continue stalling the negotiations until domestic political pressures forced Nixon to withdraw all U. S. forces from Indochina. Kissinger offered another peace proposal at Paris, a cease-fire in place, to try to move the talks forward, but Hanoi promptly rejected it.[82] The talks remained deadlocked.

As the fall 1970 midterm elections approached, Nixon campaigned energetically against his Democratic Congressional critics and denounced the antiwar protesters wherever he campaigned. The hard-pressed Administration viewed the elections as an opportunity to rally support for Vietnamization and defeat many of Nixon's prominent dovish Congressional critics. Nixon hoped to replace the doves with new people who

Figure 8.9   Hard hats on the march: Construction workers in New York City demonstrating in support of the Cambodian incursion in May 1970. Their patriotic show of support was provoked by the many college-based protests against the invasion during that troubled spring. *Source:* National Archives

would support his policies. Vice President Agnew also took to the hustings to campaign against the Nixon administration's political opponents. During the two weeks that he actively campaigned, Nixon repeatedly attacked the radical antiwar demonstrators. At a rally in San Jose, California, the president, spotting a large group of young antiwar protesters in the parking lot outside of the auditorium where he had just spoken, climbed on the hood of his limousine. He extended his arms over his head, flashing the "V-for-Victory" sign. His defiant gesture provoked the crowd into jeers, and rock-throwing.[83]

But Nixon and Agnew's efforts to strengthen administrative support in Congress mostly failed. A few prominent senatorial doves lost, but so did a few hawks. There was not much change in the House of Representatives either, and what there was not good news for the Nixon White House. Of the twelve congressmen who lost their seats, ten had been administration supporters. Several newcomers to the House were

Figure 8.10   Bob Hope and troupe entertaining soldiers of the 101st Airborne on January 8, 1971. Hope and company made Christmas tours to South Vietnam every year from 1964 through 1972. *Source:* USMI Photo Archives

avowed doves, most notably Bella Absug (New York) and Ronald Dellums (California), both outspoken peace activists. The 1970 elections turned, like most elections, on many issues besides the war. Insofar as the election could be viewed as a referendum on administration war policies, the president suffered a net loss of support. Both houses of the new Congress remained overwhelmingly Democratic, and the new Congress would prove to be slightly more dovish than its predecessor.

After two years in office, after two years of fighting and diplomatic maneuvering, the man elected president on a promise to bring an end to the Vietnam War discovered to his dismay that the American position in Southeast Asia had deteriorated. Nixon's freedom of maneuver, never very great, had diminished. He could see no way to end the war any time soon on terms that accorded with his conception of peace with honor. The Paris negotiations remained tightly deadlocked. Hanoi had not budged from its positions staked out when negotiations had begun in May 1968. The United States lacked the power to drive the North Vietnamese troops out of South Vietnam, and Kissinger had found no formula that would persuade Hanoi to withdraw them. The war had also been widened. The United States was now supporting a struggling government in Cambodia that was trying to survive a mounting insurgency backed by North Vietnam and China. In South Vietnam, the RVNAF buildup was faltering. The American troop withdrawal was accelerating. Popular support for Nixon's war policy was ebbing, Congressional opposition was growing stronger, and antiwar protest had been revitalized by the Cambodian incursion. As 1970 ended, it was evident that Nixon's improvised policy of Vietnamization was not working nor did it show any promise that it ever could work.

WIDENING THE WAR: LAOS

Although it had been a manifest failure, Nixon, perhaps as much for lack of an alternative as for any other reason, adhered to his policy of Vietnamization. Early in 1971, hoping to calm his domestic critics, he announced another speedup in the timetable of U. S. troop withdrawals. Nixon's announcement drew protests both from General Thieu, who knew that Vietnamization was not working and feared its consequences, and General Abrams, who was concerned for the security of the American forces remaining in South Vietnam. In response to stepped-up NVA infiltration, Nixon also expanded the air war against the Ho Chi Minh trail complex in Laos and resumed bombing selected targets in North Vietnam, including staging areas north of the DMZ and military targets in the Hanoi-Haiphong area. He also prepared to expand the ground war once again.

The MACV and RVNAF intelligence analysts had detected a heavy stockpiling of enemy military supplies at two sites. One site was about thirty miles west of Khe Sanh, near the Laotian town of Tchepone, and the other was along the South Vietnam-Laotian border, near the northern end of the A Shau Valley. From these two bases, the NVA units could attack the two northern provinces of South Vietnam, Quang Tri and Thua Thien, and threaten the city of Hue. It was a venerable strategy that the North Vietnamese had tried many times in the past, only to be blocked each time by U. S. troops. Some of these battles had involved some of the most intense and deadliest combat of the entire war. But now, in early 1971, the Americans were leaving Military Region I (MR1—Corps Tactical Zones were renamed Military Regions in July 1970). How would the South Vietnamese high command respond to this developing threat? Rather than wait for the NVA to attack the northern provinces of their country, General Thieu and his chief of staff, General Cao Van Vien, proposed a preemptive campaign to destroy the two supply sites to relieve the enemy pressure building in the north. The MACV Commander General Abrams approved the proposed ARVN operation, as did President Nixon. Thus, Nixon approved another expansion of the Indochina War, a ground operation into Laos.

Laos, like Cambodia, was a neutral country, its neutrality formally guaranteed by the 1962 Paris Agreement. But neither side had observed that neutrality from the day it was established, and Laos's weak coalition neutralist government, headed by Prince Souvanna Phouma, could not defend the nation's territorial integrity. The struggle for power within Laos was mainly a dimension of the Vietnam War that had spilled into that hapless country. The CIA had been waging a secret war in Laos since 1963, involving Meo tribesmen. CIA officials trained and supported the Meo in their battles against the Pathet Lao. U. S. aircraft had been bombing targets along the Ho Chi Minh trail in the Laotian corridor since 1965. The Nixon administration escalated the U. S. air war against Laos in 1969. During the first two years of Nixon's presidency, U. S. bomb tonnage dropped in Laos exceeded the totals for both the Kennedy and Johnson years. The North Vietnamese had been occupying part of Laos since the Franco-Vietminh War. They also supported and trained the Pathet Lao. By 1971, the NVA controlled all of the Laotian territory adjoining their own country and occupied the entire Laotian corridor, from which they had expelled the native Laotians, using it as one huge logistics system to support their war in South Vietnam.

General Thieu's and General Vien's main objective for the operation, code-named LAM SON 719, was the destruction of enemy logistics installations and supplies at Tchepone and at a basing area near the northern end of the A Shau Valley. The operational plan also called for holding these facilities for ninety days and for interdicting the flow of supplies down the Ho Chi Minh trail, then withdrawing from Laos before the rainy season began. The South Vietnamese military leaders calculated that a successful spoiling operation in Laos, when coupled with the destruction wrought in the Cambodian sanctuaries the previous year, would keep South Vietnam free of any enemy offensives for a year and would buy additional time for Vietnamization.[84]

Two factors made LAM SON 719 unique. It was the first major tactical operation since the American war began in 1965 in which ARVN forces would have to fight without American advisers or U. S. combat units accompanying them in battle. U. S. helicopters and strike aircraft would cover the air above Laos, but on the ground, the South Vietnamese would be on their own. The LAM SON 719 operation would be another test of Vietnamization. South Vietnamese and U. S. officials would find out if the ARVN forces were ready to be weaned from their American dependency. Could they mount a successful invasion into Laos on their own?

The second factor involved the NVA. With the closing of the port at Sihanoukville, the Ho Chi Minh trail had become the jugular of Hanoi's war in South Vietnam; it was vitally important to the NVA war effort to maintain the flow of men and materiel down the trail network. Anticipating an attack at Tchepone, the hub of the Ho Chi Minh trail complex running through the Laotian corridor, General Giap had brought in an additional 20,000 well-equipped troops and bolstered their air defense, armor, and heavy artillery capabilities. Unlike the Cambodian incursion, where the VC/NVA forces fled into the interior to avoid battle with the invaders, the PAVN forces in the vicinity of Tchepone were well-equipped, ready, and waiting to fight the South Vietnamese invaders.[85]

On February 8, 1971, after preliminary actions, units of the ARVN 1st Airborne Division and 1st Armored Brigade under the command of General Hoang Xuan Lam pushed into Laos along Route 9, west of Khe Sanh. The operation encountered trouble from the outset. North Vietnamese agents placed at high levels within the RVNAF command structure had furnished complete details of the operation to the enemy forces in advance! The element of tactical surprise was completely lacking for LAM

SON 719. Then the weather turned bad, and the American aircraft could not fly their air support missions for several days.

ARVN politics also intruded to undermine LAM SON 719's chances for success. General Thieu ordered General Lam to proceed cautiously and to not take heavy casualties. Thieu gave this order because the ARVN 1st Airborne was his palace guard; they were his coup insurance. Their destruction would leave him vulnerable to overthrow by his ARVN rivals. General Lam, a poor soldier but an astute politician, obediently stopped his columns a short distance into Laos. After the ARVN offensive stopped, the powerful NVA forces attacked. Over the next two weeks, the NVA augmented its forces and inflicted mounting casualties on the ARVN forces. Worried about the fate of his palace guard, General Thieu ordered General Lam to remove the 1st Airborne from battle altogether and to replace it with an inexperienced Marine division. Thieu's removal of the 1st Airborne further weakened LAM SON 719. The South Vietnamese president, who had originally proposed the Laotian incursion, in effect, had subverted it for reasons of state. In General Thieu's hierarchy of priorities, political self-preservation ranked well ahead of any spoiling operation into Laos against the PAVN forces.[86] Because of Thieu's meddling, LAM SON 719 achieved only a fraction of its goals. The ARVN forces destroyed some enemy supply depots and disrupted NVA logistics along the Ho Chi Minh trail for perhaps a few weeks. The South Vietnamese efforts had bought a little more time for Vietnamization.

Then came the difficult part of the operation—the tactical withdrawal of the South Vietnamese forces. The RVN forces were under intense pressure from NVA infantry, tank assaults, and artillery barrages. They had to stage their withdrawal through rugged, jungle-cloaked terrain. Between 30,000 and 40,000 NVA troops pursued 8,000 inexperienced ARVN soldiers. General Giap saw an opportunity to inflict a major defeat on the South Vietnamese forces and completely discredit Vietnamization. He ordered all-out assaults on the retreating South Vietnamese.

The ARVN's tactical retreat quickly became disorderly and then turned into a rout. In some units, discipline and order collapsed as panic-stricken troops abandoned their equipment and weapons and fled on foot in the direction of the border. Only intense use of U. S. air power and heroic efforts by American helicopter pilots that together inflicted heavy casualties on the attacking NVA forces, suppressed NVA artillery fire, knocked out enemy tanks, hauled in ammunition, and hauled out ARVN troops, kept the headlong retreat from becoming a debacle. Because of the extraordinary U. S. effort, remnants of the thoroughly demoralized ARVN forces were able to return to South Vietnam. Altogether, during operation LAM SON 719, 108 American helicopters were lost and another 618 were damaged. Eighty-nine American pilots and air crewmen were either killed or reported missing in action, and another 178 were wounded.[87]

The LAM SON 719 operation proved to be a dismal and dispiriting failure for the ARVN soldiers. The American media generally portrayed the Laotian incursion as a disaster. Television cameras showed American viewers images of panicky ARVN soldiers straggling back to South Vietnam territory. Reacting to yet another widening of the Indochina War, several senators introduced resolutions aimed at limiting presidential power to conduct military operations in Indochina and cutting off all funds for operations in Cambodia and Laos. None of them passed. "The operation revealed the inherent and incurable flaws of the RVNAF, which doomed any realistic hopes of successful Vietnamization."[88] These flaws included (1) the hopeless incompetence of the ARVN's politicized leadership, starting at the top with General Thieu; (2) the continuing inability of the static home-guard infantry divisions to meet the demands of mobile warfare; (3) the lack of professionalism, accentuated by the lack of U. S. advisers who usually coordinated helicopter flights, artillery fire, tank-infantry operations, and air strikes for the ARVN forces; (4) serious problems with communications and maintenance; (5) basic deficiencies in training and discipline; (6) the perennial lack of a fighting spirit when facing NVA troops in intensive combat; and (7) the ARVN's continuing dependence on the American forces. All of these failures again exposed Vietnamization for the illusion that it was.[89] ARVN had flunked another test.

In a televised speech delivered on the evening of April 7, 1971, President Nixon told the American people that LAM SON 719 proved that Vietnamization had succeeded. The operation had, in fact, proven exactly the opposite: Vietnamization had not succeeded and probably would never succeed. The South Vietnamese understood that they had been defeated and understood the implications of that defeat for the future of Vietnamization, even if the president of the United States did not. In Saigon, anti-American demonstrations erupted. One poster showed Nixon standing over a pile of dead South Vietnamese soldiers, with a message that Vietnamization meant the sacrifice of South Vietnamese soldiers by the United States.[90]

WAR WEARINESS

Shortly after the surviving South Vietnamese forces had come reeling back from their ill-fated Laotian incursion, Nixon instructed Henry Kissinger to offer Hanoi some new proposals in Paris that the president hoped would get the stalled peace talks moving. Nixon was motivated to make his new offers by three considerations: He understood that military operations like the Cambodian and Laotian incursions were not likely to force Hanoi to negotiate. Recent talks with the Soviets had been productive. The outlines of a major arms control agreement with the Soviets had emerged from these discussions. Work on the opening to China was promising. A foundation for detente was being structured. Nixon felt, therefore, that he could afford to be more flexible with Hanoi. He also believed that his prospects for reelection in 1972 depended mainly on his ability to end the Vietnam War. But he also knew he had to avoid the appearance of rushing to make an election year settlement of the war, so his diplomatic initiative in the spring of 1971 was well-timed.

Figure 8.11   Public domain map.

Kissinger, meeting secretly with Xuan Thuy and Le Duc Tho in Paris, offered a new seven-point peace plan. The plan contained two important concessions. Kissinger offered to set a date, December 31, 1971, for the complete withdrawal of all U. S. combat forces from South Vietnam; he also indicated that America was willing to withdraw its troops without requiring a simultaneous withdrawal of North Vietnamese forces. Since the United States had been unilaterally withdrawing its troops for two years, irrespective of Hanoi's troop deployments, Kissinger's latter proposal was not so much a concession as it was simply an aligning of the U. S. negotiating position with U. S. military reality. More important, the new proposal separated the military issues from the political issues.[91] Thus, it would be possible for Washington and Hanoi to negotiate a cease-fire and to defer settlement of the major political question over which the long war was being waged—who should rule in South Vietnam—to the postwar period.

Kissinger's new proposals ignited the first serious negotiations between Washington and Hanoi since the talks had begun. Intense secret meetings between Kissinger and Le Duc Tho took place over the next three months. Tho, responding to Kissinger's concessions, offered a nine-point plan of his own. It was the first peace plan that the North Vietnamese had ever offered the Americans, and it too contained concessions. Hanoi agreed to release the American POWs by the end of 1971, simultaneously with the departure of all U. S. troops from Vietnam. Also, for the first time, Hanoi did not ask for the removal of Thieu as a precondition for negotiations, only that the United States must stop supporting the South Vietnamese leader.

In subsequent meetings, the status of the Saigon government proved to be the sticking point between Kissinger and Le Duc Tho. Hanoi insisted that Washington disavow Thieu. Nixon refused to abandon Thieu, fearing anarchy in South Vietnam if Thieu were ousted. This latest round of secret talks broke off in September when it became obvious that the impasse could not be resolved.[92] While the new proposals made by both sides had been promising indicators, neither side was yet prepared to make the sort of concessions that would be necessary to secure an end to America's involvement in the Second Indochina War.

As the latest round of secret talks ended in failure, South Vietnam was preparing to hold its presidential election as called for under the 1967 constitution. General Thieu, acutely aware that he had won the previous election with a plurality of only 35 percent, wanted to win resoundingly this time around. He also was determined to use his considerable powers of incumbency to ensure a landslide victory. Thieu clearly grasped the first principle of South Vietnamese politics: Irrespective of constitutional principles and democratic forms, the man who controls the government always wins elections.

When the 1971 electoral campaign began, General Thieu faced serious challenges from two strong rivals, General Nguyen Cao Ky and General Doung Van "Big" Minh. Both men had considerable followings, and either might have been able to defeat Thieu in a free and fair election. General Minh had a mixed following among Buddhists, southern Catholics, non-Communist intellectuals, and civilian politicians. Minh also had obtained the support of the National Liberation Front, mainly because he had called for the creation of a coalition government that would include representatives of the Provisional Revolutionary Government (PRG), which had been created by the NLF in June 1969.[93] The mercurial Air Marshal Ky, hitherto famed for his fanatical anti-Communism, staged a remarkable *volte-face*. He called for recognition of the PRG and supported negotiating an end to the war with the Communist leaders in Hanoi.

But it did not matter what Ky and Minh stood for or who supported them; Thieu used his control of the machinery of government to eliminate them from the race. The United States took a public stance of neutrality during the election. However, behind the scenes, CIA and embassy officials worked to ensure Thieu's landslide reelection. Nixon was not about to risk losing Thieu, whose reelection he saw as imperative to U. S. interests in Indochina. The election took place on October 3, 1971. In an election that Americans helped him rig, General Thieu was the only candidate. The ballots provided space only for voting yes for Thieu. Polling was supervised by Thieu's soldiers, and the votes were counted by Thieu's officials. The result: President Thieu was reelected to another four-year term as South Vietnam's president, with 94.3 percent of the vote.[94] From their cafes along Tu Do Street, the savants observed that the man they called "The Little Dictator" had gotten his mandate. But, they asked, a mandate for what?

By 1971, most Americans, regardless of their politics, had become thoroughly sick of the Indochina War and wished only that it would go away. Yet the war and its domestic consequences continued to plague the increasingly war-weary nation. In January and February 1971, Lieutenant William Calley went on trial before a military court for his part in the notorious My Lai massacre that had taken place on March 16, 1968. While Calley was on trial, the Vietnam Veterans Against the War (VVAW), meeting in Detroit, sponsored "Winter Soldier," a forum where over 100 veterans testified that they had committed, witnessed, or heard of My-Lai-type war crimes. On March 31, 1971, a military court convicted Lieutenant William Calley of mass murder for his role in the My Lai massacre and sentenced him to life imprisonment at hard labor. For once, both hawks and doves agreed on something—that Lieutenant Calley had been given a raw deal: Hawks, because they believed that no soldier should be convicted in war time for doing his duty; doves, because they believed that Calley had been a sacrificial offering to cover up the fact that many other war criminals went free. Following Calley's conviction, in the nation's capital, VVAW staged one of the most poignant demonstrations against the war. For five days in late April 1971, disillusioned veterans who had fought the Vietnam War protested against the government that continued to wage it. Many of them threw their medals, their campaign ribbons, and their insignia of rank onto the steps of the Capitol.[95] Some in wheelchairs, some missing an arm or a leg, some in tears, some in anger—all made compelling witnesses to the anguish of a controversial war that American officials appeared to be unable to either win or end.

Following the VVAW demonstrations, hundreds of thousands of antiwar demonstrators representing a variety of perspectives, interests, and tactics descended on Washington. Peace spokesmen met with Congressional leaders, urging them to take more decisive actions to end the war and to address urgent domestic social needs. In early May, thousands of militant demonstrators rampaged through the streets of the nation's capital in a quixotic effort to shut down the government of the United States because it refused to shut down the Vietnam War. Police, National Guardsmen, and federal troops prevented any major disruptions, and thousands of protesters were arrested.[96]

Not long after the spring demonstrations in Washington had subsided, another dramatic war-related issue commanded public attention. On June 13, the *New York Times* began publishing secret government documents that had been given to the newspaper by former Department of Defense officials Daniel Ellsberg and Anthony Russo. The documents were part of a massive 1967–1968 Pentagon study that had been undertaken by Ellsberg and his colleagues, at the request of Secretary of Defense Robert McNamara. These documents amounted to an in-house secret history of the long American involvement in Indochina that had resulted in the Vietnam War. Quickly dubbed the *Pentagon Papers*, their publication caused a furor as people discovered what many dovish critics had suspected all along. Readers found that President Kennedy, President Johnson, and other high officials had consistently misled the American people about their actions and intentions concerning the war. Readers also learned that it was the United States that had often escalated the war and spurned peace initiatives. Further, readers discovered that President Kennedy had supported the military coup that had overthrown and murdered Ngo Dinh Diem and his brother on November 1, 1963. Publication of the *Pentagon Papers* widened the credibility gap. Calley's trial, the antiwar demonstrations, and the revelations of the *Pentagon Papers* helped drive popular support for the Vietnam War to an all-time low. For an increasing number of Americans, the war itself was wrong. In June, a poll recorded 61 percent of respondents stating that U. S. involvement in the war was a mistake. A July poll revealed that two-thirds of Americans believed that America should continue to withdraw its troops, even if the Saigon government collapsed.[97]

Nixon had tried hard to prevent the publication of the *Pentagon Papers*. The attorney general had secured a court injunction on the grounds that their publication represented a clear and present danger to national security. But Federal Judge Gerhardt Gesell quashed the injunction and the Supreme Court sustained him. A majority on the Supreme Court could not see how publishing the papers compromised national security; they found that publication of the *Pentagon Papers* represented a clear and present danger only to the reputations of former public officials who had conceived and implemented U. S. foreign policy in Southeast Asia. Nixon, thwarted in his efforts to stop the publication of the *Pentagon Papers* through the courts, unleashed the "Plumbers" to plug government leaks and to discredit Ellsberg.

THE NGUYEN HUE OFFENSIVE

As 1972 began, both the battlefields of Vietnam and the American home front were comparatively calm. Only about 140,000 American troops remained in Vietnam, of whom no more than 20,000 constituted combat forces, and more troops would be leaving soon. American battle deaths for 1971 had totaled 1,380, the lowest for any year since the American war had begun in 1965. The air wars continued in North Vietnam, Laos, and Cambodia, but they received little coverage in the news and entailed few U. S. casualties. Aviation warfare did not appear to concern the American public in the urgent way that U. S. ground combat in South Vietnam had in years past.

On January 25, 1972, President Nixon revealed to the American public that Henry Kissinger had been meeting secretly with North Vietnamese emissaries for six months. He also told the people that the only remaining obstacle to peace in Vietnam was Hanoi's stubborn insistence that General Thieu's government would have to be eliminated before any settlement could be reached. Simultaneously, Nixon announced a new proposal: within six months of an agreement, the United States would remove all of its forces at the same time the POWs were exchanged, a cease-fire went into effect, and new elections were held in South Vietnam under international supervision. He also indicated that the PRG could participate in these elections. But even as he announced the new proposals, he vowed once again that America would never abandon Saigon.[98] North Vietnam promptly denounced the president's decision to go public with secret negotiations and repeated its demands that the United States must stop supporting Thieu and set a final date for the removal of all of its forces from Vietnam. The peace talks collapsed soon after and were put on indefinite hold.

Even though Nixon's peace proposals did not move negotiations closer to a settlement, in fact, had gotten them suspended indefinitely, they did score domestic political points with the American public at the beginning of a presidential election year, which was their prime purpose. The president called upon all Americans to unite behind his latest offer. Many prominent dovish politicians supported his peace initiative, as did much of the influential media. Public opinion polls showed increasing popular support for the president's negotiating stance. Antiwar activists, organized and unorganized, went into another lull.

Three weeks after making his latest proposals for ending the American Vietnam War, Nixon journeyed to China for his historic state visit. Upon his return to the United States, in late February, he was delighted to find that his power and prestige as a peacemaker had been greatly enhanced. He looked forward to his trip to Moscow, scheduled for late spring. President Nixon felt confident that he and Kissinger could use his trip to China and upcoming visit to the Soviet Union to link subsequent progress toward detente to Moscow's and Beijing's willingness to pressure Hanoi into negotiating an end to the war on terms that Washington could accept.

But the Indochina War was about to resume, larger than ever. General Giap was in the final stages of planning what was going to be the largest offensive operation of the war, a spring invasion of South Vietnam that Hanoi hoped might destroy the South Vietnamese armed forces, bring down the Thieu regime, and force the Americans out of Vietnam. As events unfolded that spring, neither Nixon's diplomatic initiatives nor Hanoi's offensive could accomplish their Indochina goals in 1972, "but they did bring the war into a final, devastating phase which would ultimately lead to a compromise peace."[99]

Hanoi's decision to try once again to break the military stalemate had been reached at the 19th Plenum meeting in January 1971. The North Vietnamese leaders calculated that spring 1972 would be an opportune time to launch a major offensive against South Vietnam's military forces, for several reasons: They assumed that political necessity would force President Nixon to continue to adhere to the timetable of scheduled U. S. troop withdrawals, and he would not be able to throw the remaining American combat forces into battle against the invading NVA divisions. Hanoi also viewed a successful offensive as leading to a collapse of the Saigon regime and forcing Nixon, under pressure to end the war before the November elections, to withdraw all American forces remaining in South Vietnam. A successful offensive would also represent a major defeat for the United States. Giap perceived that, in the aftermath of its demoralizing defeat in Laos, which revealed the continuing failure of Vietnamization, South Vietnam was especially vulnerable to a powerful military assault. The six members of the Politburo were all old men, all over sixty. They had spent their lives in pursuit of their dream, the reunification of their country under their leadership. The prospect of dying with the dream unfulfilled, as had been the fate of their great leader, Ho Chi Minh, filled them with dread. They were "old men in a hurry."[100]

Hanoi's decision to seek an early end to the war also represented the response of the North Vietnamese to the changing international situation. They were wary of the growing detente between the United States and the Soviet Union that would be sealed by Nixon's journey to Moscow. They worried lest the Soviets cut their military assistance or pressure them into accepting American terms for a settlement. The North Vietnamese held memories of 1954 at Geneva, when the Soviets, concerned about improving relations with Western Europe and the United States, joined with the Chinese to force Ho Chi Minh to accept the temporary partition of Vietnam that had put reunification on indefinite hold and had led to a costly war with the United States.[101]

Hanoi also was alarmed by Nixon's opening to China, signaled by his historic journey to Beijing. China was suspicious of Soviet ties with North Vietnam and viewed the United States as a counterweight to Chinese tensions with the Soviet Union. China wanted the United States to retain a presence in Southeast Asia to offset Soviet power in that region. Hanoi sensed that, in the aftermath of the Nixon visit, the Chinese wanted an end to the Indochina War that would allow South Vietnam to survive, enable the United States to maintain a presence in Indochina, and perpetuate the partition of Vietnam indefinitely.[102]

From Hanoi's vantage point, it appeared that Nixon's and Kissinger's pursuit of a new world order based on detente with the major Communist powers was about to yield Washington a major dividend: pressure emanating from both Moscow and Beijing on the North Vietnamese to negotiate an end to the Indochina War acceptable to the Americans, that is, one that would allow the continued existence of the South Vietnam state. The aged revolutionaries in Hanoi, who had been single-mindedly pursuing the goals of revolutionary nationalism since 1945, had fretful visions of another 1954 sellout at the hands of their major allies. Hence, they viewed their imminent spring offensive as being perhaps their last opportunity to win the war, bring down the Thieu government, and force a settlement on their own terms—a settlement that would force the Americans out of Indochina and pave the way for reunification of Vietnam under the rule of the Vietnamese Communist Party leaders.[103]

But during the long interval before the offensive would be ready for launching, the Communists decided to continue their small-scale protracted war strategy, the small-unit struggle for control of villages in South Vietnam. Politburo leaders conceded that the RVN pacification programs, especially land reform, had reduced the areas controlled by the PRG and that PLAF main force levels were depleted. But the Politburo leadership also knew that in the long run it was the fighting ability of the RVN forces that mattered more than their pacification programs. Once the Americans had departed, Thieu would be forced to rely on his own forces, and Lao Dong leaders were confident that their 1972 offensive would overwhelm the ARVN.[104]

The Twentieth Plenum, meeting in February 1972, approved Giap's final plans for the spring offensive, scheduled to begin in late March. Although the Communists still considered political action important, they no longer planned for a combination general offensive/general uprising a la Tet-68. Giap hoped the VC cadres could organize rural areas where he had a greater expectation of achieving military victory, but he did not expect there to be any urban risings unless the PAVN main units were in the cities in force to support them.[105]

General Giap launched the spring attacks, called the Nguyen Hue Offensive, in three successive stages, committing altogether a dozen infantry divisions supported by tank and artillery units. About 122,000 NVA soldiers, joined by thousands of Vietcong guerrillas, were committed to action. Beginning on March 30, the first wave poured across the DMZ to strike at the ARVN positions in the two northernmost provinces of Quang Tri and Thua Thien. Three of the PAVN divisions, totaling about 30,000 men, equipped with an arsenal of modern Soviet-made weaponry that included rockets, missiles, tanks, and heavy artillery, joined in the massive assaults into the northern provinces.[106]

Once again, the Allies were caught by surprise. Although their intelligence officers had been expecting a big NVA offensive, they had not learned exactly when and where the attacks would come. They also had not anticipated their size or power. The ARVN defenses in the two northern provinces had been placed in the hands of the 1st and 3rd Divisions and bore the brunt of the NVA assaults. Within a few weeks, the situation in these provinces had become critical. The PAVN forces had overrun the ARVN defensive positions and had wiped out several of their firebases. Compounding the ARVN problems, the incompetent MRI commander, the notorious General Lam of LAM SON 719 shame, ordered the 3rd Division, probably the weakest division in the RVNAF order of battle, to counterattack in the face of superior NVA forces and under terribly unfavorable tactical circumstances. They were massacred.

On May 1, the demoralized ARVN troops, accompanied by thousands of frightened family members and panic-stricken civilians, fled in headlong fashion toward the south. The NVA gunners, firing into the fleeing masses, inflicted thousands of casualties on soldiers and civilians alike. On May 1, the provincial capital, Quang Tri City, fell. The entire province lay in NVA hands.[107] The city of Hue, forty miles south of Quang Tri City, was threatened. American officials in Saigon and Washington feared that the RVN itself might collapse from the pressures generated by the all-out North Vietnamese spring offensive.

Alarmed by the success of the PAVN forces and fearing the fall of Hue and even Danang, General Thieu replaced Lam with General Ngo Quang Truong, probably the finest general in the RVN armed forces. Apolitical, thoroughly professional, and battle-seasoned, Truong was a superb leader who could have commanded troops in any army. He organized a defense for Hue and saved the city, and perhaps saved South Vietnam as well.

Following their successful defense of Hue, the South Vietnamese made retaking Quang Tri City their major military objective of the northern campaign. General Truong built up his forces and in late June launched a counterattack. The Allied assault on Quang Tri brought massive firepower to bear, including American Naval gunfire, tactical air strikes, and B-52 bombing runs. Finally, General Thieu ordered the South Vietnamese Marines to go into the city and drive out the NVA forces. After five days of fierce hand-to-hand fighting in the streets and buildings of Quang Tri, the North Vietnamese were expelled. Although extensively damaged from the bombing, shelling, and combat, Quang Tri was officially reclaimed by the South Vietnamese on September 16. An American journalist who witnessed the Battle of Quang Tri filed this description of the aftermath:

> When it was finally recaptured Quang Tri was no longer a city but a lake of shattered masonry . . . . It was another case—on a larger scale than ever before—of destroying Vietnam to save it.[108]

The second wave of the Nguyen Hue Offensive, the NVA attacks on the central front, began in early April. Two NVA divisions penetrated the central highlands at Dak To and Tan Canh. Within a few weeks, they had beaten the ARVN defenders and had begun a series of attacks on Kontum City. At the same time the NVA forces attacked

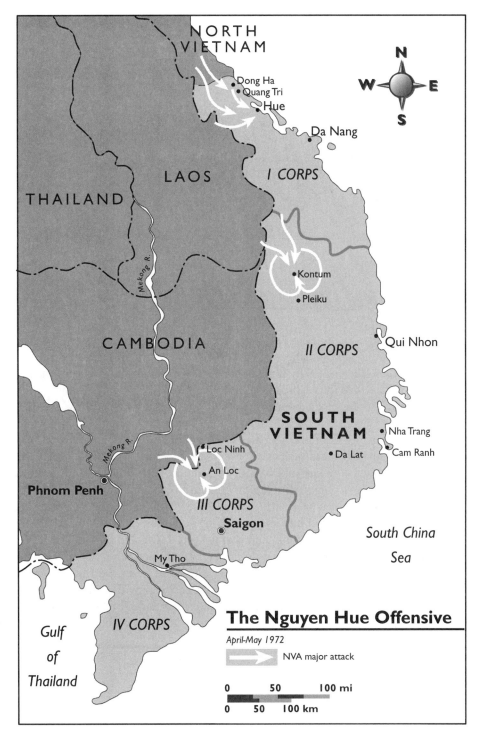

Figure 8.12 Public domain map.

Kontum, another NVA division, assisted by local VC forces, occupied most of the coastal province of Binh Dinh, a long-time Communist stronghold.[109] Once again, the perennial NVA goal, the bisection of South Vietnam, threatened. If the city of Kontum fell, the NVA forces would link up with the VC/NVA forces in Binh Dinh, and Thieu's country would be knifed in two.

The defense of Kontum City was organized and directed by the legendary John Paul Vann.[110] Vann had returned to Vietnam as a minor civilian official following his retirement from the Army in 1964. By dint of his energy, experience, intelligence, forceful personality, and total dedication to the cause, Vann had worked his way up the bureaucratic ranks to become the leading U. S. adviser in MR2 by 1972. Although a civilian, Vann held the equivalent military rank of a major general. When the RVN MR2 commander, General Ngo Dzu, an accused drug trafficker, suffered a nervous collapse under the stress of the NVA attacks, Vann personally took charge of defending Kontum City.

The Battle of Kontum raged for nearly three weeks. The NVA forces launched a series of frontal assaults on the ARVN defenders. Led by a Vann protege, Colonel Ly Tong Ba, the ARVN defenders repeatedly beat back the NVA attacks. While Colonel Ba's forces were holding the NVA attackers off, Vann called in an air armada of U. S. helicopter gunships, tactical air strikes, and B-52 bombings that decimated the attacking forces. The critical moment in the Battle of Kontum came during the night of May 28, 1972. NVA forces broke through the ARVN defenses and poured into the city. Only round-the-clock bombing by cells of B-52s finally broke the NVA assault, enabling Ba's battered 23rd Division to clear the city. American air power, especially the intensive B-52 attacks, had saved Kontum City.[111]

A few days after achieving his greatest victory, John Paul Vann died in a fiery helicopter crash a few miles south of Kontum City. Vann had given ten years, and finally his life, trying to save South Vietnam from Communist conquest. His body was recovered and flown back to the United States. John Paul Vann was given a state funeral and buried with full honors in a moving ceremony at Arlington National Cemetery. President Nixon praised him and posthumously awarded him the Medal of Freedom, the highest award a civilian could receive, for his heroic service in Vietnam.

The third wave of the Nguyen Hue Offensive struck the Tay Ninh and Binh Long Provinces northwest of Saigon in MR3. Three Vietcong divisions, the 5th, the 7th, and the 9th, manned mostly by NVA troops and commanded by North Vietnamese officers, poured into South Vietnam from their basing areas in Cambodia. The 5th VC Division took Loc Ninh, a town lying about eighty miles north of Saigon on Route 13, a highway leading straight to the South Vietnamese capital. The ARVN forces fell back to An Loc, a town nine miles south of Loc Ninh on Route 13. Failing to take An Loc by frontal assault, the NVA forces besieged the town. The Battle of An Loc raged for weeks.[112] General Thieu, determined to stop the NVA thrust at An Loc, threw in most of his strategic reserves and his elite airborne forces to bolster the defenses of the besieged town.

Figure 8.13   This photo is one of the most enduring and horrible images of the Vietnam War. Nine-year-old Phan Thi Kim Phuc running naked and screaming in agony down Route 1, from the napalm that had seared her small body. The napalm that burned Phuc and other children was dropped by a South Vietnamese pilot on Trang Bang, near a pagoda where the group had taken refuge. Staff photo by Huynh Cong "Nick" Ut. AP/Wide World Photos

The crucial battle for An Loc occurred on the morning of May 11. Units of all three enemy divisions launched attacks on the ARVN defenders. The NVA were hit immediately, first by waves of U. S. and VNAF fighter-bombers and then by B-52 strikes. Thirty B-52 strikes struck the NVA forces within twenty-four hours. Entire PAVN units, caught in the open by the big bombers, vanished in clouds of dust and debris! Although there was fighting in the vicinity of An Loc for a few more days, the battle was over. The ARVN forces had held. The key to victory at An Loc had been the effective use of Allied air power, especially the mighty B-52s.[113]

Nixon had reacted quickly and decisively to the North Vietnamese invasion. He and Kissinger both knew that the United States had to move quickly to support the South Vietnamese, or the Saigon regime might very well collapse in the face of the NVA onslaught. Both men understood that it was essential to defeat the North Vietnamese thrusts militarily. If the NVA offensive succeeded, Nixon could not expect the upcoming summit with the Soviets to be productive, nor could he hope to achieve a negotiated end to the Vietnam War on acceptable terms. He believed that a North Vietnamese victory would be a major strategic and diplomatic disaster for the United

States that could derail all of his plans for achieving a new world order based on detente with the major Communist powers. A Communist victory would also fatally undermine American credibility as a great power in the eyes of both friends and foes. Nixon also interpreted the Nguyen Hue Offensive as a DRV effort to forestall Vietnamization. He perceived that the North Vietnamese had provided Washington with an opportunity to end the war. He saw an opportunity to belatedly implement many of the DUCK HOOK operations that Kissinger's committee had drawn up during the summer of 1969. Washington moved quickly and decisively; U. S. air power could defeat the offensive and also launch a massive counterattack on the North Vietnamese heartland. Perhaps Nixon and Kissinger could compel Hanoi to accept a settlement favorable to America and the survival of South Vietnam.[114]

On April 4, 1972, in an effort to blunt it, Nixon decided to mount an all-out air war against the NVA invasion. He canceled most restrictions on bombing and revived the air war against North Vietnam that had been on hold since October 31, 1968. As the North Vietnamese had predicted, Nixon did not consider either sending American combat forces back to South Vietnam or using the few remaining maneuver battalions still serving in the country. The American forces scheduled for redeployment continued to leave South Vietnam while the battles forced by the Nguyen Hue offensive raged. On April 6, Nixon told the new commander of the 7th Air Force, General John W. Vogt, "I want you to get down there and use whatever air you need to turn this thing around. . . . "[115] From around the world, American aircraft carriers and Air Force squadrons raced toward the Indochina War. Additional B-52s flew into Andersen Air Force Base, bringing the combined total of the big strategic bombers in Thailand and Guam to 210. More than half the B-52s in the Strategic Air Command (SAC) were positioned to strike at the NVA invaders. Nixon also ordered the carriers Constellation and Kitty Hawk to join the four attack carriers already on station in the Gulf of Tonkin, giving the Navy its greatest concentration of airpower in the war.[116]

The revived air campaign against North Vietnam designed by the Navy and Air Force commanders, code-named LINEBACKER, had many diplomatic and strategic goals: (1) to send the North Vietnamese a warning that if Hanoi persisted with its offensive in an effort to win the war or to severely weaken the South Vietnamese government, the North Vietnamese could expect to get hit with the most punishing aerial offensive of the war; (2) to cut off North Vietnam from foreign sources of supply by destroying all of its railroads and harbors; (3) to destroy stockpiles of food, ammunition, weapons, and equipment already in North Vietnam; (4) to interdict as much as possible the supplies and equipment moving toward the battlefields in South Vietnam, Laos, and Cambodia; (5) to destroy all enemy transportation systems, POL facilities, and power plants; and (6) to wring concessions from the North Vietnamese so that a peace settlement would accord with U. S. and South Vietnamese desires.[117]

On April 10, U. S. aircraft struck supply storage centers near the city of Vinh, about 150 miles north of the DMZ. On April 13, B-52s flying from the large SAC base at U-Tapao in Thailand bombed oil storage sites near Hanoi and Haiphong. It was the first time in the long war that the big bombers had been used in attacks on North Vietnam's two largest cities. On April 16, American bombers accidentally hit four Soviet merchant ships lying at anchor in Haiphong Harbor, killing some Soviet seamen. The Soviets protested the bombing of their ships and the deaths of their sailors, but they did not make a big issue of these events, suggesting to Washington that the Soviets were not going to let the U. S. actions in Vietnam interfere with their upcoming summit meeting with the Americans.

Throughout the months of April and May, American military aircraft flew hundreds of sorties against military targets in North Vietnam. Air Force and Navy fighters flew most of the missions, but B-52s also participated. The LINEBACKER operation exceeded any previous U. S. aerial warfare against North Vietnam. Naval and Air Force pilots flew round-the-clock bombing missions against supply lines, storage facilities, industrial targets, power plants, and other targets considered to have military value. For the first time in the air war, American pilots dropped "smart bombs," laser-guided weapons of devastating precision. Using laser or electro-optical guidance systems, "smart bombs" could destroy targets in heavily populated areas without causing large civilian casualties.[118] In addition to reviving the air war against North Vietnam, Nixon also ordered air attacks against the invading North Vietnamese forces along their northern, central, and southern fronts in South Vietnam. Within ten days of the launching of the invasions, Allied aircraft were inflicting heavy losses on units of Hanoi's mobilized army on all three fronts. By June, the Nguyen Hue Offensive was losing its momentum.

American efforts to separate the North Vietnamese from their Chinese and Soviet sources of supply represented the most risky military move Nixon made during the Vietnam War. Nixon believed he had to take the risk to save South Vietnam from military collapse and therefore preserve detente and the chance of an acceptable settlement of the war.[119] At Nixon's request, Kissinger revived DUCK HOOK. One of DUCK HOOK's original proposals called for the mining of North Vietnam's harbors to interdict all ship traffic into Haiphong and other North Vietnamese ports. But before Nixon ordered the ports mined, he used diplomatic channels to forewarn the Chinese and Soviet leaders of his intentions. The president took these steps to preserve detente, to avoid possible reprisals by the major Communist powers, and to try to reopen secret negotiations with the North Vietnamese emissary, Le Duc Tho.[120]

As Nixon applied military pressure to Hanoi, he also applied diplomatic pressure to the Soviets, whom he and Kissinger held responsible for the NVA offensive in South Vietnam. The Americans were convinced that Hanoi could never have mounted the operation without the military hardware furnished by the Soviet Union. Kissinger met secretly with Soviet leader Leonid Brezhnev in Moscow on April 20. Before he would consent to talk to Brezhnev about any of the issues of the impending summit, Kissinger insisted that the Soviet leader agree to put pressure on Hanoi to negotiate an end to the war. The American envoy explicitly linked progress toward detente to Soviet willingness to persuade Hanoi to accept a compromise settlement of the war. Brezhnev agreed; he wanted nothing to subvert the upcoming summit. However, he protested to

Kissinger that he did not have the kind of influence with the Hanoi leadership that the Americans appeared to think he did. He also refused to ask Hanoi to call off its offensive, but he did send a high-ranking envoy to Hanoi to urge the Communist leaders to make peace with the Americans.

Brezhnev also helped Kissinger restart the talks with the North Vietnamese. Kissinger met secretly with Le Duc Tho in Paris on May 2, three weeks before the convening of the Moscow summit. At the time of the meeting, the North Vietnamese offensive was going well. Quang Tri had fallen to the NVA forces, and Kontum and An Loc were under intense attack. Le Duc Tho was confident that the Saigon government verged on collapse, and he believed American air power could not save it. Le Duc Tho was not interested in negotiations that day; confident of military victory, he rejected all of Kissinger's proposals. He was rigid, arrogant, even rude. The meeting was short, and it accomplished nothing.[121]

Disappointed and angered by Tho's response, President Nixon decided to escalate the U. S. air war against the North Vietnamese. He and Kissinger both agreed that only a massive dose of U. S. firepower could deter the North Vietnamese drive for a military victory over the South. Nixon gambled that the Chinese and Soviets both placed greater importance on improving their relations with the United States than they did on retaliating on behalf of their allies in Hanoi. The president growled to his aides, "The bastards have never been bombed like they're going to be bombed this time."[122] On May 8, in a dramatic televised speech, Nixon announced to a startled nation that he had ordered his most drastic escalations of the war: the mining of Haiphong Harbor, a naval blockade of North Vietnam, and a massive air war against that country. He also used the speech to tell the North Vietnamese that American aircraft would continue to mine ports and interdict lines of communication across the North Vietnamese heartland until Hanoi agreed to release all U. S. POWs and accept an internationally supervised cease-fire. As Nixon spoke to the American people, Navy jets were dropping mines in the narrow twelve-mile-long channel connecting the port of Haiphong with the Gulf of Tonkin. Twenty-seven freighters, mostly Soviet, were bottled up at Haiphong. For the next three days, Navy aircraft mined the approaches to North Vietnam's other ports and also several inland waterways. The blockade proved effective; it quickly cut off the sources of about 85 percent of North Vietnam's war material and disrupted all North Vietnamese naval activity.[123]

To the immense frustration of the North Vietnamese, Moscow and Beijing reacted coolly to the mining and the renewed bombing of North Vietnam. Nixon and Kissinger had gambled, and they had won. They had succeeded in isolating Hanoi from its major allies. Neither the USSR nor China did more than issue *pro forma* criticisms of the U. S. actions, and both privately put pressure on Hanoi to end the war. The two major Communist powers wanted the Vietnam War to end, lest it jeopardize the fruits of detente and the major realignment of power then taking place in the world. Hanoi's leaders bitterly observed that the Moscow summit occurred on schedule, even as Operation LINEBACKER was devastating North Vietnam and destroying their army fighting in South Vietnam.[124] Meetings in Moscow between the American and Soviet leaders proved cordial and productive. Nixon and Brezhnev signed several important agreements, including SALT 1, new trade agreements, and a new Berlin treaty.

Just as the North Vietnamese leaders worried lest their major Communist allies no longer supported their cause, Saigon's leaders feared the American commitment to their cause might also be sacrificed in the name of detente. The scale and ferocity of the fighting, the destructiveness of the renewed air war in South Vietnam, and the large numbers of casualties incurred accentuated the already intense levels of war-weariness among South Vietnam's beleaguered population. Millions of South Vietnamese had never supported the Saigon government, its war, or the American effort on its behalf. The effects of the fighting in the spring and summer of 1972 were to further diminish the ranks of South Vietnamese patriots. More and more people yearned for peace, for an end to the death and destruction afflicting their tortured country, even if it meant a Communist victory. One of the Tu Do Street savants told an American journalist, "We want peace, peace at any cost, peace with Communist rule if necessary."[125] After twenty years of precarious existence, after twenty years of American economic, political, diplomatic, military, and moral support, South Vietnam had failed to achieve a clear national identity. After twenty years, its leaders had utterly failed to project a vision, define a cause, or proclaim a goal that could inspire its citizens to fight a patriotic war.[126] The battle for Quang Tri City, which resulted in huge casualties on both sides, and the city's utter destruction, symbolized the hopeless, endless, and bloody stalemated war.

Within the United States, reaction to Nixon's dramatic war escalations proved mild. There was a flurry of protest demonstrations, but they did not attract large or militant followings. Doves introduced another round of end-the-war resolutions in the Senate, but none passed. The fact that Nixon had responded so forcefully, yet exempted the use of American ground forces and kept American casualties low, allowed more people to support his actions. The ranks of the antiwar movement had been depleted. Many peace activists were physically and morally exhausted from years of protesting a seeming endless war. Further, Vietnamization had progressed to a point where most American ground combat forces had been withdrawn from South Vietnam and those remaining in that country no longer participated in combat operations. Monthly draft calls were way down and a lottery draft was in place. One of the main energizing sources of antiwar activity had been the draft linked to a fear of being sent to fight and die in Vietnam. Now that dynamic now longer operated. Vietnamization not only gradually phased out the American ground combat role in Vietnam, it also gradually phased out much of the activist opposition to the Vietnam War.

Americans did not appear to be much moved by the spectacle of Vietnamese killing Vietnamese during the Nguyen Hue Offensive. Many Americans regarded Nixon's actions as a justifiable reaction to naked aggression, a military invasion of South Vietnam by North Vietnam. Nixon's bold response also attracted considerable popular support. The success of the Moscow summit demonstrated that military escalations did not automatically endanger detente. Polls showed strong public support for Nixon's retaliatory actions against the North Vietnamese and for his diplomatic accomplishments in Beijing and Moscow. His public approval rating climbed dramatically. In an election year, Nixon's political position had grown much stronger by June than it had been before the Nguyen Hue Offensive invasion occurred. Nixon's bold military actions, along with his and Kissinger's deft diplomacy, had paid domestic political dividends. Military escalations that did not incur many American casualties, provoke much domestic controversy, or increase Cold War tensions proved to be good presidential election-year politics.

The Nguyen Hue Offensive had petered out in September when South Vietnamese marines expelled the last NVA remnants from Quang Tri City. Nixon's decisive response had prevented a South Vietnamese military defeat and perhaps the fall of the Saigon government. Hanoi had undertaken the largest military offensive anywhere in the world since the Chinese invaded northern Korea in December 1950. But Hanoi's efforts to use massed forces to overwhelm the ARVN units had met with disaster. General Giap had miscalculated the fighting ability of the ARVN forces. U. S. air power had exacted a ghastly toll. North Vietnam lost over 100,000 troops killed in battle, most of their tanks, and much of their artillery in three months. North Vietnam had been subjected to the most intense bombing campaign of the entire war and sustained heavy damage.[127] The PAVN's inexperience and inadequacies made them vulnerable to such catastrophic destruction. Unaccustomed to mobile, mechanized warfare, they often failed to coordinate their infantry and armor attacks. Their primitive logistics capability could not provide the huge amounts of ammunition, gasoline, and spare parts required to support their offensive effectively. General Giap also appeared not to comprehend the terrible vulnerability of his mechanized forces in an operational situation where the Allied air forces enjoyed absolute control of the air. His army, by far the best the NVA had fielded to date, was destroyed.

The South Vietnamese also suffered heavy casualties—an estimated 25,000 soldiers killed in three months of fighting. Some ARVN commanders, particularly General Truong and Colonel Ba, demonstrated professional competence in battle situations. Some ARVN units, such as the airborne troops, fought courageously under fire. The VNAF pilots often gave a good account of themselves in many battles. But the PAVN offensive also revealed the continuing shortcomings of the RVNAF forces. Their helicopter and other air transport units proved inadequate. Artillery was poorly coordinated and often inaccurate. Communications and intelligence services remained poor. The ARVN logistics system could never function effectively without U. S. assistance. U. S. advisers directed most of the ARVN combat operations; they were the reinforcing steel rods that held the South Vietnamese army structures together. Too many ARVN soldiers continued to perform poorly in combat situations; their morale and nerve would desert them, and they fled in panic. The ARVN officer corps remained infested with corrupt and incompetent officers. Worse yet, South Vietnam was running out of men. The pool of draft-age men was running dry. Reserve units were depleted, and many regular units could not replace their losses. Shortages of competent officers and noncoms were more acute than ever in the aftermath of the Nguyen Hue Offensive.[128]

> The final inescapable truth to emerge from the offensive was that ARVN soldiers could neither stop the enemy without significant American air support nor could their counteroffensive have succeeded without it.[129]

Once again, Vietnamization had failed a crucial test.

On August 22, 1972, the 1st Battalion of the U. S. 7th Cavalry boarded a plane for Texas. The last U. S. ground combat forces had departed the Vietnam War. It had been seven years, five months, and fourteen days since the Marines had stormed ashore on the beaches south of Danang on March 8, 1965, to initiate the ground combat phase of the American Vietnam War. During that long interval, nearly 46,000 American soldiers had died in an effort to secure the survival of the South Vietnamese government. Now the ground combat phase of the war was over for American troops. But as the last contingent of U. S. combat soldiers departed Vietnam, the war between factions of Vietnamese nationalists raged on, its outcome not yet determined.

NEITHER PEACE NOR HONOR

Washington and Hanoi, having failed to break the diplomatic stalemate by military means during the summer of 1972, moved during the fall to break the military stalemate by diplomacy. Although confident of impending victory over George McGovern, the inept Democratic challenger, Nixon wanted to fulfill the promise he had made four years ago and to achieve a peaceful settlement of the Indochina War before the November election took place. The North Vietnamese, isolated from their major allies by Nixon and Kissinger's adroit diplomacy, their army in South Vietnam destroyed by U. S. air power and the ARVN forces fighting effectively, and their country reeling under the heaviest aerial bombardment of the war, for the first time in the long war genuinely sought a peace agreement.

The North Vietnamese were forced to abandon their efforts to achieve a military victory in South Vietnam. They were ready to accept a negotiated settlement, if it did not contravene their long-range goals of replacing the Thieu regime with a coalition government dominated by the PRG, expelling the Americans, and achieving national reunification. Although knowing McGovern had no chance to defeat Nixon, the Communist leadership in Hanoi sensed that they might get better terms from Nixon before the election than after his anticipated landslide victory. They also wanted to stop the destructive air war raining punishment on their economic and military facilities in order to rebuild for later military operations. They also sought to restrict American military operations in South Vietnam and salvage some of their forces fighting in that region.[130]

Secret meetings between Kissinger and Tho resumed in Paris in mid-July. It was evident from the first meeting that both sides genuinely wanted a negotiated settlement of the war. Tho's attitude was much altered from the May 2 meeting; he was polite, respectful, and prepared to yield concessions. The fact that Tho would bargain while American aircraft pounded his country represented a diplomatic breakthrough. Previously, Hanoi had demanded an end to the bombing of their country as a precondition for negotiations. Tho also relinquished Hanoi's other long-standing preconditions: the demand that General Thieu would have to be removed and the withdrawal of all American forces.

In August, while Tho and Kissinger and their staffs negotiated, President Nixon escalated the air war against North Vietnam. The number of daily sorties quadrupled. More and more "smart bombs" were used to allow American pilots as many precision raids as possible. In September, the Air Force introduced a new all-weather tactical bomber, the F-111, which could fly near the speed of sound (500 to 550 MPH) at tree-top level in darkness or bad weather. They could strike anytime, anywhere, and without warning.[131] The LINEBACKER operation continued until October 23, when Nixon halted all U. S. bombing of North Vietnam north of the 20th Parallel.

By October 11, Kissinger and Tho had worked out a settlement based on the U. S. concept of a two-tracked agreement that separated the military and political aspects of the conflict. Hanoi agreed to allow General Thieu to remain in power temporarily in exchange for a grant of a political status in South Vietnam to the Provisional Revolutionary Government. Within sixty days of a cease-fire, Hanoi agreed to return all of the American POWs and the United States agreed to withdraw all of its remaining troops from South Vietnam.

Both sides had made concessions. The most painful concession for the Communists had to be renouncing their demand for Thieu's removal. In effect, Hanoi accorded the Saigon government a measure of legitimacy; recognition of Thieu ran counter to the DRV's long-held goal of national reunification under the rule of the Vietnamese Communist Party. Washington's most significant concession permitted all NVA troops currently in South Vietnam to remain. That critical concession meant the Americans had accepted a basic reality of the war. Having failed to drive the North Vietnamese forces out of South Vietnam by military means, they could not hope to get them out via diplomacy. Kissinger also accepted Tho's proposal that a tripartite commission made up of delegates from the RVN, the PRG, and neutralist elements would be created to supervise elections and administer the agreement. All decisions of the tripartite commission would have to be unanimous, which meant that both the Thieu regime and the PRG representatives would retain a veto over the commission's actions.[132] Kissinger tried but failed to get Laos and Cambodia included in the proposed settlement. Significantly, the draft agreement between Kissinger and Tho deferred the key issue—who would rule in South Vietnam—to an unspecified time in the future. Presumably, that matter would be resolved by the tripartite commission after the Indochina War had ended and the Americans had gone home.

With most outstanding issues settled between Hanoi and Washington, Kissinger flew to Saigon to obtain General Thieu's approval of the mid-October agreement, only to discover that the South Vietnamese leader refused to accept it. Thieu and his associates were outraged at what they considered America's arrogant disregard of both their sensibilities and their sovereignty. Kissinger had negotiated a settlement of the war that to South Vietnamese eyes looked like an abandonment of their cause, without consulting them. General Thieu raised several strong objections to the proposed settlement and endeavored to prevent its ratification. He and his advisers drew up a lengthy list of objections and presented them to Kissinger. Thieu's two most serious concerns were the continued presence of large numbers of North Vietnamese forces in southern Vietnam after the Americans had withdrawn all of their combat forces and the proposed tripartite commission that appeared to him as a coalition government in the making. Thieu was not reassured when Kissinger told him that any North Vietnamese violation of the agreement would provoke an instant and deadly response from the United States. General Thieu preferred that the war in his country continue rather than accept a settlement he believed rendered his nation more insecure than ever.[133]

Kissinger, concerned primarily with extricating the United States from the war and skeptical of Saigon's prospects for long-term survival, probably hoped "to secure nothing more than a 'decent interval' between an American withdrawal and the resolution of the conflict in Vietnam."[134] Kissinger was angered by Thieu's strenuous opposition to the agreement and viewed the Saigon government as the main impediment to America's exit from Vietnam. When Kissinger returned to Washington following his futile efforts to get the South Vietnamese leaders to sign the agreement, he advised Nixon to sign the agreement without Thieu's approval. Kissinger also attempted to generate momentum for a preelection settlement of the Indochina conflict by announcing dramatically at a special press conference that he staged in Washington on October 26 that, "peace is at hand."[135]

But peace was not at hand, because President Nixon shared some of Thieu's objections to the mid-October agreement. Nixon had also decided that the United States would have greater leverage with both Saigon and Hanoi following his expected landslide victory over McGovern than before. In addition, Nixon discovered that former MACV Commander William Westmoreland and other American military leaders opposed the settlement. Nixon worried continually that any settlement he and Kissinger achieved that appeared to imperil South Vietnam's chances of surviving would provoke a backlash among powerful conservative forces within the United States. Consequently, Nixon backed the South Vietnamese leader's refusal to sign the agreement. Confident of winning an overwhelming victory in the upcoming election, Nixon decided to wait until after his reelection to try to forge an agreement with the North Vietnamese that would improve South Vietnam's prospects for long-term survival. Knowing that he was going to win a huge electoral victory in early November, Nixon could see his bargaining position strengthened. He would be in a position to force Hanoi to settle on American terms or "face the consequences of what we could do to them."[136] The president's support of General Thieu's intransigence guaranteed that the agreement Kissinger and Le Duc Tho had forged would fail to hold. At the same time Nixon rejected the settlement, Washington also approved a resupply operation, called ENHANCE, for Saigon: Massive amounts of military equipment were airlifted to South Vietnam—planes, tanks, trucks, APCs, and other material—to strengthen the RVNAF forces.

Nixon confronted an election-eve dilemma. A combination of diplomacy and U. S. firepower had persuaded Hanoi to negotiate an agreement acceptable to Washington. But the agreement was not acceptable to America's ally in Saigon. General Thieu demanded changes in the accord, which, in turn, were unacceptable to the North Vietnamese. Hence, the Americans viewed both Hanoi and Saigon as obstacles to "peace with honor," that is disengagement from the war while South Vietnam was still standing.

Following his landslide victory over McGovern on November 7, Nixon moved to resolve the Vietnam dilemma. Kissinger and Le Duc Tho resumed their discussions in Paris. On November 14, President Nixon sent General Thieu a secret letter informing him that Washington would try to renegotiate the pending agreement in accordance with Saigon's wishes. He also promised the South Vietnamese leader that if Hanoi refused to abide by the terms of the agreement and renewed its aggression against the Saigon government, the United States would take "swift and severe retaliatory action."[137]

In Paris, when Kissinger, responding to Nixon's and General Thieu's concerns, introduced many matters for reconsideration that the North Vietnamese assumed had been resolved, and when he also proposed major changes that would adversely affect the status of the Vietcong and the North Vietnamese forces in South Vietnam, Le Duc Tho and his colleagues, concluding that they had been tricked into approving an agreement the Americans had never intended to keep, angrily rejected Kissinger's proposals. The suspicious North Vietnamese did not believe the Saigon government would have rejected the agreement on their own; they thought, mistakenly, that the Americans had told Thieu to object to the agreement to provide a pretext for Nixon's objections and refusal to accept it.

When Kissinger warned Tho that Nixon, having just won reelection by an overwhelming margin, was prepared to take whatever action he felt necessary to protect American interests in South Vietnam, the North Vietnamese envoy boldly responded to the American's threats by hardening his position. The North Vietnamese even returned to their old stance of insisting that Thieu would have to be ousted as a precondition for any settlement. For weeks, Kissinger and Le Duc Tho negotiated, sometimes tensely, sometimes angrily. On occasion, during these talks, Tho would make concessions and appear to be trying to reach an agreement, only to retract his offer subsequently. Eventually, both sides edged toward an agreement, one similar in most of its provisions to the one they had concluded in early October, which both Thieu and Nixon had rejected.

But Kissinger decided Tho was stalling. He sensed the North Vietnamese sought to avoid an agreement; they were trying to drive a wedge between Washington and Saigon, forestall further bombing, and wait until the new American Congress convened in January 1973. The new Congress, controlled by Democrats and in a dovish mood, might cut off all funding for the war and force the Americans to get out of Vietnam. South Vietnam, abandoned by the United States, would then be vulnerable to a future NVA assault. After weeks of futile negotiation, convinced that Hanoi did not want an agreement to come out of the sessions, Nixon directed Kissinger to break off the talks on December 13.[138]

President Nixon had decided it was time to try one more big play—to try to resolve the latest Paris impasse by force. He, too, was concerned that the incoming Congress would cut off all funding for the American war, effectively ending it and handing the Communists a victory that they had not been able to win on the battle-fields of Vietnam. Once again, he resorted to air power, a campaign known as LINE-BACKER II. But LINEBACKER II differed from its predecessor; whereas LINEBACKER I was designed to destroy North Vietnam's war-making capacity, LINEBACKER II aimed to destroy Hanoi's will to fight. Nixon had concluded that he would have to strike a psychological blow, that he would have to shock the North Vietnamese into believing that Washington would not tolerate an indefinite delay in negotiating a peace settlement. The new bombing campaign would also be a spectacular show of resolve to reassure Saigon that the United States remained committed to the goal of an independent South Vietnam.[139] Nixon ordered an all-out air assault against the two largest cities of North Vietnam, Hanoi and Haiphong. He told the chairman of the Joint Chiefs, Admiral Thomas Moorer,

> I don't want any more of this crap about the fact that we couldn't hit this target or that one. This is your chance to use military power to win this war, and if you don't, I'll consider it your responsibility.[140]

To achieve maximum impact, Nixon sent no warning or ultimatum to Hanoi, nor did he go on television to tell the American public why it was necessary to renew the air war against North Vietnam. The only hint of what was to come derived from a press conference held on December 16, at which Kissinger blamed the failure to achieve a peace settlement on Communist intransigence. On that occasion, Kissinger suggested that tougher measures might be necessary to move the stalled peace talks forward, but he gave no specifics.

Starting on December 18, the sky over Hanoi and Haiphong was filled by the largest American air armada of the war. Relying mostly on the giant B-52s, the mightiest weapon in the U. S. air arsenal, U. S. aircraft dropped 15,247 tons of bombs, mostly along the sixty-mile Haiphong-Hanoi corridor, during eleven days of air attacks. The bombers struck warehouses, oil storage facilities, railyards, airfields, power plants, industrial complexes, and SAM-2 sites. Nixon had startled some of the Air

Force brass by using the B-52s to spearhead LINEBACKER II. Both Hanoi and Haiphong were well-defended; they possessed sophisticated air defense systems that could be expected to bring down a sizeable number of the big planes, which comprised an integral part of the American strategic deterrent viz-à-viz the Soviet Union. Nixon understood that the SAM-2s would claim many B-52s, but he felt he had to use them to achieve the levels of destruction and psychological impact required to persuade the North Vietnamese to return to the bargaining table. During the course of the eleven-day air war, the Soviet-supplied missile systems, some of which were manned by Soviet crews, brought down fifteen B-52s and damaged several others. Ninety-two U. S. pilots and air crewmen were killed or captured.[141]

The LINEBACKER II operation, which the American press quickly dubbed the "Christmas Bombing," provoked furious criticism within the United States and abroad. Press editorialists and Congressional opponents accused Nixon of waging a war against the civilian population of North Vietnam. Senator Edward Kennedy said the air raids "should outrage the conscience of all Americans."[142] European press and government leaders also denounced the U. S. bombing campaign. Swedish Prime Minister Olaf Palme compared the bombing to Nazi atrocities.[143] Congressional critics, on recess for the Christmas holidays, made it clear that when they returned to Washington in January they would cut off all funds to deprive the president of the ability to wage war anywhere in Indochina. Polls showed the bombing brought Nixon's approval rating down to 39 percent, the lowest rating of his presidency.

Both foreign and domestic criticism of the Christmas Bombing campaign were exaggerated. The LINEBACKER II operation was not a campaign of terror bombing that targeted cities and civilian populations. Only military targets and targets that were not located in densely populated areas were deliberately attacked. U. S. airmen went to great lengths and took grave risks to avoid hitting civilians and civilian structures. Lucrative targets sometimes escaped attack because of the concern to avoid civilian casualties. The civilian toll for Hanoi was 1,318 killed and 1,216 wounded, and for Haiphong, 305 civilians were reported killed. Considering the scale and intensity of the attacks on both cities, these casualty figures were remarkably small. Some of the civilian deaths were probably caused by SAM-2s that missed their intended targets, fell within Hanoi and Haiphong, and exploded. American journalists who visited Hanoi and Haiphong following the bombing were surprised to discover that civilian deaths and civilian property destruction were minor compared to the devastation of targeted areas.[144]

On December 22, Nixon cabled Hanoi that if the North Vietnamese agreed to resume the peace talks that the United States would stop the bombing. There was no immediate response from the North Vietnamese. On December 26, following a thirty-six-hour respite to observe the Christmas holiday, 120 B-52s, flying out of both Andersen and U-Tapao, attacked Hanoi and Haiphong. It was the most intense day of aerial bombardment in the history of aviation warfare. The next day, Hanoi signaled to Nixon that they had had enough; they were prepared to resume the Paris talks on January 8, 1973. Nixon continued the bombing for two more days. On both days, December 28 and 29, the Americans encountered feeble resistance. The North Vietnamese had expended their arsenal of about 1,000 SAM-2s, and many missile sites had been destroyed. Just as both cities lay helpless, Nixon ordered that all bombings north of the 20th Parallel cease at 7:00 P. M. local time, on December 29, 1972.[145] The LINEBACKER II operation had its successes. It temporarily reduced Hanoi's war-making capacities and again disrupted its supply lines from China and the Soviet Union. It also sent Hanoi a warning that America would unleash its aircraft in the event that the North Vietnamese violated provisions of the final treaty about to be negotiated. In addition, the firm show of U. S. resolve served to reassure the South Vietnamese and perhaps made General Thieu more willing to accept the final settlement.[146]

Negotiations between Kissinger and Tho resumed on January 8, 1973. Kissinger perceived that North Vietnam wanted to negotiate an agreement, and one was hammered out in six days. Washington again allowed the Communists to maintain an active political and military presence in South Vietnam. Hanoi again accepted the existence of the Thieu regime and allowed continuing American aid to the RVN.[147]

But the Christmas Bombing campaign had not produced a settlement that differed in any significant measure from the agreement that had been previously worked out by Kissinger and Tho in mid-October, only to be subverted by Thieu's objections, which had been backed by Nixon. Despite the pledge to Thieu, Kissinger did not try to obtain the major alterations in the agreement that the South Vietnamese leader had demanded. Nothing of substance had changed between October 1972 and January 1973. There were a few cosmetic changes, but the terms of the final agreement closely followed the October settlement that Nixon had permitted General Thieu to reject. The most important change in language occurring in the final agreement concerned the demilitarized zone. The North Vietnamese agreed to make explicit reference to it for the first time, but the U. S. negotiators accepted its description as a "provisional and not a political or territorial boundary," which conceded the substance of Hanoi's long-standing view of the DMZ.[148] More important, the Christmas Bombing campaign did not significantly alter the political or military balance between North and South Vietnam, nor did it improve the chances for the RVN's long-term survival. Whatever Nixon hoped to achieve by the intense eleven-day bombing campaign, perhaps a permanent diminution of Hanoi's war-making ability, or perhaps better terms for South Vietnam in the final settlement, all failed to transpire. For all of its sound and fury, the Christmas Bombing campaign proved to be a diplomatic irrelevance.

The president, who sensed that he had just about expended the last of his political capital with LINEBACKER II, that he had no more big plays left in his Indochina playbook, was determined to end the war. Nixon took the best settlement he could get and then imposed it on General Thieu before the new Congress itself ended the American war by cutting off all funding for military action in Indochina. Ironically, the Christmas Bombing campaign had forced Washington to accept the settlement that

Nixon had rejected in October! As John Negroponte, one of Kissinger's aides, put it, "We bombed the North Vietnamese into accepting our concessions."[149]

To make the final agreement easier for General Thieu to swallow, Nixon had vastly increased the level of military aid going to the RVN. He also gave the South Vietnamese leader a handwritten promise that the United States would continue to support the Thieu government. Nixon promised in writing that the United States would respond in full force if North Vietnam ever launched another offensive in violation of the peace treaty. But Nixon made it clear to Thieu that if he did not sign the agreement, America would cut off all further assistance to South Vietnam and that Washington would sign the treaty alone. Thieu, after failing to get the changes implemented, had no choice but to sign an agreement that he feared and loathed. Perhaps he was reassured by the increased levels of military aid going to his government, by LINEBACKER II, and by the promise of future American military intervention to preserve the agreement.[150]

To secure an accord that allowed Washington to extricatre the United States from a war that most Americans no longer supported, President Nixon had to bribe and bully the South Vietnamese leaders and bomb the North Vietnamese leaders into submission.

Representatives of all four delegations at the Paris talks, the United States, North Vietnam, South Vietnam, and the PRG signed the Agreement on Ending the War and Restoring Peace in Vietnam, usually called the Paris Accords, on January 27, 1973. The Accords had two major divisions: a set of military provisions and a set of political provisions.

According to the main military provisions of the Accords (1) a cease-fire throughout South Vietnam went into effect immediately; (2) at the same time, America ceased all acts of war against North Vietnam and agreed to remove, deactivate, or destroy immediately all of the mines that had been laid in North Vietnamese ports, harbors, and waterways; (3) the United States agreed to remove all of its remaining forces, including advisory personnel, from South Vietnam and to dismantle all of its bases in that country within sixty days (about 24,000 personnel); (4) Hanoi agreed to return all American prisoners-of-war within sixty days; (5) the 150,000 NVA troops currently inside South Vietnam were allowed to remain; (6) neither the United States nor the North Vietnamese could send more troops to South Vietnam; and (7) it created two commissions, the Joint Military Commission, made up of representatives from the ARVN and VC/NVA forces, and the International Commission on Control, made up of delegates from Hungary, Poland, Indonesia, and Canada, to enforce the cease-fire provisions of the agreement.[151]

According to the major political provisions of the Paris Accords (1) the Thieu government and the PRG were accorded legitimacy within South Vietnam; (2) both entities would establish a National Council of National Reconciliation and Concord, representing equally the RVN, the PRG, and the "third force" elements in South Vietnam (the council would implement the political aspects of the Accords, including holding elections to determine the future government of South Vietnam); (3) South Vietnam was declared to be a free and an independent nation; and (4) all signatories guaranteed that the reunification of Vietnam would be gradual, peaceful, and without coercion.[152] Few of the many military and political provisions of the Paris agreements were ever carried out.

President Nixon, in a speech from the Oval Office to the American people, given a few hours after the Accords were signed in Paris, told the American people that all remaining U. S. troops would be out of Vietnam and all American POWs would be coming home within sixty days. He also stated that:

> South Vietnam has gained the right to determine its own future. Let us be proud that America did not settle for a peace that betrayed an ally.[153]

If he truly believed his statements, President Nixon was deluding himself and his fellow citizens. The agreement that had taken so long to consummate served primarily as a vehicle that permitted the United States a more or less graceful exit from the war—we retrieved our prisoners-of-war and the Thieu government remained in power. But the graceful exit, coupled with Nixon's upbeat rhetoric, disguised a disastrous strategic defeat—withdrawal from a war that Washington could no longer hope to win, a war that no longer commanded the support of Congress, the media, or most Americans, and a war that continued on terms increasingly perilous to the survival prospects of the Saigon government. General Nguyen Cao Ky, who watched President Nixon's televised speech, had a more realistic appraisal of the Paris Accords (he also proved to be an accurate political forecaster):

> I could not stomach it, so nauseating was its hypocrisy and self-delusion. . . . This is an enormous step toward the total domination of Vietnam and there is no reason why the Communists should stop now. . . . I give them a couple of years before they invade the South.[154]

The signing of the Paris treaty occasioned no celebrations or outpourings of joy among the people of South Vietnam or within the Thieu government. The treaty permitted some 150,000 North Vietnamese troops to remain in South Vietnam. The agreement also granted the Provisional Revolutionary Government, the political dimension of the PLAF insurgency, a political status in South Vietnam, which meant that the people and areas of South Vietnam under the control of the Vietcong had been granted legitimacy and South Vietnam's internal security was further endangered by the presence of the equivalent of ten divisions of enemy troops on its soil!

The January Accords were fatally flawed; they left unresolved the fundamental issue for which the United States and North Vietnam had fought a long and bloody war, the political status, indeed the very existence of South Vietnam. Since the Geneva Accords of July 1954, since the temporary division of Vietnam at the 17th Parallel,

Washington and Hanoi had been at odds over who should rule in Southern Vietnam. Having deferred the major question for which the Vietnam War had been fought, one which would determine whether an independent South Vietnam would survive, the Paris agreement presumed that the question would be resolved by political means, sometime in an unspecified future.

But the political mechanisms created to resolve the political issues could never work; they were inherently unworkable.[155] Therefore—and all informed observers understood this reality at the time the Paris agreements were signed—the question of who would ultimately have political power in South Vietnam could only be resolved by force. The Paris Accords did not bring a cease-fire; they did not end a war. They only ensured that the Vietnam War would go on without the Americans, that Asians would continue to kill Asians.

Unable to force the Americans out of South Vietnam by military means, Hanoi opted to remove the American forces by diplomacy, which required accepting the continued existence of the RVN for a few years and according the Thieu government legitimacy. But the North Vietnamese had not renounced their long-held revolution goals. They had no intention of abiding by any terms of the Paris Accords that interfered with the attainment of their goals. Hanoi's decision to accept the Paris settlement was based on its assumption that once the Americans had left, the VC/NVA forces could defeat Thieu's regime within a few years. The North Vietnamese also understood that the

Figure 8.14 President Nixon greets Henry Kissinger upon his return from Paris, where the envoy had just negotiated the Paris Accords, ending the American Vietnam War. *Source:* National Archives

mechanisms for policing the cease-fire, like the mechanisms for resolving the political issues, were unworkable. Hanoi's leaders believed the South Vietnamese armed forces would never be able to withstand another major NVA offensive on their own; years of Vietnamization had not eliminated the RVNAF's basic flaws or given the South Vietnamese government a popular base of support. By Hanoi's reckoning, political and military reality in South Vietnam would allow the RVN to survive only as long as it would take North Vietnam to rebuild its forces and mount another offensive, about two or three years. The Paris Accords could only delay, not prevent, North Vietnam from eventually achieving its long-range military and political objectives.[156]

Only a credible threat of U. S. military retaliation could have enforced the Paris Accords and kept South Vietnam alive indefinitely. But the domestic political reaction to the Christmas Bombing campaign suggested that it had been Richard Nixon's last hurrah. Neither Congress nor the American people would likely support reentry of American naval and air power into combat anywhere in Indochina, much less advisers or ground combat forces. The Communist leaders concluded that Nixon dared not, "risk the political damage that would result from an effort to reimpose U. S. power in South Vietnam."[157] If North Vietnam could not be restrained from military action, if South Vietnam could not defend itself on its own, and if America could not intervene militarily to try to save the RVN, the demise of South Vietnam was inevitable, its days were numbered. Nixon's vaunted "peace with honor" in reality meant disguised American strategic defeat delayed by an interval of perhaps a few years' duration.

The 1973 Paris Accords, which resembled the 1954 Geneva Accords in many ways, essentially amounted to a deal between Hanoi and Washington. The United States got its POWs back and its remaining troops out of Vietnam. Hanoi got the bombing of its country and the battering of its army halted, and also got the remaining American soldiers out of Vietnam. The Thieu government got nothing, neither peace nor the realistic prospect of a political settlement that could ensure the long-term survival of South Vietnam.

The American and Vietnamese people paid a high price for the illusory peace that Nixon and Kissinger achieved after four more years of war. Four more years of war had cost more than 15,000 additional U. S. battle deaths, about 150,000 additional South Vietnamese battle deaths, and over 400,000 additional North Vietnamese battle deaths. Hundreds of thousands of civilians in South Vietnam also died during those extra years of war. Within the United States, continuing inflation weakened the economy and undermined the living standards of millions of American families. The war also perpetuated domestic pathologies, dividing Americans, polarizing politics, and poisoning the political atmosphere. The United States emerged from its lengthy involvement in Southeast Asia with its world status and prestige considerably diminished.[158] By the time America withdrew from Vietnam, the morale, discipline, and fighting spirit of its Army had seriously eroded.

The Soviet Union had used the years that the United States had entangled itself in a major war in Southeast Asia to achieve strategic parity with its major Cold War rival. By 1973, many Americans, achingly weary of war and, for that matter, of all international commitments, increasingly embraced a neoisolationist outlook. Nixon himself paid dearly for his prolongation of the Vietnam War. The Watergate scandals, which forced his resignation from the presidency in disgrace, grew out of his inability to end the Vietnam War quickly, as promised. Richard Nixon eventually joined Lyndon Johnson as one of the two most prominent American victims of the U.S. crusade to contain the expansion of Communism in Southeast Asia.

A bizarre follow-up to the Paris agreements occurred in October 1973, when a Nobel Peace Prize committee jointly awarded Henry Kissinger and Le Duc Tho the 1973 Nobel Peace Prize for their efforts to bring an end to the Vietnam War. Kissinger was uneasy about the award, and Le Duc Tho refused to accept it. Kissinger later refused to attend the awards ceremony at the University of Oslo and then donated the $65,000 cash prize he received to a scholarship fund established to help the children of American soldiers killed or missing in Vietnam. The Nobel committee had awarded its most prestigious prize to two diplomats who had negotiated a fictitious peace! There was never an effective cease-fire. Even as the committee announced its awards, the war raged on: Vietnamese continued to kill Vietnamese in South Vietnam. Former Undersecretary of State George Ball observed, "The Norwegians must have a sense of humor." A *New York Times* editorial writer called the award, "The Nobel War Prize."[159]

NOTES

1. Ambrose, Stephen E., "Nixon and Vietnam: Vietnam and Electoral Politics," in George Donelson Moss, ed., *A Vietnam Reader* (Englewood Cliffs, N. J.: 1991), 204–5.

2. Goodman, *The Lost Peace*, 79–80.

3. According to Ambrose, Richard Nixon's foremost biographer, Nixon never said, "I have a secret plan to end the war" during the 1968 campaign. The phrase was a journalistic invention. See Nixon, Richard, "Asia after Vietnam," *Foreign Affairs*, vol. 46 (October 1967), 111–25 and the excerpts from an undelivered radio speech scheduled for March 31, 1968, in Goodman, *The Lost Peace*, 80–81.

4. Kissinger, Henry, "The Vietnam Negotiations," *Foreign Affairs*, vol. 47 (January 1969), 234; Kissinger, Henry, *The White House Years* (Boston: Little, Brown, 1979), 228–32.

5. Quote is from Hess, *Vietnam*, 114.

6. Goodman, *The Lost Peace*, 81; Hess, *Vietnam*, 114–15; DeBenedetti, 277.

7. Nixon quote is found in Morris, Roger, *Uncertain Greatness: Henry Kissinger and American Foreign Policy* (New York: Harper and Row, 1977), 156. Lipsman, Samuel, Doyle, Edward, and the editors of Boston Publishing Company, *Fighting for Time* (Boston: Boston Publishing Co., 1983, 8, 27–28, a volume in the series, *The Vietnam Experience*. See Porter (ed.), *Vietnam Documents*, vol. 2, Document 289, "National Security Study Memorandum No. 1," January 21, 1969 (Extracts), 522–29).

8. Moss, *America in the Twentieth Century*, 371–3.

9. Polls cited in Mueller, *Wars, Presidents, and Public Opinion*, 92–93.

10. Quote is from Schandler, *Unmaking of a President*, 321.

11. Brandon, Henry, *The Retreat of American Power* (New York: Delta, 1972), 58–59; Goodman, *The Lost Peace*, 85.

12. Herring, George C., "The Nixon Strategy in Vietnam," in Peter Braestrup (ed.), *Vietnam as History: Ten Years after the Paris Peace Accords* (Washington, D. C.: University Press of America, 1984), 51–52; Herring, *Longest War*, 3d. ed., 245.

13. Lipsman and others, *Fighting For Time*, 30–31; Herring, *America's Longest War*, 225.

14. Kissinger, *White House Years*, 242–9; Davidson, *Vietnam at War*, 589–94.

15. Crawford, Henry B., "Operation Menu's Secret Bombing of Cambodia," in *Vietnam* (December 1996), 22–28.

16. Kissinger, *White House Years*, 252–3; Morris, *Uncertain Greatness*, 158–62. According to Morris, Kissinger approved of the wiretaps and gave the names of some officials and journalists he wanted wiretapped to FBI agents. Ambrose, Stephen E., *Nixon: The Triumph of a Politician* (New York: Simon & Schuster, 1989), 258–9.

17. Lipsman et al., *Fighting for Time*, 31–32; quote is from Hess, *Vietnam*, 115.

18. Quoted in *ibid.*, 32; Porter (ed.), *Vietnam Documents*, vol. 2, Document 291, "Address on Television By President Richard M. Nixon," May 14, 1969, (Extract), 531.

19. Kissinger, *White House Years*, 271–4; Herring, *America's Longest War*, 226.

20. Goodman, *The Lost Peace*, 87–88.

21. Duiker, *The Communist Road*, 278–83.

22. See epigraph, chapter 1, p. 5.

23. Copies of Nixon's July 15, 1969, letter to Ho Chi Minh, and the North Vietnamese leader's response, dated August 15, can be found in Szulc, Tad, *The Illusion of Peace: Foreign Policy in the Nixon Years* (New York: Viking, 1978), 137, 139. There is a story that probably originated with Harry R. "Bob" Haldeman, Nixon's former chief of staff, that Nixon developed what he himself called his "madman theory" in his efforts to end the Vietnam War on terms he could accept. He would have aides get the word to Hanoi that the new president was an extreme anti-Communist and mentally unstable, a dangerous man capable of any action in his efforts to end the war—even capable of using nuclear weapons and destroying the Red River dikes that would have flooded Vietnam's most densely populated region. Nixon thought such a ploy could frighten the North Vietnamese leaders into seeking an accommodation with the United States.

24. Quoted in Lipsman et al., *Fighting for Time*, 36.

25. Quoted in Morris, *Uncertain Greatness*, 164.

26. Hersh, Seymour M., *The Price of Power: Kissinger in the Nixon White House* (New York: Summit, 1983), 124–30; Morris, *Uncertain Greatness*, 163–4; Szulc, *Illusion of Peace*, 150–6.

27. Herring, *America's Longest War*, 228.

28. Kissinger, *White House Years*, 278–83. Henry Cabot Lodge, the head of the U. S. team at the Paris talks, had met privately many times with Xuan Thuy prior to Kissinger's August 4 meeting. These talks had all been unproductive.

29. Szulc, Tad, *Illusion of Peace*, 148–9. Nixon, like Johnson, tended to equate criticism of his war policy with subversion. He secretly ordered the FBI, the CIA, and other intelligence agencies to look for connections between the antiwar movement and the enemy.

30. Herring, *America's Longest War*, 228.

31. DeBenedetti, *An American Ordeal*, 248–53.

32. DeBenedetti, Charles, *The Peace Reform in American History* (Bloomington, Ind.: Indiana University Press, 1984),180–5; Lipsman et al., *Fighting for Time*, 36–37; DeBenedetti, *An American Ordeal*, 255–7.

33. Quoted in Lipsman et al., *Fighting for Time*, 37.

34. Transcript of Nixon's speech delivered on November 3, 1969; the speech also appears in Nixon, Richard M., *Public Papers, Richard M. Nixon, 1969* (Washington, D. C.: U. S. GPO, 1971), 901–9. Although the policy itself had been in place for a year and a half, the term "Vietnamization" was coined by Nixon's Secretary of Defense Melvin Laird. Vietnamization was always identified as Nixon's Vietnam War policy, although the policy was a creation of his predecessor.

35. Polls are cited in DeBenedetti, *An American Ordeal*, 259.

36. Quoted in Szulc, *Illusion of Peace*, 158.

37. DeBenedetti, *An American Ordeal*, 261–2.

38. *Ibid.*, pp. 262–3. One of the people who played a minor role in organizing the huge November 15 Washington protest was a 22-year-old Rhodes Scholar and future president, William Jefferson "Bill" Clinton.

39. Polls cited in *Ibid.*, 264.

40. Davidson, *Vietnam at War*, 603–6; quote is from Hess, *Vietnam*, 118.

41. Davidson, *Vietnam at War*, 606–7.

42. Quote is from *Ibid.*, 607.

43. Blaufarb, *Counterinsurgency Era*, 264–78; Sheehan, *Bright Shining Lie*, 731–6; Herring, *America's Longest War*, 231–3; and Davidson, *Vietnam at War*, 609–12; Andrade, *Ashes to Ashes*, 123–46; and Hess, *Vietnam*, 118.

44. Hess, *Vietnam*, 118–19.

45. Stanton, *Rise and Fall*, 269–70; Davidson, *Vietnam at War*, 612–13.

46. Hess, *Vietnam*, 117–19.

47. Stanton, *Rise and Fall*, 284.

48. Stanton, *Rise and Fall*, 283–8; Lipsman et al., *Fighting for Time*, 17–23; Davidson, *Vietnam at War*, 614–15.

49. Quoted in Lipsman et al., *Fighting for Time*, 22.

50. Transcript of interview with Melvin Zais, General, U. S. Army (Ret.), 1977, vol. III, 575–88, U. S. Army Military History Institute archives, Carlisle Barracks, Penn. General Zais had a son fighting in the battle of Dong Ap Bia. General Zais believed that the name, "Hamburger Hill" was suggested by a young Wire Service reporter interviewing a hysterical soldier who had participated in the battle.

51. Davidson, *Vietnam at War*, 615.

52. Davidson, *Vietnam at War*, 615–19; Stanton, *Rise and Fall*, 278–80; Lipsman et al., *Fighting For Time*, 92–115; Lewy, *America in Vietnam*, 153–61; Cincinnatus, *Self-Destruction: The Disintegration and Decay of the United States Army during the Vietnam Era* (New York: W. W. Norton, 1981). "Cincinnatus" is the pseudonym used by Cecil B. Currey.

53. Baskir and Strauss, *Chance and Circumstance*, 3–61; Moss, "The Vietnam Generation," 4–9.

54. Stanton, *Decline and Fall*, 279–80.

55. Savage, Paul L., and Gabriel, Richard A., "Cohesion and Disintegration in the American Army," *Armed Forces and Society*, vol. 2 (Spring 1976), 362–71; Baritz, *Backfire*, 294–309; Davidson, *Vietnam at War*, 617–19.

56. Lipsman et al., *Fighting for Time*, 92–96.

57. *Ibid.*, 97–100. A CBS News television documentary portrayed a combat refusal that occurred in April 1970 in War Zone C near the Cambodian border during Operation TOAN THANG 43.

58. Lewy, *America in Vietnam*, 153–8; Cincinnatus, *Self-Destruction, passim*.

59. Lewy, *America in Vietnam*, 154–5; Fiman, Bryan G., et al., "Black-White and American-Vietnamese Relations Among Soldiers in Vietnam," *Journal of Social Issues*, vol. 31 (Fall 1975), 43–46; Lipsman, *Fighting for Time*, 102. African Americans constituted approximately 15 percent of the forces sent to Vietnam from 1961 to 1972, and Vietnam was the first major foreign war in which the U. S. Armed Forces were fully integrated.

60. Moss, "Vietnam Generation," 14.

61. Cited in Lipsman, *Fighting for Time*, 103.

62. McCoy, *The Politics of Heroin in Southeast Asia* (New York: Harper and Row, 1972), 9.

63. *Ibid.*, 181–5, 217–22. McCoy accuses several high-ranking military officials in the Thieu-Ky government of drug trafficking and he names names. McCoy also charges that American embassy officials refused to investigate these charges and denied that any South Vietnamese officials were involved in drug smuggling.

64. Porter (ed.), *Vietnam Documents*, vol. 2, Document 295, "Nixon Speech," April 20, 1970 (Extract), 539–41; Herring, *Longest War*, 3d. ed, 253. Sheehan, Neil, *A Bright Shining Lie,* 741–2, makes the point that Nixon's troop withdrawals saved the Army from disintegration.

65. Kissinger, *White House Years*, 458–61; Lipsman, *Fighting for Time*, 127–30, 138–42.

66. Davidson, *Vietnam at War*, 625; Herring, "The Nixon Strategy in Vietnam," 55–56; Lipsman, *Fighting for Time*, 146–47;

67. Kissinger, *White House Years*, 468–70. William Shawcross, *Sideshow: Kissinger, Nixon and the Destruction of Cambodia* (New York: Simon and Schuster, 1979), chap. 8, "The Coup," 112–27, has suggested U. S. complicity in the coup that overthrow Sihanouk. He has been vigorously rebutted by Henry Kissinger, *White House Years*, 517–21, notes, 1484–1485. No evidence has ever surfaced connecting the United States to the anti-Sihanouk coup.

68. Davidson, *Vietnam at War*, 625–7; Palmer, *Summons of the Trumpet*, 294–6.

69. Szulc, *Illusion of Peace*, 252–60; Lipsman, *Fighting for Time*, 152–3; Herring, *America's Longest War*, 235–6.

70. Transcript of Nixon's speech, April 30, 1970; a copy of the speech is printed in Nixon, Richard M., *Public Papers, Richard Nixon, 1970* (Washington, D. C.: U. S. GPO, 1971), 405–10.

71. Stanton, *Decline and Fall*, 319–21.

72. *Ibid.*, 322–5; Palmer, *Summons of the Trumpet*, 297–301.

73. Palmer, *Summons of the Trumpet*, 299–301; Stanton, *Decline and Fall*, 324–5; Davidson, *Vietnam at War*, 627–9; Hess, *Vietnam*, 122–123. During Toan Than 43, the VC/NVA lost about 11,000 KIAs, the Allies 976, including 338 Americans. The Allies captured 16,700,000 rounds of small-arms ammunition, 23,000 individual weapons, 200,000 rounds of antiaircraft ammunition, and 14 million pounds of rice.

74. Palmer, *The 25-Year War*, 103–4; Stanton, *Decline and Fall*, 324–5; "Vietnam: A War That Is Finished," CBS television documentary first shown to the American public, August 1975.

75. DeBenedetti, *An American Ordeal*, 279.

76. *Ibid.*, 279–80.

77. Lipsman, *Fighting for Time*, 181–2; DeBenedetti, *An American Ordeal*, 280–2. During the early morning hours on May 9, 1970, President Nixon, unable to sleep, decided on impulse to visit with some of the student protesters camped near the Lincoln Memorial. He attempted to start a dialogue and explain the reasons for the Cambodian incursion. The students, amazed and embarrassed, listened, but did not respond to presidential efforts at conversation. As was his wont, Mr. Nixon was more intent on talking than he was on listening. There was no dialogue, mostly a Nixonian monologue. After an hour or so of futile efforts at communicating, Nixon went to breakfast with some members of his staff.

78. DeBenedetti, *An American Ordeal*, 281–2.

79. Morris, *Uncertain Greatness*, 199–201.

80. Young, *Vietnam Wars*, 251–2.

81. Brandon, *Retreat of American Power*, 146–9; Herring, *America's Longest War*, 238.

82. Morris, *Uncertain Greatness*, 174–5; Kissinger, *White House Years*, 968–72; Goodman, *The Lost Peace*, 105–7.

83. DeBenedetti, *An American Ordeal*, 293; Ambrose, *Nixon: The Triumph of a Politician*, 394.

84. Palmer, *Summons of the Trumpet*, 302–3; Stanton, *Decline and Fall*, 333–4; and Davidson, *Vietnam at War*, 637–41. Thieu named the proposed incursion into Laos after Lam Son, the birth place of Le Loi, a great Vietnamese national hero who, in one of the most famous military campaigns in Vietnamese history, had defeated an invading Chinese army in 1427.

85. Davidson, *Vietnam at War*, 637–42.

86. Palmer, *Summons of the Trumpet*, 304–5.

87. Davidson, *Vietnam at War*, 645–9; Stanton, *Decline and Fall*, 336–7. South Vietnamese losses were heavy: 1,146 battle deaths, 4,236 wounded.

88. Quote is from Davidson, *Vietnam at War*, 651–2.

89. *Ibid.*, 652–4; Stanton, *Rise and Fall*, 336–7.

90. Hess, *Vietnam*, 126.

91. Kissinger, *White House Years*, 1016–23.

92. Porter (ed.), *Vietnam Documents*, vol. 2, Document 300, "DRV Nine-Point Plan," June 26, 1971, 555–6; Goodman, *The Lost Peace*, pp. 111–15; Kissinger, *The White House Years*, 1023–31.

93. Fulghum, David, Maitland, Terrence, and the editors of Boston Publishing Company, *South Vietnam on Trial: Mid-1970 to 1972* (Boston: Boston Publishing Co., 1984), 102–4.

94. *Ibid.*, 104–8; Herring, *America's Longest War*, 245.

95. DeBenedetti, *An American Ordeal*, 307–8. One of the leaders of the VVAW demonstration in the nation's capital was a future U. S. senator from Massachusetts, John Kerry.

96. *Ibid.*, 309–10; Young, *Vietnam Wars*, 257–9.

97. Polls cited in DeBenedetti, *An American Ordeal*, 310.

98. DeBenedetti, *An American Ordeal*, 324.

99. Quote is from Herring, *America's Longest War*, 246.

100. Hess, *Vietnam*, 127; Clodfelter, *Limits*, 168; quote is from Thompson, Sir Robert, *Peace Is Not at Hand* (New York: David McKay, 1974), 96.

101. *Ibid.*

102. *Ibid.*, 127–8.

103. *Ibid.*

104. Duiker, *The Communist Road*, 288–92.

105. *Ibid.*, 292–3.

106. The three PAVN divisions included the 304th, the 308th, and the 324-B. Consciously emulating their heroic national past, the North Vietnamese leaders named their 1972 spring offensive after Nguyen Hue, who, in 1789, led a surprise offensive against a Chinese army, driving them out of Vietnam.

107. Davidson, *Vietnam at War*, 680–4; Stanton, *Rise and Fall*, 343; and Palmer, *Summons of the Trumpet*, 315–19.

108. Quote is from Isaacs, *Without Honor*, 26.

109. Stanton, *Rise and Fall*, 343–4; Duiker, *The Communist Road*, 293.

110. Reference note 31, chap. 4, this book; Sheehan, *A Bright Shining Lie*, 754–85. Sheehan's critically acclaimed best-seller is a superb biography of an extraordinary man who spent more time in South Vietnam than any other American civilian or military official.

111. Davidson, *Vietnam at War*, 688–93; Fulghum, *South Vietnam on Trial*, 184–9.

112. Stanton, *Rise and Fall*, 343–4; Davidson, *Vietnam at War*, 693–7.

113. Davidson, *Vietnam at War*, 706–13; Fulghum, *South Vietnam on Trial*, 150–4, 160–7.

114. Nixon, Richard, *RN: The Memoirs of Richard Nixon* (New York: Grosset and Dunlap, 1978), 587; Clodfelter, *Limits*, 153.

115. Quoted in Fulghum, *South Vietnam on Trial*, 142.

116. Clodfelter, *Limits*, 153–4.

117. *Ibid.*, 158.

118. Hess, *Vietnam*, 128–9; Clodfelter, *Limits*, 159.

119. Nixon, *Memoirs*, 590–1; Kissinger, *White House Years*, 1119–21; Fulghum, *South Vietnam on Trial*, 142–3.

120. Nixon, *Memoirs*, 588–9; Kissinger, *White House Years*, 1113–14.

121. Fulghum, *South Vietnam on Trial*, 144–5; Goodman, *The Lost Peace*, 118–19; Kissinger, *White House Years*, 1135–37, 1144–48, 1169–70.

122. Quoted in Herring, *America's Longest War*, 247.

123. Porter (ed.), *Vietnam Documents*, vol. 2, Document 305, "Address to the Nation by Nixon," May 8, 1972 (Extracts), 566–7; Nixon, *Memoirs*, 605; Clodfelter, *Limits*, 157.

124. Hess, *Vietnam*, 129.

125. Isaacs, *Without Honor*, 27.

126. Hess, *Vietnam*, 130.

127. Summers, *On Strategy*, 134–5.

128. Davidson, *Vietnam at War*, 706–12; Stanton, *Rise and Fall*, 344–5; Fulghum, *South Vietnam on Trial*, 183–4.

129. Quote is from Davidson, *Vietnam at War*, 712.

130. Duiker, *The Communist Road*, 295–6; Goodman, *The Lost Peace*, 120–1; Clodfelter, *Limits*, 170–1.

131. Clodfelter, *Limits*, 161–2, 165–7.

132. Goodman, *The Lost Peace*, 126–9; Lipsman, Samuel, Weiss, Stephen, and the editors of the Boston Publishing Co., *The False Peace; 1972–1974* (Boston: Boston Publishing Co., 1985), 9–13, in the series, *The Vietnam Experience*; Kissinger, *The White House Years*, 1331–59.

133. Kissinger, *White House Years*, 1366–92; Nixon, *Memoirs*, 702–3; Hess, *Vietnam*, 131.

134. The quote is found in Herring, *America's Longest War*, 252. Kissinger has always denied he harbored any notion of a peace agreement that would let South Vietnam survive for a decent interval, a few years, before falling to the Communists.

135. Kissinger, *White House Years*, 1395. Kissinger may have also been hoping to influence the outcome of the election with his remark.

136. Porter (ed.), *Vietnam Documents*, vol. 2, Document 315, "Letter from Richard Nixon to RVN President Nguyen Van Thieu," Nov. 14, 1972, 581–3; Nixon, *Memoirs*, 701–7. Quote is taken from Nixon's memoirs, 701.

137. Nixon is quoted in Young, *Vietnam Wars*, 277.

138. Kissinger, *White House Years*, 1415–46; Nixon, *Memoirs*, 732–3; Goodman, *The Lost Peace*, 151–60; Clodfelter, *Limits*, 179–81; and Porter, (ed.), *Vietnam Documents*, vol. 2, Document 318, "Press Conference Statement by Kissinger," Dec. 16, 1972, (Extract), 587–90.

139. Clodfelter, *Limits*, 182.

140. Quoted in Herring, *America's Longest War*, 253–4.

141. Clodfelter, *Limits*, 186–9.

142. Quoted in *Ibid.*, 191.

143. Isaacs, Arnold, *Without Honor: Defeat in Vietnam and Cambodia* (Baltimore: The Johns Hopkins University Press, 1983), 54–57; Kissinger, *White House Years*, 1453.

144. Lewy, *America in Vietnam*, 403–4.

145. Clodfelter, *Limits*, 188–9.

146. Hess, *Vietnam*, 133.

147. Duiker, *The Communist Road*, 296–7; Goodman, *The Lost Peace*, 160–4; Kissinger, *White House Years*, 1461–8. The U. S. air war against North Vietnam ended on December 29, 1972. The U. S. air war in South Vietnam ended on January 27, 1973. The U. S. air war in Laos ended on February 22, 1973. The U. S. air war against Cambodia continued until August 15, 1973.

148. Herring, *Longest War,* ed., 281.

149. Quoted in Young, *Vietnam Wars*, 279.

150. Hess, *Vietnam*, 134–5; Porter, (ed.), *Vietnam Documents*, vol. 2, Document 320, "Letter from Nixon to Thieu," January 5, 1973, 592; Nixon, *Memoirs*, 737–51. Nixon wrote two letters to Thieu, pledging U. S. support. One, dated November 14, 1972, said, "You have my absolute assurance that if Hanoi fails to abide by the terms of this agreement it is my intent to take swift and severe retaliatory action." The second letter, dated January 5, 1973, said, "We will respond with full force should the settlement be violated by North Vietnam."

151. Copies of the Agreement on Ending the War and Restoring Peace in Vietnam, January 27, 1973, are reprinted in Goodman, *The Lost Peace*, 188–99. See also Porter, (ed.), *Vietnam Documents*, vol. 2, Document 324, "Letter from Nixon to Pham Van Dong," February 1, 1973, 599–600. Article 21 of the peace agreement committed the United States to help finance the postwar reconstruction of Vietnam. In the secret February 1, 1973, letter that President Nixon sent to North Vietnam's Prime Minister Pham Van Dong, he promised $3.25 billion in reconstruction aid and another $1.5 billion in commodities.

152. *Ibid.*; Isaacs, *Without Honor*, 64–68, discusses the major political and military provisions of the treaty, mainly to show that few provisions were ever carried out.

153. Isaacs, *Without Honor*, 61; quote from Nixon's speech is from Olson and Roberts, *Where the Domino Fell*, 251.

154. General Ky's quote is from Olson and Roberts, *Where the Domino Fell*, 251.

155. Isaacs, *Without Honor,* 62–63; Herring, *America's Longest War*, 256.

156. Duiker, *The Communist Road*, 299; Davidson, *Vietnam at War*, 730–1.

157. Quote is from Duiker, *The Communist Road*, 299. The epistolary promises that President Nixon made to General Thieu to intervene militarily if the North Vietnamese violated the Paris Accords were secret, unknown to the Congress and to the American people. The commitments were never implemented because Nixon was forced to resign the presidency due to the Watergate scandals, and Congress refused to honor them.

158. Herring, *America's Longest War*, 256.

159. Quoted in Lipsman et al., *The False Peace*, 119.

9

The End of the Tunnel

The . . . lesson [of Vietnam] is that America must never commit its power and authority in defense of a country of only marginal strategic interests when that country lacks a broadly based government or the will to create one.

George Ball

INDECENT INTERVAL

The war in South Vietnam went on, despite the signing of the Paris Accords, only it now continued without direct American participation. Neither side observed the cease-fire and both ignored or deliberately violated many of the other agreements. Neither side made a serious effort to seek a political settlement. The Lao Dong leaders in Hanoi continued to seek the overthrow of the Thieu regime by both political and military means, and to reunify Vietnam under their control. South Vietnam, dependent on U. S. economic and military assistance since birth, struggled to survive after the Americans had departed. President Nixon, engulfed by the Watergate scandal from March 1973 until his forced resignation of the presidency in August 1974, could not keep the promises of support and protection that he had made to General Thieu.

Congress restricted the President's power to intervene militarily in the Indochina War. Congress also drastically curtailed the amount of American economic and military assistance to South Vietnam, which undermined both the ability and the will of the RVNAF forces to defend themselves. By the end of 1974, the United States had virtually abandoned its long-time client in southern Vietnam. The South Vietnamese economy deteriorated, its people were demoralized, and the military balance of power shifted in favor of the VC/NVA forces. During the spring of 1975, when Hanoi, confident that the United States would not intervene militarily to save the Thieu government, mounted another major offensive, the GVN defenses collapsed with stunning rapidity, and the Thieu government found itself paralyzed and helpless. Neither Kissinger nor Nixon's successor Gerald Ford could convince Congress that it should vote for additional aid funds for the dying nation. Saigon fell to the Communists on April 30, 1975, and the republic of South Vietnam ceased to exist.

A cease-fire in nearby Laos followed the January 1973 Paris agreements. The Communist Pathet Lao and the Laotian government agreed to a cease-fire on February 21, 1973. The arrangement did not bring instant peace to that country, but then the fighting in Laos had not generated the hatred or destructiveness it had in Vietnam and Cambodia. As John Kenneth Galbraith dryly observed, the people of Laos "have not learned to kill each other like the civilized nations."[1] Laotian Communist leader Prince Souphanouvong and government head Prince Souvanna Phouma were half-brothers who treated each other with respect. Following the cease-fire agreement, the fighting in Laos continued sporadically. American B-52s ended their bombing in Laos on February 22. Ground fighting gradually tapered off, and by April 1973, the long civil war in Laos had ended. On September 12, negotiators signed a protocol that cleared the way for establishing a new coalition government, a government in which the Pathet Lao was the dominant party. Under the new arrangement, the Pathet Lao retained complete control over the areas of the country where its military forces were in control and shared power to administer the rest of the country.

When Cambodia and South Vietnam fell to the Communists in the spring of 1975, the Pathet Lao formally took control in Laos. The Pathet Lao triumph meant that the North Vietnamese had considerable leverage in Laos, because the Laotian Communists had always been closely aligned with the Vietnamese Communist Party. Although the Communist takeover in Laos was kinder and gentler than the Communist triumphs in neighboring Cambodia and Vietnam, it had its violent and repressive aspects. The Pathet Lao sent thousands of supporters of the deposed Phouma government to "reeducation centers." The chief victims of the Communist triumph in Laos were the Hmong, the Meo tribesmen whom the CIA had trained and equipped to fight in the so-called "secret war" in Laos. The Hmong, abandoned by their former American patrons, were forced to flee their native land. About 100,000 Meo ended up in the United States. Most of those who stayed behind were mercilessly hunted down and killed by the Communists.[2]

In neighboring Cambodia, the Khmer Rouge and Lon Nol's forces waged a furious struggle. Lon Nol had offered the rebels a cease-fire soon after the Paris Accords had been signed, but the Khmer Rouge leaders, determined to overthrow the Cambodian government, had rejected it. In February 1973, the insurgents appeared to have victory within their grasp. They had isolated Phnom Penh, and their forces had reached the suburbs of the city, a scant five kilometers away. However, an American airlift supplied the city, and, during six months of intensive bombing, U. S. B-52s annihilated the Khmer Rouge forces attacking Phnom Penh. Having taken about 20,000 casualties, the rebels withdrew the remnants of their forces in August. The

Cambodian army mounted a counteroffensive. U. S. air power had given Lon Nol's inept army and rickety regime a reprieve. The six-month-long U. S. aerial assault had temporarily destroyed the offensive capability of the Khmer Rouge, but it also had a destructive impact on the Cambodian nation. The bombing disrupted the economy, generated 2 million refugees, and contributed to mass impoverishment and the general disintegration of Cambodian society.

Congress cut off all funds for the U. S. air war in Cambodia, and the bombing stopped on August 15, 1973. The rebels regrouped and resumed their attacks four months later. By early 1974, the Khmer Rouge once again threatened Phnom Penh. This time, Lon Nol's forces were forced to defend their capital city without American air power. The U. S. ambassador in Phnom Penh, John Gunther Dean, concluded that the government's cause was hopeless and that its military forces would be defeated.[3]

As the Indochina wars raged on, the American POWs came home. The return of the 591 American prisoners-of-war in February and March 1973 represented the only positive U. S. accomplishment to come out of any postwar negotiations held in accordance with the terms of the Paris agreements. The arrangements called for the POWs to be released in four increments, fifteen days apart. The remaining 24,000 U. S. troops on active duty in South Vietnam would depart simultaneously, in four equal-sized increments, spaced fifteen days apart. If any snags occurred that delayed the return of the POWs, the remaining U. S. troops would delay their departure from Vietnam.[4]

Called Operation HOMECOMING, the first contingent of 115 prisoners-of-war left Hanoi's Gia Lam Airport on February 12 and were flown to Clark Air Force Base in the Philippines. At Clark, the men were given medical examinations and brought up to date on family news and on their current military status. Many aviators were able to enjoy their first American-style meal in years—in this case, steaks and banana splits. They were then flown to the United States where they had to endure a media blitz as they were reunited with their families. The other returning prisoners followed in fifteen-day intervals, until the last men had been repatriated on March 29. Hundreds of small towns and cities across the United States staged heroes' welcomes for individual returnees.

The POWs had survived the longest captivity of any prisoners in American military history. As prisoners, they also had often been forced to endure deprivation, harassment, and cruel tortures inflicted by their captors. Most of the prisoners endured their agonies heroically, maintaining their military professionalism under extreme duress in accordance with the strict standards of the U. S. Code of Military Conduct.

Colonel Fred V. Cherry, the senior African American POW, set an outstanding example. He was tortured for ninety-two consecutive days after his captors failed to break him by appealing to his "blackness." Colonel Cherry's courageous patriotism earned him a broken rib and a punctured lung.[5]

Another reason for celebrating the returning POWs as heroes reflected the reality that, for most Americans, the homecoming of the POWs was the only positive

Figure 9.1   A hero's welcome at Hanoi's Gia Lam Airport: Air Force Captain William R. Schwertfeger of Caldwell, Kansas, just after his release from a North Vietnamese prison. Schwertfeger was among the last group of U. S. POWs repatriated in late March 1973. *Source:* AP/World Wide Photos

experience to come out of the long American ordeal in Vietnam. It was the only outcome of the Vietnam War that most Americans could feel any enthusiasm about or take pride in.

On March 30, the last contingent of 5,200 U. S. soldiers remaining in South Vietnam assembled at Tan Son Nhut Air Base on the outskirts of Saigon, in readiness for their flights back to the United States. By April 1, 1973, the only American military personnel remaining in South Vietnam were 159 Marines, who were serving as embassy guards, and another fifty people, who were serving in the Defense Attache Office as permitted by the provisions of the Paris agreement.

The celebrity status accorded the POWs contrasted starkly with the treatment often given to returning ground-combat veterans, particularly veterans who returned after Tet-68. They rarely received parades or official welcomes home. Few Americans appeared to appreciate their sacrifice or thanked them for a job well done. They were often ignored by a society that had carelessly sent them off to fight a war that most Americans were ambivalent about or had lost faith in completely. Returning Vietnam combat veterans found themselves to be embarrassing reminders of a war that no one wanted to think or talk about. Worse, some people, opposed to the war, took out their animus toward that conflict by insulting, harassing, or condemning the returning uniformed veterans.

The large majority of returning Vietnam combat veterans were neither war criminals nor head cases. They did not suffer from drug or alcohol addiction nor did they have acute psychological or physical disabilities. But most veterans had to struggle to come to terms with their war experiences, to readjust to civilian routines, and to reintegrate into American society. They often had trouble completing their educations, finding steady work, and maintaining stable marriages and families. They also often found that they could not discuss their war experiences, or their thoughts and feelings about the war, with their families or close friends. Many veterans retained bitter feelings that their efforts and sacrifices had been meaningless, that they had fought in the service of a losing cause that had been repudiated or forgotten by most Americans.[6]

Surveys have found that thousands of combat veterans continue to be plagued by Post-Traumatic Stress Disorder (PTSD) long after the Vietnam War. Veterans afflicted with PTSD suffer a variety of psychological dysfunctions induced by their traumatic wartime experiences. Symptoms can include (1) drug and alcohol abuse; (2) recurring nightmares, often reliving horrible war experiences; (3) chronic depression; (4) psychic numbing, the inability to feel any strong emotion; (5) guilt feelings about war actions, or having survived when buddies were killed; (6) the inability to experience intimacy; and (7) unpredictable outbursts of rage and aggressive behavior.[7]

Even as the American POWs came home, the war in Vietnam roared on.[8] Even before the cease-fire had been declared, Vietcong forces had embarked on a series of land-grabbing campaigns in various sectors of South Vietnam. General Thieu responded with offensive operations designed to reclaim these lands and enhance the total amount of territory and population under the control of the RVN. In February 1973, as the postwar war began, the military situation in South Vietnam favored Thieu's forces. U. S. aid had built up the RVNAF forces until they had become one of the largest and best-equipped armies in the world.

In the spring of 1973, the Thieu government appeared to be in a strong position. As a consequence of successful pacification efforts from 1970 to 1972, coupled with the smashing of the Communist Nguyen Hue Offensive during the summer of 1972, the RVN controlled about 75 percent of the territory and perhaps 80 percent of the 19 million inhabitants of South Vietnam. Communist holdings were confined mostly to the thinly populated western periphery of the country and scattered enclaves in the Mekong Delta, in the central highlands, and along the coast. The RVNAF totaled more than one million troops, and they were well-equipped, because of the recent lavish American resupply efforts. Both the surviving Vietcong forces and the approximately 150,000 North Vietnamese forces in southern Vietnam, still battered and short of supplies from the 1972 campaigns, were no match initially for Thieu's forces. During the first year following the Paris agreements, the South Vietnamese forces not only reclaimed most of the lands and villages grabbed by the Vietcong in the fall of 1972, but also acquired control of some areas that had been in VC hands for years. Thieu was determined to use his military advantage while he had it to try to establish his control over all the land and people of South Vietnam.[9]

Underlying political weaknesses undercut much of the military advantage that Thieu's forces enjoyed over its enemies during 1973. In some regions, authorities loyal to Saigon ruled by day; the Vietcong took over at night. The populations of many villages counted as loyal to the RVN were inhabited by villagers who did not trust or respect the Saigon government; they were secret neutralists or supporters of the National Liberation Front. Many of the Saigon government's civilian and military bureaucrats assigned to administer districts and villages came from upper-class or urban middle-class backgrounds. Sullen and resentful villagers did not identify with these alien bureaucrats or accept their authority as legitimate. The Saigon government's control over much of the rural population of South Vietnam was only nominal.[10]

Thieu remained convinced that if the Communists rebuilt their forces and launched attacks in South Vietnam that his forces could not contain, Nixon would make good on his pledge to rescue the RVN. Even though all American combat forces had been withdrawn from South Vietnam, Washington continued to provide strong military support for the Thieu government. Thousands of former American military advisers continued to work with the ARVN forces, but they had civilian statuses to circumvent treaty provisions. Powerful U. S. naval and air forces remained nearby: in the Gulf of Tonkin, in Thailand, and on the island of Guam. Nixon attempted to maintain a credible threat of U. S. reentry into the war to deter Hanoi from treaty violations and aggressive military actions. Thieu, confident he could count on U. S. forces to bail him out if he got into trouble, took a hard line toward the Communists. He pursued a policy of the "four no's": (1) no abandonment of territory in South Vietnam; (2) no coalition government with the PRG or neutralists; (3) no negotiations with the Communists; and (4) no Communist or neutralist political activities in South Vietnam.[11]

Hanoi, needing a respite from war to rebuild its shattered military forces, confined its activities in South Vietnam largely to politics during most of 1973. The Communists maintained a low level of resistance to Thieu's forces. They also modernized their logistics capability in South Vietnam. They constructed a macadamized highway and an eight-inch oil pipeline running along the border with Laos and Cambodia from the DMZ to Loc Ninh, about sixty-five miles northwest of Saigon. Hanoi also infiltrated more troops into South Vietnam in violation of the Paris Accords. During the final months of 1973, about 170,000 PAVN forces and 60,000 Vietcong could be found in South Vietnam. The Communists also decided to resume the war in the south, on a limited basis. They attacked the ARVN forces in the Mekong Delta, the Iron Triangle, and in the central highlands, inflicting heavy casualties and reclaiming some traditional strongholds.[12]

Within the United States, the burgeoning Watergate scandals had seriously eroded Nixon's ability to influence events in Indochina. During 1973, for the first time in the long war, Congress took decisive actions to end all lingering American military activity in Indochina. In June, Congress passed legislation requiring an immediate end to the bombing of Cambodia and all other U. S. military operations in Indochina. Nixon vetoed the measure and the House sustained his veto. Congress subsequently forced a reluctant president to accept a compromise proposal that halted the bombing on August 15.[13]

In November 1973, Congress enacted the War Powers Act over another presidential veto. The War Powers Act required that the president inform Congress within forty-eight hours of any decision to deploy U. S. forces overseas, and the new law further mandated that the president must remove these forces within sixty days, unless Congress specifically endorsed their deployment. The War Powers Act, in tandem with the Cambodian bombing cut-off, made it virtually impossible for President Nixon to commit U. S. forces to any further military operations in Indochina.[14]

By the end of 1973, Nixon was powerless to influence events in Indochina. All of the power and popularity that had accrued from his adroit diplomacy, the landslide victory over George McGovern, and achieving the Paris Accords had vanished; they had gone up in the smoke of the Watergate scandal and in the face of Congressional assertiveness. With his popular approval ratings reduced to historic lows, Nixon fought grimly for his political survival against a rising tide of forces determined to destroy him if evidence implicating him in the Watergate cover-up could be found. He could only watch passively as the Indochina postwar war escalated and the political settlement he had tried to forge for South Vietnam became a dead letter.[15]

During 1974, the military balance in South Vietnam turned steadily against the ARVN forces, even though paper force levels continued to favor the South Vietnamese heavily over their enemies.[16] The Communists systematically exploited strategic weaknesses of the RVNAF forces. Because of Thieu's efforts to gain control over his whole country, many of his divisions were tied down in static defensive positions. They were vulnerable to attacks wherever the VC/PAVN forces chose to strike. By the fall of 1974, Hanoi had put an estimated 285,000 troops in South Vietnam. They had also stockpiled huge quantities of war materiel brought down the Ho Chi Minh trail, which had been transformed into a rapid and efficient supply corridor for men, weapons, fuel, and supplies since the departure of U. S. air power from the war.

Meanwhile, South Vietnam's economy began to collapse from a combination of declining American support and internal weaknesses. Corruption, a chronic problem of the GVN since its inception, scaled new heights during Thieu's final years. Corruption involved most senior officials in the RVN military and civilian bureaucracies; it also involved many lower-echelon personnel. Corruption was more widespread in the military, among the officer corps, than elsewhere. Wealthy soldiers purchased safe duty assignments. Promotions were regularly sold to the highest bidders. Pilots demanded bribes before flying combat missions. Supply officers demanded bribes before furnishing food for the troops. Division commanders regularly siphoned off huge sums of money from military payrolls. Presiding at the apex of this empire of corruption, General Thieu and his senior military commanders accrued great wealth.

Thieu had allowed the corruption system to flourish in order to survive in power. "Corruption had become the glue that held the Thieu regime together."[17]

Official efforts to eliminate or slow the rate of corruption "ranged from the ineffectual to the pathetic."[18] General Thieu felt compelled to tolerate his regime's staggering corruption, since he and his cronies were the prime beneficiaries. Even had he been willing to try seriously to reform his government, he would have failed. Had Thieu tried to remove the corruption from all of his government's civilian and military agencies, the radical surgery required would have killed the patient. It also would have cut out his political power and all major sources of wealth.

Except for dismissing a few corrupt officials for cosmetic purposes, Thieu chose to cover up his regime's systemic corruption. U. S. officials, led by the last American ambassador to South Vietnam, Graham Martin, went along with the cover-up. They either denied that corruption was a serious problem in South Vietnam, or insisted that it was being eliminated. If U. S. officials were complacent about corruption, most South Vietnamese, victimized in countless ways by fraud, bribery, extortion, and graft, were not. Their anger over government corruption was intensified by economic decline, and they complained bitterly about their predicament.

By mid-1974, Thieu presided over a collapsing economy. The rate of inflation had skyrocketed. The cost of living in Saigon had risen 27 percent during the first six months of the year. The price rise for essential commodities was even sharper: rice rose 100 percent, sugar 107 percent, and cooking oil 139 percent. Hyperinflation meant that most soldiers and civil servants were not earning enough to meet the basic needs of their families. Such conditions only intensified the regime's systemic graft and corruption. "The ultimate expression of the decay of South Vietnam was the widespread black market with the Communist forces."[19] Both the Vietcong and North Vietnamese troops were able to get much of their food, medicine, and even weapons from regions under Saigon's control. The sellers' motives were usually mercenary; to make a buck, they sold their enemies what they needed.

At the same time retail prices were shooting up, unemployment was rising rapidly. In 1974, an estimated 1 million people, about one-fifth of the workforce, were without jobs. The piaster was devalued repeatedly against the American dollar; a huge trade deficit evolved that quickly wiped out the RVN's slim foreign reserves. In 1973, a poor rice harvest and an Arab oil boycott had exacerbated South Vietnam's mounting economic miseries. Rice and other food commodities had to be imported; many consumer goods were in short supply. Industries dependent on imported materials slashed their production schedules or, more often, shut down.[20] The South Vietnamese people suffered from an economic double whammy composed of hyperinflation and deep depression.

The sick South Vietnamese economy was further undermined by the effects of the American pullout. The pullout eliminated about 300,000 jobs, as well as a large annual inflow of dollars. In 1970, U. S. soldiers had spent over $500 million, and in 1971, they had spent over $400 million in South Vietnam. In 1974, they spent less than

$100 million.[21] By 1974, economic and social conditions were the worst they had ever been during South Vietnam's twenty-year existence. As corruption and economic decay destroyed the remaining morale and cohesion of South Vietnamese society, the RVNAF, its military shield, also began to give way.

One of the major causes of the RVNAF's decline in 1974 was Congress's deep reductions in the amount of U. S. military assistance going to South Vietnam. Because the huge South Vietnamese army had been trained to fight American-style battles, relying on mobility and massive fire power, it was extremely expensive to maintain and operate; requiring an annual budget of $3 to $3.5 billion to sustain it. But the United States provided only $2.3 billion during the fiscal year 1973 and $1.1 billion for 1974.[22] These drastic aid cuts severely hampered the performance of the South Vietnamese armed forces. Helicopter and air force operations had to be curtailed because of gasoline shortages and the lack of spare parts. Artillery rounds and small arms ammunition were in short supply. Unable to maneuver or to fight in the manner in which they had been trained because of equipment and ammunition shortages, the morale and confidence of the RVNAF forces, never too high under the best of circumstances, plummeted.

The Congressional aid cuts no doubt sapped the strength and morale of the RVNAF forces, but they were not the most important causes of the GVN's growing military weakness. The brute reality was that Vietnamization had never worked. Most of the RVNAF's many shortcomings that had always vitiated its fighting abilities had never been corrected. The economic deterioration of 1974 further undermined RVNAF capabilities. Desertions probably exceeded inductions in 1974, and the officer corps grew more corrupt and politicized than ever.

But the fundamental weakness of the South Vietnamese military forces could be found in the realm of politics. Thieu's government remained what it had been from its beginning, a narrowly based oligarchy dependent for its survival on the political loyalty of senior military commanders. These loyalties had to be purchased—by favors, bribery, and corruption. The Thieu regime never embodied Vietnamese nationalism. It never won the hearts and minds of most South Vietnamese civilians, nor the loyalty and devotion of most of the men serving in its military forces. Thieu's American connection and his skill at political maneuver had kept him in power for years, but neither he nor his government represented a cause or a purpose, a positive reason for which most soldiers wanted to risk their lives. South Vietnam had always been a nation made up of more cynics than believers, most of whom viewed military service as either an unavoidable disaster or an opportunity for graft. Systemic corruption, the decline of the army, and the reductions in U. S. aid combined to undermine the fragile South Vietnamese political structure. "After two decades of U. S. support, the government of South Vietnam still did not represent any genuine sense of nationhood."[23]

During August 1974, Congress slashed U. S. military aid to South Vietnam still further, and Nixon, his role in the attempted cover-up of the Watergate burglary established, was forced to resign in disgrace. It was evident by then that Thieu was running out of American friends, and Americans were running out of reasons for continuing to support his cause. Thieu soon faced the most serious challenge to his rule since taking office. On September 8, a group of Catholics led by Father Tran Huu Thanh publicly protested the extensive corruption that riddled Thieu's government. Thanh's charges set off a torrent of protest against Thieu and his corrupt regime. Militant Buddhists again took to the streets to lead popular protests against the government. Thieu made a few efforts to respond to his critics, then cracked down hard on the protesters. Thieu's police violently suppressed the protests.[24] Many citizens were bludgeoned into silence; popular support for the RVN was at an all-time low. More and more Saigonese talked openly of seeking an accommodation with the Communists.

The Communist leadership in Hanoi observed the general deterioration of South Vietnamese society and the continuing cuts in American support for Thieu's failing regime during 1974. The hawks in the Politburo believed that the time had come for another all-out war in South Vietnam. The doves took a more cautious stance. They wanted to wait and see if the new American president, Gerald Ford, could persuade Congress to restore military aid funds to Thieu's regime. They also wanted to wait and see if Ford would be willing to make good on Nixon's promise to recommit U. S. air power in South Vietnam to try to save the RVN in the event of another invasion from North Vietnam. Hanoi's hawks and doves both ruled out as politically impossible the possibility that the U. S. might once again commit ground troops to save South Vietnam.

By fall, the Hanoi hawks had won the debate. What clinched the argument favoring another North Vietnamese attack on South Vietnam was the outbreak of popular unrest in Saigon and Hanoi's perception that U. S. domestic public opinion and Congressional opposition would likely prevent Ford from ordering any further American military interventions into South Vietnam. At a key meeting held in October 1974, the Politburo approved a proposal by General Van Tien Dung, Giap's successor as chief of staff, for a new military offensive scheduled to be launched in South Vietnam in 1975. General Dung had concluded that the war in South Vietnam had reached its final stage. South Vietnam's economy, society, and government were deteriorating. The PAVN forces now enjoyed a clear advantage on the battlefield. Dung's strategic plan called for a two-year campaign that would culminate in the overthrow of the Thieu regime and the creation of a coalition government in 1976.[25]

In the fall of 1974, when Hanoi's leaders looked at the United States, they saw a nation led by an inexperienced president who had not been elected to the office and a dovish Congress that was increasingly preoccupied with the deteriorating American economy.[26] Serious internal problems generated by energy shortages and "stagflation" had a far greater urgency for most Americans than a lingering war in Indochina that no longer directly involved American troops. Washington viewed such foreign policy issues as relations with the major Communist powers, efforts to break the dismal cycle of periodic warfare between Arabs and Israelis, and the quarrels with NATO allies as all taking priority over a conflict in Southeast Asia that had already gone on far too long and had cost far more in lives and dollars than anyone had ever anticipated. Hanoi's directorate understood that the United States still possessed formidable military power and that these forces were positioned to intervene in Indochina, but they made a judgment that Washington had lost the political will to reenter the Vietnam War.

ENDGAME

In mid-December, concluding that the time had come to initiate the final phase of the postwar war, General Dung ordered two divisions of Vietcong and PAVN forces under the command of General Tran Van Tra to attack Phuoc Long, an isolated and poorly defended province near the Cambodian border northwest of Saigon. Dung would use the assault on Phuoc Long as a test, to find out whether Saigon and Washington would respond to a direct attack on South Vietnamese territory that clearly violated the Paris agreements. Dung and members of his staff knew of former President Nixon's commitments to General Thieu, and they wanted to find out if his successor intended to honor them.

Within three weeks, the Communist forces had overrun the province and captured the provincial capital, Phuoc Binh. The RVNAF forces could do little to prevent the disaster. The VNAF pilots lacked the skill to fly close air support missions. The ARVN helicopter squadrons lacked the airlift capability to fly in reinforcements. The ARVN defenders took heavy casualties during the three weeks of fighting in Phuoc Long. The Phuoc Long debacle demonstrated that Thieu's government lacked both the means and the will to defend its territory against the first major NVA offensive in three years. More important, it soon became evident to the North Vietnamese that American officials responded indifferently to this latest threat to their ally. Hanoi concluded that the Ford administration would not intervene militarily in South Vietnam, regardless of the provocation or threat.

When Hanoi's directorate perceived that Saigon could not defend Phuoc Long and that the Ford administration would not intervene, they ordered a second phase of the offensive to begin, a series of attacks to be launched in the central highlands.[27] The North Vietnamese army that General Dung prepared to unleash in the central highlands was much improved over those of 1968 and 1972. The NVA had modernized its logistics capability, had refined its tactics, and had significantly enhanced its air defense capabilities. The army that was poised to slam into the central highlands was a powerful and mobile strike force capable of defeating the RVNAF forces and overthrowing the RVN. It probably could have fought effectively even if the Americans had thrown their air power at the NVA. South Vietnam's final agony was about to begin.

On March 10, five PAVN main force divisions, joined by regiments of tanks, artillery, antiaircraft, and engineers, attacked the strategic city of Ban Me Thuot, the capital of the Darlac Province. Dung concentrated his forces to mount an overwhelming attack on the city. The outgunned ARVN defenders fought bravely, but Ban Me Thout fell to the Communists within one week. The fall of Ban Me Thuot represented a strategic disaster for the GVN. With the takeover of that city, the NVA had positioned itself to achieve its long-standing strategic goal, the bisection of South Vietnam.[28] After the fall of Ban Me Thuot, no powerful ARVN forces blocked the PAVN's march to the sea. South Vietnam was about to be cut in two.

While the battle for Ban Me Thuot was being fought, General Thieu made a fateful decision that hastened the demise of his country. He suddenly abandoned his strategy of holding as much South Vietnamese territory as possible. Convinced that the outnumbered and outgunned defenders of Pleiku and Kontum could not hold off the Communist attackers, he ordered his commanders to withdraw their forces. Thieu wanted to redeploy them to try to hold all of South Vietnam south of a line running from Tuy Hoa on the coast to the Cambodian border.[29] Most of South Vietnam's strategic resources and population lay south of this line. General Thieu decided to trade territory for time and for a chance to consolidate his defenses farther to the south. He would accept the loss of the northern half of his nation, the truncation of his country, in order to preserve the southern half. He would "lighten the top and keep the bottom."[30] Pleiku and Kontum fell to the Communists within a few days.

Thieu's military commanders in the central highlands had made no plans for a tactical retreat, and they could not execute his withdrawal orders effectively. The ARVN military discipline broke down, and the retreat quickly turned into a rout. Hundreds of thousands of terrified civilians joined the demoralized and panicked soldiers, as all fled the highlands toward the coastal city of Tuy Hoa. The two-week trek of soldiers and civilians streaming for the coast turned into a Convoy of Tears. During that hideous fortnight, two-thirds of the 60,000 RVNAF soldiers were killed or captured, and thousands of civilians perished as well. Most of the civilian casualties came from NVA fire, as the Communists continually attacked the virtually defenseless columns of intermingled soldiers, dependents, and refugees. Only about 20,000 South Vietnamese soldiers and perhaps 60,000 civilians reached their destination.[31]

Tuy Hoa provided only temporary respite for the refugees, because it too had to be abandoned to the advancing Communists. General Thieu's decision to abandon the central highlands was a strategic, political, and psychological disaster that cost his country six provinces, perhaps 200,000 civilian casualties, and more than two divisions of troops. Within two months, the NVA invaders captured most of the central provinces. During those two months there occurred the most dramatic shift in the military and political balance of power since the Vietnam War began. Thieu's decision to abandon the northern half of his country also cost him the remaining faith and confidence of the South Vietnamese people in his abilities to protect them from the enemy. Loss of the highlands "opened the way for even greater catastrophe in the coastal cities of South Vietnam."[32]

Thieu's decision to abandon the central highlands and the rapid crumbling of his armies caught the Communists by surprise. Although they were confident of ultimate victory, the North Vietnamese had anticipated stubborn resistance and hard fighting from Thieu's forces over the next two years. They had been at war with the RVN for

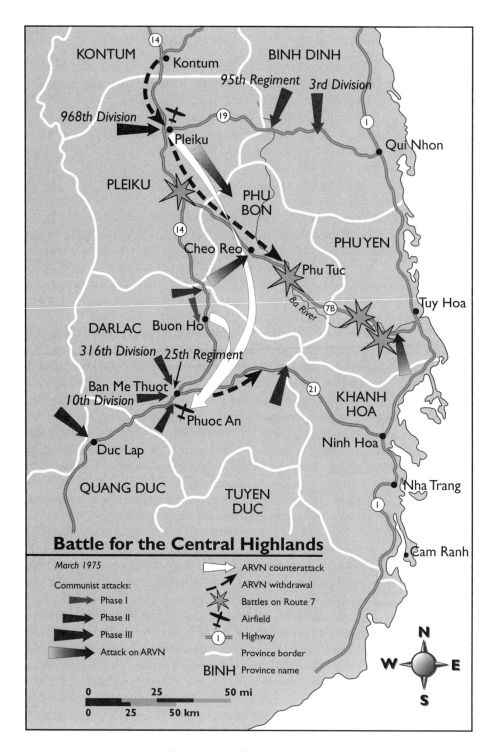

Figure 9.2 Public domain map.

nearly twenty years, and never had they enjoyed a major military victory or scored a decisive strategic breakthrough—until now. The rapid military breakdown following Thieu's fateful decision to abandon the central highlands astonished and, of course, delighted the cautious old men of the Politburo. Perceiving that their armies could probably conquer all of South Vietnam before the rainy season struck, they ordered General Dung to move up his timetable for victory by one year, from 1976 to the spring of 1975. They sensed they were getting close to achieving victory in the cause to which they had devoted their lives.

As the RVN forces abandoned the central highlands, an even greater South Vietnamese catastrophe occurred in the north. General Dung sent five NVA main force divisions, along with artillery, tank, and antiaircraft regiments, to attack key sites in the five northern provinces of South Vietnam that constituted Military Region I. In some of the battles, the outnumbered ARVN forces fought well, but the Communist quickly overpowered them. Refugees poured into Hue and Danang, the two largest cities in the region. As the PAVN forces approached these cities, the South Vietnamese defenses simply melted away. The ARVN soldiers and the militia abandoned their weapons, and many of them joined the mass air, sea, and land exodus from the doomed cities for Saigon. Chaos engulfed both cities. Hue fell on March 26. Four days later, the victorious NVA forces marched into Danang without meeting any resistance. Almost ten years to the day after the first U. S. Marines hit the beaches near Danang to initiate the American Vietnam war, South Vietnam's second largest city fell to the advancing Communist armies.

"The evacuation of Danang capped a disaster of far greater magnitude than the flight from the central highlands."[33] Only about 16,000 South Vietnamese troops were evacuated from Danang. Four infantry divisions, additional main force units, and territorial forces were either dispersed, detained, or destroyed. Of the 2 million people densely-packed into Danang at the end, over 1 million of them refugees, perhaps 50,000 got out before the Communist conquerors arrived.

The last flight out of Danang on March 29, 1975, was a World Airways 727 bound for Saigon. It was commandeered by a mob of 320 uniformed soldiers from the ARVN 1st Division who shoved aside women and children, often trampling members of their own families, in their panic-driven haste to board the plane. As pilot Ken Healy began to taxi the big plane toward the runway, crazed soldiers standing on the tarmac fired their rifles and threw grenades at the plane. One exploding grenade jammed the flaps on the left wing of the 727. Because a stalled VNAF A-37 jet fighter with bombs slung under its wings blocked the main runway, Healy was forced to use the short taxi strip for takeoff. As the overloaded plane struggled into the air, observers on the ground could see bodies hanging from the plane's undercarriage and wheel wells. Ninety minutes later, the plane, nearly empty of fuel, delivered its payload of patriots safely in Saigon.[34]

During the first week of April 1975, the coastal cities of Quang Ngai, Qui Nhon, Tuy Hoa, and Nha Trang fell to the NVA attackers as they rapidly advanced down the

South China seacoast of South Vietnam toward Saigon. The South Vietnamese defenses were collapsing so fast the Communist forces could scarcely keep pace. The PAVN forces also occupied Cam Ranh, formerly the site of the largest U. S. logistics facility in South Vietnam. Hanoi, sensing that final victory was near, ordered General Dung to marshal all of his forces for an immediate offensive against Saigon. For the North Vietnamese, time was of the essence. They had to attain final victory before the summer monsoons arrived. They also wanted to strike for the jugular while the South Vietnamese armies were demoralized and in disarray. They did not want to give the Saigon government a chance to regroup and perhaps rally the people to resist the advancing NVA forces.[35] As the Communist leaders planned the final campaign designed to bring their thirty-year war for independence and national unity to a victorious climax, they named it the Ho Chi Minh Offensive, in honor of Vietnam's late revolutionary leader.

By mid-April, advance elements of the North Vietnamese army were approaching Saigon. The last major battle of the postwar war occurred at Xuan Loc, a strategic crossroads that formed the center of Saigon's forward defenses. At Xuan Loc, about thirty miles east of the capital city astride Route 1, the main Vietnamese north-south highway, the 18th ARVN Division, under the command of General Le Minh Dao, made a gallant stand against four NVA divisions that were reinforced with tank and artillery regiments. In an epic struggle, the defenders of Xuan Loc held their positions for a week against vastly superior numbers and firepower. Although the heroic defenders of Xuan Loc could delay the North Vietnamese advance, they could not stop it. Xuan Loc was the bloodiest battle of the Second Indochina War. After the fall of Xuan Loc, the road to Bien Hoa Airport and Saigon lay open. After Xuan Loc fell, the postwar war was, for all practical purposes, over. "After Xuan Loc, it was a slide into the abyss for the South Vietnamese."[36]

As the end of the Republic of South Vietnam approached, the five-year civil war in neighboring Cambodia that had destroyed much of the country and left most of its survivors impoverished played itself out. With the defensive perimeter around the besieged capital of Phnom Penh shrinking daily, the hapless leader of the Khmer Republic, Lon Nol, was forced to resign on April 1. Efforts by Secretary of State Kissinger to arrange an eleventh-hour peace settlement were spurned by Prince Sihanouk and his Chinese patrons. On April 10, Congress refused to support a bill calling for $222 million in emergency military aid for the dying Khmer Republic. Two days later, the American evacuation of Phnom Penh began. After five years, at a cost exceeding one billion dollars, the U. S. effort to prevent a Communist takeover in Cambodia had failed. On April 17, abandoned by the Americans, the Cambodian republic fell. The Khmer Rouge occupied Phnom Penh. An eyewitness, *New York Times* reporter Sydney Schandberg, described Phnom Penh's conquerors as "grim, robot-like, brutal."[37] They immediately began evacuating the 2 million people crammed into the city. The Cambodian holocaust was about to begin.

Washington had known for months that the Khmer Republic was doomed, but the sudden collapse of the South Vietnamese armies in the central highlands and northern provinces in the spring of 1975 had stunned American officials. Intelligence reports had given them no indication that Hanoi had planned a major offensive for 1975. American officials had assumed that South Vietnam's defenses were adequate to withstand any attacks the Communists were likely to mount that year. But it soon became clear, even in the face of mounting disaster in southern Vietnam, that the Ford administration had no plans for any further U. S. military intervention in that region. Both Ford and Kissinger understood that it would be politically impossible for the United States to send in American aircraft to bomb and mine, as Nixon had done in 1972, to try to save the South Vietnamese armed forces from another NVA offensive.

On April 10, in a televised speech to the nation, Ford asked Congress to appropriate $722 million in emergency military assistance for General Thieu's imperiled government. To support his proposal, Ford sounded all of the familiar themes. He pleaded with Congress to honor a sacred American commitment, a commitment embraced by every president from Truman to Nixon. He spoke of America's "profound moral obligation" to the South Vietnamese people. He told the legislators and the American people that the United States would dishonor the sacrifices made by the tens of thousands of American soldiers who had died in Vietnam if it failed to help the people of South Vietnam in their hour of mortal danger. He raised the specter of a bloodbath in which thousands of South Vietnamese, particularly Catholics, would be slaughtered by the victorious Communists.[38]

Few Congressional leaders on either side of the aisle responded to Ford's emotional appeal with any enthusiasm. Weary of a seemingly endless war, most members of Congress were not in a generous mood. Most of them viewed the cause in Vietnam as being already lost; they were more concerned about assuring the evacuation of all Americans from Saigon than they were about sending General Thieu's failing government any more aid. On April 17, the same day Xuan Loc fell and the Khmer Rouge entered Phnom Penh, Congress rejected Ford's request for military aid for South Vietnam. Kissinger observed fatalistically, "The Vietnam debate has run its course."[39]

Most Americans, facing serious domestic economic and energy problems, and concerned about important foreign policy matters elsewhere, had long since lost their crusading enthusiasm for saving South Vietnam from Communist aggression. Opinion polls taken in April 1975 showed that a large majority of Americans opposed any further U. S. military action in South Vietnam, even if the failure to take such action resulted in a Communist takeover. Most Americans were surely unhappy about the prospect of a Communist victory in Vietnam, but they were resigned to its occurrence. Most Americans also believed that they had already sacrificed far too much of their blood and treasure in Indochina, and they refused to contribute more.

General Thieu resigned on April 21, convinced at last that the Americans were not going to send South Vietnam any more military aid, nor would they attempt an eleventh-hour military intervention to save his country. That evening, Thieu spoke for the last time to his countrymen. Most of his ninety-minute televised speech amounted to a tearful defense of his leadership and a bitter attack on his longtime ally and patron, the United States. He denounced American officials for having forced him to sign the Paris Accords and then refusing to honor former President Nixon's pledges of support when North Vietnam renewed its aggression:

> Kissinger didn't see that the agreement led the South Vietnamese people to death. . . . The United States has not respected its promises. It's unfair. It is inhumane. It is not trustworthy. It is not responsible.[40]

Four days after resigning, General Thieu fled his country.

Thieu's successor was the elderly and feeble Tran Van Huong, the RVN vice president, who, during his few days in office, tried futilely to seek a negotiated settlement of the war. The North Vietnamese, positioning their forces for a final assault on Saigon, had no time for desperate proposals for a political solution to a war that they were about to win on the battlefield. On April 22, General Dung signed the order to begin the Ho Chi Minh Campaign to conquer Saigon. At that moment, ten NVA divisions encircled the virtually defenseless city.

On April 23, speaking to a large audience at the Tulane University field house, President Ford made U. S. abandonment of South Vietnam official. He urged Americans to forget about the Vietnam War and avoid arguments about who was to blame for its disastrous outcome. He told the crowd:

> America can regain the sense of pride that existed before Vietnam. But it cannot be achieved by refighting a war that is finished as far as America is concerned.[41]

As Ford uttered the magic word, "finished," the predominantly student audience of 4,500 erupted with frenzied whistling, cheering, clapping, foot-stomping, and shouting that lasted for several minutes. The president had given voice to the national mood existing at the moment the PAVN forces readied themselves to win the final victory of the long Vietnam War.

As the Communists drove relentlessly toward their final triumph during the last days of April 1975, the contrast in the national mood with what it had been nearly ten years earlier when President Johnson had sent U. S. Armed Forces off to fight a land war in Southeast Asia could not have been greater. That combination of pride, arrogance, innocence, crusading anti-Communism, and expectations of a quick and easy triumph that had propelled the country into the war had long vanished. During those woeful and tormented days, the national mood was dominated by an overwhelming desire to be rid at last of an endless war. It was a war that had already cost far more in lives and dollars than any worst-case scenarist could have imagined at the outset of the American effort to contain the spread of Communism in Southeast Asia by thwarting the Vietnamese national revolution supported by China and the Soviet Union. A nation that had been nearly torn apart by internal divisions, and political and cultural crises, all exacerbated by the nation's longest war, wanted only for the war to cease. As the Saigon government, which the United States had essentially created and sustained for over twenty years, suffered its death agonies at the end of April 1975, most Americans averted their eyes, resigned to the bitter but inevitable failure of their errand into the wilderness of Southeast Asia to build a shining city upon a hill for all the world to see.

With the NVA forces surrounding the doomed city, thousands of Vietnamese tried desperately to escape. Everywhere, Americans were accosted by Vietnamese brandishing letters, documents, and assorted papers, pleading for a way out of their country. To facilitate the evacuation of South Vietnamese nationals, the U. S. Congress hastily approved legislation waiving entry restrictions for 150,000 Indochinese aliens, including 50,000 high-risk Vietnamese. Each day, thousands of Vietnamese flew out of Tan Son Nhut Airport on board C-141s and C-130s that formed a round-the-clock airlift to freedom.

On April 27, the Communists launched their first attack on Saigon, a rocket barrage that they deliberately aimed at densely populated areas of the city: downtown Saigon and the suburb of Cholon. The rockets killed and wounded hundreds of people. On the same day, the hapless Tran Van Huong resigned the GVN presidency. The South Vietnamese Assembly then replaced Huong with General Doung Van Minh, the man who had briefly headed the military directorate that had replaced Ngo Dinh Diem in November 1963. The Assembly charged Minh with the task of restoring peace to South Vietnam. Lest there be any doubt about this matter, the Communists quickly made it unmistakably clear that the only political settlement they would consider accepting from General Minh would be unconditional surrender.[42]

On April 28, fighting erupted along the outskirts of Saigon. Late in the day, the only NVAF air strike of the entire Vietnam War hit Tan Son Nhut Air Base. Five American-built A-37s, in a perfectly executed operation that fooled the defenders, destroyed or damaged several aircraft parked along the main runways and disrupted the U. S. airlift for several hours. The attack had been led by a VNAF defector, Lieutenant Nguyen Thanh Trung. Now a captain in the North Vietnamese Air Force, Trung had trained a group of MiG pilots to fly the A-37s that had been captured from the South Vietnamese earlier in the 1975 offensive.[43] After a three-hour delay, the airlift resumed.

Early on the morning of April 29, the NVA launched a rocket attack on Tan Son Nhut Airport. The first rockets slammed into a Marine guard post. They killed Lance Corporal Darwin Judge and Corporal Charles McMahon Jr. Corporals Judge and McMahon were the last U. S. casualties of the Vietnam War, the last of more than 58,000 who were killed. Shortly after the first rocket barrages struck, long-range artillery shells began falling on the air base. The rocket and artillery barrages forced the fixed-wing airlift operations to shut down.

President Ford then ordered the final phase of the Saigon evacuation, code-named Operation FREQUENT WIND, to begin. It was a massive helilift designed to

Figure 9.3 A young American solider assists a Vietnamese family being evacuated from Saigon during the final days before the Communist takeover on April 30, 1975. *Source*: U.S. Army Photo

remove the remaining Americans and the eligible Vietnamese and third country nationals from the surrounded city and fly them to a large fleet of U. S. naval ships anchored some forty miles out to sea. Buses navigated the crowded city streets to designated pickup sites, gathered the evacuees, and hauled them to Tan Son Nhut and the waiting helicopters. At every assembly site, the number of people waiting to board the buses vastly exceeded their carrying capacities. Many eligible Vietnamese never got evacuated.[44] By afternoon, the entire city had dissolved into chaos. Frenzied mobs roamed the streets. Vandals overturned cars and set fire to buildings. Looters ransacked homes and apartments. Thousands converged on the U. S. embassy either in the hope of finding a way out or to vent their rage at the departing Americans. Marine security guards, standing atop the compound walls, had to use their rifle butts and boots to beat back hundreds of Vietnamese trying to climb over, while at the same time helping stranded Americans inside to join the estimated 2,000 people already on the embassy grounds. Angry Vietnamese soldiers on the streets outside of the embassy grounds fired at the departing helicopters leaving them behind.

By 8:00 P. M., the evacuation from Tan Son Nhut had been completed. The last Americans to depart the airport were a detachment of Marine security guards who had been assisting the evacuees. Before the Marines boarded the last helicopter, they prepared the Defense Attache Office complex for destruction. Formerly the headquarters of the United States Military Assistance Command in Vietnam (MACV), the buildings had symbolized for a decade the U. S. commitment to defend South Vietnam. From their vantage point aboard the helicopter ascending into the night, the departing Marines watched the structures that had housed sophisticated communications equipment, secret documents, and a vault containing $3.5 million dollars in U. S. currency collapse into rubble.[45]

During the early morning hours of April 30, helicopters flying from the American embassy made the last evacuations of the Vietnam War. Just before 5:00 A. M., a weary Ambassador Martin and his senior staff members departed the embassy. But there were not nearly enough places on board the available helicopters to evacuate all of the remaining Vietnamese and third-country nationals. Between 400 and 500 people were left behind on embassy grounds. Looking down at the stranded people milling about helplessly as his helicopter headed for the open sea, one of the U. S. officials could think "of no word in any language adequate to describe the sense of shame that swept over me."[46] The last Americans to leave were the Marine security forces who had barricaded themselves on the embassy rooftop to await the final helicopters that would take them to the waiting ships. As the last American helicopter lifted off, Sergeant Juan Valdez observed Vietnamese evacuees trying to push their way through the still-barricaded door, waving papers at the sky to show that they too should be allowed to leave Vietnam.

A few hours after the last U. S. Marine had left Saigon, the thirty-year Indochina War ground to its inevitable conclusion. At about noon, North Vietnamese tanks rumbled by the American embassy, headed for Independence Palace, the South Vietnamese capitol and official residence of President Minh. Alongside the tanks rolled trucks crammed with young PAVN soldiers. All headed for the heart of the city. As it approached the palace grounds, the lead tank barreled through the steel front gate, smashing it down. The tanks gathered in a semi-circle facing the entrance to the Palace. In a gesture of triumph, a lone soldier, waving a huge blue and red flag with the yellow star of the National Liberation Front, raced up the steps of the Palace. Provisional Revolutionary Government officials announced over radio Saigon that the city had been liberated. In Paris, Communist envoys announced that Saigon had been renamed Ho Chi Minh City. Inside of Independence Palace, President Minh awaited the victors in his office. As they approached, he tried to surrender to the senior officer present, NVA Colonel Bui Tin, but Tin curtly informed him that all power had already passed into the hands of the revolution: "Your power has crumbled. You cannot give up what you do not have."[47] Minh and the other RVN officials who had assembled in his office were taken into custody.

Some of Saigon's inhabitants welcomed their conquerors. Most greeted them with indifference, or with uncertainty and fear. On May 8, a large crowd gathered in front of the presidential palace to hear the head of the new South Vietnamese provisional government, General Tran Van Tra, proclaim the success of the Vietnamese rev-

Figure 9.4   The end of the line. One of the last helicopters to depart the rooftop heliport of the U. S. Embassy in Saigon on April 30, 1975. Most of the people trying to board the small helicopter were turned away. The evacuation is one of many in the downtown area from where Americans and foreign nationals are being evacuated to waiting Navy ships off the coast. *Source: UPI/Corbis/ Bettmann Archives*

olution. Even before the cheering stopped, the victorious North Vietnamese began rounding up many Saigonese residents for "reeducation" at camps being set up in the countryside. The Republic of South Vietnam was quickly swept into the dustbin of history. America's limited war fought in Indochina to contain the expansion of Communism had failed. Kissinger observed, "We should never have been there at all. But now it's history."[48]

AFTER THE FALL

The American effort to assist in the creation of an independent South Vietnam was probably destined for failure from the outset. The Republic of South Vietnam never became, probably could never have become, a viable nation-state. It could never overcome its origins as a puppet government, an instrument of Western imperialism. From Ngo Dinh Diem's to Nguyen Van Thieu's, every one of the succession of inept, weak, and corrupt governments, all strongly supported by the United States, failed to develop a popular base of support, failed to achieve political stability, and failed to unite a politically fragmented people. They all failed to enlist the loyalties of or appeal to the

Figure 9.5   Victorious North Vietnamese forces parade through the streets of Saigon (renamed Ho Chi Minh City) on May 2, 1975, following the triumph of their revolutionary cause. The tanks are Soviet-made T-54s.

self-interest of most peasant villagers who made up the large majority of their citizenry. Failure to achieve local legitimacy ultimately doomed the South Vietnamese cause.[49] American firepower could kill and wound huge numbers of VC and NVA soldiers, but it could neither eradicate the Vietnamese national revolution nor its appeal. It could never win the hearts and minds of a majority of the Vietnamese peasantry for a succession of South Vietnamese governments.

Because they never acquired legitimacy in the eyes of the majority of their people, South Vietnam's governments never acquired the ability to defend themselves from the revolutionary war waged unrelentingly against them for nearly twenty years. With or without U. S. backing, there probably never was a viable political alternative to the revolutionary nationalism that swept Vietnam after 1945. The United States and its succession of clients could never solve the essential South Vietnamese conundrum: how to achieve a stable political order without supporting revolutionary changes.[50] There could be no long-term stability in southern Vietnam without revolutionary change, and neither the U. S. officials nor their RVN clients could accommodate the revolution.

In the early 1950s, both the Truman and Eisenhower administrations openly supported the failing French effort to reimpose colonialism on the Vietnamese people with money and arms. Following the failure of the French cause in 1954, the United States intervened to try to create a new nation-state in southern Vietnam in violation of the Geneva Accords. By the early 1960s, Americans significantly increased their support of the Republic of South Vietnam, which was trying to defend itself against the resurgent revolutionaries, now committed to winning control over the entire country and reuniting it under their rule. In 1965, perceiving that the South Vietnamese government was nearing collapse, despite massive U. S. economic and military aid, Americans assumed the major burden of the fighting against the revolutionaries. After 1969, when the American people turned against the Vietnam War, America shifted the burden of the fighting back to its South Vietnamese clients. But Vietnamization never worked, probably could never work. Until the end, the South Vietnamese state remained dependent on the United States for its security and survival. When all of the American soldiers went home and Congress drastically curtailed its support for the RVN, their cause was lost. The Communists, with relative ease, swiftly administered the *coup de grace* in the spring of 1975.

But the failure of the South Vietnamese state to establish itself and survive is not just the story of the failure of a succession of inept, corrupt, elite-based governments to develop a strong political base and the ability to defend themselves. It is not just the story of the failure of a succession of American governments, from Truman's through Ford's, to develop effective aid, counterinsurgency, and pacification programs, or effective military strategies that could neutralize the revolutionary war strategies.

To understand the outcome of the Vietnamese revolution, the focus must necessarily be on the North Vietnamese and Vietcong, and on the myriad of factors that enabled them to ultimately prevail after a decades-long struggle. The focus must be on local, particular Vietnamese realities. It was not easy; the Communists made a lot of mistakes over the years. Victory ultimately cost them dearly. The revolutionaries paid an appalling price in blood and money, and for years they governed an impoverished nation whose physical environment, economy, and social fabric had been battered by decades of war.

But they enjoyed many advantages and made skillful use of them all. The revolutionary cause attracted the best and the brightest of Vietnam's elite classes. They had able leaders—from Ho Chi Minh, Vo Nguyen Giap, and their associates—to the local cadres who organized villages, indoctrinated soldiers, and penetrated all levels of the South Vietnamese civilian and military bureaucracies. Although the revolutionary leaders were all committed Communist ideologues, they also were Vietnamese nationalists. And they harnessed the powerful patriotic feelings of most Vietnamese to their cause—reunify the fatherland under Vietnamese leadership that was independent of all foreign influences. Their social reform agenda, particularly the promise of land to poor and landless peasants who constituted the bulk of Vietnamese rural populations, enabled them to rally the masses to their cause. The revolution's appeal constituted a powerful duality: to their patriotic ideal—a reunified independent Vietnamese nation—and to their economic self-interest—land of their own.

The Vietnamese revolutionary leaders also skillfully exploited the rivalry between the major Communist powers, the Soviet Union and the Chinese, to extract the economic and military aid from both nations that the Vietnamese absolutely had to have in order to have a chance to win the war. They received the aid they required, and they played one powerful ally against the other without compromising their cause or independence.

Drawing on the rich warrior tradition of Vietnamese history, as well as on modern Chinese models of revolutionary warfare, the Vietnamese Communists fashioned a complex, sophisticated, and ultimately successful strategy of "people's warfare," a form of protracted warfare that shrewdly blended military, diplomatic, and political tactics. They heeded the lessons of their own national historical experience. They knew that if they were patient, retained the tactical initiative, avoided battles where they could suffer ruinous losses, and inflicted sizeable casualties on the invaders over a lengthy time period, that the Americans would tire of the war and go home. Just as the French did before them, and the Chinese before the French.

American officials defended the long American involvement in Vietnam as an effort to maintain political stability in Southeast Asia. The domino correlative to America's containment ideology magnified the significance of the endeavor to create a pro-Western and non-Communist alternative to revolutionary nationalism in southern Vietnam: The larger U. S. mission in Indochina was always defined as preventing the spread of Chinese and Soviet influence throughout Southeast Asia. Successive U. S. administrations perceived Vietnam as a conduit of Communist expansionism that had to be closed to keep southern Vietnam, the rest of Indochina, and the nations of Southeast Asian within the Western orbit.

But the outcome of the American Indochina war invalidated its prime ideological justifications and suggested that the containment ideology itself had been misapplied. A policy developed to contain the spread of Soviet influence into Southern and Central Europe could not be applied effectively to the regional conflicts and civil wars of Southeast Asia. Following the triumph of Communist forces in Vietnam, Laos, and Cambodia, American security was not seriously threatened. American alliances elsewhere were not weakened, nor were American allies disheartened by the outcome. After the fall of Saigon, Vientiane, and Phnom Penh, there was no deluge of Communist takeovers in Southeast Asia. Communist influence did not reach beyond Indochina. Outside of Cambodia and Laos, countries that had become integrally involved in the Second Indochina War, the dominoes never fell.

Within Indochina, the Communist dominoes soon crashed into one another. Military victory only accentuated the internal divisions within the Communist world. In Cambodia, the Khmer Rouge leadership implemented a savage reign of terror that cost at least one million lives. The Vietnamese, nursing an imperialistic agenda of their own, invaded Cambodia in 1978 and overthrew the Khmer Rouge regime it had previously helped come to power. Hanoi established a replacement regime, a puppet government in Phnom Penh supported by Vietnamese troops. China, which had close ties with Cambodia, then sent its forces into northern Vietnam in 1979 to punish Vietnam for its aggression in Cambodia. There ensued a short but bloody war between the two erstwhile Communist allies. The United States, which had gone to war in Vietnam in 1965 to contain Chinese expansionism, found itself quietly backing China's efforts to contain Vietnamese expansionism in 1979. In these intramural Communist power struggles for regional hegemony, the Soviets backed the Vietnamese against the Chinese and their Cambodian allies. Clashing perceptions of national interest and historic national rivalries consistently overrode ideological considerations in guiding the actions of Soviet, Chinese, and Indochinese Communist political leaders during the late 1970s. Such behaviors by leading members of the "international Communist conspiracy" must have been difficult for hardline American anti-Communist ideologues, with their simplistic and reductive concepts, to fathom.

In the aftermath of the Communist takeover of Indochina, the elaborate edifice of international economic and political relations that the United States had constructed in the Far East during the 1950s and 1960s did not crumble. In the years since the end of the Indochina War, the non-Communist nations of Southeast Asia have enjoyed unprecedented stability and prosperity. The Association of Southeast Asian Nations (ASEAN), which includes Thailand, Indonesia, Malaya, Singapore, and Brunei, developed strong commercial and financial ties with the United States, Japan, and Western Europe. The energetic populations and vibrant economies of the ASEAN nations contrasted starkly with the Communist-controlled nations of Vietnam, Cambodia, and Laos, which remained grim islands of poverty and repression amid a sea of prosperity long after the Indochina wars had played out.

The Communists proved to be harsh conquerors of the South Vietnamese. Although dovish critics of the American war effort scoffed at Richard Nixon's and Gerald Ford's dire predictions of a bloodbath of nightmarish proportions following the Communist takeover, a bloodbath of modest proportions did nevertheless occur. Many former high-ranking officers in the South Vietnamese armed forces and many former high government officials were executed. Perhaps as many as 65,000 executions occurred between 1975 and 1983! In addition, hundreds of thousands of minor officials and supporters of the vanished RVN were put in harsh reeducation centers.[51]

Since the Communist victory, an estimated 1.5 million Vietnamese have fled the country. Thousands perished during the attempt; additional thousands languished in squalid refugee camps in Hong Kong, Thailand, and other nations of Southeast Asia. Approximately 300,000 of these refugees resettled in France, and another 500,000 have come to the United States. Despite the horrible circumstances that brought most of the Vietnamese to the United States in the mid- and late-1970s, the new Vietnamese American population has generally done very well in its adopted land. They have replicated the oldest success story in American history; refugees from tyranny and poverty who made a fresh start in a new land. Thousands of individual success stories abound: of people arriving with little more than the clothes on their backs acquiring good educations, becoming good citizens, and achieving successful careers in business and the professions. Many of these people received help of various kinds from government and private agencies, and from compassionate individuals. They have adapted well to America, and have made it possible for their children to enjoy productive and fulfilling lives. For thousands more, however, America has remained an alien and unfriendly place. Many of these uprooted Vietnamese, victims of hate, hostility, discrimination, and prejudice, have fared poorly in their adopted land. Often they have been forced to go on welfare and have been tempted by vice and crime. They are the ultimate losers, confined to bleak lives at the social margins, victims of both Vietnamese and American history.

Within Vietnam itself, the costs of the thirty-year war were horrendous: catastrophic human loss and suffering, and extensive damage to a fragile preindustrial economic infrastructure struggling to escape the legacies of French colonial exploitation. Millions of acres of forest and crop lands were destroyed. Millions of South Vietnamese were turned into refugees, most of whom poured into the slums and back-alley labyrinths of southern cities. Twenty years of American aid programs had created an artificial consumer economy in South Vietnam that retarded commercial and industrial development. This ersatz economy collapsed during the 1974–1975 period, leaving southern Vietnam without an urban economic base.

The victors' efforts to carry out Stalinist reforms, including forced-draft industrialization and collectivized agricultural, only made terrible economic conditions worse for the people. The annual growth rate stagnated at 1 to 2 percent, and the per capita annual income hovered at around $150, making Vietnam one of the poorest countries in the world. After initially planning to create a socialist political economy in southern Vietnam, the Communist rulers made a pragmatic accommodation with the capitalistic traditions of the region. Some businesses were taken over by the state, and the land of some rich landowners was seized. But the government allowed many small and medium-sized enterprises to remain in private hands. The government also redistributed land to many poor and landless peasants and set up programs to encourage urban dwellers to return to the land.

After achieving reunification of their country in 1976, the Vietnamese were forced, in part because of continuing American official hostility, into an economic dependence on the Soviet Union. The Chinese cut off all aid to Vietnam because of Vietnamese imperialism in Cambodia and because of Vietnam's mistreatment of its Chinese minority, most of whom lived in the towns and cities of southern Vietnam and most of whom had supported the South Vietnamese governments while they lasted.

For more than a decade, thousands of Soviet advisers and technical specialists administered an elaborate range of Vietnam aid programs that cost the U. S. S. R. about $2 billion per year. With the decline of the Soviet economy in the late 1980s, the subsidies to Vietnam were reduced. They ended altogether during 1990–1991, with the collapse of the Soviet Union and the demise of Marxism-Leninism. Another cause of the mass impoverishment of the Vietnamese was Hanoi's determination to maintain a large standing army. The Peoples' Army of Vietnam is the world's fourth largest army. During the 1980s, military spending absorbed approximately half of the government's annual budget, representing about 20 percent of the annual GNP and making Vietnam one of the most militarized societies in the world.

The loss of Soviet economic assistance caused severe hardship for the Vietnamese, who had been able to attract little in the way of foreign investment or trade. A new generation of younger pragmatic leaders, many of them southerners, came to power in Vietnam during the mid-1980s; they replaced the old hardline revolutionaries who defeated the French and the Americans, and redeemed Vietnamese nationhood. The old leaders, vintage Stalinist and Maoist ideologues, proved to be more adept at defeating Western imperialism than they were at promoting economic development and managing economic affairs.

Since the mid-1980s, Vietnam's new rulers have cautiously implemented a program of *do moi* (renewal). Do moi included introducing market incentives to stimulate industrial production and trying to attract foreign investment. Meanwhile, the Communist Party retained its monopoly of state power. The agricultural economy, based on rice-growing, revived, and Vietnam became one of the world's leading exporters of rice. The rate of foreign investment increased, and the annual growth rate jumped to the 5 to 7 percent range. Foreign trade also rose.[52]

Despite the modest economic gains occurring as a result of *do moi*, the Vietnamese economy of the 1990s continued to suffer a plague of serious problems. Vietnam remained one of the world's poorest countries. Its people, two-thirds of whom still lived in villages and hamlets, although most of them were remarkably hardworking and literate, and certainly desirous of better lives for themselves and their children, were forced to work long hours for low wages. They also continued to be denied basic human, legal, and political rights. Trade unions were controlled by the government and opposition political parties were illegal. Infrastructure industries and services were antiquated and inadequate. Vietnam appeared to be rich in politicians and military leaders, but poor in capable personnel trained to develop and operate a modern, high-tech industrial economy. Inept and corrupt management, lack of investment capital and banks, and backward technologies hindered economic development. A rapidly growing population threatened to undercut any economic progress that occurred. The gap between rich and poor was widening in the 1990s, and the government suffered from a corruption that some critics claimed was as bad as any in South Vietnam during the war.[53] For the great mass of Vietnamese people, their revolution was both a great national achievement, and, at least in the short-term, a political and economic disaster.

THE WOUNDS WITHIN

Within the United States, following the fall of Saigon, there was no bitter "who lost Vietnam?" debate or a resurgence of McCarthyite red-baiting. Instead, historical amnesia set in, symptomatic of moral and political exhaustion. Most Americans did not want to think or talk about Vietnam for years, much less fight about it or indulge in recriminations. Amnesia persisted until the early 1980s, when there was a revival of interest in the war and controversy over its lessons and legacies. Conferences and symposia of concerned scholars, journalists who had covered the Vietnam beat, and former civilian and military officials involved in the war convened to examine and explain the war from multiple perspectives. A veritable flood of scholarly and popular literature on the war was suddenly issued. Hollywood and network television discovered Vietnam, and the war quickly became a staple topic of popular culture. Amnesia and a conspiracy of silence rapidly gave way to an obsessive interest in the first major foreign war the United States ever lost.

The fallacies of U. S. Cold War ideology may have been exposed by the internecine Communist wars in Indochina and the absence of a McCarthyite backlash at home. Vital American foreign policy interests in the Far East may have suffered no permanent setbacks following the U.S. withdrawal and defeat. However, the damage done to the United States by the Vietnam ordeal was nevertheless severe and lasting. George Kennan, the principal theorist of America's Cold War foreign policy, based on containing Communism's expansionist tendencies, has called the Vietnam War "the most disastrous of all America's undertakings over the whole two hundred years of its history."

The fall of Saigon in April 1975 was a severe blow to the pride and self-confidence of a nation whose fondest boast had been that it had never lost a major war. The tragic outcome of the long war on the eve of the Bicentennial dampened many

Americans' enthusiasm for celebrating their nation's 200th birthday. The Vietnam War had consumed over 58,000 American lives and left another 300,000 soldiers wounded.

In addition to the human costs of the war, the economic and financial costs were high. The Vietnam War cost more than any other war in American history, except for World War II, an estimated $167 billion. President Johnson's efforts to finance simultaneously a major war and Great Society reform programs without imposing major tax increases or economic controls ignited inflation and undermined the value of the dollar. The long-term economic costs of the Vietnam War were even more serious. Historically, the American economy reached its peak in about 1965, and by the early 1970s it had entered an era of relative decline. The Vietnam War was one of the major causes of American economic decline, and accelerated it. The war helped launch and sustain the great inflation that ravaged the American economy, weakened many important industries, and eroded living standards from the late 1960s through the early 1980s.[54]

The Vietnam War also exacted a high political price. It undermined public faith in the competency and honesty of elected officials and forced two strong presidents out of office prematurely. It enlarged the administrative state in a nation that lauded private initiative and private sector solutions to problems. It weakened the value of public service and engendered fear, suspicion, and hatred of government. Military service was discredited for years. Americans lost respect, trust, and goodwill for the nation's Armed Forces.

The Vietnam War shattered the bipartisan consensus that had guided American foreign policy since the late 1940s, and it inaugurated an era of confusion and conflict that has never been entirely resolved. The losing war also proved that America's vast wealth and powerful military technology could not defeat a poor Third World nation determined to achieve national reunification, nor could the United States support forever an ineffective regime that lacked a popular base of support and the will to fight. Americans also discovered that there were limits to American power and limits to the burdens the American people would shoulder in pursuit of foreign policy objectives. For the first time since the Cold War began, many Americans questioned the validity of their global mission to contain Communism. The Vietnam War represented an economic, political, and military disaster for the United States. American stature in the world declined as a consequence of U. S. involvement in the Vietnam War.

There were other costs of war. A bitter controversy erupted over whether hundreds of thousands of draft evaders and resisters, and deserters, should be granted amnesty or severely punished for their violations of Selective Service laws. The debate perpetuated the war-sown divisions between doves and hawks. The Vietnam War was the most controversial and least popular war in U. S. history. It divided Americans more deeply than any conflict since their own civil war 100 years earlier. Most Americans had become disillusioned with the national crusade to save South Vietnam from Communism and had stopped supporting the U. S. war effort long before it ended. Millions of Americans opposed the Vietnam War, and many of those opponents actively demonstrated their opposition.

The gravest damage done to America by the Vietnam War occurred in the realm of the spirit. It was a deep wound within the national psyche. The ultimate domino was America's mythic conception of itself. Before Vietnam, America's most cherished vision of itself was expressed in the famed metaphor of the city upon a hill. America's mission in the world was to redeem history. In secular terms, America's mission was to set a democratic example to guide and inspire the rest of the world. America's post-World War II foreign policy was founded on the principle of thwarting the spread of Communism to preserve the sphere of freedom, the empire of liberty, in the world. The redeemer-nation sent its citizens-soldiers to southern Vietnam to save its inhabitants from the evil embrace of expanding Communism. But once launched upon their errand into the wilderness of Vietnam, Americans made the horrible discovery that the red-white-and-blue alternative to revolutionary nationalism was only death and destruction and, ultimately, defeat for their soldiers and for the Vietnamese people that they had tried so hard for so long to help. The lofty American conception of itself as the world's redeemer civilization perished in the jungles, swamps, and rice paddies of Vietnam.

Within the nation, some healing has occurred from the trauma of Vietnam with the passage of time and with much study and reflection about the war experience. In the case of Vietnam veterans, Americans gradually understood that most of them had not committed atrocities against helpless peasants, that most of them were not junkies, alcoholics, or crazies. Despite encountering some difficulties deriving from their war service, most Vietnam veterans completed school, obtained jobs, went to college, entered the professions, married, had families, and became solid and productive citizens in their communities. It also was gradually understood and accepted that dysfunctional veterans were not weaklings, losers, or criminals, but that they suffered from serious medical and psychological disorders. They needed sympathy and support, and above all they needed medical attention, not moral condemnation.

Doves who had previously denounced Vietnam veterans as racist killers of babies now viewed them as nineteen-year-old boys drafted and sent to fight an immoral war. They realized that many veterans themselves were victims of a war policy that was misguided and wrong. Hawks belatedly acknowledged that most Vietnam veterans had fought with valor and tenacity under circumstances that precluded the possibility of victory. They had fought bravely, they had won all of the major battles, and they had always inflicted far greater casualties than they took; however, politicians had denied them victory. Both hawks and doves, in simple moral terms, in time accepted the Vietnam veterans. They agreed that they had been good soldiers in a bad war, although "bad war" still meant something quite different to a dove than it did to a hawk.

The most compelling symbol of the new esteem accorded the Vietnam veterans was the Vietnam Veterans' Memorial in Washington, D. C. The memorial was conceived by a small group of Vietnam veterans and built entirely with private contributions. It was dedicated in a moving ceremony on November 23, 1982. It stands in a grassy meadow near the Lincoln Memorial. It was designed by Maya Ling Lin, an undergraduate architecture student at Yale University. The memorial is stark and simple; it consists of two wings of black granite rising out of the earth and then sinking back into it. On the reflecting panels are carved the names of the 58,201 men and women who died in the Vietnam War. The memorial is a shrine to honor the war dead.

In the years since its opening, the Memorial has become one of the most often visited of Washington's many monuments. The wall of names exerts enormous emotional power over all who come to see it. As one approaches the granite slabs, one has the distinct sensation of descending into a valley of death, a valley of death consecrated by the blood of fallen heroes—of nineteen year-old-boys who died in a strange, faraway place for a murky cause.

On a warm summer day, a bearded man in a wheelchair, dressed in battle fatigues and carrying his two children in his burly arms, comes to find the name of a fallen comrade. A mother comes to touch the name of her son and a widow comes to touch the name of her husband. They leave mementos—flowers, combat decorations, photographs, and a teddy bear. Those visitors who had known none of the dead, who had lost no one in Vietnam, even those who protested against the war, are deeply moved by the wall of names. They too are filled with grief and sadness at the loss, and perhaps rage at the waste and futility of an unnecessary and pointless war.

THE SPECTRE OF VIETNAM

The spectre of Vietnam lurked in the background of every American foreign policy debate of the 1970s, 1980s, and 1990s. There was a manifest unwillingness to intervene militarily in Third World countries for fear of being sucked into another Vietnam-like quagmire. An arrogance about the uses of American military power that existed before the Vietnam War had been succeeded by a diffident neoisolationist postwar yearning to avoid all military involvement in the world. Former President Nixon labeled this neoisolationist tendency "the Vietnam syndrome."

The ghost of Vietnam influenced the public debate over President Reagan's controversial interventionist policies in Nicaragua in the early 1980s. The Reagan administration vigorously waged a proxy war against the Sandinista government by arming and training a counterrevolutionary army, "the Contras," to overthrow them. Democratic Congressional opponents of the Contra policy cried, "No more Vietnams in Central America!" Defenders of the Reagan policy insisted that Nicaragua was different from Vietnam and that they would not make the same mistakes that had allegedly undermined the U. S. effort in Southeast Asia. They were not sending American ground combat forces to get bogged down in a stalemated war; they were training, equipping, and supporting Nicaraguan "freedom fighters" who could defeat the Sandinista forces and liberate Nicaragua without a direct American military intervention. In this debate, both critics and defenders of the American intervention in Nicaragua revealed that they drew different lessons from the Vietnam experience. The

Figure 9.6 Vietnam Veterans" Memorial. The memorial was conceived by a small group of Vietnam veterans and built entirely with private funds. On its stark granite walls are engraved the names of the 58,201 soldiers who lost their lives in Vietnam. It is one of the most powerful and moving monuments in the nation's capital. Note the items visitors have left to memorialize lost comrades, friends, spouses, and relatives. *Source:* Smithsonian Institution

debate also suggested that its participants were more interested in using the history of Vietnam to score debaters' points in the present than they were in coming to terms with what really happened in Indochina.[55]

Memories of Vietnam dominated public debate over the Persian Gulf War and shaped the Bush administration's war policy during the period 1990–1991. Congressional opponents of President Bush's plan to use military force to drive the Iraqi army out of Kuwait warned of the dangers of getting bogged down in a lengthy and costly war in a Third World country. These critics preferred to use economic sanctions to drive the Iraqis out. Mindful of the fears of millions of his fellow citizens, when President Bush launched the Gulf War, he pledged that "this will not be another Vietnam. Our troops will . . . not be asked to fight with one hand tied behind their back."[56] The military's handling of the media coverage of the Gulf War reflected its mistaken belief that uncensored and biased media coverage of the Vietnam War had contributed to the American defeat in Indochina. The heroes' welcome given to the returning Desert Storm veterans was shaped, in part, by guilty memories of the shabby treatment given to returning Vietnam War veterans. In fact, many Vietnam-era veterans joined the parades honoring the returning Gulf War veterans. It was, for many of them, a long-overdue celebratory reception. After the victorious outcome of the Gulf War, President Bush proclaimed that Americans had once and for all licked the Vietnam syndrome.

The Vietnam spectre surfaced once again during the 1992 presidential election. Democratic candidate William "Bill" Clinton was attacked repeatedly by George Bush for having evaded the draft while the Vietnam War was raging and for having helped to organize antiwar demonstrations in London in 1969 while he was a Rhodes Scholar at Oxford. Although less was made of it, Bush's running mate, Vice President Dan Quayle, had to rebut the charges against him that had surfaced at the time he was chosen to be Bush's running mate in 1988: that Quayle allegedly used family political connections to land a prized slot in an Indiana National Guard unit in 1969 to sidestep a possible tour of duty in Vietnam. Neither Quayle nor Clinton appeared to suffer much political damage from these attacks, but the fact that they were made attested to the continuing troublesome legacy of Vietnam. The charges dredged up bad memories of bad times and of a controversial war that created dilemmas for many young men and forced them to make hard choices, in many instances, morally ambiguous choices about the war.

"The ghosts of Vietnam still lingered"[57] during the 1990s. President Clinton was forced to withdraw U. S. forces from Somalia in 1993 when they expanded their humanitarian mission to include efforts to shape the political destiny of that impoverished land. Eighteen American Marines got killed in the cross fire of two factions fighting for control of Somalia, and Clinton had no choice but to withdraw all U. S. forces lest Somalia would become the latest Vietnam.

Americans were divided over whether to intervene militarily in the brutal ethnically driven civil wars in Bosnia-Herzegovina from 1993 to 1995. Opponents of U. S. intervention once again evoked the spectre of another Vietnam-like quagmire. Many of Clinton's advisers warned him of the political fate that awaited presidents who got their country bogged down in an unpopular war. Polls showed that a majority of Congressional members and a large majority of the American people opposed the Clinton administration's decision in December 1995 to broker a political agreement in Bosnia that included sending 20,000 U. S. combat troops as part of a 60,000-person NATO contingent assigned to keep the peace and try to regenerate a national rebirth in that tortured land.

In 1997, Vietnam remains a metaphor, a cautionary tale of the catastrophe that awaits a nation, however rich and powerful, that ever again allows its crusading idealism to override its realistic sense of limits.

THE ENDLESS WAR

Although the American war in Vietnam ended in early 1973 with the signing of the Paris Accords, the removal of all remaining U. S. troops, and the return of the POWs, the United States did not normalize relations with its former enemies for over twenty years. For over twenty years, the United States, embarrassed and embittered by the outcome of the Second Indochina War, regarded the Vietnamese government as an enemy. It rejected all requests to normalize relations or develop commercial ties. The United States also endeavored to keep Vietnam isolated from the world family of nations and outside of the developing world economic system.

In the immediate aftermath of the war, the Ford administration took a hard line toward its former enemies. A wartime embargo that had applied only to North Vietnam was extended to include all of Vietnam, Cambodia, and Laos. Henry Kissinger claimed that Hanoi's violations of the Paris Accords provided a legal basis for U. S. actions. The Ford administration also refused to pay any of the $3.25 billion that former President Nixon had promised in writing to Prime Minister Pham Van Dong at the time of the signing of the Paris Accords to help pay for the postwar reconstruction of Vietnam. President Ford "made normalization contingent on Vietnam's restraint toward its neighbors and a full accounting of U. S. soldiers missing in action (MIAs)."[58]

The Vietnamese had an opportunity to achieve normal relations with the United States in 1977, when Jimmy Carter, who favored normalizing relations, took office. He made normalizing relations conditional upon Vietnam giving a full and proper accounting of the 2,387 American servicemen who were listed as "missing in action" (MIAs) from the Indochina wars. But the Vietnamese failed to provide a full accounting of the MIAs and insisted on payment of the $3.25 billion that was promised to them by Nixon. The Carter administration, acknowledging no legal obligation to pay reparations, severed negotiations with the Vietnamese. No reparations were ever paid, and the boycott continued for nearly twenty years.

The two major obstacles to normalizing relations between the United States and Vietnam were the Vietnamese occupation of Cambodia and the POW/MIA issue. Most of the MIAs were flyers whose planes had gone down over water or over Vietnam, Laos, or Cambodia during the war and whose fate was yet unknown. A few were POWs apparently not accounted for at the time most U. S. POWs were repatriated in March and April 1973.

Under the terms of the Paris agreements, the responsibility for resolving the question of the MIAs devolved upon the Four-Party Joint Military Team (JMT) made up of members from America, South Vietnam, North Vietnam, and the PRG. The Americans on the Joint Military Team quickly discovered that the Communists were in no hurry to resolve the MIA issue. Hanoi preferred to use the information that its officials had on the fate of some of the men missing in action as bargaining chips. The Communists linked providing information on the fate of MIAs to progress on unrelated issues. Little progress had been made, and the fate of only a few of the MIAs had been resolved when the Communist delegates started boycotting the JMT meetings in June 1974.[59]

The emotionally charged MIA issue lingered long after the Vietnam War ended, even though all but one of the MIAs had been declared legally dead. The exception was maintained to symbolize continuing official efforts to extract a full account of the fate of the MIAs from the recalcitrant Vietnamese. When Ronald Reagan took office in 1981, he promised the families of the missing men that he would make a vigorous effort to resolve the troubling, lingering matter. But American government officials repeatedly stated that they had no evidence that any American servicemen were alive or were being held against their will anywhere in Indochina. The National League of Families of American Prisoners and Missing in Southeast Asia continued to demand an account from Hanoi and from the American government for the 2,393 people they regarded as missing. There were many raids, searches, and expeditions over the years into Indochina to try to find or account for some of the missing men. Many people insisted that they saw or heard of live American POWs being held in Laos or Vietnam, although no live Americans were ever found. Relatives of MIAs charged the U. S. government with covering up evidence it had of Americans still being held in Indochina prisons. The Vietnamese have repeatedly denied that they kept any POWs at the time of the repatriation or that they had any MIAs in custody. They have also offered to cooperate with U. S. officials to account for the missing people.[60]

Some progress toward resolving the issues dividing Americans and Vietnamese was made in the early 1990s. All Vietnamese troops were withdrawn from Cambodia by the end of 1990. Following U. S. leadership, the United Nations provided for a peace-keeping force in Cambodia to prevent a recurrence of hostilities and the return of the Khmer Rouge to power. In the summer of 1991, the United States opened a special liaison office in Hanoi, headed by John W. Vessey Jr., a retired Army general, to work with the Vietnamese in resolving the cases of the 2,265 Americans still listed as MIAs. There also were dozens of people combing Vietnam, checking out so-called "live sighting" reports, and interviewing villagers.

In the summer of 1992, a Senate Select Committee chaired by Massachusetts Senator John Kerry, a Vietnam veteran, held extensive hearings into the POW/MIA matter. In sensational testimony before the committee, former Secretary of Defense James Schlesinger acknowledged that at the time of the return of the POWs, there may have been some unaccounted-for POWs who were left behind in Laos. Ross Perot, a maverick billionaire from Texas, who ran for president as an independent candidate in 1992 and 1996, who had a long record of involvement with the POW/MIA issue, told the committee that he had evidence of Americans still being held in Laos and Vietnam. Appearing before the same select committee, an angry Henry Kissinger emphatically denied Schlesinger's and Perot's charges, claiming that had he or President Nixon had any evidence that even one American POW had been left behind in January 1973, they would "have moved heaven and earth" to retrieve that individual.

A major breakthrough occurred in October 1992, when the Vietnamese announced that they were determined to bring the long-running dispute with the Americans over the MIA situation to a close. They pledged to work with Americans to render a full report. Although for years they had denied having such materials in their archives, the Vietnamese suddenly turned over more than 5,000 black-and-white photographs of American servicemen and their personal effects. They also released thousands of supporting documents to accompany the photographs. This treasure trove of photos and documents enabled Washington to resolve many of the MIA cases. However, nothing has been found in these pictures and papers that suggests there are any live POWs anywhere in Southeast Asia.

President Bush praised the Vietnamese for providing the materials, and he promised a review of American policy toward Vietnam. The Vietnamese leader responsible for his country's new cooperativeness and for the release of the photographs and documents was the new president of Vietnam, Le Duc Anh. Anh's primary goal was to signal to the United States that it was ready to meet Washington's prime requirement for establishing diplomatic relations and for lifting the boycott. In December 1992, Bush granted permission for American companies to open offices in Vietnam.

Polls taken over the years showed that a large majority of Americans supported the policy of nonrecognition of Vietnam and the efforts to isolate that country from the international community. Critics of the policy contended that nonrecognition had not served American interests: It drove the Vietnamese into the hands of the Soviets, and it deprived the American business community of profitable trade and investment opportunities in a Third World country where U. S. capital and technology were sorely needed. In addition to its geopolitical advantages, others, including many veterans of the Vietnam War, insisted that diplomatic recognition was a prerequisite for the reconciliation between the Americans and the Vietnamese that must come after the long war between them. Many Vietnamese, both officially and privately, indicated that they bore Americans no ill-will and wanted them to return as friends and investors.

Some groups within the United States continued to actively oppose normalizing relations with Vietnam, including many members of the large Vietnamese-American community. Many of these people remain bitter enemies of the government and economic system in power in their former homeland. Some emigres even talked of returning to Vietnam to liberate the Vietnamese people from Communist tyranny. Many Vietnamese have indicated that they would like to return, but only to a free Vietnam. Before the United States normalized relations with Vietnam, these Vietnamese Americans wanted to see Washington prod Hanoi to democratize its government and privatize its economy. Some U. S. veterans, still bitter about the humiliation and defeat the Vietnamese inflicted on the United States, opposed any movement toward normalizing relations. Many Americans simply saw no advantage in normalizing relations with Vietnam nor any harm in not. In their eyes, Vietnam was a small, poor, and unimportant place in the world, and they did not care what relations, if any, the United States had with the country.

By 1993, the Clinton administration cautiously moved toward normalization. Vietnam had clearly met the U. S. standards for recognition. The boycott was ineffective, and other nations were investing capital in many Vietnamese enterprises and developing trade ties with that country. Wall Street pressured Washington to lift the failing embargo and to allow U. S. companies a crack at a major Asian market. A public opinion poll taken in 1993 showed for the first time that a majority of Americans supported normalization of relations with Vietnam.

Clinton finally lifted the embargo in February 1994. Thirty U. S. corporations opened branch offices in Vietnam the day after the boycott ended. Thus began, in historian George Herring's words, "the battle for Vietnamese hearts and wallets."[61] But U. S. trade and investment prospects in Vietnam appeared modest. The efforts of a few U. S. oil companies to become involved in developing Vietnam's offshore oil wells have not been promising to date. The proven oil reserves are modest, the oil is apparently not of high-grade quality, and there is a glut of oil on world markets for the foreseeable future. Inept and corrupt Vietnamese bureaucrats are more of a hindrance than a help in promoting foreign trade and investment. Vietnamese industries do not currently produce goods that American consumers are likely to buy, nor can the Vietnamese people, with an annual per capita income of $180, buy many U. S. products. Even though most of its leaders and most of its people want it, it is going to take Vietnam many years to develop a modern industrial economy and a society of consumers.

In January 1995, as a symbolic gesture, the Vietnamese returned the embassy compound in Ho Chi Minh City to the United States. Representatives of the two nations signed an agreement opening liaison offices in their respective capitals. In a brief White House ceremony held on the morning of July 11, 1995, President Clinton, who as a graduate student had opposed the Vietnam War and avoided military service, with Arizona Senator John McCain, a former Naval aviator and POW, standing at his side, officially extended diplomatic recognition to the Democratic Republic of Vietnam. In making the announcement, the President said:

> This moment offers us an opportunity to bind up our wounds. They have resisted time for so long. We can now move on to common ground.[62]

On May 9, 1997, Pete Peterson, a former U. S. Air Force pilot shot down over North Vietnam in 1966, who spent six and one-half years as a prisoner-of-war in Hanoi, arrived at that city's Noi Bai Airport en route to assuming his duties as the new ambassador to Vietnam. Peterson was the first American envoy ever posted to that Communist country. Ambassador Peterson was warmly greeted by a friendly crowd waving both U. S. and Vietnamese flags.

The endless war had finally ended. A new era, with a potential for peace and prosperity, had begun.

NOTES

1. Quoted in Lipsman et al., *The False Peace*, 51.
2. Isaacs, *Without Honor*, 173–80; Hess, *Vietnam*, 145–7.
3. Isaacs, *Without Honor*, 217–40; Lipsman et al., *The False Peace*, 53–57, 118–22, 124–33, 171–2.
4. Kissinger linked the return of the POWs to the departure of the final contingents of U. S. ground forces to ensure that these provisions of the Paris agreements were carried out.
5. Terry, Wallace (ed.), *Bloods: An Oral History of the Vietnam War By Black Veterans* (New York: Ballantine, 1984), 281–3.
6. Frey-Wouters, Ellen, and Laufer, Robert S., *Legacy of War: The American Soldier in Vietnam* (Armonk, N. Y.: M. E. Sharpe, 1986), 39–72. Lifton, Robert J., *Home from the War: Vietnam Veterans: Neither Victims nor Executioners* (New York: Simon and Schuster, 1973).
7. During 1986–1988, the Veterans' Administration funded an extensive survey of the mental health of Vietnam War veterans. Researchers found that about 15 percent of all Vietnam combat veterans still suffered from PTSD.
8. Herring, *America's Longest War*, 257.
9. Turley, *The Second Indochina War*, 162–5.
10. Hess, *Vietnam*, 136.
11. Szulc, *The Illusion of Peace*, 672–6; Duiker, *The Communist Road*, 301–2.
12 Porter (ed.), "Statement by the Provisional Revolutionary Government Foreign Ministry," Nov. 2, 1973, *Vietnam Documents*, vol. 2, Document #345, 642–5; Duiker, *The Communist Road*, 302–5.
13. Porter (ed.), "Fulbright-Aiken Amendment—Public Law 93–52, Section 108, July 1, 1973, *Vietnam Documents*, vol. 2, Document # 341, 639; Isaacs, *Without Honor*, 143, 226–8, 234–7.
14. Davidson, *Vietnam at War*, 741–2; Turley, *The Second Indochina War*, 173–4.
15. Herring, *America's Longest War*, 261–2.
16. In mid-1974, total RVNAF forces numbered about 1.1 million. The Vietcong and PAVN forces in the South totaled about 240,000.
17. Quote is from Turley, *The Second Indochina War*, 167; Hess, 136–7.
18. Lipsman et al., *The False Peace*, 138.

19. Quote is from Hess, *Vietnam*, 137.

20. Turley, *The Second Indochina War*, 173–4; Lipsman et al., *The False Peace*, 140–1.

21. Lipsman et al., *The False Peace*, 182–3.

22. Isaacs, *Without Honor*, 313–21; Lewy, *America in Vietnam*, 207–9.

23. Quote is from Hess, 138.

24. Snepp, Frank, *Decent Interval: An Insider's Account of Saigon's Indecent End Told by the CIA's Chief Strategy Analyst in Vietnam* (New York: Vintage, 1977), 116–24.

25. Porter (ed.), "General Dung's Account of the October Political Bureau Conference," *Vietnam Documents*, vol. 2, Document # 351 (Extract), 658–9. Dung conceded that U. S. intervention remained a possibility, but he also stated that even if Americans did reenter the war, they could not save Thieu's government from collapse; Duiker, *The Communist Road*, 306–8.

26. Lipsman et al., *The False Peace*, 182–3.

27. Duiker, *The Communist Road*, 308–9; Davidson, *Vietnam at War*, 762–4; Isaacs, *Without Honor*, 331–5.

28. Isaacs, *Without Honor*, 345–52; Davidson, *Vietnam at War*, 770–4; Dougan, Clark, Fulghum, David, and the editors of Boston Publishing Company, *The Fall of the South* (Boston: Boston Publishing Co., 1985), 48–52.

29. Davidson, *Vietnam at War*, 774–7; Isaacs, *Without Honor*, 353–6; Turley, *The Second Indochina War*, 179–81.

30. Quoted in Hess, *Vietnam*, 139.

31. Davidson, *Vietnam at War*, 777–9; Dougan et al., *Fall of the South*, 56–63.

32. Quote is from Herring, *America's Longest War*, 265.

33. Quote is from Dougan et al., *Fall of the South*, 83.

34. Isaacs, *Without Honor*, 366–71; Dougan et al., *Fall of the South*, 81–82; CBS television documentary, "Vietnam: A War that is Finished," first shown in August 1975.

35. Hess, *Vietnam*, 138.

36. Davidson, *Vietnam at War*, 790.

37. Quoted in Isaacs, *Without Honor*, 281–2. Isaacs has a riveting account of the final days of the Khmer Republic. See his chapter 8, "Fall of the Khmer Republic," 241–89.

38. *Ibid.*, 407–13; Dougan et al., *Fall of the South*, 107–8, 118–21, 127–9. Although Congress rejected Ford's request for $722 million, it authorized a final $300 million the president had requested to provide humanitarian aid and to pay the costs of the evacuation from South Vietnam.

39. Quoted in Herring, *America's Longest War*, 266.

40. Thieu's remarks quoted in Hess, 140; Snepp, *Decent Interval*, 392–7.

41. Ford's remarks were recorded on the CBS video "Vietnam: A War that is Finished."

42. Dougan et al., *Fall of the South*, 154–5.

43. *Ibid.*, 157–8.

44. *Ibid.*, 163–4.

45. Isaacs, *Without Honor*, 447–68.

46. Quoted in Dougan et al., *Fall of the South*, 171.

47. Colonel Tin's remarks are quoted in Hess, *Vietnam*, 140. Isaacs, *Without Honor*, 447–8; Hosmer, Stephen T., Kellen, Konrad, and Jenkins, Brian M., *The Fall of South Vietnam: Statements by Vietnamese Military and Civilian Leaders* (New York: Crane, Russak, 1980), 252–3.

48. Quoted in Isaacs, *Without Honor*, 485.

49. Herring, *Longest War*, 3d. ed., 298; Bergerud, Eric M., *The Dynamics of Defeat: The Vietnam War in Hau Nghia Province*. Boulder, Colo: Westview, 1991. In detailing the various South Vietnamese and American pacification efforts in a specific locale, Begerud discovered that nothing they could do could overcome the Saigon government's lack of local legitimacy. The Phoenix program badly damaged the NFL infrastructure in the Hau Nghia Province, but the Saigon government could never replace it. To quote Bergerud, p. 3: "The difficulties Americans faced were virtually beyond solution."

50. *Ibid.*

51. Hess, *Vietnam*, 150. The source for the estimated numbers of Vietnamese executed by the Communists is a study based on the testimony of Vietnamese immigrants to the United States.

52. Herring, *Longest War*, 3d. ed., 303.

53. *Ibid.*

54. Galambos, Louis, "Separating the Wheat from the Chaff: Vietnam's Implications for the Future," unpub. paper delivered at the Fourteenth Military Symposium on "Vietnam, 1964–1975: An American Dilemma," held at the United States Air Force Academy, October 19, 1990.

55. O'Keefe, Kevin, "The Vietnamization of Nicaragua," in George Donelson Moss, ed., *A Vietnam Reader: Sources and Essays* (Englewood Cliffs, N. J.: Prentice Hall, 1991), 301–13.

56. Quoted in Kiernan, Ben, "The Vietnam War: Alternative Endings," *American Historical Review*, vol. 97, no. 4 (October 1992), 1136.

57. Herring, *Longest War*, 3d. ed., 312.

58. *Ibid.*, 316.

59. Lipsman et al., *The False Peace*, 76–79; *New York Times*, August 30, 1988, A6.

60. *New York Times*, August 31, 1988, A6.

61. Herring, *Longest War*, 3d. ed., 320.

62. Quoted in Olson and Roberts, *Where the Domino Fell*, 282.

Tables

TABLE A. UNITED STATES MILITARY PERSONNEL SERVING IN SOUTH VIETNAM

December 31, 1960	900
December 31, 1961	3,205
December 31, 1962	9,000
December 31, 1963	16,500
December 31, 1964	23,300
December 31, 1965	184,300
June 30, 1966	267,500
December 31, 1966	385,300
June 30, 1967	448,800
December 31, 1967	485,600
June 30, 1968	534,700
December 31, 1968	536,100
April 30, 1969	543,400
June 30, 1969	538,700
December 31, 1969	475,200
June 30, 1970	414,900
December 31, 1970	334,600
June 30, 1971	239,200
December 31, 1971	156,800
June 30, 1972	47,000
December 31, 1972	24,200
March 30, 1973	240

Source: U. S. Department of Defense official records.

Table B.   Comparative Military Casualty Figures

Year	KIA		WIA	
	U. S.	RVNAF	U. S.	RVNAF
1960	0	2,223	0	2,788
1961	11	4,004	2	5,449
1962	31	4,457	41	7,195
1963	78	5,665	218	11,488
1964	147	7,457	522	17,017
1965	1,369	11,242	3,308	23,118
1966	5,008	11,953	16,526	20,975
1967	9,377	12,716	32,370	29,448
1968	14,589	27,915	46,797	70,696
1969	9,414	21,833	32,940	65,276
1970	4,221	23,346	15,211	71,582
1971	1,381	22,738	4,767	60,939
1972	300	39,587	587	109,960
1973	237	27,901	24	131,936
1974	207	31,219	0	155,735
Totals	46,370	254,256	153,313	783,602

Source: Jeffrey J. Clarke, *Advice and Support: The Final Years*, p. 275.

Table C.   Casualties from January 1, 1961 to January 28, 1973

United States
- Killed in action..45,941
- Wounded..300,635
- Missing...2,330
- Killed or died, noncombat-related 10,420

South Vietnam
- Military: Killed in action 220,357
- Military: Wounded 499,026

Vietcong/North Vietnam
- Military: Killed 851,000
- Civilian: North Vietnam...65,000

Third-Country Forces
- Military: Killed in action
- Korea 4,407
- Australia/New Zealand..469
- Thailand..351

Sources: Lewy, Gunther, *America in Vietnam*; O'Ballance, Edgar, *The Wars in Vietnam*; Thayer, Thomas C., *War Without Fronts: The American Experience in Vietnam.*

TABLE D. STATISTICAL PORTRAIT OF U. S. CASUALTIES IN INDOCHINA

1. Killed in combat...45,941
2. Wounded in combat...300,635
3. Died in non-combat situations 10,420
4. 90% of combat deaths were enlisted men 41,003
5. 10% of combat deaths were officers..4,938
6. 60% of combat deaths were aged 19–21 26,931
7. 22% of combat deaths were aged 22–25 10,421
8. 18% of combat deaths were aged 26+..8,589
9. 33% of the dead had served less than 1 year......................................14,995
10. 33% of the dead had served between 1 and 2 years 14,853
11. Blacks accounted for 12% of the combat deaths..................................5,662
12. Other non-whites accounted for 1% of the combat deaths........................469
13. Whites accounted for 87% of the combat deaths 39,827
14. Draftees accounted for 33% of the combat deaths 15,404

Source: Thayer, *War Without Fronts.*

TABLE E. CAUSES OF COMBAT AND NON-COMBAT DEATHS

Combat Deaths...45,941
Aircraft loss...4,178
Gunshot or small arms fire 18,385
Artillery/rocket/other explosion...12,350
Multiple fragmentation wounds..8,465
Other causes/unknown 2,563
Non-Combat Deaths...10,420
Accidents...8,483
Illness 929
Murder...190
Suicide...379
Other..439

Source: Thayer, *War Without Fronts.*

TABLE F. A STATISTICAL PORTRAIT OF U. S. VIETNAM VETERANS

Service during Vietnam Era, 1964–1975 8,700,000
Service in South Vietnam...2,700,000
Combat in South Vietnam 870,000
Vital Statistics (1978)
Median age ....32 years
Median education ....12.9 years
Median income, ages 20–39 ....$12,680
Unemployment rate, ages 20–34 ....5.5 %
In VA hospitals...9,652

Source: Veterans' Administration and Department of Defense official reports.

Glossary

A Teams: Twelve-man Special Forces units

AID: Agency for International Development (also USAID)

Airborne: People or materiel delivered by helicopters or fixed-wing aircraft

AK-47: A Russian and Chinese assault rifle used extensively by the Vietcong and PAVN forces

Amtrack: An armored amphibious vehicle used by Marines

APC: Armored Personnel Carrier

ARVN: Army of the Republic of Vietnam; the regular South Vietnamese national forces

Base camp: Field headquarters for a maneuver unit, usually a battalion

Body bags: Plastic bags used for the retrieval of bodies of soldiers killed in the field

CAP: Combined Action Program

Charlie: GI slang for the Vietcong, a short version of Victor Charlie, from the U. S. military phonetic alphabet for VC

Chieu Hoi: Literally "Open Arms," a program set up to encourage Vietcong and NVA soldiers to defect to the South Vietnamese side

Chinook: CH-47 transport helicopter

CIDG: Civilian Irregular Defense Groups, teams devised by CIA operatives that combined defense functions with social and economic development programs designed to win the allegiance of the Montagnards

CINCPAC: Commander-in-Chief, United States Pacific Command

Clear and hold: U. S. military operation in which troops would hold an area permanently after killing, dispersing, or capturing all enemy soldiers in the area

Cobra: Bell AH-1G fast-attack helicopter, armed with machine guns, grenade launchers, and rockets

COMUSMACV: Commander, United States Military Assistance Command, Vietnam

CONUS: Military acronym for the Continental United States

CORDS: Civil Operations and Revolutionary Development Support

Corps: Two divisions assigned to defend a military region

COSVN: Central Office, South Vietnam, the headquarters controlling all Vietcong political and military operations in southern Vietnam

CTZ: Corps Tactical Zone

DAO: Defense Attache Office, an agency that was part of the U. S. mission sent to South Vietnam following the January 1973 Accords that ended the American war. It was a replacement for MACV; DAO administered the U. S. military assistance program to the GVN from 1973 to 1975

DEROS: Date eligible for return from overseas; the date a soldier's tour of duty in Vietnam ended, usually one year after arriving in the country

DESOTO: U. S. Navy destroyer patrols in the South China Sea

DMZ: Demilitarized Zone

DOD: Department of Defense

DRV: Democratic Republic of Vietnam (North Vietnam), created by Ho Chi Minh on September 2, 1945

EAGLE PULL: Code-name of the U. S. evacuation of Phnom Penh in April 1975

FAC: Forward Air Controller, a forward spotter who coordinated air strikes, usually airborne

FMFPAC: Fleet Marine Force, Pacific Command

Fragging: The murder of a commissioned or non-commissioned officer by an enlisted man of lower rank, usually with a fragmentation grenade

Free-fire zones: Territory considered completely under enemy control. South Vietnamese officials authorized the use of unlimited firepower in such zones

FREQUENT WIND: Code-name of the U. S. evacuation of Saigon in April 1975

FSB: Fire support base, a protected forward artillery base

Green Berets: Famed nickname of soldiers serving in the U. S. Army Special Forces trained for counterinsurgency operations; the named derived from the green berets worn by these elite forces

Grunt: The most frequent nickname given to Army and Marine ground combat forces

GVN: The Government of Vietnam (South Vietnam)

HES: Hamlet Evaluation System; a monthly statistical report that provided the CORDS with information on rural security

Hot Pursuit: The policy, occasionally authorized, of allowing U. S. soldiers cross-border pursuit of retreating Vietcong or NVA forces into Cambodia

Huey: Nickname given to the UH-1 series helicopter

ICC: International Control Commission, created by the Geneva Accords (1954) to supervise implementation of the agreements

ICCS: International Commission of Control and Supervision; agency responsible for administering the January 1973 Paris agreement

JCS: Joint Chiefs of Staff

JGS: Joint General Staff, the South Vietnamese equivalent of the U. S. Joint Chiefs

JMC: Joint Military Commission, consisting of members from North Vietnam, South Vietnam, the PRG, and the United States, responsible for implementing the military provisions of the Paris agreement

JMT: Joint Military Team, consisting of members from North Vietnam, South Vietnam, the PRG, and the United States, responsible for accounting for all prisoners of war and MIAs

KIA: Killed in Action

Lao Dong: The Vietnamese Worker's Party, the North Vietnamese Communist party founded in 1951; the ruling party of North Vietnam until 1975; thereafter it ruled the entire country.

LINEBACKER I: Code-name for U. S. bombing of North Vietnam, resumed in April 1972 in response to the Nguyen Hue Offensive

LINEBACKER II: Code-name for the U. S. bombing of North Vietnam during December 1972, the "Christmas Bombing"

LST: Landing Ship Tank, a large, shallow-draft cargo-hauling and landing craft

LZ: Landing Zone, for helicopters

M-16:   The standard issue U. S. automatic rifle used in the Vietnam War from 1966

MAAG: Military Assistance Advisory Group, the forerunner of MACV, 1955 to 1964

MACV: Military Assistance Command, Vietnam, formed in 1962, lasted until 1973

Main Force: Regular army forces of the North Vietnamese and Vietcong

MAP: Military Assistance Program

Medevac: Helicopters with the mission of transporting wounded soldiers quickly from the battlefield to forward hospitals

MENU: Code-name for the secret B-52 bombing missions in Cambodia

MIA: Missing in Action

MR: Military Region, formerly a CTZ, Corps Tactical Zone

Napalm: A jellied incendiary weapon used by the French and the Americans during the Indochina wars

NCO: Noncommissioned Officer

Neutralize: Word used by Phoenix/Phung Hoang operatives to define putting the VCI out of action; neutralize could mean killing, capturing, or going into the Chieu Hoi program

NLF: The National Liberation Front, formed on December 20, 1960

NSAM: National Security Action Memorandum

NSC: National Security Council

NVA: North Vietnamese Army

NVN: North Vietnam or North Vietnamese

OB: Order of Battle, a comprehensive arrangement and disposition of military units deployed in battle

OCS: Officers' Candidate School

Operation VULTURE: A planned U. S. operation to relieve the siege at Dien Bien Phu in April 1954; it was never implemented

OPLAN: Operations Plan

OSS: Office of Strategic Services, a World War II intelligence organization, forerunner of the CIA

PACAF: United States Pacific Air Force

PACFLT: United States Pacific Fleet

Pathet Lao: Laotian Communist insurgents who came to power in 1974–75

PAVN: People's Army of Vietnam, the North Viertnamese army

PF: Popular Forces

PHOENIX: A joint U. S./South Vietnamese program to detect and neutralize the Vietcong infrastructure

Phung Hoang: The South Vietnamese-run program to destroy the VCI; it paralleled the PHOENIX program

PLA: People's Liberation Army of South Vietnam, the military arm of the Vietcong

PLAF: People's Liberation Armed Forces of South Vietnam, a. k. a. the PLA

POW: Prisoner of War

PRG: Provisional Revolutionary Government, formed by the NLF in 1969

PRP: People's Revolutionary Party, the Communist Party apparatus that controlled the National Liberation Front, founded in 1962

PSYOP: Pyschological Operations, a form of psychological warfare

PTSD: Post-Traumatic Stress Disorder

RANCH HAND: Code-name for the Air Force aerial defoliation program to deny ground cover and food crops to the Vietcong

RDC: Revolutionary Development Cadres, teams of South Vietnamese pacification workers trained to carry out various missions

RF: Regional Forces

ROK: Republic of Korea (South Korea)

ROTC: Reserve Officer Training Corps

Ruff-puffs: South Vietnamese regional and local forces used for village security

RVN: Republic of Vietnam (South Vietnam)

RVNAF: Republic of Vietnam Armed Forces, all South Vietnamese military forces including ARVN, Regional Forces, and Popular Forces

SAC: Strategic Air Command

SAM: Surface to air missile

SAM-2: Medium-range Communist surface to air missile, effective up to 60,000 feet, speed about Mach 2.5

SANE: Committee for a Sane Nuclear Policy, an organization opposed to the nuclear arms race active in the late 1950s and early 1960s

Sappers: Vietcong commandos, used for demolition and sabotage operations

Search and Destroy: Large-scale Allied offensive operations designed to find, fix, and destroy enemy forces; a form of attrition warfare

SEATO: Southeast Asia Treaty Organization

Seventeenth (17th) Parallel: Temporary dividing line separating northern and southern Vietnam, created by Geneva Accords (1954), pending unification elections scheduled for July 1956, which were never held

SOG: Studies and Observation Group, MACV

Sortie: An operational flight by one aircraft

Special Forces: U. S. Army personnel trained to carry out counterinsurgency operations, often covert and unconventional; they also trained Montagnards and South Vietnamese Special Forces

SVN: South Vietnam

Tet: The Vietnamese lunar New Year and their most important holiday

Third Countries: U. S. Allies that furnished military forces for the Vietnam War: South Korea, Thailand, the Philippines, Australia, and New Zealand

USAID: United States Agency for International Development

VC: Vietcong, a derogatory contraction meaning a Vietnamese who is a Communist

VCI: Vietcong infrastructure, the political leaders of the Vietcong, also responsible for logistic support of the military forces

VNAF: Vietnamese Air Force (the South Vietnamese Air Force)

WIA: Wounded in Action

Chronology of U. S. Involvement in Vietnam, 1942–1975

1942
U. S. pilots attached to the Flying Tigers fly combat missions in Vietnam against Japanese military installations

1944–1945
The OSS funds Vietminh actions against the Japanese in Vietnam, and OSS operatives work with the Vietnamese to rescue downed U. S. flyers and go on espionage and sabotage missions with them

September 1945
America supports the French efforts to reimpose colonialism in Vietnam

May 8, 1950
The United States signs an agreement with France to provide the French Associated States of Vietnam with military assistance

August 3, 1950
A U. S. Military Assistance Advisory Group (MAAG) of thirty-five men arrives in Vietnam to teach troops receiving U. S. weapons how to use them

December 30, 1950
The United States signs a Mutual Defense Assistance Agreement with France, Vietnam, Cambodia, and Laos

September 7, 1951
The Truman administration signs an agreement with Saigon to provide direct military aid to South Vietnam

September 30, 1953
President Eisenhower approves $785 million in military aid for South Vietnam

April 7, 1954

At a news conference, President Eisenhower, stressing the importance of defending Dien Bien Phu, enunciates the domino theory

July 21, 1954

The American observer at Geneva, General Walter Bedell Smith, issues a unilateral declaration stating that the United States will refrain from the threat or the use of force to prevent implementation of the Geneva Accords

August 1, 1954

An exodus of about 900,000 refugees from northern Vietnam traveling to southern Vietnam begins

September 8, 1954

The Manila Treaty is concluded creating SEATO; a separate protocol extends the SEATO umbrella to include Laos, Cambodia, and "the free territory under the jurisdiction of the State of Vietnam" (South Vietnam)

October 24, 1954

President Eisenhower sends a letter to the new leader in southern Vietnam, Ngo Dinh Diem, pledging U. S. support and agreeing to send $100 million to build up Diem's military forces. Eisenhower begins the U. S. commitment to maintaining a non-Communist government in South Vietnam

April 28, 1955

Under severe pressure from a coalition of political enemies, Diem's fledgling regime almost falls; he is saved by the actions of Air Force Colonel Edwin Landsdale, who is also a CIA operative

October 26, 1955

Diem, after defeating Bao Dai in a rigged election, declares himself to be president of the Republic of South Vietnam; his government is instantly recognized by the United States

July 20, 1956

The deadline for holding reunification elections in accordance with the Geneva Accords passes; America supports Diem's refusal to hold elections.

May 8, 1957

Diem makes a triumphant visit to the United States; Eisenhower praises him lavishly and reaffirms American support for his government.

October, 1957

Small-scale civil war begins in South Vietnam between Diem's forces and cadres of Vietminh, who have remained in South Vietnam after the partition at Geneva

April 4, 1959

Eisenhower delivers a speech in which he links American vital national interests to the survival of a non-Communist state in South Vietnam.

December 20, 1960
The National Liberation front is formed. It is the Vietminh reborn. The Communist-controlled NLF takes charge of the growing insurgency against the Diem regime. Diem dubs the NLF the "Vietcong," meaning Vietnamese who are Communists.

January 6, 1961
Soviet Premier Khrushchev announces support for all "wars of national liberation" around the world. His speech influences the incoming Kennedy administration's decision to support counterinsurgency in Vietnam.

April 1961
The Kennedy administration confronts a crisis in Laos. Kennedy considers military intervention, then decides to seek a political solution.

May 1961
Kennedy approves sending Special Forces to South Vietnam and authorizes clandestine warfare against North Vietnam and a secret war in Laos.
Vice President Lyndon B. Johnson visits South Vietnam and recommends a strong commitment to South Vietnam's head of state Ngo Dinh Diem.

June 1961
Kennedy and Khrushchev, meeting in Vienna, agree to support a neutral and independent Laos; Kennedy rejects neutrality for Vietnam.

November 1961
Special Forces are deployed to the central highlands in the vicinity of Pleiku to work with Montagnards; they begin developing the CIDGs

December 1961
The *New York Times* reports that some of the 3,200 U. S. advisers are operating in battle areas and are authorized to fire back if fired on.

January 1962
The Air Force launches Operation RANCHHAND, the aerial spraying of defoliating herbicides to deny cover to the Vietcong and destroy their crops.

February 8, 1962
The MACV is established in Saigon; its first commander is General Paul D. Harkins.

March 22, 1962
The Strategic Hamlet Program is launched.

July 23, 1962
The Geneva Accords on Laos is signed.

December 1962
There are now about 9,000 U. S. advisory and support personnel in South Vietnam; 109 Americans were killed or wounded in 1962.

January 2, 1963
At Ap Bac in the Mekong Delta, the ARVN 7th Division, equipped with American weapons and accompanied by U. S. advisers, cannot defeat a lightly armed Vietcong battalion of 300 soldiers. The battle demonstrates that government troops cannot match the tactics or the fighting spirit of the insurgents.

May 8, 1963
In Hue, 20,000 Buddhists celebrating the birthday of Gautama Siddhartha Buddha are fired on by government forces; this action begins a series of events that will bring the downfall of the Diem regime.

June 11, 1963
Thich Quang Duc, an elderly Buddhist monk, immolates himself by fire at a busy Saigon intersection to protest Diem's suppression of the Buddhists

August 21, 1963
Military forces loyal to Diem and to his brother Nhu attack Buddhist temples; President Kennedy denounces these actions. Meanwhile, a coup to overthrow Diem is being planned by dissident ARVN generals.

September 2, 1963
President Kennedy strongly reaffirms the American commitment to Vietnam; he also criticizes Diem's attacks on the Buddhists and calls for reform.

Nov. 1, 1963
A coup, led by General Tran Van Don and General Duong Van Minh, with the foreknowledge and encouragement of American officials, overthrows the Diem regime; a military directorate, led by General Minh, succeeds Diem

Nov. 2, 1963
Diem and his brother Nhu are murdered on the order of one of the coup leaders

Nov. 22, 1963
President John F. Kennedy is assassinated by Lee Harvey Oswald in Dallas, Texas

Nov. 24, 1963
President Lyndon Johnson affirms U. S. support of the new South Vietnamese government

December 31, 1963
There are about 16,500 U. S. soldiers in South Vietnam at year's end; 489 have been killed or wounded during 1963

January 2, 1964
President Johnson approves covert military operations against North Vietnam to be carried out by South Vietnamese and Asian mercenaries; called OPLAN 34A, they include espionage, sabotage, psychological warfare, and intelligence gathering

January 30, 1964
Minh's government is overthrown in a bloodless coup by General Nguyen Khanh

March 8–12, 1964
Secretary of Defense Robert McNamara visits South Vietnam; he affirms that America will remain in South Vietnam for as long as it takes to win the war

April 1964
North Vietnam decides to infiltrate units of the NVA into South Vietnam

June 20, 1964

General Harkins is succeeded by General William C. Westmoreland as COMUS-MACV; three days later, Henry Cabot Lodge resigns as the U. S. ambassador to the GVN and is replaced by General Maxwell Taylor

July 1964

Both sides are engaged in covert warfare in violation of the 1954 Geneva Accords; North Vietnam is using the Ho Chi Minh trail to infiltrate NVA troops south and to supply the Vietcong. America implements the OPLAN 34A operations; one OPLAN 34A operation uses U. S. destroyers to conduct surveillance missions off the North Vietnamese coast; these operations are called DESOTO Missions.

August 2, 1964

North Vietnamese patrol boats attack the U. S. S. *Maddox*, which was on a DESOTO Mission in waters near the North Vietnamese coast.

August 3, 1964

South Vietnamese PT boats carry out OPLAN 34A raids, attacking North Vietnamese radar installations in the same area

August 4–5, 1964

Both U. S. S. *Maddox* and another destroyer, U. S. S. *Turner Joy*, which has joined the *Maddox*, report that they are under attack at sea. Carrier-based U. S. naval aircraft fly reprisal raids, ordered by President Johnson, are flown against North Vietnamese targets.

August 7, 1964

At Johnson's request, Congress enacts the Gulf of Tonkin resolution granting President Johnson the power to "to take all necessary measures to repel any armed attack against the forces of the United States and to prevent further aggression . . . including the use of armed force. . . . " Johnson will later use this resolution as a post-dated declaration of war.

October 1964

General Khanh resigns and is replaced by a civilian, Tran Van Huong

Nov. 1, 1964

Vietcong forces attack Bien Hoa Air Base. Five U. S. soldiers are killed and six B-57 bombers are destroyed. It is the first direct attack on a U. S. military installation signaling a major shift in Vietcong tactics.

December 31, 1964

About 23,000 Americans are now serving in South Vietnam. There is now a full-scale undeclared war raging in South Vietnam, and there is also fighting in Laos and Cambodia. There have been 1,278 U. S. casualties for the year.

January 4, 1965

In his State of the Union address, President Johnson reaffirms the American commitment to South Vietnam. He states that American security is tied to peace in Southeast Asia.

January 27–28, 1965
Tran Van Huong is ousted and General Khanh returns to power.

February 7, 1965
The Vietcong attack a U. S. helicopter base and other installations near Pleiku in the central highlands. Eight Americans are killed and 126 wounded. Johnson orders retaliatory air strikes on targets in North Vietnam.

February 13, 1965
Johnson orders a sustained bombing campaign against North Vietnam that has been long-planned by his advisers. Called Operation ROLLING THUNDER, it will continue, with occasional pauses, until October 31, 1968. The American air war against North Vietnam begins on March 2.

February 25, 1965
General Khanh is forced out by Air Marshal Nguyen Cao Ky

March 8, 1965
The first U. S. combat troops arrive in Vietnam

April 6, 1965
President Johnson authorizes U. S. forces to take the offensive to support ARVN forces

June 19, 1965
Air Marshal Ky becomes premier of the eighth South Vietnamese government since Diem was overthrown

June 28–30, 1965
U. S. forces undertake the first major American offensive against the Vietcong in War Zone D, twenty miles northeast of Saigon

July 21–28, 1965
President Johnson makes a series of decisions that amount to committing the United States to a major war in Vietnam. Among the decisions he makes: draft calls will be raised to 35,000 per month, 50,000 additional troops will be sent to Vietnam with additional increases as the situation demands, and the air war against North Vietnam is expanded. Johnson also makes it clear that he wants these decisions implemented in low-key fashion so as not to excite or alarm either Congress or the American people. These decisions began the seven-and-one-half-year U. S. war in Indochina

August 7, 1965
The Chinese government warns the United States that it will send troops to fight in Vietnam if necessary

October 23 to November 20, 1965
In the largest battle of the war to date, the U. S. 1st Air Cavalry defeats NVA forces in the Ia Drang valley, in a remote corner of the Pleiku Province

December 31, 1965
This was a pivotal year of the war. America began a sustained air war against North Vietnam. It also committed large numbers of forces to ground combat operations in South Vietnam. At year's end, there are 184,000 U. S. troops in South Vietnam;

U. S. casualties for the year, 1,369 KIA and 5,300 WIA; 1965 is year one of the American war in Vietnam.

February 4, 1966
Senate Foreign Relations Committee, chaired by Senator J. William Fulbright, holds televised hearings on the Vietnam War and allows critics of the developing war to present their views

February 6, 1966
President Johnson convenes a conference on the Vietnam War in Honolulu

March 9, 1966
The U. S. Department of State issues a White Paper claiming that American intervention in Vietnam is legal under international law, the U. N. Charter, and the U. S. Constitution

April 7, 1966
President Johnson makes a speech at Johns Hopkins University defending his war policy against both hawkish and dovish critics

June 29, 1966
U. S. aircraft strike North Vietnamese petroleum storage facilities near Haiphong and Hanoi

October 15 to November 26, 1966
U. S. forces are involved in one of the biggest operations of the war in the Tay Ninh Province near the Cambodian border, fifty miles northwest of Saigon

December 31, 1966
The Vietnam War has become the dominant event in world affairs. During the year, the United States increased its forces in Vietnam from 184,000 to 385,000. The air war against North Vietnam has been expanded significantly; 5,008 Americans were killed and 30,093 were wounded during the year.

January 8–26, 1967
American troops are involved in the largest offensive of the war; about 16,000 American troops participate in Operation CEDAR FALLS to disrupt Vietcong operations in the Iron Triangle region northeast of Saigon.

February 22 to April 1, 1967
The largest Allied offensive of the war to date takes place, Operation JUNCTION CITY, involving thirty-four U. S. battalions. Its goal is to smash the VC stronghold in War Zone C near the Cambodian border and ease pressure on Saigon.

March 10–11, 1967
U. S. aircraft bomb the Thai Nguyen steel works near Hanoi; they are the first bombing raids on a major industrial target.

May 14–16, 1967
A U. S. newspaper reports that Chinese Premier Chou En-lai threatened to send Chinese troops into North Vietnam if the United States invaded that country

July 30, 1967
A Gallup poll shows that 52 percent of Americans disapprove of Johnson's Vietnam War policy; 56 percent believe America is in a stalemate.

September 29, 1967
President Johnson offers to stop the bombing of North Vietnam if it will agree to start negotiations; offer becomes known as the "San Antonio Formula"

October 16–21, 1967
Antiwar activists hold antidraft demonstrations throughout the United States; the largest occurs at the Army Induction Center in Oakland, California

October 21–23, 1967
Fifty thousand demonstrate against the Vietnam War in Washington, D. C.

October 25–30, 1967
The air war against North Vietnam intensifies. Sustained attacks are carried out on targets near Hanoi and Haiphong.

November 2, 1967
President Johnson meets privately with a group of distinguished former leaders; dubbed the "Wise Men," they generally support his war policy

November 3–22, 1967
One of the bloodiest and fiercest battles of the war between American and North Vietnamese troops occurs at Dak To in the central highlands

November 22, 1967
President Johnson brings General Westmoreland home to rally support for the war; Westmoreland tells his audiences that the United States is winning the war

November 30, 1967
Senator Eugene J. McCarthy announces that he will challenge President Johnson for the Democratic presidential nomination in 1968; he will run on a platform calling for a negotiated settlement of the Vietnam War.

December 31, 1967
At year's end, there are about 500,000 U. S. troops in Vietnam. For the year, the war cost taxpayers about $21 billion; casualties, 9,353 KIA and 99,742 WIA

January 20 to April 14, 1968
One of the most famous battles of the war takes place at Khe Sanh, an American Marine base just south of the DMZ; NVA forces besiege Khe Sanh. It is feared that Khe Sanh will become an American Dien Bien Phu, but U. S. airpower eventually breaks the siege, and the Communists are forced to withdraw.

January 30 to February 10, 1968
On the first day of the Tet truce, Vietcong forces, supported by NVA troopers, launch the largest offensive of the war. Simultaneous attacks are mounted in South Vietnam's largest cities and many provincial capitals. The offensive is crushed by American and GVN forces. Tet is a decisive military victory for the Allies, but it turns out to be a psychological and political disaster.

February 28, 1968

General Earle Wheeler, chairman of the Joint Chiefs, tells Johnson that General Westmoreland needs an additional 206,000 troops; a crucial point in the war has been reached—if Johnson does not send the troops, he will be conceding that the United States cannot win a military victory; but if he sends the troops, it will require a reserve call-up, and significantly raise the costs and casualties of war. Johnson delays a decision and asks his new Secretary of Defense Clark Clifford to conduct a thorough reappraisal of U. S. Vietnam policy.

March 12, 1968

Senator Eugene McCarthy, in the New Hampshire primary, makes a strong showing in a hawkish state; four days later, Senator Robert Kennedy announces that he too will seek the Democratic nomination and run on an antiwar platform

March 16, 1968

In what will become the most notorious atrocity committed by American soldiers during the Vietnam War, a platoon of troopers slaughter hundreds of unarmed villagers in the hamlet of My Lai-4

March 25–26, 1968

Johnson reconvenes the "Wise Men"; most advise against any more troop increases and recommend that the United States seek a negotiated peace in Vietnam

March 31, 1968

Johnson announces a unilateral halt to all U. S. bombing north of the 20th Parallel and that he will seek to start negotiations with North Vietnam; he also stuns the nation with an announcement that he will not seek reelection

April 22, 1968

Clifford announces that GVN is going to take responsibility for more and more of the fighting; this is the first announcement of a policy that under President Nixon will come to be called Vietnamization.

May 3, 1968

America and North Vietnam agree to begin formal negotiations in Paris on May 10; peace talks begin on May 12

June 10, 1968

General Creighton W. Abrams succeeds General Westmoreland as COMUSMACV

August 5–8, 1968

The Republican National Convention, held in Miami, nominates Richard M. Nixon for president; the Republican platform calls for an honorable negotiated peace in Vietnam and for the progressive "de-Americanization" of the war.

August 26–29, 1968

The Democratic National Convention is held in Chicago; Democrats adopt a platform endorsing the administration's war policy and nominate Vice President Hubert H. Humphrey for president. On the evening of August 28, there is a full-scale riot in the streets, between Chicago police and antiwar radicals.

October 31, 1968
In a televised address to the nation, President Johnson announces a complete bombing halt over North Vietnam; Operation ROLLING THUNDER ends.

November 5, 1968
Richard Nixon is elected President of the United States.

December 31, 1968
The major turning point of the American Vietnam War occurred in 1968. After Tet, Johnson had to abandon his policy of measured escalation in search of military victory and replace it with an early version of Vietnamization looking to a negotiated settlement. Richard Nixon was elected president, and the general sense at the time was that he had a plan for bringing the war to an early end; 1968 is the largest and costliest year of the American war—14,314 KIAs and 150,000 WIAs, costing about $30 billion.

January 25, 1969
The first plenary session of the four-way Paris peace talks among the Americans, the North Vietnamese, the South Vietnamese, and the National Liberation Front occurs

March 18, 1969
President Nixon orders the secret bombing of Communist base camps and supply depots in Cambodia to commence; Operation MENU begins.

May 10–20, 1969
The battle for Hamburger Hill takes place near the A Shau Valley. In ten days of intense fighting and heavy casualties, Allied forces take the hill. The hill is abandoned soon thereafter.

June 8, 1969
President Nixon announces that 25,000 U. S. troops will be withdrawn by the end of August and that they will be replaced by South Vietnamese forces; the gradual phase-out of the American war in Vietnam has begun.

June 10, 1969
The NLF announces the formation of a Provisional Revolutionary Government (PRG) to rule in South Vietnam; it amounts to a formal challenge to the Thieu regime for political control of South Vietnam.

August 4, 1969
Secret negotiations begin in Paris between U. S. special envoy Henry Kissinger and North Vietnam's Xuan Thuy

September 3, 1969
Ho Chi Minh dies

September 23, 1969
Eight antiwar leaders go on trial in Chicago for their part in organizing the antiwar demonstrations in Chicago at the time of the Democratic Convention, August 26–29, 1968

October 15, 1969
The largest antiwar demonstrations in American history take place at many sites across the country

November 3, 1969

President Nixon makes his most successful speech in defense of his Vietnam War policies; Congress and public opinion overwhelmingly support Vietnamization as he successfully blunts the efforts of the antiwar movement.

November 15, 1969

More than 250,000 people come to Washington, D. C., to protest the Vietnam War; it is the largest single antiwar demonstration to date.

November 16, 1969

First public discourse about the My Lai massacre appears in U. S. press

December 31, 1969

At year's end, there are 479,000 U. S. troops in Vietnam. GVN forces have increased and now number over 900,000. Fighting continued during the year on a large-scale. American KIAs totaled 9,414 for the year. The U. S. forces are beginning to show signs of declining morale, discipline, and fighting spirit.

February 19–20, 1970

All defendants in the Chicago trial are convicted of conspiracy to incite rioting and receive maximum sentences of five years in prison and $5,000 fines; all will be acquitted on appeal.

March 18, 1970

In a bloodless coup in Cambodia, pro-Western General Lon Nol ousts Prince Norodom Sihanouk as head of state

April 11, 1970

Polls show that only 48 percent of Americans support Vietnamization, down from 70 percent in November 1969.

April 20, 1970

President Nixon promises to withdraw 150,000 more U. S. troops over the next year if Vietnamization continues to make progress.

May 1, 1970

American forces totaling about 30,000 invade the Fishhook region of Cambodia. The Cambodian incursion is the last major offensive of the Indochina War involving U. S. ground combat forces

May 4, 1970

Ohio National Guard troops fire into a crowd of student demonstrators on the campus of Kent State University, killing four and wounding eleven

May 6, 1970

More than 100 colleges and universities across the nation shut down because of student protests and rioting in response to the Cambodian invasion and killings at Kent State

May 8–20, 1970

In New York City, construction workers attack antiwar student demonstrators on Wall Street; an estimated 80,000 young people, mostly college students, demonstrate peacefully in the nation's capital, protesting the "Kent State Massacre" and calling for the immediate withdrawal of all U. S. troops from Indochina. In New York City, more than 100,000 workers march in support of Nixon's war policies.

June 24, 1970

The Senate, by a vote of 81 to 10, repeals the Gulf of Tonkin resolution; President Nixon states that the legal basis for the American war in Vietnam is not the Gulf of Tonkin resolution, but the constitutional authority of the president as commander-in-chief to protect the lives of U. S. military forces in Vietnam.

August 19, 1970

America signs a pact with Cambodia to provide Lon Nol's government with military aid

November 9, 1970

The Supreme Court refuses to hear a case brought by the state of Massachusetts challenging the constitutionality of the Vietnam War

November 11, 1970

On this day, for the first time in more than five years, no American soldier is killed in Vietnam

December 22, 1970

Congress prohibits U. S. combat forces or advisers in Cambodia or Laos

December 31, 1970

The U. S. war in Vietnam is winding down. At year's end, there are about 335,000 U. S. troops in South Vietnam; U. S. KIAs for the year number 4,221, but the war has spread to Cambodia and no progress is reported at the Paris peace talks

January 1, 1971

Congress forbids the use of U. S. ground troops in either Laos or Cambodia

March 6–24, 1971

The ARVN forces invade Laos to interdict enemy supply routes down the Ho Chi Minh trail complex; Communist counterattacks drive the invaders out of Laos and inflict heavy casualties

March 29, 1971

Lt. William Calley is convicted of mass murder.

April 19–23, 1971

Vietnam Veterans Against the War stage a demonstration in Washington, D. C., ending with veterans throwing combat ribbons and medals on the Capitol's steps

June 13, 1971

The *New York Times* begins publication of the stolen portions of the 47-volume Pentagon analysis of the U. S. involvement in Vietnam through 1967.

July 1, 1971

The 26th Amendment to the Constitution, granting the vote to eighteen to twenty-one year-olds, is ratified.

November 12, 1971

President Nixon orders that, henceforth, U. S. soldiers serving in Vietnam will be assigned only to defensive roles.

December 26, 1971

President Nixon orders U. S. bombing of North Vietnam to resume

December 31, 1971

The American war in Vietnam is ending; 156,800 U. S. troops remain. There were 1,380 KIAs that year. As the Americans withdraw, the Communists intensify their attacks in Laos, Cambodia, and parts of South Vietnam.

February 21–27, 1972

President Nixon makes his historic visit to China; the North Vietnamese fear that China and the United States will make a deal behind their backs, Taiwan for peace in Vietnam.

March 30 to April 8, 1972

A major NVA offensive begins as Communist forces attack South Vietnamese towns and bases just south of the DMZ. The Communists open a second front with a drive into the Binh Long Province, about seventy miles north of Saigon. Communists forces open a third front with drives into the central highlands. The fighting in South Vietnam between GVN and Communist forces is the most intense of the entire war.

April 10, 1972

America responds with air attacks, as B-52s strike targets in North Vietnam for the first time since November 1967. The B-52s and tactical bombers also strike targets in South Vietnam. America is waging an air war over all of Vietnam.

May 8, 1972

Nixon announces he has ordered the mining of all North Vietnamese ports

May 20, 1972

The summit conference between President Nixon and Leonid Brezhnev takes place on schedule in Moscow

June 28, 1972

President Nixon announces that no more draftees will be sent to Vietnam unless they volunteer

July 13, 1972

The Paris peace talks resume after a hiatus of about ten weeks

August 11, 1972

The last U. S. combat unit is withdrawn from South Vietnam; there are now 44,000 American servicemen in South Vietnam.

August 16, 1972

U. S. aircraft fly a record 370 sorties against North Vietnam; most American aircraft fly from carriers in the Gulf of Tonkin or from bases in Thailand.

September 15, 1972

The ARVN forces recapture Quang Tri City; the fighting destroys most of the city, which formerly had a population of 300,000.

October 8–11, 1972

Lengthy secret meetings in Paris between Henry Kissinger and Le Duc Tho produce a tentative settlement of the war. The substance of the agreement is a cease-fire, to be followed by both sides working out a political settlement

October 22, 1972

President Thieu rejects the proposed settlement

November 7, 1972

Richard Nixon is reelected president by a landslide margin. He promises that he will achieve "peace with honor" in Vietnam.

November 11, 1972

The U. S. Army turns over its giant headquarters base at Long Binh to the South Vietnamese, symbolizing the end of the direct American participation in the war after more than seven years.

December 14, 1972

The U. S. breaks off peace talks with the North Vietnamese that have been going on since Nixon's reelection.

December 18–31, 1972

President Nixon announces the resumption of the bombing and mining of North Vietnam. The most concentrated air offensive of the war begins, mostly aimed at targets in the vicinity of Hanoi and Haiphong.

December 28, 1972

Hanoi announces that it is willing to resume negotiations if the United States will stop bombing above the 20th Parallel. The bombing ends on December 31.

December 31, 1972

At year's end, there are about 24,000 U. S. troops remaining in South Vietnam; 312 Americans were killed in action.

January 8–18, 1973

Henry Kissinger and Le Duc Tho resume negotiations in Paris, and they quickly reach an agreement that is similar to the one that had been rejected previously by General Thieu

January 19–26, 1973

Heavy fighting occurs in South Vietnam between the GVN and Communist forces, as both sides try to gain as much territory as they can before the cease-fire.

January 23, 1973

Nixon announces that the Paris Accords will go into effect at 7:00 P. M. EST, on January 27, 1973. He says "peace with honor" has been achieved.

January 27, 1973

The draft ends; for the first time since 1949, America has no conscription.

February 12–27, 1973

American POWs begin to come home

February 21, 1973

A cease-fire formally ends the 20-year war in Laos

March 29, 1973

The last U. S. troops and POWs leave South Vietnam. Only a DAO contingent and Marine embassy guards remain. About 8,500 U. S. civilian officials stay on.

June 4 to August 15, 1973
The Senate blocks all funds for any U. S. military activities in Indochina. The House concurs. The Nixon administration works out a compromise agreement with Congress to permit continued U. S. bombing in Cambodia until August 15. The cessation marks the end of twelve years of American military action in Indochina.

November 7, 1973
Congress enacts the War Powers Act over President Nixon's veto.

December 31, 1973
The war in Vietnam continues without U. S. involvement. Most of the provisions of the Paris agreements are not observed by either side. During the year, there were 13,788 RVNAF KIAs and 45,057 Communist KIAs.

August 5, 1974
Congress makes sharp cuts in the amount of military aid going to the South Vietnamese government

August 9, 1974
Richard M. Nixon resigns the U. S. presidency; Gerald R. Ford is sworn in as president

September 16, 1974
President Ford offers clemency to draft evaders and deserters

December 31, 1974
During 1974, 80,000 people, both civilians and soldiers, have been killed in the war. This is the highest total for any year of the wars that began in 1945

January 6, 1975
The NVA forces overrun the Phuoc Long Province. When the Americans do not react, Hanoi concludes that America will not reintroduce its military forces to save the GVN.

January 28, 1975
President Ford requests an additional $722 million in military aid for South Vietnam. Congress refuses his request.

March 1975
The NVA forces launch an offensive in the central highlands; in a desperate effort to save the southern half of his country, General Thieu orders his forces to abandon their central highlands positions.

March 24, 1975
Hanoi launches its Ho Chi Minh campaign to "liberate" South Vietnam before the rains begin

April 8–21, 1975
The last major battle of the Vietnam War is fought at Xuan Loc, about thirty miles from Saigon. After hard fighting, the Communists win.

April 12, 1975
President Nguyen Van Thieu resigns and flees South Vietnam

April 16, 1975
The Cambodian government surrenders to the Khmer Rouge, who promptly occupy the capital city of Phnom Penh

April 23, 1975
President Ford pronounces the Vietnam War "finished as far as America is concerned."

April 29–30, 1975
The last Americans and thousands of South Vietnamese are evacuated from Saigon

April 30, 1975
The Communists conquer Saigon. The Vietnam War ends in victory for the VC/NVA forces. The long American effort to create a non-Communist state in southern Vietnam fails

MAJOR SOURCES FOR THE CHRONOLOGY

Bowman, John, General Editor, *The World Almanac of the Vietnam War* (New York: A Bison Books, 1985).

Davidson, Phillip B., *Vietnam at War: The History, 1946–1975* (Novato, Ca.: Presidio, 1988).

Gravel, Mike (ed.), *The Pentagon Papers: The Defense Department History of U. S. Decision Making in Vietnam*, 4 vols. (Boston: Beacon, 1971).

Summers, Harry G. Jr., *The Vietnam War Almanac* (New York: Facts on File, 1985).

Bibliography

BOOKS

ACHESON, DEAN. *Present at the Creation*. New York: Norton, 1969.

AMBROSE, STEPHEN E. *Eisenhower*, vol. 2: *The President*. New York: Simon and Schuster, 1984.

———. *Nixon: The Education of a Politician*. New York: Simon and Schuster, 1987.

———. *Nixon: The Triumph of a Politician*. New York: Simon and Schuster, 1989.

———. *Nixon: Ruin and Recovery*. New York: Simon and Schuster, 1991.

———. *Rise to Globalism: American Foreign Policy since 1938*. 2d rev. ed. New York: Penguin, 1985.

ANDERSON, DAVID L. *Trapped by Success: The Eisenhower Administration and Vietnam, 1953–1961*. New York: Columbia University Press, 1991.

———. ed. *Shadow on the White House: Presidents and the Vietnam War*. Lawrence, Kans.: University of Kansas Press, 1993.

ANDRADE, DALE. *Ashes to Ashes: The Phoenix Program and the Vietnam War*. Lexington, Mass.: Lexington Books, 1990.

APPY, CHRISTIAN G. *Working Class War: American Combat Soldiers and Vietnam*. Chapel Hill, N.C.: University of North Carolina Press, 1993.

ARLEN, MICHAEL J. *The Living Room War*. New York: Viking, 1969.

ARNOLD, JAMES R. *The First Domino: Eisenhower, the Military, and America's Intervention in Vietnam*. New York: Morrow, 1991.

BAIN, CHESTER A. *Vietnam: The Roots of Conflict*. Englewood Cliffs, N. J.: Prentice-Hall, 1967.

BAKER, MARK (ed.). *NAM: The Vietnam War in the Words of the Soldiers Who Fought There*. New York: Berkeley, 1981.

BALL, GEORGE. *Diplomacy for a Crowded World*. Boston: Little, Brown, 1976.

————. *The Past Has Another Pattern*. New York: W. W. Norton, 1982.

BARITZ, LOREN. *Backfire: A History of How American Culture Led Us into Vietnam and Made Us Fight the Way We Did*. New York: Ballantine, 1985.

BARNET, RICHARD J. *The Roots of War*. New York: Atheneum, 1972.

————. *Intervention and Revolution*. New York: New American Library, 1972.

BARRETT, DAVID M. *Uncertain Warriors: Lyndon Johnson and His Vietnam Advisers*. Lawrence, Kans.: University of Kansas Press, 1993.

BASKIR, LAWRENCE M., and STRAUSS, WILLIAM A. *Chance and Circumstance: The Draft, the War, and the Vietnam Generation*. New York: Vintage, 1978.

BECKER, ELIZABETH. *America's Vietnam War*. New York: Clarion Books, 1992.

BECKER, ELIZABETH. *When the War Was Over: The Voices of Cambodia's Revolution and Its People*. New York: Simon & Schuster, 1986.

BECKETT, IAN F. W., and PIMLOTT, JOHN, eds. *Armed Forces and Modern Counterinsurgency*. New York: St. Martin's Press, 1985.

BERESFORD, MELANIE. *Vietnam: Politics, Economics, and Society*. London: Pinter Publishers, 1988.

BERGER, CARL (ed.). *The United States Air Force in Southeast Asia, 1961–1973*. Washington, D. C.: U. S. Government Printing Office, 1977.

BERGERUD, ERIC M. *The Dynamics of Defeat: The Vietnam War in Hau Nghia Province*. Boulder, Colo.: Westview Press, 1991.

BERMAN, LARRY. *Lyndon Johnson's War*. New York: W. W. Norton, 1989.

————. *Planning a Tragedy*. New York: W. W. Norton, 1982.

BERMAN, WILLIAM C. *William Fulbright and the Vietnam War: The Dissent of a Political Realist*. Kent, Ohio: Kent State University Press, 1988.

BESCHLOSS, MICHAEL R. *The Crisis Years: Kennedy & Khrushchev, 1960–1963*. New York: Edward Burlingame Books, 1991.

BILLINGS-YUN, MELANIE. *Decision Against War: Eisenhower and Dien Bien Phu, 1954*. New York: Columbia University Press, 1988.

BILLS, SCOTT, L. (ed.). *Kent State/May 4: Echoes Through a Decade*. Kent, Ohio: Kent State University Press, 1982.

BILTON, MICHAEL, and SIM, KEVIN. *Four Hours in My Lai: The Soldiers of Charlie Company*. New York: Viking, 1992.

BLAUFARB, DOUGLAS S. *The Counterinsurgency Era: U. S. Doctrines and Performance*. New York: The Free Press, 1977.

BLUM, ROBERT. *Drawing the Line: The Origins of the American Containment Policy in East Asia*. New York: W. W. Norton, 1982.

BODARD, LUCIEN. *The Quicksand War: Prelude to Vietnam*. Boston: Little, Brown, 1967.

BOETTCHER, THOMAS D. *Vietnam: The Valor and the Sorrow*. Boston: Little Brown, 1985.

BORDEN, WILLIAM S. *The Pacific Alliance: United States Foreign Economic Policy and Japanese Trade Recovery, 1947–1955*. Madison, Wisc.: University of Wisconsin Press, 1984.

BORNET, VAUGHN. *The Presidency of Lyndon Johnson*. Lawrence, Kans.: University of Kansas Press, 1983.

BOUSCAREN, ANTHONY TRAWICK. *The Last of the Mandarins: Diem of Vietnam*. Pittsburgh: Duquesne University Press, 1965.

BRADLEE, BENJAMIN C. *Conversations with Kennedy*. New York: Norton, 1975.

BRAESTRUP, PETER. *Big Story*, 2 vols. Boulder, Colo.: Westview, 1977.

———. (ed.). *Vietnam as History: Ten Years After the Paris Peace Accords*. Washington, D. C.: University Press of America, 1984.

BRANDON, HENRY. *The Retreat of American Power*. Garden City, N. Y.: Doubleday, 1973.

———. *The Anatomy of Error*. Boston: Bambit, 1969.

BRODIE, BERNARD. *War and Politics*. New York: Macmillan, 1973.

BROWNE, MALCOLM W. *The New Face of War*. Indianapolis: Bobbs Merrill, 1965.

BRYAN, C. D. B. *Friendly Fire*. New York: Putnam, 1976.

BUCKINGHAM, WILLIAM A. JR. *Operation Ranch Hand: The Air Force and Herbicides in Southeast Asia, 1961–1971*. Washington, D. C.: U. S. Government Printing Office, 1982.

BURCHETT, WILFRED G. *Vietnam: Inside Story of a Guerrilla War*. New York: International Publishers, 1965.

BURKE, JOHN P., and FRED I. GREENSTEIN, in collaboration with LARRY BERMAN and RICHARD IMMERMAN. *How Presidents Test Reality: Decisions on Vietnam, 1954 and 1965*. New York: Richard Sage Foundation, 1989.

BUTLER, DAVID. *The Fall of Saigon*. New York: Simon and Schuster, 1985.

BUTTINGER, JOSEPH. *A Dragon Defiant: A Short History of Vietnam*. New York: Praeger, 1972.

———. *The Smaller Dragon: A Political History of Vietnam*. New York: Praeger, 1958.

———. *Vietnam: A Dragon Embattled*, 2 vols. New York: Praeger, 1967.

———. *Vietnam: The Unforgettable Tragedy*. New York: Horizon, 1977.

CABLE, JAMES. *The Geneva Conference on Indochina*. New York: St. Martin's Press, 1986.

CABLE, LARRY E. *Conflict of Myths: The Development of Counterinsurgency Doctrine and the Vietnam War*. New York: New York University Press, 1988.

———. *Unholy Grail: The US and the Wars in Vietnam, 1965–1968*. London: Routledge, 1991.

CADY, JOHN F. *The Roots of French Imperialism in Eastern Asia*. Ithaca, N.Y.: Cornell University Press, 1954.

———. *Southeast Asia: Its Historical Development*. New York: McGraw-Hill, 1964.

CAMPAGNA, ANTHONY S. *The Economic Conseqeunces of the Vietnam War*. Westport, Conn.: Greenwood, 1991.

CAPPS, WALTER H. *The Unfinished War: Vietnam and the American Conscience*. Boston: Beacon, 1982.

————, ed. *The Vietnam Reader*. New York: Routledge, 1991.

CASH, JOHN A. *Seven Firefights in Vietnam*. Washington, D. C.: U. S. Government Printing Office, 1970.

CASTLE, TIMOTHY N. *At War in the Shadow of Vietnam: U. S. Military Aid to the Royal Lao Government, 1955–1975*. New York: Columbia University Press, 1993.

CECIL, PAUL FREDERICK. *Herbicidal Warfare: The RANCH HAND Project in Vietnam*. New York: Praeger, 1986.

CHANDA, NAYAN. *Brother Enemy: The War after the War*. San Diego, CA: Harcourt Brace Jovanovich, 1986.

CHANDLER, DAVID P. *The Tragedy of Cambodian History*. New Haven, Conn.: Yale University Press, 1992.

CHANDLER, ROBERT W. *War of Ideas: The U. S. Propaganda Campaign in Vietnam*. Boulder, Colo.: Westview Press, 1981.

CHANOFF, DAVID, and DOAN VAN TOAI. *Portrait of the Enemy*. New York: Random House, 1986.

CHARLTON, MICHAEL, and MONCRIEFF, ANTHONY. *Many Reasons Why: The American Involvement in Vietnam*. New York: Hill and Wang, 1978.

CHEN, KING C. *Vietnam and China, 1938–1954*. Princeton, N. J.: Princeton University Press, 1969.

CHINH, TRUONG. *The Resistance Will Win*. Hanoi: Foreign Language Publishing House, 1960.

CHOMSKI, NOAM. *American Power and the New Mandarins*. New York: Vintage Books, 1969.

CINCINNATUS. *Self-Destruction: The Disintegration and Decay of the United States Army During the Vietnam Era*. New York: W. W. Norton, 1981.

CLARKE, JEFFREY J. *United States Army in Vietnam: Advice and Support: The Final Years, 1965–1973*. Washington, D. C.: U. S. Government Printing Office, 1988.

VON CLAUSEWITZ, KARL. *On War*. Edited by Michael Howard and Peter Paret. Princeton, N. J.: Princeton University Press, 1976.

CLIFFORD, CLARK, and RICHARD HOLBROOKE. *Counsel to the President: A Memoir*. New York: Random House, 1991.

CLODFELTER, MARK. *The Limits of Air Power: The American Bombing of North Vietnam*. New York: The Free Press, 1989.

COHEN, STEVEN, (ed.). *Vietnam: Anthology and Guide to A Television History*. New York: Knopf, 1983.

COHEN, WARREN I. *Dean Rusk*. New York: Cooper Square, 1980.

COLBY, WILLIAM E. *Lost Victory: A First Hand Account of America's Sixteen Year Involvement in Vietnam*. Chicago: Contemporary Books, 1989.

COLBY, WILLIAM E., and FORBATH, PETER. *Honorable Men: My Life in the CIA*. New York: Simon and Schuster, 1978.

COLLINS, JOHN M. *The Vietnam War in Perspective*. Washington, D. C.: Strategic Research Group, 1972.

COOPER, CHESTER L. *The Lost Crusade: America in Vietnam*. N. Y.: Dodd, Mead, 1970.

CORNELL UNIVERSITY STUDY GROUP. *The Air War in Vietnam*. Ithaca, New York: Cornell University Press, 1972.

CORSON, WILLIAM R. *Consequences of Failure*. New York: W. W. Norton, 1974.

CURREY, CECIL B. *Edward Landsdale: The Unquiet American*. Boston: Houghton Mifflin, 1988.

DAVIDSON, PHILLIP B. *Vietnam at War: The History 1946–1975*. Novato, Calif.: Presidio, 1988.

————. *Secrets of the Vietnam War*. Novato, Calif.: Presidio Press, 1991.

DAWSON, ALAN. *55 Days: The Fall of South Vietnam*. Englewood Cliffs, N. J.: Prentice Hall, 1977.

DeBENEDETTI, CHARLES, assisted by CHARLES CHATFIELD. *An American Ordeal: The Antiwar Movement of the Vietnam Era*. Syracuse, N. Y.: Syracuse University Press, 1990.

DE RIENCOURT, AMAURY. *The American Empire*. New York: Dell, 1968.

DEVILLERS, PHILIPPE. *Histoire du Viet-Nam, de 1940 à 1952*. Paris: Editions du Seuil, 1952.

————, and LACOUTURE, JEAN. *The End of A War: Indochina, 1954*. New York: Praeger, 1969.

DIEM, BUI, with CHANOFF, DAVID. *In the Jaws of History*. Boston: Houghton Mifflin, 1987.

DIETZ, TERRY. *Republicans and Vietnam, 1961–1968*. Westport, Conn.: Greenwood, 1986.

DiLEO, DAVID L. *George Ball, Vietnam, and the Rethinking of Containment*. Chapel Hill, N. C.: University of North Carolina Press, 1991.

DOUGHAN, CLARK, FULGHUM, DAVID, and the editors of Boston Publishing Company. *The Fall of the South*. Boston: Boston Publishing Co., 1985, a volume in the series, *The Vietnam Experience*, a 26-volume series on the Vietnam War.

DOYLE, EDWARD, LIPSMAN, SAMUEL, and the editors. *America Takes Over*. Boston: Boston Publishing Co., 1982, a volume in the series *The Vietnam Experience*.

————, LIPSMAN, SAMUEL, and the editors. *Setting the Stage*. Boston: Boston Publishing Co., 1981, a volume in the series, *The Vietnam Experience*.

————, LIPSMAN, MAITLAND, TERRENCE, and the editors. *The North*. Boston: Boston Publishing Co., 1982, a volume in the series, *The Vietnam Experience*.

————, LIPSMAN, WEISS, STEPHEN, and the editors. *Passing the Torch*. Boston: Boston Publishing Co., 1981, a volume in the series, *The Vietnam Experience*.

————, MAITLAND, and the editors. *The Aftermath, 1975–1985*. Boston: Boston Publishing Co., 1985, a volume in the series, *The Vietnam Experience*.

DRACHMAN, EDWARD R. *United States Policy Toward Vietnam, 1940–1945*. Rutherford, N. J.: Fairleigh-Dickinson University Press, 1970.

DRENDEL, LOU. *The Air War in Vietnam*. New York: Arco, 1968.

DUIKER, WILLIAM J. *The Communist Road to Power*. Boulder, Colo.: Westview, 1981.

———. *The Rise of Nationalism in Vietnam, 1900–1941*. Ithaca, N. Y.: Cornell University Press, 1975.

———. *Sacred War: Nationalism and Revolution in a Divided Nation*. New York: McGraw-Hill, 1995.

———. *U. S. Containment Policy and the Conflict in Indochina*. Stanford, CA: Stanford University Press, 1994.

———. *Vietnam: Nation in Revolution*. Boulder, Colo.: Westview, 1983.

———. *Vietnam Since the Fall of Saigon*. Athens, Ohio: Ohio University, Center for International Studies, 1980.

DUNN, PETER M. *The First Vietnam War*. New York: St. Martin's Press, 1985.

EDELMAN, BERNARD, (ed.). *Dear America: Letters Home from Vietnam*. New York: Pocket Books, 1985.

EISENHOWER, DWIGHT DAVID. *The White House Years: Mandate for Change, 1953–1956*. Garden City, N. Y.: Doubleday, 1963.

ELLSBERG, DANIEL. *Papers on the War*. New York: Simon and Schuster, 1972.

EMERSON, GLORIA. *Winners and Losers: Battles, Retreats, Gains, Losses, and Ruins from a Long War*. New York: Harcourt, Brace, 1976.

ENTHOVEN, ALAIN C., and SMITH, K. WAYNE. *How Much Is Enough: Shaping the Defense Program, 1961–1968*. New York: Harper & Row, 1971.

EPSTEIN, EDWARD JAY. *News from Nowhere: Television and the News*. New York: Vintage, 1973.

ERRINGTON, ELIZABETH J., and MCKERCHER, B. J. C., eds. *The Vietnam War As History*. Westport, Conn: Praeger, 1990.

ESPER, GEORGE. *The Eyewitness History of the Vietnam War, 1961–1975*. New York: Ballantine, 1983.

FAIRLIE, HENRY. *The Kennedy Promise: The Politics of Expectation*. Garden City, N.Y.: Doubleday, 1973.

FALL, BERNARD. *The Anatomy of a Crisis: The Laotian Crisis of 1960–61*. Garden City, N. Y.: Doubleday, 1960.

———. *Hell in a Very Small Place: The Siege of Dien Bien Phu*. New York: Lippincott, 1967.

———, (ed.). *Ho Chi Minh on Revolution, Selected Writings, 1920–1966*. New York: Harper Colophon, 1971.

———. *Last Reflections on a War*. New York: Doubleday, 1967.

———. *Street Without Joy*. Harrisburg, Penn.: The Stackpole Co., 1967.

———. *The Two Vietnams: A Political and Military Analysis*. New York: Praeger, 1964).

———. *Vietnam Witness, 1953–1966*. New York: Praeger, 1966.

FARBER, DAVID. *Chicago '68*. Chicago: University of Chicago Press, 1988.

FERBER, MICHAEL, and LYND, STAUGHTON. *The Resistance*. Boston: Beacon, 1971.

FISHEL, WESLEY R., (ed.). *Vietnam: Anatomy of a Conflict*. Itasca, Ill.: F. E. Peacock, 1968.

FITZGERALD, FRANCES. *Fire in the Lake: The Vietnamese and the Americans in Vietnam*. New York: Random House, 1972.

FRANKLAND, NOBLE, and DOWLING, (eds.). *Decisive Battles of the Twentieth Century*. London: Sidgwick & Jackson, 1976.

FRANKLIN, H. BRUCE. *M. I. A. or Mythmaking in America*. New Brunswick, N.J.: Rutgers University Press, 1992.

FREY-WOUTERS, ELLEN, and LAUFER, ROBERT S. *Legacy of a War: The American Soldier in Vietnam*. Armonk, N. Y.: M. E. Sharpe, 1986.

FULBRIGHT, J. WILLIAM. *The Arrogance of Power*. New York: Random House, 1967.

FULGHUM, DAVID, MAITLAND, TERRENCE, and the editors. *South Vietnam on Trial*. Boston: Boston Publishing Co., 1984, a volume in the series, *The Vietnam Experience*.

FURGUSON, ERNEST B. *Westmoreland: The Inevitable General*. Boston: Little, Brown, 1968.

GABRIEL, RICHARD, and SAVAGE, PAUL. *Crisis in Command*. New York: Hill and Wang, 1978.

GALBRAITH, JOHN KENNETH. *Ambassador's Journal: A Personal Account of the Kennedy Years*. Boston: Houghton Mifflin, 1969.

GALLOWAY, JOHN. *The Gulf of Tonkin Resolution*. Rutherford, N. J.: Fairleigh Dickinson University Press, 1970.

GALLUCCI, ROBERT L. *Neither Peace nor Honor: The Politics of American Military Policy in Vietnam*. Baltimore: Johns Hopkins University Press, 1975.

GARDNER, LLOYD C. *Approaching Vietnam: From World War II through Dienbienphu*. New York: W. W. Norton, 1988.

———. *Pay Any Price: Lyndon Johnson and the Wars for Vietnam*. Chicago: Ivan R. Dees, 1995.

GELB, LESLIE, with BETTS, RICHARD. *The Irony of Vietnam: The System Worked*. Washington, D. C.: The Brookings Institution, 1979.

GETTLEMAN, MARVIN E., (ed.). *Viet Nam: History, Documents, and Opinions on a Major World Crisis*. Greenwich, Conn.: Fawcett, 1965.

———, FRANKLIN, JANE, YOUNG, MARILYN, and FRANKLIN, H. BRUCE, (eds.). *Vietnam and America: A Documentary History*. New York: Grove Press, 1985.

GEYELIN, PHILIP. *Lyndon B. Johnson and the World*. New York: Praeger, 1966.

GIAP, VO NGUYEN. *Big Victory, Great Task*. New York: Praeger, 1967.

———. *People's War, People's Army*. Hanoi: Foreign Language Publishing House, 1961.

GIBBONS, WILLIAM CONRAD. *The U. S. Government and the Vietnam War: Executive and Legislative Roles and Relationships.* Part I: 1945–1960. Princeton, N. J.: Princeton University Press, 1986.

———. Part II: 1961–1964.

GIBSON, JAMES WILLIAM. *The Perfect War: The War We Couldn't Lose and How We Did.* New York: Vintage, 1986.

GIGLIO, JAMES N. *The Presidency of John F. Kennedy.* Lawrence, Kans.: University of Kansas Press, 1991.

GITLIN, TODD. *The Sixties: Years of Hope: Days of Rage.* New York: Bantam, 1987.

———. *The Whole World Is Watching: Mass Media in the Making and Unmaking of the New Left.* Berkeley, Calif.: University of California Press, 1980.

GOLDMAN, ERIC. *The Tragedy of Lyndon Johnson.* New York: Dell, 1968.

GOLDSTEIN, JOSEPH, MARSHALL, BURKE, and SCHWARTZ, JACK. *The My Lai Massacre and Its Cover-Up.* New York: Free Press, 1976.

GOLDSTEIN, MARTIN E. *American Policy Toward Laos.* Teaneck, N. J.: Fairleigh-Dickinson University Press, 1986.

GOODMAN, ALLEN E. *The Lost Peace: America's Search for a Negotiated Settlement of the Vietnam War.* Stanford, Calif.: Hoover Institution Press, 1978.

———. *Politics in War.* Cambridge, Mass.: Harvard University Press, 1973.

GRAEBNER, NORMAN, (ed.). *Nationalism and Communism in Asia.* Lexington, Mass.: Heath, 1977.

GRAFF, HENRY. *The Tuesday Cabinet: Deliberation and Decision on Peace and War under Lyndon B. Johnson.* Englewood Cliffs, N. J.: Prentice Hall, 1970.

GRANT, ZALIN. *Facing the Phoenix: The CIA and the Political Defeat of the United States in Vietnam.* New York: Norton, 1991.

GRINTER, LAWRENCE E., and PETER DUNN, eds. *The American War in Vietnam: Lessons, Legacies, and Implications for the Future.* New York: Greenwood Press, 1987.

GUTHMAN, EDWIN O., and SHULMAN, JEFFREY. *Robert Kennedy in His Own Words, the Unpublished Recollections of the Kennedy Years.* New York: Bantam Press, 1988.

HACKWORTH, DAVID H., and SHERMAN, JULIE. *About Face.* New York: Simon and Schuster, 1989.

HALBERSTAM, DAVID. *The Best and the Brightest.* New York: Random House, 1964.

———. *The Making of a Quagmire: America and Vietnam during the Kennedy Era.* Rev. ed. New York: Knopf, 1988.

HALDEMAN, HARRY R. *The Ends of Power.* New York: *New York Times* Book, 1978.

———. *The Haldeman Diaries: Inside the Nixon White House,* with editorial assistance from Steven Ambrose. New York: G. P. Putnam's, 1994.

HALEY, P. EDWARD. *Congress and the Fall of South Vietnam and Cambodia.* London: Associated University Presses, 1982.

HALL, DANIEL G. E. *A History of Southeast Asia.* 2d ed. New York: Macmillan, 1963.

HALLIN, DANIEL C. *The Uncensored War: The Media and Vietnam.* New York: Oxford University Press, 1986.

HAMILTON-MERRITT, JANE. *Tragic Mountains: The Hmong, the Americans, and the Secret Wars for Laos, 1942–1992.* Bloomington, Ind.: University of Indiana Press, 1993.

HAMMEL, ERIC. *The Battle for Hue, Tet 1968.* Chicago: Contemporary Books, 1991.

HAMMER, ELLEN J. *A Death in November: America in Vietnam, 1963.* New York: E. P. Dutton, 1987.

———. *The Struggle for Indochina, 1940–1955.* Palo Alto, Calif.: Stanford University Press, 1966.

———. *Vietnam, Yesterday and Today.* New York: Holt, Rinehart, and Winston, 1966.

HAMMER, RICHARD J. *The Court Martial of Lt. Calley.* New York: Coward-McCann and Geoghegan, 1972.

———. *One Morning in the War: The Tragedy at Son My.* New York: Coward-McCann, 1970.

HAMMOND, WILLIAM. *Public Affairs: The Military and the Media, 1962–1968.* Washington, D. C.: U. S. Government Printing Office, 1989.

———. *Public Affairs: The Military and the Media, 1968–1973.* Washington, D. C.: U. S. Government Printing Office, 1996.

HANH, NHAT. *Vietnam: Lotus in a Sea of Fire.* New York: Hill and Wang, 1962.

HANNAH, NORMAN B. *The Key to Failure: Laos and the Vietnam War.* Washington, D. C.: University Press of America, 1988.

HARRIMAN, AVERELL. *America and Russia in a Changing World: A Half Century of Personal Observation.* Garden City, N.Y.: Doubleday, 1971.

HARRISON, JAMES PINCKNEY. *The Endless War: Fifty Years of Struggle in Vietnam.* New York: Free Press, 1982.

HASKINS, JAMES. *The War and the Protest: Vietnam.* Garden City, N.Y.: Doubleday, 1971.

HATCHER, PATRICK LLOYD. *The Suicide of an Elite: American Internationalists and Vietnam.* Stanford, Calif.: Stanford University Press, 1990.

HAVENS, THOMAS R. H. *Fire Across the Sea: The Vietnam War and Japan, 1965–1975.* Princeton, N. J.: Princeton University Press, 1987.

HEARDEN, PATRICK J. *The Tragedy of Vietnam.* New York: Harper Collins, 1991.

———, ed. *Vietnam: Four American Perspectives.* West Lafayette, Ind.: Purdue University Press, 1990.

HELLER, CHARLES E., and STOFFT, WILLIAM A. *America's First Battles.* Lawrence, Kans.: University of Kansas Press, 1986.

HELLMAN, JOHN. *American Myth and the Legacy of Vietnam.* New York: Columbia University Press, 1986.

HELMER, JOHN. *Bringing the War Home: The American Soldier in Vietnam and After.* New York: Free Press, 1974.

HERRING, GEORGE C. *America's Longest War: The United States and Vietnam, 1950–1975,* 2d ed. New York: Knopf, 1986.

——. *America's Longest War: The United States and Vietnam, 1950–1975*, 3d. ed., New York: McGraw Hill, 1996.

——. *LBJ and Vietnam: A Different Kind of War*. Austin, Tex.: University of Texas Press, 1994.

——, ed. *The Secret Diplomacy of the Vietnam War: The Negotiating Volumes of the Pentagon Papers*. Austin, Tex.: University of Texas Press, 1983.

HERRINGTON, STUART A. *Peace with Honor?: An American Reports on Vietnam, 1973–1975*. Novato, Calif.: Presidio, 1983.

——. *Silence Was a Weapon: The Vietnam War in the Villages*. Novato, Calif.: Presidio Press, 1982.

HERSH, SEYMOUR M. *Cover-up: The Army's Secret Investigation of the Massacre at My-Lai 4*. New York: Random House, 1972.

——. *My Lai 4: A Report on the Massacre and Its Aftermath*. New York: Vintage, 1970.

——. *The Price of Power: Kissinger in the Nixon White House*. New York: Summit Books, 1983.

HERZ, MARTIN F. *The Prestige Press and the Christmas Bombings, 1972*. Washington, D. C.: Ethics and Public Policy Center, 1980.

——. *The Vietnam War in Retrospect*. Lanham, Md.: University Press of America, 1984.

HESS, GARY R. *The United States' Emergence as a Southeast Asian Power, 1940–1956*. New York: Columbia University Press, 1987.

——. *Vietnam and the United States: Origins and Legacy of War*. Boston: Twayne Publishers, 1990.

HILSMAN, ROGER. *To Move a Nation: The Politics of Foreign Policy in the Administration of John F. Kennedy*. Garden City, N.Y.: Doubleday, 1967.

HOBART, MARK, and TAYLOR, ROBERT H., (eds.). *Context, Meaning, and Power in Southeast Asia*. Ithaca, N. Y.: Cornell University Press, 1986.

HODGSON, GEOFFREY. *America in Our Time: From World War II to Nixon, What Happened and Why*. New York: Vintage, 1976.

HOOPES, TOWNSEND. *The Devil and John Foster Dulles*. Boston: Little Brown, 1973.

——. *The Limits of Intervention: An Inside Account of How the Johnson Policy of Escalation in Vietnam was Reversed*. Rev. ed., New York: McKay, 1973.

HORNE, A. D., (ed.). *The Wounded Generation*. Englewood Cliffs, N. J.: Prentice Hall, 1986.

HOSMER, STEPHEN, et al., *The Fall of South Vietnam*. Santa Monica, Calif.: Rand Corporation, 1978.

HUE-TAM, HO TAI. *Radicalism and the Origins of the Vietnamese Revolution*. Cambridge: Harvard University Press, 1992.

HUMPHREY, HUBERT H. *The Education of a Public Man: My Life and Politics*. Garden City, N. Y.: Doubleday, 1976.

HUNT, RICHARD A., and SCHULTZ, RICHARD H., eds. *Lessons from an Unconventional War: Reassessing U. S. Strategies for Future Conflicts*. New York: Pergamon Press, 1982.

IRVING, R. E. M. *The First Indochina War: French and American Policy, 1945–1954*. London: C. Helm, 1975.

ISAACS, ARNOLD. *Without Honor: Defeat in Vietnam and Cambodia*. Baltimore: The Johns Hopkins University Press, 1983.

ISAACS, HAROLD. *No Peace for Asia*. New York: Macmillan, 1947.

ISAACSON, WALTER. *Kissinger: A Biography*. New York: Simon & Schuster, 1992.

ISAACSON, WALTER, and THOMAS, EVAN. *The Wise Men: Six Friends and the World They Made*. New York: Simon & Schuster, 1986.

ISSERMAN, MAURICE. *If I Had a Hammer: The Death of the Old Left and the Birth of the New Left*. New York: Basic Books, 1987.

JAMIESON, NEIL L. *Understanding Vietnam*. Berkeley: University of California Press, 1993.

JANIS, IRVING. *Victims of Groupthink: A Psychological Study of Foreign Policy Decisions and Fiascos*. Boston: Houghton-Mifflin, 1972.

JENSEN-STREVENSON. *Spite House: The Last Secret of the Vietnam War*. New York: Norton, 1997.

JOHNSON, LYNDON. *The Vantage Point: Perspectives of the Presidency, 1963–1969*. New York: Holt, Rinehart, and Winston, 1971.

JOINER, CHARLES A. *The Politics of Massacre: Political Processes in South Vietnam*. Philadelphia: Temple University Press, 1974.

JOSEPH, PAUL. *Cracks in the Empire: State Politics in the Vietnam War*. Boston: South End Press, 1981.

JOYAUX, FRANCOIS. *La Chine et le reglement du premier conflit d'Indochine, Geneve 1954*. Paris: University of Sorbonne, 1954.

KAHIN, GEORGE. *Intervention: How American Became Involved in Vietnam*. New York: Knopf, 1986.

———, and LEWIS, JOHN. *The United States in Vietnam*. Rev. ed., New York: Delta, 1967; 1969.

KALB, BERNARD, and KALB, MARVIN. *Kissinger*. Boston: Little, Brown, 1974.

KALB, MARVIN, and ABEL, ELIE. *Roots of Involvement, The United States in Asia, 1784–1971*. New York: W. W. Norton, 1971.

KAPLAN, LAWRENCE S., ARTAUD, DENISE, and RUBIN, MARK R., (eds.). *Dien Bien Phu and the Crisis of Franco-American Relations, 1954–1955*. Wilmington, Del.: University of Delaware Press, 1990.

KARNOW, STANLEY. *Vietnam: A History*. New York: Viking, 1983.

KATTENBURG, PAUL M. *The Vietnam Trauma in American Foreign Policy, 1945–1975*. New Brunswick, N. J.: Transaction, 1980.

KEARNS, DORIS. *Lyndon Johnson and the American Dream*. New York: Signet, 1976.

KENDRICK, ALEXANDER. *The Wound Within: America in the Vietnam Years, 1954–1974*. Boston: Little, Brown, 1974.

KENNEDY, PAUL. *The Rise and Fall of the Great Powers: Economic Change and Military Conflict from 1500 to 2000.* New York: Random House, 1987.

KHANH, HUYNH KIM. *Vietnamese Communism, 1925–1945.* Ithaca, N. Y.: Cornell University Press, 1976.

KHOI, LE TRANH. *Le Viet-Nam: Historie et Civilisation.* Paris: Editions de Minuit, 1955.

KINNARD, DOUGLAS. *The War Managers.* Hanover, N. H.: University Press of New England, 1977.

———. *The Certain Trumpet: Maxwell Taylor and the American Experience in Vietnam.* Washington, D. C.: U. S. Government Printing Office, 1991.

KISSINGER, HENRY A. *Nuclear Weapons and Foreign Policy.* Garden City, N. Y.: Doubleday, 1957.

———. *The White House Years.* Boston: Little, Brown, 1979.

———. *Years of Upheaval.* Boston: Little, Brown, 1982.

KLARE, MICHAEL. *War Without End: American Planning for the Next Vietnam.* New York: Alfred A. Knopf, 1972.

KNIGHTLEY, PHILLIPP. *The First Casualty: From the Crimea to Vietnam: The War Correspondent as Hero, Propagandist, and Myth Maker.* New York: Harcourt, Brace, Jovanovich, 1975.

KNOLL, ERWIN, and McFADDEN, JUDITH NIES, (eds.). *War Crimes and American Conscience.* New York: Holt, Rinehart, and Winston, 1970.

KOLKO, GABRIEL. *Anatomy of a War: Vietnam, the United States, and Modern Historical Experience.* New York: Pantheon, 1985.

KOMER, ROBERT W. *Bureaucracy at War: U. S. Performance in the Vietnam Conflict.* Boulder, Colo.: Westview Press, 1986.

———. *Bureaucracy Does Its Thing: Institutional Constraints on U. S.-GVN Performance in Vietnam.* Santa Monica, Calif.: Rand Corp., 1973.

KRASLOW, DAVID, and LOORY, STUART H. *The Secret Search for Peace in Vietnam.* New York: Random House, 1968.

KREPINEVICH, ANDREW F. JR. *The Army and Vietnam.* Baltimore: The Johns Hopkins University Press, 1986.

LACOUTURE, JEAN. *Ho Chi Minh: A Political Biography.* New York: Random House, 1968.

———, and DEVILLERS, PHILIPPE. *La Fin d'une Guerre: Indochine, 1954.* Paris: Editions du Seuil, 1960. There is an English translation of this book: *End of a War: Indochina, 1954.* New York: Praeger, 1969.

LAFEBER, WALTER. *America, Russia, and the Cold War, 1945–1975.* 3d ed., New York: John Wiley, 1976.

———. *Inevitable Revolutions: The United States in Central America.* New York: W. W. Norton, 1984.

LAKE, ANTHONY (ed.). *The Vietnam Legacy.* New York: New York University Press, 1976.

LANCASTER, DONALD. *The Emancipation of French Indo-China*. London: Oxford University Press, 1961.

LANDSDALE, EDWARD GEARY. *In the Midst of Wars: An American's Mission to Southeast Asia*. New York: Harper and Row, 1972.

LANNING, MICHAEL LEE, and DAN CRAGG. *Inside the VC and the NVA: The Real Story of North Vietnam's Armed Forces*. New York: Fawcett, 1992.

LARSEN, STANLEY R., and JAMES L. COLLINS JR. *Allied Participation in Vietnam*. Washington, D. C.: Department of the Army, 1975.

LE GRO, WILLIAM E. *Vietnam from Cease-Fire to Capitulation*. Washington, D. C.: U. S. Army Center of Military History, 1981.

LEHRACH, OTTO J., ed. *No Shining Armor: The Marines at War in Vietnam*. Lawrence, Kans.: University of Kansas Press, 1992.

LEVINE, ALAN J. *The United States and the Struggle for Southeast Asia, 1945–1975*. Westport, Conn.: Prager, 1995.

LEVY, DAVID L. *The Debate over Vietnam*. Baltimore: Johns Hopkins University Press, 1991.

LEWIS, CHESTER, HODGSON, GODFREY, and PAGE, BRUCE. *An American Melodrama: The Presidential Campaign of 1968*. New York: Viking, 1969.

LEWY, GUENTHER. *America in Vietnam*. New York: Oxford University Press, 1978.

LIFTON, ROBERT L. *Home from the War: Vietnam Veterans: Neither Victims nor Executioners*. New York: Simon and Schuster, 1973.

LIPSMAN, SAMUEL, DOYLE, EDWARD, and the editors. *Fighting for Time*. Boston: Boston Publishing Co., 1983, a volume in the series, *The Vietnam Experience*.

———, WEISS, STEPHEN, and the editors. *The False Peace*. Boston: Boston Publishing Co., 1985, a volume in the series, *The Vietnam Experience*.

LITTAUER, RAPHAEL, and UPHOFF, NORMAN, (eds.). *The Air War in Indochina*. Rev. ed., Boston: Beacon, 1972.

LOCKHART, GREG. *Nation in Arms: The Origins of the People's Army of Vietnam*. Boston: Allen & Unwin, 1989.

LODGE, HENRY CABOT JR. *As It Was*. New York: W. W. Norton, 1976.

———. *The Storm Has Many Eyes: A Personal Narrative*. New York: W. W. Norton, 1973.

LOMPERIS, TIMOTHY J. *Reading the Wind*. Durham, N. C.: Duke University Press, 1987.

———. *The War Everyone Lost—and Won: America's Intervention in Viet Nam's Twin Struggles*. Baton Rouge, La.: Louisiana State University Press, 1984.

MACDONALD, J. FRED. *Television and the Red Menace: The Video Road to Vietnam*. New York: Praeger, 1985.

MACLEAR, MICHAEL. *The Ten Thousand Day War: Vietnam, 1945–1975*. New York: Avon, 1981.

MCALEAVY, HENRY. *Black Flags in Vietnam: The Story of Chinese Intervention*. London: Allen and Unwin, 1968.

MCALISTER, JOHN T. JR. *Vietnam: The Origins of Revolution.* New York: Knopf, 1969.

———, and MUS, PAUL. *The Vietnamese and Their Revolution.* New York: Harper and Row, 1970.

MCCARTHY, EUGENE J. *The Year of the People.* Garden City, N. Y.: Doubleday, 1969.

MCCORMICK, THOMAS. *America's Half Century: United States Foreign Policy in the Cold War.* Baltimore: Johns Hopkins University Press, 1989.

MCCOY, ALFRED W., with READ, CATHLEEN B., and ADAMS, LEONARD P. II. *The Politics of Heroin in Southeast Asia.* New York: Harper and Row, 1972.

MCDONALD, PETER. *Giap: Victor in Vietnam.* New York: 1993.

MCGLOTHLEN, RONALD. *Controlling the Waves: Dean Acheson and U. S. Foreign Policy in Asia.* New York: Norton, 1993.

MCGOVERN, GEORGE. *Grassroots: The Autobiography of George McGovern.* New York: Random House, 1977.

MCNAMARA, ROBERT STRANGE, with BRIAN VAN DE MARK. *In Retrospect: The Tragedy and Lessons of Vietnam.* New York: Time Books, 1995.

MCPHERSON, HARRY. *A Political Education.* Boston: Little, Brown, 1971.

MCPHERSON, MYRA, ed. *Longtime Passing: Vietnam and the Haunted Generation.* New York: Doubleday, 1984.

MAITLAND, WEISS, and the editors. *Raising the Stakes.* Boston: Boston Publishing Co., 1982, a volume in the series, *The Vietnam Experience.*

MANGOLD, TOM, and PENYCATE, JOHN. *The Tunnels of Cu Chi.* New York: Berkley Books, 1985.

MAROLDA, EDWARD J., and FITZGERALD, OSCAR P. *The United States Navy and the Vietnam Conflict*, vol. 2: *From Military Assistance to Combat, 1959–1965.* Washington, D. C.: U. S. Government Printing Office, Naval Historical Center, 1986.

MARR, DAVID G. *Vietnamese Anti-Colonialism, 1885–1925.* Berkeley, Calif.: University of California Press, 1971.

———. *Vietnamese Tradition on Trial.* Berkeley: University of California Press, 1982.

MARSHALL, KATHRYN. *In the Combat Zone.* New York: Penguin, 1987.

MARSHALL, S. L. A. *Vietnam: Three Battles.* New York: Da Capo Press, 1971.

MATTHEWS, LLOYD J. and BROWN, DALE E., (eds.). *Assessing the Vietnam War.* Washington, D. C.: Pergamon-Brassup, 1987.

MAURER, HARRY. *Strange Ground: Americans in Vietnam, 1945–1975.* New York: Holt, 1988.

MEAD, WALTER RUSSELL. *Mortal Splendor: The American Empire in Transition.* Boston: Houghton Mifflin, 1987.

MERSKY, PETER B., and POLMAR, NORMAN. *The Naval Air War in Vietnam.* New York: Kensington, 1981.

MEYERSON, HARVEY. *Vinh Long.* Boston: Houghton Mifflin, 1970.

MICHENER, JAMES. *Kent State: What Happened and Why*. New York: Random House, 1971.

MILLET, ALLAN R. (ed.). *A Short History of the Vietnam War*. Bloomington, Ind.: Indiana University Press, 1978.

MILLETT, ALLAN R., and MASLOWSKI, PETER. *For the Common Defense: A Military History of the United States of America*. New York: The Free Press, 1984.

MINH, HO CHI. *Prison Diary*. Hanoi: Foreign Language Publishing House, 1966.

MIROFF, BRUCE. *Pragmatic Illusions: The Presidential Politics of John F. Kennedy*. New York: David McKay, 1976.

MOISE, EDWIN E. *Land Reform in China and North Vietnam: Consolidating the Revolution at the Village Level*. Chapel Hill, N. C.: University of North Carolina Press, 1983.

MOORE, HAROLD G., and GALLOWAY, JOSEPH L. *We Were Soldiers Once . . . And Young*. New York: Random House, 1992.

MORRIS, ROGER. *An Uncertain Greatness: Henry Kissinger and American Foreign Policy*. New York: Harper and Row, 1977.

MORROCCO, JOHN, and the editors. *Thunder from Above*. Boston: Boston Publishing Co., 1984, a volume in the series, *The Vietnam Experience*.

———. *Rain of Fire: Air War, 1969–1973*. Boston: Boston Publishing Co., 1985, a volume in the series, *The Vietnam Experience*.

MOSS, GEORGE DONELSON. *America in the Twentieth Century*, 3d edition. Englewood Cliffs, N. J.: Prentice Hall, 1997.

———. *Moving On: The American People Since 1945*. Englewood Cliffs, N. J.: Prentice Hall, 1994.

———. *A Vietnam Reader: Sources and Essays*. Englewood Cliffs, N. J.: Prentice Hall, 1991.

MROZEK, DONALD J. *Air Power and the Ground War in Vietnam: Ideas and Actions*. Washington, D. C.: U. S. Government Printing Office, 1989.

MUELLER, JOHN E. *War, Presidents, and Public Opinion*. New York: John Wiley, 1973.

NEWMAN, JOHN M. *JFK and Vietnam: Deception, Intrigue, and the Struggle for Power*. New York: Warner Books, 1992.

NGO, VINH LONG. *Before the Revolution: The Vietnamese Peasants under the French*. New York: Columbia University Press, 1973, 1991.

NGUYEN, CAO KY. *Twenty Years and Twenty Days*. New York: Stein and Day, 1976.

NGUYEN, GREGORY TIEN HUNG. *Economic Development of Socialist Vietnam, 1955–1980*. New York: Praeger, 1977.

———, and SCHECHTER, JERROLD L. *The Palace File*. New York: Harper and Row, 1986.

NIGHSWONGER, WILLIAM A. *Rural Pacification in Vietnam*. New York: Praeger, 1966.

NIXON, RICHARD M. *RN: The Memoirs of Richard Nixon*. New York: Grosset & Dunlap, 1978.

———. *No More Vietnams*. New York: Avon, 1985.

———. *The Real War*. New York: Warner, 1980.

O'BALLANCE, EDGAR. *The Indo-China War, 1945–1954*. London: Faber and Faber, 1964.

————. *The Wars in Vietnam, 1954–1980*. New York: Hippocrene, 1981.

OBERDORFER, DON. *Tet! The Turning Point in the Vietnam War*. Garden City, N. Y.: Doubleday, 1971.

O'DONNELL, KENNETH P., and POWERS, DAVID F., with JOE MCCARTHY. *Johnny, We Hardly Knew Ye: Memories of John Fitzgerald Kennedy*. Boston: Little, Brown, 1972.

OLSON, JAMES S., ed. *Dictionary of the Vietnam War*. New York: Greenwood, 1988.

————, and ROBERTS, RANDY. *Where the Domino Fell: America and Vietnam, 1945–1990*. New York: St. Martin's Press, 1991.

O'NEILL, ROBERT J. *General Giap: Politician and Strategist*. Australia: Cassell, 1969.

O'NEILL, WILLIAM. *Coming Apart: An Informal History of America in the 1960s*. New York: Quadrangle, 1971.

OSGOOD, ROBERT E. *America and the World: From the Truman Doctrine to Vietnam*. Baltimore: Johns Hopkins University Press, 1970.

————. *Limited War Revisited*. Boulder, Colo.: Westview, 1979.

OUDES, BRUCE, ed. *From: The President: Richard Nixon's Secret Files*. New York: Harper and Row, 1989.

PALMER, BRUCE, JR. *The 25-Year War: America's Military Role in Vietnam*. New York: Simon and Schuster, 1985.

PALMER, DAVE RICHARD. *Summons of the Trumpet: A History of the Vietnam War from a Military Man's Viewpoint*. New York: Ballantine, 1978.

PALMER, GREGORY. *The McNamara Strategy and the Vietnam War: Program Budgeting in the Pentagon, 1960–1968*. Westport, Conn.: Greenwood, 1978.

PALMER, LAURA. *Shrapnel in the Heart: Letters and Remembrances from the Vietnam Veterans Memorial*. New York: Vintage, 1987.

PARET, PETER, and SHY, JOHN W. *Guerrillas in the 1960s*. Rev. ed. New York: Praeger, 1962.

PARMET, HERBERT. *JFK: The Presidency of John F. Kennedy*. New York: Penguin, 1983.

PATERSON, THOMAS G., et al., *American Foreign Policy*. Lexington, Mass.: D. C. Heath, 1977.

————. *Kennedy's Quest for Victory: American Foreign Policy, 1961–1963*. New York: Oxford University Press, 1989.

PATTI, ARCHIMEDES L. *Why Vietnam? Prelude to America's Albatross*. Berkeley, Calif.: University of California Press, 1980.

PEARSON, WILLIARD. *The War in the Northern Provinces, 1966–1968*. Washington, D. C.: Department of the Army, 1975.

PEERS, WILLIAM R. *My Lai Inquiry*. New York: W. W. Norton, 1979.

PETTIT, CLYDE EDWIN. *The Experts*. Secaucus, N. J.: Lyle Stuart, 1975.

PIKE, DOUGLAS. *History of Vietnamese Communism, 1925–1976*. Stanford, Calif.: Hoover Institution Press, 1978.

————. *PAVN: People's Army of Vietnam*. Novato, Calif.: Presidio, 1986.

————. *Vietcong: The Organization and Technique of the National Liberation Front of South Vietnam.* Rev. ed. Cambridge, Mass.: MIT Press, 1972.

————. *The Vietcong Strategy of Terror.* Cambridge, Mass.: MIT Press, 1970.

————. *Vietnam and the Soviet Union: Anatomy of an Alliance.* Boulder, Colo.: Westview, 1985.

————. *War, Peace, and the Vietcong.* Cambridge, Mass.: The MIT Press, 1969.

PILGER, JOHN. *The Last Day: America's Final Hours in Vietnam.* New York: Vintage, 1975.

PISOR, ROBERT. *The End of the Line: The Siege of Khe Sanh.* New York: W. W. Norton, 1982.

PODHORETZ, NORMAN. *Why We Were in Vietnam.* New York: Simon and Schuster, 1982.

POLNER, MURRAY. *No Victory Parades: The Return of the Vietnam Veterans.* New York: Holt, Rinehart, and Winston, 1971.

POPKIN, SAMUEL. *The Rational Peasant: The Political Economy of Rural Society in Vietnam.* Berkeley, Calif.: University of California Press, 1979.

PORTER, GARETH. *The Myth of the Bloodbath: North Vietnam's Land Reform Program Reconsidered.* Ithaca, N. Y.: Cornell University Press, 1972.

————. *A Peace Denied: The United States, Vietnam, and the Paris Agreements.* Bloomington, Ind.: Indiania University Press, 1975.

————, and EMERSON, GLORIA, eds., *Vietnam: A History in Documents.* New York: New American Library, 1981.

POWERS, THOMAS. *Vietnam: The War at Home.* Boston: G. K. Hall, 1984.

PRADOS, JOHN. *The Sky Would Fall: Operation Vulture: The U. S. Bombing Mission in Indochina.* New York: Dial, 1982.

————, and STUBBE, ROY. *Valley of Decision: The Siege of Khe Sanh.* New York: Houghton Mifflin, 1991.

PRATT, JOHN CLARK, ed. *Vietnam Voices: Perspectives on the War Years, 1941–1982.* New York: Viking Press, 1984.

PRICE, RAYMOND. *With Nixon.* New York: Viking Press, 1977.

PROACHNAU, WILLIAM. *Once Upon A Distant War.* New York: Time Books, 1995.

RACE, JEFFREY. *War Comes to Long An: Revolutionary Conflict in a Vietnamese Province.* Berkeley, Calif.: University of California Press, 1972.

RANDLE, ROBERT. *Geneva 1954: The Settlement of the Indochinese War.* Princeton, N. J.: Princeton University Press, 1969.

RAPPAPORT, ARMIN, (ed.). *Sources in American Diplomatic History.* New York: Macmillan, 1966.

RASKIN, MARCUS G., and FALL, BERNARD B., (eds.). *The Viet-nam Reader: Articles and Documents on American Foreign Policy and the Vietnam Crisis.* New York: Vintage, 1965.

REEDY, GEORGE E. *Lyndon B. Johnson, A Memoir.* New York: Andrews and McMeel, 1982.

REEVES, RICHARD. *President Kennedy: A Profile of Power*. New York: Simon & Schuster, 1993.

REISCHAUER, EDWIN O. *Beyond Vietnam: The United States and Asia*. New York: Vintage, 1967.

RESTON, JAMES JR. *Sherman's March and Vietnam*. New York: Macmillan, 1984.

ROBBINS, CHRISTOPHER. *Air America*. New York: Avon, 1979.

ROBERTS, STEPHEN H. *History of French Colonial Policy: 1870–1925*. Two vols. London: P. S. King and Son, 1929.

ROGERS, BERNARD W. *Cedar Falls-Junction City: A Turning Point*. Washington, D. C.: U. S. Government Printing Office, 1974.

ROSTOW, WALT W. *The Diffusion of Power: An Essay in Recent History*. New York: Macmillan, 1972.

ROTTER, ANDREW J. *The Path to Vietnam: Origins of the American Commitment to Southeast Asia*. Ithaca, N. Y.: Cornell University Press, 1987.

ROY, JULES. *The Battle of Dienbienphu*. New York: Harper and Row, 1965.

RUSK, DEAN, as told to RUSK, RICHARD. *As I Saw It*. New York: Norton, 1990.

RUST, WILLIAM J. *Kennedy in Vietnam: American Vietnam Policy 1960–1963*. New York: Da Capo, 1985.

RUTLEDGE, PAUL JAMES. *The Vietnamese Experience in America*. Bloomington, Ind.: University of Indiana Press, 1992.

SAFIRE, WILLIAM. *Before the Fall: An Insider's View of the Pre-Watergate White House*. Garden City, N. Y.: Doubleday, 1975.

SAINTENY, JEAN. *Histoire d'une paix manque*. Paris: Amoit Dumont, 1953.

SALE, KIRKPATRICK. *SDS*. New York: Vintage, 1973.

SALISBURY, HARRISON. *Behind the Lines: Hanoi, Dec. 23, 1966–January 7, 1967*. New York: Harper and Row, 1967.

———, (ed.). *Vietnam Reconsidered: Lessons from a War*. New York: Harper and Row, 1983.

SANSOME, ROBERT L. *The Economics of Insurgency in the Mekong Delta of Vietnam*. Cambridge, Mass.: MIT Press, 1970.

SANTOLI, AL. *To Bear Any Burden*. New York: Ballantine, 1985.

———. *Everything We Had*. New York: Random House, 1981.

SCHALLER, MICHAEL. *The American Occupation of Japan: The Origins of the Cold War in Asia*. New York: Oxford University Press, 1985.

SCHANDLER, HERBERT Y. *The Unmaking of a President: Lyndon Johnson and Vietnam*. Princeton, N. J.: Princeton University Press, 1977.

SCHEER, ROBERT. *How the United States Got Involved in Vietnam*. Santa Barbara, Calif.: Center for the Study of Democratic Institutions, 1965.

SCHELL, JONATHAN. *The Real War: The Classic Reporting on the Vietnam War*. New York: Pantheon, 1988.

——. *The Time of Illusion*. New York: Knopf, 1976.

——. *The Village of Ben Suc*. New York: Knopf, 1967.

SCHLESINGER, ARTHUR M. JR. *The Bitter Heritage: Vietnam and American Democracy 1941–1966*. New York: Fawcett, 1966.

——. *The Imperial Presidency*. Boston: Houghton Mifflin, 1973.

——. *Robert Kennedy and His Times*. Boston: Houghton Mifflin, 1978.

——. *A Thousand Days: John F. Kennedy in the White House*. Greenwich, Conn.: Fawcett, 1965.

SCHLIGHT, JOHN, ed. *Second Indochina War Symposium*. Washington, D. C.: Department of the Army, 1986.

——. *The United States Air Force in Southeast Asia: The War in South Vietnam: The Years of the Offensive, 1965–1968*. Washington, D. C.: U. S. Government Printing Office, 1988.

SCHOENBAUM, THOMAS J. *Waging Peace and War: Dean Rusk in the Truman, Kennedy, and Johnson Years*. New York: Simon and Schuster, 1988.

SCIGLIANO, ROBERT. *South Vietnam: Nation Under Stress*. Boston: Houghton Mifflin, 1964.

SHAFER, D. MICHAEL. *Deadly Paradigms: The Failure of U. S. Counterinsurgency Policy*. Princeton, N. J.: Princeton University Press, 1988.

——, ed. *The Legacy; The Vietnam War in the American Imagination*. Boston: Beacon Press, 1990.

SHAPLEN, ROBERT. *Bitter Victory*. New York: Harper & Row, 1986.

——. *The Lost Revolution: The U. S. in Vietnam, 1946–1966*. Rev. ed. New York: Harper & Row, 1966.

——, ed. *The Road from War: Vietnam, 1965–1971*. New York: Harper & Row, 1970.

——. *Time Out of Hand: Revolution and Reaction in Southeast Asia*. New York: Harper & Row, 1969.

SHAPLEY, DEBORAH. *Promise and Power: The Life and Times of Robert S. McNamara*. Boston: 1993.

SHARP, ULYSSES S. GRANT. *Strategy for Defeat*. San Rafael, Calif.: Presidio, 1978.

SHAWCROSS, WILLIAM. *Sideshow: Kissinger, Nixon and the Destruction of Cambodia*. New York: Simon & Schuster, 1979.

SHEEHAN, NEIL. *A Bright Shining Lie: John Paul Vann and America in Vietnam*. New York: Random House, 1989.

——. *After the War Was Over: Hanoi and Saigon*. New York: Random House, 1991.

SHORT, ANTHONY. *The Origins of the Vietnam War*. London: Longman, 1989.

SHULIMSON, JACK. *U. S. Marines in Vietnam: 1966*. Washington, D. C.: U. S. Marine Corps, 1982.

SMALL, MELVIN. *Covering Dissent: The Media and the Anti-Vietnam War Movement*. New Brunswick, N. J.: Rutgers University Press, 1994.

————, and WILLIAM D. HOOVER, eds. *Give Peace a Chance: Exploring the Vietnam Antiwar Movement. Essays from the Charles DeBenedetti Memorial Conference.* Syracuse, N. Y.: Syracuse University Press, 1992.

————. *Johnson, Nixon, and the Doves.* New Brunswick, N. J.: Rutgers University Press, 1988.

SMITH, RALPH BERNARD. *An International History of the Vietnam War.* vol. 1. *Revolution versus Containment, 1955–1961.* New York: St. Martin's Press, 1983.

————. vol. 2, *The Kennedy Strategy.* New York: St. Martin's Press, 1985.

————. vol. 3, *The Making of A Limited War, 1965–1966.* New York: St. Martin's Press, 1991.

SNEPP, FRANK. *Decent Interval: An Insider's Account of the Saigon's Indecent End.* New York: Random House, 1977.

SORENSEN, THEODORE C. *Kennedy.* New York: Harper and Row, 1965.

SORLEY, LEWIS. *Thunderbolt: General Creighton Abrams and the Army of His Times.* New York: Simon & Schuster, 1992.

SPECTOR, RONALD H. *After Tet: The Bloodiest Year in Vietnam.* New York: Macmillan, 1993.

————. *Researching the Vietnam Experience.* Washington, D. C.: Analysis Branch of the U. S. Army Center of Military History, 1984.

————. *United States Army in Vietnam: Advice and Support: The Early Years, 1941–1960.* Washington, D. C.: Center for Military History, 1984.

STANTON, SHELBY L. *The Rise and Fall of An American Army: U. S. Ground Forces in Vietnam, 1965–1973.* New York: Dell, 1985.

————. *Vietnam Order of Battle.* New York: Galahad, 1987.

STEEL, RONALD. *Pax Americana: The Cold War Empire and the Politics of Counter-Revolution.* Rev. ed. New York: Viking, 1970.

STEVENS, RICHARD L. *The Trail: A History of the Ho Chi Minh Trail and the Role of Nature in the War in Viet Nam.* New York: Garland Pub., 1993.

STEVENS, ROBERT W. *Vain Hopes, Grim Realities: The Economic Consequences of the Vietnam War.* New York: New Viewpoints, 1976.

STEVENSON, CHARLES A. *The End of Nowhere: American Policy Toward Laos since 1954.* Boston: Beacon, 1972.

STOCKDALE, JAMES B., and SYBIL. *In Love and War.* New York: Harper and Row, 1984.

SUMMERS, HARRY G. JR. *Historical Atlas of the Vietnam War.* Boston: Houghton Mifflin, 1995.

————. *On Strategy: A Critical Analysis of the Vietnam War.* New York: Dell, 1982.

————. *Vietnam War Almanac.* New York: Facts on File, 1985.

SZULC, TAD. *The Illusion of Peace: Foreign Policy in the Nixon-Kissinger Years.* New York: Viking, 1979.

TANG, TRUONG NHU. *A Vietcong Memoir.* San Diego: Harcourt Brace Jovanovich, 1983.

TAYLOR, MAXWELL D. *Swords and Ploughshares.* New York: W. W. Norton, 1972.

————. *The Uncertain Trumpet*. New York: Harper and Row, 1959.

TAYLOR, TELFORD. *Nuremberg and Vietnam: An American Tragedy*. New York: Quadrangle, 1967.

TERRY, WALLACE, ed. *Bloods: An Oral History of the War By Black Veterans*. New York: Random House, 1984.

THAYER, CARLYLE. *War By Other Means: National Liberation and Revolution in Vietnam*. Boston: Allen & Unwin, 1989.

THAYER, THOMAS C. *War without Fronts: The American Experience in Vietnam*. Boulder, Colo.: Westview, 1985.

THEOHARIS, ATHAN. *Spying in America: Political Surveillance from Hoover to the Huston Plan*. Philadelphia: Temple University Press, 1978.

THIES, WALLACE J. *When Governments Collide: Coercion and Diplomacy in the Vietnam Conflict, 1964–1968*. Berkeley, Calif.: University of California Press, 1980.

THO, TRAN DINH. *The Cambodian Incursion*. Washington, D. C.: U. S. Army Center of Military History, 1983.

————. *Pacification*. Washington, D. C.: U. S. Army Center of Military History, 1980.

THOMPSON, JAMES CLAY. *Rolling Thunder: Understanding Policy and Program Failure*. Chapel Hill, N. C.: University of North Carolina Press, 1980.

THOMPSON, KENNETH W., ed. *The Kennedy Presidency: Seventeen Intimate Perspectives of John F. Kennedy*. Lanham, Md.: University Press of America, 1985.

THOMPSON, ROBERT G. K. *Defeating Communist Insurgency: The Lessons of Malaya and Vietnam*. New York: Praeger, 1966.

————. *No Exit from Vietnam*. New York: David McKay, 1969.

————. *Peace Is Not at Hand*. New York: David McKay, 1974.

THOMPSON, VIRGINIA M. *French Indochina*. London: Allen and Unwin, 1937.

THOMPSON, W. SCOTT, and FRIZZELL, DONALDSON D., (eds.). *The Lessons of Vietnam*. New York: Crane, Ruzzak, 1977.

THOMSON, JAMES C. JR., STANLEY, PETER W., and PERRY, JOHN CURTIS. *Sentimental Imperialists: The American Experience in East Asia*. New York: Harper & Row, 1981.

TILFORD, EARL H. JR. *Setup—What the Air Force Did in Vietnam and Why*. Maxwell Air Force Base, Alabama, 1991.

TOLLEFSON, JAMES W., ed. *The Strength Not to Fight*. Boston: Beacon, 1993.

TONNESSON, STEIN. *The Vietnamese Revolution of 1945: Roosevelt, Ho Chi Minh, and de Gaulle in a World At War*. London: Sage Publications, 1991.

TRA, TRAN VAN. *Vietnam: History of the Bulwark B-2 Theater*. Vol. 5: *Concluding the 30-Years' War*. Ho Chi Minh City: Van Nghe Publishing Plant, 1982.

TRAGER, FRANK N., (ed.). *Marxism in Southeast Asia*. Palo Alto, Calif.: Stanford University Press, 1959.

TRAN, VAN DON. *Our Endless War: Inside South Vietnam*. San Rafael, Calif.: Presidio Press, 1978.

TRAN, VAN TRA. *Ending the Thirty Year War*. Washington, D. C.: U. S. Government Printing Office, 1983.

TREGASKIS, RICHARD B. *Vietnam Diary*. New York: Holt, Rinehart, and Winston, 1963.

TREWHITT, HENRY L. *McNamara: His Ordeal in the Pentagon*. New York: Harper and Row, 1971.

TRUONG, NGO QUANG. *The Easter Offensive of 1972*. Washington, D. C.: U. S. Army Center of Military History, 1980.

TRUONG, NHU TANG, with CHANOFF, DAVID, and DOAN, VAN TOAI. *A Vietcong Memoir*. San Diego, Calif.: Harcourt, Brace, 1985.

TUCHMAN, BARBARA. *The March of Folly*. New York: Ballantine, 1984.

TURLEY, WILLIAM S. *The Second Indochina War: A Short Political and Military History, 1954–1975*. New York: New American Library, 1986.

TURNER, KATHLEEN. *Lyndon Johnson's Dual War: Vietnam and the Press*. Chicago: University of Chicago Press, 1985.

UNGER, IRWIN. *The Movement: A History of the American New Left 1959–1972*. New York: Dodd, Mead, 1974.

UNGER, IRWIN, and DEBI UNGER. *Turning Point: 1968*. New York: Charles Scribner's Sons, 1988.

VADNEY, T. E. *The World Since 1945*. London: Penguin Books, 1987.

VALENTINE, DOUGLAS. *The Phoenix Program*. New York: Morrow, 1990.

VANDEMARK, BRIAN. *Into the Quagmire: Lyndon Johnson and the Escalation of the Vietnam War*. New York: Oxford University Press, 1991.

VAN DYKE, JOHN M. *North Vietnam's Strategy for Survival*. Palo Alto, Calif.: Stanford University Press, 1972.

VAN, TIEN DUNG. *Our Great Spring Victory: An Account of the Liberation of South Vietnam*. New York: Monthly Review Press, 1977.

VIEN, CAO VAN. *The Final Collapse*. Washington, D. C.: U. S. Army Center of Military History, 1982.

——, and KHUYEN, DONG VAN. *Reflections on the Vietnam War*. Washington, D. C.: U. S. Army Center of Military History, 1980.

VIETNAM VETERANS AGAINST THE WAR. *The Winter Soldier Investigations*. Boston: Beacon, 1972.

VO, NGUYEN GIAP. *People's War, People's Army*. New York: Praeger, 1962.

WALT, LEWIS W. *Strange War, Strange Strategy*. New York: Funk and Wagnalls, 1969.

WALTON, RICHARD J. *Cold War and Counter-Revolution: The Foreign Policy of John F. Kennedy*. Baltimore: Penguin, 1972.

WARNER, DENIS. *The Last Confucian*. New York: Macmillan, 1963.

WEIGLEY, RUSSELL. *The American Way of War: A History of United States Military Strategy and Policy*. New York: Macmillan, 1973.

WELLS, TOM. *The War Within: America's Battle over Vietnam*. Berkeley, Calif.: University of California Press, 1994.

WERNER, JAYNE S., and LUU DOAN HUYNH, (eds.). *The Vietnam War: Vietnamese and American Perspectives*. New York: M. E. Sharpe, 1993.

WESTMORELAND, WILLIAM C. *A Soldier Reports*. New York: Dell, 1976.

WHEELER, JOHN. *Touched with Fire: The Future of the Vietnam Generation*. New York: Avon, 1984.

WHITE, RALPH K. *Nobody Wanted War: Misperceptions in Vietnam and Other Wars*. Garden City, N. Y.: Doubleday, 1968.

WHITE, THEODORE H. *Breach of Faith: The Fall of Richard Nixon:*. New York: Atheneum, 1975.

———. *The Making of the President 1960*. New York: Atheneum, 1961.

———. *The Making of the President 1964*. New York: New American Library, 1965.

———. *The Making of the President 1968*. New York: Atheneum, 1969.

———. *In Search of History*. New York: Harper and Row, 1978.

WICKER, TOM. *JFK and LBJ: The Influence of Personality on Politics*. New York: William Morrow, 1968.

WILLENSON, KIM. *The Bad War: An Oral History of the Vietnam Conflict*. New York: New American Library, 1987.

WILLIAMS, WILLIAM APPLEMAN, et al., (eds.). *America in Vietnam: A Documentary History*. Garden City, N. Y.: Doubleday, 1985.

WILLS, GARRY. *The Kennedy Imprisonment: A Meditation on Power*. Boston: Little, Brown, 1982.

———. *Nixon Agonistes: The Crisis of the Self-Made Man*. New York: New American Library, 1970.

WILSON, JAMES C. *Vietnam in Prose and Film*. Jefferson, N. C.: McFarland, 1982.

WINDCHY, EUGENE. *Tonkin Gulf*. Garden City, N. Y.: Doubleday, 1971.

WINTER SOLDIER ARCHIVE. *Soldiering in Vietnam: The Short-Timer's Journal*. Berkeley, Calif.: Winter Soldier Archive, 1980.

WIRTZ, JAMES J. *The Tet Offensive: Intelligence Failure in War*. Ithica, N. Y.: Cornell University Press, 1991.

WITCOVER, JULES. *85 Days: The Last Campaign of Robert Kennedy*. New York: Atheneum, 1969.

WOODSIDE, ALEXANDER. *Community and Revolution in Modern Vietnam*. Cambridge, Mass.: Houghton Mifflin, 1976.

———. *Vietnam and the Chinese Model: A Comparative Study of Vietnamese and Chinese Government in the First Half of the Nineteenth Century*. Cambridge, Mass.: Harvard University Press, 1971.

The World Almanac of the Vietnam War, JOHN S. BOWMAN, General Editor, with introduction by Fox Butterfield. New York: Bison, 1985.

WYATT, CLARENCE R. *Paper Soldiers: The American Press and the Vietnam War*. New York: Norton, 1993.

YARMOLINSKI, ADAM. *The Military Establishment: Its Impact on American Society*. New York: Harper and Row, 1971.

YOUNG, MARILYN B. *The Vietnam Wars, 1945–1990*. New York: Harper Collins, 1991.

YUEN, FOONG KHONG. *Analogies At War: Korea, Munich, Dien Bien Phu, and the Vietnam Decisions of 1965*. Princeton, N. J.: Princeton University Press, 1992.

ZAFFIRI, SAMUEL. *Hamburger Hill, May 11–20, 1969*. Novato, CA: Presidio Press, 1988.

———. *Westmoreland: A Biography of General William C. Westmoreland*. New York: Morrow, 1994.

ZAROULIS, NANCY, and SULLIVAN, GERALD. *Who Spoke Up? American Protest Against the War in Vietnam*. Garden City, N. Y.: Doubleday, 1984.

ZASLOFF, JOSEPH J. *Origins of the Insurgency in South Vietnam, 1954–1960: The Role of the Southern Vietminh Cadres*. Santa Monica, Calif.: Rand Corporation, 1968.

———. *Postwar Indochina: Old Enemies and New Allies*. Washington, D. C.: U. S. Government Printing Office, 1988.

———, and BROWN, MACALISTER, eds. *Communism in Indochina: New Perspectives*. Lexington, Mass.: D. C. Heath, 1975.

ZUMWALT, ELMO R. JR. *On Watch: A Memoir*. New York: Times Book Co., 1976.

ARTICLES

ADAMS, SAMUEL, "Vietnam Cover-up: Playing with Numbers," *Harper's Magazine* (May 1975): 41.

BADILLO, GILBERT, and CURRY, G. DAVID, "The Social Incidence of Vietnam Casualties: Social Class or Race?" *Armed Forces and Society*, vol. 2 (spring 1976): 397–406.

BAILEY, GEORGE A., "Television War: Trends in Network Coverage of Vietnam 1965–1970," *Journal of Broadcasting*, vol. 20 (Spring 1976), 147–57.

BAILEY, GEORGE A., and LICHTY, LAWRENCE W., "Rough Justice on a Saigon Street: A Gatekeeper Study of NBC's Tet Execution Film," *Journalism Quarterly* 49 (summer 1972): 221–9.

BALL, GEORGE, "The Light that Failed," *Atlantic Monthly* (July 1973): 33–49.

———, "Top Secret: The Prophecy the President Rejected," *Atlantic*, vol. 230 (July 1972): 35–49.

BASSETT, LAWRENCE J., and PELZ, STEPHEN E., "The Failed Search for Victory: Vietnam and the Politics of War," in Paterson, Thomas G., ed., *Kennedy's Quest for Victory: American Foreign Policy, 1961–1963*. New York: Oxford Univ. Press, 1989.

BELLHOUSE, MARY L., and LITCHFIELD, LAWRENCE, "Vietnam and the Loss of Innocence: An Analysis of the Political Implications of the Popular Literature of the Vietnam War," *Journal of Popular Culture*, vol. 16 (winter 1982): 157–74.

BRODIE, BERNARD, "The Tet Offensive," in Frankland, Noble, and Dowling, Christopher (eds.), *Decisive Battles of the Twentieth Century*. (London: Sidgwick & Jackson, 1976).

———, "Why We Were So (Strategically) Wrong," *Foreign Policy* (winter 1971–1972): 151–62.

CANNON, MICHAEL, "Raising the Stakes: The Taylor-Rostow Mission," *Journal of Strategic Studies* 12 (June 1989).

CHEN, KING C., "Hanoi's Three Decisions and the Escalation of the Vietnam War," *Political Science Quarterly*, vol. 90 (summer 1975): 239–59.

CHESNEAUX, JEAN, "The Historical Background of Vietnamese Communism," in *Government and Opposition*, vol. 4 (winter 1969): 119–35.

CLIFFORD, CLARK, "A Vietnam Reappraisal," *Foreign Affairs*, vol. 47 (July 1969): 601–22.

COLLINS, ROBERT M., "The Economic Crisis of 1968 and the Waning of the 'American Century,'" *American Historical Review*, vol. 101, no. 2 (April 1996): 396–422.

CONVERSE, PHILIP E., MILLER, WARREN E., RUSK, JEROLD G., and WOLFE, ARTHUR C., "Continuity and Change in American Politics: Parties and Issues in the 1968 Election," *American Political Science Review*, vol. 63 (December 1969): 1083–1105.

———, and SCHUMAN, HOWARD, "'Silent Majorities' and the Vietnam War," *Scientific American*, vol. 222 (June 1970): 17–24.

CRAWFORD, HENRY B., "Operation Menu's Secret Bombing of Cambodia," *Vietnam* (December 1966): 22–28.

DEBENEDETTI, CHARLES, "A CIA Analysis of the Anti-Vietnam War Movement: October, 1967," *Peace and Change*, vol. 9 (spring 1983): 31–42.

———, "On the Significance of Citizen Peace Activism: America, 1961–1975," *Peace and Change*, vol. 9 (summer 1983): 6–20.

DUNN, PETER M., "The American Army: the Vietnam War, 1965–1973," in *Armed Forces and Modern Counter-insurgency*, edited by Ian F. W. Beckett and John Pimlott. London: Croom Helm, 1985.

ELEGANT, ROBERT, "How to Lose a War: Reflections of a Foreign Correspondent," *Encounter* (August 1981).

ESZTERHOZ, JOSEPH, et al., "The Massacre at My Lai," *Life* (December 5, 1969).

GELB, LESLIE, "The Essential Domino: American Politics and Vietnam," *Foreign Affairs*, vol. 50 (April 1972): 459–72.

———, "The System Worked," *Foreign Policy*, vol. 3 (summer 1971): 140–67.

GREENE, DANIEL O'C., "John Foster Dulles and the End of the Franco-American Entente in Indochina," *Diplomatic History,* 16 (fall 1992).

GREENSTEIN, FRED. I., and IMMERMAN, RICHARD H., "What Did Eisenhower Tell Kennedy about Indochina? The Politics of Misperception," *The Journal of American History*, vol. 79, no. 2 (September 1992): 568–87.

HALBERSTAM, DAVID, "Getting the Story in Vietnam," *Commentary*, vol. 39 (January 1968): 30–34.

———, "Return to Vietnam," *Harpers*, 235 (December 1967).

———, "The Ugliest American in Vietnam," *Esquire*, vol. 62 (November 1964): 37–40.

———, "Vietnamese Reds Gain in Key Area" in *New York Times*, (August 15, 1963), A1, A3.

HEINL, ROBERT, "The Collapse of the Armed Forces," *Armed Forces Journal*, vol. 19 (June 1971): 30–38.

HERRING, GEORGE C., "American Strategy in Vietnam: The Postwar Debate," *Military Affairs*, vol. 46 (April 1982): 57–63.

———, "'Cold Blood:' LBJ's Conduct of Limited War in Vietnam," The Harmon Memorial Lectures in Military History, Washington, D. C.: U. S. Government Printing Office, 1990.

———, and IMMERMAN, RICHARD H., "Eisenhower, Dulles, and Dienbienphu: 'The Day We Didn't Go to War' Revised," *Journal of American History*, vol. 71 (September 1984); 343–63.

———, "The 1st Cavalry and the Ia Drang Valley, 18 October–24 November 1965," in Heller, Charles E., and Stofft, William A., *America's First Battles*, 300–26. Lawrence, Kans.: University of Kansas Press, 1986.

———, "The Nixon Strategy in Vietnam," in *Vietnam as History*, edited by Peter Braestrup, Washington, D. C.: University Press of America, 1984, 51–58.

———, HESS, GARY R., and IMMERMAN, RICHARD H., "Passage of Empire: The U. S., France, and South Vietnam, 1954–1955," in *Dien Bien Phu and the Crisis of Franco–American Relations, 1954–1955*, eds. Lawrence Kaplan, Denise Artaud, and Mark Rubin (Lanham, 1990).

———, "'Peoples Quite Apart': Americans, South Vietnamese, and the War in Vietnam," *Diplomatic History* 14 (winter, 1990).

———, "The Truman Administration and the Restoration of French Sovereignty in Indochina," *Diplomatic History*, vol. 1 (spring 1977): 97–117.

———, "Vietnam, El Salvador, and the Uses of History," in *The Central American Crisis*, edited by Kenneth Coleman and George C. Herring. Wilmington, Del.: Scholarly Resources, 1985.

HESS, GARY R., "Franklin D. Roosevelt and Indochina," *Journal of American History*, vol. 59 (September 1972): 353–68.

———, "The Military Perspective on Strategy in Vietnam: Harry G. Summers's *On Strategy* and Bruce Palmer's *The 25-Year War*," *Diplomatic History*, vol. 1, no. 1 (winter 1986), 91–106.

———, "The Unending Debate: Historians and the Vietnam War," *Diplomatic History*, vol. 18, no. 2 (spring 1994): 239–64.

JACOBS, JAMES B., and MCNAMARA, DENNIS, "Vietnam Veterans and Agent Orange," *Armed Forces and Society*, vol. 13 (fall 1986): 57–79.

———, "The Pentagon Papers: A Critical Evaluation," *American Political Science Review*, vol. 69 (June 1975): 675–84.

JIAN CHEN, "China and the First Indochina War, 1950–1954," *China Quarterly* (March 1993): 85–110.

KAHIN, GEORGE MCT., "Political Polarization in South Vietnam: U. S. Policy in the Post-Diem Period," *Pacific Affairs* 52 (winter 1979–1980): 647–73.

KATTENBURG, PAUL M., "Vietnam and U. S. Diplomacy, 1940–1970," *Orbis*, vol. 15 (fall 1971): 818–41.

KIMBALL, JEFFREY P., "How Wars End: The Viet Nam War," *Peace and Change*, vol. 20, no. 2 (April 1995): 183–202.

———, " 'Peace with Honor:' Richard Nixon and the Diplomacy of Threat and Symbolism," in Anderson, David L., ed., *Shadows on the White House*. Lawrence, Kans.: University of Kansas Press, 1993, 152–83.

———, "The Stab-in-the-Back Legend and the Vietnam War," *Armed Forces and Society*, vol. 14 (spring 1988): 433–58.

KISSINGER, HENRY A., "The Viet Nam Negotiations," *Foreign Affairs*, vol. 47 (January 1969): 211–34.

KOMER, ROBERT W., "Pacification: A Look Back," *Army* (June 1970): 20–29.

LAFEBER, WALTER, "The Rise and Fall of American Power, 1963–1975," in Williams, William Appleton, McCormick, Thomas, Gardner, Lloyd, and LaFeber, Walter, (eds.), *America in Vietnam: A Documentary History*. Garden City, N. Y.: Doubleday, 1985.

———, "Roosevelt, Churchill, and Indochina, 1942–1945," *American Historical Review*, vol. 80 (December 1975): 1277–89.

LICHTY, LAWRENCE W., and BAILEY, GEORGE A., "Violence in Television News: A Case Study of Audience Response," *Central States Speech Journal*, vol. 23 (winter 1972): 225–9.

LINDEN, EUGENE, "The Demoralization of an Army: Fragging and Other Withdrawal Symptoms," *Saturday Review* (January 8, 1972): 12–17, 55.

MILTON, T. R., "The Lessons of Vietnam," *Air Force Magazine*, no. 66 (March 1983).

———, "USAF and the Vietnam Experience," *Air Force Magazine*, no. 58 (June 1975).

MOISE, EDWIN E., "Land Reform and Land Reform Errors in North Vietnam," *Pacific Affairs*, vol. 49 (spring 1976): 70–92.

MOSKOS, CHARLES C., "Success Story: Blacks in the Military," *Atlantic Monthly*, vol. 257 (May 1986): 64–72.

MUELLER, JOHN E., "Reflections on the Vietnam Antiwar Movement and the Curious Calm at War's End," in *Vietnam as History*, edited by Peter Braestrup. Washington, D. C.: The University Press of America, 1984, 151–7.

————, "The Search for the 'Breaking Point' in Vietnam: The Statistics of a Deadly Quarrel," *International Studies Quarterly*, vol. 4 (December 1980), 497–519.

————, "A Summary of Public Opinion and the Vietnam War," in *Vietnam as History*, edited by Peter Braestrup. Washington, D. C.: University Press of America, 1984, appendixes.

————, "Trends in Popular Support for the Wars in Korea and Vietnam," *American Political Science Quarterly* 65 (June 1971): 358–75.

NIXON, RICHARD M., "Asia after Vietnam," *Foreign Affairs*, vol. 46 (October 1967): 111–25.

PARKER, MAYNARD, "Vietnam: The War that won't End," *Foreign Affairs*, vol. 53 (January 1975): 352–74.

PATERSON, THOMAS G., "Bearing the Burden: A Critical Look at JFK's Foreign Policy," *Virginia Quarterly Review*, vol. 54 (spring 1978): 193–212.

PATTERSON, OSCAR, III, "An Analysis of Television Coverage of the Vietnam War," *Journal of Broadcasting*, vol. 28 (fall 1984): 397–404.

PELZ, STEPHEN, "John F. Kennedy's 1961 Vietnam War Decisions," *Journal of Strategic Studies* vol. 4 (December 1981): 356–85.

POPKIN, SAMUEL, "Pacification: Politics and the Village," *Asian Survey*, vol. 10 (August 1970): 662–71.

PORTER, GARETH, "The 1968 'Hue Massacre,'" *Indochina Chronicle* 33 (June 24, 1974).

PROSTERMAN, ROY L., "Land-to-the-Tiller in South Vietnam: The Tables Turn," *Asian Survey*, vol. 10 (August 1970): 751–64.

QIANG ZHAI, "Transplanting the Chinese Model: Chinese Military Advisers and the First Vietnam War, 1950–1954," *Journal of Military History* 57 (October 1993): 689–715.

RACE, JEFFREY, "How They Won," *Asian Survey*, vol. 10 (August 1970): 628–50.

————, "The Origins of the Second Indochina War," *Asian Survey*, vol. 10 (May 1960): 359–82.

ROBERTS, CHALMERS, "Foreign Policy and a Paralyzed Presidency," *Foreign Affairs*, vol. 52 (July 1974).

SALTER, MacDONALD, "The Broadening Base of Land Reform in South Vietnam," *Asian Survey*, vol. 10 (August 1970): 724–37.

SASAKI, DR. CLARENCE T., "Holding Death at Bay," *Vietnam*, vol. V, no. 2 (August 1992): 35–40.

SAVAGE, PAUL, and GABRIEL, RICHARD A., "Cohesion and Disintegration in the American Army," *Armed Forces and Society*, vol. 2 (spring 1976): 340–76.

SCHALLER, MICHAEL, "Securing the Great Crescent: Occupied Japan and the Origins of Containment in Southeast Asia," *Journal of American History* 69 (September 1982): 392–413.

SCHANDLER, HERBERT Y., "America and Vietnam: The Failure of Strategy, 1964–1967," in *Vietnam as History*, Braestrup, Peter, (ed.). Washington, D. C.: University Press of America, 1984.

SCHUMAN, HOWARD, "Two Sources of Antiwar Sentiment in America," *American Journal of Sociology*, vol. 78 (November 1972): 519–35.

SHEEHAN, NEIL, "In Vietnam, the Birth of the Credibility Gap," *New York Times* (Oct. 1, 1988): A15.

———, four articles about the life, military career, and Vietnam service of John Paul Vann appeared in consecutive issues of the *New Yorker*, under the general title of "Annals of War: An American Soldier in Vietnam," vol. 44, nos. 19–22, (June 20, June 27, July 4, and July 11, 1988).

SMALL, MELVIN, "The Impact of the Antiwar Movement on Lyndon Johnson, 1965–1968," *Peace and Change*, vol. 10 (spring 1984): 1–22.

SPERLICH, PETER W., and LUNCH, WILLIAM L., "American Public Opinion and the War in Vietnam," *Western Political Quarterly* 32 (March 1979): 21–44.

SUMMERS, HARRY G. JR., "The Bitter Triumph of Ia Drang," *American Heritage* (January–February 1984): 51–58.

SZULC, TAD, "Behind the Vietnam Cease Fire Agreement," *Foreign Policy*, vol. 15 (summer 1974): 21–69.

THOMSON, JAMES C., "Getting Out and Speaking Out," *Foreign Policy* 13 (winter 1973–1974).

———, "How Could Vietnam Happen?" *Atlantic* Monthly, vol. 22 (April 1968), 47–53.

U. S. News and World Report, "'The Phantom Battle' that Led to War," (July 23, 1984): 56–67.

VERBA, SIDENY, *et alia*, "Public Opinion and the War in Vietnam," *American Political Science Review* 61 (June 1967): 317–33.

WARD, RICHARD, "The Origins of United States Interest in Vietnam," *Vietnam Quarterly*, no. 1 (winter 1976).

WARNER, GEOFFREY, "The United States and the Fall of Diem," "The Coup That Never Was," *Australian Outlook*, vol. 28 (December 1974): 245–58; "The Death of Diem," *Australian Outlook*, vol. 29 (March 1975): 3–17.

WOODSIDE, ALEXANDER, "Decolonization and Agricultural Reform in Northern Vietnam," *Asian Survey*, vol. 10 (August 1970): 705–23.

———, "Some Southern Vietnamese Writers Look At the War," *Bulletin of Concerned Asian Scholars*, vol. 2 (October 1969): 53–58.

WYATT, CLARENCE R., " 'At the Cannon's Mouth:' The American Press and the Vietnam War," *Journalism History* 13 (autumn–winter 1986): 104–13.

DOCUMENTS

Citizen's Commission of Inquiry (eds.), *The Dellums Committee Hearings on War Crimes in Vietnam*. New York: Vintage, 1972.

GRAVEL, MIKE, (ed.), *The Pentagon Papers: The Defense Department History of U. S. Decisionmaking in Vietnam*. Boston: Beacon, 1971.

EISENHOWER, DWIGHT D., *Public Papers of the President, Dwight D. Eisenhower, 1953–1961*. Washington, D. C.: U. S. Government Printing Office, 1962.

JOHNSON, LYNDON B., *Public Papers of Lyndon B. Johnson, 1968–1969*. Washington, D. C.: U. S. Government Printing Office, 1970.

KENNEDY, JOHN F., *John F. Kennedy: Public Papers*. Washington, D. C.: U. S. Government Printing Office, 1963.

MINH, HO CHI, *Selected Writings, 1920–1969*. Hanoi: People's Publishing House, 1973.

NIXON, RICHARD M., *Public Papers, Richard Nixon, 1969 and 1970*. Washington, D. C.: U. S. Government Printing Office, 1971.

PORTER, GARETH, *Vietnam: The Definitive Documentation of Human Decisions*. Stanfordville, N. Y.: Earl M. Coleman, 1979.

Report of the Department of Army Review of Preliminary Investigations into My Lai Incident. (Peers Report) Washington, D. C.: U. S. Government Printing Office, 1976.

SHEEHAN, NEIL, SMITH, HEDRICK, KENWORTHY, E. W., and BUTTERFIELD, FOX, *The Pentagon Papers: The Secret History of the Vietnam War*. New York: Bantam, 1971.

United States Congress, House, Committee on Armed Services, *United States-Vietnam Relations, 1945–1967: A Study Prepared by the Department of Defense*. Washington, D. C.: U. S. Government Printing Office, 1971.

United States, Department of State, *American Foreign Policy, 1950–1955: Basic Documents*. Vol. 1.Washington, D. C.: U. S. Government Printing Office, 1957.

United States, Department of State. Several volumes in the Foreign Relations of the United States series, including *Foreign Relations of the United States 1946, vol. 8, The Far East*. Washington, D. C.: U. S. Government Printing Office, 1971. *Foreign Relations of the United States 1947, vol. 6, The Far East*. Washington, D. C.: U. S. Government Printing Office, 1972. *Foreign Relations of the United States, 1952–1954, vol. 13, Indochina*. Washington, D. C.: U. S. Government Printing Office, 1982. *Foreign Relations of the United States, 1955–1957, vol. 3*, John P. Glennon, general editor. Washington, D. C.: U. S. Government Printing Office, 1971.

United States, Department of State, *White Paper: A Threat to Peace: North Viet Nam's Effort to Conquer South Viet Nam*. Washington, D. C.: U. S. Government Printing Office, 1961.

ARCHIVAL AND UNPUBLISHED SOURCES

HARKINS, PAUL D., "Oral History," 1974, U. S. Army Military History Institute Archives, Carlisle Barracks, Penn.

HUNT, DAVID, "U. S. Scholarship and the National Liberation Front," unpublished essay, April 1992.

MOSS, GEORGE DONELSON, "The Vietnam Generation: The Impact of the War and the Draft on the Generation Called to Fight in Southeast Asia," unpublished essay, 1984.

OFFNER, ARNOLD A., "The Truman Myth Revealed: From Parochial Nationalist to Cold Warrior," unpublished essay, 1988.

O'KEEFE, KEVIN, "Media Coverage of Gulf of Tonkin," unpublished essay, 1988.

PEERS, WILLIAM R., "Oral History," U. S. Army Military History Institute Archives, Carlisle Barracks, Penn.

VANN, JOHN PAUL, papers, Archives of the U. S. Army Military Institute, Carlisle Barracks, Penn.

ZAIS, MELVIN, Oral History Interview, pp. 575–83, Archives of the U. S. Army Military History Institute, Carlisle Barracks, Penn.

LITERATURE: POETRY, NOVELS, NOVELISTIC MEMOIRS, NOVELISTIC JOURNALISM

BUTLER, ROBERT OLEN. *A Good Scent from a Strange Mountain: Stories*. New York: H. Holt, 1992.

CANO, DANIEL. *Shifting Loyalties*. Houston, Tex.: Arte Publico Press, 1995.

CAPUTO, PHILLIP. *A Rumor of War*. New York: Ballantine, 1977.

DEL VECCHIO, JOHN M. *The 13th Valley*. New York: Bantam, 1982.

DONOVAN, DAVID. *Once a Warrior King: Memories of an Officer in Vietnam*. New York: McGraw Hill, 1985.

EHRHART, W. D., ed. *Carrying the Darkness: American Indochina—The Poetry of the Vietnam War*. New York: Avon Books, 1985.

GREENE, GRAHAM. *The Quiet American*. New York: Penguin, 1977.

HEINEMAN, LARRY. *Close Quarters*. New York: Farrar, Straus, & Giroux, 1977.

HERR, MICHAEL. *Dispatches*. New York: Knopf, 1977.

KAIKO, TAKESHI; translated by CECILIA SEGAWA SEIGLE. *Into a Black Sun*. Tokyo: Kadansha, 1980. (Distributed in the United States by Kadansha through Harper and Row, 1980.)

KOVIC, RON. *Born on the Fourth of July*. New York: McGraw-Hill, 1976.

LE, LY HAYSLIP. *When Heaven and Earth Changed Places*. New York: Doubleday, 1989.

LEDERER, WILLIAM, J., and BURDICK, EUGENE. *The Ugly American*. New York: W. W. Norton, 1958.

MAILER, NORMAN. *Armies of the Night*. Cleveland: World, 1968.

MASON, BOBBIE ANN. *In Country*. New York: Harper and Row, 1985.

MASON, ROBERT. *Chickenhawk*. New York: Penguin, 1983.

O'BRIEN, TIM. *Going after Cacciato*. New York: Delacorte, 1978.

———. *If I Die in a Combat Zone*. New York: Dell, 1969.

———. *The Things They Carried*. New York: Penguin Books, 1990.

SMITH, STEVEN PHILLIP. *American Boys*. New York: Avon, 1978.

STONE, ROBERT. *Dog Soldiers*. Boston: Houghton Mifflin, 1974.

WEBB, JAMES. *Fields of Fire*. Englewood Cliffs, N. J.: Prentice Hall, 1978.

WILLSON, DAVID A. *REMF Diary*. Seattle: 1988.

TELEVISION DOCUMENTARIES AND TELEVISION PROGRAMS

Accuracy in Media (AIM), "Television's Vietnam. Part 1: The Real Story; Part 2: The Impact of Media," 1984 and 1985, television documentary transcripts.

CBS News, "The Uncounted Enemy: A Vietnam Deception," January 23, 1982, television documentary transcript.

CBS News, "Vietnam: A War That is Finished," July, 1975, television documentary transcript.

CBS News, "Vietnam: the Deadly Decision," CBS televsion documentary shown on April 1, 1964.

CBS News, "The World of Charlie Company," television documentary transcript.

"Vietnam: A Television History," 13-part video documentary series first shown on PBS in October 1983–March 1984.

FILMS

Apocalypse Now, fiction film

Coming Home, fiction film

The Deer Hunter, fiction film

Full Metal Jacket, fiction film

Hamburger Hill, fiction film based on the Battle of Dong Ap Bia, fought along the rim of the A Shau Valley, May 11–20, 1969

Hearts and Minds, documentary

JFK, a fiction film released in 1991, written and directed by Oliver Stone. The film suggests that Kennedy was assassinated by a conspiracy of government officials because he was going to phase out the American Vietnam war.

The Killing Fields, fiction film based on the experiences of Sydney Schrandberg and Dith Pran

Platoon, fiction film based on the Vietnam experiences of Oliver Stone

Index

"Doves," 189
Draft resistance, 258–59
Drug abuse in U. S. Army, 355
DRV (*see* Democratic Republic of Vietnam)
DUCK HOOK, 342, 382, 383
Dulles, John Foster:
    becomes Secretary of State, 60
    orchestrates SEATO, 78–79
    snubs Zhou En-Lai, 64
Durbrow, Elbridge, 107

E

Eden, Anthony, 62, 64
Eisenhower, Dwight David:
    assumes office of president, 60
    backs Diem, 81
    makes decision to intervene in Vietnam, 65
    quoted, 62, 95
    refuses French request for military
        intervention, 63
    supports the French war, 60–61
Elections:
    in South Vietnam:
        1955, 85
        1967, 247–48
    in the United States:
        1964, 175–76
        1968, 318–24
        1970, 364–66
    in Vietnam:
        1946, 37
Elegant, Robert, 305
Ellsberg, Daniel, 339, 374
Ely, Paul, 61
Enthoven, Alain, 289–90
European Defense Community (EDC), 48,
    52, 61, 64, 81

F

FACs, 238
First Air Cavalry (Air Mobile), 215–18
First Indochina War (1945–1946), 36

First Logistical Command, 212
FLAMING DART, 182
"Flying Tigers," 24
Ford, Gerald R., 415, 421, **quoted**, 422
Foreign Ministers Council, 60
Formosa (Taiwan), 44
Fowler, Henry, 297
"Fragging," 354
France:
    colonial rule of Vietnam, 14–16
    colonial rule of Vietnam ends, 26
    colonizes Vietnam, 11–12
    conquered by Germany, 35
    defeated at Dien Bien Phu, 58
    departs Vietnam, 85
    establishes French Indochina, 12
    fights war in Indochina, 41–46, 53–60
Franco-Vietminh War, 40–46, 53–58
Fulbright, William J., 172, 241, 255, 293

G

Galbraith, John K., **quoted**, 407
General Offensive—General Uprising (TCK-
    TKN), 276
Geneva Accords, 66, 67, 78–79, 81, 100, 395
Geneva Conference (1954), 59, 60, 63, 64–66
Geneva Agreement (1962), 121
Gia Long (*see* Nguyen, Anh)
Gingrich, Newt, **quoted**, 333
Goldwater, Barry, 173
Gracey, Douglas D., 35
Great Britain, 64–65
Great Society, 198
Green Berets (*see* Special Forces)
Gruening, Ernest, 172, **quoted**, 173
Gulf of Tonkin Resolution, 173, 363
GVN (*see* Republic of Vietnam)

H

Ha Dong, 40
Haiphong, 290, 382, 383, 391
Halberstam, David, 135, 136